Lecture Notes in Computer Science 9779

Commenced Publication in 1973
Founding and Former Series Editors:
Gerhard Goos, Juris Hartmanis, and Jan van Leeuwen

More information about this series at http://www.springer.com/series/7407

Swarat Chaudhuri · Azadeh Farzan (Eds.)

Computer Aided Verification

28th International Conference, CAV 2016
Toronto, ON, Canada, July 17–23, 2016
Proceedings, Part I

 Springer

Editors
Swarat Chaudhuri
Rice University
Houston, TX
USA

Azadeh Farzan
University of Toronto
Toronto, ON
Canada

ISSN 0302-9743   ISSN 1611-3349   (electronic)
Lecture Notes in Computer Science
ISBN 978-3-319-41527-7   ISBN 978-3-319-41528-4   (eBook)
DOI 10.1007/978-3-319-41528-4

Library of Congress Control Number: 2015943799

LNCS Sublibrary: SL1 – Theoretical Computer Science and General Issues

This Springer imprint is published by Springer Nature
The registered company is Springer International Publishing AG Switzerland

Preface

It is our pleasure to welcome you to the proceedings of CAV 2016, the 28th International Conference on Computer-Aided Verification, held in Toronto, Ontario, during July 17–23, 2016.

The CAV conference series is dedicated to the advancement of the theory and practice of computer-aided formal analysis of hardware and software systems. The conference covers the spectrum from theoretical results to concrete applications, with an emphasis on practical verification tools and the algorithms and techniques that are needed for their implementation. CAV considers it vital to continue spurring advances in hardware and software verification while expanding to new domains such as biological systems and computer security.

The CAV 2016 program included four invited keynote talks, four invited tutorials, 58 technical papers (consisting of 46 regular papers and 12 tool papers) accepted out of 195 submissions, and briefings from the SYNTCOMP and SYGUS synthesis competitions. The conference was accompanied by six co-located events: VSTTE (Verified Software: Theories, Tools, and Experiments), NSV (Numerical Software Verification), SYNT (Synthesis), EC^2 (Exploiting Concurrency Efficiently and Correctly), HCCV (High-Consequence Control Verification), and VMW (Verification Mentoring Workshop).

Our invited keynote speakers were Gilles Barthe (IMDEA Software Institute), Gerwin Klein (NICTA and University of New South Wales), and Moshe Vardi (Rice University). Parosh Aziz Abdulla (Uppsala University), Vitaly Chipounov (EPFL), Paulo Tabuada (UCLA), and Martin Vechev (ETH Zurich) gave invited tutorials.

We introduced three significant changes to CAV's review process this year. First, CAV 2016 employed a lightweight double-blind reviewing process. This meant that committee members did not have access to the names and affiliations of the authors as they reviewed a paper, and were able to produce an unbiased initial reivew. However, author names were revealed late in the online discussion process to permit calibration against the authors' prior work. Second, we introduced an External Review Committee, consisting of reviewers committed to producing four to five reviews, and also increased the size of the main Program Committee. These changes significantly reduced the number of papers that a committee had to review. Third, CAV 2016 had a two-phase evaluation process. Each paper received three reviews by the end of the first phase; considering the reviews and accounting for feedback from the reviewers, we solicited up to two additional reviews for papers for which consensus did not exist or further expertise was considered necessary.

Many people worked hard to make CAV 2016 a success. We thank the authors and the invited speakers for providing the excellent technical material, the Program Committee and the External Review Committee for their thorough reviews and the time spent on evaluating all the submissions and discussing them during the online discussion period, and the Steering Committee for their guidance.

We thank Pavol Černý, Sponsorship Chair, for helping to bring much-needed financial support to the conference; Zachary Kincaid, Workshop Chair, and all the organizers of the co-located events for bringing their events to the CAV week; Roopsha Samanta, Publicity Chair, for diligently publicizing the event; and Aws Albarghouthi, Artifact Evaluation Chair, and the Artifact Evaluation Committee for their work on evaluating the artifacts submitted. We gratefully acknowledge NSF for providing financial support for student participants. We sincerely thank the sponsors of CAV 2016 for their generous contributions.

We also thank the University of Toronto and Rice University for their support. Finally, we hope you find the proceedings of CAV 2016 intellectually stimulating and practically valuable.

July 2016

Swarat Chaudhuri
Azadeh Farzan

Organization

Program Committee

Rajeev Alur	University of Pennsylvania, USA
Christel Baier	Technische Universität Dresden, Germany
Clark Barrett	New York University, USA
Roderick Bloem	Graz University of Technology, Austria
Pavol Cerny	University of Colorado, Boulder, USA
Adam Chlipala	MIT, USA
Swarat Chaudhuri	Rice University, Houston, USA
Alessandro Cimatti	Fondazione Bruno Kessler, Italy
Loris D'Antoni	University of Wisconsin, Madison, USA
Constantin Enea	University of Paris Diderot (Paris 7), France
Javier Esparza	Technische Universität München, Germany
Kousha Etessami	University of Edinburgh, UK
Azadeh Farzan	University of Toronto, Toronto, Canada
Susanne Graf	VERIMAG, France
Orna Grumberg	Technion, Israel
Franjo Ivancic	Google, USA
Somesh Jha	University of Wisconsin, Madison, USA
Ranjit Jhala	University of California, San Diego, USA
Joost-Pieter Katoen	RWTH Aachen University, Germany
Zachary Kincaid	University of Toronto, Canada
Laura Kovacs	Chalmers University of Technology, Sweden
Viktor Kuncak	EPFL, Switzerland
Marta Kwiatkowska	Oxford University, UK
Shuvendu Lahiri	Microsoft Research, Redmond, USA
Akash Lal	Microsoft Research, Bangalore, India
Pete Manolios	Northeastern University, USA
Kenneth McMillan	Microsoft Research, Redmond, USA
David Monniaux	VERIMAG, France
Kedar Namjoshi	Bell Labs, Alcatel-Lucent, USA
David Parker	University of Birmingham, UK
Corina Pasareanu	Carnegie Mellon Silicon Valley; NASA Ames, USA
Ruzica Piskac	Yale University, USA
Andreas Podelski	University of Freiburg, Germany
Shaz Qadeer	Microsoft Research, Redmond, USA
Andrey Rybalchenko	Microsoft Research, Cambridge, UK
Mooly Sagiv	Tel Aviv University, Israel
Sriram Sankaranarayanan	University of Colorado, Boulder, USA

Sanjit Seshia	University of California, Berkeley, USA
Natasha Sharygina	University of Lugano, Switzerland
Sharon Shoham	Academic College of Tel Aviv-Yaffo, Israel
Fabio Somenzi	University of Colorado, Boulder, USA
Serdar Tasiran	Koç University, Turkey
Mahesh Viswanathan	University of Illinois, Urbana-Champaign, USA
Bow-Yaw Wang	Academia Sinica, Taiwan
Thomas Wies	New York University, USA
Lenore Zuck	University of Illinois, Chicago, USA

External Review Committee

Aws Albarghouthi	University of Wisconsin, Madison, USA
Jade Alglave	Microsoft Research Cambridge; University College London, UK
Sagar Chaki	Software Engineering Institute, Carnegie Mellon University, USA
Hana Chockler	King's College London, UK
Byron Cook	University College London; Amazon, UK
Deepak D'Souza	Indian Institute of Science, India
Thao Dang	CNRS, France
Cezara Dragoi	Inria, France
Pierre Ganty	IMDEA, Spain
Ganesh Gopalakrishnan	University of Utah, USA
Arie Gurfinkel	Software Engineering Institute, Carnegie Mellon University, USA
Jan Hoffmann	Carnegie Mellon University, USA
William Hung	Synopsys, USA
Joxan Jaffer	National University of Singapore
Naoki Kobayashi	University of Tokyo, Japan
Igor Konnov	Vienna University of Technology, Austria
Hillel Kugler	Bar-Ilan University, Israel
Rupak Majumdar	Max Planck Institute for Software Systems, Germany
Sayan Mitra	University of Illinois at Urbana Champaign, USA
Peter Mueller	ETH Zurich, Switzerland
Tim Nelson	Brown University, USA
Jan Otop	University of Wroclaw, Poland
Gennaro Parlato	University of Southampton, UK
Madhusudan Parthasarathy	University of Illinois at Urbana Champaign, USA
Doron Peled	Bar Ilan University, Israel
Pavithra Prabhakar	Kansas State University, USA
Arjun Radhakrishna	University of Pennsylvania, USA
Zvonimir Rakamaric	University of Utah, USA
Nishant Sinha	IBM Research, Bangalore, India
Ana Sokolova	University of Salzburg, Austria
Armando Solar-Lezama	MIT, USA

Viktor Vafeiadis   Max Planck Institute for Software Systems, Germany
Martin Vechev   ETH Zurich, Switzerland
Willem Visser   Stellenbosch University, South Africa
Tomas Vojnar   Brno University of Technology, Czech Republic
Thomas Wahl   Northeastern University, USA
Eran Yahav   Technion, Israel
Karen Yorav   IBM Haifa Research Lab, Israel
Florian Zuleger   Vienna University of Technology, Austria

Additional Reviewers

Houssam Abbas   University of Pennsylvania, USA
Stavros Aronis   Uppsala University, Sweden
Amir Ben-Amram   The Academic College of Tel Aviv-Yaffo, Israel
Dirk Beyer   University of Passau, Germany
Armin Biere   Johannes Kepler University, Austria
David Binkley   Loyola University, USA
James Brotherston   University College London, UK
Domenico Cantone   University of Catania, Italy
Ernie Cohen   Amazon, USA
Sylvain Conchon   LRI, Univesité Paris-Sud 11, France
Chris Hawblitzel   Microsoft Research, Redmond, USA
Jean-François Raskin   Université Libre de Bruxelles, Belgium
Antoine Miné   UPMC University, France
Anders Møller   Aarhus University, Denmark
Andrew Reynolds   University of Iowa, USA
Ulrich Schmid   Vienna University of Technology, Austria
Margus Veanes   Microsoft Research, Redmond, USA

Contents – Part I

Model Checking I

Program Analysis

Timed and Hybrid Systems

Contents – Part II

Model Checking II

Probabilistic Systems

Termination Analysis of Probabilistic Programs Through Positivstellensatz's

Krishnendu Chatterjee[1]([✉]), Hongfei Fu[1,2], and Amir Kafshdar Goharshady[1]

[1] IST Austria, Vienna, Austria
{krishnendu.Chatterjee,hongfei.fu,goharshady}@ist.ac.at
[2] State Key Laboratory of Computer Science, Institute of Software,
Chinese Academy of Sciences, Beijing, People's Republic of China

Abstract. We consider nondeterministic probabilistic programs with the most basic liveness property of termination. We present efficient methods for termination analysis of nondeterministic probabilistic programs with polynomial guards and assignments. Our approach is through synthesis of polynomial ranking supermartingales, that on one hand significantly generalizes linear ranking supermartingales and on the other hand is a counterpart of polynomial ranking-functions for proving termination of nonprobabilistic programs. The approach synthesizes polynomial ranking-supermartingales through Positivstellensatz's, yielding an efficient method which is not only sound, but also semi-complete over a large subclass of programs. We show experimental results to demonstrate that our approach can handle several classical programs with complex polynomial guards and assignments, and can synthesize efficient quadratic ranking-supermartingales when a linear one does not exist even for simple affine programs.

1 Introduction

Probabilistic Programs. Classic imperative programs extended with *random-value generators* give rise to probabilistic programs. Probabilistic programs provide the appropriate framework to model applications ranging from randomized algorithms [17,38], to stochastic network protocols [5,34], to robot planning [30,33], etc. Nondeterminism plays a crucial role in modeling, such as, to model behaviors over which there is no control, or for abstraction. Thus nondeterministic probabilistic programs are crucial in a huge range of problems, and hence their formal analysis has been studied across disciplines, such as probability theory and statistics [18,28,32,39,42], formal methods [5,34], artificial intelligence [30,31], and programming languages [10,19,21,43].

Basic Termination Questions. Besides safety properties, the most basic property for analysis of programs is the liveness property. The most basic and widely used notion of liveness for programs is *termination*. In absence of probability (i.e., for

---

A full version is available in [11].

© Springer International Publishing Switzerland 2016
S. Chaudhuri and A. Farzan (Eds.): CAV 2016, Part I, LNCS 9779, pp. 3–22, 2016.
DOI: 10.1007/978-3-319-41528-4_1

nonprobabilistic programs), the synthesis of *ranking functions* and proof of termination are equivalent [22], and numerous approaches exist for synthesis of ranking functions for nonprobabilistic programs [8,13,40,48]. The most basic extension of the termination question for probabilistic programs is the *almost-sure termination* question which asks whether a program terminates with probability 1. Another fundamental question is about *finite termination* (aka positive almost-sure termination [7,21]) which asks whether the expected termination time is finite. The next interesting question is the *concentration* bound computation problem that asks to compute a bound M such that the probability that the termination time is below M is concentrated, or in other words, the probability that the termination time exceeds the bound M decreases exponentially.

Previous Results. We discuss the relevant previous results for termination analysis of probabilistic programs.

- *Probabilistic Programs.* First, quantitative invariants was introduced to establish termination of discrete probabilistic programs with demonic nondeterminism [35,36], This was extended in [10] to *ranking supermartingales* resulting in a sound (but not complete) approach to prove almost-sure termination of probabilistic programs without nondeterminism but with integer- and real-valued random variables from distributions like uniform, Gaussian, and Poison, etc. For probabilistic programs with countable state-space and without nondeterminism, the Lyapunov ranking functions provide a sound and complete method for proving finite termination [7,23]. Another sound method is to explore bounded-termination with exponential decrease of probabilities [37] through abstract interpretation [15]. For probabilistic programs with nondeterminism, a sound and complete characterization for finite termination through ranking-supermartingale is obtained in [21]. Ranking supermartingales thus provide a very powerful approach for termination analysis of probabilistic programs.
- *Ranking Functions/Supermartingales Synthesis.* Synthesis of linear ranking-functions/ranking-supermartingales has been studied extensively in [10,12,13,40]. In context of probabilistic programs, the algorithmic study of synthesis of linear ranking supermartingales for probabilistic programs (cf. [10]) and probabilistic programs with nondeterminism (cf. our previous result [12]) has been studied. The major technique adopted in these results is Farkas' Lemma [20] which serves as a complete reasoning method for linear inequalities. Beyond linear ranking functions, polynomial ranking functions have also been considered. Heuristic synthesis method of polynomial ranking-functions is studied in [4,9]: Babic *et al.* [4] checked termination of deterministic polynomial programs by detecting divergence on program variables and Bradley *et al.* [9] extended to nondeterministic programs through an analysis on finite differences over transitions. More general methods for deterministic polynomial programs are given by [14,47] where Cousot [14] uses Lagrangian Relaxation, and Shen *et al.* [47] use Putinar's Positivstellensatz [41]. Complete methods of synthesizing polynomial ranking-functions for nondeterministic programs are studied by Yang *et al.* [50], where a complete method through root

classification/real root isolation of semi-algbebraic systems and quantifier elimination is proposed.

To summarize, while many different approaches has been studied, the algorithmic study of synthesis of ranking supermartingales for probabilistic programs has only been limited to linear ranking supermartingales (cf. [10,12]). Hence there is no algorithmic approach to handle nonlinear ranking supermartingales even for probabilistic programs without nondeterminism.

Our Contributions. Our contributions are as follows:

1. *Polynomial Ranking Supermartingales.* First, we extend the notion of linear ranking supermartingales (LRSM) to polynomial ranking supermartingales (pRSM). We show (by a straightforward extension of LRSM) that pRSM implies both almost-sure as well as finite termination.
2. *Positivstellensatz's.* Second, we conduct a detailed investigation on the application of Positivstellensatz's (German for "positive-locus-theorem" which is related to polynomials over semialgebraic sets) (cf. Sect. 5.1) to synthesis of pRSMs over nondeterministic probabilistic programs. To the best of our knowledge, this is the first result which demonstrates the synthesis of a polynomial subclass of ranking supermartingales through Positivstellensatz's.
3. *New Approach for Non-probabilistic Programs.* Our results also extend existing results for nonprobabilistic programs. We present the first result that uses Schmüdgen's Positivstellensatz [45] and Handelman's Theorem [25] to synthesize polynomial ranking-functions for nonprobabilistic programs.
4. *Efficient Approach.* The previous complete method [50] suffers from high computational complexity due to the use of quantifier elimination. In contrast, our approach (sound but not complete) is efficient since the synthesis can be accomplished through linear or semi-definite programming, which can mostly be solved in polynomial time in the problem size [24]. In particular, our approach does not require quantifier elimination, and works for nondeterministic probabilistic programs.
5. *Experimental Results.* We demonstrate the effectiveness of our approach on several classical examples. We show that on classical examples, such as Gambler's Ruin, and Random Walk, our approach can synthesize a pRSM efficiently. For these examples, LRSMs do not exist, and many of them cannot be analysed efficiently by previous approaches.

In summary, while Farkas' Lemma and Motzkin's Transposition Theorem are standard techniques to linear ranking functions or linear ranking supermartingales, they are not sufficient for synthesizing polynomial ranking-supermartingales. To address this problem, we study the use of Positivstellensatz's for the first time to synthesize polynomial ranking-supermartingales for probabilistic programs, for some of them even the first time for nonprobabilistic programs, and show that how they can be used for efficient termination analysis over programs. Due to space restrictions, some technical details are available only in the full version [11].

2   Probabilistic Programs

2.1   Basic Notations and Concepts

For a set A, we denote by $|A|$ the cardinality of A. We denote by $\mathbb{N}$, $\mathbb{N}_0$, $\mathbb{Z}$, and $\mathbb{R}$ the sets of all positive integers, non-negative integers, integers, and real numbers, respectively. We use boldface notation for vectors, e.g. $\boldsymbol{x}$, $\boldsymbol{y}$, etc., and we denote an i-th component of a vector $\boldsymbol{x}$ by $\boldsymbol{x}[i]$.

Polynomial Predicates. Let X be a finite set of variables endowed with a fixed linear order under which we have $X = \{x_1, \ldots, x_{|X|}\}$. We denote the set of real-coefficient polynomials by $\mathfrak{R}[x_1, \ldots, x_{|X|}]$ or $\mathfrak{R}[X]$. A *polynomial constraint* over X is a logical formula of the form $g_1 \bowtie g_2$, where g_1, g_2 are polynomials over X and $\bowtie \in \{<, \leq, >, \geq\}$. A *propositional polynomial predicate* over X is a propositional formula whose all atomic propositional literals are either *true, false* or polynomial constraints over X. The validity of the satisfaction assertion $\boldsymbol{x} \models \phi$ between a vector $\boldsymbol{x} \in \mathbb{R}^{|X|}$ (interpreted in the way that the value for x_j ($1 \leq j \leq |X|$) is $\boldsymbol{x}[j]$) and a propositional polynomial predicate ϕ is defined in the standard way w.r.t polynomial evaluation and normal semantics for logical connectives. The satisfaction set of a propositional polynomial predicate ϕ is defined as $[\![\phi]\!] := \{\boldsymbol{x} \in \mathbb{R}^{|X|} \mid \boldsymbol{x} \models \phi\}$. For more on polynomials (e.g., polynomial evaluation and arithmetic over polynomials), we refer to the textbook [29, Chapter 3].

Probability Space. A *probability space* is a triple $(\Omega, \mathcal{F}, \mathbb{P})$, where Ω is a non-empty set (so-called *sample space*), $\mathcal{F}$ is a *σ-algebra* over Ω (i.e., a collection of subsets of Ω that contains the empty set $\emptyset$ and is closed under complementation and countable union), and $\mathbb{P}$ is a *probability measure* on $\mathcal{F}$, i.e., a function $\mathbb{P} \colon \mathcal{F} \to [0, 1]$ such that (i) $\mathbb{P}(\Omega) = 1$ and (ii) for all set-sequences $A_1, A_2, \cdots \in \mathcal{F}$ that are pairwise-disjoint (i.e., $A_i \cap A_j = \emptyset$ whenever $i \neq j$) it holds that $\sum_{i=1}^{\infty} \mathbb{P}(A_i) = \mathbb{P}(\bigcup_{i=1}^{\infty} A_i)$.

Random Variables and Filtrations. A *random variable* X in a probability space $(\Omega, \mathcal{F}, \mathbb{P})$ is an $\mathcal{F}$-measurable function $X \colon \Omega \to \mathbb{R} \cup \{-\infty, +\infty\}$, i.e., a function satisfying the condition that for all $d \in \mathbb{R} \cup \{+\infty, -\infty\}$, the set $\{\omega \in \Omega \mid X(\omega) \leq d\}$ belongs to $\mathcal{F}$. The *expected value* of a random variable X, denote by $\mathbb{E}(X)$, is defined as the Lebesgue integral of X with respect to $\mathbb{P}$, i.e., $\mathbb{E}(X) := \int X \, d\mathbb{P}$; the precise definition of Lebesgue integral is somewhat technical and is omitted here (cf. [6, Chapter 5] for a formal definition). A *filtration* of a probability space $(\Omega, \mathcal{F}, \mathbb{P})$ is an infinite sequence $\{\mathcal{F}_n\}_{n \in \mathbb{N}_0}$ of σ-algebras over Ω such that $\mathcal{F}_n \subseteq \mathcal{F}_{n+1} \subseteq \mathcal{F}$ for all $n \in \mathbb{N}_0$.

2.2   Probabilistic Programs

The Syntax. The class of probabilistic programs we consider encompasses basic programming mechanisms such as assignment statement (indicated by ':='), while-loop, if-branch, basic probabilistic mechanisms such as probabilistic branch (indicated by 'prob') and random sampling, and demonic nondeterminism indicated by '$\star$'. Variables (or identifiers) of a probabilistic program are of *real* type, i.e., values of the variables are real numbers; moreover, variables are classified into *program* and *sampling* variables, where program variables receive their values through assignment statements and sampling variables do through random samplings. We consider that each sampling variable r is *bounded*, i.e., associated with a one-dimensional cumulative distribution function Υ_r and a non-empty bounded interval $supp_r$ such that any random variable z which respects Υ_r satisfies that z lies in the bounded interval with probability 1. Due to space restriction, details (e.g., grammar) are relegated to the full version [11]. An example probabilistic program is illustrated in Example 1.

Example 1. Consider the running example depicted in Fig. 1, where r is a sampling variable with the two-point distribution $\{1 \mapsto 0.5, -1 \mapsto 0.5\}$ where the probability to take values 1 and -1 are both 0.5. The probabilistic program models a scenario of Gambler's Ruin where the gambler has initial money x and repeats gambling until he wins more than 10 or loses all his money. The result of a gamble is nondeterministic: either win 1 with probability 0.5 (nondeterministic branch); or lose with probability 0.51 (the probabilistic branch). The numbers 1–7 on the left are the program counters for the program, where 1 is the initial program counter and 7 the terminal program counter.

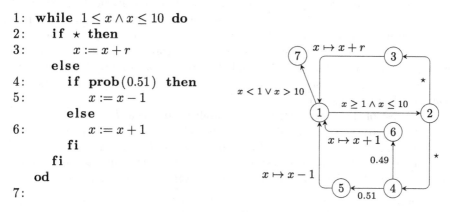

1: **while** $1 \leq x \wedge x \leq 10$ **do**
2:     **if** $\star$ **then**
3:         $x := x + r$
     else
4:         **if** $\mathbf{prob}(0.51)$ **then**
5:             $x := x - 1$
         else
6:             $x := x + 1$
         fi
     fi
     od
7:

Fig. 1. Running example: Gambler Ruin   **Fig. 2.** The CFG of the running example

The Semantics. We use control flow graphs to capture the semantics of probabilistic programs, which we define below.

Definition 1 (Control Flow Graph). *A control flow graph (CFG) is a tuple* $\mathcal{G} = (L, \perp, (X, R), \mapsto)$ *with the following components:*

– *L is a finite set of* labels *partitioned into four pairwise-disjoint subsets* L_d, L_p, L_c *and* L_a *of demonic, probabilistic, conditional-branching (branching for short) and assignment labels, resp.; and* $\perp$ *is a special label not in L called the* terminal label;

- *X and R are disjoint finite sets of real-valued* program *and* sampling variables *respectively;*
- $\mapsto$ *is a* transition relation *in which every member (called* transition*) is a tuple of the form* (ℓ, α, ℓ') *for which* ℓ *(resp.* ℓ'*) is the* source label *(resp.* target label*) in* L *and* α *is either a real number in* $(0,1)$ *if* $\ell \in L_{\mathrm{p}}$*, or* $\star$ *if* $\ell \in L_{\mathrm{d}}$*, or a propositional polynomial predicate if* $\ell \in L_{\mathrm{c}}$*, or an* update function $f \colon \mathbb{R}^{|X|} \times \mathbb{R}^{|R|} \to \mathbb{R}^{|X|}$ *if* $\ell \in L_{\mathrm{a}}$*.*

W.l.o.g, we assume that $L \subseteq \mathbb{N}_0$. Intuitively, labels in L_{d} correspond to demonic statements indicated by '$\star$'; labels in L_{p} correspond to probabilistic-branching statements indicated by '**prob**'; labels in L_{c} correspond to conditional-branching statements indicated by some propositional polynomial predicate; labels in L_{a} correspond to assignments indicated by ':='; and the terminal label $\bot$ denotes the termination of a program. The transition relation $\mapsto$ specifies the transitions between labels together with the additional information specific to different types of labels. The update functions are interpreted as follows: we first fix two linear orders on X and R so that $X = \{x_1, \ldots, x_{|X|}\}$ and $R = \{r_1, \ldots, r_{|R|}\}$, interpreting each vector $\boldsymbol{x} \in \mathbb{R}^{|X|}$ (resp. $\boldsymbol{r} \in \mathbb{R}^{|R|}$) as a *valuation* of program (resp. sampling) variables in the sense that the value of x_j (resp. r_j) is $\boldsymbol{x}[j]$ (resp. $\boldsymbol{r}[j]$); then each update function f is interpreted as a function which transforms a valuation $\boldsymbol{x} \in \mathbb{R}^{|X|}$ before the execution of an assignment statement into $f(\boldsymbol{x}, \boldsymbol{r})$ after the execution of the assignment statement, where $\boldsymbol{r}$ is the valuation on R obtained from a sampling before the execution of the assignment statement.

It is intuitively clear that any probabilistic program can be naturally transformed into a CFG. Informally, each label represents a program location in an execution of a probabilistic program for which the statement of the program location is the next to be executed (see Fig. 2).

In the rest of the section, we fix a probabilistic program P with the set $X = \{x_1, \ldots, x_{|X|}\}$ of program variables and the set $R = \{r_1, \ldots, r_{|R|}\}$ of sampling variables, and let $\mathcal{G} = (L, \bot, (X, R), \mapsto)$ be its associated CFG. We also fix ℓ_0 and resp. $\boldsymbol{x}_0$ to be the label corresponding to the first statement to be executed in P and resp. the initial valuation of program variables.

The Semantics. A *configuration* (for P) is a tuple $(\ell, \boldsymbol{x})$ where $\ell \in L \cup \{\bot\}$ and $\boldsymbol{x} \in \mathbb{R}^{|X|}$. A *finite path* (of P) is a finite sequence of configurations $(\ell_0, \boldsymbol{x}_0), \cdots, (\ell_k, \boldsymbol{x}_k)$ such that for all $0 \le i < k$, either (i) $\ell_{i+1} = \ell_i = \bot$ and $\boldsymbol{x}_i = \boldsymbol{x}_{i+1}$ (i.e., the program terminates); or (ii) there exist $(\ell_i, \alpha, \ell_{i+1}) \in \mapsto$ and $\boldsymbol{r} \in \{\boldsymbol{r}' \mid \forall r \in R.\ \boldsymbol{r}'(r) \in \mathrm{supp}_r\}$ such that one of the following conditions hold: (a) $\ell_i \in L_{\mathrm{p}} \cup L_{\mathrm{d}}$ and $\boldsymbol{x}_i = \boldsymbol{x}_{i+1}$ (probabilistic or demonic transitions), (b) $\ell_i \in L_{\mathrm{c}}$, $\boldsymbol{x}_i = \boldsymbol{x}_{i+1}$ and $\boldsymbol{x}_i \models \alpha$ (conditional-branch transitions), (c) $\ell_i \in L_{\mathrm{a}}$ and $\boldsymbol{x}_{i+1} = \alpha(\boldsymbol{x}_i, \boldsymbol{r})$ (assignment transitions). A *run* (of P) is an infinite sequence of configurations whose all finite prefixes are finite paths over P. A configuration $(\ell, \boldsymbol{x})$ is *reachable* from the initial configuration $(\ell_0, \boldsymbol{x}_0)$ if there exists a finite path $(\ell_0, \boldsymbol{x}_0), \cdots, (\ell_k, \boldsymbol{x}_k)$ such that $(\ell, \boldsymbol{x}) = (\ell_k, \boldsymbol{x}_k)$.

The probabilistic feature of P can be captured by constructing a suitable probability measure over the set of all its runs. However, before this can be done, nondeterminism in P needs to be resolved by some *scheduler*.

Definition 2 (Scheduler). *A scheduler (for P) is a function which assigns to every finite path* $(\ell_0, \boldsymbol{x}_0), \dots, (\ell_k, \boldsymbol{x}_k)$ *with* $\ell_k \in L_d$ *a transition in* $\mapsto$ *with source label* ℓ_k.

The behaviour of P under a scheduler σ is standard: at each step, P first samples a real number for each sampling variable and then evolves to the next step according to its CFG or the scheduler choice. In this way, the scheduler and random choices/samplings produce a run over P. Moreover, each scheduler σ induces a unique probability measure $\mathbb{P}^\sigma$ over the runs of P. In the sequel, we will use $\mathbb{E}^\sigma(\cdot)$ to denote the expected values of random variables under $\mathbb{P}^\sigma$.

Random Variables and Filtrations over Runs. We define the following (vectors of) random variables on the set of runs of P: $\{\theta_n^P\}_{n \in \mathbb{N}_0}$, $\{\overline{\boldsymbol{x}}_n^P\}_{n \in \mathbb{N}_0}$ and $\{\overline{\boldsymbol{r}}_n^P\}_{n \in \mathbb{N}_0}$: each θ_n^P is the random variable representing the (integer-valued) label at the n-th step; each $\overline{\boldsymbol{x}}_n^P$ is the vector of random variables such that each $\overline{\boldsymbol{x}}_n^P[i]$ is the random variable representing the value of the program variable x_i at the n-th step; and each $\overline{\boldsymbol{r}}_n^P[i]$ is the random variable representing the sampled value of the sampling variable r_i at the n-th step. The filtration $\{\mathcal{H}_n^P\}_{n \in \mathbb{N}_0}$ is defined such that each σ-algebra $\mathcal{H}_n^P$ is the smallest σ-algebra that makes all random variables in $\{\theta_k^P\}_{0 \le k \le n}$ and $\{\overline{\boldsymbol{x}}_k^P\}_{0 \le k \le n}$ measurable. We will omit the superscript P in all the notations above if it is clear from the context.

Remark 1. Under the condition that each sampling variable is bounded, using an inductive argument it follows that each $\overline{\boldsymbol{x}}_n$ is a vector of bounded random variables. Thus $\mathbb{E}^\sigma(|\overline{\boldsymbol{x}}_n[i]|)$ exists for each random variable $\overline{\boldsymbol{x}}_n[i]$.

Below we define the notion of *polynomial invariants* which logically captures all reachable configurations. A polynomial invariant may be obtained through abstract interpretation [15].

Definition 3 (Polynomial Invariant). *A polynomial invariant (for P) is a function I assigning a propositional polynomial predicate over X to every label in $\mathcal{G}$ such that for all configurations $(\ell, \boldsymbol{x})$ reachable from $(\ell_0, \boldsymbol{x}_0)$ in $\mathcal{G}$, it holds that $\boldsymbol{x} \models I(\ell)$.*

3 Termination over Probabilistic Programs

In this section, we first define the notions of almost-sure/finite termination and concentration bounds over probabilistic programs, and then describe the computational problems studied in this paper. Below we fix a probabilistic program P with its associated CFG $\mathcal{G} = (L, \perp, (X, R), \mapsto)$ and an initial configuration $(\ell_0, \boldsymbol{x}_0)$ for P.

Definition 4 (Termination [7,12,21]). *A run $\omega = \{(\ell_n, \boldsymbol{x}_n)\}_{n \in \mathbb{N}_0}$ over P is terminating if $\ell_n = \perp$ for some $n \in \mathbb{N}_0$. The termination time of P is a random variable T_P such that for each run $\omega = \{(\ell_n, \boldsymbol{x}_n)\}_{n \in \mathbb{N}_0}$, $T_P(\omega)$ is the least number n such that $\ell_n = \perp$ if such n exists, and ∞ otherwise. The program P is said to be almost-sure terminating (resp. finitely terminating) if $\mathbb{P}^\sigma(T_P < \infty) = 1$ (resp. $\mathbb{E}^\sigma(T_P) < \infty$) for all schedulers σ (for P).*

Note that $\mathbb{E}^\sigma(T_P) < \infty$ implies that $\mathbb{P}^\sigma(T_P < \infty) = 1$, but the converse does not necessarily hold (see [10, Example 5] for an example). To measure the expected values of the termination time under all (demonic) schedulers, we further define the quantity $\mathsf{ET}(P) := \sup_\sigma \mathbb{E}^\sigma(T_P)$.

Definition 5 (Concentration on Termination Time [12,37]). *A concentration bound for P is a non-negative integer M such that there exist real constants $c_1 \geq 0$ and $c_2 > 0$, and for all $N \geq M$ we have $\mathbb{P}(T_P > N) \leq c_1 \cdot e^{-c_2 \cdot N}$.*

Informally, a concentration bound characterizes exponential decrease of probability values of non-termination beyond the bound. On one hand, it can be used to give an upper bound on probability of non-termination beyond a large step; and on the other hand, it leads to an algorithm that approximates $\mathsf{ET}(P)$ (cf. [12, Theorem 5]).

In this paper, we consider the algorithmic analysis of the following problems:

- **Input:** a probabilistic program P, a polynomial invariant I for P and an initial configuration $(\ell_0, \boldsymbol{x}_0)$ for P;
- **Output (Almost-Sure/Finite Termination):** "yes" if the algorithm finds that P is almost-sure/finite terminating and "*fail*" otherwise;
- **Output (Concentration on Termination):** a concentration bound if the algorithm finds one and "*fail*" otherwise.

4 Polynomial Ranking-Supermartingale

In this section, we develop the notion of polynomial ranking-supermartingale which is an extension of linear ranking-supermartingale [10,12]. We fix a probabilistic program P, a polynomial invariant I for P and an initial configuration $(\ell_0, \boldsymbol{x}_0)$ for P. Let $\mathcal{G} = (L, \bot, (X, R), \mapsto)$ be the associated CFG of P, with $X = \{x_1, \ldots, x_{|X|}\}$ and $R = \{r_1, \ldots, r_{|R|}\}$. We first present the general notion of *ranking supermartingale*, and then define *polynomial ranking supermartingale*.

Definition 6 (Ranking Supermartingale [12,21]). *A discrete-time stochastic process $\{X_n\}_{n \in \mathbb{N}_0}$ w.r.t a filtration $\{\mathcal{F}_n\}_{n \in \mathbb{N}_0}$ is a ranking supermartingale (RSM) if there exist $K < 0$ and $\epsilon > 0$ such that for all $n \in \mathbb{N}_0$, we have $\mathbb{E}(|X_n|) < \infty$ and it holds almost surely (with probability 1) that $X_n \geq K$ and $\mathbb{E}(X_{n+1} \mid \mathcal{F}_n) \leq X_n - \epsilon \cdot \mathbf{1}_{X_n \geq 0}$, where $\mathbb{E}(X_{n+1} \mid \mathcal{F}_n)$ is the conditional expectation of X_{n+1} given $\mathcal{F}_n$ (cf. [49, Chapter 9]).*

Informally, a polynomial ranking-supermartingale over P is a polynomial instantiation of an RSM through certain function $\eta : (L \cup \{\bot\}) \times \mathbb{R}^{|X|} \to \mathbb{R}$ which satisfies that each $\eta(\ell, \cdot)$ (for all $\ell \in L \cup \{\bot\}$) is essentially a polynomial function over X. Given such a function η, the intuition is to have conditions that make the stochastic process $X_n = \eta(\theta_n, \overline{\boldsymbol{x}}_n)$ an RSM. To ensure this, we consider the conditional expectation $\mathbb{E}^\sigma(X_{n+1} \mid \mathcal{H}_n)$; this is captured by an extension of *pre-expectation* [10,12] from the linear to the polynomial case. Below we define $L_\bot := L \cup \{\bot\}$. For a function $g : \mathbb{R}^{|X|} \times \mathbb{R}^{|R|} \to \mathbb{R}$, we let $\mathbb{E}_R(g, \cdot) : \mathbb{R}^{|X|} \to \mathbb{R}$

be the function such that each $\mathbb{E}_R(g, \boldsymbol{x})$ is the expected value $\mathbb{E}(g(\boldsymbol{x}, \hat{\boldsymbol{r}}))$, where $\hat{\boldsymbol{r}}$ is any vector of independent random variables such that each $\hat{\boldsymbol{r}}[i]$ is a random variable that respects the cumulative distribution function Υ_{r_i}.

Definition 7 (Pre-Expectation). *Let* $\eta : L_\perp \times \mathbb{R}^{|X|} \to \mathbb{R}$ *be a function such that each* $\eta(\ell, \cdot)$ *(for all* $\ell \in L_\perp$*) is a polynomial function over* X*. The function* $\mathrm{pre}_\eta : L_\perp \times \mathbb{R}^{|X|} \to \mathbb{R}$ *is defined by:*

- $\mathrm{pre}_\eta(\ell, \boldsymbol{x}) := \sum_{(\ell, z, \ell') \in \mapsto} z \cdot \eta(\ell', \boldsymbol{x})$ *if* $\ell \in L_\mathrm{p}$ *(probabilistic transitions);*
- $\mathrm{pre}_\eta(\ell, \boldsymbol{x}) := \max_{(\ell, \star, \ell') \in \mapsto} \eta(\ell', \boldsymbol{x})$ *if* $\ell \in L_\mathrm{d}$ *(nondeterministic transitions);*
- $\mathrm{pre}_\eta(\ell, \boldsymbol{x}) := \eta(\ell', \boldsymbol{x})$ *if* $\ell \in L_\mathrm{c}$ *and* (ℓ, ϕ, ℓ') *is the only transition in* $\mapsto$ *such that* $\boldsymbol{x} \models \phi$ *(conditional transitions);*
- $\mathrm{pre}_\eta(\ell, \boldsymbol{x}) := \mathbb{E}_R(g, \boldsymbol{x})$ *if* $\ell \in L_\mathrm{a}$*, where* g *is the function such that* $g(\boldsymbol{x}, \boldsymbol{r}) = \eta(\ell', f(\boldsymbol{x}, \boldsymbol{r}))$ *and* (ℓ, f, ℓ') *is the only transition in* $\mapsto$ *(assignment transitions); and*
- $\mathrm{pre}_\eta(\ell, \boldsymbol{x}) := \eta(\ell, \boldsymbol{x})$ *if* $\ell = \perp$ *(terminal location).*

The following lemma establishes the relationship between pre-expectation and conditional expectation.

Lemma 1. *Let* $\eta : L_\perp \times \mathbb{R}^{|X|} \to \mathbb{R}$ *be a function such that each* $\eta(\ell, \cdot)$ *(for all* $\ell \in L_\perp$*) is a polynomial function over* X*, and* σ *be any scheduler. Let the stochastic process* $\{X_n\}_{n \in \mathbb{N}_0}$ *be defined by:* $X_n := \eta(\theta_n, \bar{\boldsymbol{x}}_n)$*. Then for all* $n \in \mathbb{N}_0$*, we have* $\mathbb{E}^\sigma(X_{n+1} \mid \mathcal{H}_n) \leq \mathrm{pre}_\eta(\theta_n, \bar{\boldsymbol{x}}_n)$*.*

Example 2. Consider the running example in Example 1 with CFG in Fig. 2. Let η be the function specified in the second and fifth column of Table 1, where $g(x) := (x - 1)(10 - x)$. Then pre_η is given in the third and sixth column of Table 1. Note that the case for $i = 2$ is obtained from $\mathrm{pre}_\eta(2, x) = \max\{g(x) + 9.6, g(x) + 9.6\}$, and the case for $i = 3$ is from $\mathrm{pre}_\eta(3, x) = \mathbb{E}_R(h, x)$, where h is the function $h(y, r) = g(y) - (2y - 11)r - r^2 + 10$.

We now define the notion of polynomial ranking-supermartingale. The intuition is that we encode the RSM-difference condition as a logical formula, treat zero as the threshold between terminal and non-terminal labels, and use the invariant I to over-approximate the set of reachable configurations at each label. Below for each $\ell \in L_\mathrm{c}$, we define $\mathsf{PP}(\ell)$ to be the propositional polynomial predicate $\bigvee_{(\ell, \phi, \ell') \in \mapsto, \ell' \neq \perp} \phi$; and for $\ell \in L \backslash L_\mathrm{c}$, we let $\mathsf{PP}(\ell) := \mathrm{true}$.

Table 1. η and pre_η for Example 1 and Fig. 2

i	$\eta(i, x)$	$\mathrm{pre}_\eta(i, x)$	i	$\eta(i, x)$	$\mathrm{pre}_\eta(i, x)$
1	$g(x) + 10$	$\mathbf{1}_{1 \leq x \leq 10} \cdot (g(x) + 9.8)$ $+ \mathbf{1}_{x < 1 \vee x > 10} \cdot (-0.2)$	5	$g(x) + 2x - 1.8$	$g(x) + 2x - 2$
2	$g(x) + 9.8$	$g(x) + 9.6$	6	$g(x) - 2x + 20.2$	$g(x) - 2x + 20$
3	$g(x) + 9.6$	$g(x) + 9$	7	-0.2	-0.2
4	$g(x) + 9.6$	$g(x) + 0.04x + 8.98$			

Definition 8 (Polynomial Ranking-Supermartingale). *A d-degree polynomial ranking-supermartingale map (in short, d-pRSM) w.r.t (P, I) is a function $\eta : L_{\perp} \times \mathbb{R}^{|X|} \to \mathbb{R}$ satisfying that there exist $\epsilon > 0$ and $K \le -\epsilon$ such that for all $\ell \in L_{\perp}$ and all $\boldsymbol{x} \in \mathbb{R}^{|X|}$, the conditions (C1-C4) hold:*

- *C1: the function $\eta(\ell, \cdot) : \mathbb{R}^{|X|} \to \mathbb{R}$ is a polynomial over X of order at most d;*
- *C2: if $\ell \ne \perp$ and $\boldsymbol{x} \models I(\ell)$, then $\eta(\ell, \boldsymbol{x}) \ge 0$;*
- *C3: if $\ell = \perp$, then $\eta(\ell, \boldsymbol{x}) = K$;*
- *C4: if $\ell \ne \perp$ and $\boldsymbol{x} \models I(\ell) \wedge \mathsf{PP}(\ell)$, then $\mathrm{pre}_{\eta}(\ell, \boldsymbol{x}) \le \eta(\ell, \boldsymbol{x}) - \epsilon$.*

Note that C2 and C3 together separate non-termination and termination by the threshold 0, and C4 is the *RSM difference* condition which is intuitively related to the ϵ difference in the RSM definition (cf. Definition 6). By generalizing our previous proofs in [12] (from LRSM to pRSM), we establish the soundness of pRSMs w.r.t both almost-sure and finite termination.

Theorem 1. *If there exists a d-pRSM η w.r.t (P, I) with constants ϵ, K (cf. Definition 8), then P is a.s. terminating and $\mathsf{ET}(P) \le \mathsf{UB}(P) := \frac{\eta(\ell_0, \boldsymbol{x}_0) - K}{\epsilon}$.*

Example 3. Consider the running example (cf. Example 1) and the function η given in Example 2. Assuming that the initial valuation satisfies $1 \le x \wedge x \le 10$, we assign the trivial invariant I such that $I(1) = 0 \le x \wedge x \le 11$, $I(j) = 1 \le x \wedge x \le 10$ for $2 \le j \le 6$ and $I(7) = x < 1 \vee x > 10$. It is straightforward to verify that η is a 2-pRSM with $\epsilon = 0.2$ and $K = -0.2$ (cf. Definition 8 for ϵ, K). Hence by Theorem 1, the program in Example 1 terminates almost-surely under any scheduler and its expected termination time is at most $5 \cdot (x_0 - 1) \cdot (10 - x_0) + 51$, given the initial value x_0.

Remark 2. The running example (cf. Example 1) does not admit a linear (i.e. 1-) pRSM since $\mathbb{E}_R(r) = 0$ at label 3. This indicates that linear pRSMs may not exist even over simple affine programs like Example 1. Thus, this motivates the study of pRSMs even for simple affine programs.

Remark 3. The non-strict inequality symbol '$\ge$' in C2 can be replaced by its strict counterpart '$>$' since $\eta + c$ ($c > 0$) remains to be a pRSM if η is a pRSM and K (in C3) is sufficiently small. (By definition, $\mathrm{pre}_{\eta+c} = \mathrm{pre}_{\eta} + c$.) Moreover, the non-strict inequality symbol '$\le$' in C4 can be replaced by '$<$' since a pRSM η and a constant K (for C3) can be scaled by a constant factor (e.g. 1.1) so that strict inequalities are ensured. Moreover, one can also assume that $K = -1$ and $\epsilon = 1$ in Definition 8. This is because one can first scale a pRSM with constants ϵ, K by a positive scalar to ensure that $\epsilon = 1$, and then safely set $K = -1$ due to C2.

Theorem 1 answers the questions of almost-sure and finite termination in a unified fashion. Generalizing our approach in [12], we show that by restricting a pRSM to have *bounded difference*, we also obtain concentration results.

Definition 9 (Difference-Bounded pRSM). *A d-pRSM η is difference-bounded w.r.t a non-empty interval $[a, b] \subseteq \mathbb{R}$ if the following conditions hold:*

- for all $\ell \in L_d \cup L_p$ and $(\ell, \alpha, \ell') \in \mapsto$, and for all $\boldsymbol{x} \in \llbracket I(\ell) \rrbracket$, it holds that $a \le \eta(\ell', \boldsymbol{x}) - \eta(\ell, \boldsymbol{x}) \le b$;
- for all $\ell \in L_c$ and $(\ell, \phi, \ell') \in \mapsto$, and for all $\boldsymbol{x} \in \llbracket I(\ell) \wedge \phi \rrbracket$, it holds that $a \le \eta(\ell', \boldsymbol{x}) - \eta(\ell, \boldsymbol{x}) \le b$;
- for all $\ell \in L_a$ and $(\ell, f, \ell') \in \mapsto$, for all $\boldsymbol{x} \in \llbracket I(\ell) \rrbracket$ and for all $\boldsymbol{r} \in \{\boldsymbol{r}' \mid \forall r \in R.\ \boldsymbol{r}'[r] \in \mathrm{Supp}_r\}$, it holds that $a \le \eta(\ell', f(\boldsymbol{x}, \boldsymbol{r})) - \eta(\ell, \boldsymbol{x}) \le b$.

Note that if a d-pRSM η with constants ϵ, K (cf. Definition 8) is difference-bounded w.r.t $[a, b]$, then from definition $a \le -\epsilon$; one can further assume that $-\epsilon \le b$ since otherwise one can reset $\epsilon := -b$. By definition, the stochastic process $X_n := \eta(\theta_n, \overline{\boldsymbol{x}}_n)$ defined through a difference-bounded pRSM w.r.t $[a, b]$ satisfies that $a \le X_{n+1} - X_n \le b$; then using Hoeffding's Inequality [12,26], we establish a concentration bound.

Theorem 2. Let η be a difference-bounded d-pRSM w.r.t $[a, b]$ with constants ϵ and K. For all $n \in \mathbb{N}$, if $\epsilon(n-1) > \eta(\ell_0, \boldsymbol{x}_0)$, then $\mathbb{P}(T_P > n) \le e^{-\frac{2(\epsilon(n-1)-\eta(\ell_0, \boldsymbol{x}_0))^2}{(n-1)(b-a)^2}}$.

From Theorem 2, a difference-bounded d-pRSM η implies a concentration bound $\frac{\eta(\ell_0, \boldsymbol{x}_0)}{\epsilon} + 2$.

Example 4. Consider again our running example in Example 1 with invariant given in Example 3. Let η be the function illustrated in Table 1. One can verify that the interval $[-10.2, 8.6]$ satisfies the conditions specified in Definition 9 for η, as the following hold:

- for all $x \in [1, 10]$, $\eta(2, x) - \eta(1, x) = -0.2$;
- for all $x \in [0, 1) \cup (10, 11]$, $-10.2 \le \eta(7, x) - \eta(1, x) \le -0.2$;
- for all $x \in [1, 10]$ and $i \in \{3, 4\}$, $\eta(i, x) - \eta(2, x) = -0.2$;
- for all $x \in [1, 10]$ and $i \in \{5, 6\}$, $-9.4 \le \eta(i, x) - \eta(4, x) \le 8.6$;
- for all $x \in [1, 10]$, $\eta(1, x-1) - \eta(5, x) = -0.2$;
- for all $x \in [1, 10]$, $\eta(1, x+1) - \eta(6, x) = -0.2$;
- for all $x \in [1, 10]$ and $r \in \{-1, 1\}$, $-9.6 \le \eta(1, x+r) - \eta(3, x) \le 8.4$.

Then by Theorem 2, assuming that the program have initial value $x_0 = 5$, one can deduce that $\mathbb{P}(T_P > 50000) \le e^{-\frac{2 \cdot (0.2 \cdot 49999 - 30)^2}{49999 \cdot 18.8^2}} \approx 1.3016 \cdot 10^{-5}$.

We end this section with a result stating that whether a (difference-bounded) d-pRSM exists can be decided (using quantifier elimination).

Theorem 3. *For any fixed natural number $d \in \mathbb{N}$, the problem whether a (difference-bounded) d-pRSM w.r.t an input pair (P, I) exists is decidable.*

5 The Synthesis Algorithm

In this section, we present an efficient algorithmic approach for solving almost-sure/finite termination and concentration questions through synthesis of pRSMs. Instead of computationally-expensive quantifier elimination (cf. Theorem 3) we use Positivstellensatz, which is sound but not complete. Note that by Theorem 1, the existence of a pRSM implies both almost-sure and finite termination of a probabilistic program.

The General Framework. To synthesize a pRSM, the algorithm first sets up a polynomial template with unknown coefficients. Next, the algorithm finds values for the unknown coefficients, ϵ, K (cf. Definition 8) and $[a, b]$ (cf. Definition 9) so that C2-C4 in Definition 8 and concentration conditions in Definition 9 are satisfied. Note that from Definition 7, each $\mathrm{pre}_\eta(\ell, \cdot)$ is a (piecewise) polynomial over X whose coefficients are *linear combinations* of unknown coefficients from the polynomial template. Instead of using quantifier elimination (cf. e.g. [50] or Theorem 3), we use Positivstellensatz's [44]. We observe that each universally-quantified formula described in C2, C4 and Definition 9 can be decomposed (through disjunctive normal form of propositional polynomial predicate or transformation of max in Definition 7 into two conjunctive clauses) into a conjunction of formulae of the following pattern (†)

$$\forall \boldsymbol{x} \in \mathbb{R}^{|X|}. \left[(g_1(\boldsymbol{x}) \geq 0 \wedge \cdots \wedge g_m(\boldsymbol{x}) \geq 0) \rightarrow g(\boldsymbol{x}) > 0 \right] \qquad (\dagger)$$

where each g_i is a polynomial with constant coefficients and g is one with unknown coefficients from the polynomial template. In the pattern, we over-approximate any possible '$g_j(\boldsymbol{x}) > 0$' by '$g_j(\boldsymbol{x}) \geq 0$'. By Remark 3, the difference between '$g(\boldsymbol{x}) > 0$' and '$g(\boldsymbol{x}) \geq 0$' does not matter.

Example 5. Consider again the program in Example 1 with its CFG. Consider the invariant specified in Example 3. The instances of the pattern for termination of this program are listed as follows, where each instance is represented by a pair (Γ, g) where Γ and g corresponds to $\{g_1, \ldots, g_m\}$ and resp. g described in (†).

- (C4, label 1) $(\{x - 1, 10 - x, x, 11 - x\}, \eta(1, x) - \eta(2, x) - \epsilon)$;
- (C4, label 2) $(\{x - 1, 10 - x\}, \eta(2, x) - \eta(3, x) - \epsilon)$ and $(\{x - 1, 10 - x\}, \eta(2, x) - \eta(4, x) - \epsilon)$;
- (C4, label 3) $(\{x - 1, 10 - x\}, \eta(3, x) - \mathbb{E}_R((y, r) \mapsto \eta(1, y + r), x) - \epsilon)$;
- (C4, label 4) $(\{x - 1, 10 - x\}, \eta(4, x) - 0.51\eta(5, x) - 0.49\eta(6, x) - \epsilon)$;
- (C4, label 5) $(\{x - 1, 10 - x\}, \eta(5, x) - \eta(1, x - 1) - \epsilon)$;
- (C4, label 6) $(\{x - 1, 10 - x\}, \eta(6, x) - \eta(1, x + 1) - \epsilon)$;
- (C2) $(\{x, 11 - x\}, \eta(1, x))$ and $(\{x - 1, 10 - x\}, \eta(j, x))$ for $2 \leq j \leq 6$.

In the next part, we show that such pattern can be solved by Positivstellensatz's.

5.1   Positivstellensatz's

We fix a linearly-ordered finite set X of variables and a finite set $\Gamma = \{g_1, \ldots, g_m\} \subseteq \mathfrak{R}[X]$ of polynomials. Let $\llbracket \Gamma \rrbracket$ be the set of all vectors $\boldsymbol{x} \in \mathbb{R}^{|X|}$ satisfying the propositional polynomial predicate $\bigwedge_{i=1}^m g_i \geq 0$. We first define pre-orderings and sums of squares as follows.

Definition 10 (Sums of Squares). *Define Θ to be the set of sums-of-squares, i.e.,*

$$\Theta := \left\{ \sum_{i=1}^k h_i^2 \mid k \in \mathbb{N} \text{ and } h_1, \ldots, h_k \in \mathfrak{R}[X] \right\}.$$

Definition 11 (Preordering). *The* preordering *generated by Γ is defined by:*

$$PO(\Gamma) := \left\{ \sum_{w \in \{0,1\}^m} h_w \cdot \prod_{i=1}^{m} g_i^{w_i} \mid \forall w.\ h_w \in \Theta \right\}.$$

Remark 4. It is well-known that a real-coefficient polynomial g of degree $2d$ is a sum of squares iff there exists a k-dimensional positive semi-definite real square matrix Q such that $g = \boldsymbol{y}^{\mathsf{T}} Q \boldsymbol{y}$, where k is the number of monomials of degree no greater than d and $\boldsymbol{y}$ is the column vector of all such monomials (cf. [27, Corollary 7.2.9]). This implies that the problem whether a given polynomial (with real coefficients) is a sum of squares can be solved by semi-definite programming [24].

Now we present the first Positivstellensatz, called Schmüdgen's Positivstellensatz.

Theorem 4 (Schmüdgen's Positivstellensatz [45]). *Let $g \in \mathfrak{R}[X]$. If the set $[\![\Gamma]\!]$ is compact and $g(\boldsymbol{x}) > 0$ for all $\boldsymbol{x} \in [\![\Gamma]\!]$, then $g \in PO(\Gamma)$.*

From Schmüdgen's Positivstellensatz, any polynomial g which is positive on $[\![\Gamma]\!]$ can be represented by

$$(\ddagger) : g = \sum_{w \in \{0,1\}^m} h_w \cdot g_w \ ,$$

where $g_w := \prod_{i=1}^{m} g_i^{w_i}$ and $h_w \in \Theta$ for each $w \in \{0,1\}^m$. To apply Schmüdgen's Positivstellensatz, the degrees of those h_w's are restricted to be no greater than a fixed natural number. Then from Remark 4 and by equating the coefficients of the same monomials between the two polynomials, Eq. $(\ddagger)$ results in a system of linear equalities that involves coefficients of g and variables (grouped as 2^m square matrices) under semi-definite constraints.

Example 6. Consider that $X = \{x\}$ and $\Gamma = \{1 - x, 1 + x\}$. Choose the maximal degree for sums of squares to be 2. Then from Remark 4, the form of Eq. $(\ddagger)$ can be written as:

$$g = \sum_{i=1}^{4} \left[(1\ x) \cdot \begin{pmatrix} a_{i,1,1} & a_{i,1,2} \\ a_{i,2,1} & a_{i,2,2} \end{pmatrix} \cdot \begin{pmatrix} 1 \\ x \end{pmatrix} \right] \cdot u_i$$

where $u_1 = 1$, $u_2 = 1 - x$, $u_3 = 1 + x$, $u_4 = 1 - x^2$ and each matrix $(a_{i,j,k})_{2 \times 2}$ $(1 \le i \le 4)$ is a matrix of variables subject to be positive semi-definite.

Theorem 4 can be further refined by a weaker version of Putinar's Positivstellensatz.

Theorem 5 (Putinar's Positivstellensatz [41]). *Let $g \in \mathfrak{R}[X]$. If (i) there exists some $g_i \in \Gamma$ such that the set $\{\boldsymbol{x} \in \mathbb{R}^{|X|} \mid g_i(\boldsymbol{x}) \ge 0\}$ is compact and (ii) $g(\boldsymbol{x}) > 0$ for all $\boldsymbol{x} \in [\![\Gamma]\!]$, then*

$$(\S) \qquad g = h_0 + \sum_{i=1}^{m} h_i \cdot g_i$$

for some sums of squares $h_0, \ldots, h_m \in \Theta$.

Similar to Eqs. (‡) and (§) results in a system of linear equalities that involves variables for synthesis of a pRSM and matrices of variables under semi-definite constraints, provided that an upper bound on the degrees of sums of squares is enforced.

Example 7. Consider that $X = \{x\}$ and $\Gamma = \{1 - x^2, 0.5 - x\}$. Choose the maximal degree for sums of squares to be 2. Then the form of Eq. (§) can be written as:

$$g = \sum_{i=1}^{3} \left[(1\ x) \cdot \begin{pmatrix} a_{i,1,1} & a_{i,1,2} \\ a_{i,2,1} & a_{i,2,2} \end{pmatrix} \cdot \begin{pmatrix} 1 \\ x \end{pmatrix} \right] \cdot u_i$$

where $u_1 = 1$, $u_2 = 1 - x^2$, $u_3 = 0.5 - x$ and each matrix $(a_{i,j,k})_{2\times 2}$ $(1 \le i \le 3)$ is a matrix of variables subject to be positive semi-definite.

In the following, we introduce a Positivstellensatz entitled Handelman's Theorem when Γ consists of only linear (degree one) polynomials. For Handelman's Theorem, we assume that Γ consists of only linear (degree 1) polynomials and $[\![\Gamma]\!]$ is non-empty. (Note that whether a system of linear inequalities has a solution is decidable in PTIME [46].)

Definition 12 (Monoid). *The* monoid *of Γ is defined by:*

$$Monoid(\Gamma) := \left\{ \prod_{i=1}^{k} h_i \mid k \in \mathbb{N}_0 \text{ and } h_1, \ldots, h_k \in \Gamma \right\} .$$

Theorem 6 (Handelman's Theorem [25]). *Let $g \in \mathfrak{R}[X]$ be a polynomial such that $g(\boldsymbol{x}) > 0$ for all $\boldsymbol{x} \in [\![\Gamma]\!]$. If $[\![\Gamma]\!]$ is compact, then*

$$(\#) \qquad g = \sum_{i=1}^{d} a_i \cdot u_i$$

for some $d \in \mathbb{N}$, real numbers $a_1, \ldots, a_d \ge 0$ and $u_1, \ldots, u_d \in Monoid(\Gamma)$.

To apply Handelman's theorem, we consider a natural number which serves as a bound on the number of multiplicands allowed to form an element in $Monoid(\Gamma)$; then Eq. (#) results in a system of linear equalities involving $a_1, \ldots, a_d$. Unlike previous Positivstellensatz's, the form of Handelman's theorem allows us to construct a system of linear equalities free from semi-definite constraints.

Example 8. Consider that $X = \{x\}$ and $\Gamma = \{1 - x, 1 + x\}$. Fix the maximal number of multiplicands in an element of $Monoid(\Gamma)$ to be 2. Then the form of Eq. (#) can be rewritten as $g = \sum_{i=1}^{6} a_i \cdot u_i$ where $u_1 = 1$, $u_2 = 1-x$, $u_3 = 1+x$, $u_4 = 1 - x^2$, $u_5 = 1 - 2x + x^2$, $u_6 = 1 + 2x + x^2$ and each a_i $(1 \le i \le 6)$ is subject to be a non-negative real number.

5.2   The Algorithm for pRSM Synthesis

Based on the Positivstellensatz's introduced in the previous part, we present our algorithm for synthesis of pRSMs. Below, we fix an input probabilistic program P, an input polynomial invariant I and an input initial configuration (ℓ_0, x_0) for P. Let $\mathcal{G} = (L, \perp, (X, R), \mapsto)$ be the associated CFG of P.

Description of the Algorithm PRSMSYNTH. We present a succinct description of the key ideas. The description of the key steps of the algorithm is as follows.

1. *Template η for a pRSM.* The algorithm fixes a natural number d as the maximal degree for a pRSM, constructs $\mathcal{M}_d$ as the set of all monomials over X of degree no greater than d, and set up a template d-pRSM η such that each $\eta(\ell, \cdot)$ is the polynomial $\sum_{h \in \mathcal{M}_d} a_{h,\ell} \cdot h$ where each $a_{h,\ell}$ is a (distinct) scalar variable (cf. C1).
2. *Bound for Sums of Squares and Monoid Multiplicands.* The algorithm fixes a natural number k as the maximal degree for a sum of squares (cf. Schmüdgen's and Putinar's Positivstellensatz) or as the maximal number of multiplicands in a monoid element (cf. Handelman's Theorem).
3. *RSM-Difference and Terminating-Negativity.* From Remark 3, the algorithm fixes ϵ to be 1 (cf. condition C3) and K to be -1 (cf. condition C4).
4. *Computation of pre-expectation* pre_η. With ϵ, K fixed to be resp. $1, -1$ in the previous step, the algorithm computes pre_η by Definition 7, whose all involved coefficients are linear combinations from $a_{h,\ell}$'s.
5. *Pattern Extraction.* The algorithm extracts instances conforming to pattern (†) from C2, C4 and formulae presented in Definition 9, and translates them into systems of linear equalities over variables among $a_{h,\ell}$'s, ϵ, K, and extra matrices of variables assumed to be positive semi-definite (cf. Schmüdgen's and Putinar's Positivstellensatz) or scalar variables assumed to be non-negative (cf. Handelman's Theorem) through Eqs. (‡), (§) and (#).
6. *Solution via Semidefinite or Linear Programming.* The algorithm calls semi-definite programming (for Schmüdgen's and Putinar's Positivstellensatz) or linear programming (for Handelman's Theorem) in order to check the feasibility or to optimize $\mathsf{UB}(P)$ (cf. Theorem 1 for upper bound of $\mathsf{ET}(P)$) over all variables among $a_{h,\ell}$'s and extra matrix/scalar variables from Eqs. (‡), (§) and (#). Note that the feasibility implies the existence of a (difference-bounded) d-pRSM; the existence of a d-pRSM in turn implies finite termination, and the existence of a difference-bounded d-pRSM in turn implies a concentration bound through Theorem 2.

The soundness of our algorithm is as follows.

Theorem 7 (Soundness). *Any function η synthesized through the algorithm* PRSMSYNTH *is a valid pRSM.*

Remark 5 (Efficiency). It is well-known that for semi-definite programs with a positive real number R to bound the Frobenius norm of any feasible solution, an approximate solution upto precision ϵ can be computed in polynomial time in the size of the semi-definite program (with rational numbers encoded in binary), $\log R$ and $\log \epsilon^{-1}$ [24]. Thus, our sound approach presents an efficient method for analysis of many probabilistic programs. Moreover, when each propositional polynomial predicate in the probabilistic program involves only linear polynomials, then the sound form of Handelman's theorem can be applied, resulting in feasibility checking of systems of linear inequalities rather than semi-definite constraints. By polynomial-time algorithms for solving systems of linear inequalities [46], our approach is polynomial time (and thus efficient) over such programs.

Remark 6 (Semi-Completeness). Consider probabilistic programs of the following form: **while** ϕ **do if** $\star$ **then** P_1 **else** P_2 **od**, where P_1, P_2 are single assignments, $[\![\phi]\!]$ is compact, and invariants which assign to each label a propositional polynomial predicate is in DNF form that involves no strict inequality (i.e. no '$<$' or '$>$'). Upon such inputs, our approach is *semi-complete* in the sense that by raising the upper bounds for the degree of a sum of squares and the number of multiplicands in a monoid element, the algorithm PRSMSYNTH will eventually find a pRSM if it exists. This is because Theorems 4 to 6 are "semi-complete" when $[\![\Gamma]\!]$ is compact, as the terminal label can be separately handled by PP($\cdot$) so that only compact Γ's for Positivstellensatz's may be formed, and the difference between strict and non-strict inequalities does not matter (cf. Remark 3).

6   Experimental Results

In this section, we present experimental results for our algorithm through the semi-definite programming tool SOSTOOLS [3] (that uses SeDuMi [1]) and the linear programming tool CPLEX [2]. Due to space constraints, the detailed description of the input probabilistic programs are in [11].

Experimental Setup. We consider six classical examples of probabilistic programs that exhibit distinct types non-linear behaviours. Our examples are, namely, *Logistic Map* adopted in [14] which was previously handled by Lagrangian relaxation and semi-definite programming whereas our approach uses linear programming, *Decay* that models a sequence of points converging stochastically to the origin, *Random Walk* that models a random walk within a bounded region defined through non-linear curves, *Gambler's Ruin* which is our running example (Example 1), *Gambler's Ruin Variant* which is a variant of Example 1, and *Nested Loop* which is a nested loop with stochastic increments. Except for *Gambler's Ruin Variant* and *Nested Loop*, our approach is semi-complete for all other examples (cf. Remark 6). In all the examples the invariants are straightforward and was manually integrated with the input. Since SOSTOOLS only produces numerical results, we modify "$\eta(\ell, \boldsymbol{x}) \geq 0$" in C2 to "$\eta(\ell, \boldsymbol{x}) \geq 1$" for Putinar's or Schmüdgen's Positivstellensatz and check whether the maximal numerical error of all equalities added to SOSTOOLS is sufficiently small over a bounded region. In our examples, the bounded region is $\{(x, y) \mid x^2 + y^2 \leq 2\}$ and the maximal numerical error should not exceed 1. Note that 1 is also our fixed ϵ in C4, and by Remark 3, the modification on C2 is not restrictive. Instead, one may also pursue Sylvester's Criterion (cf. [27, Theorem 7.2.5]) to check membership of sums of squares through checking whether a square matrix is positive semi-definite or not.

Experimental Results. In Table 2, we present the experimental results, where 'Method' means that whether we use either Handelman's Theorem, Putinar's Positivstellensatz or Schmüdgen's Positivstellensatz to synthesize pRSMs, 'SOS-TOOLS/CPLEX' means the running time for CPLEX/SOSTOOLS in seconds, 'error' is the maximal numerical error of equality constraints added into SOS-TOOLS (when instantiated with the solutions), and $\eta(\ell_0, \cdot)$ is the polynomial for the initial label in the synthesized pRSM. The synthesized pRSMs (in the last column) refer to the variables of the program. All numbers except errors are rounded to 10^{-4}. For all the examples, our translation to the optimization problems are linear. We report the running times of the optimization tools and synthesized pRSMs. The experimental results were obtained on Intel Core i7-2600 machine with 3.4 GHz and 16 GB RAM.

Table 2. Experimental results

Example	Method	SOSTOOLS	error	$\eta(\ell_0, \cdot)$
Decay	Putinar	0.1248s	$\leq 10^{-9}$	$5282.3435x^2 + 5282.3435y^2 + 1$
Random Walk	Schmüdgen	0.7176s	$\leq 10^{-7}$	$-300x^2 - 300y^2 + 601$
Example	Method	CPLEX	-	$\eta(\ell_0, \cdot)$
Gambler's Ruin	Handelman	$\leq 10^{-2}$s	-	$33x - 3x^2$
Gambler's Ruin V	Handelman	$\leq 10^{-2}$s	-	$-21 + 100x - 70y - 100x^2 + 100xy$
Logistic Map	Handelman	$\leq 10^{-2}$s	-	$1000500.7496x$
Nested Loop	Handelman	$\leq 2 \cdot 10^{-2}$s	-	$48 + 160n + (m - x)(800n + 240)$

For all the examples we consider except Logistic Map, their almost-sure termination cannot be answered by previous approaches. For the Logistic-Map example, our reduction is to linear programming whereas existing approaches [14,47] reduce to semidefinite programming.

7 Conclusion and Future Work

In this paper, we extended linear ranking supermartingale (LRSM) for probabilistic programs proposed in [10,12] to polynomial ranking supermartingales (pRSM) for nondeterministic probabilistic programs. We developed the notion of (difference bounded) pRSM and proved that it is sound for almost-sure and finite termination, as well as for concentration bound (Theorems 1 and 2). Then we developed an efficient (sound but not complete) algorithm for synthesizing pRSMs through Positivstellensatz's (cf. Sect. 5.1), proved its soundness (Theorem 7) and argued its semi-completeness (Remark 6) over an important class of programs. Finally, our experiments demonstrate the effectiveness of our synthesis approach over various classical probabilistic programs, where LRSMs do not exist (cf. Example 1 and Remark 2). Directions of future work are to explore (a) more elegant methods for numerical problems related to semi-definite programming, and (b) other forms of RSMs for more general class of probabilistic programs.

Acknowledgements. We thank anonymous referees for valuable comments. We also thank Hui Kong for his help on SOSTOOLS. The research was partly supported by Austrian Science Fund (FWF) NFN Grant No. S11407-N23 (RiSE/SHiNE), ERC Start grant (279307: Graph Games), ERC Advanced Grant (267989: QUAREM), and Natural Science Foundation of China (NSFC) under Grant No. 61532019.

References

1. SeDuMi 1.3 (2008). http://sedumi.ie.lehigh.edu/
2. IBM ILOG CPLEX Optimizer Interactive Optimizer Community Edition 12.6.3.0 (2010). http://www-01.ibm.com/software/integration/optimization/cplex-optimizer/
3. SOSTOOLS v3.00 (2013). http://www.cds.caltech.edu/sostools/
4. Babic, D., Cook, B., Hu, A.J., Rakamaric, Z.: Proving termination of nonlinear command sequences. Form. Asp. Comput. **25**(3), 389–403 (2013)
5. Baier, C., Katoen, J.P.: Principles of Model Checking. MIT Press, Cambridge (2008)
6. Billingsley, P.: Probability and Measure, 3rd edn. Wiley, New York (1995)
7. Bournez, O., Garnier, F.: Proving positive almost-sure termination. In: Giesl, J. (ed.) RTA 2005. LNCS, vol. 3467, pp. 323–337. Springer, Heidelberg (2005)
8. Bradley, A.R., Manna, Z., Sipma, H.B.: Linear ranking with reachability. In: Etessami, K., Rajamani, S.K. (eds.) CAV 2005. LNCS, vol. 3576, pp. 491–504. Springer, Heidelberg (2005)
9. Bradley, A.R., Manna, Z., Sipma, H.B.: Termination of polynomial programs. In: Cousot [16], pp. 113–129
10. Chakarov, A., Sankaranarayanan, S.: Probabilistic program analysis with Martingales. In: Sharygina, N., Veith, H. (eds.) CAV 2013. LNCS, vol. 8044, pp. 511–526. Springer, Heidelberg (2013)
11. Chatterjee, K., Fu, H., Goharshady, A.K.: Termination analysis of probabilistic programs through positivstellensatz's (2016). arXiv CoRR: http://arxiv.org/abs/1604.07169
12. Chatterjee, K., Fu, H., Novotný, P., Hasheminezhad, R.: Algorithmic analysis of qualitative and quantitative termination problems for affine probabilistic programs. In: POPL, pp. 327–342. ACM (2016)
13. Colón, M.A., Sipma, H.B.: Synthesis of linear ranking functions. In: Margaria, T., Yi, W. (eds.) TACAS 2001. LNCS, vol. 2031, pp. 67–81. Springer, Heidelberg (2001)
14. Cousot, P.: Proving program invariance and termination by parametric abstraction, Lagrangian relaxation and semidefinite programming. In: Cousot [16], pp. 1–24
15. Cousot, P., Cousot, R.: Abstract interpretation: a unified Lattice model for static analysis of programs by construction or approximation of fixpoints. In: POPL, pp. 238–252. ACM (1977)

16. Cousot, R. (ed.): VMCAI 2005. LNCS, vol. 3385. Springer, Heidelberg (2005)
17. Dubhashi, D., Panconesi, A.: Concentration of Measure for the Analysis of Randomized Algorithms, 1st edn. Cambridge University Press, New York (2009)
18. Durrett, R.: Probability: Theory and Examples, 2nd edn. Duxbury Press, Belmont (1996)
19. Esparza, J., Gaiser, A., Kiefer, S.: Proving termination of probabilistic programs using patterns. In: Madhusudan, P., Seshia, S.A. (eds.) CAV 2012. LNCS, vol. 7358, pp. 123–138. Springer, Heidelberg (2012)
20. Farkas, J.: A fourier-féle mechanikai elv alkalmazásai (Hungarian). Mathematikaiés Természettudományi Értesitö **12**, 457–472 (1894)
21. Fioriti, L.M.F., Hermanns, H.: Probabilistic termination: soundness, completeness, and compositionality. In: POPL, pp. 489–501. ACM (2015)
22. Floyd, R.W.: Assigning meanings to programs. Math. Asp. Comput. Sci. **19**, 19–33 (1967)
23. Foster, F.G.: On the stochastic matrices associated with certain queuing processes. Ann. Math. Stat. **24**(3), 355–360 (1953)
24. Grötschel, M., Lovasz, L., Schrijver, A.: Geometric Algorithms and Combinatorial Optimization. Springer, Heidelberg (1993)
25. Handelman, D.: Representing polynomials by positive linear functions on compact convex polyhedra. Pacific J. Math. **132**, 35–62 (1988)
26. Hoeffding, W.: Probability inequalities for sums of bounded random variables. J. Am. Stat. Assoc. **58**(301), 13–30 (1963)
27. Horn, R.A., Johnson, C.R.: Matrix Analysis, 2nd edn. Cambridge University Press, Cambridge (2013)
28. Howard, H.: Dynamic Programming and Markov Processes. MIT Press, Cambridge (1960)
29. Hungerford, T.W.: Algebra. Springer, Heidelberg (1974)
30. Kaelbling, L.P., Littman, M.L., Cassandra, A.R.: Planning and acting in partially observable stochastic domains. Artif. intell. **101**(1), 99–134 (1998)
31. Kaelbling, L.P., Littman, M.L., Moore, A.W.: Reinforcement learning: a survey. J. Artif. Intell. Res. **4**, 237–285 (1996)
32. Kemeny, J., Snell, J., Knapp, A.: Denumerable Markov Chains. D. Van Nostrand Company, Princeton (1966)
33. Kress-Gazit, H., Fainekos, G.E., Pappas, G.J.: Temporal-logic-based reactive mission and motion planning. IEEE Trans. Robot. **25**(6), 1370–1381 (2009)
34. Kwiatkowska, M., Norman, G., Parker, D.: PRISM 4.0: verification of probabilistic real-time systems. In: Gopalakrishnan, G., Qadeer, S. (eds.) CAV 2011. LNCS, vol. 6806, pp. 585–591. Springer, Heidelberg (2011)
35. McIver, A.K., Morgan, C.: Developing and reasoning about probabilistic programs in $pGCL$. In: Cavalcanti, A., Sampaio, A., Woodcock, J. (eds.) PSSE 2004. LNCS, vol. 3167, pp. 123–155. Springer, Heidelberg (2006)
36. McIver, A., Morgan, C.: Abstraction, Refinement and Proof for Probabilistic Systems. Monographs in Computer Science. Springer, New York (2005)
37. Monniaux, D.: An abstract analysis of the probabilistic termination of programs. In: Cousot, P. (ed.) SAS 2001. LNCS, vol. 2126, pp. 111–126. Springer, Heidelberg (2001)
38. Motwani, R., Raghavan, P.: Randomized Algorithms. Cambridge University Press, New York (1995)
39. Paz, A.: Introduction to Probabilistic Automata. Computer Science and Applied Mathematics. Academic Press, New York (1971)

40. Podelski, A., Rybalchenko, A.: A complete method for the synthesis of linear rank-
    ing functions. In: Steffen, B., Levi, G. (eds.) VMCAI 2004. LNCS, vol. 2937, pp.
    239–251. Springer, Heidelberg (2004)
41. Putinar, M.: Positive polynomials on compact semi-algebraic sets. Indiana Univ.
    Math. J. **42**, 969–984 (1993)
42. Rabin, M.: Probabilistic automata. Inf. Control **6**, 230–245 (1963)
43. Sankaranarayanan, S., Chakarov, A., Gulwani, S.: Static analysis for probabilistic
    programs: inferring whole program properties from finitely many paths. In: PLDI,
    pp. 447–458 (2013)
44. Scheiderer, C.: Positivity and sums of squares: a guide to recent results. In: Putinar,
    M., Sullivant, S. (eds.) Emerging Applications of Algebraic Geometry. IMAVMA,
    vol. 149, pp. 271–324. Springer, New York (1996)
45. Schmüdgen, K.: The K-moment problem for compact semi-algebraic sets. Math.
    Ann. **289**, 203–206 (1991)
46. Schrijver, A.: Theory of Linear and Integer Programming. Wiley-Interscience Series
    in Discrete Mathematics and Optimization. Wiley, New York (1999)
47. Shen, L., Wu, M., Yang, Z., Zeng, Z.: Generating exact nonlinear ranking functions
    by symbolic-numeric hybrid method. J. Syst. Sci. Comput. **26**(2), 291–301 (2013)
48. Sohn, K., Gelder, A.V.: Termination detection in logic programs using argument
    sizes. In: PODS, pp. 216–226. ACM Press (1991)
49. Williams, D.: Probability with Martingales. Cambridge University Press, Cam-
    bridge (1991)
50. Yang, L., Zhou, C., Zhan, N., Xia, B.: Recent advances in program verification
    through computer algebra. Front. Comput. Sci. China **4**(1), 1–16 (2010)

Markov Chains and Unambiguous Büchi Automata

Christel Baier[1], Stefan Kiefer[2], Joachim Klein[1], Sascha Klüppelholz[1],
David Müller[1(✉)], and James Worrell[2]

[1] Technische Universität Dresden,
Dresden, Germany
david.mueller2@tu-dresden.de

[2] University of Oxford, Oxford, United Kingdom

Abstract. Unambiguous automata, i.e., nondeterministic automata with the restriction of having at most one accepting run over a word, have the potential to be used instead of deterministic automata in settings where nondeterministic automata can not be applied in general. In this paper, we provide a polynomially time-bounded algorithm for probabilistic model checking of discrete-time Markov chains against unambiguous Büchi automata specifications and report on our implementation and experiments.

1 Introduction

Unambiguity is a widely studied generalization of determinism with many important applications in automata-theoretic approaches, see e.g. [12,13]. A nondetermistic automaton is said to be unambiguous if each word has at most one accepting run. In this paper we consider unambiguous Büchi automata (UBA) over infinite words. Not only are UBA as expressive as the full class of nondeterministic Büchi automata (NBA) [2], they can also be exponentially more succinct than deterministic automata. For example, the language "eventually b occurs and a appears k steps before the first b" over the alphabet $\{a, b, c\}$ is recognizable by a UBA with $k+1$ states (see the UBA on the left of Fig. 1), while a deterministic automaton requires at least 2^k states, regardless of the acceptance condition, as it needs to store the positions of the a's among the last k input symbols. Languages of this type arise in a number of contexts, e.g., absence of unsolicited response in a communication protocol – if a message is received, then it has been sent in the recent past.

C. Baier, J. Klein, S. Klüppelholz and D. Müller—The authors are supported by the DFG through the Collaborative Research Center SFB 912 – HAEC, the Excellence Initiative by the German Federal and State Governments (cluster of excellence cfAED and Institutional Strategy), and the Research Training Groups QuantLA (GRK 1763) and RoSI (GRK 1907).

S. Kiefer is supported by a University Research Fellowship of the Royal Society. J. Worrell is supported by EPSRC grant EP/M012298/1.

© Springer International Publishing Switzerland 2016
S. Chaudhuri and A. Farzan (Eds.): CAV 2016, Part I, LNCS 9779, pp. 23–42, 2016.
DOI: 10.1007/978-3-319-41528-4_2

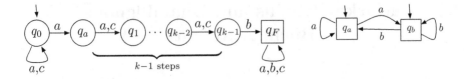

Fig. 1. Two UBA (where final states are depicted as boxes)

Furthermore, the NBA for linear temporal logic (LTL) formulas obtained by applying the classical closure algorithm of [39,40] are unambiguous. The generated automata moreover enjoy the separation property: the languages of the states are pairwise disjoint. Thus, while the generation of deterministic ω-automata from LTL formulas involves a double exponential blow-up in the worst case, the translation of LTL formulas into separated UBA incurs only a single exponential blow-up. This fact has been observed by several authors, see e.g. [16,34], and recently adapted for LTL with step parameters [11,41].

These nice properties make UBA a potentially attractive alternative to deterministic ω-automata in those applications for which general nondeterministic automata are not suitable. However reasoning about UBA is surprisingly difficult. While many decision problems for unambiguous finite automata (UFA) are known to be solvable in polynomial time [37], the complexity of several fundamental problems for unambiguous automata over infinite words is unknown. This, for instance, applies to the universality problem, which is known to be in P for deterministic Büchi automata (DBA) and PSPACE-complete for NBA. However, the complexity of the universality problem for UBA is a long-standing open problem. Polynomial-time solutions are only known for separated UBA and other subclasses of UBA [9,26].

In the context of probabilistic model checking, UFA provide an elegant approach to compute the probability for a regular safety or co-safety property in finite-state Markov chains [7]. The use of separated UBA for a single exponential-time algorithm that computes the probability for an LTL formula in a Markov chain has been presented in [16]. However, separation is a rather strong condition and non-separated UBA (and even DBA) can be exponentially more succinct than separated UBA, see [9]. This motivates the design of algorithms that operate with general UBA rather than the subclass of separated UBA. Algorithms for the generation of (possibly non-separated) UBA from LTL formulas that are more compact than the separated UBA generated by the classical closure-algorithm have been realized in the tool `Tulip` [32,33] and the automata library `SPOT` [17].

The main theoretical contribution of this paper is a polynomial-time algorithm to compute the probability measure $\Pr^{\mathcal{M}}(\mathcal{L}_\omega(\mathcal{U}))$ of the set of infinite paths generated by a finite-state Markov chain $\mathcal{M}$ that satisfy an ω-regular property given by a (not necessarily separated) UBA $\mathcal{U}$. The existence of such an algorithm has previously been claimed in [6,7,33] (see also [32]). However these previous works share a common fundamental error. Specifically they rely on the claim that if $\Pr^{\mathcal{M}}(\mathcal{L}_\omega(\mathcal{U})) > 0$ then there exists a state s of the Markov chain $\mathcal{M}$ and a state q of the automaton $\mathcal{U}$ such that q accepts almost all trajectories emanating from s (see [7, Lemma 7.1], [6, Theorem 2][1], and [33, Sect. 3.3.1]). While this claim is true in case $\mathcal{U}$ is deterministic [14], it need not hold when $\mathcal{U}$ is merely unambiguous. Indeed, as we explain in Remark 3, a counterexample is obtained by taking $\mathcal{U}$ to be the automaton on the right in Fig. 1 and $\mathcal{M}$ the Markov chain that generates the uniform distribution on $\{a,b\}^\omega$. The long version of this paper [4] gives a more detailed analysis of the issue, describing precisely the nature of the errors in the proofs of [6,7,33]. To the best of our knowledge these errors are not easily fixable, and the present paper takes a substantially different approach.

Our algorithm involves a two-phase method that first analyzes the strongly connected components (SCCs) of a graph obtained from the product of $\mathcal{M}$ and $\mathcal{U}$, and then computes the value $\mathrm{Pr}^{\mathcal{M}}(\mathcal{L}_\omega(\mathcal{U}))$ using linear equation systems. The main challenge is the treatment of the individual SCCs. For a given SCC we have an equation system comprising a single variable and equation for each vertex (s,q), with s a state of $\mathcal{M}$ and q a state of $\mathcal{U}$. We use results in the spectral theory of non-negative matrices to argue that this equation system has a non-zero solution just in case the SCC makes a non-zero contribution to $\mathrm{Pr}^{\mathcal{M}}(\mathcal{L}_\omega(\mathcal{U}))$. In order to compute the exact value of $\mathrm{Pr}^{\mathcal{M}}(\mathcal{L}_\omega(\mathcal{U}))$ the key idea is to introduce an additional normalization equation. To obtain the latter we identify a pair (s,R), where s is a state of the Markov chain $\mathcal{M}$ and R a set of states of automaton $\mathcal{U}$ such that almost all paths starting in s have an accepting run in $\mathcal{U}$ when the states in R are declared to be initial. The crux of establishing a polynomial bound on the running time of our algorithm is to find such a pair (s,R) efficiently (in particular, without determinizing $\mathcal{U}$) by exploiting structural properties of unambiguous automata.

As a consequence of our main result, we obtain that the *almost universality* problem for UBA, which can be seen as probabilistic variant of the universality problem for UBA and which asks whether a given UBA accepts almost all infinite words, is solvable in polynomial time.

The second contribution of the paper is an implementation of the new algorithm as an extension of the model checker PRISM, using the automata library SPOT [17] for the generation of UBA from LTL formulas and the COLT library [25] for various linear algebra algorithms. We evaluate our approach using the bounded retransmission protocol case study from the PRISM benchmark suite [31] as well as specific aspects of our algorithm using particularly "challenging" UBA.

Outline. Section 2 summarizes our notations for Büchi automata and Markov chains. The theoretical contribution will be presented in Sect. 3. Section 4 reports on the implementation and experimental results. Section 5 contains concluding remarks. The full version of this paper [4] contains an appendix with the counterexamples for the previous approaches, proofs and further details on the implementation and results of experimental studies. Further information is available on the website [1] as well.

---

[1] As the flaw is in the handling of the infinite behavior, the claim and proof of Lemma 1 in [6], dealing with unambiguous automata over finite words, remain unaffected.

2   Preliminaries

We suppose the reader to be familiar with the basic notions of ω-automata and Markov chains, see e.g. [22,29]. In what follows, we provide a brief summary of our notations for languages and the uniform probability measure on infinite words, Büchi automata as well as Markov chains.

Prefixes, Cylinder Sets and Uniform Probability Measure for Infinite Words. Throughout the document, we suppose Σ is a finite alphabet with two or more elements. If $w = a_1 a_2 a_3 \ldots \in \Sigma^\omega$ is an infinite word then $Pref(w)$ denotes the set of finite prefixes of w, i.e., $Pref(w)$ consists of the empty word and all finite words $a_1 a_2 \ldots a_n$ where $n \geqslant 1$. Given a finite word $x = a_1 a_2 \ldots a_n \in \Sigma^*$, the cylinder set of x, denoted $Cyl(x)$, is the set of infinite words $w \in \Sigma^\omega$ such that $x \in Pref(w)$. The set Σ^ω of infinite words over Σ is supposed to be equipped with the σ-algebra generated by the cylinder sets of the finite words and the probability measure given by $\mathrm{Pr}\big(Cyl(a_1 a_2 \ldots a_n) \big) = 1/|\Sigma|^n$ where $a_1, \ldots, a_n \in \Sigma$. Note that all ω-regular languages over Σ are measurable. We often make use of the following lemma (see [4] for its proof):

Lemma 1. *If $L \subseteq \Sigma^\omega$ is ω-regular and $\mathrm{Pr}(L) > 0$ then there exists $x \in \Sigma^*$ such that $\mathrm{Pr}\big\{ w \in \Sigma^\omega : xw \in L \big\} = 1$.*

Büchi Automata. A nondeterministic Büchi automaton is a tuple $\mathcal{A} = (Q, \Sigma, \delta, Q_0, F)$ where Q is a finite set of states, $Q_0 \subseteq Q$ is a set of initial states, Σ denotes the alphabet, $\delta : Q \times \Sigma \to 2^Q$ denotes the transition function, and F is a set of accepting states. We extend the transition function $\delta : 2^Q \times \Sigma \to 2^Q$ in the standard way for subsets of Q and finite words over Σ. Given states $q, p \in Q$ and a finite word $x = a_1 a_2 \ldots a_n \in \Sigma^*$ then a run for x from q to p is a sequence $q_0 q_1 \ldots q_n \in Q^+$ with $q_0 = q$, $q_n = p$ and $q_{i+1} \in \delta(q_i, a_{i+1})$ for $0 \leqslant i < n$. A run in $\mathcal{A}$ for an infinite word $w = a_1 a_2 a_3 \ldots \in \Sigma^\omega$ is an infinite sequence $\rho = q_0 q_1 \ldots \in Q^\omega$ such that $q_{i+1} \in \delta(q_i, a_{i+1})$ for all $i \in \mathbb{N}$ and $q_0 \in Q_0$. Run ρ is called accepting, if $q_i \in F$ for infinitely many $i \in \mathbb{N}$. The language $\mathcal{L}_\omega(\mathcal{A})$ of accepted words consists of all infinite words $w \in \Sigma^\omega$ that have at least one accepting run. If $R \subseteq Q$ then $\mathcal{A}[R]$ denotes the automaton $\mathcal{A}$ with R as set of initial states. For $q \in Q$, $\mathcal{A}[q] = \mathcal{A}[\{q\}]$. If $\mathcal{A}$ is understood from the context, then we write $\mathcal{L}_\omega(R)$ rather than $\mathcal{L}_\omega(\mathcal{A}[R])$ and $\mathcal{L}_\omega(q)$ rather than $\mathcal{L}_\omega(\mathcal{A}[q])$. $\mathcal{A}$ is called deterministic if Q_0 is a singleton and $|\delta(q, a)| \leqslant 1$ for all states q and symbols $a \in \Sigma$ and unambiguous if each word $w \in \Sigma^\omega$ has at most one accepting run in $\mathcal{A}$. Clearly, each deterministic automaton is unambiguous. We use the shortform notations NBA, DBA and UBA for nondeterministic, deterministic and unambiguous Büchi automata, respectively.

Markov Chains. In this paper we only consider finite-state discrete-time Markov chains. Formally, a Markov chain is a triple $\mathcal{M} = (S, P, \iota)$ where S is a finite set of states, $P : S \times S \to [0, 1]$ is the transition probability function satisfying $\sum_{s' \in S} P(s, s') = 1$ for all states $s \in S$ and ι an initial distribution on S. We write $\mathrm{Pr}^{\mathcal{M}}$ to denote the standard probability measure on the infinite paths of $\mathcal{M}$.

For $s \in S$, the notation $\Pr_s^{\mathcal{M}}$ will be used for $\Pr^{\mathcal{M}_s}$ where $\mathcal{M}_s = (S, P, \mathrm{Dirac}[s])$ and $\mathrm{Dirac}[s] : S \to [0, 1]$ denotes the Dirac distribution that assigns probability 1 to state s and 0 to all other states. If $L \subseteq S^\omega$ is measurable then $\Pr^{\mathcal{M}}(L)$ is a short-form notation for the probability for $\mathcal{M}$ to generate an infinite path π with $\pi \in L$.

Occasionally, we also consider Markov chains with transition labels in some alphabet Σ. These are defined as triples $\mathcal{M} = (S, P, \iota)$ where S and ι are as above and the transition probability function is of the type $P : S \times \Sigma \times S \to [0, 1]$ such that $\sum_{(a,s') \in \Sigma \times S} P(s, a, s') = 1$ for all states $s \in S$. If $L \subseteq \Sigma^\omega$ is measurable then $\Pr^{\mathcal{M}}(L)$ denotes the probability measure of the set of infinite paths π where the projection to the transition labels constitutes a word in L. Furthermore, if $\mathcal{M}[\Sigma] = (S, P, \iota)$ is a transition-labeled Markov chain where $S = \{s\}$ is a singleton and $P(s, a, s) = 1/|\Sigma|$ for all symbols $a \in \Sigma$, then $\Pr^{\mathcal{M}[\Sigma]}(L) = \Pr(L)$ for all measurable languages L.

3   Analysis of Markov Chains Against UBA-specifications

The task of the *probabilistic model-checking problem* for a given Markov chain $\mathcal{M}$ and NBA $\mathcal{A}$ is to compute $\Pr^{\mathcal{M}}(\mathcal{L}_\omega(\mathcal{A}))$ where $\mathcal{M}$ is either a plain Markov chain and the alphabet of $\mathcal{A}$ is the state space of $\mathcal{M}$ or the transitions of $\mathcal{M}$ are labeled by symbols of the alphabet of $\mathcal{A}$. The *positive model-checking problem* for $\mathcal{M}$ and $\mathcal{A}$ asks whether $\Pr^{\mathcal{M}}(\mathcal{L}_\omega(\mathcal{A})) > 0$. Likewise, the *almost-sure model-checking problem* for $\mathcal{M}$ and $\mathcal{A}$ denotes the task to check whether $\Pr^{\mathcal{M}}(\mathcal{L}_\omega(\mathcal{A})) = 1$. While the positive and the almost-sure probabilistic model-checking problems for Markov chains and NBA are both known to be PSPACE-complete [14,38], the analysis of Markov chains against UBA-specification can be carried out efficiently as stated in the following theorem:

Theorem 2. *Given a Markov chain $\mathcal{M}$ and a UBA $\mathcal{U}$, the value $\Pr^{\mathcal{M}}(\mathcal{L}_\omega(\mathcal{U}))$ is computable in time polynomial in the sizes of $\mathcal{M}$ and $\mathcal{U}$.*

Remark 3. The statement of Theorem 2 has already been presented in [5] (see also [6,33]). However, the presented algorithm to compute $\Pr^{\mathcal{M}}(\mathcal{L}_\omega(\mathcal{U}))$ is flawed. This approach, rephrased for the special case where the task is to compute $\Pr(\mathcal{L}_\omega(\mathcal{U}))$ for a given positive UBA $\mathcal{U}$ (which means a UBA where $\Pr(\mathcal{L}_\omega(\mathcal{U})) > 0$) relies on the mistaken belief that there is at least one state q in $\mathcal{U}$ such that $\Pr(\mathcal{L}_\omega(\mathcal{U}[q])) = 1$. However, such states need not exist. To illustrate this, we consider the UBA $\mathcal{U}$ with two states q_a and q_b and $\delta(q_a, a) = \delta(q_b, b) = \{q_a, q_b\}$ and $\delta(q_a, b) = \delta(q_b, a) = \varnothing$. (See the UBA on the right of Fig. 1.) Both states are initial and final. Clearly, $\mathcal{L}_\omega(\mathcal{U}[q_a]) = a\Sigma^\omega$ and $\mathcal{L}_\omega(\mathcal{U}[q_b]) = b\Sigma^\omega$. Thus, $\mathcal{U}$ is universal and $\Pr(\mathcal{L}_\omega(\mathcal{U})) = 1$, while $\Pr(\mathcal{L}_\omega(\mathcal{U}[q_a])) = \Pr(\mathcal{L}_\omega(\mathcal{U}[q_b])) = \frac{1}{2}$.

Outline of Section 3. The remainder of Sect. 3 is devoted to the proof of Theorem 2. We first assume that the Markov chain $\mathcal{M}$ generates all words according to a uniform distribution and explain how to compute the value $\Pr(\mathcal{L}_\omega(\mathcal{U}))$ for a given UBA $\mathcal{U}$ in polynomial time. For this, we first address the case of strongly connected UBA (Sect. 3.1) and then lift the result to the general case

(Sect. 3.2). The central idea of the algorithm relies on the observation that each positive, strongly connected UBA has "recurrent sets" of states, called *cuts*. We exploit structural properties of unambiguous automata for the efficient construction of a cut and show how to compute the values $\Pr(\mathcal{L}_\omega(\mathcal{U}[q]))$ for the states of $\mathcal{U}$ by a linear equation system with one equation per state and one equation for the generated cut. Furthermore, positivity of a UBA $\mathcal{U}$ (i.e., $\Pr(\mathcal{L}_\omega(\mathcal{U})) > 0$) is shown to be equivalent to the existence of a positive solution of the system of linear equations for the states. Finally, we explain how to adapt these techniques to general Markov chains (Sect. 3.3).

3.1 Strongly Connected UBA

We start with some general observations about strongly connected Büchi automata under the probabilistic semantics. For this, we suppose $\mathcal{A} = (Q, \Sigma, \delta, Q_0, F)$ is a strongly connected NBA where Q_0 and F are nonempty. Clearly, $\mathcal{L}_\omega(q) \neq \varnothing$ for all states q and

$$\Pr(\mathcal{L}_\omega(\mathcal{A})) > 0 \quad \text{iff} \quad \Pr(\mathcal{L}_\omega(q)) > 0 \text{ for some state } q$$
$$\text{iff} \quad \Pr(\mathcal{L}_\omega(q)) > 0 \text{ for all states } q$$

Moreover, almost all words $w \in \Sigma^\omega \setminus \mathcal{L}_\omega(\mathcal{A})$ have a finite prefix x with $\delta(Q_0, x) = \varnothing$ (for the proof see [4]):

Lemma 4 (Measure of strongly connected NBA). *For each strongly connected NBA $\mathcal{A}$ with at least one final state, we have:*

$$\Pr(\mathcal{L}_\omega(\mathcal{A})) \;=\; 1 - \Pr\big\{\, w \in \Sigma^\omega \,:\, w \text{ has a finite prefix } x \text{ with } \delta(Q_0, x) = \varnothing \,\big\}$$

In particular, $\mathcal{A}$ is almost universal if and only if $\delta(Q_0, x) \neq \varnothing$ for all finite words $x \in \Sigma^*$. This observation will be crucial at several places in the soundness proof of our algorithm for UBA, but can also be used to establish PSPACE-hardness of the positivity (probabilistic nonemptiness) and almost universality problem for strongly connected NBA, see [4]. For computing $\Pr(\mathcal{L}_\omega(\mathcal{U}))$ given a UBA $\mathcal{U}$, it suffices to compute the values $\Pr(\mathcal{L}_\omega(q))$ for the (initial) states of $\mathcal{U}$ as we have

$$\Pr(\mathcal{L}_\omega(\mathcal{U})) = \sum_{q \in Q_0} \Pr(\mathcal{L}_\omega(q))$$

Furthermore, in each strongly connected UBA, the accepting runs of almost all words $w \in \mathcal{L}_\omega(\mathcal{U})$ visit each state of $\mathcal{U}$ infinitely often (see [4]).

Deciding Positivity for Strongly Connected UBA. The following lemma provides a criterion to check positivity of a strongly connected UBA in polynomial time using standard linear algebra techniques.

Lemma 5. *Let $\mathcal{U}$ be a strongly connected UBA with at least one initial and one final state, and*

$$(*) \qquad \zeta_q = \frac{1}{|\Sigma|} \cdot \sum_{a \in \Sigma} \sum_{p \in \delta(q,a)} \zeta_p \qquad \text{for all } q \in Q$$

Then, the following statements are equivalent:

(1) $\Pr(\mathcal{L}_\omega(\mathcal{U})) > 0$,
(2) *the linear equation system (*) has a strictly positive solution, i.e., a solution $(\zeta_q^*)_{q \in Q}$ with $\zeta_q^* > 0$ for all $q \in Q$,*
(3) *the linear equation system (*) has a non-zero solution.*

Given the strongly connected UBA $\mathcal{U}$ with at least one final state, we define a matrix $M \in [0,1]^{Q \times Q}$ by $M_{p,q} = \frac{1}{|\Sigma|}|\{a \in \Sigma : q \in \delta(p,a)\}|$ for all $p,q \in Q$. Since $\mathcal{U}$ is strongly connected, M is irreducible. Write $\rho(M)$ for the spectral radius of M. We will use the following Lemma in the proof of Lemma 5.

Lemma 6. *We have $\rho(M) \leq 1$. Moreover $\rho(M) = 1$ if and only if $\Pr(\mathcal{L}_\omega(\mathcal{U})) > 0$.*

Proof. For $p,q \in Q$ and $n \in \mathbb{N}$, let $E_{p,n,q} \subseteq \Sigma^\omega$ denote the event of all words $w = a_1 a_2 \ldots$ such that $q \in \delta(p, a_1 a_2 \ldots a_n)$. Its probability under the uniform distribution on Σ^ω is an entry in the n-th power of M:

$$\Pr(E_{p,n,q}) = (M^n)_{p,q} \tag{1}$$

In particular, $M_{p,q}^n \leq 1$ for all n. From the boundedness of M^n it follows (e.g., by [24, Corollary 8.1.33]) that $\rho(M) \leq 1$. The same result implies that

$$\rho(M) = 1 \quad \Longleftrightarrow \quad \limsup_{n \to \infty} (M^n)_{p,q} > 0 \quad \text{for all } p,q \in Q$$
$$\Longleftrightarrow \quad \limsup_{n \to \infty} (M^n)_{p,q} > 0 \quad \text{for some } p,q \in Q \tag{2}$$

For the rest of the proof, fix some state $p \in Q$. By the observations from the beginning of Sect. 3.1 it suffices to show that $\Pr(\mathcal{L}_\omega(p)) > 0$ if and only if $\rho(M) = 1$. To this end, consider the event $E_{p,n} := \bigcup_{q \in Q} E_{p,n,q}$. Notice that $(E_{p,n})_{n \in \mathbb{N}}$ forms a decreasing family of sets. We have:

$$\Pr(\mathcal{L}_\omega(p)) = \lim_{n \to \infty} \Pr(E_{p,n}) \qquad \text{by Lemma 4}$$

$$= \lim_{n \to \infty} \Pr\left(\bigcup_{q \in Q} E_{p,n,q}\right) \qquad \text{definition of } E_{p,n} \tag{3}$$

Assuming that $\rho(M) = 1$, we show that $\Pr(\mathcal{L}_\omega(p)) > 0$. Let $q \in Q$. We have:

$$\Pr(\mathcal{L}_\omega(p)) \geq \limsup_{n \to \infty} \Pr(E_{p,n,q}) \qquad \text{by (3)}$$

$$= \limsup_{n \to \infty} (M^n)_{p,q} \qquad \text{by (1)}$$

$$> 0 \qquad \text{by (2)}$$

Conversely, assuming that $\rho(M) < 1$, we show that $\Pr(\mathcal{L}_\omega(p)) = 0$.

$$
\begin{aligned}
\Pr(\mathcal{L}_\omega(p)) &= \lim_{n\to\infty} \Pr\left(\bigcup_{q\in Q} E_{p,n,q}\right) & \text{by (3)} \\
&\le \limsup_{n\to\infty} \sum_{q\in Q} \Pr(E_{p,n,q}) & \text{union bound} \\
&= \limsup_{n\to\infty} \sum_{q\in Q} (M^n)_{p,q} & \text{by (1)} \\
&= 0 & \text{by (2)}
\end{aligned}
$$

This concludes the proof. $\qquad\square$

Proof (of Lemma 5). "(1) $\Longrightarrow$ (2)": Suppose $\Pr(\mathcal{L}_\omega(\mathcal{U})) > 0$. Define the vector $(\zeta_q^*)_{q\in Q}$ with $\zeta_q^* = \Pr(\mathcal{L}_\omega(q))$. It holds that

$$
\mathcal{L}_\omega(q) = \bigcup_{a\in\Sigma} \bigcup_{p\in\delta(q,a)} \{aw : w \in \mathcal{L}_\omega(p)\}
$$

Since $\mathcal{U}$ is unambiguous, the sets $\{aw : w \in \mathcal{L}_\omega(p)\}$ are pairwise disjoint. So, the vector $(\zeta_q^*)_{q\in Q}$ is a solution to the equation system.

As $\Pr(\mathcal{L}_\omega(\mathcal{U})) > 0$ and $\mathcal{U}$ is strongly connected, the observation at the beginning of Sect. 3.1 yields that $\Pr(\mathcal{L}_\omega(q)) > 0$ for all states q. Thus, the vector $(\zeta_q^*)_{q\in Q}$ is strictly positive.

"(2) $\Longrightarrow$ (3)" holds trivially.

"(3) $\Longrightarrow$ (1)": Suppose ζ^* is a non-zero solution of the linear equation system. Then, $M\zeta^* = \zeta^*$. Thus, 1 is an eigenvalue of M. This yields $\rho(M) \geqslant 1$. But then $\rho(M) = 1$ and $\Pr(\mathcal{L}_\omega(\mathcal{U})) > 0$ by Lemma 6. $\qquad\square$

Computing Pure Cuts for Positive, Strongly Connected UBA. The key observation to compute the values $\Pr(\mathcal{L}_\omega(q))$ for the states q of a positive, strongly connected UBA $\mathcal{U}$ is the existence of so-called cuts. These are sets C of states with pairwise disjoint languages such that almost all words have an accepting run starting in some state $q \in C$. More precisely:

Definition 7 ((Pure) cut). *Let $\mathcal{U}$ be a UBA and $C \subseteq Q$. C is called a* cut *for $\mathcal{U}$ if $\mathcal{L}_\omega(q) \cap \mathcal{L}_\omega(p) = \varnothing$ for all $p, q \in C$ with $p \neq q$ and $\mathcal{U}[C]$ is almost universal. A cut is called* pure *if it has the form $\delta(q, z)$ for some state q and some finite word $z \in \Sigma^*$.*

Obviously, $\mathcal{U}$ is almost universal iff Q_0 is a cut. If $q \in Q$ and K_q denotes the set of finite words $z \in \Sigma^*$ such that $\delta(q, z)$ is a cut then $\Pr(\mathcal{L}_\omega(q))$ equals the probability measure of the language L_q consisting of all infinite words $w \in \Sigma^\omega$ that have a prefix in K_q, see [4].

Lemma 8 (Characterization of pure cuts). *Let $\mathcal{U}$ be a strongly connected UBA. For all $q \in Q$ and $z \in \Sigma^*$ we have: $\delta(q,z)$ is a cut iff $\delta(q,zy) \neq \varnothing$ for each word $y \in \Sigma^*$. Furthermore, if $\mathcal{U}$ is positive then for each cut C:*

$$C \text{ is pure, i.e., } C = \delta(q,z) \text{ for some state-word pair } (q,z) \in Q \times \Sigma^*$$

iff for each state $q \in Q$ there is some word $z \in \Sigma^*$ with $C = \delta(q,z)$

iff for each cut C' there is some word $y \in \Sigma^*$ with $C = \delta(C',y)$

The proof of Lemma 8 is provided in [4]. By Lemmas 1 and 8 we get:

Corollary 9. *If $\mathcal{U}$ is a strongly connected UBA then $\Pr(\mathcal{L}_\omega(\mathcal{U})) > 0$ iff $\mathcal{U}$ has a pure cut.*

For the rest of Sect. 3.1, we suppose that $\mathcal{U}$ is positive and strongly connected. The second part of Lemma 8 yields that the pure cuts constitute a bottom strongly connected component of the automaton obtained from $\mathcal{U}$ using the standard powerset construction. The goal is now to design an efficient (polynomially time-bounded) algorithm for the generation of a pure cut. For this, we observe that if $q, p \in Q$, $q \neq p$, then $\{q,p\} \subseteq C$ for some pure cut C iff there exists a word y such that $\{q,p\} \subseteq \delta(q,y)$, see [4].

Definition 10 (Extension). *A word $y \in \Sigma^*$ is an extension for a state-word pair $(q,z) \in Q \times \Sigma^*$ iff there exists a state $p \in Q$ such that $q \neq p$, $\delta(p,z) \neq \varnothing$ and $\{q,p\} \subseteq \delta(q,y)$.*

It is easy to see that if y is an extension of (q,z), then $\delta(q,yz)$ is a proper superset of $\delta(q,z)$ (see [4]). Furthermore, for all state-word pairs $(q,z) \in Q \times \Sigma^*$ (see [4]):

$$\delta(q,z) \text{ is a cut} \quad \text{iff} \quad \text{there is no extension for } (q,z)$$

These observations lead to the following algorithm for the construction of a pure cut. We pick an arbitrary state q in the UBA and start with the empty word $z_0 = \varepsilon$. The algorithm iteratively seeks for an extension for the state-word pair (q, z_i). If an extension y_i for (q, z_i) has been found then we switch to the word $z_{i+1} = y_i z_i$. If no extension exists then (q, z_i) is a pure cut. In this way, the algorithm generates an increasing sequence of subsets of Q,

$$\delta(q,z_0) \subsetneq \delta(q,z_1) \subsetneq \delta(q,z_2) \subsetneq \ldots \subsetneq \delta(q,z_k),$$

which terminates after at most $|Q|$ steps and yields a pure cut $\delta(q,z_k)$.

It remains to explain an efficient realization of the search for an extension of the state-word pairs (q, z_i). The idea is to store the sets $Q_i[p] = \delta(p, z_i)$ for all states p. The sets $Q_i[p]$ can be computed iteratively by:

$$Q_0[p] = \{p\} \quad \text{and} \quad Q_{i+1}[p] = \bigcup_{r \in \delta(p,y_i)} Q_i[r]$$

To check whether (q, z_i) has an extension we apply standard techniques for the intersection problem for the languages $H_{q,q} = \{y \in \Sigma^* : q \in \delta(q,y)\}$ and

$H_{q,F_i} = \{y \in \Sigma^* : \delta(q,y) \cap F_i \neq \varnothing\}$ where $F_i = \{p \in Q \setminus \{q\} : Q_i[p] \neq \varnothing\}$. Then, for each word $y \in \Sigma^*$ we have: $y \in H_{q,q} \cap H_{q,F_i}$ if and only if y is an extension of (q, z_i). The languages $H_{q,q}$ and H_{q,F_i} are recognized by the NFA $\mathcal{U}_{q,q} = (Q, \Sigma, \delta, q, q)$ and $\mathcal{U}_{q,F_i} = (Q, \Sigma, \delta, q, F_i)$. Thus, to check the existence of an extension and to compute an extension y (if existent) where the word y has length at most $|Q|^2$, we may run an emptiness check for the product-NFA $\mathcal{U}[q, q] \otimes \mathcal{U}[q, F_i]$. We conclude:

Corollary 11. *Given a positive, strongly connected UBA $\mathcal{U}$, a pure cut can be computed in time polynomial in the size of $\mathcal{U}$.*

Computing the Measure of Positive, Strongly Connected UBA. We suppose that $\mathcal{U} = (Q, \Sigma, \delta, Q_0, F)$ is a positive, strongly connected UBA and C is a cut. (C might be a pure cut that has been computed by the techniques explained above. However, in Theorem 12 C can be any cut.) Consider the linear equation system of Lemma 5 with variables ζ_q for all states $q \in Q$ and add the constraint that the variables ζ_q for $q \in C$ sum up to 1.

Theorem 12. *Let $\mathcal{U}$ be a positive, strongly connected UBA and C a cut. Then, the probability vector $(\Pr(\mathcal{L}_\omega(q)))_{q \in Q}$ is the unique solution of the following linear equation system:*

$$(1) \quad \zeta_q = \frac{1}{|\Sigma|} \cdot \sum_{a \in \Sigma} \sum_{p \in \delta(q,a)} \zeta_p \qquad \text{for all states } q \in Q$$

$$(2) \quad \sum_{q \in C} \zeta_q = 1$$

Proof. Let $n = |Q|$. Define a matrix $M \in [0,1]^{Q \times Q}$ by $M_{q,p} = |\{a \in \Sigma : p \in \delta(q,a)\}|/|\Sigma|$ for all $q, p \in Q$. Then, the n equations (1) can be written as $\zeta = M\zeta$, where $\zeta = (\zeta_q)_{q \in Q}$ is a vector of n variables. It is easy to see that the values $\zeta_q^* = \Pr(\mathcal{L}_\omega(q))$ for $q \in Q$ satisfy the equations (1). That is, defining $\zeta^* = (\zeta_q^*)_{q \in Q}$ we have $\zeta^* = M\zeta^*$. By the definition of a cut, those values also satisfy Eq. (2).

It remains to show uniqueness. We employ Perron-Frobenius theory as follows. Since $\zeta^* = M\zeta^*$, the vector ζ^* is an eigenvector of M with eigenvalue 1. Since ζ^* is strictly positive (i.e., positive in all components), it follows from [8, Corollary 2.1.12] that $\rho = 1$ for the spectral radius ρ of M. Since $\mathcal{U}$ is strongly connected, matrix M is irreducible. By [8, Theorem 2.1.4 (b)] the spectral radius $\rho = 1$ is a simple eigenvalue of M, i.e., all solutions of $\zeta = M\zeta$ are scalar multiples of ζ^*. Among those multiples, only ζ^* satisfies Eq. (2). Uniqueness follows. ∎

Together with the criterion of Lemma 5 to check whether a given strongly connected UBA is positive, we obtain a polynomially time-bounded computation scheme for the values $\Pr(\mathcal{L}_\omega(q))$ for the states q of a given strongly connected UBA. The next section shows how to lift these results for arbitrary UBA.

3.2   Computing the Measure of Arbitrary UBA

In what follows, let $\mathcal{U} = (Q, \Sigma, \delta, Q_0, F)$ be a (possibly not strongly connected) UBA. We assume that all states are reachable from Q_0 and that F is reachable from all states. Thus, $\mathcal{L}_\omega(q) \neq \varnothing$ for all states q.

Let $\mathcal{C}$ be a strongly connected component (SCC) of $\mathcal{U}$. $\mathcal{C}$ is called non-trivial if $\mathcal{C}$ viewed as a direct graph contains at least one edge, i.e., if $\mathcal{C}$ is cyclic. $\mathcal{C}$ is called bottom if $\delta(q, a) \subseteq \mathcal{C}$ for all $q \in \mathcal{C}$ and all $a \in \Sigma$. We define Q_{BSCC} to be the set of all states $q \in Q$ that belong to some bottom SCC (BSCC) of $\mathcal{U}$. If $\mathcal{C}$ is a non-trivial SCC of $\mathcal{U}$ and $p \in \mathcal{C}$ then the sub-NBA

$$\mathcal{U}\big|_{\mathcal{C},p} = (\mathcal{C}, \Sigma, \delta|_\mathcal{C}, \{p\}, \mathcal{C} \cap F)$$

of $\mathcal{U}$ with state space $\mathcal{C}$, initial state p and the transition function $\delta|_\mathcal{C}$ given by $\delta|_\mathcal{C}(q, a) = \delta(q, a) \cap \mathcal{C}$ is strongly connected and unambiguous. Let L_p be the accepted language, i.e., $L_p = \mathcal{L}_\omega(\mathcal{U}\big|_{\mathcal{C},p})$. The values $\Pr(L_p)$, $p \in \mathcal{C}$, can be computed using the techniques for strongly connected UBA presented in Sect. 3.1. A non-trivial SCC $\mathcal{C}$ is said to be positive if $\Pr(L_p) > 0$ for all/some state(s) p in $\mathcal{C}$.

We perform the following preprocessing. As before, for any $p \in Q$ we write $\mathcal{L}_\omega(p)$ for $\mathcal{L}_\omega(\mathcal{U}[p])$, and call p zero if $\Pr(\mathcal{L}_\omega(p)) = 0$. First we remove all states that are not reachable from any initial state. Then we run standard graph algorithms to compute the directed acyclic graph (DAG) of SCCs of $\mathcal{U}$. By processing the DAG bottom-up we can remove all zero states by running the following loop: If all BSCCs are marked (initially, all SCCs are unmarked) then exit the loop; otherwise pick an unmarked BSCC $\mathcal{C}$.

- If $\mathcal{C}$ is trivial or does not contain any final state then we remove it: more precisely, we remove it from the DAG of SCCs, and we modify $\mathcal{U}$ by deleting all transitions $p \xrightarrow{a} q$ where $q \in \mathcal{C}$.
- Otherwise, $\mathcal{C}$ is a non-trivial BSCC with at least one final state. We check whether $\mathcal{C}$ is positive by applying the techniques of Sect. 3.1. If it is positive, we mark it; otherwise we remove it as described above.

Note that this loop does not change $\Pr(\mathcal{L}_\omega(p))$ for any state p.

Let Q_{BSCC} denote the set of states in $\mathcal{U}$ that belong to some BSCC. The values $\Pr(\mathcal{L}_\omega(p))$ for the states $p \in Q_{BSCC}$ can be computed using the techniques of Sect. 3.1. The remaining task is to compute the values $\Pr(\mathcal{L}_\omega(q))$ for the states $q \in Q \setminus Q_{BSCC}$. For $q \in Q \setminus Q_{BSCC}$, let $\beta_q = 0$ if $\delta(q, a) \cap Q_{BSCC} = \varnothing$ for all $a \in \Sigma$. Otherwise:

$$\beta_q = \frac{1}{|\Sigma|} \cdot \sum_{a \in \Sigma} \sum_{p \in \delta(q,a) \cap Q_{BSCC}} \Pr(\mathcal{L}_\omega(p))$$

In [4] we show:

Theorem 13. *If all BSCCs of $\mathcal{U}$ are non-trivial and positive, then the linear equation system*

$$\zeta_q = \frac{1}{|\Sigma|} \cdot \sum_{a \in \Sigma} \sum_{\substack{r \in \delta(q,a) \\ r \notin Q_{BSCC}}} \zeta_r + \beta_q \qquad for q \in Q \setminus Q_{BSCC}$$

has a unique solution, namely $\zeta_q^* = \Pr(\mathcal{L}_\omega(q))$.

This yields that the value $\Pr(\mathcal{L}_\omega(\mathcal{U}))$ for given UBA $\mathcal{U}$ is computable in polynomial time.

Remark 14. For the special case where $\delta(q,a) = \{q\}$ for all $q \in F$ and $a \in \Sigma$, the language of $\mathcal{U}$ is a co-safety property and $\Pr(\mathcal{L}_\omega(q)) = 1$ if $q \in F = Q_{BSCC}$, when we assume that all BSCCs are non-trivial and positive. In this case, the linear equation system in Theorem 13 coincides with the linear equation system presented in [7] for computing the probability measure of the language of $\mathcal{U}$ viewed as an UFA.

Remark 15. As a consequence of our results, the positivity problem ("does $\Pr(\mathcal{L}_\omega(\mathcal{U})) > 0$ hold?") and the almost universality problem ("does $\Pr(\mathcal{L}_\omega(\mathcal{U})) = 1$ hold?") for UBA are solvable in polynomial time. This should be contrasted with the standard (non-probabilistic) semantics of UBA and the corresponding results for NBA. The non-emptiness problem for UBA is in P (this already holds for NBA), while the complexity-theoretic status of the universality problem for UBA is a long-standing open problem. For standard NBA, it is well known that the non-emptiness problem is in P and the universality problem is PSPACE-complete. However, the picture changes when switching to NBA with the probabilistic semantics as both the positivity problem and the almost universality problem for NBA are PSPACE-complete, even for strongly connected NBA (see [4]).

3.3 Probabilistic Model Checking of Markov Chains Against UBA

To complete the proof of Theorem 2, we show how the results of the previous section can be adapted to compute the value $\Pr^{\mathcal{M}}(\mathcal{L}_\omega(\mathcal{U}))$ for a Markov chain $\mathcal{M} = (S, P, \iota)$ and a UBA $\mathcal{U} = (Q, \Sigma, \delta, Q_0, F)$ with alphabet $\Sigma = S.$[2] The necessary adaptions to the proofs are detailed in [4].

If $\mathcal{A}$ is an NBA over the alphabet S and $s \in S$, then $\Pr_s^{\mathcal{M}}(\mathcal{A})$ denotes the probability $\Pr_s^{\mathcal{M}}(\Pi)$ with Π being the set of infinite paths $\pi = s_0 s_1 \ldots \in S^\omega$

---

[2] In practice, e.g., when the UBA is obtained from an LTL formula, the alphabet of the UBA is often defined as $\Sigma = 2^{AP}$ over a set of atomic propositions AP and the Markov chain is equipped with a labeling function from states to the atomic propositions that hold in each state. Clearly, unambiguity w.r.t. the alphabet 2^{AP} implies unambiguity w.r.t. the alphabet S when switching from the original transition function $\delta : Q \times 2^{AP} \to 2^Q$ to the transition function $\delta_S : Q \times S \to 2^Q$ given by $\delta_S(q,s) = \delta(q, L(s))$, where $L : S \to 2^{AP}$ denotes the labeling function of $\mathcal{M}$.

starting with $s_0 = s$ and such that $s_1 s_2 \ldots \in \mathcal{L}_\omega(\mathcal{A})$. Our algorithm relies on the observation that

$$\mathrm{Pr}^{\mathcal{M}}(\mathcal{L}_\omega(\mathcal{U})) = \sum_{s \in S} \iota(s) \cdot \mathrm{Pr}_s^{\mathcal{M}}(\mathcal{U}[\delta(Q_0, s)])$$

As the languages of the UBA $\mathcal{U}[q]$ for $q \in \delta(Q_0, s)$ are pairwise distinct (by the unambiguity of $\mathcal{U}$), we have $\mathrm{Pr}_s^{\mathcal{M}}(\mathcal{U}[\delta(Q_0, s)]) = \sum_{q \in \delta(Q_0, s)} \mathrm{Pr}_s^{\mathcal{M}}(\mathcal{U}[q])$.

Thus, the task is to compute the values $\mathrm{Pr}_s^{\mathcal{M}}(\mathcal{U}[q])$ for $s \in S$ and $q \in Q$. As a first step, we build a UBA $\mathcal{P} = \mathcal{M} \otimes \mathcal{U}$ that arises from the synchronous product of the UBA $\mathcal{U}$ with the underlying graph of the Markov chain $\mathcal{M}$. Formally, $\mathcal{P} = (S \times Q, \Sigma, \Delta, Q_0', S \times F)$ where Q_0' consists of all pairs $\langle s, q \rangle \in S \times Q$ where $\iota(s) > 0$ and $q \in \delta(Q_0, s)$. Let $s, t \in S$ and $q \in Q$. If $P(s, t) = 0$ then $\Delta(\langle s, q \rangle, t) = \varnothing$, while for $P(s, t) > 0$, the set $\Delta(\langle s, q \rangle, t)$ consists of all pairs $\langle t, p \rangle$ where $p \in \delta(q, s)$. We are only concerned with the reachable fragment of the product.

Given that $\mathcal{M}$ viewed as an automaton over the alphabet S behaves deterministically and we started with an unambiguous automaton $\mathcal{U}$, the product $\mathcal{P}$ is unambiguous as well. Let $\mathcal{P}[s, q]$ denote the UBA resulting from $\mathcal{P}$ by declaring $\langle s, q \rangle$ to be initial. It is easy to see that $\mathrm{Pr}_s^{\mathcal{M}}(\mathcal{P}[s, q]) = \mathrm{Pr}_s^{\mathcal{M}}(\mathcal{U}[q])$ for all states $\langle s, q \rangle$ of $\mathcal{P}$, as the product construction only removes transitions in $\mathcal{U}$ that can not occur in the Markov chain. Our goal is thus to compute the values $\mathrm{Pr}_s^{\mathcal{M}}(\mathcal{P}[s, q])$. For this, we remove all states $\langle s, q \rangle$ from $\mathcal{P}$ that can not reach a state in $S \times F$. Then, we determine the non-trivial SCCs of $\mathcal{P}$ and, for each such SCC $\mathcal{C}$, we analyze the sub-UBA $\mathcal{P}|_{\mathcal{C}}$ obtained by restricting to the states in $\mathcal{C}$. An SCC $\mathcal{C}$ of $\mathcal{P}$ is called positive if $\mathrm{Pr}_s^{\mathcal{M}}(\mathcal{P}|_{\mathcal{C}}[s, q]) > 0$ for all/any $\langle s, q \rangle \in \mathcal{C}$. As in Sect. 3.2, we treat the SCCs in a bottom-up manner, starting with the BSCCs and removing them if they are non-positive. Clearly, if a BSCC $\mathcal{C}$ of $\mathcal{P}$ does not contain a final state or is trivial, then $\mathcal{C}$ is not positive. Analogously to Lemma 5, a non-trivial BSCC $\mathcal{C}$ in $\mathcal{P}$ containing at least one final state is positive if and only if the linear equation system

$$(*) \qquad \zeta_{s,q} = \sum_{t \in \mathrm{Post}(s)} \sum_{p \in \delta_{\mathcal{C}}(q, t)} P(s, t) \cdot \zeta_{t,p} \quad \text{for all } \langle s, q \rangle \in \mathcal{C}$$

has a strictly positive solution if and only if $(*)$ has a non-zero solution. Here, $\mathrm{Post}(s) = \{t \in S : P(s, t) > 0\}$ denotes the set of successors of state s in $\mathcal{M}$ and $\delta_{\mathcal{C}}(q, t) = \{p \in \delta(q, t) : \langle t, p \rangle \in \mathcal{C}\}$.

We now explain how to adapt the cut-based approach of Sect. 3.1 for computing the probabilities in a positive BSCC $\mathcal{C}$ of $\mathcal{P}$. For $\langle s, q \rangle \in \mathcal{C}$ and $t \in S$, let $\Delta_{\mathcal{C}}(\langle s, q \rangle, t) = \Delta(\langle s, q \rangle, t) \cap \mathcal{C}$. A pure cut in $\mathcal{C}$ denotes a set $C \subseteq \mathcal{C}$ such that $\mathrm{Pr}_s^{\mathcal{M}}(\mathcal{P}[C]) = 1$ and $C = \Delta_{\mathcal{C}}(\langle s, q \rangle, z)$ for some $\langle s, q \rangle \in \mathcal{C}$ and some finite word $z \in S^*$ such that $s z$ is a cycle in $\mathcal{M}$. (In particular, the last symbol of z is s, and therefore $C \subseteq \{\langle s, p \rangle \in \mathcal{C} : p \in Q\}$.) To compute a pure cut in $\mathcal{C}$, we pick an arbitrary state $\langle s, q \rangle$ in $\mathcal{C}$ and successively generate path fragments $z_0, z_1, \ldots, z_k \in S^*$ in $\mathcal{M}$ by adding prefixes. More precisely, $z_0 = \varepsilon$

and z_{i+1} has the form yz_i for some $y \in S^+$ such that (1) sy is a cycle in $\mathcal{M}$ and (2) there exists a state $p \in Q \setminus \{q\}$ in $\mathcal{U}$ with $\Delta_{\mathcal{C}}(\langle s, p \rangle, z_i) \neq \varnothing$ and $\{\langle s, q \rangle, \langle s, p \rangle\} \subseteq \Delta_{\mathcal{C}}(\langle s, q \rangle, y)$. Each such word y is called an extension of $(\langle s, q \rangle, z_i)$, and $\Delta_{\mathcal{C}}(\langle s, q \rangle, z_{i+1}) = \Delta_{\mathcal{C}}(\langle s, q \rangle, yz_i)$ is a proper superset of $\Delta_{\mathcal{C}}(\langle s, q \rangle, z_i)$. The set $C = \Delta_{\mathcal{C}}(\langle s, q \rangle, z)$ is a pure cut if and only if $(\langle s, q \rangle, z_i)$ has no extension. The search for an extension can be realized efficiently using a technique similar to the one presented in Sect. 3.1. Thus, after at most $\min\{|\mathcal{C}|, |Q|\}$ iterations, we obtain a pure cut C.

Having computed a pure cut C of $\mathcal{C}$, the values $\mathrm{Pr}_s^{\mathcal{M}}(\mathcal{P}[s, q])$ for $\langle s, q \rangle \in C$ are then computable as the unique solution of the linear equation system consisting of equations (*) and the additional equation $\sum_{\langle s, q \rangle \in C} \zeta_{s,q} = 1$.

In this way we adapt Theorem 12 to obtain the values $\mathrm{Pr}_s^{\mathcal{M}}(\mathcal{P}[s, q])$ for the states $\langle s, q \rangle$ belonging to some positive BSCC of $\mathcal{P}$. It remains to explain how to adapt the equation system of Theorem 13. Let Q_{BSCC} be the set of BSCC states of $\mathcal{P}$ and $Q_?$ be the states of $\mathcal{P}$ not contained in Q_{BSCC}. For $\langle s, q \rangle \in Q_?$, let $\beta_{s,q} = 0$ if $\Delta(\langle s, q \rangle, t) \cap Q_{BSCC} = \varnothing$ for all $t \in S$. Otherwise:

$$\beta_{s,q} = \sum_{t \in \mathrm{Post}(s)} \sum_{\substack{p \in \delta(q, t) \text{ s.t.} \\ \langle t, p \rangle \in Q_{BSCC}}} P(s, t) \cdot \mathrm{Pr}_t^{\mathcal{M}}(\mathcal{P}[t, p])$$

Then, the vector $(\mathrm{Pr}_s^{\mathcal{M}}(\mathcal{P}[s, q]))_{\langle s, q \rangle \in Q_?}$ is the unique solution of the linear equation system

$$\zeta_{s,q} = \sum_{t \in \mathrm{Post}(s)} \sum_{\substack{p \in \delta(q, t) \text{ s.t.} \\ \langle t, p \rangle \notin Q_{BSCC}}} P(s, t) \cdot \zeta_{t,p} + \beta_{s,q} \qquad \text{for } \langle s, q \rangle \in Q_?$$

This completes the proof of Theorem 2.

4   Implementation and Experiments

We have implemented a probabilistic model checking procedure for Markov chains and UBA specifications using the algorithm detailed in Sect. 3 as an extension to the probabilistic model checker PRISM [30,35].[3] Our implementation is based on the explicit engine of PRISM, where the Markov chain is represented explicitly. An implementation for the symbolic, MTBDD-based engines of PRISM is planned as future work.

Our implementation supports UBA-based model checking for handling the LTL fragment of PRISM's PCTL*-like specification language as well as direct verification against a path specification given by a UBA provided in the HOA format [3]. For LTL formulas, we rely on external LTL-to-UBA translators. For the purpose of the benchmarks we employ the ltl2tgba tool from SPOT [18] to generate UBA for a given LTL formula.

---

[3] More details are available at [1]. All experiments were carried out on a computer with two Intel E5-2680 8-core CPUs at 2.70 GHz with 384 GB of RAM running Linux.

For the linear algebra parts of the algorithms, we rely on the COLT library [25]. We considered two different variants for the SCC computations as detailed in [4]. The first variant relies on COLT to perform a QR decomposition of the matrix for the SCC to compute the rank, which allows for deciding the positivity of the SCC. The second approach relies on a variant of the power iteration method for iteratively computing an eigenvector. This method has the benefit that, in addition to deciding the positivity, the computed eigenvector can be directly used to compute the values for a positive SCC, once a cut has been found. (As the proof of Theorem 12 shows: $\Pr(\mathcal{L}_\omega(q)) = \zeta_q^* / \sum_{p \in C} \zeta_p^*$ if ζ^* is an eigenvector of the matrix M for eigenvalue 1.) We have evaluated the performance and scalability of the cut generation algorithm together with both approaches for treating SCCs with selected automata specifications that are challenging for our UBA-based model checking approach, see [4]. As the power iteration method performed better, our benchmark results presented in this section use this method for the SCC handling.

We report here on benchmarks using the bounded retransmission protocol (BRP) case study of the PRISM benchmark suite [31]. The model from the benchmark suite covers a single message transmission, retrying for a bounded number of times in case of an error. We have slightly modified the model to allow the transmission of an infinite number of messages by restarting the protocol once a message has been successfully delivered or the bound for retransmissions has been reached. We consider the LTL property

$$\varphi^k = (\neg\texttt{sender\_ok})\ \mathcal{U}\ \big((\texttt{retransmit} \wedge (\neg\texttt{sender\_ok}\ \mathcal{U}^{=k}\ \texttt{sender\_ok})\big),$$

ensuring that k steps before an acknowledgment the message was retransmitted. To remove the effect of selecting specific tools for the LTL to automaton translation (ltl2tgba for UBA, the Java-based PRISM reimplementation of ltl2dstar [28] to obtain a deterministic Rabin automaton (DRA) for the standard PRISM approach), we also consider direct model checking against automata specifications. As the language of φ^k is equivalent to the UBA depicted in Fig. 1 (on the left) when $a = \texttt{retransmit} \wedge \neg\texttt{sender\_ok}$, $b = \texttt{sender\_ok}$ and $c = \neg\texttt{retransmit} \wedge \neg\texttt{send\_ok}$, we use this automaton and the minimal DBA for the language (this case is denoted by $\mathcal{A}$). We additionally consider the UBA and DBA obtained by replacing the self-loop in the last state with a switch back to the initial state (denoted by $\mathcal{B}$), i.e., roughly applying the ω-operator to $\mathcal{A}$.

Table 1 shows results for selected k (with a timeout 30 min), demonstrating that for this case study and properties our UBA-based implementation is generally competitive with the standard approach of PRISM relying on deterministic automata. For φ and $\mathcal{A}$, our implementation detects that the UBA has a special shape where all final states have a true-self loop, which allows for skipping the SCC handling. Without this optimization, t_{Cut} and t_{Pos} are in the sub-second range for φ and $\mathcal{A}$ for all considered k. At a certain point, the implementation of the standard approach in PRISM becomes unsuccessful, either due to timeouts in

Table 1. Statistics for DBA/DRA- and UBA-based model checking of the BRP case study (parameters $N = 16$, $MAX = 128$), a DTMC with 29358 states, depicting the number of states for the automata and the product and the time for model checking (t_{MC}). For φ, t_{MC} includes the translation to the automaton, for $\mathcal{B}$ the time for checking positivity (t_{Pos}) and cut generation (t_{Cut}) are included in t_{MC}. The mark − stands for "not available" or timeout (30 min).

	PRISM standard			PRISM UBA				
	DRA	Product	t_{MC}	UBA	Product	t_{MC}	t_{Pos}	t_{Cut}
$k = 4$, φ	118	62, 162	0.8 s	6	34, 118	0.6 s		
$\mathcal{A}$	33	61, 025	0.8 s	6	34, 118	0.5 s		
$\mathcal{B}$	33	75, 026	0.7 s	6	68, 474	1.9 s	1.1 s	< 0.1 s
$k = 6$, φ	4, 596	72, 313	3.2 s	8	36, 164	0.9 s		
$\mathcal{A}$	129	62, 428	1.1 s	8	36, 164	0.9 s		
$\mathcal{B}$	129	97, 754	1.1 s	8	99, 460	3.1 s	1.5 s	< 0.1 s
$k = 8$, φ	297, 204	−	−	10	38, 207	0.8 s		
$\mathcal{A}$	513	64, 715	1.1 s	10	38, 207	0.7 s		
$\mathcal{B}$	513	134, 943	1.3 s	10	136, 427	4.5 s	2.5 s	< 0.1 s
$k = 14$, φ	−	−	−	16	44, 340	12.8 s	0.0 s	0.0 s
$\mathcal{A}$	32, 769	83, 845	5.3 s	16	44, 340	1.0 s		
$\mathcal{B}$	32, 769	444, 653	6.0 s	16	246, 346	10.2 s	6.5 s	< 0.1 s
$k = 16$, φ	−	−	−	18	46, 390	115.0 s		
$\mathcal{A}$	131, 073	−	−	18	46, 390	1.0 s		
$\mathcal{B}$	131, 073	−	−	18	282, 699	12.3 s	8.6 s	< 0.1 s
$k = 48$, $\mathcal{A}$	−	−	−	50	79, 206	1.8 s		
$\mathcal{B}$	−	−	−	50	843, 414	88.4 s	71.1 s	< 0.1 s

the DRA construction (φ: $k \geq 10$) or PRISM size limitations in the deterministic product construction (φ: $k \geq 8$, $\mathcal{A}/\mathcal{B}$: $k \geq 16$). For $k \geq 18$, ltl2tgba was unable to construct the UBA for φ within the given time limit, for $k = 16$, 114.4 s of the 115.0 s were spent on constructing the UBA. As can be seen, using the UBA approach we were able to successfully scale the parameter k beyond 48 when dealing directly with the automata-based specifications ($\mathcal{A}/\mathcal{B}$) and within reasonable time required for model checking.

5   Conclusion

The main contribution of the paper is a polynomial-time algorithm for the quantitative analysis of Markov chains against UBA-specifications, and an implementation thereof. This yields a single exponential-time algorithm for the probabilistic model-checking problem for Markov chains and LTL formulas, and thus an alternative to the double exponential-time classical approach with deterministic automata that has been implemented in PRISM and other tools. Other single exponential algorithms for Markov chains and LTL are known, such as the automata-less method of [14] and the approaches with weak alternating automata [10] or separated UBA [16]. To the best of our knowledge, no implementations of these algorithms are available.[4]

The efficiency of the proposed UBA-based analysis of Markov chains against LTL-specifications crucially depends on sophisticated techniques for the generation of UBA from LTL formulas. Compared to the numerous approaches for the generation of compact nondeterministic or deterministic automata, research on for efficient LTL-to-UBA translators is rare. The tool Tulip [33] uses a variant of the LTL-to-NBA algorithm by Gerth et al. [21] for the direct construction of UBA from LTL formulas, while SPOT's LTL-to-UBA generator relies on an adaption of the Couvreur approach [15]. A comparison of NBA versus UBA sizes for LTL benchmark formulas from [19, 20, 36] (see [4]) using SPOT suggests that requiring unambiguity does not necessarily lead to a major increase in NBA size. An alternative to the direct translation of LTL formulas into UBA are standard LTL-to-NBA translators combined with disambiguation approaches for NBA (e.g. of [27]). However, we are not aware of tool support for these techniques.

Besides the design of efficient LTL-to-UBA translators that exploit the additional flexibility of unambiguous automata compared to deterministic ones, our future work will include a symbolic implementation of our algorithm and more experiments to evaluate the UBA-based approach against the classical approach with deterministic automata (e.g. realized in PRISM [30, 35] and IscasMC [23] and using state-of-the-art generators for deterministic automata such as Rabinizer) or other single exponential-time algorithms [10, 14, 16], addressing the complex interplay between automata sizes, automata generation time, size of the (reachable fragment of the) product and the cost of the analysis algorithms that all influence the overall model checking time.

Acknowledgments. The authors would like to thank Théodore Lopez for his comments on a draft of this paper.

References

1. Website with additional material for this paper. http://wwwtcs.inf.tu-dresden.de/ALGI/PUB/CAV16/
2. Arnold, A.: Deterministic and non ambiguous rational omega-languages. In: Nivat, M., Perrin, D. (eds.) Automata on Infinite Words, Ecole de Printemps d'Informatique Théorique, Le Mont Dore. LNCS, vol. 192, pp. 18–27. Springer, Heidelberg (1985)

---

[4] The paper [16] reports on experiments with a prototype implementation, but this implementation seems not to be available anymore. As briefly explained in [4], our algorithm can be seen as a generalization of the approach of [16] with separated UBA. The tool Tulip [33] also has an engine for analysis of Markov chains against UBA-specifications, but it relies on the flawed algorithm of [7].

3. Babiak, T., Blahoudek, F., Duret-Lutz, A., Klein, J., Křetínský, J., Müller, D., Parker, D., Strejček, J.: The Hanoi omega-automata format. In: Kroening, D., Păsăreanu, C.S. (eds.) CAV 2015. LNCS, vol. 9206, pp. 479–486. Springer, Heidelberg (2015)
4. Baier, C., Kiefer, S., Klein, J., Klüppelholz, S., Müller, D., Worrell, J.: Markov chains and unambiguous Büchi automata (extended version) (2016). http://arxiv.org/abs/1605.00950
5. Benedikt, M., Lenhardt, R., Worrell, J.: LTL model checking of interval Markov chains. In: Piterman, N., Smolka, S.A. (eds.) TACAS 2013 (ETAPS 2013). LNCS, vol. 7795, pp. 32–46. Springer, Heidelberg (2013)
6. Benedikt, M., Lenhardt, R., Worrell, J.: Model checking Markov chains against unambiguous Büchi automata (2014). arXiv:1405.4560
7. Benedikt, M., Lenhardt, R., Worrell, J.: Two variable vs. linear temporal logic in model checking and games. Log. Methods Comput. Sci. 9(2), 1–37 (2013)
8. Berman, A., Plemmons, R.J.: Nonnegative Matrices in the Mathematical Sciences. Academic Press, Cambridge (1979)
9. Bousquet, N., Löding, C.: Equivalence and inclusion problem for strongly unambiguous Büchi automata. In: Dediu, A.-H., Fernau, H., Martín-Vide, C. (eds.) LATA 2010. LNCS, vol. 6031, pp. 118–129. Springer, Heidelberg (2010)
10. Bustan, D., Rubin, S., Vardi, M.Y.: Verifying ω-regular properties of Markov Chains. In: Alur, R., Peled, D.A. (eds.) CAV 2004. LNCS, vol. 3114, pp. 189–201. Springer, Heidelberg (2004)
11. Chakraborty, S., Katoen, J.-P.: Parametric LTL on Markov chains. In: Diaz, J., Lanese, I., Sangiorgi, D. (eds.) TCS 2014. LNCS, vol. 8705, pp. 207–221. Springer, Heidelberg (2014)
12. Colcombet, T.: Forms of determinism for automata (invited talk). In: 29th International Symposium on Theoretical Aspects of Computer Science, (STACS), LIPIcs, vol. 14, pp. 1–23. Schloss Dagstuhl - Leibniz-Zentrum fuer Informatik (2012)
13. Colcombet, T.: Unambiguity in automata theory. In: Shallit, J., Okhotin, A. (eds.) DCFS 2015. LNCS, vol. 9118, pp. 3–18. Springer, Heidelberg (2015)
14. Courcoubetis, C., Yannakakis, M.: The complexity of probabilistic verification. J. ACM 42(4), 857–907 (1995)
15. Couvreur, J.-M.: On-the-fly verification of linear temporal logic. In: Wing, J.M., Woodcock, J. (eds.) FM 1999. LNCS, vol. 1708, pp. 253–271. Springer, Heidelberg (1999)
16. Couvreur, J.-M., Saheb, N., Sutre, G.: An optimal automata approach to LTL model checking of probabilistic systems. In: Vardi, M.Y., Voronkov, A. (eds.) LPAR 2003. LNCS, vol. 2850, pp. 361–375. Springer, Heidelberg (2003)
17. Duret-Lutz, A.: Manipulating LTL formulas using spot 1.0. In: Van Hung, D., Ogawa, M. (eds.) ATVA 2013. LNCS, vol. 8172, pp. 442–445. Springer, Heidelberg (2013)
18. Duret-Lutz, A.: LTL translation improvements in Spot 1.0. Int. J. Crit. Comput.-Based Syst. 5(1/2), 31–54 (2014)
19. Dwyer, M.B., Avrunin, G.S., Corbett, J.C.: Patterns in property specifications for finite-state verification. In: 21th International Conference on Software Engineering (ICSE), pp. 411–420. ACM (1999)
20. Etessami, K., Holzmann, G.J.: Optimizing Büchi automata. In: Palamidessi, C. (ed.) CONCUR 2000. LNCS, vol. 1877, pp. 153–168. Springer, Heidelberg (2000)

21. Gerth, R., Peled, D., Vardi, M.Y., Wolper, P.: Simple on-the-fly automatic verification of linear temporal logic. In: Fifteenth IFIP WG6.1 International Symposium on Protocol Specification (PSTV), IFIP Conference Proceedings, vol. 38, pp. 3–18. Chapman & Hall (1995)
22. Grädel, E., Thomas, W., Wilke, T. (eds.): Automata, Logics, Infinite Games: A Guide to Current Research. LNCS, vol. 2500. Springer, Heidelberg (2002)
23. Hahn, E.M., Li, Y., Schewe, S., Turrini, A., Zhang, L.: ISCASMC: a web-based probabilistic model checker. In: Jones, C., Pihlajasaari, P., Sun, J. (eds.) FM 2014. LNCS, vol. 8442, pp. 312–317. Springer, Heidelberg (2014)
24. Horn, R.A., Johnson, C.R.: Matrix Analysis, 2nd edn. Cambridge University Press, Cambridge (2013)
25. Hoschek, W.: The colt distribution: open source libraries for high performance scientific and technical computing in Java (2004)
26. Isaak, D., Löding, C.: Efficient inclusion testing for simple classes of unambiguous ω-automata. Inf. Process. Lett. **112**(14–15), 578–582 (2012)
27. Kähler, D., Wilke, T.: Complementation, disambiguation, and determinization of Büchi automata unified. In: Aceto, L., Damgård, I., Goldberg, L.A., Halldórsson, M.M., Ingólfsdóttir, A., Walukiewicz, I. (eds.) ICALP 2008, Part I. LNCS, vol. 5125, pp. 724–735. Springer, Heidelberg (2008)
28. Klein, J., Baier, C.: Experiments with deterministic ω-automata for formulas of linear temporal logic. Theoret. Comput. Sci. **363**(2), 182–195 (2006)
29. Kulkarni, V.G.: Modeling and Analysis of Stochastic Systems. Chapman & Hall, London (1995)
30. Kwiatkowska, M., Norman, G., Parker, D.: PRISM 4.0: verification of probabilistic real-time systems. In: Gopalakrishnan, G., Qadeer, S. (eds.) CAV 2011. LNCS, vol. 6806, pp. 585–591. Springer, Heidelberg (2011)
31. Kwiatkowska, M.Z., Norman, G., Parker, D.: The PRISM benchmark suite. In: 9th International Conference on Quantitative Evaluation of SysTems (QEST), pp. 203–204. IEEE Computer Society (2012)
32. Lenhardt, R.: Tulip: model checking probabilistic systems using expectation maximisation algorithm. In: Joshi, K., Siegle, M., Stoelinga, M., D'Argenio, P.R. (eds.) QEST 2013. LNCS, vol. 8054, pp. 155–159. Springer, Heidelberg (2013)
33. Lenhardt, R.: Two variable and linear temporal logic in model checking and games. Ph.D. thesis, University of Oxford (2013)
34. Morgenstern, A.: Symbolic controller synthesis for LTL specifications. Ph.D. thesis, Technische Universität Kaiserslautern (2010)
35. The PRISM model checker. http://www.prismmodelchecker.org/
36. Somenzi, F., Bloem, R.: Efficient Büchi automata from LTL formulae. In: Emerson, E.A., Sistla, A.P. (eds.) Computer Aided Verification. LNCS, vol. 1855, pp. 248–263. Springer, Heidelberg (2000)
37. Stearns, R.E., Hunt, H.B.: On the equivalence and containment problem for unambiguous regular expressions, grammars, and automata. SIAM J. Comput. **14**(3), 598–611 (1985)
38. Vardi, M.Y.: Automatic verification of probabilistic concurrent finite-state programs. In: 26th IEEE Symposium on Foundations of Computer Science (FOCS), pp. 327–338. IEEE Computer Society (1985)

39. Vardi, M.Y., Wolper, P.: An automata-theoretic approach to automatic program verification (preliminary report). In: 1st Symposium on Logic in Computer Science (LICS), pp. 332–344. IEEE Computer Society Press (1986)
40. Wolper, P., Vardi, M.Y., Sistla, P.A.: Reasoning about infinite computation paths (extended abstract). In: 24th Annual Symposium on Foundations of Computer Science (FOCS), pp. 185–194. IEEE Computer Society (1983)
41. Zimmermann, M.: Optimal bounds in parametric LTL games. Theoret. Comput. Sci. **493**, 30–45 (2013)

Synthesizing Probabilistic Invariants via Doob's Decomposition

Gilles Barthe[1(✉)], Thomas Espitau[2], Luis María Ferrer Fioriti[3],
and Justin Hsu[4]

[1] IMDEA Software Institute, Madrid, Spain
`gilles.barthe@imdea.org`
[2] ENS Cachan, Cachan, France
[3] Saarland University, Saarbrücken, Germany
[4] University of Pennsylvania, Philadelphia, USA

Abstract. When analyzing probabilistic computations, a powerful approach is to first find a *martingale*—an expression on the program variables whose expectation remains invariant—and then apply the optional stopping theorem in order to infer properties at termination time. One of the main challenges, then, is to systematically find martingales.

We propose a novel procedure to synthesize martingale expressions from an arbitrary initial expression. Contrary to state-of-the-art approaches, we do not rely on constraint solving. Instead, we use a symbolic construction based on *Doob's decomposition*. This procedure can produce very complex martingales, expressed in terms of conditional expectations.

We show how to *automatically* generate and simplify these martingales, as well as how to apply the *optional stopping theorem* to infer properties at termination time. This last step typically involves some simplification steps, and is usually done manually in current approaches. We implement our techniques in a prototype tool and demonstrate our process on several classical examples. Some of them go beyond the capability of current semi-automatic approaches.

1 Introduction

Probabilistic computations are a key tool in modern computer science. They are ubiquitous in machine learning, privacy-preserving data mining, cryptography, and many other fields. They are also a common and flexible tool to model a broad range of complex real-world systems. Not surprisingly, probabilistic computations have been extensively studied from a formal verification perspective. However, their verification is particularly challenging.

In order to understand the difficulty, consider the standard way to infer properties about the final state of a non-probabilistic program using a strong invariant (an assertion which is preserved throughout program execution) and a proof of termination. This proof principle is not easily adapted to the probabilistic case. First, probabilistic programs are interpreted as distribution transformers [25]

© Springer International Publishing Switzerland 2016
S. Chaudhuri and A. Farzan (Eds.): CAV 2016, Part I, LNCS 9779, pp. 43–61, 2016.
DOI: 10.1007/978-3-319-41528-4_3

rather than state transformers. Accordingly, assertions (including strong invariants) must be interpreted over distributions. Second, the notion of termination is different for probabilistic programs. We are usually not interested in proving that *all* executions are finite, but merely that the probability of termination is 1, a slightly weaker notion. Under this notion, there may be no finite bound on the number of steps over all possible executions. So, we cannot use induction to transfer local properties to the end of the program—more complex limiting arguments are needed.

We can avoid some of these obstacles by looking at the *average* behavior of a program. That is, we can analyze numerical expressions (over program variables) whose average value is preserved. These expressions are known as martingales, and have several technical advantages. First, martingales are easy to manipulate symbolically and can be checked locally. Second, the average value of martingale is preserved at termination, even if the control-flow of the program is probabilistic. This fact follows from the *optional stopping theorem* (OST), a powerful result in martingale theory.

While martingales are quite useful, they can be quite non-obvious. Accordingly, recent investigation has turned to automatically synthesizing martingales. State-of-the-art frameworks are based on constraint solving, and require the user to provide either a template expression [6,22] or a limit on the search space [7,10]. The main advantage of such approaches is that they are generally complete— they find *all* possible martingales in the search space. However, they have their drawbacks: a slightly wrong template can produce no invariant at all, and a lot of search space may be needed to arrive at the martingale.

We propose a framework that *complements* current approaches—we rely on purely symbolic methods instead of solving constraints or searching. We require the user to provide a "seed" expression, from which we *always* generate a martingale. Our approach uses *Doob's decomposition theorem*, which gives a symbolic method to construct a martingale from any sequence of random values. Once we have the martingale, we can apply optional stopping to reason about the martingale at loop termination. While the martingale and final fact may be quite complex, we can use non-probabilistic invariants and symbolic manipulations to automatically simplify them.

We demonstrate our techniques in a prototype implementation, implementing Doob's decomposition and the Optional Stopping Theorem. Although these proof principles have been long known to probability theory, we are the first to incorporate them into an automated program analysis. Given basic invariants and hints, our prototype generates martingales and facts for a selection of examples.

2 Mathematical Preliminaries

We briefly introduce some definitions from probability theory required for our technical development. We lack the space to discuss the definitions in-depth, but we will explain informally what the various concepts mean in our setting. Interested readers can find a more detailed presentation in any standard probability theory textbook (e.g., Williams [33]).

First, we will need some basic concepts from probability theory.

Definition 1. *Let Ω be the set of outcomes.*

- *A sigma algebra is a set $\mathcal{F}$ of subsets of Ω, closed under complements and countable unions, and countable intersections.*
- *A probability measure is a countably additive mapping $\mathbb{P} : \mathcal{F} \to [0, 1]$ such that $\mathbb{P}(\Omega) = 1$.*
- *A probability space is a triple $(\Omega, \mathcal{F}, \mathbb{P})$.*

Next, we can formally define stochastic processes. These constructions are technical but completely standard.

Definition 2. *Let $(\Omega, \mathcal{F}, \mathbb{P})$ be a probability space.*

- *A (real) random variable is a function $X : \Omega \to \mathbb{R}$. X is $\mathcal{F}$-measurable if $X^{-1}((a, b]) \in \mathcal{F}$ for every $a, b \in \mathbb{R}$.*
- *A filtration is a sequence $\{\mathcal{F}_i\}_{i \in \mathbb{N}}$ of sigma algebras such that $\mathcal{F}_i \subseteq \mathcal{F}$ and $\mathcal{F}_{i-1} \subseteq \mathcal{F}_i$ for every $i > 0$. When there is a fixed filtration on $\mathcal{F}$, we will often abuse notation and write $\mathcal{F}$ for the filtration.*
- *A stochastic process adapted to filtration $\mathcal{F}$ is a sequence of random variables $\{X_i\}_{i \in \mathbb{N}}$ such that each X_i is $\mathcal{F}_i$-measurable.*

Intuitively, we can think of Ω as a set where each element represents a possible outcome of the samples. In our setting, grouping samples according to the loop iteration gives a natural choice for the filtration: we can take $\mathcal{F}_i$ to be the set of events that are defined by samples in iteration i or before. A stochastic process X is adapted to this filtration if X_i is defined in terms of samples from iteration i or before. Sampled variables at step i are independent of previous steps, so they are not $\mathcal{F}_{i-1}$-measurable.

Expectation. To define martingales, we need to introduce expected values and conditional expectations. The *expected value* of a random variable is defined as

$$\mathbf{E}[X] \triangleq \int_{\Omega} X \cdot d\mathbb{P}$$

where $\int$ is the Lebesgue integral [33]. We say that a random variable is *integrable* if $\mathbf{E}[|X|]$ is finite. Given a integrable random variable X and a sigma algebra $\mathcal{G}$, a *conditional expectation* of X with respect to $\mathcal{G}$ is a random variable Y such that Y is $\mathcal{G}$-measurable, and $\mathbf{E}[X \cdot \mathbb{1}_{\{A\}}] = \mathbf{E}[Y \cdot \mathbb{1}_{\{A\}}]$ for all events $A \in \mathcal{G}$. (Recall that the *indicator function* $\mathbb{1}_{\{A\}}$ of an event A maps $\omega \in A$ to 1, and all other elements to 0.) Since one can show that this Y is essentially unique, we denote it by $\mathbf{E}[X \mid \mathcal{G}]$.

Moments. Our method relies on computing higher-order moments. Suppose X is a random variable with distribution d. If X takes numeric values, the *kth moment* of d is defined as

$$G(d)_k \triangleq \mathbf{E}[X^k]$$

for $k \in \mathbb{N}$. If X ranges over tuples, the *correlations* of d are defined as

$$G(d, \{a, b\})_{p,q} \triangleq \mathbf{E}[\pi_a(X)^p \cdot \pi_b(X)^q],$$

for $p, q \in \mathbb{N}$, and similarly for products of three or more projections. Here, the *projection* $\pi_i(X)$ for X a tuple-valued random variable is the marginal distribution of the ith coordinate of the tuple.

Martingales. A martingale is a stochastic process with a special property: the average value of the current step is equal to the value of the previous step.

Definition 3. *Let $\{X_i\}$ be a stochastic process adapted to filtration $\{\mathcal{F}_i\}$. We say that X is a* martingale *with respect to $\mathcal{F}$ if it satisfies the property*

$$\mathbf{E}[X_i \mid \mathcal{F}_{i-1}] = X_{i-1}.$$

For a simple example, consider a symmetric random walk on the integers. Let $X \in \mathbb{Z}$ denote the current position of the walk. At each step, we flip a fair coin: if heads, we increase the position by 1, otherwise we decrease the position by 1. The sequence of positions $X_0, X_1, \ldots$ forms a martingale since the average position at time i is simply the position at time $i - 1$:

$$\mathbf{E}[X_i \mid \mathcal{F}_{i-1}] = X_{i-1}.$$

Doob's Decomposition. One important result in martingale theory is Doob's decomposition. Informally, it establishes that any integrable random process can be written uniquely as a sum of a martingale and a predictable process. For our purposes, it gives a constructive and purely symbolic method to extract a martingale from any arbitrary random process.

Theorem 1 (Doob's Decomposition). *Let $X = \{X_i\}_{i \in \mathbb{N}}$ be a stochastic process adapted to filtration $\{\mathcal{F}_i\}_{i \in \mathbb{N}}$ where each X_i has finite expected value. Then, the following process is a martingale:*

$$M_i = \begin{cases} X_0 & : i = 0 \\ X_0 + \sum_{j=1}^{i} X_j - \mathbf{E}[X_j \mid \mathcal{F}_{j-1}] & : i > 0 \end{cases}$$

If X is already a martingale, then $M = X$.

We will think of the stochastic process X as a seed process which generates the martingale. While the definition of the martingale involves conditional expectations, we will soon see how to automatically simplify these expectations.

Optional Stopping Theorem. For any martingale M, it is not hard to show that the expected value of M remains invariant at each time step. That is, for any fixed value $n \in \mathbb{N}$, we have

$$\mathbf{E}[M_n] = \mathbf{E}[M_0].$$

The optional stopping theorem extends this equality to situations where n itself may be random, possibly even a function of the martingale.

Definition 4. *Let* $(\Omega, \mathcal{F}, \mathbb{P})$ *be a probability space with filtration* $\{\mathcal{F}_i\}_{i \in \mathbb{N}}$. *A random variable* $\tau : \Omega \to \mathbb{N}$ *is a* stopping time *if the subset* $\{w \in \Omega \mid \tau(w) \leq i\}$ *is a member of* $\mathcal{F}_i$ *for each* $i \in \mathbb{N}$.

Returning to our random walk example, the first time that the position is farther than 100 from the origin is a stopping time since this time depends only on past samples. In contrast, the last time that a position is farther than 100 from the origin is *not* a stopping time, since this time depends on future samples. More generally, the iteration count when we exit a probabilistic loop is a stopping time since termination is a function of past samples only.

If we have a stopping time and a few mild conditions, we can apply the optional stopping theorem.[1]

Theorem 2 (Optional Stopping) *Let* τ *be a stopping time, and let* M *be a martingale. If the expected value of* τ *is finite, and if* $|M_i - M_{i-1}| \leq C$ *for all* $i > 0$ *and some constant* C, *then*

$$\mathbf{E}[M_\tau] = \mathbf{E}[M_0].$$

To see this theorem in action, consider the random walk martingale S and take the stopping time τ to be the first time that $|S| \geq 100$. It is possible to show that τ has finite expected value, and clearly $|S_i - S_{i-1}| \leq 1$. So, the optional stopping theorem gives

$$\mathbf{E}[S_\tau] = \mathbf{E}[S_0] = 0.$$

Since we know that the position is ± 100 at time τ, this immediately shows that the probability of hitting $+100$ is equal to the probability of hitting -100. This intuitive fact can be awkward to prove using standard probabilistic invariants, but falls out directly from a martingale analysis.

3 Overview of Method

Now that we have seen the key technical ingredients of our approach, let us see how to combine these tools into an automated program analysis. We will take an imperative program specifying a stochastic process and a seed expression,

---

[1] A basic version of the optional stopping theorem will suffice for our purposes, but there are alternative versions that don't require finite expected stopping time and bounded increments.

and we will automatically synthesize a martingale and an assertion that holds at termination. We proceed in three stages: extracting a polynomial representing the stochastic process in the program, applying Doob's decomposition to the polynomial representation, and applying optional stopping. We perform symbolic manipulations to simplify the martingale and final fact.

Programs. We consider programs of the form:[2]

$$I; \mathsf{while}\ e\ \mathsf{do}\ (S; B)$$

where I and B are sequences of deterministic assignments (of the form $\mathcal{X} \leftarrow \mathcal{E}$), and S is a sequence of probabilistic samplings (of the form $S \xleftarrow{\$} \mathcal{DE}$).

Note that we separate *sample variables* $s \in \mathcal{S}$, which are the target of random samplings, from *process variables* $x \in \mathcal{X}$, which are the target of deterministic assignments. This distinction will be important for our simplifications: we know the moments and correlations of sample variables, while we have less information for process variables. We require that programs assign to sample variables before assigning to process variables in each loop iteration; this restriction is essentially without loss of generality.

We take $\mathcal{DE}$ to be a set of standard distributions over the integers or over finite tuples of integers, to model joint distributions. For instance, we often consider the distribution $\mathsf{Bern}(1/2, \{-1, 1\}) \in \mathcal{DE}$ that returns -1 and $+1$ with equal probability. We assume that all distributions in $\mathcal{DE}$ have bounded support; all moments and correlations of the primitive distributions are finite. We will also assume that distributions do not depend on the program state.

The set $\mathcal{E}$ of expressions is mostly standard, with a few notational conveniences for defining stochastic processes:

$$
\begin{aligned}
\mathcal{E} ::=\ &\mathcal{X} \mid \mathcal{S} \mid \mathcal{X}[-n] &&\text{process/sample/history variables} \\
&\mid\ \mathbb{Z} &&\text{constants} \\
&\mid\ \pi_a(\mathcal{E}) &&\text{projections} \\
&\mid\ \mathcal{E} + \mathcal{E} \mid \mathcal{E} \cdot \mathcal{E} &&\text{arithmetic} \\
&\mid\ \mathcal{E} < \mathcal{E} \mid \mathcal{E} \wedge \mathcal{E} \mid \neg\mathcal{E} &&\text{guards}
\end{aligned}
$$

History variables $\mathcal{X}[-n]$ are indexed by a positive integer n and are used inside loops. The variable $x[-n]$ refers to the value of x assigned n iterations before the current iteration. If the loop has run for fewer than n iterations, $x[-n]$ is specified by the initialization step of our programs:

$$I \triangleq x_1[-n_1] \leftarrow e_1; \cdots ; x_k[-n_k] \leftarrow e_k.$$

---

[2] We focus on programs for which our method achieves full automation. For instance, we exclude conditional statements because it is difficult to fully automate the resulting simplifications. We note however that there are standard transformations for eliminating conditionals; one such transformation is *if-conversion*, a well-known compiler optimization [1].

Extracting the Polynomial. For programs in our fragment, each variable assigned in the loop determines a stochastic process: x is the most recent value, $x[-1]$ is the previous value, etc. In the first stage of our analysis, we extract polynomial representations of each stochastic process from the input program.

We focus on the variables that are mutated in B—each of these variables determines a stochastic process. To keep the notation light, we will explain our process for *first-order* stochastic processes: we only use history variables $x[-1]$ from the past iteration. We will also suppose that there is just one process variable and one sample variable, and only samples from the current iteration are used.

Since our expression language only has addition and multiplication as operators, we can represent the program variable x as a polynomial of other program variables:

$$x = P_x(x[-1], s) \tag{1}$$

Next, we pass to a symbolic representation in terms of (mathematical) random variables. To variable x, we associate the random variable $\{X_i\}_{i\in\mathbb{N}}$ modeling the corresponding stochastic process, and likewise for the sample variable s. By convention, $i = 0$ corresponds to the initialization step, and $i > 0$ corresponds to the stochastic process during the loop. In other words,

$$x[0] \leftarrow 0; \mathsf{while}\ e\ \mathsf{do}\ s \overset{\$}{\leftarrow} d; x \leftarrow x[-1] + s$$

desugars to

$$x[0] \leftarrow 0; i \leftarrow 0; \mathsf{while}\ e\ \mathsf{do}\ i \leftarrow i + 1; s \overset{\$}{\leftarrow} d; x[i] \leftarrow x[i-1] + s$$

in a language with arrays instead of history variables. Then, the program variable $x[i]$ corresponds to the random variable X_i.

Then, Eq. (1) and the initial conditions specified by the command I give an inductive definition for the stochastic process:

$$X_i = P_x(X_{i-1}, S_i). \tag{2}$$

Applying Doob's Decomposition. The second stage of our analysis performs Doob's decomposition on the symbolic representation of the process. We know that the seed expression e must be a polynomial, so we can form the associated stochastic process $\{E_i\}_{i\in\mathbb{N}}$ by replacing program variables by their associated random variable:

$$E_i = P_e(X_i, S_i). \tag{3}$$

(Recall that the initial conditions X_0 and S_0, which define E_0, are specified by the initialization portion I of the program.)

Then, Doob's decomposition produces the martingale:

$$M_i = \begin{cases} E_0 & : i = 0 \\ E_0 + \sum_{j=1}^{i} E_j - \mathbf{E}[E_j \mid \mathcal{F}_{j-1}] & : i > 0. \end{cases}$$

$$\mathbf{E}[c \cdot f + c' \cdot g \mid -] \mapsto c \cdot \mathbf{E}[f \mid -] + c' \cdot \mathbf{E}[g \mid -]$$

$$\mathbf{E}[X_{i-n} \cdot f \mid \mathcal{F}_{i-1}] \mapsto X_{i-n} \cdot \mathbf{E}[f \mid \mathcal{F}_{i-1}] \qquad (n > 0)$$

$$\mathbf{E}[S_i \cdot S_i' \mid \mathcal{F}_{i-1}] \mapsto \mathbf{E}[S_i \mid \mathcal{F}_{i-1}] \cdot \mathbf{E}[S_i' \mid \mathcal{F}_{i-1}] \qquad (S \neq S')$$

$$\mathbf{E}[S_i^k \mid \mathcal{F}_{i-1}] \mapsto G(d)_k \qquad (S \sim d)$$

$$\mathbf{E}[\pi_a(S_i)^p \cdot \pi_b(S_i)^q \mid \mathcal{F}_{i-1}] \mapsto G(d_{a,b})_{p,q} \qquad (S \sim d)$$

Fig. 1. Selection of simplification rules

To simplify the conditional expectation, we unfold E_j via Eq. (3) and unroll the processes X_i by one step with Eq. (2).

Now, we apply our simplification rules; we present a selection in Fig. 1. The rules are divided into three groups (from top): linearity of expectation, conditional independence, and distribution information. The first two groups reflect basic facts about expectations and conditional expectations. The last group encodes the moments and correlations of the primitive distributions. We can pre-compute these quantities for each primitive distribution d and store the results in a table.

By the form of Eq. (3), the simplification removes all expectations and we can give an explicit definition for the martingale:

$$M_i = \begin{cases} E_0 & : i = 0 \\ Q_e(X_{i-1}, \ldots, X_0, S_i, \ldots, S_1) & : i > 0, \end{cases} \qquad (4)$$

where Q_e is a polynomial.

Applying Optional Stopping. With the martingale in hand, the last stage of our analysis applies the optional stopping theorem. To meet the technical conditions of the theorem, we need two properties of the loop:

- The expected number of iterations must be finite.
- The martingale must have bounded increments.

These side conditions are non-probabilistic assertions that can already be handled using existing techniques. For instance, the first condition follows from the existence of a *bounded variant* [19]: an integer expression v such that

- $0 \leq v < K$;
- $v = 0$ implies the guard is false; and
- the probability that v decreases is strictly bigger than ϵ

throughout the loop, for ϵ and K positive constants. However in general, finding a bounded variant may be difficult; proving finite expected stopping time is an open area of research which we do not address here.

The second condition is also easy to check. For one possible approach, one can replace stochastic sampling by non-deterministic choice over the support of the distribution, and verify that the seed expression e is bounded using standard techniques [13,14,28]. This suffices to show that the martingale M_i has bounded increments. To see why, suppose that the seed expression is always bounded by a constant C. By Doob's decomposition, we have

$$|M_i - M_{i-1}| = \left| \left(\sum_{j=1}^{i} E_j - \mathbf{E}[E_j \mid \mathcal{F}_{j-1}] \right) - \left(\sum_{j=1}^{i-1} E_j - \mathbf{E}[E_j \mid \mathcal{F}_{j-1}] \right) \right|$$

$$= |E_i - \mathbf{E}[E_i \mid \mathcal{F}_{j-1}]| \leq 2C,$$

so the martingale has bounded increments.

Thus, we can apply the optional stopping theorem to Eq. (4) to conclude:

$$E_0 = \mathbf{E}[M_0] = \mathbf{E}[M_\tau] = \mathbf{E}[Q_e(X_{\tau-1}, \ldots, X_0, S_\tau, \ldots, S_1)]$$

Unlike the simplification step after applying Doob's decomposition, we may not be able to eliminate all expected values. For instance, there may be expected values of X at times before τ. However, if we have additional invariants about the loop, we can often simplify the fact with basic symbolic transformations.

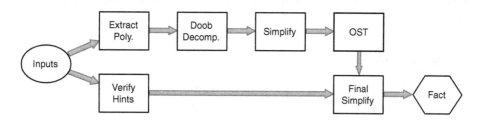

Fig. 2. Tool pipeline

Implementation. We have implemented our process in a Python prototype using the **sympy** library for handling polynomial and summation manipulations [20]. Figure 2 shows the entire pipeline. There are three parts of the input: the program describing a stochastic process, the seed expression, and hint facts. The output is a probabilistic formula that holds at termination.

The most challenging part of our analysis is the last stage: applying OST. First, we need to meet the side conditions of the optional stopping theorem: finite expected iteration count and bounded increments. Our prototype does not verify these side conditions automatically since available termination tools are either not fully automatic [17] or can only synthesize linear ranking supermartingales [6,9] that are insufficient for the majority of our case studies[3]. Furthermore, the

---

[3] Although most of the ranking supermatingales needed in our case studies are non-linear, the bounded variants are always linear.

final fact typically cannot be simplified without some basic information about the program state at loop termination. We include this information as *hints*. Hints are first-order formulae over the program variables and the loop counter (represented by the special variable t), and are used as auxiliary facts during the final simplification step. Hints can be verified using standard program verification tools since they are non-probabilistic. In our examples, we manually translate the hints and the program into the input language of EasyCrypt [4], and perform the verifications there. Automating the translation poses no technical difficulty and is left for future work.

We note that the performance of the tool is perfectly reasonable for the examples considered in the next section. For instance, it handles the "ABRA-CADABRA" example in less than 2 s on a modern laptop.

4   Examples

Now, we demonstrate our approach on several classic examples of stochastic processes. In each case, we describe the code, the seed expression, and any hints needed for our tool to automatically derive the final simplified fact.

Geometric Distribution. As a first application, we consider a program that generates a draw from the geometric distribution by running a sequence of coin flips.

```
x[0] ← 0;
while (z ≠ 0) do
    z ←$ Bern(p, {1, 0});
    x ← x[−1] + z;
end
```

Here, Bern(p, {1, 0}) is the distribution that returns 1 with probability $p > 0$, and 0 otherwise. The program simply keeps drawing until we sample 0, storing the number of times we sample 1 in x.

We wish to apply our technique to the seed expression x. First, we can extract the polynomial equation:

$$X_i = X_{i-1} + Z_i.$$

Applying Doob's decomposition, our tool constructs and reduces the martingale:

$$M_i = \begin{cases} X_0 & : i = 0 \\ X_i - p \cdot i & : i > 0. \end{cases}$$

To apply optional stopping, we first need to check that the stopping time τ is integrable. This follows by taking z as a bounded variant—it remains in $\{0, 1\}$ and decreases with probability $p > 0$. Also, the martingale M_i has bounded increments: $|M_i - M_{i-1}|$ should be bounded by a constant. But this is clear since we can use a loop invariant to show that $|X_i - X_{i-1}| \le 1$, and the increment is

$$|M_i - M_{i-1}| = |X_i - X_{i-1} - p| \le |X_i - X_{i-1}| + p \le 1 + p.$$

So, optional stopping shows that

$$0 = \mathbf{E}[X_\tau - p \cdot \tau].$$

With the hint $x = t - 1$—which holds at termination—our tool replaces X_τ by $\tau - 1$ and automatically derives the expected running time:

$$0 = \mathbf{E}[\tau - 1 - p \cdot \tau]$$
$$\mathbf{E}[\tau] = 1/(1 - p).$$

Gambler's Ruin. Our second example is the classic *Gambler's ruin* process. The program models a game where a player starts with $a > 0$ dollars and keeps tossing a fair coin. The player wins one dollar for each head and loses one dollar for each tail. The game ends either when the player runs out of money, or reaches his target of $b > a$ dollars. We can encode this process as follows:

```
x[0] ← a;
while  (0 < x < b)  do
    z ←$ Bern(1/2, {-1, 1});
    x ← x + z;
end
```

We will synthesize two different martingales from this program, which will yield complementary information once we apply optional stopping. For our first martingale, we use x as the seed expression. Our tool synthesizes the martingale

$$M_i = \begin{cases} X_0 & : i = 0 \\ X_i & : i > 0. \end{cases}$$

So in fact, x is already a martingale.

To apply optional stopping, we first note that x is a bounded variant: it remains in $(0, b)$ and decreases with probability $1/2$ at each iteration. Since the seed expression x is bounded, the martingale M_i has bounded increments. Thus, optional stopping yields

$$a = \mathbf{E}[X_0] = \mathbf{E}[X_\tau].$$

If we give the hint

$$(x = 0) \vee (x = b) \tag{5}$$

at termination, our prototype automatically derives

$$a = \mathbf{E}[X_\tau \cdot \mathbb{1}_{\{X_\tau=0 \vee X_\tau=b\}}]$$
$$= \mathbf{E}[X_\tau \cdot \mathbb{1}_{\{X_\tau=0\}}] + \mathbf{E}[X_\tau \cdot \mathbb{1}_{\{X_\tau=b\}}]$$
$$= 0 \cdot \Pr[X_\tau = 0] + b \cdot \Pr[X_\tau = b] = b \cdot \Pr[X_\tau = b],$$

so the probability of exiting at b is exactly a/b.

Now, let us take a look at a different martingale generated by the seed expression x^2. Our prototype synthesizes the following martingale:

$$M'_i = \begin{cases} X_0^2 & : i = 0 \\ X_i^2 - i & : i > 0 \end{cases}$$

Again, we can apply optional stopping: x is a bounded variant, and the seed expression x^2 remains bounded in $(0, b^2)$. So, we get

$$a^2 = \mathbf{E}[M_0] = \mathbf{E}[X_\tau^2 - \tau].$$

By using the same hint Eq. (5), our prototype automatically derives

$$
\begin{aligned}
a^2 &= \mathbf{E}[X_\tau^2 \cdot \mathbb{1}_{\{X_\tau = 0 \vee X_\tau = b\}}] - \mathbf{E}[\tau] \\
&= \mathbf{E}[X_\tau^2 \cdot \mathbb{1}_{\{X_\tau = 0\}}] + \mathbf{E}[X_\tau^2 \cdot \mathbb{1}_{\{X_\tau = b\}}] - \mathbf{E}[\tau] \\
&= 0 \cdot \Pr[X_\tau = 0] + b^2 \cdot \Pr[X_\tau = b] - \mathbf{E}[\tau] = b^2 \cdot \Pr[X_\tau = b] - \mathbf{E}[\tau].
\end{aligned}
$$

Since we already know that $\Pr[X_\tau = b] = a/b$ from the first martingale $\{M_i\}_{i \in \mathbb{N}}$, this implies that the expected running time of the Gambler's ruin process is

$$\mathbf{E}[\tau] = a(b - a).$$

Gambler's Ruin with Momentum. Our techniques extend naturally to stochastic processes that depend on variables beyond the previous iteration. To demonstrate, we'll consider a variant of Gambler's ruin process with momentum: besides just the coin flip, the gambler will also gain profit equal to the difference between the *previous two* dollar amounts. Concretely, we consider the following process:

```
x[0] ← a;
x[1] ← a;
while (0 < x < b) do
    z ←$ Bern(p, {-1, 1});
    x ← x[-1] + (x[-1] - x[-2]) + z;
end
```

Note that we must now provide the initial conditions for two steps, since the process is second-order recurrent. Given seed expression x, our tool synthesizes the following martingale:

$$
M_i = \begin{cases}
X_0 & : i = 0 \\
X_0 + X_i - X_{i-1} & : i > 0
\end{cases}
$$

Identical to the Gambler's ruin process, we can verify the side conditions and apply optional stopping, yielding

$$a = \mathbf{E}[M_0] = \mathbf{E}[M_\tau] = \mathbf{E}[X_0 + X_\tau - X_{\tau-1}].$$

Unfolding $X_0 = a$ and simplifying, our tool derives the fact

$$\mathbf{E}[X_\tau] = \mathbf{E}[X_{\tau-1}].$$

We are not aware of existing techniques that can prove this kind of fact—reasoning about the expected value of a variable in the iteration *just prior* to termination.

Abracadabra. Our final example is a classic application of martingale reasoning. In this process, a monkey randomly selects a character at each time step, stopping when he has typed a special string, say "ABRACADABRA". We model this process as follows:

```
match₀ [0]  ←  1;
match₁ [0]  ←  0;
. . .
match₁₁ [0]  ←  0;
while ( match₁₁ == 0 ) do
    s  ⇐ UnifMatches ;
    match₁₁  ←  match₁₀ [ −1 ]  ∗  π₁₁ ( s ) ;
    match₁₀  ←  match₉ [ −1 ]  ∗  π₁₀ ( s ) ;
    . . .
    match₁  ←  match₀ [ −1 ]  ∗  π₁ ( s ) ;
end
```

Here, UnifMatches is a distribution over tuples that represents a uniform c draw from the letters, where the kth entry is 1 if the c matches the kth word and 0 if not. The variables $match_i$ record whether the i most recent letters match the first i letters of target word; $match_0$ is always 1, since we always match 0 letters.

Now, we will apply Doob's decomposition. Letting L be the number of possible letters and taking the seed expression

$$e \triangleq 1 + L \cdot \mathtt{match_1} + \cdots + L^{11} \cdot \mathtt{match_{11}},$$

our tool synthesizes the following martingale:

$$M_i = \begin{cases} 1 + L \cdot X_i^{(1)} + \cdots + L^{11} \cdot X_i^{(11)} & : i = 0 \\ \sum_{j=1}^{i} \left(L \cdot X_j^{(1)} + \cdots + L^{11} \cdot X_j^{(11)} - L^0 \cdot X_{j-1}^{(0)} + \cdots + L^{10} \cdot X_{j-1}^{(10)} \right) & : i > 0, \end{cases}$$

where $X^{(j)}$ is the stochastic process corresponding to $match_j$. The dependence on L is from the expectations of projections of UnifMatches, which are each $1/L$—the probability of a uniformly random letter matching any fixed letter.

To apply the optional stopping theorem, note that the seed expression e is bounded in $(0, L^{12})$, and $1 + L + \cdots + L^{11} - e$ serves as a bounded variant: take the highest index j such that $match_j = 1$, and there is probability $1/L$ that we increase the match to get $match_{j+1} = 1$, decreasing the variant. So, we have

$$1 = \mathbf{E}[M_0] = \sum_{j=1}^{\tau} \mathbf{E}[L \cdot X_j^{(1)} + \cdots + L^{11} \cdot X_j^{(11)}] - \mathbf{E}[L^0 \cdot X_{j-1}^{(0)} + \cdots + L^{10} \cdot X_{j-1}^{(10)}].$$

Our tool simplifies and uses the hints $X_j^{(11)} = 0$ and $X_j^{(0)} = 1$ for $j < \tau$ to derive

$$1 = L^0 \cdot \mathbf{E}[X_\tau^{(0)}] + \cdots + L^{11} \cdot \mathbf{E}[X_\tau^{(11)}] - \mathbf{E}[\tau].$$

For the target string "ABRACADABRA", we use hints

$$(\texttt{match}_{11} = 1) \implies (\texttt{match}_4 = 1)$$
$$(\texttt{match}_{11} = 1) \implies (\texttt{match}_1 = 1)$$
$$(\texttt{match}_{11} = 1) \implies (\texttt{match}_0 = 1)$$
$$(\texttt{match}_{11} = 1) \implies (\texttt{match}_j = 0). \qquad (\text{for } j \neq 0, 1, 4, 11)$$

For example, if $\texttt{match}_{11}$ is set then the full string is matching "ABRA-CADABRA", so the most recently seen four characters are "ABRA". This matches the first four letters of "ABRACADABRA", so $\texttt{match}_4$ is also set. The hint can be proved from a standard loop invariant.

Our tool derives the expected running time:

$$\mathbf{E}[\tau] = L^1 + L^4 + L^{11}.$$

Benchmarks. To give an idea of the efficiency of our tool, we present some benchmarks for our examples in Table 1. We measured timing on a recent laptop with a 2.4 GHz Intel Core processor with 8 GB of RAM. We did not optimize for the performance; we expect that the running time could be greatly improved with some tuning.

The example MINIABRA is a smaller version of the ABRACADABRA example, where the alphabet is just $\{0, 1\}$, and we stop when we sample the sequence 111; FULLABRA is the full ABRACADABRA example.

While there is a growing body of work related to martingale techniques for program analysis (see the following section), it is not obvious how to compare benchmarks. Existing work focuses on searching for martingale expressions within some search space; this is a rather different challenge than synthesizing a single martingale from a programmer-provided seed expression. In particular, if the seed expression happens to already be a martingale by some lucky guess, our tool will simply return the seed expression after checking that it is indeed a martingale.

Table 1. Preliminary benchmarks.

Example	Running time (s)
GEOM	0.14
GAMBLE	0.11
GAMBLE2	0.17
MINIABRA	0.87
FULLABRA	3.58

5   Related Work

Martingales. Martingale theory is a central tool in fields like statistics, applied mathematics, control theory, and finance. When analyzing randomized algorithms, martingales can show tight bounds on tail events [30]. In the verification community, martingales are used as invariant arguments, and as variants arguments to prove almost sure termination [5,6,9,18]. Recently, martingale approaches were extended to prove more complex properties. Chakarov, Voronin, and Sankaranarayanan [8] propose proof rules for proving persistence and recurrence properties. Dimitrova, Ferrer Fioriti, Hermanns, and Majumdar [16] develop a deductive proof system for PCTL*, with proof rules based on martingales and supermartingales.

Probabilistic Hoare Logic. McIver and Morgan [27] propose a Hoare-like logic that is quite similar to our approach of using martingales and OST. Their approach is based on *weakest pre-expectations*, which are an extension of Dijkstra's weakest preconditions [15] based on "backward" conditional expectations. Their probabilistic invariants are similar to submartingales, as the expected value of the invariant at the beginning of the execution lower bounds the expected value of the invariant at termination. Their proof rule also requires an additional constraint to ensure soundness, but it requires a limiting argument that is more difficult to automate compared to our bounded increment condition. We could relax our condition using a weaker version of OST that generalizes their condition [33]. Another substantial difference with our approach is that their logic supports non-deterministic choices—ours does not. It is not obvious how we can extend our synthesis approach to the non-probabilistic case as we heavily rely on the concept of filtration, not applicable in the presence of non-determinism.

Probabilistic Model Checking. In the last twenty years, model checking technology for probabilistic models have made impressive strides [11,23,26] (Baier and Katoen [3] provide overview). The main advantage of model checking is that it requires nothing from the user; our technique requires a seed expression. However, model checking techniques suffer from the state explosion problem—the time and memory consumption of the model checking algorithm depends on the number of reachable states of the program. Our approach can be used to verify infinite and parametric programs without any performance penalty, as we work purely symbolically. For example, a probabilistic model checker can find the expected running time of the gambler's ruin process for concrete values of a and b but they cannot deduce the solution for the general case, unlike our technique.

Invariant Synthesis. There are several approaches for synthesizing probabilistic invariants. Katoen et al. [22] propose the first complete method for the synthesis of McIver and Morgan's probabilistic linear invariants. It is an extension of the constraint solving approach by Colón, Sankaranarayanan, and Sipma [12] for the synthesis of (non-probabilistic) linear invariants. Chakarov and Sankaranarayanan [6] later extended this work to martingales and ranking supermartingales. Chakarov and Sankaranarayanan [7] propose a new notion of probabilistic invariants that generalizes the notion of supermatingales. They give a synthesis approach based on abstract interpretation, but it is not clear how their techniques can prove properties at termination time. Chen et al. [10] propose a synthesis tool for verifying Hoare triples in the McIver and Morgan logic, using a combination of Lagrange's interpolation, sampling, and counterexample guided search. One of the novelties is that they can synthesize non-linear invariants. The main disadvantages is that one must manually check the soundness condition, and one must provide a pre-expectation. For instance, we can apply the method of Chen et al. [10] to the gambler's ruin process only if we already know that the expected running time is $a(b - a)$. In contrast, we can deduce $\mathbf{E}[\tau] = a(b - a)$ knowing only that $\mathbf{E}[\tau]$ is finite.

Expected Running Time. As the termination time of a probabilistic program is a random quantity, it is natural to measure its performance using the average running time. Rough bounds can be obtained from martingale-based termination proofs [18]. Recently, Chatterjee et al. [9] showed that arbitrary approximations can be obtained from such proofs when the program is linear. They use Azuma's inequality to obtain a tail distribution of the running time, and later they model check a finite unrolling of the loop. Monniaux [29] propose a similar approach that uses abstract interpretation to obtain the tail distribution of the running time. Kaminski, Katoen, Matheja, and Olmedo [21] extend Nielson's proof system [31] to bound the expected running time of probabilistic programs.

Recurrence Analysis. Our synthesis approach is similar to the use of recurrences relations for the synthesis of non-probabilistic invariants [2,24,32]. The main idea is to find syntactic or semantic recurrences relations, and later simplify them using known closed forms to obtain loop invariants. In essence, we apply algebraic identities to simplify the complex martingales from Doob's decomposition. The difference is that our simplifications are more complex as we cannot always obtain a closed form but a simpler summation. However, we obtain the same closed form when we apply Doob's decomposition to inductive variables. Another difference is that we rely on the syntactic criteria to identify which values are predictable and which values are random.

6   Conclusion

We proposed a novel method for automatically synthesizing martingales expressions for stochastic processes. The basic idea is to transform any initial expression supplied by the user into a martingale using Doob's decomposition theorem. Our method complements the state-of-the-art synthesis approaches based on constraint solving. On one hand, we always output a martingale expression, we are able to synthesize non-inductive martingales, and since we do not rely on quantifier elimination, we can synthesize polynomial expression of very high degree. On the other hand, we do not provide any completeness result, and the shape of martingale is difficult to predict.

We considered several classical case studies from the literature, combining our synthesis method with the optional stopping theorem and non-probabilistic invariants to infer properties at termination time in a fully automatic fashion.

Future work includes extending our approach to programs with arrays and improving the tool with automated procedures for checking side-conditions. It would also be interesting to consider richer programs, say distributions with parameters that depend on program state. Another possible direction would be improving the simplification procedures; possibly, the tool could produce simpler facts. Experimenting with more advanced computer-algebra systems and designing simplification heuristics specialized to handling the conditional expectations synthesized by Doob's decomposition are both promising future directions. It would also be interesting to integrate our method as a special tool in systems for interactive reasoning about probabilistic computations.

Acknowledgments. We thank the anonymous reviewers for their helpful comments. This work was partially supported by NSF grants TWC-1513694 and CNS-1065060, and by a grant from the Simons Foundation (#360368 to Justin Hsu).

References

1. Allen, J.R., Kennedy, K., Porterfield, C., Warren, J.: Conversion of control dependence to data dependence. In: ACM Symposium on Principles of Programming Languages (POPL), Austin, Texas, pp. 177–189. ACM, New York (1983). ISBN 0-89791-090-7
2. Ammarguellat, Z., Harrison III, W.L.: Automatic recognition of induction variables and recurrence relations by abstract interpretation. In: ACM SIGPLAN Conference on Programming Language Design and Implementation (PLDI), White Plains, New York, pp. 283–295 (1990)
3. Baier, C., Katoen, J.: Principles of Model Checking. MIT Press, Cambridge (2008). ISBN 978-0-262-02649-9
4. Barthe, G., Grégoire, B., Heraud, S., Béguelin, S.Z.: Computer-aided security proofs for the working cryptographer. In: Rogaway, P. (ed.) CRYPTO 2011. LNCS, vol. 6841, pp. 71–90. Springer, Heidelberg (2011)
5. Bournez, O., Garnier, F.: Proving positive almost-sure termination. In: Giesl, J. (ed.) RTA 2005. LNCS, vol. 3467, pp. 323–337. Springer, Heidelberg (2005)
6. Chakarov, A., Sankaranarayanan, S.: Probabilistic program analysis with martingales. In: Sharygina, N., Veith, H. (eds.) CAV 2013. LNCS, vol. 8044, pp. 511–526. Springer, Heidelberg (2013)
7. Chakarov, A., Sankaranarayanan, S.: Expectation invariants for probabilistic program loops as fixed points. In: Müller-Olm, M., Seidl, H. (eds.) Static Analysis. LNCS, vol. 8723, pp. 85–100. Springer, Heidelberg (2014)
8. Chakarov, A., Voronin, Y.-L., Sankaranarayanan, S.: Deductive proofs of almost sure persistence and recurrence properties. In: Chechik, M., Raskin, J.-F. (eds.) TACAS 2016. LNCS, vol. 9636, pp. 260–279. Springer, Heidelberg (2016). doi:10. 1007/978-3-662-49674-9_15

9. Chatterjee, K., Fu, H., Novotný, P., Hasheminezhad, R.: Algorithmic analysis of qualitative and quantitative termination problems for affine probabilistic programs. In: ACM SIGPLAN–SIGACT Symposium on Principles of Programming Languages (POPL), St. Petersburg, Florida, pp. 327–342 (2016)

10. Chen, Y.-F., Hong, C.-D., Wang, B.-Y., Zhang, L.: Counterexample-guided polynomial loop invariant generation by lagrange interpolation. In: Kroening, D., Păsăreanu, C.S. (eds.) CAV 2015. LNCS, vol. 9206, pp. 658–674. Springer, Heidelberg (2015)

11. Ciesinski, F., Baier, C.: LiQuor: a tool for qualitative and quantitative linear time analysis of reactive systems. In: Third International Conference on the Quantitative Evaluation of Systems (QEST), Riverside, California, pp. 131–132 (2006)

12. Colón, M.A., Sankaranarayanan, S., Sipma, H.B.: Linear invariant generation using non-linear constraint solving. In: Hunt Jr., W.A., Somenzi, F. (eds.) CAV 2003. LNCS, vol. 2725, pp. 420–432. Springer, Heidelberg (2003)

13. Cousot, P., Halbwachs, N.: Automatic discovery of linear restraints among variables of a program. In: ACM Symposium on Principles of Programming Languages (POPL), Tucson, Arizona, pp. 84–96 (1978)

14. de Moura, L., Bjørner, N.S.: Z3: an efficient SMT solver. In: Ramakrishnan, C.R., Rehof, J. (eds.) TACAS 2008. LNCS, vol. 4963, pp. 337–340. Springer, Heidelberg (2008)

15. Dijkstra, E.W.: Guarded commands, nondeterminacy and formal derivation of programs. Commun. ACM 18(8), 453–457 (1975)

16. Dimitrova, R., Ferrer Fioriti, L.M., Hermanns, H., Majumdar, R.: Probabilistic CTL*: the deductive way. In: Chechik, M., Raskin, J.-F. (eds.) TACAS 2016. LNCS, vol. 9636, pp. 280–296. Springer, Heidelberg (2016). doi:10.1007/978-3-662-49674-9_16

17. Esparza, J., Gaiser, A., Kiefer, S.: Proving termination of probabilistic programs using patterns. In: Madhusudan, P., Seshia, S.A. (eds.) CAV 2012. LNCS, vol. 7358, pp. 123–138. Springer, Heidelberg (2012)

18. Ferrer Fioriti, L.M., Hermanns, H.: Probabilistic termination: soundness, completeness, and compositionality. In: ACM SIGPLAN-SIGACT Symposium on Principles of Programming Languages (POPL), Mumbai, India, pp. 489–501 (2015)

19. Hart, S., Sharir, M., Pnueli, A.: Termination of probabilistic concurrent program. ACM Trans. Program. Lang. Syst. 5(3), 356–380 (1983)

20. Joyner, D., Čertík, O., Meurer, A., Granger, B.E.: Open source computer algebra systems: SymPy. ACM Commun. Comput. Algebra 45(3–4), 225–234 (2012)

21. Kaminski, B.L., Katoen, J.-P., Matheja, C., Olmedo, F.: Weakest precondition reasoning for expected run–times of probabilistic programs. In: Thiemann, P. (ed.) ESOP 2016. LNCS, vol. 9632, pp. 364–389. Springer, Heidelberg (2016). doi:10.1007/978-3-662-49498-1_15

22. Katoen, J.-P., McIver, A.K., Meinicke, L.A., Morgan, C.C.: Linear-invariant generation for probabilistic programs: automated support for proof-based methods. In: Cousot, R., Martel, M. (eds.) SAS 2010. LNCS, vol. 6337, pp. 390–406. Springer, Heidelberg (2010)

23. Katoen, J., Zapreev, I.S., Hahn, E.M., Hermanns, H., Jansen, D.N.: The ins and outs of the probabilistic model checker MRMC. Perform. Eval. 68(2), 90–104 (2011)

24. Kovács, L.: Reasoning algebraically about P-solvable loops. In: Ramakrishnan, C.R., Rehof, J. (eds.) TACAS 2008. LNCS, vol. 4963, pp. 249–264. Springer, Heidelberg (2008)

25. Kozen, D.: Semantics of probabilistic programs. J. Comput. Syst. Sci. **22**(3), 328–350 (1981)
26. Kwiatkowska, M., Norman, G., Parker, D.: PRISM 4.0: verification of probabilistic real-time systems. In: Gopalakrishnan, G., Qadeer, S. (eds.) CAV 2011. LNCS, vol. 6806, pp. 585–591. Springer, Heidelberg (2011)
27. McIver, A., Morgan, C.: Abstraction, Refinement and Proof for Probabilistic Systems. Monographs in Computer Science. Springer, New York (2005)
28. Miné, A.: The octagon abstract domain. High.-Order Symb. Comput. **19**(1), 31–100 (2006)
29. Monniaux, D.: An abstract analysis of the probabilistic termination of programs. In: Cousot, P. (ed.) SAS 2001. LNCS, vol. 2126, pp. 111–126. Springer, Heidelberg (2001)
30. Motwani, R., Raghavan, P.: Randomized Algorithms. Cambridge University Press, Cambridge (1995). ISBN 0-521-47465-5
31. Nielson, H.R.: A hoare-like proof system for analysing the computation time of programs. Sci. Comput. Program. **9**(2), 107–136 (1987)
32. Rodríguez-Carbonell, E., Kapur, D.: Generating all polynomial invariants in simple loops. J. Symb. Comput. **42**(4), 443–476 (2007)
33. Williams, D.: Probability with Martingales. Cambridge University Press, Cambridge (1991)

PSI: Exact Symbolic Inference
for Probabilistic Programs

Timon Gehr[1]([⊠]), Sasa Misailovic[1,2], and Martin Vechev[1]

[1] ETH Zurich, Zurich, Switzerland
tgehr@student.ethz.ch, {misailo,martin.vechev}@inf.ethz.ch
[2] University of Illinois at Urbana-Champaign, Champaign and Urbana, USA

Abstract. Probabilistic inference is a key mechanism for reasoning about probabilistic programs. Since exact inference is theoretically expensive, most probabilistic inference systems today have adopted approximate inference techniques, which trade precision for better performance (but often without guarantees). As a result, while desirable for its ultimate precision, the practical effectiveness of exact inference for probabilistic programs is mostly unknown.

This paper presents PSI (http://www.psisolver.org), a novel symbolic analysis system for exact inference in probabilistic programs with both continuous and discrete random variables. PSI computes succinct symbolic representations of the joint posterior distribution represented by a given probabilistic program. PSI can compute answers to various posterior distribution, expectation and assertion queries using its own backend for symbolic reasoning.

Our evaluation shows that PSI is more effective than existing exact inference approaches: (i) it successfully computed a precise result for more programs, and (ii) simplified expressions that existing computer algebra systems (e.g., Mathematica, Maple) fail to andle.

1 Introduction

Many statistical learning applications make decisions under uncertainty. Probabilistic languages provide a natural way to model uncertainty by representing complex probability distributions as programs [8,12,19–21,25,32,39,46]. Exact probabilistic inference for programs with only discrete random variables is already a #P-hard computational problem [13]. Programs which have both discrete and continuous variables reveal additional challenges, such as representing discrete and continuous components of the joint distribution, computing integrals, and managing a large number of terms in the joint distribution.

For these reasons, most existing probabilistic languages implement inference algorithms that calculate numerical approximations. The general approaches include sampling-based Monte Carlo methods [19–21,32,39,40,46] and projections to convenient probability distributions, such as variational inference [8,34] or discretization [12,31]. While these methods scale well, they typically come with no accuracy guarantees, since providing such guarantees is NP-hard [15].

© Springer International Publishing Switzerland 2016
S. Chaudhuri and A. Farzan (Eds.): CAV 2016, Part I, LNCS 9779, pp. 62–83, 2016.
DOI: 10.1007/978-3-319-41528-4_4

At the same time, there has been a renewed research interest in symbolic inference methods due to their promise for computing more precise inference results. Existing symbolic inference works fall into different categories:

- *Approximate symbolic inference:* Several analyses of graphical models approximate continuous distribution functions with a mixture of base functions, such as truncated exponentials or polynomials, which can be integrated more easily [11,36,43–45]. For instance, SVE [43] approximates distributions as piecewise low-rank polynomials.
- *Interactive symbolic inference:* A user can write down the inference steps within modern computer algebra systems, such as Mathematica [3] and Maple [1]. These tools can help the user by automating parts of the integration and/or simplification of distribution expressions.
- *Exact symbolic inference:* Bhat et al. [7] presents a type-based analysis translating programs with mixed discrete/continuous variables into symbolic distribution expressions, but does not simplify integral terms symbolically and instead computes them using a numerical integration library. Most recently, Hakaru [10,38] optimizes probabilistic programs by translating a program into a distribution expression in a DSL within Maple's expression language, and simplifying this expression utilizing Maple's engine, before running (if necessary) the optimized program within a MCMC simulation.

While these works are promising steps, the practical effectiveness of exact symbolic inference in hybrid probabilistic models (with *both* discrete and continuous distributions) remains unknown, dictating the need for further investigation.

This Work. We present the PSI (Probabilistic Symbolic Inference) system, a comprehensive approach for automating exact probabilistic inference via program analysis. PSI's analysis performs an *end-to-end symbolic inference* for probabilistic programs with discrete and/or continuous random variables. PSI analyzes a probabilistic program using a symbolic domain which captures the program's probability distribution in a precise manner. PSI comes with its own symbolic optimization engine which generates compact expressions that represent *joint probability density functions* using various optimizations, including algebraic simplification and symbolic integration. The symbolic domain and optimizations are designed to strike a balance between the expressiveness of the probability density expressions and the efficiency of automatically computing integrals and generating compact densities.

Our symbolic analysis (Sect. 3) generalizes existing analyzers for exact inference on discrete programs (e.g., those that operate at the level of concrete states [12]). Our optimization engine (Sect. 4) can also automatically simplify many integrals in density expressions and thus directly improve the performance of works that generate unoptimized expressions, such as [7], without requiring the full complexity of a general computer algebra system, as in [10,38]. As a result, PSI is able to compute precise and compact inference results even when the existing approaches fail (Sect. 5).

Contributions. Our main contributions are:

– *Symbolic inference for programs with continuous/discrete variables:* A novel approach for fully symbolic probabilistic inference. The algorithm represents the posterior distribution within a symbolic domain.
– *Probabilistic inference system:* PSI, an implementation of our algorithm together with optimizations that simplify the symbolic representation of the posterior distribution. PSI is available at http://www.psisolver.org.
– *Evaluation:* The paper shows an experimental evaluation of PSI against state-of-the-art symbolic inference techniques – Hakaru, Maple, Mathematica, and SVE – on a corpus of 21 benchmarks selected from the literature. PSI produced correct and compact distribution expressions for more benchmarks than the alternatives. In addition, we compare PSI to state-of-the-art approximate inference engines, Infer.NET [34] and R2 [39], and show the benefits of exact inference.

Based on our results, we believe that PSI is the most effective exact symbolic inference engine to date and is useful for understanding the potential of exact symbolic inference for probabilistic programs.

2   Overview

Figure 1 presents the ClickGraph probabilistic program, adapted from a Fun language program from [34]. It describes an information retrieval model that calculates the posterior distribution of the similarity of two files, conditioned on the users' access patterns to these files.

The program first specifies the prior distribution on the document similarity (line 2) and the recorded accesses to A and B for each user (lines 4–5). It then specifies a trial in which the variable sim is the similarity of the documents for an issued query (line 7). If the documents are similar, the probabilities of accessing them (p1 and p2) are the same, otherwise p1 and p2 are independent (lines 9–14). Finally, the variables clickA and clickB represent outcomes of the users accessing the documents (lines 16–17), and each trial produces a specific observation using the observe statements (lines 18–19). The return statement specifies that PSI should compute the posterior distribution of simAll.

2.1   Analysis

To compute the posterior distribution, PSI analyzes the probabilistic program via a symbolic domain that captures probability distributions, and applies optimizations to simplify the resulting expression after each analysis step.

Symbolic Analysis: For each statement, the analysis computes a symbolic expression that captures the program's probability distribution at that point. The analysis operates forward, starting form the beginning of the function. As a pre-processing step, the analysis unrolls all loops and lowers the array elements into a sequence of scalars or inlined constants. The state of the analysis at each program point captures (1) the correct execution of the program as a map that relates live program variables $x_1, \ldots, x_n$ to a symbolic expression e representing a *probability density* of the computation at this point in the program, and (2) erroneous executions (e.g., due to an assertion violation) represented by an aggregate error probability expression $\bar{e}$.

```
1   def ClickGraph(){
2       simAll := Uniform(0,1);
3
4       clicksA := [1, 1, 1, 0, 0];
5       clicksB := [1, 1, 1, 0, 0]
6       for i in [0..5) {
7           sim := Bernoulli(simAll);
8
9           p1:=0; p2:=0;
10          if sim {
11              p1 = Uniform(0,1); p2 = p1;
12          } else {
13              p1 = Uniform(0,1); p2 = Uniform(0,1);
14          }
15
16          clickA := Bernoulli(p1);
17          clickB := Bernoulli(p2);
18          observe(clickA==clicksA[i]);
19          observe(clickB==clicksB[i]);
20      }
21      return simAll;
22  }
```

Fig. 1. ClickGraph Example

The analysis of the first statement (line 2) identifies that the state consists of the variable simAll, which has the Uniform$(0, 1)$ distribution. In general, for $x := $ Uniform(a, b), the analysis generates the expression $[a \leq x] \cdot [x \leq b]/(b - a)$, which denotes the density of this distribution. The factors $[a \leq x]$ and $[x \leq b]$ are *Iverson brackets*, guard functions that equal 1 if their conditions are true, or equal 0 otherwise. Therefore, this density has a non-zero value only if $x \in [a, b]$. In particular, for simAll, the analysis generates $e_{L.2} = [0 \leq \text{simAll}] \cdot [\text{simAll} \leq 1]$.

Since the constant arrays are inlined, the analysis next processes the statement on line 7 (in the first loop iteration). The analysis adds the variable sim to the state, and multiplies the expression $e_{L.2}$ with the density function for the distribution Bernoulli(simAll):

$$e_{L.7} = [0 \leq \text{simAll}] \cdot [\text{simAll} \leq 1] \cdot (\text{simAll} \cdot \delta(1 - \text{sim}) + (1 - \text{simAll}) \cdot \delta(\text{sim}))$$
$$\bar{e}_{L.7} = 0$$

The expression $e_{L.7}$ represents a generalized joint probability density over simAll and sim. To encode discrete distributions like Bernoulli, the analysis uses *Dirac deltas*, $\delta(e)$, which specify a distribution with point masses at the zeros of e.

Optimizations: After analyzing each statement, the analysis simplifies the generated distribution expression by applying equivalence-preserving optimizations:

- basic algebraic manipulations (e.g., in the previous expression, an optimization can distribute multiplication over addition);
- removal of factors with trivial or unsatisfiable guards (e.g., in this example the analysis checks whether a product $[0 \leq \text{simAll}] \cdot [\text{simAll} \leq 1]$ is always equal to zero, and since it is not, leaves the expression unchanged);
- symbolic integration of the distribution expressions; for instance, at the end of the each loop iteration, the analysis expression $e_{L.19}$ contains several loop-local variables: sim, p1, p2, clickA, and clickB. The analysis integrates out these local variables because they will not be referenced by the subsequent computation. It first removes the discrete variables sim, clickA, and clickB by exploiting the properties of Dirac deltas. For the continuous variables p1 and p2, it computes the antiderivative (indefinite integral) using PSI's integration engine, finds the integration bounds, and evaluates the antiderivative on these bounds. After the analysis of the first loop iteration, this optimization reduces the size of the distribution expression from 22 to 6 summands.

Result of the Analysis: After analyzing the entire program, the analysis produces the final posterior probability density expression for the variable simAll:

$$e_{L.21} \quad = \quad [0 \leq \text{simAll}] \cdot [\text{simAll} \leq 1] \cdot \frac{6(\text{simAll} + 3)^5}{3367}$$

The analysis also computes that the final error probability $\bar{e}_{L.21}$ is 0. This is the exact posterior distribution for this program. We present this posterior density function graphically in Fig. 8.

2.2   Applications of PSI

PSI's source language (with conditional and bounded loop statements) has the expressive power to represent arbitrary Bayesian networks, which encode many probabilistic models relevant in practice [22]. PSI's analysis is analogous to the variable elimination algorithm for inference in graphical models. We anticipate that PSI can be successfully deployed in several contexts:

Probabilistic Inference: PSI allows a developer to specify several classes of queries. For joint posterior distribution, a user may return multiple variables in the return statement. The special operators FromMarginal(e) and Expectation(e) return the marginal distribution and the expectation of an expression e, respectively. A developer can also specify assertions using the assert(e) statement.

Testing and Debugging: The exact inference results produced by PSI can be used as reference versions for debugging and testing approximate inference engines. It can also be used to test existing computer algebra systems – using PSI, we found errors in Maple's simplifier (see Sect. 5).

Sampling from Optimized Probabilistic Programs: Optimized distribution expressions generated by PSI's symbolic optimizer can be used, in principle, for computing proposal distributions in MCMC simulations, as done by [7,38].

Uncertainty Propagation Analysis: PSI's analysis can serve as a basis for static analyses that propagate uncertainty through computations and determine error bars for the result. This provides a powerful alternative to existing analyses that are primarily sampling-based [9,41], with at most limited support for simplifying algebraic identities that involve random variables [41].

$$n \in \mathbb{Z} \qquad bop \in \{+, -, *, /, \hat{\ }\} \qquad lop \in \{\&\&, ||\} \qquad cop \in \{==, \neq, <, >, \leq, \geq\}$$

$r \in \mathbb{R}$ $\text{Dist} \in \{\texttt{Bernoulli}, \texttt{Gauss}, \dots\} \; \text{SOp} \in \{\texttt{Expectation}, \texttt{FromMarginal}, \texttt{SampleFrom}\}$

$x \in \text{Var}$ $p \in \text{Prog} \to \text{Func}^+$

$a \in \text{ArrVar}$ $f \in \text{Func} \to \texttt{def} \; Id(Var^*) \; \{\text{Stmt}; \; \texttt{return} \; Var^*\}$

$se \in \text{Expr} \to$ $n \mid r \mid x \mid a\,[\text{Expr}] \mid \text{Expr} \; bop \; \text{Expr} \mid \text{Expr} \; cop \; \text{Expr} \mid \text{Expr} \; lop \; \text{Expr} \mid$
              $\text{Dist}(\text{Expr}^+) \mid \text{SOp}(\text{Expr}) \mid f(\text{Expr}^*)$

$s \in \text{Stmt} \to$ $x := \text{Expr} \mid a := \texttt{array}(\text{Expr}) \mid x = \text{Expr} \mid a\,[\text{Expr}] = \text{Expr} \mid$
              $\texttt{observe} \; \text{Expr} \mid \texttt{assert} \; \text{Expr} \mid \texttt{skip} \mid \text{Stmt}; \; \text{Stmt} \mid$
              $\texttt{if} \; \text{Expr} \; \{\text{Stmt}\} \; \texttt{else} \; \{\text{Stmt}\} \mid \texttt{for} \; x \; \texttt{in} \; [\text{Expr}..\text{Expr}) \; \{\text{Stmt}\}$

Fig. 2. PSI's source language syntax

3 Symbolic Inference

In this section we describe our core analysis: the procedure analyzes each statement in the program and produces a corresponding expression in our symbolic domain which captures probability distributions.

3.1 Source Language

Figure 2 presents the syntax of PSI's source language. This is a simple imperative language that operates on real-valued scalar and array data. The language defines probabilistic assignments, which can assign a random value drawn from a distribution Dist, and **observe** statements, which allow constraining the values of probabilistic expressions. The language also supports the standard sequence, conditional statement, and bounded loop statement.

3.2 Symbolic Domain for Probability Distributions

Figure 3 presents the syntax of our symbolic domain. The domain can succinctly describe joint probability distributions with discrete and continuous components:

$$e \in E ::= \quad x \mid n \mid r \mid \log(e) \mid \varphi(e_1, \ldots, e_n) \mid -e \mid e_1 + \ldots + e_n \mid e_1 \cdot \ldots \cdot e_n \mid e_1^{e_2} \mid$$

$$\delta(e) \mid [e_1 = e_2] \mid [e_1 \le e_2] \mid [e_1 \ne e_2] \mid [e_1 < e_2] \mid$$

$$\sum_{x \in \mathbb{Z}} e[\![x]\!] \mid \int_{\mathbb{R}} \mathrm{d}x \, e[\![x]\!] \mid (\mathrm{d}/\mathrm{d}x)^{-1}[e^{-x^2}](e)$$

Fig. 3. Symbolic domain for probability distributions

- *Basic terms* include variables, numerical constants (such as e and π), logarithms and uninterpreted functions. These terms can form sums, products, or exponents. Division is handled using the rewrite $a/b \to a \cdot b^{-1}$.
- *Dirac deltas* represent distributions that have weight in low-dimensional sets (such as single points). In our analysis, they encode variable definitions and assignments, and linear combinations of Dirac deltas specify discrete distributions.
- *Iverson brackets* represent functions that are 1 if the condition within the brackets is satisfied and 0 otherwise. In our analysis, they encode comparison operators and certain primitive probability distributions (e.g., Uniform).
- *Integrals and infinite sums* are used during the analysis to represent marginalization of variables and UniformInt distributions respectively.
- *Gaussian antiderivative* – $(\mathrm{d}/\mathrm{d}x)^{-1}[e^{-x^2}](e)$ – used to denote the function $\int_{-\infty}^{e} \mathrm{d}x \, e^{-x^2}$, which cannot be decomposed into simpler elementary functions.

We use the notation $e[\![x_1, \ldots, x_n]\!]$ to denote that a symbolic distribution expression e may contain free variables $x_1, \ldots, x_n$ that are bound by an outer operator (such as a sum or integral).

Our design of the symbolic domain aims to strike a balance between *expressiveness* – the kinds of distributions it can represent – and *efficiency* – the ability of the analysis to automatically integrate functions and find simple equivalent expressions. In particular, our symbolic domain enables us to define most discrete and continuous distributions from the exponential family and other well-known primitive distributions, such as Student-t and Laplace (see the Appendix A).

Primitive Distributions: For each primitive distribution Dist, we define two mappings, PDF$_{\text{Dist}}$, and Conditions$_{\text{Dist}}$ to respectively specify the probability density function, and valid parameter and input ranges. For instance, the Bernoulli distribution with a parameter e_p has PDF$_{\text{Bern}}(x, e_p) = e_p \cdot \delta(1 - x) + (1 - e_p) \cdot \delta(x)$ and Conditions$_{\text{Bern}} = [0 \le e_p] \cdot [e_p \le 1]$. We present the encodings of several other primitive distributions in the Appendix A. Additionally, PSI allows the developer to specify an arbitrary density function of the resulting distribution using the `SampleFrom` (`sym_expr, ...`) primitive, which takes as inputs a distribution expression and a set of its parameters.

Program State: A symbolic program state σ denotes a probability distribution over the program variables with an additional error state:

$$\sigma \in \Sigma ::= \lambda M. \textbf{case } M \textbf{ of } (x_1, \ldots, x_n) \Rightarrow e_1 \llbracket x_1, \ldots, x_n \rrbracket, \ \bot \Rightarrow e_2 \qquad (1)$$

In a regular execution, the state is represented with the variables $x_1, \ldots, x_n$ and the posterior distribution expression e_1. We represent the error state as a symbol $\bot$ and the expression for the probability of error e_2. Conceptually, the map σ associates a probability density with each concrete program state M, which is either a tuple of values of program variables or the error state.

3.3   Analysis of Expressions

Figure 4 presents the analysis of expressions. The function A_e converts each expression of the source language to a transformer $t \in \Sigma \rightarrow \Sigma \times E$ on the symbolic representation. The transformer returns both a new state ($\sigma \in \Sigma$) and a result of expression evaluation ($e \in E$), thus capturing side effects (e.g., sampling values from probability distributions or exhibiting errors such as division by zero).

Operations: The first five rules transform source language variables to distribution expression variables (including operators via the helper function *SymbolicOp*). The rules are standard, with Boolean constants `true` and `false` encoded as numbers 1 and 0, respectively. The rules compose the side effects of the operands. The division rule additionally uses the Assert helper function to add the guard $[e_2 \neq 0]$ to the distribution expression and aggregate the probability of $e_2 = 0$ to the overall error probability.

Distribution Sampling: The expression $\text{Dist}(se_1, \ldots, se_n)$ accepts distribution parameters $se_1, \ldots, se_n$, which can be arbitrary expressions. For a primitive distribution Dist, the analysis obtains expressions from the mappings PDF_{Dist} and $\text{Conditions}_{\text{Dist}}$ (Sect. 3.2).

The rule first analyzes all of the distribution's parameters (which can represent random quantities). To iterate over the parameters, the rule uses the helper function A_e^*, defined inductively as:

$$A_e^*([]) \quad := \lambda \sigma . (\sigma, [])$$
$$A_e^*(se : t) := \lambda \sigma . \textbf{let } (\sigma_1, e) = A_e(se)(\sigma) \textbf{ and } (\sigma_2, t') = A_e^*(t)(\sigma_1) \textbf{ in } (\sigma_2, e : t').$$

To ensure that distribution parameters have the correct values, the rule invokes a helper function Assert, which adds guards from the $\text{Conditions}_{\text{Dist}}$. Finally, the rule declares a *fresh* temporary variable τ (specified by a predicate FreshVar), which is then distributed according to the density function PDF_{Dist}, using the helper function Distribute. In the definitions of Assert and Distribute, we specified the states in their expanded forms (Eq. 1).

$$A_e : \text{Expr} \rightarrow (\Sigma \rightarrow \Sigma \times E)$$

$$A_e(x) := \lambda \sigma. \, (\sigma, x)$$

$$A_e(\text{se}_1 \, bop \, \text{se}_2) := \lambda \sigma. \, \textbf{let} \, (\sigma_1, e_1) = A_e(\text{se}_1)(\sigma) \, \textbf{and} \, (\sigma_2, e_2) = A_e(\text{se}_2)(\sigma_1)$$
$$\textbf{in} \, (\sigma_2, e_1 \, SymbolicOp(bop) \, e_2), \quad bop \in \{+, -, *\}$$

$$A_e(\text{se}_1/\text{se}_2) := \lambda \sigma. \, \textbf{let} \, (\sigma_1, e_1) = A_e(\text{se}_1)(\sigma) \, \textbf{and} \, (\sigma_2, e_2) = A_e(\text{se}_2)(\sigma_1)$$
$$\textbf{in} \, (\text{Assert}([e_2 \neq 0])(\sigma_2), e_1 \cdot e_2^{-1})$$

$$A_e(\text{se}_1 \&\& \text{se}_2) := \lambda \sigma. \, \textbf{let} \, (\sigma_1, e_1) = A_e(\text{se}_1)(\sigma) \, \textbf{and} \, (\sigma_2, e_2) = A_e(\text{se}_2)(\sigma_1)$$
$$\textbf{in} \, (\sigma_2, [e_1 \neq 0] \cdot [e_2 \neq 0])$$

$$A_e(\text{se}_1 \, || \, \text{se}_2) := \lambda \sigma. \, \textbf{let} \, (\sigma_1, e_1) = A_e(\text{se}_1)(\sigma) \, \textbf{and} \, (\sigma_2, e_2) = A_e(\text{se}_2)(\sigma_1)$$
$$\textbf{in} \, (\sigma_2, [\, [e_1 \neq 0] + [e_2 \neq 0] \neq 0 \,])$$

$$A_e(\text{Dist}(\text{se}_1, \ldots, \text{se}_n)) := \lambda \sigma. \, \textbf{let} \, (\sigma_1, [e_1, \ldots, e_n]) = A_e^*([\text{se}_1, \ldots, \text{se}_n])(\sigma) \, \textbf{and} \, \text{FreshVar}(\tau)$$
$$\textbf{and} \, (P, C) = (\text{PDF}_{\text{Dist}}(\tau, e_1, \ldots, e_n), \text{Conditions}_{\text{Dist}}(e_1, \ldots, e_n))$$
$$\textbf{in let} \, \sigma_2 = (\text{Distribute}(\tau, P) \circ \text{Assert}(C))(\sigma_1) \, \textbf{in} \, (\sigma_2, \tau),$$

$$\text{Assert}(e[\![x_1, \ldots, x_n]\!])(\lambda M. \, \textbf{case} \, M \, \textbf{of} \, (x_1, \ldots, x_n) \Rightarrow e_1[\![x_1, \ldots, x_n]\!], \bot \Rightarrow e_2) :=$$
$$\lambda M. \, \textbf{case} \, M \, \textbf{of} \, (x_1, \ldots, x_n) \Rightarrow (e_1 \cdot [e \neq 0])[\![x_1, \ldots, x_n]\!],$$
$$\bot \Rightarrow e_2 + \text{MarginalizeAll}([e = 0] \cdot e_1)$$

$$\text{Distribute}(x, e[\![x_1, \ldots, x_n, x]\!])(\lambda M. \, \textbf{case} \, M \, \textbf{of} \, (x_1, \ldots, x_n) \Rightarrow e_1[\![x_1, \ldots, x_n]\!], \bot \Rightarrow e_2) :=$$
$$\lambda M. \, \textbf{case} \, M \, \textbf{of} \, (x_1, \ldots, x_n, x) \Rightarrow e_1[\![x_1, \ldots, x_n]\!] \cdot e[\![x_1, \ldots, x_n, x]\!], \, \bot \Rightarrow e_2$$

Fig. 4. Symbolic snalysis of expressions

Marginalization: Marginalization aggregates the probability by summing up over the variables in an expression (e.g., local variables at the end of scope or variables in an error expression). To marginalize all variables, we define the function

$$\text{MarginalizeAll}(e[\![x_1, \ldots, x_n]\!]) := \int_{\mathbb{R}} dx_1 \cdots \int_{\mathbb{R}} dx_n e[\![x_1, \ldots, x_n]\!].$$

The function KeepOnly performs selective marginalization. It takes as input the variables $x_1' \ldots, x_m'$ to keep and the input state σ, and marginalizes out the remaining variables in σ's distribution expressions:

$$\text{KeepOnly}(x_1', \ldots, x_m')(\lambda M. \, \textbf{case} \, M \, \textbf{of} \, (x_1, \ldots, x_n) \Rightarrow e_1[\![x_1, \ldots, x_n]\!], \bot \Rightarrow e_2) =$$
$$\textbf{let} \, \{x_1'', \ldots, x_l''\} = \{x_1, \ldots, x_n\} \setminus \{x_1', \ldots, x_m'\}$$
$$\textbf{in} \, \lambda M. \, \textbf{case} \, M \, \textbf{of} \, (x_1', \ldots, x_m') \Rightarrow \int_{\mathbb{R}} dx_1'' \cdots \int_{\mathbb{R}} dx_l'' e_1[\![x_1, \ldots, x_n]\!], \bot \Rightarrow e_2$$

3.4 Analysis of Statements

Figure 5 presents the definition of function A_s: it analyzes each statement and produces a transformer of states: $\Sigma \rightarrow \Sigma$. The initial analysis state σ_0 is defined

$$A_s : \text{Stmt} \to (\Sigma \to \Sigma)$$

$$A_s(\textbf{skip}) := \lambda\sigma.\sigma$$

$$A_s(x := \text{se}) := \lambda\sigma.\,\textbf{let}\ (\sigma', e) = A_e(\text{se})(\sigma)\ \textbf{in}\ \text{Distribute}(x, \delta(x - e))(\sigma')$$

$$A_s(x = \text{se}) := A_s(x := \text{se}[\![\tau/x]\!]) \circ \text{Rename}(x, \tau),\ \text{with FreshVar}(\tau)$$

$$A_s(s_1; s_2) := A_s(s_2) \circ A_s(s_1)$$

$$A_s(\textbf{assert}(\text{se})) := \lambda\sigma.\,\textbf{let}\ (\sigma', e) = A_e(\text{se})(\sigma)\ \textbf{in}\ \text{Assert}([e \neq 0])(\sigma')$$

$$A_s(\textbf{observe}(\text{se})) := \lambda\sigma.\,\textbf{let}\ (\sigma', e) = A_e(\text{se})(\sigma)\ \textbf{in}\ \text{Observe}([e \neq 0])(\sigma')$$

$$A_s(\textbf{if se}\ \{s_1\}\ \textbf{else}\ \{s_2\}) := \lambda\sigma.\,\textbf{let}\ (\sigma_0, e) = A_e(\text{se})(\sigma)$$
$$\textbf{and}\ \sigma_1 = (A_s(s_1) \circ \text{Observe}([e \neq 0]))(\sigma_0)$$
$$\textbf{and}\ \sigma_2 = (A_s(s_2) \circ \text{Observe}([e = 0]))(\sigma_0)$$
$$\textbf{in}\ \text{Join}(\sigma, \sigma_1, \sigma_2)$$

$$A_s(\textbf{return}\ (x_1, \ldots, x_n)) := \text{KeepOnly}(x_1, \ldots, x_n)$$

Fig. 5. Symbolic analysis of statements

as follows: $\sigma_0 = (\lambda M.\,\textbf{case}\ M\ \textbf{of}\ \vec{x} \Rightarrow \varphi(\vec{x}), \bot \Rightarrow 0)$. Here, the function F under analysis has parameters $\vec{x} = (x_1, \ldots x_n)$ where φ is an uninterpreted function representing the joint probability density of $\vec{x}$. If F has no parameters, we replace $\varphi()$ with 1.

Definitions: The statement $x := \text{se}$ declares a new variable x and distributes it as a point mass centered at e (the symbolic expression corresponding to se), i.e. the analysis binds x by multiplying the joint probability density by $\delta(x - e)$.

Assignments: Analysis of assignments to existing variables ($x = \text{se}$) consistently renames these variable and introduces a new variable with the previous name. The substitution $\text{se}[\![\tau/x]\!]$ renames x to τ in the source expression se, since the variable being assigned may itself occur in se. The function $\text{Rename}(x, \tau)$ alpha-renames all occurrences of the variable x to τ in an existing state (σ) to avoid capture (Fig. 6). It is necessary to rename x in se separately, because se is a source program expression, while Rename renames variables in the analysis state.

Observations: Observations are handled by a call to the helper function Observe (Fig. 6), which conditions the probability distribution on the given expression being true. We do not renormalize the distribution after an observation, but only once, before reporting the final result (Sect. 3.5). Therefore, observations do not immediately change the error part of the distribution.

Conditionals: The analysis of conditionals first analyzes the condition, and then creates two copies of the resulting state σ_0. In one of the copies, the condition is then observed to be true, and in the other copy, the condition is observed to be false. Analysis of the 'then' and 'else' statements s_1 and s_2 in the corresponding states yields σ_1 and σ_2. Finally, σ_1 and σ_2 are joined together by marginalizing

$\mathrm{Rename}(x, x')(\lambda M.\,\mathbf{case}\ M\ \mathbf{of}\ (x_1, ..., x, ..., x_n) \Rightarrow e_1[\![x_1, ..., x, ..., x_n]\!], \bot \Rightarrow e_2) :=$
$\quad \lambda M.\,\mathbf{case}\ M\ \mathbf{of}\ (x_1, ..., x', ..., x_n) \Rightarrow e_1[\![x_1, ..., x', ..., x_n]\!], \bot \Rightarrow e_2$

$\mathrm{Observe}(e[\![\vec{x}]\!])(\lambda M.\,\mathbf{case}\ M\ \mathbf{of}\ (\vec{x}) \Rightarrow e_1[\![\vec{x}]\!], \bot \Rightarrow e_2) :=$
$\quad \lambda M.\,\mathbf{case}\ M\ \mathbf{of}\ (\vec{x}) \Rightarrow e_1[\![\vec{x}]\!] \cdot e[\![\vec{x}]\!], \bot \Rightarrow e_2$

$\mathrm{Join}((\lambda M.\,\mathbf{case}\ M\ \mathbf{of}\ (\vec{x}) \Rightarrow e_1[\![\vec{x}]\!], \bot \Rightarrow e_2), \sigma_{\mathrm{then}}, \sigma_{\mathrm{else}}) :=$
$\quad \mathbf{let}\ (\lambda M.\,\mathbf{case}\ M\ \mathbf{of}\ (\vec{x}) \Rightarrow e_1'[\![\vec{x}]\!], \bot \Rightarrow e_2') = \mathrm{KeepOnly}(\vec{x})(\sigma_{\mathrm{then}})$
$\quad \mathbf{and}\ (\lambda M.\,\mathbf{case}\ M\ \mathbf{of}\ (\vec{x}) \Rightarrow e_1''[\![\vec{x}]\!], \bot \Rightarrow e_2'') = \mathrm{KeepOnly}(\vec{x})(\sigma_{\mathrm{else}})$
$\quad \mathbf{in}\ \lambda M.\,\mathbf{case}\ M\ \mathbf{of}\ (\vec{x}) \Rightarrow e_1'[\![\vec{x}]\!] + e_1''[\![\vec{x}]\!], \bot \Rightarrow e_2'[\![\vec{x}]\!] + e_2''[\![\vec{x}]\!] - e_2[\![\vec{x}]\!]$

Fig. 6. Analysis of statements - helper functions

all locally scoped variables, including temporaries created during the analysis of the condition, and then adding the distribution and the error terms (Join; Fig. 6). We subtract the error probability in the original state to avoid counting it twice.

3.5   Final Result and Renormalization

We obtain the final result by applying the state transformer obtained from analysis of the function body to the initial state and *renormalizing* it. We define the renormalization function as:

$\mathrm{Renormalize}(\lambda M.\,\mathbf{case}\ M\ \mathbf{of}\ (x_1, \ldots, x_n) \Rightarrow e_1[\![x_1, \ldots, x_n]\!], \bot \Rightarrow e_2) :=$
$\quad \mathbf{let}\ e_Z = \mathrm{MarginalizeAll}(e_1) + e_2$
$\quad \mathbf{in}\ \lambda M.\,\mathbf{case}\ M\ \mathbf{of}\ (x_1, \ldots, x_n) \Rightarrow [e_Z \neq 0] \cdot e_1[\![x_1, \ldots, x_n]\!] \cdot e_Z^{-1},$
$$\bot \Rightarrow [e_Z \neq 0] \cdot e_2 \cdot e_Z^{-1} + [e_Z = 0]$$

The function obtains a normalization expression e_Z, such that the renormalized distribution expression of the resulting state integrates to 1. This way, PSI computes a normalized joint probability distribution for the function results that depends symbolically on the initial joint distribution of the function's arguments.

3.6   Discussion

Loop Analysis: PSI analyzes loops like `for i in [0..N){...}` (as mentioned in Sect. 2.1) by unrolling the loop body a constant N number of times. This approach also extends to loops where the number of iterations N is a random program variable. If N can be bounded from above by a constant N_{max}, a developer can encode the loop as

```
assert(N <= Nmax);
for i in [0..Nmax) {
    if(i < N) {  /* loop body */  }
}
```

To handle `for`-loops with unbounded random variables and general `while`-loops, a developer can select N_{max} such that the probability of error (i.e., probability that the loop runs for more than N_{max} iterations) is small enough. We anticipate that this approach can be readily automated. Related techniques such as [18,42] employ similar approximation techniques.

Function Call Analysis: PSI can analyze multiple functions, generating for each function $f(x_1, ..., x_n)$ the density expression of its m outputs, parameterized by the unknown distribution of the function's n inputs. The distribution of the function inputs is represented by an uninterpreted function $\varphi(x_1, ..., x_n)$ which appears as a subterm in the output density expression.

The rule for the analysis of function calls (see Appendix B) first creates temporary variables $a_1, ..., a_n$ for each argument of f, and variables $r_1, ..., r_m$ for each result returned by f. The variables $a_1, ..., a_n$ are then initialized by the actual parameters $e_1, ..., e_n$ by multiplying the density of the caller by $\prod_i \delta(a_i - e_i)$. The result variables in f's density expression are renamed to match $r_1, ..., r_m$, and the uninterpreted function φ within f's density expression is replaced with the new density of the caller (avoiding variable capture).

Formal Argument: A standard approach to prove that the translation from the source language to the target domain (in our case, the symbolic domain) is correct is to show that the transformation preserves semantics, as in [17]. This requires a specification of semantics for both the source language and the symbolic domain language. Below, we outline how one might approach such a formal proof using denotational semantics that map programs and distribution expressions to measure transformers.

Denotational semantics for the source language is easy to define by extending [30], but defining the measure semantics for distribution expressions is more challenging. Defining measure semantics for most expression terms in the symbolic domain is simple (e.g., the measure corresponding to a sum of terms is the sum of the measures of the terms). However, the semantics of expressions containing Dirac deltas is less immediate, since there is no general pointwise product when Dirac delta factors have overlapping sets of free variables.

To assign semantics to a product expression with Dirac delta factors, we therefore (purely formally) integrate the expression against the indicator function of the measured set and simplify it using Dirac delta identities until no Dirac deltas are left. The resulting term can then be easily interpreted as a measure. A formal proof will also need to show that this is a well-formed definition, i.e., that all ways of eliminating Dirac deltas lead to the same measure. Once the semantics for distribution expressions has been defined, the correctness proof proceeds as a straightforward induction over the source language production rules. We consider a complete formalized proof to be an interesting future work item.

4 Symbolic Optimizations

After each step of the analysis from Sect. 3, PSI's symbolic engine simplifies the joint posterior distribution expressions. The algorithm of this optimization engine is a fixed point computation, which applies various symbolic transformations. We selected these transformations by their ability to optimize expressions that typically arise when analyzing probabilistic programs and that have demonstrated their efficiency for practical programs (as we discuss in Sect. 5). We next describe three main groups of the transformations.

4.1 Algebraic Optimizations

These optimizations implement basic algebraic identities. Some examples include removing zero-valued terms in addition expressions, removing one-valued terms in multiplication expressions, distributing exponents over products, or condensing equivalent summands and factors.

4.2 Guard Simplifications

For each term in an expression with multiple Iverson brackets and/or Dirac deltas, these optimizations analyze the constraints in the bracket factors and delta factors using sound but incomplete heuristics. PSI can then (1) remove the whole term if the constraints are inconsistent and therefore the term is always zero, (2) remove a factor if it is always satisfied, e.g., if both sides of an inequality are constants, or (3) remove a bracket factor if it is implied by other factors.

Guard Linearization: Guard linearization analyzes complex Iverson brackets and Dirac deltas with the goal to rewrite expressions in such a way that all included constraints (expressions in Iverson brackets and Dirac deltas) depend on a specified variable x in a linear way. It handles constraints that are easily recognizable as compositions of quadratic polynomials, multiplications with only one factor depending on x and integer and fractional powers (including in particular multiplicative inverses).

One aspect that requires special care is that the integral of a Dirac delta along x depends on the partial derivative of its argument in the direction of x. For example, we have $\delta(2x) = \frac{1}{2}\delta(x)$, and in general we have $\delta(f(x)) = \sum_i \frac{\delta(x - x_i)}{|f'(x_i)|}$ for $f(x_i) = 0$, whenever $f'(x_i) \neq 0$. We ensure the last constraint by performing a case split on $f'(x) = 0$, and substituting the solutions for x into the delta expression in the "equals" case. For example, $\delta(y - x^2)$ is linearized to

$$[-y \leq 0] \cdot ([x = 0] \cdot \delta(y) + [x \neq 0] \cdot \frac{1}{2\sqrt{y}}(\delta(x - \sqrt{y}) + \delta(x + \sqrt{y}))).$$

We present the details of the guard linearization algorithm in the Appendix C.

4.3   Symbolic Integration

These optimizations replace the integration terms with equivalent terms that do not contain integration symbols. If the integrated term is a sum, the symbolic engine integrates each summand separately and pulls all successfully integrated summands out of the integral. If the integrated term is a product, the symbolic engine pulls out all factors that do not contain the integration variable before performing the integration.

Integration of Terms with Deltas: The integration engine first attempts to eliminate the integration variable with a factor that is a Dirac delta, by applying the rule $f(e) = \int_{\mathbb{R}} dx f(x) \cdot \delta(x - e)$. The engine can often transform deltas that depend on the integration variable x in more complicated ways into equivalent expressions only containing x-dependent deltas of the above form, using guard linearization. This transformation is applied when evaluating the integral.

Integration of Continuous Terms: The symbolic engine integrates continuous terms (without Dirac deltas) in several steps. First, it multiplies out all terms that contain the integration variable and groups together all Iverson bracket terms in a single term. Second, it computes the lower and upper bounds of integration by analyzing the Iverson bracket term. If necessary, it first rewrites the term into an equivalent term within which all Iverson brackets specify the constraints on the integration variable in a direct fashion, using guard linearization. This is necessary as in general, a single condition inside a bracket might not be equivalent to a single lower or upper bound for the integration variable. The integration bounds are then computed as the minimum of all upper bounds and the maximum of all lower bounds, where minimum and maximum are again encoded using Iverson brackets. Third, the symbolic engine applies a number of standard rules for obtaining antiderivatives, including integration of power terms, natural logaritms and exponential functions, and integration by parts. We present the details of PSI's integration rules in the Appendix C.

5   Evaluation

This section presents an experimental evaluation of PSI and its effectiveness compared to the state-of-the-art symbolic and approximate inference techniques.

Implementation: We implemented PSI using the D programming language. PSI can produce resulting query expressions in several formats including Matlab, Maple, and Mathematica. Our system and additional documentation, including the Appendix, is available at: http://www.psisolver.org.

Benchmarks: We selected two sets of benchmarks distributed with existing inference engines. Specifically, we used examples from R2 [39] and Fun programs from Infer.NET 2.5 [34]. We describe these benchmarks in the Appendix D. We use the data sets and queries provided with the original computations. Out of 21 benchmarks, 10 have bounded loops. The loop sizes are usually equal to the sizes of the data sets (up to 784 data points in `DigitRecognition`). Since several benchmarks have data sets that are too large for any of the symbolic tools to successfully analyze, we report the results with truncated data sets.

Table 1. Comparison of Exact and Interactive Symbolic Inference Approaches.

Benchmark	Type	Dataset	PSI	Mathem.	Maple	Hakaru
`BurglarAlarm`	D	–	●	●	●	●
`ClinicalTrial1`	DC	100/1000	●	–	–	××
`CoinBias`	DC	5/5	●	t/o	t/o	●^{n}
`DigitRecognition`	D	784/784	●	–	–	×
`Grass`	D	–	●	●	××	●
`HIV`	C0	10/369	◐^{n}	–	–	–
`LinearRegression1`	C0	100/1000	◐$^\int$	–	–	–
`NoisyOr`	D	–	●	●	●	●
`SurveyUnbias`	DC	5/5	●^{n}	t/o	×	●^{n}
`TrueSkill`	C	3/3	◐$^\int$	t/o	t/o	◐^{n}
`TwoCoins`	D	–	●	●	●	–
`AddFun/max`	C	–	●	○	×	○
`AddFun/sum`	C	–	●	●	●	◐^{n}
`BayesPointMachine`	C	6/6	●^{n}	t/o	t/o	◐^{n}
`ClickGraph`	DC	5/5	●	t/o	t/o	●^{n}
`ClinicalTrial2`	DC	5/5	●	t/o	t/o	●^{n}
`Coins`	D	–	●	●	××	●
`Evidence/model1`	D	–	●	○	××	●
`Evidence/model2`	D	–	●	●	××	●
`LearningGaussian`	C0	100/100	◐^{n}	–	–	–
`MurderMystery`	D	–	●	●	●	●

Legend: **Type:** Discrete (D), Continuous (C), Zero-probability observations (0).

Dataset: Full (a/a), no input (–), or the first a out of b inputs (a/b).

Tools: Fully simplified (●) Partially simplified (◐), Not simplified (○), Not normalized (●^{n}, ◐^{n}), Remaining Integrals (◐$^\int$), Incorrect (××), Crash (×), Timeout (t/o).

5.1 Comparison with Exact Symbolic Inference Engines

Experimental Setup: For comparison with Mathematica 2015 and Maple 2015, we instruct PSI to skip symbolic integration and automatically generate distribution expressions in the formats of the two tools. We run Mathematica's

Simplify() and Maple's simplify() commands. For Hakaru [10,38] (commit e61cc72009b5cae1dee33bee26daa53c0599f0bc), we implemented the benchmarks as Hakaru terms in Maple, using the API exposed by the NewSLO.mpl simplifier (as recommended by the Hakaru developers). For each benchmark, we set a timeout of 10 minutes and manually compared the results of the tools.

Results: Table 1 presents the results of symbolic inference. For each benchmark, we present the types of variables it has and whether it has zero-probability observations. We also report the size of the data set provided by the benchmark (if applicable) and the size of the subset we used. For each tool we report the observed inference result. We mark a result as fully simplified (●) if it does not have any integrals remaining and has a small number of remaining terms. We mark results that have some integral terms remaining (◐$^\int$), and partially simplified results (◐). We mark a result as not normalized (●^{n}, ◐^{n}) if a tool does not fully simplify the normalization constant. We marked specifically if execution of a tool experienced a crash (×) a timeout (t/o) or a tool produced an incorrect result (××). For five benchmarks, the automatic conversion of PSI's expressions could not produce Mathematica and Maple expressions, because of the complexity of the benchmarks. We marked those entries as '–'. Hakaru's simplifier does not handle zero-probability observations and expectation queries, and therefore we have not encoded these benchmarks (also marked as '–').

PSI: PSI was able to fully symbolically evaluate many of the benchmark programs and generate compact symbolic distributions. Running PSI took less than a second for most benchmarks. The most time consuming benchmark was DigitRecognition, which PSI analyzed in 37 s. For two benchmarks, PSI was not able to remove all integral terms, although it simplified and removed many intermediate integrals.

Mathematica and Maple: For several benchmarks, both Mathematica and Maple did not produce a result before the timeout, or returned a non-simplified expression as the result. This indicates that the distribution expressions of these benchmarks are too complex, causing general computer algebra systems to navigate a huge search space. However, we note that these results are obtained for a mechanized translation of programs with the specific encoding we described in this paper. It is possible that a human-driven interactive inference with an alternative encoding may result in more simplified distribution expressions.

Maple crashed for addFun/max and addFun/sum. We identified that the crashes were caused by an infinite recursion and subsequent stack overflow during simplification. Four benchmarks – Coins, Evidence/model1, Evidence/model2, and Grass produce results that are different from those produced by the other tools. For instance, Maple simplifies the density function of Coins to 0 (which is incorrect). We attribute this incorrectness to the way Maple integrates Dirac deltas and how it defines Heaviside functions (by default, they are undefined at input 0, but a user can provide a different setting [2]). In our evaluation, none of the alternative settings could yield the correct results. We reported these bugs to the

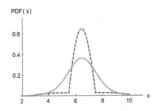 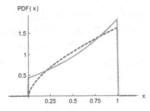 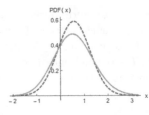

Fig. 7. Tracking.query2: PSI (solid; exact) and SVE (dashed).

Fig. 8. ClickGraph: PSI (solid; exact) and Infer.NET (dashed).

Fig. 9. AddFun/max: PSI (solid; exact) and Infer.NET (dashed).

Maple developers. These examples indicate that users should be cautious when using general computer algebra systems to analyze probabilistic programs.

Hakaru: For the `ClinicalTrial1` benchmark, Hakaru produced a result differing from PSI's. To get a reference result, we ran R2's simulation to compute an approximate result and found that this result is substantially closer to PSI's. For the `DigitRecognition` benchmark, Hakaru overflowed Maple's stack limit. Hakaru does not simplify the `AddFun/max` benchmark, but unlike Maple (which it uses), it does not crash.

Performance: Summed over all examples where Hakaru produced correct but possibly unsimplified results except `BayesPointMachine`, PSI and Hakaru ran for about the same time (8.7 s and 8.8 s, respectively). `BayesPointMachine` is an outlier, for which Hakaru requires 41.9 s, while PSI finds a solution in 1.24 s. Mathematica and Maple are 10–300 times slower than PSI. We present the detailed time measurements for each benchmark in the Appendix E.

5.2 Comparison with Approximate Symbolic Inference Engine

Experimental Setup: We compared PSI with SVE [43] by running posterior distribution queries on the models from the SVE distribution (from the commit `f4cea111f7d489933b36a43c753710bd14ef9f7f`). We included models `tracking` (with 7 provided posterior distribution queries) and `radar` (with 5 posterior distribution queries). We excluded the `competition` model because SVE crashes on it. We did not evaluate SVE on R2 and Infer.NET benchmarks as SVE does not encode some distributions (e.g., Beta or Gamma) and lacks support for Dirac deltas, significantly limiting its ability to represent assignment statements.

Results: PSI fully optimized the posterior distributions for all seven queries of the `tracking` model. PSI fully optimized one query from the `radar` benchmark and experienced timeout for the remaining queries. Figure 7 presents the posterior density functions (PDFs) for one of the `tracking` queries. SVE's polynomial approximation yields a less precise shape of the distribution compared to PSI.

5.3   Comparison with Approximate Numeric Inference Engines

Experimental Setup: We also compared the precision and performance of PSI's exact inference with the approximate inference engines Infer.NET [34] and R2 [39] for a subset of their benchmarks. Specifically, we compared PSI to Infer.NET on ClickGraph, ClinicalTrial, AddFun/max, AddFun/sum, and MurderMystery and compared PSI to R2 on BurglarAlarm, CoinBias, Grass, NoisyOR, and TwoCoins. We executed both approximate engines with their default parameters.

Results: Infer.NET produces less precise approximate distributions for ClickGraph and AddFun/max (Figs. 8 and 9), Infer.NET's approximate inference is imprecise in representing the tails of the distributions, although the means of the two distributions are similar (e.g., differing by 0.7 % for both benchmarks). PSI and Infer.NET produced identical distributions for the remaining benchmarks. Because of its efficient variational inference algorithms, Infer.NET computed results 5–200 times faster than PSI. The precision loss of R2 on Burglar alarm is 20 % (R2's output burglary probability is 0.0036 compared to the exact probability 0.00299). For the other benchmarks, the difference between the results of PSI and R2 is less than 3 %. The run times of PSI and R2 were similar, e.g., PSI was two times faster on TwoCoins, and R2 was two times faster on NoisyOR. We present details of the comparison in the Appendix F.

The examples in Figs. 7, 8, and 9 illustrate that the choice of inference method depends on the context in which the inference results are used. While inferences about expectations in machine learning applications may often tolerate imprecision in return for faster or more scalable computation, many uses of probabilistic inference in domains such as security, privacy, and reliability engineering need to reason about a richer set of queries, while requiring correct and precise inference. We believe that the PSI system presented in this paper is particularly suited for such settings and is an important step forward in making automated exact inference feasible.

6   Related Work

This section discusses related work in symbolic inference and probabilistic program analysis.

6.1   Symbolic Inference

Graphical Models: Early research in the machine learning community focused on symbolic inference in Bayesian networks with discrete distributions [44] and combinations of discrete and linearly-dependent Gaussian distributions [11]. For more complex hybrid models, researchers proposed projecting distributions to mixtures of base functions, which can be easily integrated, such as truncated exponentials [36] and piecewise polynomials [43,45]. In contrast to these approximate approaches, PSI's algorithm performs exact symbolic integration.

Probabilistic Programs: Claret et al. [12] present a data flow analysis for symbolically computing exact posterior distributions for programs with discrete variables. This analysis operates on the program's concrete state, while efficiently storing the states using ADD diagrams.

Bhat et al. [6] present a type system for programs with continuous probability distributions. This approach is extended in [7] to programs with discrete and continuous variables (but only discrete observations). Like PSI, the density compiler from [7] computes posterior distribution expressions, but instead of symbolically simplifying and removing integrals, it generates a C program that performs numerical integration (which may, in general, be expensive to run).

The Hakaru probabilistic language [10,38] runs inference tasks by combining symbolic and sampling-based methods. To optimize MCMC sampling for probabilistic programs, Hakaru's symbolic optimizer (1) translates the programs to probability density expressions in Maple's language, (2) calls an extended version of Maple's simplifier, (3) uses these results to generate an optimized Hakaru program, and, if necessary, (4) calls a MCMC sampler with the optimized program. While Maple's expression language is more expressive than PSI's, it also creates a more complex search space for expression optimizations. PSI further reduces the search space by optimizing expressions after each analysis step, while in Hakaru's workflow, the distribution expression is optimized only after translating the whole program.

6.2 Probabilistic Program Analysis

Verification: Researchers presented various static analyses that verify probabilistic properties of programs, including safety, liveness, and/or expectation queries. These verification techniques have been based on abstract interpretation [14,16,33,35], axiomatic reasoning [5,29,37], model checking [26], and symbolic execution [18,42]. Many of the existing approaches compute exact probabilities of failure only for discrete distributions or make approximations when analyzing computations with both discrete and continuous distributions.

Researchers have also formalized fragments of probability theory inside general-purpose theorem provers, including reasoning about discrete [4,28] and continuous distributions [17,24]. The focus of these works is on human-guided interactive verification of (possibly recursive) programs. In contrast, PSI performs fully automated inference of hybrid discrete and continuous distributions for programs with bounded loops.

Transformation: R2 [39] transforms probabilistic programs by moving observe statements next to the sampling statement of the corresponding variable to improve performance of MCMC samplers. Gretz et al. [23] generalize this transformation to move observations arbitrarily through a program. Probabilistic program slicing [27] removes statements that are not necessary for computing a user-provided query. These transformations simplify program structure, while preserving semantics. In comparison, PSI directly transforms and simplifies the probability distribution that underlies a probabilistic program.

7 Conclusion

We presented PSI, an approach for end-to-end exact symbolic analysis of probabilistic programs with discrete and continuous variables. PSI's symbolic nature provides the necessary flexibility to answer various queries for non-trivial probabilistic programs. More precise and reliable probabilistic inference has the potential to improve the quality of the results in various application domains and help developers when testing and debugging their probabilistic models and inference algorithms. With its rich symbolic domain and optimization engine, we believe that PSI is a useful tool for studying the design of precise and scalable probabilistic inference based on symbolic reasoning.

References

1. Maple (2015). www.maplesoft.com/products/maple/
2. Maple Heaviside Function (2015). http://www.maplesoft.com/support/help/Maple/view.aspx?path=Heaviside
3. Mathematica (2015). https://www.wolfram.com/mathematica/
4. Audebaud, P., Paulin-Mohring, C.: Proofs of randomized algorithms in Coq. Sci. Comput. Program. **74**(8), 568–589 (2009)
5. Barthe, G., Köpf, B., Olmedo, F., Zanella Béguelin, S.: Probabilistic relational reasoning for differential privacy. In: ACM POPL (2012)
6. Bhat, S., Agarwal, A., Vuduc, R., Gray, A.: A type theory for probability density functions. In: ACM POPL (2012)
7. Bhat, S., Borgström, J., Gordon, A.D., Russo, C.: Deriving probability density functions from probabilistic functional programs. In: Piterman, N., Smolka, S.A. (eds.) TACAS 2013 (ETAPS 2013). LNCS, vol. 7795, pp. 508–522. Springer, Heidelberg (2013)
8. Borgström, J., Gordon, A.D., Greenberg, M., Margetson, J., Van Gael, J.: Measure transformer semantics for bayesian machine learning. In: Barthe, G. (ed.) ESOP 2011. LNCS, vol. 6602, pp. 77–96. Springer, Heidelberg (2011)
9. Bornholt, J., Mytkowicz, T., McKinley, K.S.: Uncertain<T>: a first-order type for uncertain data. In: ASPLOS (2014)
10. Carette, J., Shan, C.-C.: Simplifying probabilistic programs using computer algebra. In: Gavanelli, M., et al. (eds.) PADL 2016. LNCS, vol. 9585, pp. 135–152. Springer, Heidelberg (2016). doi:10.1007/978-3-319-28228-2_9
11. Chang, K.C., Fung, R.: Symbolic probabilistic inference with both discrete and continuous variables. IEEE Trans. Syst. Man Cybern. **25**(6), 910–916 (1995)
12. Claret, G., Rajamani, S.K., Nori, A.V., Gordon, A.D., Borgström, J.: Bayesian inference using data flow analysis. In: ESEC/FSE (2013)
13. Cooper, G.F.: The computational complexity of probabilistic inference using Bayesian belief networks. Artif. Intell. **42**(2), 393–405 (1990)
14. Cousot, P., Monerau, M.: Probabilistic abstract interpretation. In: Seidl, H. (ed.) Programming Languages and Systems. LNCS, vol. 7211, pp. 169–193. Springer, Heidelberg (2012)
15. Dagum, P., Luby, M.: Approximating probabilistic inference in Bayesian belief networks is NP-hard. Artif. Intell. **60**(1), 141–153 (1993)

16. Di Pierro, A., Wiklicky, H.: Probabilistic abstract interpretation and statistical testing (extended abstract). In: Hermanns, H., Segala, R. (eds.) PROBMIV 2002, PAPM-PROBMIV 2002 and PAPM 2002. LNCS, vol. 2399, p. 211. Springer, Heidelberg (2002)

17. Eberl, M., Hölzl, J., Nipkow, T.: A verified compiler for probability density functions. In: Vitek, J. (ed.) ESOP 2015. LNCS, vol. 9032, pp. 80–104. Springer, Heidelberg (2015)

18. Filieri, A., Păsăreanu, C.S., Visser, W.: Reliability analysis in symbolic pathfinder. In: ICSE (2013)

19. Gelman, A., Lee, D., Guo, J.: Stan a probabilistic programming language for Bayesian inference and optimization. J. Educ. Behav. Stat. **40**, 530–543 (2015)

20. Gilks, W.R., Thomas, A., Spiegelhalter, D.J.: A language and program for complex Bayesian modelling. Statistician **43**, 169–177 (1994)

21. Goodman, N., Mansinghka, V., Roy, D., Bonawitz, K., Tenenbaum, J.: Church: a language for generative models. In: UAI (2008)

22. Gordon, A.D., Henzinger, T.A., Nori, A.V., Rajamani, S.K.: Probabilistic programming. In: Proceedings of Future of Software Engineering (2014)

23. Gretz, F., Jansen, N., Kaminski, B.L., Katoen, J.P., McIver, A., Olmedo, F.: Conditioning in probabilistic programming. arXiv preprint (2015). arXiv:1504.00198

24. Hasan, O.: Formalized Probability Theory and Applications Using Theorem Proving. IGI Global, Hershey (2015)

25. Hershey, S., Bernstein, J., Bradley, B., Schweitzer, A., Stein, N., Weber, T., Vigoda, B.: Accelerating inference: towards a full language, compiler and hardware stack. arXiv preprint (2012). arXiv:1212.2991

26. Hinton, A., Kwiatkowska, M., Norman, G., Parker, D.: PRISM: a tool for automatic verification of probabilistic systems. In: Hermanns, H., Palsberg, J. (eds.) TACAS 2006. LNCS, vol. 3920, pp. 441–444. Springer, Heidelberg (2006)

27. Hur, C.K., Nori, A.V., Rajamani, S.K., Samuel, S.: Slicing probabilistic programs. In: ACM PLDI (2014)

28. Hurd, J.: Formal verification of probabilistic algorithms. Ph.D. thesis, University of Cambridge (2001)

29. Katoen, J.-P., McIver, A.K., Meinicke, L.A., Morgan, C.C.: Linear-invariant generation for probabilistic programs. In: Cousot, R., Martel, M. (eds.) SAS 2010. LNCS, vol. 6337, pp. 390–406. Springer, Heidelberg (2010)

30. Kozen, D.: Semantics of probabilistic programs. J. Comput. Syst. Sci. **22**(3), 328–350 (1981)

31. Kozlov, A.V., Koller, D.: Nonuniform dynamic discretization in hybrid networks. In: UAI (1997)

32. Mansinghka, V., Selsam, D., Perov, Y.: Venture: a higher-order probabilistic programming platform with programmable inference. arXiv preprint (2014). arXiv:1404.0099

33. Mardziel, P., Magill, S., Hicks, M., Srivatsa, M.: Dynamic enforcement of knowledge-based security policies using probabilistic abstract interpretation. J. Comput. Secur. **21**(4), 463–532 (2013)

34. Minka, T., Winn, J., Guiver, J., Webster, S., Zaykov, Y., Yangel, B., Spengler, A., Bronskill, J.: Infer.NET 2.5 (2013). http://research.microsoft.com/infernet

35. Monniaux, D.: Abstract interpretation of probabilistic semantics. In: SAS (2000)

36. Moral, S., Rumí, R., Salmerón, A.: Mixtures of truncated exponentials in hybrid Bayesian networks. In: Benferhat, S., Besnard, P. (eds.) ECSQARU 2001. LNCS (LNAI), vol. 2143, pp. 156–167. Springer, Heidelberg (2001)

37. Morgan, C., McIver, A., Seidel, K.: Probabilistic predicate transformers. ACM Trans. Program. Lang. Syst. (TOPLAS) **18**(3), 325–353 (1996)
38. Narayanan, P., Carette, J., Romano, W., Shan, C.C., Zinkov, R.: Probabilistic inference by program transformation in Hakaru (system description), http://homes.soic.indiana.edu/ccshan/rational/system.pdf
39. Nori, A.V., Hur, C.K., Rajamani, S.K., Samuel, S.: R2: an efficient MCMC sampler for probabilistic programs. In: AAAI (2014)
40. Pfeffer, A.: IBAL: a probabilistic rational programming language. In: Proceedings of 17th International Joint Conference on Artificial Intelligence, vol. 1, pp. 733–740. Morgan Kaufmann Publishers Inc. (2001)
41. Sampson, A., Panchekha, P., Mytkowicz, T., McKinley, K.S., Grossman, D., Ceze, L.: Expressing and verifying probabilistic assertions. In: ACM PLDI (2014)
42. Sankaranarayanan, S., Chakarov, A., Gulwani, S.: Static analysis for probabilistic programs: inferring whole program properties from finitely many paths. In: ACM PLDI (2013)
43. Sanner, S., Abbasnejad, E.: Symbolic variable elimination for discrete and continuous graphical models. In: AAAI (2012)
44. Shachter, R.D., D'Ambrosio, B., Del Favero, B.: Symbolic probabilistic inference in belief networks. In: AAAI (1990)
45. Shenoy, P.P., West, J.C.: Inference in hybrid Bayesian networks using mixtures of polynomials. Int. J. Approx. Reason. **52**(5), 641–657 (2011)
46. Wood, F., van de Meent, J.W., Mansinghka, V.: A new approach to probabilistic programming inference. In: AISTATS (2014)

PSCV: A Runtime Verification Tool for Probabilistic SystemC Models

Van Chan Ngo[1]([✉]), Axel Legay[2], and Vania Joloboff[2]

[1] Carnegie Mellon University, Pittsburgh, PA 15213, USA
channgo@cmu.edu
[2] Inria Rennes - Bretagne Atlantique, 35042 Rennes, France

Abstract. This paper describes PSCV, a runtime verification tool for a class of SystemC models which have inherent probabilistic characteristics. The properties of interest are expressed using bounded linear temporal logic. The various features of the tool including automatic monitor generation for producing execution traces of the model-under-verification, mechanism for automatically instrumenting the model, and the interaction with statistical model checker are presented.

1 Introduction

SystemC[1], a C^{++} library [6], has been become increasingly prominent in modeling hardware and embedded systems at the level of transactions. Models can be used to simulate the system behavior with a single-core reference event-driven simulation kernel [2]. A SystemC model is a complex and multi-threaded program where scheduling is cooperative and thread execution is mutually exlusive. In many cases, models include probabilistic characteristics, i.e., random data, reliability of the system's components. Hence, it is crucial to evaluate quantitative and qualitative analyses of system property probabilities. Many algorithms [4,7,10] with the corresponding mature tools based on model checking techniques, i.e., *Probabilistic Model Checking* (PMC), are created, in which they compute probability by a numerical approach. However, they are infeasible for large real-life systems due to *state space explosion* and cannot work directly with SystemC source code.

In this paper we present PSCV a new tool for checking properties expressed in *Bounded Linear Temporal Logic* (BLTL) [14] of probabilistic SystemC models. It uses *Statistical Model Checking* (SMC) [7–9,14,16–18] techniques, a simulation-based approach. Simulation-based approaches use a finite set of system executions to produce an approximation of the value to be evaluated. Since these techniques do not construct all reachable states of the model-under-verification (MUV), execution time and memory space required are far less than numerical approaches.

The tool supports a rich set of properties, a wide range of abstractions from statement level to system level, and a more fine-grained model of time than

---

[1] IEEE Standard 1666-2005.

© Springer International Publishing Switzerland 2016
S. Chaudhuri and A. Farzan (Eds.): CAV 2016, Part I, LNCS 9779, pp. 84–91, 2016.
DOI: 10.1007/978-3-319-41528-4_5

a coarse-grained cycle-based simulation provided by the current SystemC kernel [2]. Given a property, a user-defined absolute error and confidence, the tool implements the *statistical estimation* and *hypothesis testing* techniques [8,16] for computing probability that the property is satisfied by the model or asserting that this probability is at least equal to a threshold. The theoretical and algorithmic foundations of the tool are based on Ngo et al.'s work [12].

2   Verification Flow

The verification flow using PSCV consists of three steps, as shown in Fig. 1, in which the *Monitor and Advice Generator* (MAG), AspectC++, the modified SystemC kernel, and SystemC plugin are components of PSCV. In the first step, users write a configuration file containing a set of typed variables called *observed variables*, a Boolean expression called *temporal resolution*, and all properties to be verified. MAG translates the configuration file into a C++ monitor and a set of aspect-advices. In the second step, the set of aspect-advices is used as an input of AspectC++ to automatically instrument the MUV for exposing the user model states and syntax. The instrumented model and the generated monitor are compiled and linked together with the modified SystemC kernel to produce an executable model.

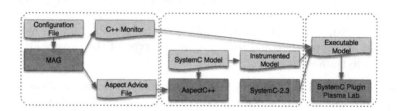

Fig. 1. The verification flow

Finally, the SystemC plugin independently simulates the executable model in order to make the monitor produce execution traces with inputs provided by the user. The inputs can be generated using any standard stimuli-generation technique. These traces are finite in length since the BLTL semantics [14] is defined with respect to finite execution traces. The number of simulations is determined by the statistic algorithm used by the plugin. Given these execution traces and the user-defined absolute error and confidence, the SystemC plugin employs SMC to produce an estimation of the probability that the property is satisfied or an assertion that this probability is at least equal to a threshold.

3   Expressing Properties

The tool accepts input properties of the forms $\Pr(\varphi)$, $\Pr_{\geq\theta}(\varphi)$, and $X_{\leq T}(rv)$, where φ is a BLTL formula. The first is used to compute the probability that

φ satisfied by the model. The second asserts that this probability is at least equal to the threshold θ. The last returns the mean value of random variable rv. The set of atomic propositions in the logic describes SystemC code features and the simulation semantics. It is a set of Boolean expressions defined over a set of typed variables called *observed variables* with the standard operators $(+, -, *, /, >, \geq, <, \leq, !=, =)$. The semantics of the temporal operators in BLTL formulas interpreted over states is defined by a *temporal resolution* that defines at which time points the states are sampled in order to make the transition from one state to another state. A temporal resolution is a logical disjunction over a set of Boolean observed variables, in which the tool should sample a new state whenever the temporal resolution is evaluated to true. For example, assume that we want the satisfaction of the underlying formula φ to be checked either at the end of every delta-cycle or every time immediately after the event e is notified. Hence, the temporal resolution is defined by the following disjunction (MON_DELTA_CYCLE_END | e.notified), where MON_DELTA_CYCLE_END and e.notified are Boolean observed variables that have the value *true* whenever the kernel phase is at the end of delta-cycle and e is notified, respectively. The observed variables used to describe SystemC code features, the simulation semantics, and temporal resolution are summarized below; see [12,13] for the full syntax and semantics.

Attribute. Users can define an observed variable whose value and type are equal to the value and type of a module's attribute in the user code. Attributes can be public, protected, or private. For example, $a.t\ a\_t$ defines a variable named a_t whose value and type are equal to the value and type of the private attribute t of the module instance a.

Function. Let f be a C^{++} function with k arguments in the user code. Users can refer to locations in the source code that contain the function call, immediately after the function call, immediately before the first executable statement, and immediately after the last executable statement in f by using the Boolean observed variables $f()$:call, $f()$:return, $f()$:entry, and $f()$:exit, respectively. Moreover, users define an observed variable $f()$:i, $i = 0, \cdots, k$, whose value and type are equal to the value and type of the return object (with $i = 0$) or i^{th} argument of function f before executing the first statement in the function body. For example, if the function int div(int x, int y) is defined in the user code, then the formula $G_{\leq T}(div()$:entry $\rightarrow div()$:2 $!= 0)$ asserts that the divisor is nonzero whenever the div function starts execution.

Simulation phase. There are 18 predefined Boolean observed variables which refer to the 18 kernel states [13]. These variables are usually used to define a temporal resolution. For example, the formula $G_{\leq T}(p = 0)$ which is accompanied by the temporal resolution (MON_DELTA_CYCLE_END) requires the value of variable p to be zero at the end of every delta-cycle.

Event. For each SystemC event e, PSCV provides a Boolean observed variable e.notified that is true only when the simulation kernel actually notifies e. For example, the formula $G_{\leq T}(e.\text{notified} \rightarrow (a = 0))$ says that whenever the event e is notified, a equals to 0.

4   Architecture

PSCV, available as an open-source software [13], implements SMC for probabilistic SystemC models. The main components are depicted in Fig. 2. It consists of off-the-self, modified and original components: (1) an off-the-self component, AspectC++ [5], a C++ aspect compiler for instrumenting the MUV, (2) a modified component, a patched SystemC-2.3.0 kernel for facilitating the communication between the kernel and the monitor and implementing a random scheduler, and (3) two original components are MAG, a C++ tool for automatically generating monitor and aspect-advices for instrumentation, and SystemC plugin, a plugin of the statistical model checker Plasma Lab [3].

4.1   Execution Trace Extraction

In PSCV, based on the techniques in [15], the set of observed variables and temporal resolution are converted into a C++ monitor class and a set of aspect-advices. MAG generates three files: aspect_definitions.ah, monitor.h, and monitor.cc, in which they contain a set of AspectC++ *aspect* definitions, one monitor class, and a class called *local_observer* that is responsible for invoking the callback functions, which invoke the sampling function at the right time point during the MUV simulation.

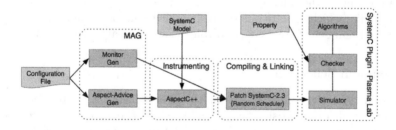

Fig. 2. The architecture of PSCV

The monitor has a *step* function, sampling function, that waits for a request from the SystemC plugin. If the request is stopping the current simulation, it then terminates the MUV execution. If the plugin requests a new state, then the current values of all observed variables and the simulation time are sent. The *step* function is called at every time point defined by temporal resolution. These time points can be kernel phases, event notifications, or locations in the MUV code control flow. In such cases, the patched kernel needs to communicate with the *local_observer*, i.e., when a delta-cycle ends, via a class called *mon_observer* to invoke the *step* function of the monitor. In case of locations in the MUV code, the advice code generated by MAG will call the callback function to invoke the *step* function.

The aspect is an extension of the class concept of C^{++}, to collect advice code implementing a common crosscutting concern in a modular way. For example, to access all attributes of a module called A and the location that occurs immediately before the first executable statement of the function *foo* in A (defined in the configuration file as $\% A::foo()$:entry), MAG generates the following aspect definition.

```
aspect Automatic {
  pointcut reveal() = "A"; //Pointcut for accessing private data of A
  advice reveal() : slice class {
    friend class monitor_A; //Generated monitor is friend class of A
  };
  advice execution("% A::foo()"): before() { //Instrumentation code
    mon_observer* observer = local_observer::getInstance();
    monitor_A* mon = (monitor_A*) observer->get_monitor_by_index(0);
    mon->callback_userloc_loc1(); //Invoke callback function
  }
};
```

4.2 Statistical Model Checker

The statistical model checker is implemented as a plugin of Plasma Lab. It establishes a communication, in which the generated monitor transmits execution traces of the MUV. In the current version, the communication is done via the standard input and output. When a new state is requested, the monitor reports the current state containing current observed variable values and the simulation time to the plugin. The length of traces depends on the satisfaction of the formula, which is finite due to the bounded temporal operators. Similarly, the required number of traces depends on the statistic algorithms in use.

4.3 Random Scheduler

Verification does not only depend on the probabilistic characteristics of the MUV, but it also can be significantly affected by the *scheduling policy*. Consider a simple module A that consists of two thread processes as shown in the following listing, where x is initialized to be 1.

```
void A::t1() {               void A::t2() {               SC_CTOR(A) {
  if (x <= 0)                  if (x > 0)                    SC_THREAD(t1);
    x := x + 1;                 x := x - 1;                  SC_THREAD(t2);
}                            }                            }
```

Assume that we want to compute the probability that x is always equal to 1. Obviously, x depends on the execution order of two threads, i.e., the value is 1 if $t2$ is executed before the execution of $t1$ and 0 if the order is $t1$ then $t2$. The current scheduling policy is deterministic as it always picks the process that is first added into the queue, the implementation uses a queue to store a set of runnable processes. Hence, only one execution order, $t1$ then $t2$, is verified instead of two possible orders. As a result, the probability to be verified is 0, however, it should be 0.5. Therefore, it is more interesting if a verification is performed on all possible execution orders than a fixed one. In many cases, there is no decision or an a-priori knowledge of the scheduling to be implemented. Moreover, verification of a specification should be independent of the scheduling policy to be finally implemented.

To perform our verification on possible execution orders of the MUV, we implemented a random scheduler. The source of the process scheduler is the evaluation phase, in which one of the runnable processes is executed. Given a set of N runnable processes in the queue at the evaluation phase, the scheduler randomly chooses one of these processes to execute. The random algorithm is implemented by generating a random integer number uniformly over a range $[0, N - 1]$. For more simulation efficiency and implementation simplicity, we employ the $rand()$ function and % operator in C/C++.

5   Experimental Results

We report the experimental results for several examples including a running example, a case study of dependability analysis of a large control system (i.e., the number of states is 2^{155}), and random scheduler examples. We used the 2-sided Chernoff bound with the absolute error $\varepsilon = 0.02$ and the confidence $\alpha = 0.98$. The experiments were run on machine with Intel Core i7 2.67 GHz processor and 4GB RAM under the Linux OS. The analysis of the control system takes almost 2 h, in which 90 liveness properties were verified. The full experiments can be found at the website [13]. For example, the first property we checked is the probability that the message latency from the producer to the consumer within T_1 time units over a period of T time of operation using the formula $\varphi = G_{\leq T}((c\_read = \ '\&') \rightarrow F_{\leq T_1}(c\_read = \ '@'))$, where c_read, &, and @ are the current received character, special starting and ending delimiters, respectively. The second property we tried to determine which kind of component is more likely to cause the failure of the control system. It is expressed in BLTL as $\neg$shutdown $U_{\leq T}$ failure$_i$, where shutdown $= \bigvee_{i=1}^{4}$ failure$_i$. The results are plotted in Figs. 3 and 4.

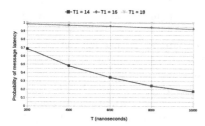

Fig. 3. Message latency (Color figure online)

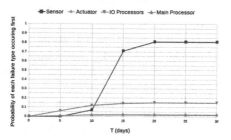

Fig. 4. Each component fails first (Color figure online)

For the random scheduler, it seems that the implementation with the pseudo random number generator (PRNG), by using the *rand()* function and % operator is not efficient. We are planning to investigate the Mersenne Twister generator [11] that is by far the most widely used general-purpose PRNG in order to deal with this issue.

6 Conclusion

We present PSCV an SMC-based verification tool for checking properties expressed in BLTL of probabilistic SystemC models. The tool supports a rich set of properties, a wide range of abstractions from statement level to system level, and a more fine-grained model of time. In the feature we plan to make the verification process more automated by eliminating the user interaction with AspectC^{++} and embedding the checker inside the tool such as [1].

References

1. Abarbanel, Y., Beer, I., Glushovsky, L., Keidar, S., Wolfsthal, Y.: Focs: automatic generation of simulation checkers from formal specifications. In: Emerson, E.A., Sistla, A.P. (eds.) CAV 2000. LNCS, vol. 1855, pp. 538–542. Springer, Heidelberg (2000)
2. Accellera. http://www.accellera.org/downloads/standards/systemc
3. Boyer, B., Corre, K., Legay, A., Sedwards, S.: PLASMA-lab: a flexible, distributable statistical model checking library. In: Joshi, K., Siegle, M., Stoelinga, M., D'Argenio, P.R. (eds.) QEST 2013. LNCS, vol. 8054, pp. 160–164. Springer, Heidelberg (2013)
4. Ciesinski, F., Größer, M.: On probabilistic computation tree logic. In: Baier, C., Haverkort, B.R., Hermanns, H., Katoen, J.-P., Siegle, M. (eds.) Validation of Stochastic Systems. LNCS, vol. 2925, pp. 147–188. Springer, Heidelberg (2004)
5. Gal, A., Schroder-Preikschat, W., Spinczyk, O.: AspectC++: language proposal and prototype implementation. In: OOPSLA (2001)
6. Grotker, T., Liao, S., Martin, G., Swan, S.: System Design with SystemC. Kluwer Academic Publishers, Berlin (2002)
7. Hermanns, H., Wachter, B., Zhang, L.: Probabilistic CEGAR. In: Gupta, A., Malik, S. (eds.) CAV 2008. LNCS, vol. 5123, pp. 162–175. Springer, Heidelberg (2008)
8. Hoeffding, W.: Probability inequalities for sums of bounded random variables. J. Am. Stat. Assoc. **58**, 13–30 (1963)
9. Katoen, J., Hahn, E., Hermanns, H., Jansen, D., Zapreev, I.: The Ins and Outs of the probabilistic model checker MRMC. In: QEST (2009)
10. Kwiatkowska, M., Norman, G., Parker, D.: Controller dependability analysis by probabilistic model checking. Control Eng. Pract. **15**, 1427–1434 (2007)
11. Matsumoto, M., Nishimura, T.: Mersenne twister: a 623-dimensionally equidistributed uniform pseudo-random number generator. ACM Trans. Model. Comput. Simul. **8**, 3–30 (1998)
12. Ngo, V.C., Legay, A., Quilbeuf, J.: Statistical model checking for SystemC models. In: HASE (2016)

13. PSCV (2016). https://project.inria.fr/pscv/
14. Sen, K., Viswanathan, M., Agha, G.: On statistical model checking of stochastic systems. In: Etessami, K., Rajamani, S.K. (eds.) CAV 2005. LNCS, vol. 3576, pp. 266–280. Springer, Heidelberg (2005)
15. Tabakov, D., Vardi, M.: Monitoring temporal SystemC properties. In: Formal Methods and Models for Codesign (2010)
16. Younes, H.: Verification and planning for stochastic processes with asynchronous events. Ph.D. thesis, Carnegie Mellon (2005)
17. Younes, H., Kwiatkowska, M., Norman, G., Parker, D.: Numerical vs. statistical probabilistic model checking. Int. J. Softw. Tools Technol. Transfer **8**, 216–228 (2006)
18. Zuliani, P., Platzer, A., Clarke, E.M.: Bayesian statistical model checking with application to Simulink/Stateflow verification. Formal Methods Syst. Des. **43**, 338–367 (2013)

Synthesis I

Structural Synthesis for **GXW** Specifications

Chih-Hong Cheng[(⊠)], Yassine Hamza, and Harald Ruess

fortiss - An-Institut Technische Universität München,
Guerickestr. 25, 80805 Munich, Germany
{cheng,ruess}@fortiss.org,
yassine.hamza@in.tum.de

Abstract. We define the **GXW** fragment of linear temporal logic (**LTL**) as the basis for synthesizing embedded control software for safety-critical applications. Since **GXW** includes the use of a *weak-until* operator we are able to specify a number of diverse programmable logic control (**PLC**) problems, which we have compiled from industrial training sets. For **GXW** controller specifications, we develop a novel approach for synthesizing a set of synchronously communicating actor-based controllers. This synthesis algorithm proceeds by means of recursing over the structure of **GXW** specifications, and generates a set of dedicated and synchronously communicating sub-controllers according to the formula structure. In a subsequent step, 2QBF constraint solving identifies and tries to resolve potential conflicts between individual **GXW** specifications. This structural approach to **GXW** synthesis supports traceability between requirements and the generated control code as mandated by certification regimes for safety-critical software. Our experimental results suggest that **GXW** synthesis scales well to industrial-sized control synthesis problems with 20 input and output ports and beyond.

1 Introduction

Embedded control software in the manufacturing and processing industries is usually developed using specialized programming languages such as ladder diagrams or other IEC 61131-3 defined languages. Programming in these rather low-level languages is not only error-prone but also time- and resource-intensive. Therefore we are addressing the problem of correct-by-construction and automated generation of embedded control software from high-level requirements, which are expressed in a suitable fragment of linear temporal logic.

Moreover, an explicit correspondence between the high-level requirements and the generated control code is essential, since embedded control software is usually an integral part of safety-critical systems such as supervisory control and data acquisition (**SCADA**) systems for controlling critical machinery or infrastructure. In particular current industrial standards for safety-related development such as IEC 61508, DO 178C for avionics, and ISO 26262 for automotive applications mandate traceability between the control code and it requirements. Controllers generated by state-of-the-art **LTL** synthesis algorithms and tools such as generalized reactivity(1) (**GR(1)**) [15,25] or bounded LTL synthesis [8,11,28],

© Springer International Publishing Switzerland 2016
S. Chaudhuri and A. Farzan (Eds.): CAV 2016, Part I, LNCS 9779, pp. 95–117, 2016.
DOI: 10.1007/978-3-319-41528-4_6

however, usually do not explicitly support such traceability requirements. For example, the GR(1) synthesis tool Anzu generates circuit descriptions in Verilog from BDDs [15].

We are therefore proposing a novel approach for synthesizing structured control software. In essence, the control code is generated by means of structural recursion on the given LTL formulas. Therefore, the structure of the control code corresponds closely to the syntactic structure of the given requirements, and there is a direct correspondence between controller components and subformulas of the specification.

In a first step towards this goal, we identify a fragment of LTL for specifying the input-output behavior of typical embedded control components. Besides the specification of input assumptions, invariance conditions on outputs, and transition-like reactions of the form $\mathbf{G}(\text{input} \rightarrow \mathbf{X}^i\text{output})$, this fragment also contains specifications of reactions of the form $\mathbf{G}(\text{input} \rightarrow \mathbf{X}^i(\text{output } \mathbf{W} \text{ release}))$, where input is an LTL formula whose validity is determined by the next i input valuations. The latter reaction formula states that if there is a temporal input event satisfying the constraint input, then the output constraint should hold on output events until there is a release event (or output always holds). The operator $\mathbf{G}$ is the universal path quantifier, $\mathbf{X}^i$ abbreviates i consecutive next-steps, $\mathbf{W}$ denotes the *weak until* temporal operator, the constraint output contains no temporal operator, and the subformula release may contain certain numbers of consecutive next-steps but no other temporal operators. The resulting fragment of LTL is called GXW. So far we have successfully modelled more than 70 different embedded control scenarios in GXW. The main source for this set of benchmarking problems are publicly available collections of industrial training materials for PLCs (including CODESYS 3.0 and AC500) [2,16,24]. The proposed GXW fragment of LTL is also similar to established requirements templates for specifying embedded control software in the aerospace domain, such as EARS [23].

Previous work on LTL synthesis (e.g., [5,7,8,10,11,14,15,25,28,31]) usually generates gate-level descriptions for the synthesized control strategies. In contrast, we generate controller in an actor language with high-level behavioral constructs and synchronous dataflow communication between connected actors. This choice of generating *structured controllers* is motivated by current practice of programming controllers using, say, Matlab Simulink [4], continuous function charts (IEC 61131-3), and Ptolemy II [12], which also supports synchronous dataflow (SDF) models [19]. Notice that the usual notions of LTL synthesis also apply to synthesis for SDF, since the composition of actors in SDF may also be viewed as Mealy machines with synchronous cycles [30].

Synthesis of structured controllers from GXW specifications proceeds in two subsequent phases. In the first phase, the procedure recurses on the structure of the given GXW formulas for generating dedicated actors for monitoring inputs events, for generating corresponding control events, and for wiring these actors according to the structure of the given GXW formulas. In the second phase, appropriate values for unknown parameters are synthesized in order to realize the conjunction of all given GXW specifications. Here we use satisfiability checking for quantified Boolean formula (2QBF) for examining if there exists such conflicts between multiple GXW specifications. More precisely, existential variables of generated 2QBF problems capture the remaining design freedom when an output variable is not constrained by any trigger of low-level events. We demonstrate that controller synthesis for the GXW fragment is in PSPACE as compared to the 2EXPTIME -completeness result of full-fledged LTL [27]. Under some further reasonable syntactic restrictions on the GXW fragment we show that synthesis is in coNP .

An implementation of our GXW structural synthesis algorithm and application to our benchmark studies demonstrates a substantial speed-up compared to existing LTL synthesis tools. Moreover, the structure of the generated control code in SDF follows the structure of the given GXW specifications, and is more compact and, arguably, also more readable and understandable than commonly used gate-level representations for synthesized control strategies.

The paper is structured as follows. We introduce in Sect. 2 some basic notation for LTL synthesis, a definition of the GXW fragment of LTL and SDF actor systems together with the problem of actor-based LTL synthesis under GXW fragment. Section 3 illustrates GXW and actor-based control for such specifications by means of an example. Section 4 includes the main technical contributions and describes algorithmic workflow for generating structured controllers from GXW, together with soundness and complexity results for GXW synthesis. A summary of our experimental results is provided in Sect. 5, and a comparison of GXW synthesis with closely related work on LTL synthesis is included in Sect. 6. The paper closes with concluding remarks in Sect. 7. Due to space limits, some details are moved to an extended report [1].

2   Problem Formulation

We present basic concepts and notations of LTL synthesis, and we define the GXW fragment of LTL together with the problem of synthesizing actor-based synchronous dataflow controllers for GXW.

2.1   LTL Synthesis

Given two disjoint sets of Boolean variables V_{in} and V_{out}, the *linear temporal logic* (LTL) formulae over $2^{V_{in} \cup V_{out}}$ is the smallest set such that (1) $v \in 2^{V_{in} \cup V_{out}}$ is an LTL formula, (2) if ϕ_1, ϕ_2 are LTL-formulae, then so are $\neg\phi_1, \neg\phi_2, \phi_1 \vee \phi_2, \phi_1 \wedge \phi_2, \phi_1 \rightarrow \phi_2$, and (3) if ϕ_1, ϕ_2 are LTL-formulae, then so are $\mathbf{G}\phi_1, \mathbf{X}\phi_1, \phi_1\mathbf{U}\phi_2$. Given an ω-word σ, define $\sigma(i)$ to be the i-th element in σ, and define σ^i to be the suffix ω-word of σ obtained by truncating $\sigma(0)\ldots\sigma(i-1)$. The satisfaction relation $\sigma \vDash \phi$ between an ω-word σ and an LTL formula ϕ is defined in the usual way. The *weak until* operator, denoted $\mathbf{W}$, is similar to the *until* operator but the stop condition is not required to occur; therefore $\phi_1\mathbf{W}\phi_2$ is simply defined as $(\phi_1\mathbf{U}\phi_2) \vee \mathbf{G}\phi_1$. Also, we use the abbreviation $\mathbf{X}^i\phi$ to abbreviate i consecutive $\mathbf{X}$ operators before ϕ.

Table 1. Patterns defined in GXW specifications

ID	Meaning	Pattern
P1	Initial-until	$\varrho_{out} \mathbf{W} \phi_{in}^i$
P2	Trigger-until	$\mathbf{G}(\phi_{in}^i \rightarrow$ $\mathbf{X}^i(\varrho_{out} \mathbf{W} (\varphi_{in}^j \vee \rho_{out}^0)))$
P3	If-then	$\mathbf{G}(\phi_{in}^i \rightarrow \mathbf{X}^i \varrho_{out})$
P4	Iff	$\mathbf{G}(\phi_{in}^i \leftrightarrow \mathbf{X}^i \varrho_{out})$
P5	Invariance	$\mathbf{G}(\phi_{out}^0)$
P6	Assumption	$\mathbf{G}(\phi_{in}^0)$

Table 2. Specification patterns and corresponding skeleton specification.

Pattern ID	High-level control specification
P1	output $\mathbf{W}$ input
P2	$\mathbf{G}(\text{input} \rightarrow (\text{output} \mathbf{W} \text{release}))$
P3	$\mathbf{G}(\text{input} \rightarrow \text{output})$

A deterministic *Mealy machine* is a finite automaton $\mathcal{C} = (Q, q_0, 2^{V_{in}}, 2^{V_{out}}, \delta)$, where Q is set of (Boolean) state variables (thus 2^Q is the set of states), $q_0 \in 2^Q$ is the initial state, $2^{V_{in}}$ and $2^{V_{out}}$ are sets of all input and output assignments defined by two disjoint sets of variables V_{in} and V_{out}. $\delta = 2^Q \times 2^{V_{in}} \rightarrow 2^{V_{out}} \times 2^Q$ is the transition function that takes (1) a state $q \in 2^Q$ and (2) input assignment $v_{in} \in 2^{V_{in}}$, and returns (1) an output assignment $v_{out} \in 2^{V_{out}}$ and (2) the successor state $q' \in 2^Q$. Let δ_{out} and δ_s be the projection of δ which considers only output assignments and only successor states. Given a sequence $a_0 \ldots a_k$ where $\forall i = 0 \ldots k, a_i \in 2^{V_{in}}$, let $\delta_s^k(q_0, a_0 \ldots a_k)$ abbreviate the output state derived by executing $a_0 \ldots a_k$ as an input sequence on the Mealy machine.

Given a set of input and output Boolean variables V_{in} and V_{out}, together with an LTL formula ϕ on V_{in} and V_{out} the *LTL synthesis problem* asks the existence of a controller as a deterministic Mealy machine $\mathcal{C}_\phi$ such that, for every input sequence $a = a_0 a_1 \ldots$, where $a_i \in 2^{V_{in}}$: (1) given the prefix a_0 produce $b_0 = \delta_{out}(q_0, a_0)$, (2) given the prefix $a_0 a_1$ produce $b_1 = \delta_{out}(\delta_s(q_0, a_0), a_1)$, (3) given the prefix $a_0 \ldots a_k a_{k+1}$, produce $b_{k+1} = \delta_{out}(\delta_s^k(q_0, a_0 \ldots a_k), a_{k+1})$, and (4) the produced output sequence $b = b_0 b_1 \ldots$ ensures that the word $\sigma = \sigma_1 \sigma_2 \ldots$, where $\sigma_i = a_i b_i \in 2^{V_{in} \cup V_{out}}$, $\sigma \models \phi$.

2.2 GXW Synthesis

We formally define the GXW fragment of LTL . Let ϕ^i, φ^i, ψ^i be LTL formulae over input variables V_{in} and output variables V_{out}, where all formulas are (without loss of generality) assumed to be in disjunctive normal form (DNF), and each literal is of form $\mathbf{X}^j v$ or $\neg \mathbf{X}^j v$ with $0 \leq j \leq i$ and $v \in V_{in} \cup V_{out}$. Clauses in DNF are also called *clause formulae*. Moreover, a formula ϕ_{in}^i is restricted to contain only input variables in V_{in}, and similarly, ϕ_{out}^i contains only output variables in V_{out}. Finally, ϱ_{out} denotes either v_{out} or $\neg v_{out}$, where v_{out} is an output variable.

For given input variables V_{in} and output variables V_{out}, a GXW *formula* is an LTL formula of one of the forms (P1)–(P6) as specified in Table 1. For example,

GXW formulas of the form (P2) stop locking ϱ_{out} as soon as $(\varphi_{in}^j \vee \rho_{out}^0)$ holds. *GXW specifications* are of the form

$$\varrho \rightarrow \bigwedge_{m=1...k} \eta_m \; , \tag{1}$$

where ϱ matches the GXW pattern (P6), and η_m matches one of the patterns (P1) through (P5) in Table 1. Furthermore, the notation "." is used for projecting subformulas from η_m, when it satisfies a given type. For example, assuming that sub-specification η_m is of pattern P3, i.e., it matches $\mathbf{G}(\phi_{in}^i \rightarrow \mathbf{X}^i \varrho_{out})$, $\eta_m.\varrho_{out}$ specifies the matching subformula for ϱ_{out}. Notice also that GXW specifications, despite including the $\mathbf{W}$ operator, have the *finite model property*, since the smallest number of unrolling steps for disproving the existence of an implementation is linear with respect to the structure of the given formula (cmp. Sect. 4.4).

Instead of directly synthesizing a Mealy machine as in standard LTL synthesis, we are considering here the generation of *actor-based controllers* using the computational model of *synchronous dataflow* (SDF) without feedback loops. An *actor-based controller* is a tuple $\mathcal{S} = (\mathcal{V}_{in}, \mathcal{V}_{out}, Act, \tau)$, where $\mathcal{V}_{in}$ and $\mathcal{V}_{out}$ are disjoint sets of external input and output ports. Each port is a variable which may be assigned a Boolean value or undefined if no such value is available at the port. In addition, actors $\mathcal{A} \in Act$ may be associated with internal input ports U_{in} and output ports U_{out} (all named apart), which are also three-valued. The projection $\mathcal{A}.u$ denotes the port u of $\mathcal{A}$. An actor $\mathcal{A} \in Act$ defines Mealy machine $\mathcal{C}$ whose input and output assignments are based on $2^{U_{in}}$ and $2^{U_{out}}$, i.e., the output update function of $\mathcal{C}$ sets each output port to true or false, when each input port has value in {true, false}. Lastly, $\mathcal{A}^{(i)}$ denotes a *copy* of $\mathcal{A}$ which is indexed by i.

Let $Act.U_{in}$ and $Act.U_{out}$ be the set of all internal input and output ports for Act. The wiring $\tau \subseteq (\mathcal{V}_{in} \cup Act.U_{out}) \times (\mathcal{V}_{out} \cup Act.U_{in})$ connects one (external, internal) input port to one or more (external, internal) output ports. For convenience, denote the wiring from port out of $\mathcal{A}_1$ to port in of $\mathcal{A}_2$ as $(\mathcal{A}_1.\text{out} \dashrightarrow \mathcal{A}_2.\text{in})$. All ports are supposed to be connected, and every internal input port and every external output port is only connected to one wire (thus a port does not receive data from two different sources). Also, we do not consider actor systems with feedback loops here (therefore no cycles such as the one in Fig. 1(c)), since systems without feedback loops can be statically scheduled [18].

Evaluation cycles are triggered externally under the semantics of synchronous dataflow. In each such cycle, the data received at the external input ports is processed and corresponding values are transferred to external output ports. Notice also that the composition of actors under SDF acts cycle-wise as a Mealy machine [30]. We illustrate the *operational semantics* of actor-based systems under SDF by means of the example in Fig. 1(a), with input ports in1, in2, output port out, and actors f_1, f_2, f_3, f_4 (see also Fig. 1(b))[1]. Now, assume that

---

[1] The formal operational semantics, as it is standardized notation from SDF, is relegated to [1].

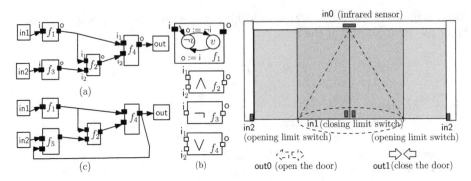

Fig. 1. An actor system allowing functional composition and corresponding actors f_1 (a)(b), feedback loops such as (c) are not considered here.

Fig. 2. Control of automatic door switch.

in the first cycle, the input ports in1 and in2 receive the value (false, true) and in the second cycle the value (false, true). The false value in in1 is copied to f_1.i. As f_1 is initially at state where $v =$ false, it creates the output value true (places it to f_1.o) and changes its internal state to $v =$ true. The value true from f_1.o is then transferred to f_4.i$_1$ and f_2.i$_1$. However, at this stage one cannot evaluate f_2 or f_4, as the i$_2$ port is not yet filled with a value. f_3 receives the value from in2 and produces f_3.o to false. Continuing this process, at the end of first cycle out is set to true, while in the second cycle, out is set to false.

As we do not consider feedback loops between actors in *Act*, from input read to output write, one can, using the enumeration method as exemplified above, create a static linear list Ξ of size $|Act| + |\tau|$, where each element $\xi_{ind} \in \Xi$ is either in *Act* or in τ, for specifying the linear order (from the partial order) how data is transferred between wires and actors. Such a total order Ξ is also called an *evaluation ordering* of the actor system $\mathcal{S}$.

One may wrap any Mealy machine $\mathcal{C}$ as an actor $\mathcal{A}(\mathcal{C})$ by simply creating corresponding ports in $\mathcal{A}(\mathcal{C})$ and by setting the underlying Mealy machine of $\mathcal{A}(\mathcal{C})$ to $\mathcal{C}$. Therefore, actor-based controllers may be synthesized for a given LTL specification ϕ by first synthesizing a Mealy machine $\mathcal{C}$ realizing ϕ, followed by the wrapping $\mathcal{C}$ as $\mathcal{A}(\mathcal{C})$, creating external I/O ports, and connecting external I/O ports with $\mathcal{A}(\mathcal{C})$.

Given a GXW specification ϕ over the input variables V_{in} and output variables V_{out}, the problem of GXW *synthesis* is to generate an actor-based SDF controller $\mathcal{S}$ realizing ϕ. As one can always synthesize a Mealy machine followed by wrapping it to an actor-based controller, GXW synthesis has the same complexity for Mealy machine and for actor-based controllers.

3   Example

We exemplify the use of GXW specifications and actor-based synthesis for these kinds of specification by means of an automatic sliding door[2], which is visualized in Fig. 2. Inputs and outputs are as follows: in0 is true when someone enters the sensing field; in1 denotes a closing limit switch - it is true when two doors touch each other; in2 denotes an opening limit switch - it is true when the door reaches the end; out0 denotes the opening motor - when it is set to true the motor rotates clockwise, thereby triggering the door opening action; and out1 denotes closing motor - when it is set to true the motor rotates counter-clockwise, thereby triggering the door closing action. Finally, the triggering of a timer t0 is modeled by means a (controllable) output variable t0start and the expiration of a timer is modeled using an (uncontrollable) input variable t0expire.

Before stating the formal GXW specification for the example we introduce some mnemonics.

- entering^1 := ¬in0 ∧ **X** in0
- expired^1 := ¬t0expire ∧ (**X**t0expire)
- lim_reached^1 := ¬in2 ∧ **X**in2
- closing_stopped := in1 ∨ in0 ∨ out0

The superscripts denote the maximum number of consecutive next-steps. Now the automatic sliding door controller is formalized in GXW as follows.

S1: **G**(entering^1 → **X**(out0 **W** in2))
S2: **G**(expired^1 → **X**(out1 **W** closing_stopped))
S3: ¬out0 **W** entering^1
S4: **G**(in2 → ¬out0)

S5: **G**(lim_reached^1 ↔ **X**(t0start))
S6: **G**(in0 → ¬out1)
S7: **G**(¬(out0 ∧ out1))

In particular, formula (S1) expresses the requirement that the opening of the door should continue (out0 = true) until the limit is reached (in2), and formulas (S3) and (S7) specify the expected initial behavior of the automatic sliding door. The GXW specifications for the sliding door example are classified as follows: formulas (S1), (S2) are of type (P2), (S3) is of type (P1), (S4), (S6) is of type (P3), (S5) is of type (P4), and (S7) of type (P5) according to Table 1.

Figure 3 visualizes an actor-based automatic sliding door controller which realizes the GXW specification (S1)-(S7). It is constructed from a small number of building blocks, which are also described in Fig. 3. Monitor actors, for example, are used for monitoring when the entering, expired, and lim_reached constraints are fulfilled, the OR actor is introduced because of the closing_stopped release condition in specification (S1), and the two copies of the *trigger-until* actors are introduced because of the (P2) shape of the specifications (S1) and (S2). The input and output ports of the *trigger-until* actor are in accordance with the namings for (P2) in Table 2. *Resolution actors* are used for resolving potential conflicts between individual GXW formulas in a specification. These actors are parameterized with respect to a Boolean A, which is the output of the resolution actor in case all inputs of this actor may be in {true, false} (this set is denoted by the shorthand "–" in Fig. 3). The presented algorithm sets up a 2QBF problem for

---

[2] The automatic door example is adapted from http://plc-scada-dcs.blogspot.com/ 2014/08/basic-plc-ladder-programming-training_20.html.

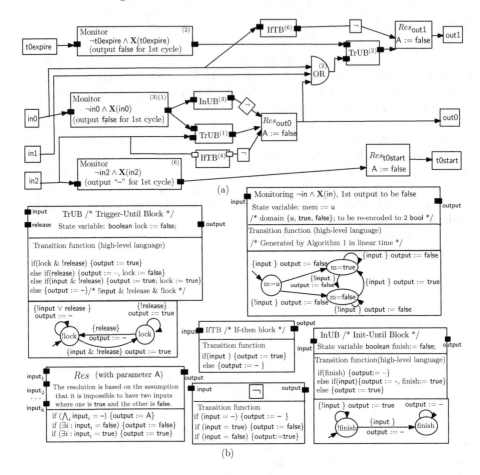

Fig. 3. Actor-based controller realizing automatic sliding door.

synthesizing possible values for these parameters. Because of the constraint (S7) on possible outputs out0 and out1, the parameter A for the resolution actor for output out0, for example, needs to be set to A:=false . Figure 3 also includes the operational behavior of selected actors in terms of high-level transitions and/or Mealy machines. The internal state and behavior for monitor actors, however, is synthesized, in linear time, from a given GXW constraint on inputs (see Sect. 4).

Finally, the structural correspondence of the actor-based controller in Fig. 3 with the given GXW specification of the sliding door example is being made explicit by superscripting actors with index (i) whenever the actor has been introduced due to the i-th specification.

4   Structural Synthesis

We now describe the algorithmic details for generating structured controllers from the GXW specifications of the form $\varrho \rightarrow \bigwedge_{m=1...k} \eta_m$. The automated sliding door is used as running example for illustrating the result of each step.

First, our algorithm prepares I/O ports, iterates through every formula η_m for creating high-level controllers (Step 1) based on the appropriate GXW pattern. For specifications of types P1 to P3, Table 2 lists the corresponding LTL specification (as high-level control objective), where input and release are input Boolean variables, output is an output Boolean variable.

Then, for each GXW formula, the algorithm constructs actors and wirings for monitoring low-level events by mimicking the DNF formula structure (Steps 2 and 3). On the structural level of clause formulas in DNF, the algorithm constructs corresponding controllers in linear time (Algorithm 1). Finally, the algorithm applies 2QBF satisfiability checking (and synthesis of parameters for resolution actors) for guaranteeing nonexistence of potential conflicts between different formulas in the GXW specifications (Step 4).

4.1   High-Level Control Specifications and Resolution Actors

The initial structural recursion over GXW formulas is described in Step 1.

Step 1.1 - Controller for high-level control objectives. Line 1 associates the three high-level controller actors InUB, TrUB, IfTB with their corresponding pattern identifier. Implementations for the actors InUB, TrUB, IfTB are listed in Fig. 3(b). For example, the actor IfTB is used for realizing $\mathbf{G}(\text{input} \rightarrow \text{output})$ in Table 2. When input equals false, the output produced by this actor equals "–". This symbol is used as syntactic sugar for the set {true, false}. Therefore the output is unconstrained, that is, it is feasible for output to be either true or false. The value "–" is transferred in the dataflow, thereby allowing the delay of decisions when considering multiple specifications influencing the same output variable.

Step 1.2 - External I/O ports. Line 2 and 3 are producing external input and output port for each input variable $v_{in} \in V_{in}$ and output variable $v_{out} \in V_{out}$.

Step 1.3 - High-level control controller instantiation. Lines 4 and 5 iterate through each specification η_m to find the corresponding pattern (using Detect-Pattern). Based on the corresponding type, line 6 creates a high-level controller by copying the content stored in the map. If there exists a specification which does not match one of the patterns, immediately reject (line 7). Notice that pattern P4 is handled separately in Step 3. For the door example, the controller in Fig. 3(a) contains the two copies $TrUB^{(1)}$ and $TrUB^{(2)}$ of the trigger-until actor $TrUB$; the subscripts of these copies are tracing the indices of the originating formulas (S1) and (S2).

Step 1. Initiate external I/O ports, high-level controller and resolution controllers

> **Input**   : LTL specification $\phi = \varrho \rightarrow \bigwedge_{m=1...k} \eta_m$, input and output variables V_{in}, V_{out}
>
> **Output**: Actor-based (partial) ctrl implementation $\mathcal{S} = (\mathcal{V}_{in}, \mathcal{V}_{out}, Act, \tau)$, map_{out}

1 **let** $\mathsf{map}_{pattern} := \{\text{P1} \mapsto \text{InUB}, \text{P2} \mapsto \text{TrUB}, \text{P3} \mapsto \text{IfTB}\}$
2 $\mathcal{V}_{in} := \{\, \boxed{v_{in}} \mid v_{in} \in V_{in} \}$
3 $\mathcal{V}_{out} := \{\, \boxed{v_{out}} \mid v_{out} \in V_{out} \}$
4 **foreach** η_m, $m = 1 \ldots k$ **do**
5 $\quad$ **if** $(p := \mathsf{DetectPattern}(\eta_m)) \in \{P1, P2, P3\}$ **then**
6 $\quad\quad$ Create actor $\mathcal{A}^{(m)}$ from $\mathcal{A} := \mathsf{map}_{pattern}.\mathsf{get}(p)$, and add to $\mathcal{S}$;
7 $\quad$ **else if** $(p := \mathsf{DetectPattern}(\eta_m)) \notin \{P4, P5, P6\}$ **then return error** ;
8 **let** $\mathsf{map}_{out} := \mathsf{NewEmptyMap}()$;
9 **foreach** $v_{out} \in V_{out}$ **do** $\mathsf{map}_{out}.\mathsf{put}(v_{out}, \mathsf{NewEmptyList}())$; ;
10 **foreach** η_m, $m = 1 \ldots k$ **do**
11 $\quad$ $\mathsf{map}_{out}.\mathsf{get}(v_{out}).\mathsf{add}(m)$, where v_{out} is the output variable used in $\tau_m.\varrho_{out}$;
12 **foreach** $v_{out} \in V_{out}$ **do** Add actor $Res_{v_{out}} :=$ $\mathsf{CreateResActor}(\mathsf{map}_{out}.\mathsf{get}(v_{out}).\mathsf{size}())$ to Act ;
13 **foreach** η_m, $m = 1 \ldots k$ **do**
14 $\quad$ **let** v_{out} be the variable used in $\tau_m.\varrho_{out}$, $\mathsf{ind} := \mathsf{map}_{out}.\mathsf{get}(v_{out}).\mathsf{indexOf}(m)$;
15 $\quad$ **if** $\neg v_{out}$ equals $\tau_m.\varrho_{out}$ **then** // negation is used in literal
16 $\quad\quad$ Create a negation actor $\boxed{\neg}^{(m)}$ and add it to Act;
17 $\quad\quad$ $\tau := \tau \cup \{(\mathcal{A}^{(m)}.\mathsf{output} \dashrightarrow \boxed{\neg}^{(m)}.\mathsf{input}), (\boxed{\neg}^{(m)}.\mathsf{output} \dashrightarrow Res_{v_{out}}.\mathsf{input}_{\mathsf{ind}})\}$;
18 $\quad$ **else** $\tau := \tau \cup \{(\mathcal{A}^{(m)}.\mathsf{output} \dashrightarrow Res_{v_{out}}.\mathsf{input}_{\mathsf{ind}})\}$;
19 **foreach** $v_{out} \in V_{out}$ **do** $\tau := \tau \cup \{(Res_{v_{out}}.\mathsf{output} \dashrightarrow \boxed{v_{out}})\}$;

Step 1.4 - Resolution Actors. This step is to consider all sub-specifications that influence the same output variable v_{out}. Line 9 to 11 adds, for each specification η_m using v_{out}, its index m maintained by $\mathsf{map}_{out}.\mathsf{get}(v_{out})$. E.g., for the door example, specifications S1, S3 and S4 all output out0. Therefore after executing line 10 and 11, we have $\mathsf{map}_{out}.\mathsf{get}(\mathsf{out0}) = \{1, 3, 4\}$, meaning that for variable out0, the value is influenced by S1, S3 and S4.

For each output variable v_{out}, line 12 creates one *Resolution Actor* $Res_{v_{out}}$ which contains one parameter equaling the number of specifications using v_{out} in ϱ_{out}. Here we make it a simple memoryless controller as shown in Fig. 3(b) - $Res_{v_{out}}$ outputs true when one of its inputs is true, outputs false when one of its inputs is false, and outputs A (which is currently an unknown value to be synthesized later) when all inputs are "−". The number of input pins is decided by calling the map. E.g., for Res_{out0} in Fig. 3(a), three inputs are needed because $\mathsf{map}_{out}.\mathsf{get}(\mathsf{out0}).\mathsf{size}() = 3$. The output of the high-level controller $\mathcal{A}^{(m)}$ is connected to the input of $Res_{v_{out}}$. When negation is needed due to the negation symbol in ϱ_{out} (line 15), one introduces a negation actor $\boxed{\neg}$ which

Step 2. Synthesize monitoring controllers (for pattern P1, P2, P3)

Input : $\phi = \varrho \rightarrow \bigwedge_{m=1\ldots k} \eta_m$, V_{in}, V_{out}, $\mathcal{S} = (\mathcal{V}_{in}, \mathcal{V}_{out}, Act, \tau)$ from Step 1.

Output: (partial) controller $\mathcal{S} = (V_{in}, V_{out}, Act, \tau)$ by adding more elements

1 **foreach** η_m, $m = 1 \ldots k$ **do**

2 $\quad$ $p :=$ DetectPattern(η_m);

3 $\quad$ **if** $p \in \{P1, P2, P3\}$ **then** // Work on subformula ''input '' of η_m, defined by ϕ_{in}^i

4 $\quad\quad$ Add an OR-gate actor $\mathsf{OR}_{\phi_{in}^i}$ with size($\eta_m.\phi_{in}^i$) inputs to Act;

5 $\quad\quad$ **foreach** *clause formula* χ_{in}^i *from DNF of* $\eta_m.\phi_{in}^i$ **do**

6 $\quad\quad\quad$ Add $\mathcal{A}(\mathcal{C})$ to Act, where $\mathcal{C} :=$ Syn($\mathbf{G}(\chi_{in}^i \leftrightarrow \mathbf{X}^i\mathsf{out}) \wedge \bigwedge_{z=0}^{i-1} \mathbf{X}^z\neg\mathsf{out}$, $\mathsf{In}(\chi_{in}^i)$, {out });

7 $\quad\quad\quad$ **foreach** $v_{in} \in \mathit{In}(\chi_{in}^i)$ **do** $\tau := \tau \cup \{(\boxed{v_{in}} \dashrightarrow \mathcal{A}(\mathcal{C}).v_{in})\}$;

8 $\quad\quad\quad$ $\tau := \tau \cup \{(\mathcal{A}(\mathcal{C}).\mathsf{out} \dashrightarrow \mathsf{OR}_{\phi_{in}^i}.\mathsf{in}_{\mathsf{Index}(\chi_{in}^i, \phi_{in}^i)})\}$;

9 $\quad\quad$ $\tau := \tau \cup \{(\mathsf{OR}_{\phi_{in}^i}.\mathsf{out} \dashrightarrow \mathcal{A}^{(m)}.\mathsf{input})\}$;

10 $\quad$ **if** $p \in \{P2\}$ **then** // Work on subformula ''release '' of η_m, defined by $\varphi_{in}^j \vee \rho_{out}^0$

11 $\quad\quad$ Add an OR-gate actor $\mathsf{OR}_{\varphi_{in}^j \vee \rho_{out}^0}$ with size($\eta_m.(\varphi_{in}^j \vee \rho_{out}^0)$) inputs to Act;

12 $\quad\quad$ **foreach** *clause formula* χ_{in}^h *from DNF* $\eta_m.\varphi_{in}^j$ **do**

13 $\quad\quad\quad$ Add $\mathcal{A}(\mathcal{C})$ to Act, where $\mathcal{C} :=$ Syn($\mathbf{G}(\chi_{in}^h \leftrightarrow \mathbf{X}^h\mathsf{out}) \wedge \bigwedge_{z=0}^{h-1} \mathbf{X}^z\neg\mathsf{out}$, $\mathsf{In}(\chi_{in}^h)$, {out });

14 $\quad\quad\quad$ **foreach** $v_{in} \in \mathit{In}(\chi_{in}^i)$ **do** $\tau := \tau \cup \{(\boxed{v_{in}} \dashrightarrow \mathcal{A}(\mathcal{C}).v_{in})\}$;

15 $\quad\quad\quad$ **if** $h = 0$ **then** Add $(\mathcal{A}(\mathcal{C}).\mathsf{out} \dashrightarrow \mathsf{OR}_{\varphi_{in}^j \vee \rho_{out}^0}.\mathsf{in}_{\mathsf{Index}(\chi_{in}^z, \varphi_{in}^j \vee \rho_{out}^0)})$ to τ ;

16 $\quad\quad\quad$ **else**

17 $\quad\quad\quad\quad$ Add $\mathcal{A}(\mathcal{C}_{\Theta_h})$ to Act, where $\mathcal{C}_{\Theta_h} :=$ CreateThetaCtrl(h);

18 $\quad\quad\quad\quad$ $\tau := \tau \cup \{(\mathsf{OR}_{\phi_{in}^i}.\mathsf{out} \dashrightarrow \mathcal{A}(\mathcal{C}_{\Theta_h}).\mathsf{set}), (\mathcal{A}(\mathcal{C}).\mathsf{out} \dashrightarrow \mathcal{A}(\mathcal{C}_{\Theta_h}).\mathsf{in}), (\mathcal{A}(\mathcal{C}_{\Theta_h}).\mathsf{out} \dashrightarrow \mathsf{OR}_{\varphi_{in}^j \vee \rho_{out}^0}.\mathsf{in}_{\mathsf{Index}(\chi_{in}^z, \varphi_{in}^j \vee \rho_{out}^0)})\}$;

19 $\quad\quad$ **foreach** *clause formula* χ_{out}^0 *from DNF of* $\eta_m.\rho_{out}^0$ **do**

20 $\quad\quad\quad$ Add an AND-gate actor $\mathsf{AND}_{\eta_m \cdot \chi_{out}^0}$ with size(χ_{out}^0) inputs to Act;

21 $\quad\quad\quad$ **foreach** *literal* ω_{out} *of* χ_{out}^0 **do**

22 $\quad\quad\quad\quad$ **let** v_{out} be the variable used in ω_{out};

23 $\quad\quad\quad\quad$ **if** ω_{out} *equals* $\neg v_{out}$ **then** // negation is used in literal

24 $\quad\quad\quad\quad\quad$ Create $\boxed{\neg}_{Res_{v_{out}}}$ and add to Act, if not exists;

25 $\quad\quad\quad\quad\quad$ Add $(Res_{v_{out}}.\mathsf{output} \dashrightarrow \boxed{\neg}_{Res_{v_{out}}}.\mathsf{input})$ to τ, if not exists;

26 $\quad\quad\quad\quad\quad$ Add $(\boxed{\neg}_{Res_{v_{out}}}.\mathsf{output} \dashrightarrow \mathsf{AND}_{\chi_{out}^0}.\mathsf{in}_{\mathsf{Index}(\omega_{out}, \chi_{out}^0)})$ to τ;

27 $\quad\quad\quad\quad$ **else** $\tau := \tau \cup \{Res_{v_{out}}.\mathsf{output} \dashrightarrow \mathsf{AND}_{\chi_{out}^0}.\mathsf{in}_{\mathsf{Index}(\omega_{out}, \chi_{out}^0)}\}$;

28 $\quad\quad\quad$ $\tau := \tau \cup \{\mathsf{AND}_{\chi_{out}^0}.\mathsf{out} \dashrightarrow \mathsf{OR}_{\varphi_{in}^j \vee \rho_{out}^0}.\mathsf{in}_{\mathsf{Index}(\chi_{out}^0, \varphi_{in}^j \vee \rho_{out}^0)}\}$

29 $\quad\quad$ $\tau := \tau \cup \{\mathsf{OR}_{\phi_{in}^j \vee \rho_{out}^0}.\mathsf{out} \dashrightarrow \mathcal{A}^{(m)}.\mathsf{release}\}$;

negates $A^{(m)}$.output when $A^{(m)}$.input is true or false (line 16, 17). To ensure that connections are wired appropriately, map_{out} is used such that the number "ind" records the precise input port of the Res_{out} (line 14). Consider again the door example. Due to the maintained list $\{1, 3, 4\}$, $TrUB^{(1)}$.output is connected to $Res_{v_{out}}$.input$_1$, i.e., the first input pin of $Res_{v_{out}}$. Also, as $\neg$out0 is used in S3 and S4, the wiring from $InUB^{(3)}$ and $IfTB^{(4)}$ to Res_{out0} in Fig. 3(a) has a negation actor in between.

Lastly, line 19 connects the output port of a resolution actor to the corresponding external output port. If $Res_{v_{out}}$ receives simultaneously true and false from two of its input ports, then $Res_{v_{out}}$.output needs to be simultaneously true and false. These kinds of situations are causing unrealizability of GXW specification, and Step 4 is used for detecting these kinds of inconsistencies.

4.2 Monitors and Phase Adjustment Actors

The second step of the algorithm synthesizes controllers for monitoring the appearance of an event matching the subformula, and connects these controllers to previously created actors for realizing high-level control objectives. For a formula ϕ in DNF form, let $\mathsf{size}(\phi)$ return the number of clauses in ϕ. For clause formula χ_{in}^i in ϕ, let $\mathsf{In}(\chi_{in}^i)$ return the set of all input variables and $\alpha = \mathsf{Index}(\chi_{in}^i, \phi_{in}^i)$ specify that χ_{in}^i is the α-th clause in ϕ_{in}^i.

Step 2.1 - Realizing "input" part for pattern P1, P2, P3. In Step 2, from line 3 to 9, the algorithm synthesizes controller realizing the portion input listed in Table 2, or equivalently, the ϕ_{in}^i part listed in Table 1. Line 4 first creates an OR gate, as the formula is represented in DNF. Then synthesize a controller for monitoring each clause formula (line 5, 6) using function Syn, with input variables defined in $\mathsf{In}(\chi_{in}^i)$ and a newly introduced output variable $\{\mathsf{out}\}$[3]. The first attempt is to synthesize $\mathbf{G}(\chi_{in}^i \leftrightarrow \mathbf{X}^i\mathsf{out})$. By doing so, the value of χ_{in}^i is reflected in out. However, as the output of the synthesized controller is connected to the input of an OR-gate (line 8) and subsequently, passed through the port "input" of the high-level controller (line 9), one needs to also ensure that from time 0 to $i-1$, out remains false, such that the high-level controller $\mathcal{A}_m$ for specification η_m will not be "unintentionally" triggered and subsequently restrict the output. To this end, the specification to be synthesized is $\mathbf{G}(\chi_{in}^i \leftrightarrow \mathbf{X}^i\mathsf{out}) \wedge \bigwedge_{z=0...i-1} \mathbf{X}^z \neg\mathsf{out}$, being stated in line 6.

For above mentioned property that needs to be synthesized in line 6, one does not need to use full LTL synthesis algorithms. Instead, we present a simpler algorithm (Algorithm 1) which creates a controller in time linear to the number of variables times the maximum number of $\mathbf{X}$ operators in the formula. Here again for simplicity, each state variable is three-valued (true, false, u); in implementation every 3-valued state variable is translated into 2 Boolean variables. In the

---

[3] For pattern type P2 or P3, one needs to have each clause formula of ϕ_{in}^i be of form χ_{in}^i, i.e., the highest number of consecutive $\mathbf{X}$ should equal i. The purpose is to align χ_{in}^i with the preceding $\mathbf{X}^i$ in $\mathbf{G}(\phi_{in}^i \rightarrow \mathbf{X}^i(\varrho_{out} \mathbf{W} (\varphi_{in}^j \vee \rho_{out}^0)))$ or $\mathbf{G}(\phi_{in}^i \rightarrow \mathbf{X}^i\varrho_{out})$. If a clause formula in DNF contains no literal starting with $\mathbf{X}^i$, one can always pad a conjunction $\mathbf{X}^i$ true to the clause formula. The padding is not needed for P1.

Algorithm 1. Realizing Syn without full LTL synthesis

Input : LTL specification $\mathbf{G}(\chi_{in}^i \leftrightarrow \mathbf{X}^i\text{out}) \wedge \bigwedge_{z=0}^{i-1} \mathbf{X}^z\neg\text{out})$, input variables $\mathsf{In}(\chi_{in}^i)$, output variables $\{\text{out}\}$

Output: Mealy machine $\mathcal{C} = (Q, q_0, 2^{V_{in}}, 2^{V_{out}}, \Delta)$ for realizing the specification

1 $V_{out} := \{\text{out}\}$, $V_{in} := \mathsf{In}(\chi_{in}^i)$;

2 **foreach** *Variable* $v_{in} \in \mathsf{In}(\chi_{in}^i)$ **do** // Create all state variables in the Mealy machine

3 $\quad$ **for** $j = 1 \ldots i$ **do** $Q := Q \cup \{v_{in}[j]\}$, where $v_{in}[j]$ is three-valued (true , false , u) ;

4 $q_0 := \bigwedge_{v_{in} \in \mathsf{In}(\chi_{in}^i), j \in \{1, \ldots i\}} v_{in}[j] := \mathsf{u}$ /* Initial state */;

5 **let** Cd := true /* Cd for output condition */;

6 **foreach** *literal* $\mathbf{X}^k v_{in}$ in χ_{in}^i **do**

7 $\quad$ **if** $k = i$ **then** Cd := Cd $\wedge (v_{in} = \text{true})$ **else** Cd := Cd $\wedge (v_{in}[i-k] = \text{true})$;

8 **foreach** *literal* $\mathbf{X}^k \neg v_{in}$ in χ_{in}^i **do**

9 $\quad$ **if** $k = i$ **then** Cd := Cd $\wedge (v_{in} = \text{false})$ **else** Cd := Cd $\wedge (v_{in}[i-k] = \text{false})$;

10 $\delta_{out} := (\text{out} := \text{Cd})$ /* Output assignment should follow the value of Cd */;

11 $\delta_s := (\bigwedge_{v_{in} \in \mathsf{In}(\chi_{in}^i), j=1 \ldots i-1} v_{in}[j+1] := v_{in}[j]) \wedge (\bigwedge_{v_{in} \in \mathsf{In}(\chi_{in}^i)} v_{in}[1] := v_{in})$;

---

algorithm, state variable $v_{in}[i]$ is used to store the i-step history of for v_{in}, and $v_{in}[i] = \mathsf{u}$ means that the history is not yet recorded. Therefore, for the initial state, all variables are set to u (line 4). The update of state variable $v_{in}[i+1]$ is based on the current state of $v_{in}[i]$, but for state variable $v_{in}[1]$, it is updated based on current input v_{in} (line 11). With state variable recording previously seen values, monitoring the event is possible, where the value of out is based on the condition stated from line 6 to 10.

Consider a controller realizing $\chi_{in}^i := \neg\text{in1} \wedge \mathbf{X}\text{in1} \wedge \mathbf{X}\text{in2} \wedge \mathbf{XX}\neg\text{in2}$, being executed under a run prefix (false, false)(true, true)(true, false). As shown in Fig. 4, the update of state variables is demonstrated by a left shift. The first and the second output are false. After receiving the third input, the controller is able to detect a rising edge of in1 (via in1[2]=false and in1[1]=true) is immediately followed by a falling edge of in2 (via in2[1]=true and in2 =false).

Step 2.2 - Realizing "release" part for pattern P2. Back to Step 2, the algorithm from line 10 to 29 synthesizes a controller realizing the portion release listed in Table 2, or equivalently, the $\varphi_{in}^j \vee \rho_{out}^0$ part listed in Table 1. The DNF structure is represented as an OR-actor (line 11), taking input from φ_{in}^j (line 12–18) and ρ_{out}^0 (line 19–28).

For ρ_{out}^0 (line 19–28), first create an AND-gate for each clause in DNF. Whenever output variable v_{out} is used, the wiring is established by a connection to the output port of $Res_{v_{out}}$ (line 27). Negation in the literal is done by adding a wire to connect $Res_{v_{out}}$ to a dedicated negation actor $\boxed{\neg}_{Res_{v_{out}}}$ to negate the output (line 23 to 26). Consider, for example, specification $S2$ of the automatic door running example, where the "release" part (in1 $\vee$ in0 $\vee$ out0) is a disjunction of literals using output variable out0. As a consequence, one creates an AND-gate (line 20) which takes one input Res_{out0}.output (line 27), and connects this AND-gate to the OR-gate (line 28). Figure 3(a) displays an optimized version of this construction, since the single-input AND-gate may be removed and Res_{out0}.output is directly wired with the OR-gate.

For φ_{in}^j (line 12 to 23), similar to Step 2.1, one needs to synthesize a controller which tracks the appearance of χ_{in}^h (line 13). However, the start of tracking is triggered by ϕ_{in}^i (the input subformula). That is, whenever ϕ_{in}^i is true, start monitoring if φ_{in}^j has appeared true. This is problematic when χ_{in}^h contains $\mathbf{X}$ operators (i.e., $h > 0$). To realize this mechanism, at line 17, the function CreateThetaCtrl additionally initiates a controller which guarantees the following: Whenever input variable set turns true, the following h values of output variable out are set to false. After that, the value of output variable out is the same as the input variable in. This property can be formulated as Θ_h (to trigger consecutive h false value over out after seeing set = true) listed in Eq. 2, with implementation shown in Fig. 6. By observing the Mealy machine and the high-level transition function, one infers that the time for constructing such a controller in symbolic form is again linear in h.

$$\Theta_h := (\neg\text{out}\,\mathbf{W}\,\text{set}) \wedge \mathbf{G}(\text{set} \rightarrow (\bigwedge_{z=0}^{h-1} \neg\mathbf{X}^z\text{out} \wedge \mathbf{X}^h((\text{in} \leftrightarrow \text{out})\,\mathbf{W}\,\text{set}))) \quad (2)$$

The overall construction in Step 2 is illustrated using the example in Fig. 5, which realizes the formula

$$\mathbf{G}((\neg\text{in1} \wedge \mathbf{X}\text{in1}) \rightarrow \mathbf{X}(\text{out1}\,\mathbf{W}(\neg\text{in2} \wedge \mathbf{X}\text{in2}))) \quad (3)$$

with $V_{in} = \{\text{in1}, \text{in2}\}$ and $V_{out} = \{\text{out1}\}$. This specification requires to set output out1 to true when a rising edge of in1 appears, and after that, out1 should remain true until detecting a raising edge of in2. Using the algorithm listed in Step 2, line 6 synthesizes the monitor for the input part (i.e., detecting rising edge of in1), line 13 synthesizes the monitor for the release part (i.e., detecting rising edge of in2), line 14 creates the wiring from input port to the monitor. As $h = 1$ (line 16), line 17 creates $\mathcal{A}(\mathcal{C}_{\Theta_1})$, and line 18 establishes the wiring to and from $\mathcal{A}(\mathcal{C}_{\Theta_1})$.

The reader may notice that it is incorrect to simply connect the monitor controller for $\neg\text{in2} \wedge \mathbf{X}\text{in2}$ directly to TrUB.release, as, when both $\neg\text{in1} \wedge \mathbf{X}\text{in1}$ and $\neg\text{in2} \wedge \mathbf{X}\text{in2}$ are true at the same time, TrUB.output is unconstrained. On the contrary, in Fig. 5, when $\neg\text{in1} \wedge \mathbf{X}\text{in1}$ is true and the value is passed through TrUB.input, $\mathcal{A}(\mathcal{C}_{\Theta_1})$ enforces to invalidate the incoming value of TrUB.release for 1 cycle by setting it to false.

Step 3 - Realizing "input" for pattern P4. For pattern P4, in contrast to pattern P1, P2, and P3, the synthesized monitoring element is directly connected to a Resolution Actor (see Fig. 3(a) for example). To maintain maximum freedom over output variable, one synthesizes the event monitor from the specification allowing the first consecutive i output to be "–". The monitor construction is analogous to Algorithm 1 and we refer readers to [1] for details.

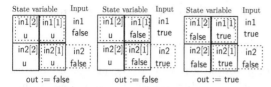

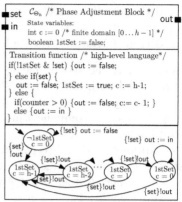

Fig. 4. Executing monitor with $\chi_{in}^{i} := \neg in1 \wedge$ **X**$in1 \wedge$ **X**$in2 \wedge$ **XX**$\neg in2$, by taking first three inputs (false, false)(true, true)(true, false).

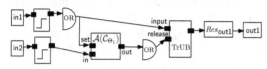

Fig. 5. Correct controller construction for specification satisfying pattern P2.

Fig. 6. Implementing Θ_h (state variables not mentioned in update remain the same value).

Optimizations. Runtimes for Steps 2 and 3 may be optimized by using simple pattern matching and hashing of previously synthesized controllers. We are listing three different opportunities for optimized *generation of monitors.* First, the controller in Fig. 3(a) for monitoring $\neg in0 \wedge$ **X** $in0$ is connected to two high-level controllers. The second case can be observed in Fig. 5, where by rewriting in1 and in2 to in, the controller being synthesized is actually the same. Therefore, one can also record the pattern for individual monitor and perform synthesis once per pattern. A third opportunity for optimization occurs when Algorithm 1 takes $i = 0$ (i.e., no **X** operator is used). In this case there is no need to create a controller at all and one may proceed by directly building a combinatorial circuit, similar to the constructions of line 19 to 28 in Step 2. For example, for specification S2 of the automatic door, the release part is in1 $\vee$ in0 $\vee$ out0; since no **X** operator occurs, a combinatorial circuit is created by wiring directly $\boxed{in1}$ and $\boxed{in0}$ to the OR-gate.

4.3 Parameter Synthesis for 2QBF Without Unroll

Previous steps construct actors as building blocks and wires the actors according to the structure of the given GXW specification from type P1 to P4. The resulting (partial) controller, however, does not yet realize this specification as it may still contain unknowns in the resolution actors. Further checks are necessary, and a controller is rejected if one of the following conditions holds.

(**Condition 1**) The wiring forms a directed loop in the constructed actor-based controller.

(**Condition 2**) It is possible for a resolution actor $Res_{v_{out}}$ to receive true and false simultaneously.

(**Condition 3**) Outputs violate invariance conditions of pattern P5.

Condition 1 is checked by means of a simple graph analysis: (1) let all ports be nodes and wirings be edges; (2) for each actor, create directed edges from each of its input ports to each of its output ports; (3) check if there exists a strongly connected component in the resulting graph using, for example, Tarjan's algorithm [29].

Conditions 2 and 3 are checked by means of creating corresponding 2QBF satisfiability problems. Recall that each resolution actor $Res_{v_{out}}$ is parameterized with respect to the output A when all incoming inputs for $Res_{v_{out}}$ are "–". The corresponding parameter assignment problem is encoded as a 2QBF[4] formula, where existential variables are the parameters to be synthesized, universal variables are input variables, and the quantifier-free body is a logical implication specifying that the encoding of the system guarantees condition 2 and 3.

Step 4 shows a simplified algorithm for generating 2QBF constraints which does not perform unrolling. Stated in line 15, the quantifier free formula is of form $\Upsilon_a \rightarrow \Upsilon_g$, where Υ_a are input assumptions and system dynamics, and Υ_g are properties to be guaranteed. First, unknown parameters are added to the set of existential variables $V_\exists$ (line 2). All other variables are universal variables. Then based on the evaluation ordering of S, perform one of the following tasks:

- When an element ξ in the execution ordering Ξ is a wire (line 5), we add source and dest as universal variables (as $V_\forall$ is a set, repeated variables will be neglected), and establish the logical constraint (source $\leftrightarrow$ dest) (lines 6 to 8).
- When an element ξ in the execution ordering Ξ is an actor, we use function EncodeTransition to encode the transition (pre-post) relation as constraints (line 11), and add all state variables (for pre and post) in the actor (recall our definition of Mealy machine is based on state variables) to $V_\forall$ using function GetStateVariable (line 10).

Υ_a is initially set to ϱ (line 1) to reflect the allowed input patterns regulated by the specification (specification type P6). Line 12 creates the constraint stating that no two inputs of a resolution actor should create contradicting conditions. As the number of input ports for any resolution actor is finite, the existential quantifier is only an abbreviation which is actually rewritten to a quantifier-free formula describing relations between input ports of a resolution actor.

The encoding presented in Step 4 does not involve unroll (it encodes the transition relation, but not the initial condition). Therefore, by setting all variables to be universally quantified, one approximates the behavior of the system dynamics without considering the relation between two successor states. Therefore, using

---

[4] Quantified Boolean Formula with one top-level quantifier alternation.

Step 4. Parameter synthesis by generating 2QBF constraints

Input   : LTL specification $\phi = \varrho \rightarrow \bigwedge_{m=1\ldots k} \eta_m$, input variables V_{in}, output variables V_{out}, partial implementation $\mathcal{S} = (V_{in}, V_{out}, Act, \tau)$ with unknown parameters

Output: Controller implementation $\mathcal{S}$ or "unknown"

1 let $\Upsilon_a := \varrho, \Upsilon_g :=$ true, $V_\exists, V_\forall :=$ NewEmptySet();
2 **foreach** $v_{out} \in V_{out}$ **do** $V_\exists := V_\exists \cup \{Res_{v_{out}}.\text{A}\}$;
3 let Ξ be the evaluation ordering of $\mathcal{S}$;
4 **foreach** $\xi \in \Xi$ **do**
5 $\quad$ **if** $\xi \in \tau$ **then** // ξ is a wire; encode using biimplication
6 $\quad\quad$ Let ξ be (source $\dashrightarrow$ dest);
7 $\quad\quad$ $V_\forall.add(\text{source})$, $V_\forall.add(\text{dest})$;
8 $\quad\quad$ $\Upsilon_a := \Upsilon_a \wedge (\text{source} \leftrightarrow \text{dest})$;
9 $\quad$ **else** // ξ is an actor; encode transition
10 $\quad\quad$ $V_\forall.add(\text{GetStateVariable}(\xi))$;
11 $\quad\quad$ $\Upsilon_a := \Upsilon_a \wedge (\text{EncodeTransition}(\xi))$ /* $\xi \in Act$ */ ;
12 **for** $v_{out} \in V_{out}$ **do**
$\quad$ $\Upsilon_g := \Upsilon_g \wedge (\nexists i, j : (Res_{v_{out}}.\text{input}_i = \text{true}) \wedge (Res_{v_{out}}.\text{input}_j = \text{false}))$;
13 **foreach** η_m, $m = 1\ldots k$ **do**
14 $\quad$ **if** DetectPattern$(\eta_m) \in \{P5\}$ **then** $\Upsilon_g := \Upsilon_g \wedge \eta_m$;
15 **if** Solve2QBF$(V_\exists, V_\forall, \Upsilon_a \rightarrow \Upsilon_g)$.isSatisable **then**
16 $\quad$ **return** $\mathcal{S}$ by replacing each $Res_{out}.\text{A}$ by the value of witness in 2QBF;
17 **else** **return** unknown ;

Step 4 only guarantees *soundness*: If the formula is satisfiable, then the specification is realizable (line 15, 16). Otherwise, unknown is returned (line 17).[5]

As each individual specification of one of the types {P1, P2, P3, P4} is trivially realizable, the reason for rejecting a specification is (1) simultaneous true and false demanded by different sub-specifications, (2) violation of properties over output variables (type P5), and (3) feedback loop within $\mathcal{S}$. Therefore, as Steps 1-4 guarantees non-existence of above three situations, the presented method is *sound*.

Theorem 1. (Soundness) *Let ϕ be a GXW specification, and $\mathcal{S}$ be an actor-based controller as generated by Steps 1-4 from ϕ; then $\mathcal{S}$ realizes ϕ.*

---

[5] Even without unroll, one can infer relations over universal variables via statically analyzing the specification. As an example, consider two sub-specifications $S1$: $\mathbf{G}(\text{in1} \rightarrow (\text{out}\,\mathbf{W}\,\text{in2}))$ and $S2$: $\mathbf{G}(\text{in2} \rightarrow (\neg\text{out}\,\mathbf{W}\,\text{in1}))$. One can infer that it is impossible for $TrUB^{(1)}$ and $TrUB^{(2)}$ to be simultaneously have state variable $lock = $ true, as both starts with $lock = $ false, and if $S1$ first enters lock ($lock = $ true) due to in1, the $S2$ cannot enter, as release part of $S2$ is also in1. Similar argument follows vice versa.

The GXW synthesis algorithm as described above, however is *incomplete*, as controllers with feedback loops are rejected; that is, whenever output variables listed in the release part of P2 necessitate simultaneous reasoning over two or more output variables. Figure 7 display a controller (with feedback loop) for realizing

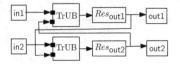

Fig. 7. Incompleteness example.

the specification $\mathbf{G}(\text{in1} \rightarrow (\text{out1}\,\mathbf{W}\,\text{out2})) \wedge \mathbf{G}(\text{in2} \rightarrow (\text{out2}\,\mathbf{W}\,\text{out1}))$. However, our workflow rejects such a controller even though the given specification is realizable. With further structural restriction over GXW (which guarantees no feedback loop in during construction) and by using unrolling of the generated actor-based controllers, the workflow as presented here can be made to be *complete*, as demonstrated in Sect. 4.4.

4.4   General Properties for GXW Synthesis

Since unrealizability of a GXW specification is due to the conditions (1) simultaneous true and false demanded by different sub-specifications, and (2) violation of properties over output variables (type P5)[6], one can build a counter-strategy[7] by first building a tree that provides input assignments to lead all runs to undesired states violating (1) or (2), then all leafs of the tree violating (1) or

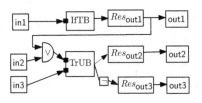

Fig. 8. Control implementation.

(2) are connected to a self-looped final state, in order to accept ω-words. As the input part listed in Table 2 does not involve any output variable, a counter-strategy, if exists, can lead to violation of (1) or (2) within Ω cycles, where Ω is a number sufficient to let each input part of the sub-specification be true in a run.

Lemma 1. For GXW specification $\varrho \rightarrow \bigwedge_{m=1\ldots k} \eta_m$, if (a) ρ_{out}^0 is false for all η_m of type P2 and (b) no specification of type P5 exists, then if the specification is not realizable, then there exists a counter-strategy which leads to violation of (1) or (2) in Ω steps, where Ω is bounded by the sum of (i) the number of specifications k, and (ii) the sum of all i value defined within each ϕ_{in}^i of η_m.

When ρ_{out}^0 is false for all η_m of type P2, our presented construction guarantees no feedback loop. As no specification of type P5 exists, the selection of

---

[6] Rejecting feedback loops on the controller structure is only a restriction of our presented method and is not the reason for unrealizability; similar to Fig. 7, feedback loop can possibly be resolved by merging all actors involving feedback to a single actor.

[7] A counter-strategy in LTL synthesis a state machine where the environment can enforce to violate the given property, regardless of all possible moves by the controller [27].

A never influences whether the specification is realizable. Therefore, quantifier alternation is removed. To this end, checking unrealizability is equivalent to non-deterministically guessing Ω input assignments and subsequently, checking if a violation of (1) or (2) appears by executing $\mathcal{S}$. This brings the co-NP result stated in Lemma 2. This also means that under the restriction from Lemma 1, a slight modification of Step 4 to perform unrolling the computation Ω-times makes our synthesis algorithm *complete*.

Lemma 2. Deciding whether a given GXW specification, which also obeys the additional restrictions as stated in Lemma 1, is realizable or not is in co-NP.

For the general case, the bound in Lemma 1 remains valid (as input part is not decided by the output variable). Complexity result is achieved by, without using our construction, directly using finite memory to store and examine all possible control strategies in Ω steps.

Lemma 3. For GXW specification $\varrho \rightarrow \bigwedge_{m=1\ldots k} \eta_m$, if the specification is not realizable, then there exists a counter-strategy which leads to violation of (1) or (2) in Ω steps, where Ω is bounded by condition similar to Lemma 1.

Lemma 4. Deciding whether a given GXW specification is realizable or not is in PSPACE.

The above mentioned bounds are only conditions to detect realizability of a GXW specification, while our presented workflow in Sect. 4 targets generating structured implementations. Still, by unrolling the computation Ω-times, one can detect if a controller, following our regulated structure, exists.

4.5   Extensions

One can extend the presented workflow to allow richer specification than previously presented GXW fragment. Here we outline how these extensions are realized by considering the following sample specification: $\mathbf{G}(\text{in1} \rightarrow \text{out1}) \wedge \mathbf{G}((\text{in2} \vee \text{out1}) \rightarrow ((\text{out2} \wedge \neg\text{out3})\mathbf{W}\,\text{in3}))$. The SDF controller implementation is shown in Fig. 8. First, conjunctions in ϱ_{out} can be handled by considering each output variable separately. E.g., for $\varrho_{out} \equiv \text{out2} \wedge \neg\text{out3}$, in Fig. 8 both are connected to the same TrUB. Second, the use of output variables in "input" part for pattern P1, P2, P3 is also supported, provided that in effect a combinatorial circuit is created (i.e., output variables should always proceed with $\mathbf{X}^i$), and the generated system does not create a feedback loop. E.g., for the antecedent (in2 $\vee$ out1), it is created by wiring the Res_{out1}.out to an OR-gate.

5   Experimental Evaluation

We implemented a tool for GXW synthesis in Java, which invokes DepQBF [21] (Version 5.0) for QBF solving. Table 3 includes experimental results for a representative subset of our PLC benchmark examples. Execution times is recorded using Ubuntu VM (Virtual Box with 3 GB RAM) running on an Intel i7-3520M 2.9 GHz CPU and 8 GB RAM). Most control problems are solved in less than a second[8]. GXW synthesis always generated a controller without feedback loops for all examples.

Table 3 lists a comparison of execution times of GXW synthesis and the bounded LTL synthesis tool Acacia+ [8] (latest version 2.3). We used the option --player 1 of Acacia+ for forcing the environment to take a first move, but we did not do manual annotation in order to support compositional synthesis in Acacia+, as it is not needed by our tool. For many of the simpler case studies, the reported runtimes of Acacia+ are similar to GXW synthesis. However, GXW seems to scale much better to more complex case studies with a larger number of input and output variables such as examples 5, 9, 11, 12, 13, 15, 16, 17, 18, 19 in Table 3. The representation of the generated controller in terms of a system of interacting actors in GXW synthesis, however, allows the engineer to trace each sub-specification with corresponding partial implementation. In fact the structure of the controllers generated by GXW is usually similar to reference implementations by the case study providers. In contrast, a controller expressed in terms of single Mealy machine is rather difficult to grasp and to maintain for problems such as example 18 with 13 input and 13 output variables.

6 Related Work

Here we compare GXW synthesis with related GR(1) synthesis (e.g., [5,15,25,31]) and bounded LTL synthesis (e.g., [8,11,28]) techniques.

Synthesis for the GR(1) fragment of LTL is in time polynomial to the number of nodes of a generated game, which is PSPACE when considering exponential blow-up caused by input and output variables. GXW is also in PSPACE, where GXW allows **W** and GR(1) allows **F**. Even though it has been demonstrated that the expressiveness of GR(1) is enough to cover many practical examples, the use of an until logical operator, which is not included in GR(1), proved to be essential for encoding a majority of our PLC case studies. Also, implementations of GR(1) synthesis such as Anzu [15] do not generate structured controllers. Since GR(1) synthesis, however, includes a round-robin arbiter for circulating among sub-specifications, the systematic structuring of controllers underlying GXW synthesis may be applicable for synthesizing structured GR(1) controllers.

Bounded synthesis supports full LTL and is based on a translation of the LTL synthesis problem to safety games. By doing so, one solves the safety game and finds smaller controllers (as demonstrated in synthesis competitions via tools like Simple BDD solver [13], AbsSynthe [9], Demiurge [17]). The result of solving safety games in bounded LTL synthesis usually is a monolithic Mealy (or Moore) machine, whereas our GXW synthesis method of creating SDF actors may be understood as a way of avoiding the expensive construction of the product of machines. Instead, we are generating controllers by means of wiring smaller

---

[8] Approximately 0.25 seconds is used for initializing JVM in every run.

sub-controllers for specific monitoring and event triggering tasks. The structure of the resulting controllers seem to be very close to what is happening in practice, as a number of our industrial benchmark examples are shipped with reference implementation which are usually structured in a similar way. The size of the representations of generated controllers is particularly important when considering resource-bounded embedded computing devices such as a PLCs. LTL component synthesis, however, has the same worst-case complexity as full LTL synthesis [22].

Table 3. Experimental Result

ID	Description	Source	I/O vars	GXW time (s)	Acacia+ time (s)
1	Automatic door	Ex15 [2]	(4,3)	0.389	0.180
2	Simple conveyor belt	Ex7.1.19 [24]	(3,3)	0.556	0.637
3	Hydraulic ramp	Ex7.1.3 [24]	(5,2)	0.642	0.451
4	Waste water treatment V1	Ex7.1.8 [24]	(6,3)	0.471	0.323
5	Waste water treatment V2	Ex7.1.9 [24]	(8,9)	0.516	5.621
6	Container fusing	Ex10 [2]	(7,6)	0.444	0.425
7	Elevator control mixing plant	Ex7.1.4 [24]	(10,5)	0.484	2.902
8	Lifting platform	Ex21 [16]	(6,3)	0.350	0.645
9	Control of reversal	Ex36 [16]	(7,7)	0.395	2.901
10	Gear wheel	Ex19 [16]	(4,6)	0.447	0.302
11	Two directional conveyor (simplified)	Ex7.1.31.1 [24]	(9,5)	0.789	6.552
12	Garage door control	Ex7.1.25 [24]	(13,5)	0.574	7.002
13	Contrast agent injection	Ex7.1.18 [24]	(6,8)	0.458	3.209
14	Identification	Ex39 [16]	(5,5)	0.430	0.392
15	Monitoring chain elevator	Ex7.1.15 [24]	(10,9)	0.429	9.647
16	Two directional conveyor	Ex7.1.31.1 [24]	(12,5)	0.890	51.553
17	Control of single torque drive (simplified)	Ex7.1.26 [24]	(12,8)	0.538	38.010
18	Gravel transportation via 3 conveyors (simplified)	Ex7.1.31.4 [24]	(13,13)	1.227	> 600 (t.o.)
19	Control of two torque drives (simplified)	Ex7.1.26 [24]	(22,16)	0.790	> 600 (t.o.)

7   Conclusion

We have identified a useful subclass GXW of LTL for specifying a large class of embedded control problems, and we developed a novel synthesis algorithm (in PSPACE) for automatically generating structured controllers in a high-level programming language with synchronous dataflow without cycles. Our experimental results suggest that GXW synthesis scales well to industrial-sized control problems with around 20 input and output ports and beyond.

In this way, GXW synthesis can readily be integrated with industrial design frameworks such as CODESYS [3], Matlab Simulink, and Ptolemy II, and the generated SDF controllers (without cycles) can be statically scheduled and implemented on single and multiple processors [18]. It would also be interesting to use our synthesis algorithms to automatically generate control code from established requirement frameworks for embedded control software such as EARS [23]. Moreover, our presented method supports traceability between specifications and the generated controller code as required by safety-critical applications. Traceability is also the basis for an incremental development methodology.

One of the main impediments of using synthesis in engineering practice, however, is the lack of useful and automated feedback in case of unrealizable specifications [6,10,20] or realizable specifications with unintended realizations. The use of a stylized specification languages such as GXW seems to be a good starting point for supporting design engineers in identifying and analyzing unrealizable specifications, since there are only a relatively small number of potential sources of unrealizability in GXW specifications. Finally, hierarchical SDF may also be useful for modular synthesis [30].

Acknowledgement. We thank Lacramioara Aştefănoaei for her fruitful feedback during the development of the paper, and CAV reviewers for their constructive comments. This work is supported by the H2020 project openMOS, GA no. 680735.

References

1. Full version available at http://arxiv.org/abs/1605.01153
2. Online training material for PLC programming. http://plc-scada-dcs.blogspot. com/
3. CODESYS - industrial IEC 61131-3 programming framework. http://www. codesys.com/
4. Matlab Simulink. http://www.mathworks.com/products/simulink/
5. Bloem, R., Cimatti, A., Greimel, K., Hofferek, G., Könighofer, R., Roveri, M., Schuppan, V., Seeber, R.: RATSY – a new requirements analysis tool with synthesis. In: Touili, T., Cook, B., Jackson, P. (eds.) CAV 2010. LNCS, vol. 6174, pp. 425–429. Springer, Heidelberg (2010)
6. Bloem, R., Ehlers, R., Jacobs, S., Knighofer, R.: How to handle assumptions in synthesis. In: SYNT, pp. 34–50 (2014). EPTCS 157
7. Bloem, R., Könighofer, B., Könighofer, R., Wang, C.: Shield synthesis: runtime enforcement for reactive systems. In: Baier, C., Tinelli, C. (eds.) TACAS 2015. LNCS, vol. 9035, pp. 533–548. Springer, Heidelberg (2015)
8. Bohy, A., Bruyère, V., Filiot, E., Jin, N., Raskin, J.-F.: Acacia+, a tool for LTL synthesis. In: Madhusudan, P., Seshia, S.A. (eds.) CAV 2012. LNCS, vol. 7358, pp. 652–657. Springer, Heidelberg (2012)
9. Brenguier, R., Prez, G.A., Raskin, J.-F., Sankur, O.: AbsSynthe: abstract synthesis from succinct safety specifications. In: SYNT, pp. 100–116 (2014). EPTCS 157
10. Cheng, C.-H., Huang, C.-H., Ruess, H., Stattelmann, S.: G4LTL – ST: automatic generation of PLC programs. In: Biere, A., Bloem, R. (eds.) CAV 2014. LNCS, vol. 8559, pp. 541–549. Springer, Heidelberg (2014)
11. Ehlers, R.: Unbeast: symbolic bounded synthesis. In: Abdulla, P.A., Leino, K.R.M. (eds.) TACAS 2011. LNCS, vol. 6605, pp. 272–275. Springer, Heidelberg (2011)
12. Eker, J., Janneck, J., Lee, E.A., Liu, J., Liu, X., Ludvig, J., Sachs, S., Xiong, Y.: Taming heterogeneity - the Ptolemy approach. Proc. IEEE **91**(1), 127–144 (2003)

13. Jacobs, S., Bloem, R., Brenguier, R., Ehlers, R., Hell, T., Knighofer, R. Prez, G.A., Raskin, J.-F., Ryzhyk, L., Sankur, O., Seidl, M., Tentrup, L., Walker, A.: The first reactive synthesis competition. In: SYNTCOMP 2014 (2014). http://arxiv.org/abs/1506.08726
14. Jobstmann, B., Bloem, R.: Optimizations for LTL synthesis. In: FMCAD, pp. 117–124. IEEE (2006)
15. Jobstmann, B., Galler, S., Weiglhofer, M., Bloem, R.: Anzu: a tool for property synthesis. In: Damm, W., Hermanns, H. (eds.) CAV 2007. LNCS, vol. 4590, pp. 258–262. Springer, Heidelberg (2007)
16. Kaftan, J.: Praktische Beispiele mit AC500 von ABB: 45 Aufgaben und Lsungen mit CoDeSys (2014). http://pwww.kaftan-media.com/. ISBN 978-3-943211-05-4
17. Knighofer, R., Seidl, M.: Demiurge 1.2: A SAT-Based Synthesis Tool. Tool description for the SyntComp 2015 competition. http://www.iaik.tugraz.at/content/research/opensource/demiurge/
18. Lee, E.A., Messerschmitt, D.G.: Static scheduling of synchronous data flow programs for digital signal processing. IEEE Trans. Comput. 36(1), 24–35 (1987)
19. Lee, E.A., Messerschmitt, D.G.: Synchronous data flow. Proc. IEEE 75(9), 1235–1245 (1987)
20. Li, W.-C.: Specification mining: new formalisms, algorithms and applications. Ph.D. thesis. UC Berkeley (2015)
21. Lonsing, F., Biere, A.: DepQBF: a dependency-aware QBF solver. J. Satisfiability Boolean Model. Comput. 7, 71–76 (2010)
22. Lustig, Y., Vardi, M.Y.: Synthesis from component libraries. STTT 15(5–6), 603–618 (2013)
23. Mavin, A., Wilkinson, P., Harwood, A., Novak, M.: Easy Approach to Requirements Syntax (EARS). In: RE, pp. 317–322. IEEE (2009)
24. Petry, J.: IEC 61131–3 mit CoDeSys V3: Ein Praxisbuch fuer SPS-Programmierer. Eigenverlag 3S-Smart Software Solutions. ISBN 978-3-000465-08-6 (2011)
25. Piterman, N., Pnueli, A., Sa'ar, Y.: Synthesis of reactive(1) designs. In: Emerson, E.A., Namjoshi, K.S. (eds.) VMCAI 2006. LNCS, vol. 3855, pp. 364–380. Springer, Heidelberg (2006)
26. Pnueli, A.: The temporal logic of programs. In: FOCS, pp. 46–57. IEEE (1977)
27. Pnueli, A., Rosner, R.: On the synthesis of a reactive module. In: POPL, pp. 179–190. IEEE (1989)
28. Schewe, S., Finkbeiner, B.: Bounded synthesis. In: Namjoshi, K.S., Yoneda, T., Higashino, T., Okamura, Y. (eds.) ATVA 2007. LNCS, vol. 4762, pp. 474–488. Springer, Heidelberg (2007)
29. Tarjan, R.E.: Depth-first search and linear graph algorithms. SIAM J. Comput. 1(2), 146–160 (1972)
30. Tripakis, S., Bui, D., Geilen, M., Rodiers, B., Lee, E.A.: Compositionality in synchronous data flow: modular code generation from hierarchical SDF graphs. ACM Trans. Embed. Comput. Syst. 12(3), 83:1–83:26 (2013). http://doi.acm.org/10.1145/2442116.2442133, articleno 83, ISSN = 1539-9087
31. Wong, K.-W., Ehlers, R., Kress-Gazit, H.: Correct high-level robot behavior in environments with unexpected events. In: Robotics: Science and Systems X (RSS X) (2014)

Bounded Cycle Synthesis

Bernd Finkbeiner and Felix Klein[(✉)]

Reactive Systems Group, Saarland University, Saarbrücken, Germany
{finkbeiner,fklein}@cs.uni-saarland.de

Abstract. We introduce a new approach for the synthesis of Mealy machines from specifications in linear-time temporal logic (LTL), where the number of cycles in the state graph of the implementation is limited by a given bound. Bounding the number of cycles leads to implementations that are structurally simpler and easier to understand. We solve the synthesis problem via an extension of SAT-based bounded synthesis, where we additionally construct a witness structure that limits the number of cycles. We also establish a triple-exponential upper and lower bound for the potential blow-up between the length of the LTL formula and the number of cycles in the state graph.

1 Introduction

There has been a lot of recent progress in the automatic synthesis of reactive systems from specifications in temporal logic [4,6,7,9,12]. From a theoretical point of view, the appeal of synthesis is obvious: the synthesized implementation is guaranteed to satisfy the specification. No separate verification is needed.

From a practical point of view, the value proposition is not so clear. Instead of writing programs, the user of a synthesis procedure now writes specifications. But many people find it much easier to understand the precise meaning of a program than to understand the precise meaning of a temporal formula. Is it really justified to place higher trust into a program that was synthesized automatically, albeit from a possibly ill-understood specification, than in a manually written, but well-understood program? A straightforward solution would be for the programmer to *inspect* the synthesized program and confirm that the implementation is indeed as intended. However, current synthesis tools fail miserably at producing readable code.

Most research on the synthesis problem has focused on the problem of finding *some* implementation, not necessarily a high-quality implementation. Since specification languages like LTL restrict the behavior of a system, but not its structure, it is no surprise that the synthesized implementations are often much larger and much more complex than a manual implementation. There has been some progress on improving other quality measures, such as the runtime performance [4], but very little has been done to optimize the *structural quality* of

---

Partially supported by the DFG project "AVACS" (SFB/TR 14). The second author was supported by an IMPRS-CS PhD Scholarship.

S. Chaudhuri and A. Farzan (Eds.): CAV 2016, Part I, LNCS 9779, pp. 118–135, 2016.
DOI: 10.1007/978-3-319-41528-4_7

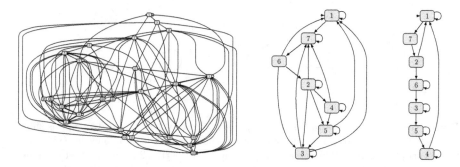

Fig. 1. Three implementations of the TBURST4 component of the AMBA bus controller. Standard synthesis with Acacia+ produces the state graph on the left with 14 states and 61 cycles. Bounded synthesis produces the graph in the middle with 7 states and 19 cycles. The graph on the right, produced by our tool, has 7 states and 7 cycles, which is the minimum.

the synthesized implementations (cf. [14]). Can we develop synthesis algorithms that produce implementations that are small, structurally simple, and therefore easy to understand?

A first step into this direction is *Bounded Synthesis* [9]. Here, we bound the number of states of the implementation and can therefore, by incrementally increasing the bound, ensure that the synthesized solution has minimal size.

In this paper, we go one step further by synthesizing implementations where, additionally, the number of *(simple) cycles* in the state graph is limited by a given bound. Reducing the number of cycles makes an implementation much easier to understand. Compare the three implementations of the TBURST4 component of the AMBA bus controller shown in Fig. 1: standard synthesis with Acacia+ produces the state graph on the left with 14 states and 61 cycles. Bounded Synthesis produces the middle one with 7 states and 19 cycles. The graph on the right, produced by our tool, has 7 states and 7 cycles, which is the minimum.

An interesting aspect of the number of cycles as a parameter of the implementations is that the number of cycles that is potentially needed to satisfy an LTL specification explodes in the size of the specification: we show that there is a triple exponential lower and upper bound on the number of cycles that can be enforced by an LTL specification. The impact of the size of the specification on the number of cycles is thus even more dramatic than on the number of states, where the blow-up is double exponential.

Our synthesis algorithm is inspired by Tiernan's cycle counting algorithm from 1970 [17]. Tiernan's algorithm is based on exhaustive search. From some arbitrary vertex v, the graph is unfolded into a tree such that no vertices repeat on any branch. The number of vertices in the tree that are connected to v then corresponds to the number of cycles through v in the graph. Subsequently, v is removed from the graph, and the algorithm continues with one of the remaining vertices until the graph becomes empty. We integrate Tiernan's algorithm into the Bounded Synthesis approach. Bounded Synthesis uses a SAT-solver to

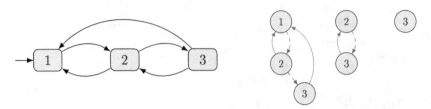

Fig. 2. Witness for an example state graph with three cycles. The state graph is shown on the left. The first graph on the right proves that vertex 1 is on two cycles (via vertex 2 and vertices 2 and 3). The second graph proves that vertex 2 is on a further cycle not, containing vertex 1, namely via vertex 3. There are no further cycles through vertex 3.

simultaneously construct an implementation and a *witness* for the correctness of the implementation [9]. For the standard synthesis from an LTL specification φ, the witness is a finite graph which describes an accepting run of the universal tree automaton corresponding to φ. To extend the idea to Bounded Cycle Synthesis, we define a second witness that proves the number of cycles, as computed by Tiernan's algorithm, to be equal to or less than the given bound. An example state graph with three cycles is shown on the left in Fig. 2. The witness consists of the three graphs shown on the right in Fig. 2. The first graph proves that vertex 1 is on two cycles (via vertex 2 and vertices 2 and 3). The second graph proves that vertex 2 is on a further cycle, not containing vertex 1, namely via vertex 3. There are no further cycles through vertex 3.

Our experiments show that Bounded Cycle Synthesis is comparable in performance to standard Bounded Synthesis. The specifications that can be handled by Bounded Cycle Synthesis are smaller than what can be handled by tools like Acacia+, but the quality of the synthesized implementations is much better. Bounded Cycle Synthesis could be used in a development process where the programmer decomposes the system into modules that are small enough so that the implementation can still be inspected comfortably by the programmer (and synthesized reasonably fast by using the Bounded Cycle Synthesis approach). Instead of manually writing the code for such a module, the programmer has the option of writing a specification, which is then automatically replaced by the best possible implementation.

2   Preliminaries

The non-negative integers are denoted by $\mathbb{N}$. An alphabet Σ is a non-empty finite set. Σ^ω denotes the set of infinite words over Σ. If $\alpha \in \Sigma^\omega$, then α_n accesses the n-th letter of α, starting at α_0. For the rest of the paper we assume $\Sigma = 2^{\mathcal{I} \cup \mathcal{O}}$ to be partitioned into sets of input signals $\mathcal{I}$ and output signals $\mathcal{O}$.

A *Mealy machine* $\mathcal{M}$ is a tuple $(\mathcal{I}, \mathcal{O}, T, t_I, \delta, \lambda)$ over input signals $\mathcal{I}$ and output signals $\mathcal{O}$, where T is a finite set of states, $t_I \in T$ is the initial state, $\delta\colon T \times 2^{\mathcal{I}} \to T$ is the transition function, and $\lambda\colon T \times 2^{\mathcal{I}} \to 2^{\mathcal{O}}$ is the output function. Thereby, the output only depends on the current state and the last input letter. The size of $\mathcal{M}$, denoted by $|\mathcal{M}|$, is defined as $|T|$. A path p of a Mealy machine M is an infinite sequence $p = (t_0, \sigma_0)(t_1, \sigma_1)(t_2, \sigma_2) \ldots \in (T \times \Sigma)^\omega$ such that $t_0 = t_I$, $\delta(t_n, \mathcal{I} \cap \sigma_n) = t_{n+1}$ and $\lambda(t_n, \mathcal{I} \cap \sigma_n) = \mathcal{O} \cap \sigma_n$ for all $n \in \mathbb{N}$. We use $\pi_1(p) = \sigma_0 \sigma_1 \sigma_2 \ldots \in \Sigma^\omega$, to denote the projection of p to its second component. $\mathcal{P}(M)$ denotes the set of all paths of a Mealy machine M.

Specifications are given in *Linear-time Temporal Logic* (LTL). The atomic propositions of the logic consist of the signals $\mathcal{I} \cup \mathcal{O}$, resulting in the alphabet $\Sigma = 2^{\mathcal{I} \cup \mathcal{O}}$. The syntax of an LTL specification φ is defined as follows:

$$\varphi := true \mid a \in \mathcal{I} \cup \mathcal{O} \mid \neg \varphi \mid \varphi \vee \varphi \mid \bigcirc \varphi \mid \varphi \mathcal{U} \varphi$$

The size of a specification φ is denoted by $|\varphi|$ and is defined to be the number of sub-formulas of φ. The semantics of LTL are defined over infinite words $\alpha \in \Sigma^\omega$. We define the satisfaction of a word α at a position $n \in \mathbb{N}$ and a specification φ, denoted by $\alpha, n \vDash \varphi$, for the different choices of φ, respectively, as follows:

- $\alpha, n \vDash true$
- $\alpha, n \vDash a$ iff $a \in \alpha_i$
- $\alpha, n \vDash \neg \varphi$ iff $\alpha, n \nvDash \varphi$
- $\alpha, n \vDash \varphi_1 \vee \varphi_2$ iff $\alpha, n \vDash \varphi_1$ or $\alpha, i \vDash \varphi_2$
- $\alpha, n \vDash \bigcirc \varphi$ iff $\alpha, n + 1 \vDash \varphi$
- $\alpha, n \vDash \varphi_1 \mathcal{U} \varphi_2$ iff $\exists m \geq n. \; \alpha, m \vDash \varphi_2$ and $\forall n \leq i < m. \; \alpha, i \vDash \varphi_1$.

An infinite word α satisfies φ, denoted by $\alpha \vDash \varphi$, iff $\alpha, 0 \vDash \varphi$. The language $\mathcal{L}(\varphi)$ is the set of all words that satisfy φ, i.e., $\mathcal{L}(\varphi) = \{\alpha \in \Sigma^\omega \mid \alpha \vDash \varphi\}$. Beside the standard operators, we have the standard derivatives of the boolean operators, as well as $\Diamond \varphi \equiv true \, \mathcal{U} \, \varphi$ and $\Box \varphi \equiv \neg \Diamond \neg \varphi$. A Mealy machine M is an implementation of φ iff $\pi_1(\mathcal{P}(M)) \subseteq \mathcal{L}(\varphi)$.

Let $G = (V, E)$ be a directed graph. A *(simple) cycle* c of G is a tuple (C, η), consisting of a non-empty set $C \subseteq V$ and a bijection $\eta \colon C \mapsto C$ such that

- $\forall v \in C. \; (v, \eta(v)) \in E$ and
- $\forall v \in C. \; n \in \mathbb{N}. \; \eta^n(v) = v \Leftrightarrow n \bmod |C| = 0$,

where η^n denotes n times the application of η. In other words, a cycle of G is a path through G that starts and ends at the same vertex and visits every vertex of V at most once. We say that a cycle $c = (C, \eta)$ has length n iff $|C| = n$.

We extend the notion of a cycle of a graph G to Mealy machines $M = (\mathcal{I}, \mathcal{O}, T, t_I, \delta, \lambda)$, such that c is a cycle of M iff c is a cycle of the graph (T, E) for $E = \{(t, t') \mid \exists \nu \in 2^{\mathcal{I}}. \; \delta(t, \nu) = t\}$. Thus, we ignore the input labels of the edges of M. The set of all cycles of a Mealy machine M is denoted by $\mathcal{C}(M)$.

A *universal co-Büchi automaton* $\mathcal{A}$ is a tuple $(\Sigma, Q, q_I, \Delta, R)$, where Σ is the alphabet, Q is a finite set of states, $q_0 \in Q$ is the initial state, $\Delta \subseteq Q \times \Sigma \times Q$ is the transition relation and $R \subseteq Q$ is the set of rejecting states. A run $r = (q_0, \sigma_0)(q_1, \sigma_1)(q_2, \sigma_2) \ldots \in (Q \times \Sigma)^\omega$ of $\mathcal{A}$ is an infinite sequence such that $q_0 = q_I$ and $(q_n, \sigma_n, q_{n+1}) \in \Delta$ for all $n \in \mathbb{N}$. A run r is accepting if it has a suffix $q_n q_{n+1} q_{n+2} \ldots \in (Q \setminus R)^\omega$ for some $n \in \mathbb{N}$. An infinite word $\alpha \in \Sigma^\omega$ is accepted by $\mathcal{A}$ if all corresponding runs, i.e., all runs $r = (q_0, \sigma_0)(q_1, \sigma_1)(q_2, \sigma_2) \ldots$ with $\alpha = \sigma_0 \sigma_1 \sigma_2 \ldots$, are accepting. The language $\mathcal{L}(\mathcal{A})$ of $\mathcal{A}$ is the set of all $\alpha \in \Sigma^\omega$, accepted by $\mathcal{A}$.

The *run graph* G of a universal co-Büchi automaton $\mathcal{A} = (2^{\mathcal{I} \cup \mathcal{O}}, Q, q_I, \Delta, R)$ and a Mealy machine $\mathcal{M} = (\mathcal{I}, \mathcal{O}, T, t_I, \delta, \lambda)$ is a directed graph $G = (T \times Q, E)$, with $E = \{((t, q), (t', q')) \mid \exists \sigma. \, \delta(t, \mathcal{I} \cap \sigma) = t', \, \lambda(t, \mathcal{I} \cap \sigma) = \mathcal{O} \cap \sigma, \, (q, \sigma, q') \in \Delta\}$. A vertex (t, q) of G is rejecting iff $q \in R$. A run graph is accepting iff there is no cycle of G, which contains a rejecting vertex. If the run graph is accepting, we say, $\mathcal{M}$ is accepted by $\mathcal{A}$.

3   Bounds on the Number of Cycles

Our goal is to synthesize systems that have a simple structure. System quality most certainly has other dimensions as well, but structural simplicity is a property of interest for most applications.

The purpose of this section is to give theoretical arguments why the number of cycles is a good measure: we show that the number of cycles may explode even in cases where the number of states is small, and even if the specification enforces a large implementation, there may be a further explosion in the number of cycles. This indicates that bounding the number of cycles is important, if one wishes to have a structurally simple implementation. On the other hand, we observe that bounding the number of states alone is not sufficient in order to obtain a simple structure.

Similar observations apply to modern programming languages, which tend to be much better readable than transition systems, because their control constructs enforce a simple cycle structure. Standard synthesis techniques construct transition systems, not programs, and therefore loose this advantage. With our approach, we get closer to the control structure of a program, without being restricted to a specific programming language.

3.1   Upper Bounds

First, we show that the number of cycles of a Mealy machine $\mathcal{M}$, implementing an LTL specification φ, is bounded triply exponential in the size of φ. To this end, we first bound the number of cycles of an arbitrary graph G with bounded outdegree.

On graphs with arbitrary outdegree, the maximal number of cycles is given by a fully connected graph, where each cycle describes a permutation of states, and vice versa. Hence, using standard math we obtain an upper bound of $2^{n \log n}$ cycles for a graph with n states. However, our proof uses a more involved argument to improve the bound even further down to $2^{n \log(m+1)}$ for graphs with bounded outdegree m. Such an improvement is desirable, as for LTL the state graph explodes in the number of states, while the outdegree is constant in the number of input and output signals.

Lemma 1. *Let $G = (V, E)$ be a directed graph with $|V| = n$ and with maximal outdegree m. Then G has at most $2^{n \log(m+1)}$ cycles.*

Proof. We show the result by induction over n. The base case is trivial, so let $n > 1$ and let $v \in V$ be some arbitrary vertex of G. By induction hypothesis, the subgraph G', obtained from G by removing v, has at most $2^{(n-1)\log(m+1)}$ cycles. Each of these cycles is also a cycle in G, thus it remains to consider the cycles of G containing v. In each of these remaining cycles, v has one of m possible successors in G' and from each such successor v' we have again $2^{(n-1)\log(m+1)}$ possible cycles in G' returning to v'. Hence, if we *redirect* these cycles to v instead of v', i.e., we insert v before v' in the cycle, then we cover all possible cycles of G containing v^1. All together, we obtain an upper bound of $2^{(n-1)\log(m+1)} + m \cdot 2^{(n-1)\log(m+1)} = 2^{n\log(m+1)}$ cycles in G. □

We obtain an upper bound on the number of cycles of a Mealy machine $\mathcal{M}$.

Lemma 2. *Let $\mathcal{M}$ be a Mealy machine. Then $|\mathcal{C}(\mathcal{M})| \in O(2^{|\mathcal{M}| \cdot |\mathcal{I}|})$.*

Proof. The Mealy machine $\mathcal{M}$ has an outdegree of $2^{|\mathcal{I}|}$ and, thus, by Lemma 1, the number of cycles is bounded by $2^{|\mathcal{M}|\log(2^{|\mathcal{I}|}+1)} \in O(2^{|\mathcal{M}| \cdot |\mathcal{I}|})$. □

Finally, we are able to derive an upper bound on the implementations realizing a LTL specification φ.

Theorem 1. *Let φ be a realizable LTL specification. Then there is a Mealy machine $\mathcal{M}$, realizing φ, with at most triply exponential many cycles in $|\varphi|$.*

Proof. From [9,15,16] we obtain a doubly exponential upper bound in $|\varphi|$ on the size of $\mathcal{M}$. With that, applying Lemma 2 yields the desired result. □

3.2 Lower Bounds

It remains to prove that the bound of Theorem 1 is tight. To this end, we show that for each $n \in \mathbb{N}$ there is a realizable LTL specification φ with $|\varphi| \in \Theta(n)$, such that every implementation of φ has at least triply exponential many cycles in n. The presented proof is inspired by [1], where a similar argument is used to prove a lower bound on the distance of the longest path through a synthesized implementation $\mathcal{M}$. We start with a gadget, which we use to increase the number of cycles exponentially in the length of the longest cycle of $\mathcal{M}$.

Lemma 3. *Let φ be a realizable LTL specification, for which every implementation $\mathcal{M}$ has a cycle of length n. Then there is a realizable specification ψ, such that every Mealy machine $\mathcal{M}'$ implementing ψ contains at least 2^n many cycles.*

Proof. Let a and b be a fresh input and output signals, respectively, which do not appear in φ, and let $\mathcal{M} = (\mathcal{I}, \mathcal{O}, T, t_I, \delta, \lambda)$ be an arbitrary implementation of φ. We define $\psi ::= \varphi \wedge \Box(a \leftrightarrow \bigcirc b)$ and construct the implementation $\mathcal{M}'$ as

$$\mathcal{M}' = (\mathcal{I} \cup \{a\}, \mathcal{O} \cup \{b\}, T \times 2^{\{b\}}, (t_I, \emptyset), \delta', \lambda'),$$

where $\lambda'((t,s),\nu) = \lambda(t, \mathcal{I} \cap \nu) \cup s$ and

$$\delta'((t,s),\nu) = \begin{cases} (\delta(t, \mathcal{I} \cap \nu), \emptyset) & \text{if } a \in \nu \\ (\delta(t, \mathcal{I} \cap \nu), \{b\}) & \text{if } a \notin \nu \end{cases}$$

---

^{1} Note that not every such edge needs to exist for a concrete given graph. However, in our worst-case analysis, every possible cycle is accounted for.

We obtain that $\mathcal{M}'$ is an implementation of ψ. The implementation remembers each input a for one time step and then outputs the stored value. Thus, it satisfies $\square(a \leftrightarrow \bigcirc b)$. Furthermore, $\mathcal{M}'$ still satisfies φ. Hence, ψ must be realizable, too.

Next, we pick an arbitrary implementation $\mathcal{M}''$ of ψ, which must exist according to our previous observations. Then, after projecting away the fresh signals a and b from $\mathcal{M}''$, we obtain again an implementation for φ, which contains a cycle (C, η) of length n, i.e., $C = \{t_1, t_2, \ldots, t_n\}$. We obtain that $\mathcal{M}''$ contains at least the cycles

$$\mathbb{C} = \{(\{(t_i, f(t_i)) \mid i \in \{1, 2, \ldots n\}\}, (t, s) \mapsto (\eta(t), f(\eta(t)))) \mid f: C \to 2^{\{b\}}\},$$

which concludes the proof, since $|\mathbb{C}| = 2^n$. □

Now, with Lemma 3 at hand, we are ready to show that the aforementioned lower bounds are tight. The final specification only needs the temporal operators $\bigcirc$, $\square$ and $\diamondsuit$, i.e., the bound already holds for a restricted fragment of LTL.

Theorem 2. *For every $n > 1$, there is a realizable specification φ_n with $|\varphi_n| \in \Theta(n)$, for which every implementation $\mathcal{M}_n$ has at least triply exponential many cycles in n.*

Proof. According to Lemma 3, it suffices to find a realizable φ_n, such that φ_n contains at least one cycle of length doubly exponential in n. We choose

$$\varphi_n \quad ::= \quad \square(\diamondsuit \underbrace{\bigwedge_{i=1}^{n} (a_i \to \diamondsuit b_i)}_{\varphi_n^{prem}} \to \diamondsuit \underbrace{\bigwedge_{i=1}^{n} (c_i \to \diamondsuit d_i)}_{\varphi_n^{con}}) \leftrightarrow \square\diamondsuit s$$

with $\mathcal{I} = \mathcal{I}_a \cup \mathcal{I}_b \cup \mathcal{I}_c \cup \mathcal{I}_d$ and $\mathcal{O} = \{s\}$, where $\mathcal{I}_x = \{x_1, x_2, \ldots, x_n\}$. The specification describes a monitor, which checks whether the invariant $\diamondsuit\varphi_n^{prem} \to \diamondsuit\varphi_n^{con}$ over the input signals $\mathcal{I}$ is satisfied or not. Thereby, satisfaction is signaled by the output s, which needs to be triggered infinitely often, as long as the invariant stays satisfied.

In the following, we denote a subset $x \subseteq \mathcal{I}_x$ by the n-ary vector $\vec{x}$ over $\{0, 1\}$, where the i-th entry of $\vec{x}$ is set to 1 if and only if $x_i \in x$.

The specification φ_n is realizable. First, consider that to check the fulfillment of φ_n^{prem} (φ_n^{con}), an implementation $\mathcal{M}$ needs to store the set of all requests $\vec{a}$ ($\vec{c}$), whose 1-positions have not yet been released by a corresponding response $\vec{b}(\vec{d})$. Furthermore, to monitor the complete invariant $\diamondsuit\varphi_n^{prem} \to \diamondsuit\varphi_n^{con}$, $\mathcal{M}$ has to guess at each point in time, whether φ_n^{prem} will be satisfied in the future (under the current request $\vec{a}$), or not. To realize this guess, $\mathcal{M}$ needs to store a mapping f, which maps each open request $\vec{a}$ to the corresponding set of requests $\vec{c}$.[2] This way, $\mathcal{M}$ can look up the set of requests $\vec{c}$, tracked since the last occurrence of $\vec{a}$, whenever $\vec{a}$ gets released by a corresponding vector $\vec{b}$. If this is the case, it continues to monitor the satisfaction of φ_n^{con} (if not already satisfied) and finally adjusts the output

---

[2] Our representation is open for many optimizations. However, they will not affect the overall complexity result. Thus, we ignore them for the sake of readability here.

signal s, correspondingly. Note that $\mathcal{M}$ still has to continuously update and store the mapping f, since the next satisfaction of φ_n^{prem} may already start while the satisfaction of current φ_n^{con} is still checked. There are double exponential many such mappings f, hence, $\mathcal{M}$ needs to be at least doubly exponential in n.

It remains to show that every such implementation $\mathcal{M}$ contains a cycle of at least doubly exponential length. By the aforementioned observations, we can assign each state of $\mathcal{M}$ a mapping f, that maps vectors $\vec{a}$ to sets of vectors $\vec{c}$. By interpreting the vectors as numbers, encoded in binary, we obtain that $f\colon \{1, 2, \ldots, 2^n\} \mapsto 2^{\{1,2,\ldots,2^n\}}$. Next, we again map each such mapping f to a binary sequence $b_f = b_0 b_1 \ldots b_m \in \{0,1\}^m$ with $m = 2^n$. Thereby, a bit b_i of b_f is set to 1 if and only if $i \in f(i)$. It is easy to observe, that if two binary sequences are different, then their related states have to be different as well.

To conclude the proof, we show that the environment has a strategy to manipulate the bits of associated sequences b_f via the inputs $\mathcal{I}$.

To set bit b_i, the environment chooses the requests $\vec{a}$ and $\vec{c}$ such that they represent i in binary. The remaining inputs are fixed to $\vec{b} = \vec{d} = \vec{0}$. Hence, all other bits are not affected, as possible requests of previous $\vec{a}$ and $\vec{c}$ remain open.

To reset bit b_i, the environment needs multiple steps. First, it picks $\vec{a} = \vec{c} = \vec{d} = \vec{0}$ and $\vec{b} = \vec{1}$. This does not affect any bit of the sequence b_f, since all requests introduced through vectors $\vec{c}$ are still open. Next, the environment executes the aforementioned procedure to set bit b_j for every bit currently set to 1, except for the bit b_i, it wants to reset. This refreshes the requests introduced by previous vectors $\vec{a}$ for every bit, except for b_i. Furthermore, it does not affect the sequence b_f. Finally, the environment picks $\vec{a} = \vec{b} = \vec{c} = \vec{0}$ and picks $\vec{d}$ such that it represents i in binary. This removes i from every entry in f, but only resets b_i, since all other bits are still open due to the previous updates.

With these two operations, the environment can enforce any sequences of sequences b_f, including a binary counter counting up to 2^{2^n}. As different states are induced by the different sequences, we obtain a cycle of doubly exponential length in n by resetting the counter at every overflow. □

3.3   The Trade-Off Between States and Cycles

We conclude this section with some observations regarding tradeoffs between the problem of synthesizing implementations, which are minimal in the number of states, versus the problem of synthesizing implementations, which are minimal in the number of cycles. The main question we answer, is whether we can achieve both: minimality in the number of states and minimality in the number of cycles. Unfortunately, this is not possible, as shown by Theorem 3.

Theorem 3. *For every $n > 1$, there is a realizable LTL specification φ_n with $|\varphi| \in \Theta(n)$, such that*

- *there is an implementation of φ consisting of n states and*
- *there is an implementation of φ containing m cycles,*
- *but there is no implementation of φ with n states and m cycles.*

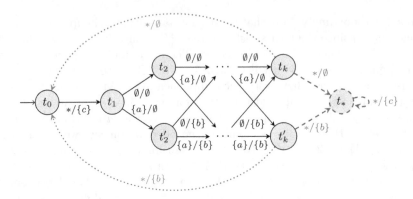

Fig. 3. The Mealy automata $\mathcal{M}_n$ (red/dotted) and $\mathcal{M}'_n$ (blue/dashed). Solid edges are shared between both automata.

Consider the specification

$$\varphi_n = (\neg b \wedge c) \wedge \bigcirc^{k+2}(\neg b \wedge c) \wedge \bigwedge_{i=1}^{k} \bigcirc^i(\neg c \wedge \bigcirc \neg c \wedge (a \leftrightarrow \bigcirc b))$$

over $\mathcal{I} = \{a\}$ and $\mathcal{O} = \{b, c\}$, where $\bigcirc^i$ denotes i times the application of $\bigcirc$. The specification φ_n is realizable with at least $n = 2k + 1$ states. The corresponding Mealy machine $\mathcal{M}_n$ is depicted in Fig. 3. However, $\mathcal{M}_n$ has $m = 2^k$ many cycles. This blowup can be avoided by spending the implementation at least one more state, which reduces the number of cycles to $m = 1$. The result $\mathcal{M}'_n$ is also depicted in Fig. 3.   □

Our results show that the number of cycles can explode (even more so than the number of states), and that sometimes this explosion is unavoidable. However, the results also show that there are cases, where the cycle count can be improved by choosing a better structured solution. Hence, it is desirable to have better control over the number of cycles that appear in an implementation. In the remainder of the paper, we show how to achieve this control.

4 Bounding the Cycles

In this section, we show how to synthesize an implementation $\mathcal{M}$ from a given LTL specification φ, while giving a guarantee on the size and the number of cycles of $\mathcal{M}$. We first show how to guarantee a bound on the number of states of $\mathcal{M}$, by reviewing the classical Bounded Synthesis approach. Our encoding uses Mealy machines as implementations, and Boolean Satisfiability (SAT) as the underlying constraint system.

We then review the classical algorithm to count the cycles of $\mathcal{M}$ and show how this algorithm gets embedded into a constraint system, such that we obtain a guarantee on the number of cycles of $\mathcal{M}$.

4.1   Bounded Synthesis

In the bounded synthesis approach [9], we first translate a given LTL specification φ into an equivalent universal co-Büchi automaton $\mathcal{A}$, such that $\mathcal{L}(\mathcal{A}) = \mathcal{L}(\varphi)$. Thus, we reduce the problem to finding an implementation $\mathcal{M}$ that is accepted by $\mathcal{A}$, i.e., we look for an implementation $\mathcal{M}$ such that the run graph of $\mathcal{M}$ and $\mathcal{A}$ contains no cycle with a rejecting vertex. This property is witnessed by a ranking function, which annotates each vertex of G by a natural number that bounds the number of possible visits to rejecting states. The annotation itself is bounded by $n \cdot k$, where n is the size bound on $\mathcal{M}$ and k denotes the number or rejecting states of $\mathcal{A}$.

Fix some set of states T with $|T| = n$ and let $\mathcal{A} = (2^{\mathcal{I} \cup \mathcal{O}}, Q, q_I, \Delta, R)$. Then, to guess a solution within SAT, we introduce the following variables:

- TRANS(t, ν, t') for all $t, t' \in T$ and $\nu \in 2^{\mathcal{I}}$, for the transition relation of $\mathcal{M}$.
- LABEL(t, ν, x) for all $t \in T$, $\nu \in 2^{\mathcal{I}}$ and $x \in \mathcal{O}$, for the labels of each transition.
- RGSTATE(t, q) for all $t \in T$ and $q \in Q$, to denote the reachable states of the run graph G of $\mathcal{M}$ and $\mathcal{A}$. Only reachable states have to be annotated.
- ANNOTATION(t, q, i) for all $t \in T$, $q \in Q$ and $0 < i \leq \log(n \cdot k)$, denoting the annotation of a state (t, q) of G. Thereby, we use a logarithmic number of bits to encode the annotated value in binary. We use ANNOTATION$(t, q) \circ m$ for $\circ \in \{<, \leq, =, \geq, >\}$, to denote an appropriate encoding of the relation of the annotation to some value m or other annotations ANNOTATION(t', q').

Given a universal co-Büchi automaton $\mathcal{A}$ and a bound n on the states of the resulting implementation, we encode the Bounded Synthesis problem via the SAT formula $\mathcal{F}_{BS}(\mathcal{A}, n)$, consisting of the following constraints:

- The target of every transition is unambiguous:

$$\bigwedge_{t \in T, \nu \in 2^{\mathcal{I}}} exactlyOne(\{\text{TRANS}(t, v, t') \mid t' \in T\})$$

where $exactelyOne : X \mapsto \mathbb{B}(X)$ returns a SAT query, which ensures that among all variables of the set X exactly one is *true* and all others are *false*.
- The initial state (t_I, q_I) of the run graph for some arbitrary, but fix, $t_I \in T$ is reachable and annotated by one. Furthermore, all annotations are bounded by $n \cdot k$:

$$\text{RGSTATE}(1, 1) \wedge \text{ANNOTATION}(1, 1) = 1 \wedge \bigwedge_{t \in T, q \in Q} \text{ANNOTATION}(t, q) \leq n \cdot k$$

- Each annotation of a vertex of the run graph bounds the number of visited accepting states, not counting the current vertex itself:

$$\bigwedge_{t \in T, q \in Q} \text{RGSTATE}(t, q) \rightarrow \bigwedge_{\sigma \in 2^{\Sigma}} label(t, \sigma) \rightarrow \bigwedge_{t' \in T} \text{TRANS}(t, \mathcal{I} \cap \sigma, t') \rightarrow$$

$$\bigwedge_{q' \in \Delta(q,\sigma)} \text{RGSTATE}(t',q') \wedge \text{ANNOTATION}(t,q) \prec_q \text{ANNOTATION}(t',q')$$

where $\prec_q$ equals $<$ if $q \in R$ and equals $\leq$ otherwise. Furthermore, we use the function $label(t,\sigma)$ to fix the labeling of each transition, i.e., $label(t,\sigma) = \bigwedge_{x \in \mathcal{O} \cap \sigma} \text{LABEL}(t, \mathcal{I} \cap \sigma, x) \wedge \bigwedge_{x \in \mathcal{O} \smallsetminus \sigma} \neg \text{LABEL}(t, \mathcal{I} \cap \sigma, x)$.

Theorem 4 (Bounded Synthesis [9]). *For each bound $n \in \mathbb{N}$ and each universal co-Büchi automaton $\mathcal{A}$, the SAT formula $\mathcal{F}_{BS}(\mathcal{A}, n)$ is satisfiable if and only if there is a Mealy machine $\mathcal{M}$ with $|\mathcal{M}| = n$, which is accepted by $\mathcal{A}$.*

4.2 Counting Cycles

Before we bound the number of cycles of a Mealy machine $\mathcal{M}$, we review Tiernan's classical algorithm [17] to count the number of cycles of a directed graph G. The algorithm not only gives insights into the complexity of the problem, but also contains many inspirations for our latter approach.

Algorithm 1. Given a directed graph $G = (V, E)$, we count the cycles of G using the following algorithm:

(1) Initialize the cycle counter c to $c := 0$ and some set P to $P := \emptyset$.
(2) Pick some arbitrary vertex v_r of G, set $v := v_r$ and $P := \{v_r\}$.
(3) For all edges $(v, v') \in E$, with $v' \notin P \setminus \{v_r\}$:
   (3a) If $v' = v_r$, increase c by one.
   (3b) Otherwise, add v' to P and recursively execute (3). Afterwards, reset P to its value before the recursive call.
(4) Obtain the sub-graph G', by removing v_r from G:
   (4a) If G' is empty, return c.
   (4b) Otherwise, continue from (2) with G'.

The algorithm starts by counting all cycles that contain the first picked vertex v_r. This is done by an unfolding of the graph into a tree, rooted in v_r, such that there is no repetition of a vertex on any path from the root to a leaf. The number of vertices that are connected to the root by an edge of E then represents the corresponding number of cycles through v_r. The remaining cycles of G do not contain v_r and, thus, are cycles of the sub-graph G' without v_r, as well. Hence, we count the remaining cycles by recursively counting the cycles of G'. The algorithm terminates as soon as G' gets empty.

The algorithm is correct [17], but has the drawback, that the unfolded trees, may become exponential in the size of the graph, even if none of their vertices is connected to the root, i.e., even if there is no cycle to be counted. For an example consider the induced graph of $\mathcal{M}'_n$, as depicted in Fig. 3. However, this drawback can be avoided by first reducing the graph to all its strongly connected components (SCCs) and then by counting the cycles of each SCC separately [13,18]. A cycle never leaves an SCC of the graph.

As a result, we obtain an improved algorithm, which is exponential in the size of G, but linear in the number of cycles m. Furthermore, the time between two detections of a cycle, during the execution, is bounded linear in the size of the graph G.

4.3   Bounded Cycle Synthesis

We combine the insights of the previous sections to obtain a synthesis algorithm, which not only bounds the number of states of the resulting implementation $\mathcal{M}$ but also bounds the number of cycles of $\mathcal{M}$. We use the unfolded trees from the previous section as our witnesses.

We call a tree that witnesses m cycles in G, all containing the root r of the tree, a witness-tree $\mathcal{T}_{r,m}$ of G. Formally, a *witness-tree* $\mathcal{T}_{r,m}$ of $G = (V, E)$ is a labeled graph $\mathcal{T}_{r,m} = ((W, B \cup R), \tau)$, consisting of a graph $(W, B \cup R)$ with $m = |R|$ and a labeling function $\tau : W \to V$, such that:

1. The edges are partitioned into blue edges B and red edges R.
2. All red edges lead back to the root:
   $$R \subseteq W \times \{r\}$$
3. No blue edges lead back to the root:
   $$B \cap W \times \{r\} = \emptyset$$
4. Each non-root has at least one blue incoming edge:
   $$\forall w' \in W \setminus \{r\}. \ \exists w \in W. \ (w, w') \in B$$
5. Each vertex has at most one blue incoming edge:
   $$\forall w_1, w_2, w \in W. \ (w_1, w) \in B \wedge (w_2, w) \in B \Rightarrow w_1 = w_2$$
6. The graph is labeled by an unfolding of G:
   $$\forall w, w' \in B \cup R. \ (\tau(w), \tau(w')) \in E,$$
7. The unfolding is complete:
   $$\forall w \in W. \ \forall v' \in V. \ (\tau(w), v') \in E \Rightarrow \exists w' \in W. \ (w, w') \in B \cup R \wedge \tau(w') = v'$$
8. Let $w_i, w_j \in W$ be two different vertices that appear on a path from the root to a leaf in the r-rooted tree $(W, B)^3$. Then the labeling of w_i and w_j differs, i.e., $\tau(v_i) \neq \tau(v_j)$.
9. The root of the tree is the same as the corresponding vertex of G, i.e., $\tau(r) = r$.

Lemma 4. *Let $G = (V, E)$ be a graph consisting of a single SCC, $r \in V$ be some vertex of G and m be the number of cycles of G containing r. Then there is a witness-tree $\mathcal{T}_{r,m} = ((W, B \cup R), \tau)$ of G with $|W| \leq m \cdot |V|$.*

Proof. We construct $\mathcal{T}_{r,m}$ according to the strategy induced by *Algorithm 1*, where an edge is colored red if and only if it leads back to the root. The constructed tree satisfies all conditions 1–9. By correctness of *Algorithm 1*, we have that $|R| = m$.

Now, for the sake of contradiciton, assume $|W| > m \cdot |V|$. First we observe, that the depth of the tree (W, B) must be bounded by $|V|$ to satisfy Condition 8. Hence, as there are at most m red edges in $\mathcal{T}_{r,m}$, there must be a vertex $w \in W$ without any outgoing edges. However, since G is a single SCC, this contradicts the completeness of $\mathcal{T}_{r,m}$ (Condition 7). ☐

Lemma 5. *Let $G = (V, E)$ be a graph consisting of a single SCC and let $\mathcal{T}_{r,m}$ be a witness-tree of G. Then there are at most m cycles in G that contain r.*

---

^{3} Note that the tree property is enforced by Conditions 3–5.

Proof. Let $\mathcal{T}_{r,m} = ((W, R \cup B), \tau)$. Assume for the sake of contradiction that G has more than m cycles and let $c = (C, \eta)$ be an arbitrary such cycle. By the completeness of $\mathcal{T}_{r,m}$, there is path $w_0 w_1 \ldots w_{|C|-1}$ with $w_0 = r$ and $\tau(w_i) = \eta^i(r)$ for all $0 \leq i < |C|$. From $w_i \neq r$ and Condition 2, it follows $(w_{i-1}, w_i) \in B$ for all $0 < i < |C|$. Further, $\eta^{|C|}(r) = r$ and thus $(w_{|C|-1}, w_0) \in R$. Hence, by the tree shape of (W, B), we get $|R| > m$, yielding the desired contradiction. $\square$

From Lemmas 4 and 5 we derive that $\mathcal{T}_{r,m}$ is a suitable witness to bound the number of cycles of an implementation $\mathcal{M}$. Furthermore, from Lemma 4 we also obtain an upper bound on the size of $\mathcal{T}_{r,m}$.

We proceed with our final encoding. Therefore, we first construct a simple directed graph G out of the implementation $\mathcal{M}$. Then, we guess all the subgraphs, obtained from G via iteratively removing vertices, and split them into their corresponding SCCs. Finally, we guess the witness-tree for each such SCC.

To keep the final SAT encoding compact, we even introduce some further optimizations. First, we do not need to introduce a fresh copy for each SCC, since the SCC of a vertex is always unique. Thus, it suffices to guess an annotation for each vertex, being unique for each SCC. Second, we have to guess n trees $\mathcal{T}_{i,r_i}$, each one consisting of at most $i \cdot n$ vertices, such that the sum of all i is equal to the overall number of cycles m. One possible solution would be to overestimate each i by m. Another possibility would be to guess the exact distribution of the cycles over the different witness-trees $\mathcal{T}_{i,r_i}$. However, there is a smarter solution: we guess all trees together in a single graph bounded by $m \cdot n$. Additionally, to avoid possible interleavings, we add an annotation of each vertex by its corresponding witness-tree $\mathcal{T}_{i,r_i}$. Hence, instead of bounding the number of each $\mathcal{T}_{i,r_i}$ separately by i, we just bound the number of all red edges in the whole forest by m. This way, we not only reduce the size of the encoding, but also skip the additional constrains, which would be necessary to sum the different witness-tree bounds i to m, otherwise.

Let T be some ordered set with $|T| = n$ and $S = T \times \{1, 2, \ldots, m\}$. We use T to denote the vertices of G and S to denote the vertices of the forest of $\mathcal{T}_{i,r_i}$ s. Further, we use $M = T \times \{1\}$ to denote the roots and $N = S \setminus M$ to denote the non-roots of the corresponding trees. We introduce the following variables:

- EDGE(t, t') for all $t, t' \in T$, denoting the edges of the abstraction of $\mathcal{M}$ to G.
- BEDGE(s, s') for all $s \in S$ and $s' \in N$, denoting a blue edge.
- REDGE(s, s') for all $s \in S$ and $s' \in M$, denoting a red edge.
- WTREE(s, i) for all $s \in S$, $0 < i \leq \log n$, denoting the witness-tree of each s. As before, we use WTREE$(s) \circ x$ to relate values with the underlying encoding.
- VISITED(s, t) for all $s \in S$ and $t \in T$, denoting the set of all vertices t, already visited at s, since leaving the root of the corresponding witness-tree.
- RBOUND(c, i) for all $0 < c \leq m$, $0 < i \leq \log(n \cdot m)$, denoting an ordered list of all red edges, bounding the red edges of the forest.
- SCC(k, t, i) for all $0 < k \leq n$, $t \in T$, and $0 \leq i < \log n$, denoting the SCC of t in the k-th sub-graph of G. The sub-graphs are obtained by iteratively removing vertices of T, according to the pre-defined order. This way, each sub-graph contains exactly all vertices that are larger than the root.

Note that by the definition of S we introduce m explicit copies for each vertex of G. This is sufficient, since each cycle contains each vertex at most once. Thus, the labeling τ of a vertex s can be directly derived from the first component of s.

Given a universal co-Büchi automaton $\mathcal{A}$, a bound n on the states of the resulting implementation $\mathcal{M}$, and a bound m on the number of cycles of $\mathcal{M}$, we encode the Bounded Cycle Synthesis problem via the SAT formula $\mathcal{F}_{BS}(\mathcal{A}, n) \wedge \mathcal{F}_{CS}(\mathcal{A}, n, m) \wedge \mathcal{F}_{SCC}(n)$. The constraints of $\mathcal{F}_{CS}(\mathcal{A}, n, m)$, bounding the cycles of the system, are given by Table 1. The constraints of $\mathcal{F}_{SCC}(n)$, enforcing that each vertex is labeled by a unique SCC, can be found in the technical report [8].

Theorem 5. *For each pair of bounds $n, m \in \mathbb{N}$ and each universal co-Büchi automaton $\mathcal{A}$ with $|\mathcal{A}| = k$, the formula $\mathcal{F} = \mathcal{F}_{BS}(\mathcal{A}, n) \wedge \mathcal{F}_{CS}(\mathcal{A}, n, m) \wedge \mathcal{F}_{SCC}$ is satisfiable if and only if there is a Mealy machine $\mathcal{M}$ with $|\mathcal{M}| = n$ and $|\mathcal{C}(\mathcal{M})| = m$, accepted by $\mathcal{A}$. Furthermore, $\mathcal{F}$ consists of x variables with $x \in O(n^3 + n^2(m^2 + 2^{|\mathcal{I}|}) + n|\mathcal{O}| + nk \log(nk))$ and $|\mathcal{F}| \in O(n^3 + n^2(m^2 + k|\Sigma|))$.*

5   Experimental Results

We have implemented the Bounded Cycle Synthesis approach in our tool *BoWSer*, the Bounded Witness Synthesizer, and compared it against standard Bounded Synthesis and *Acacia+* (v2.3) [6,7]. To ensure a common encoding, we used *BoWSer* for both, the Bounded Synthesis and the Bounded Cycle Synthesis approach. Our tool uses *LTL3BA* (v1.0.2) [3] to convert specifications to universal co-Büchi automata. The created SAT queries are solved by *MiniSat* (v.2.2.0) [5] and *clasp* (v.3.1.4) [10], where the result of the faster solver is taken.

The benchmarks are given in TLSF [11] and represent a decomposition of ARM's *Advanced Microcontroller Bus Architecture* (AMBA) [2]. They are created from the assumptions and guarantees presented in [12], which were split into modules, connected by new signals. A detailed description of the benchmarks is given in [11].

All experiments were executed on a Unix machine, operated by a 64-bit kernel (v4.1.12) running on an Intel Core i7 with 2.8 GHz and 8 GB RAM. Each experiment had a time limit of 1000 s and a memory limit of 8 GB. When counting cycles of a solution, the limit was set to 10000000 cycles.

The results of the evaluation are shown in Table 2, which displays the sizes of the intermediate universal co-Büchi tree automata $\mathcal{A}_{UCT}$, the sizes of the synthesized implementations $\mathcal{M}$, the number of cycles of each implementation $\mathcal{M}$, and the overall synthesis time. Thereby, for each instance, we guessed the minimal number of states for the Bounded Synthesis approach and, additionally, the minimal number of cycles for the Bounded Cycle Synthesis approach, to obtain a single satisfiable instance. Further, to verify the result, we also created the unsatisfiable instance, where the state bound was decreased by one in the case of Bounded Synthesis and the cycle bound was decreased by one in the case of Bounded Cycle Synthesis. Note that these two instances already give an almost complete picture, since for increased and decreased bounds the synthesis times

Table 1. Constraints of the SAT formula $\mathcal{F}_{CS}(\mathcal{A}, n, m)$.

$\bigwedge\limits_{t,t'\in T,\nu\in 2^I}$ $\text{TRANS}(t,\nu,t') \to \text{EDGE}(t,t')$	Construction of G from $\mathcal{M}$.
$\bigwedge\limits_{t,t'\in T}$ $\text{EDGE}(t,t') \to \bigvee\limits_{\nu\in 2^I} \text{TRANS}(t,\nu,t')$	
$\bigwedge\limits_{r\in T}$ $\text{WTREE}((r,1)) = r$	Roots indicate the witness-tree.
$\bigwedge\limits_{s\in S,\,(r,1)\in M}$ $\text{REDGE}(s,(r,1)) \to \text{WTREE}(s) = r$	Red edges only connect vertices of the current T_{i,r_i}.
$\bigwedge\limits_{s\in S,\,s'\in N}$ $\text{BEDGE}(s,s')$ $\to \text{WTREE}(s) = \text{WTREE}(s')$	Blue edges only connect vertices of the current T_{i,r_i}.
$\bigwedge\limits_{s'\in N}$ $exactlyOne($ $\{\text{BEDGE}(s,s') \mid s \in S\}$ $)$	Every non-root has exactly one blue incoming edge.
$\bigwedge\limits_{(t,c)\in S,\,r\in T,}$ $\text{REDGE}((t,c),(r,1)) \to \text{EDGE}(t,r)$	Red edges are related to the edges of the graph G.
$\bigwedge\limits_{(t,c)\in S,\,(t',c')\in N}$ $\text{BEDGE}((t,c),(t',c')) \to \text{EDGE}(t,t')$	Blue edges are related to the edges of the graph G.
$\bigwedge\limits_{\substack{(t,c)\in S,\,r\in T,\\ t\geq r}}$ $\text{EDGE}(t,r) \wedge \text{SCC}(r,t) = \text{SCC}(r,r) \wedge$ $\text{WTREE}((t,c)) = r$ $\to \text{REDGE}((t,c),(r,1))$	Every possible red edge must be taken.
$\bigwedge\limits_{\substack{(t,c)\in S,\,r,t'\in T,\\ t\geq t'}}$ $\text{EDGE}(t,t') \wedge \text{SCC}(r,t) = \text{SCC}(r,t') \wedge$ $\text{WTREE}((t,c)) = r \wedge \text{VISITED}((t,c),t')$ $\to \bigvee\limits_{0<c'\leq m} \text{BEDGE}((t,c),(t',c'))$	Every possible blue edge must be taken.
$\bigwedge\limits_{r\in T}$ $\bigwedge\limits_{t\leq r} \neg\text{VISITED}((r,1),t) \wedge$ $\bigwedge\limits_{t>r} \text{VISITED}((r,1),t)$	Only non-roots of the corresponding sub-graph can be successors of a root.
$\bigwedge\limits_{(t,c)\in S,\,s\in N}$ $\text{BEDGE}((t,c),s)$ $\to \neg\text{VISITED}(s,t) \wedge$ $(\text{VISITED}(s,t')$ $\leftrightarrow \text{VISITED}((t,c),t'))$	Every vertex appears at most once on a path from the root to a leaf.
$\bigwedge\limits_{s\in S,\,s'\in M}$ $\text{REDGE}(s,s')$ $\to \bigvee\limits_{0<c\leq m} \text{RBOUND}(c) = f(s)$	The list of red edges is complete. ($f(s)$ maps each state of S to a unique number in $\{1,\dots,n\cdot m\}$)
$\bigwedge\limits_{0<c\leq m}$ $\text{RBOUND}(c) < \text{RBOUND}(c+1)$	Red edges are strictly ordered.

behave monotonically. Hence, increasing the bound beyond the first realizable instance increases the synthesis time. Decreasing it below the last unsatisfiable instance decreases the synthesis time. The results for the TBURST4 component are additionally depicted in Fig. 1.

On most benchmarks, Acacia+ solves the synthesis problem the fastest, followed by Bounded Synthesis and our approach. (On some benchmarks, Bounded

Table 2. Results of the tools *LTL3BA*, *Aca(cia)+* and *BoWSer*. The *LTL3BA* tool was used to generate the universal co-Büchi tree automata $\mathcal{A}_{UCT}$. The Bo(unded) Sy(nthesis) and Bo(unded) Cy(cle Synthesis) encodings were generated by BoWSer.

Benchmark	Size			Cycles			Time (s)				
	$\mathcal{A}_{UCT}$	Aca+	BoSy/ BoCy	Aca+	BoSy	BoCy	Aca+	SAT		UNSAT	
								BoSy	BoCy	BoSy	BoCy
ARBITER[2]	6	26	2	5439901	3	3	0.261	0.847	0.868	0.300	0.836
ARBITER[3]	20	111	3	> 9999999	8	4	0.511	9.170	9.601	3.916	9.481
ARBITER[4]	64	470	4	> 9999999	8	5	12.981	105.527	109.180	56.853	106.803
LOCK[2]	12	4	3	12	6	5	0.459	0.395	0.522	0.165	0.487
LOCK[3]	20	4	3	12	5	5	55.917	1.037	1.245	0.433	1.107
LOCK[4]	36	–	3	–	6	5	> 999	4.419	4.761	1.407	3.726
ENCODE[2]	3	6	2	41	3	3	0.473	0.071	0.089	0.048	0.084
ENCODE[3]	5	16	3	90428	8	8	1.871	0.292	0.561	0.200	0.503
ENCODE[4]	5	20	4	> 9999999	24	24	4.780	1.007	16.166	0.579	> 999
DECODE	1	4	1	8	1	1	0.328	0.055	0.051	–	–
SHIFT	3	6	2	31	3	3	0.387	0.060	0.072	0.041	0.071
TBURST4	103	14	7	61	19	7	0.634	8.294	206.604	6.261	> 999
TINCR	43	5	3	7	5	2	0.396	2.262	2.279	0.845	2.221
TSINGLE	22	8	4	12	5	4	0.372	1.863	2.143	1.165	2.067

Synthesis outperforms Acacia+.) Comparing the running times of Bounded Synthesis and Bounded Cycle Synthesis, the overhead for bounding the number of cycles is insignificant on most benchmarks. The two exceptions are ENCODE, which requires a fully connected implementation, and TBURST4, where the reduction in the number of cycles is substantial. In terms of states and cycles, our tool outperforms Bounded Synthesis on half of the benchmarks and it outperforms Acacia+ on all benchmarks.

The results of Acacia+ show that the number of cycles is indeed an explosive factor. However, they also show that this explosion can be avoided effectively.

6   Conclusions

We have introduced the Bounded Cycle Synthesis problem, where we limit the number of cycles in an implementation synthesized from an LTL specification. Our solution is based on the construction of a witness structure that limits the number of cycles. The existence of such a witness can be encoded as a SAT problem. Our experience in applying Bounded Cycle Synthesis to the synthesis of the AMBA bus arbiter shows that the approach leads to significantly better implementations. Furthermore, the performance of our prototype implementation is sufficient to synthesize the components (in a natural decomposition of the specification) in reasonable time.

Both Bounded Synthesis and Bounded Cycle Synthesis can be seen as the introduction of structure into the space of implementations. Bounded Synthesis structures the implementations according to the number of states, Bounded Cycle Synthesis additionally according to the number of cycles. The double exponential blow-up between the size of the specification and the number of states, and the triple exponential blow-up between the size and the number of cycles indicate that, while both parameters provide a fine-grained structure, the number of cycles may even be the superior parameter. Formalizing this intuition and finding other useful parameters is a challenge for future work.

Our method does not lead to a synthesis algorithm in the classical sense, where just a specification is given and an implementation or an unsatisfiability result is returned. In our setting, the bounds are part of the input, and have to be determined beforehand. In Bounded Synthesis, the bound is usually eliminated by increasing the bound incrementally. With multiple bounds, the choice which parameter to increase becomes non-obvious. Finding a good strategy for this problem is a challenge on its own and beyond the scope of this paper. We leave it open for future research.

References

1. Alur, R., La Torre, S.: Deterministic generators and games for LTL fragments. ACM Trans. Comput. Log. **5**(1), 1–25 (2004). http://doi.acm.org/10.1145/963927.963928
2. ARM Ltd.: AMBA Specification (rev. 2) (1999). www.arm.com
3. Babiak, T., Křetínský, M., Řehák, V., Strejček, J.: LTL to Büchi automata translation: fast and more deterministic. In: Flanagan, C., König, B. (eds.) TACAS 2012. LNCS, vol. 7214, pp. 95–109. Springer, Heidelberg (2012). http://dx.doi.org/10.1007/978-3-642-28756-5_8
4. Bloem, R., Chatterjee, K., Henzinger, T.A., Jobstmann, B.: Better quality in synthesis through quantitative objectives. In: Bouajjani, A., Maler, O. (eds.) CAV 2009. LNCS, vol. 5643, pp. 140–156. Springer, Heidelberg (2009). http://dx.doi.org/10.1007/978-3-642-02658-4_14
5. Eén, N., Sörensson, N.: An extensible SAT-solver. In: Giunchiglia, E., Tacchella, A. (eds.) SAT 2003. LNCS, vol. 2919, pp. 502–518. Springer, Heidelberg (2004). http://dx.doi.org/10.1007/978-3-540-24605-3_37
6. Filiot, E., Jin, N., Raskin, J.: Antichains and compositional algorithms for LTL synthesis. Form. Methods Syst. Des. **39**(3), 261–296 (2011). http://dx.doi.org/10.1007/s10703-011-0115-3
7. Filiot, E., Jin, N., Raskin, J.: Exploiting structure in LTL synthesis. STTT **15**(5–6), 541–561 (2013). http://dx.doi.org/10.1007/s10009-012-0222-5
8. Finkbeiner, B., Klein, F.: Bounded cycle synthesis. CoRR abs/1605.01511 (2016). http://arxiv.org/abs/1605.01511
9. Finkbeiner, B., Schewe, S.: Bounded synthesis. STTT **15**(5–6), 519–539 (2013). http://dx.doi.org/10.1007/s10009-012-0228-z
10. Gebser, M., Kaufmann, B., Neumann, A., Schaub, T.: *clasp*: a conflict-driven answer set solver. In: Baral, C., Brewka, G., Schlipf, J. (eds.) LPNMR 2007. LNCS (LNAI), vol. 4483, pp. 260–265. Springer, Heidelberg (2007). http://dx.doi.org/10.1007/978-3-540-72200-7_23

11. Jacobs, S., Klein, F.: A high-level LTL synthesis format: TLSF v1.1 (Extended Version). CoRR abs/1604.02284 (2016). http://arxiv.org/abs/1604.02284
12. Jobstmann, B.: Applications and optimizations for LTL synthesis. Ph.D. thesis, Graz University of Technology, March 2007
13. Johnson, D.B.: Finding all the elementary circuits of a directed graph. SIAM J. Comput. 4(1), 77–84 (1975). http://dx.doi.org/10.1137/0204007
14. Kupferman, O.: Recent challenges and ideas in temporal synthesis. In: Bieliková, M., Friedrich, G., Gottlob, G., Katzenbeisser, S., Turán, G. (eds.) SOFSEM 2012. LNCS, vol. 7147, pp. 88–98. Springer, Heidelberg (2012). doi:10.1007/978-3-642-27660-6_8
15. Kupferman, O., Vardi, M.Y.: Safraless decision procedures. In: 46th Annual IEEE Symposium on Foundations of Computer Science (FOCS 2005), 23–25 October 2005, Pittsburgh, PA, USA, Proceedings, pp. 531–542. IEEE Computer Society (2005). http://dx.doi.org/10.1109/SFCS.2005.66
16. Piterman, N.: From nondeterministic Büchi and Streett automata to deterministic parity automata. Log. Methods Comput. Sci. 3(3) (2007). http://dx.doi.org/10.2168/LMCS-3(3:5)2007
17. Tiernan, J.C.: An efficient search algorithm to find the elementary circuits of a graph. Commun. ACM 13(12), 722–726 (1970). http://doi.acm.org/10.1145/362814.362819
18. Weinblatt, H.: A new search algorithm for finding the simple cycles of a finite directed graph. J. ACM 19(1), 43–56 (1972). http://doi.acm.org/10.1145/321679.321684

Fast, Flexible, and Minimal CTL Synthesis via SMT

Tobias Klenze[1,2(✉)], Sam Bayless[1], and Alan J. Hu[1]

[1] University of British Columbia, Vancouver, Canada
{sbayless,ajh}@cs.ubc.ca
[2] Technische Universität München, Munich, Germany
tobias.klenze@mytum.de

Abstract. CTL synthesis [8] is a long-standing problem with applications to synthesising synchronization protocols and concurrent programs. We show how to formulate CTL model checking in terms of "monotonic theories", enabling us to use the *SAT Modulo Monotonic Theories* (SMMT) [5] framework to build an efficient SAT-modulo-CTL solver. This yields a powerful procedure for CTL synthesis, which is not only faster than previous techniques from the literature, but also scales to larger and more difficult formulas. Additionally, because it is a constraint-based approach, it can be easily extended with further constraints to guide the synthesis. Moreover, our approach is efficient at producing *minimal* Kripke structures on common CTL synthesis benchmarks.

1 Introduction

Computation Tree Logic (CTL) is widely used in the context of model checking, where a CTL formula specifying a temporal property, such as safety or liveness, is checked for validity in a program or algorithm (represented by a Kripke structure). Both the branching time logic CTL and its application to model checking were first proposed by Clarke and Emerson [8]. In that work, they also introduced a decision procedure for CTL satisfiability, which they applied to the synthesis of *synchronization skeletons*, abstractions of concurrent programs which are notoriously difficult to construct manually. Though CTL model checking has been a phenomenal success, there have been fewer advances in the field of CTL synthesis, due to its high complexity.

In CTL synthesis, a system is specified by a CTL formula, and the goal is to find a model of the formula — a Kripke structure in the form of a transition system in which states are annotated with sets of atomic propositions (so called *state properties*). The most common motivation for CTL synthesis remains the synthesis of synchronization for concurrent programs, such as mutual exclusion protocols. In this setting, the Kripke structure is interpreted as a global state

Electronic supplementary material The online version of this chapter (doi:10. 1007/978-3-319-41528-4_8) contains supplementary material, which is available to authorized users.

© Springer International Publishing Switzerland 2016
S. Chaudhuri and A. Farzan (Eds.): CAV 2016, Part I, LNCS 9779, pp. 136–156, 2016.
DOI: 10.1007/978-3-319-41528-4_8

machine in which each global state contains every process's internal local state. The CTL specification in this setting consists of both structural intra-process constraints on local structures, and inter-process behavioral constraints on the global structure (for instance, starvation freedom). If a Kripke structure is found which satisfies the CTL specification, then one can derive from it the guarded commands that make up the corresponding synchronization skeleton [4,8].

In this paper, we introduce a novel method for CTL synthesis. We build on the recent introduction of SAT modulo Monotonic Theories (SMMT) [5], creating a CTL satisfiability procedure for the case where the number of states in the Kripke structure is bounded in advance. (Note, however, that the underlying CTL model checking theory is for the standard, unbounded semantics of CTL.) Due to the CTL small model property [12], in principle a bounded CTL-SAT procedure yields a complete decision procedure for unbounded CTL-SAT, but in practice, neither bounded approaches, nor classical tableau approaches, have been scalable enough for completeness to be a practical concern. Rather, our approach (like similar constraint-solver based techniques for CTL [10,14] and LTL [15,17]) is appropriate for the case where a formula is expected to be satisfiable by a Kripke structure with a modest number of states (∼100). Nevertheless, we will show that our approach solves larger and more complex satisfiable CTL formulas, including ones with a larger numbers of states, much faster than existing bounded and unbounded synthesis techniques. This makes our approach particularly appropriate for CTL synthesis.

In addition to being more efficient than existing techniques, our approach is also capable of synthesizing minimal models. As we will discuss below, previous CTL synthesis approaches were either incapable of finding minimal models [3,8], or could not do so with comparable scalability to our technique [10,14].

The paper is structured as follows: We begin with a review of related work in Sect. 2. To make this paper self-contained, we go over the theory behind SAT Modulo Monotonic Theories in Sect. 3 and some challenges in applying it to CTL. In the same section, we show how to utilize this framework for bounded CTL synthesis. Section 4 explains the most important implementation details and optimizations. The experimental results of Sect. 5 demonstrate that our implementation, based on the open-source SMT solver MONOSAT[1] for Boolean monotonic theories, is able to outperform other approaches in two families of synthesis benchmarks: one derived from mutual exclusion protocols, and the other derived from readers-writers protocols.

2   Related Work

The original 1981 Clarke and Emerson paper introducing CTL synthesis [8] proposed a tableau-based synthesis algorithm, and used this algorithm to construct a 2-process mutex in which each process was guaranteed mutually exclusive access to the critical section, with starvation freedom.

Subsequently, although there has been steady progress on the general CTL synthesis problem, the most dramatic gains have been with techniques that

---

[1] http://www.cs.ubc.ca/labs/isd/Projects/monosat/

are structurally-constrained, taking a CTL formula along with some additional 'structural' information about the desired Kripke structure, not specified in CTL, which is then leveraged to achieve greater scalability than generic CTL synthesis techniques. For example, in 1998, Attie and Emerson [2,3] introduced a CTL synthesis technique for the case where the Kripke structure is known to be composed of multiple similar communicating processes. They used this technique to synthesize a Kripke structure for a specially constructed 2-process version of the CTL formula (a 'pair-program') in such a way that the produced Kripke structure could be safely generalized into an N-process solution. This allowed them to produce a synchronization skeleton for a mutex with 1000 or more processes, far larger than other techniques. However, while this process scales very well, only certain CTL properties can be guaranteed to be preserved in the resulting Kripke structure, and in general the Kripke structure produced this way may be much larger than the minimal solution to the instance. In particular, EX and AX properties are not preserved in this process [2].

The similar-process synthesis techniques of Attie and Emerson rely on a generic CTL synthesis method to synthesize these pair-programs. As such, improvements to the scalability or expressiveness of generic CTL synthesis methods can be directly applied to improving this pair-program synthesis technique. Their use of the synthesis method from [8] yields an initially large Kripke structure that they minimize in an intermediate step. We note that our approach is particularly suited for synthesizing such pair-programs, not merely for performance reasons, but also because it is able to synthesize minimal models directly.

On the topic of finding minimal models, Bustan and Grumberg [7] introduced a technique for minimizing Kripke structures. However, the minimal models that our technique produces can in general be smaller than what can be achieved by starting with a large Kripke structure and subsequently minimizing it. This is because minimization techniques which are applied on an existing Kripke structure *after* its synthesis only yield a structure minimal with respect to equivalent structures (for some definition of equivalence, *e.g.*, strong or weak bisimulation). This does not necessarily result in a structure that is the overall minimal model of the original CTL formula. For this reason, techniques supporting the direct synthesis of minimal models, such as ours, have an advantage over post-synthesis minimization techniques.

In 2005, Heymans et al. [14] introduced a novel, constraint-based approach to the general CTL synthesis problem. They created an extension of answer set programming (ASP) that they called 'preferential ASP' and used it to generate a 2-process mutex with the added property of being 'maximally parallel', meaning that each state has a (locally) maximal number of outgoing transitions (without violating the CTL specification). They argued that this formalized a property that was implicit in the heuristics of the original 1981 CTL synthesis algorithm, and that it could result in Kripke structures that were easier to implement as efficient concurrent programs. As the formulation in their paper does not require additional structural constraints (though it can support them), it is a general CTL synthesis method. Furthermore, being a constraint-based method, one can flexibly add structural or other constraints to guide the synthesis. However, the scalability of their method was poor.

Subsequently, high performance ASP solvers [13] built on techniques from Boolean satisfiability solvers were introduced, allowing ASP solvers to solve much larger and much more difficult ASP formulas. In 2012, De Angelis, Pettorossi, and Proietti [10] showed that (unextended) ASP solvers could also be used to perform efficient bounded CTL synthesis, allowing them to use the high performance ASP solver Clasp [13]. Similar to [3], they introduced a formulation for doing CTL synthesis via ASP in the case where the desired Kripke structure is composed of multiple similar processes. Using this approach, they synthesized 2-process and 3-process mutexes with properties at least as strong as the original CTL specification from [3]. The work we introduce in this paper is also a constraint-solver-based, bounded CTL-synthesis technique. However, we will show that our approach scales to larger and more complex specifications than previous work, while simultaneously avoiding the limitations that prevent those approaches from finding minimal models.

Our approach is based on *SAT Modulo Monotonic Theories* (SMMT), introduced by Bayless et al. in 2015 [5]. This is a technique for building lazy SMT solvers [11,18] for a class of theories they defined as *Boolean monotonic theories*. The restriction to Boolean monotonic theories appears rather limiting, but in this paper, we will show how SMMT can be used to build an SMT solver for the theory of CTL model checking. We will then show that this 'SAT modulo CTL' solver can perform efficient and scalable CTL synthesis. We provide experimental comparisons to state-of-the-art techniques showing that this SMT-approach can find solutions to larger and more complex CTL formulas than comparable techniques, and does so without the limitations and extra expert knowledge that previous approaches require.

3   SAT Modulo Monotonic Theories for CTL

Bayless et al. [5] introduced techniques for building efficient SMT solvers for *Boolean monotonic theories* (SMMT), which are defined as follows:

Definition 1 (Boolean Monotonic Theory). *A theory T with signature Σ is Boolean monotonic if and only if:*

1. *The only sort in Σ is Boolean;*
2. *all predicates in Σ are monotonic; and*
3. *all functions in Σ are monotonic.*

   A predicate $P: \{0,1\}^n \mapsto \{0,1\}$ is Boolean positive monotonic iff, for all i:
   $$P(\ldots, s_{i-1}, 0, s_{i+1}, \ldots) \rightarrow P(\ldots, s_{i-1}, 1, s_{i+1}, \ldots)$$
   A predicate $P: \{0,1\}^n \mapsto \{0,1\}$ is Boolean negative monotonic iff, for all i:
   $$P(\ldots, s_{i-1}, 1, s_{i+1}, \ldots) \rightarrow P(\ldots, s_{i-1}, 0, s_{i+1}, \ldots)$$
   The definition of monotonicity for a function $F: \{0,1\}^n \mapsto \mathcal{P}(S)$ (for some set S) is the same as above, but with "$\subseteq$" instead of "$\rightarrow$".

Theories operating over only Booleans are atypical in the SMT literature, and would appear at first glance to be highly restrictive. However, [5] showed that many common graph properties, such as reachability and maximum flow, can be expressed as Boolean monotonic theories, and that the resulting SMT solver (implemented in the lazy SMT solver MONOSAT) performs well in practice. Subsequently, MONOSAT has been extended to support theories of finite state machines, bit-vectors, and additional graph properties including acyclicity and connected component counts.

To see how [5] uses Boolean monotonic theories, consider the theory of graph reachability as an example. In that theory, a set of Boolean atoms determine which edges are included (*enabled*) in a finite graph. Reachability over such a graph is monotonic with respect to those edge atoms: given a graph in which node a reaches node b, a must still reach b after adding additional edges to the graph. One challenge of implementing lazy SMT solvers is that efficient solvers typically include theory propagation procedures that make deductions from partial assignments. However, because reachability is Boolean monotonic, two concrete graphs are sufficient to capture the space of possible graphs under a partial assignment: G_{under}, containing only edges that are enabled by the partial assignment, and G_{over}, in which additionally all unassigned edges are enabled. If a reachability predicate does not hold in G_{over}, then it can safely be deduced that it does not hold in any extension of the partial assignment. Similarly, if it holds in G_{under}, then it holds in all extensions of the partial assignment. These facts are used by MONOSAT to implement efficient theory propagation.

Below, we show that MONOSAT can be extended to support a theory of CTL model checking, allowing MONOSAT to express predicates of the form $Model_{\phi,K}(T, A)$, where ϕ is a CTL formula over atomic propositions P, and K is a Kripke structure with a fixed set S of states, T is a vector of $|S|^2$ Booleans controlling which transitions are in K, and A is a vector of $|S||P|$ Booleans controlling which atomic propositions hold in each state. $Model_{\phi,K}(T, A)$ is TRUE if and only if the Kripke structure K is a model for ϕ under assignment to these transition and state property variables.

However, we face an immediate challenge: CTL model checking is neither monotonic with respect to the set T of transitions in the Kripke structure, nor with respect to the set A of property assignments in each state. Consider, for example, a two state Kripke structure with transitions between both states. $\phi = (\mathbf{EF}\, a \land \neg(\mathbf{AG}\, a))$ evaluates to FALSE if atomic proposition a is in neither state, evaluates to TRUE if a is in one, but not the other state, and evaluates to FALSE if a is in both states (a similar argument can be made for the non-monotonicity of $Model_{\phi,K}(T, A)$ with respect to T).

Our solution begins with the observation that each individual CTL operator, considered on its own in a non-nested formula, is monotonic. We will use this observation to construct an alternative predicate, $ModelApprox_{\phi,K}(T_1, A_1, T_2, A_2)$, over two separate assignments of transitions and states to K. Unlike $Model_{\phi,K}$, $ModelApprox_{\phi,K}$ is Boolean monotonic, and we will show that it can be used either to safely over-approximate the semantics of CTL, or to safely under-approximate them. By combining this new monotonic predicate with additional constraints on its arguments, we will then recover the semantics required to support our original CTL model checking predicate $Model_{\phi,K}(T, A)$.

3.1 A Monotonic Approximation of CTL

Below, we restrict our attention to the existentially quantified CTL operators EX, EG and EU, along with propositional operators $(\neg, \wedge, \vee)$, as well as TRUE and FALSE, which are well known to form an adequate set. Any CTL formula can be efficiently converted into a logically equivalent existential normal form (ENF) in terms of these operators, linear in the size of the original formula [16].

First, we show that CTL formulas consisting of a single operator EX p, EG p or p EU q have each, individually, a Boolean positive monotonic satisfiability predicate (where p, q are atomic propositions). We let $solve_{s,\phi}(T, A)$ be the predicate that denotes whether or not the formula ϕ holds in the initial state s of the Kripke structure determined by the vector of Booleans T (transitions) and A (state properties).

Lemma 1. $solve_{s,\phi}(T, A)$ *is positive Boolean monotonic if ϕ is one of EX p, EG p, or p EU q.*

Proof. Take any T, A that determine a structure K for which the predicate holds. Let K' be a structure determined by some T', A' such that K' has the same states, state properties and transitions as K, except for one transition that is enabled in K' but not in K, or one state property which holds in K' but not in K. Formally, there is exactly one argument in either T' or A' that is 0 in T (or A respectively) and 1 in T' (or A' respectively). Then either (a) one of the states satisfies one of the atomic propositions in K', but not in K, or (b) there is a transition in K', but not in K.

We assume $solve_{s,\phi}(T, A)$ holds. Then, there must exist a witnessing infinite sequence starting from s in K. If (b), the exact same sequence must exist in K', since it has a superset of the transitions in K. Thus we can conclude $solve_{s,\phi}(T', A')$ holds. If (a), then the sequence will only differ in at most one state, where p holds instead of $\neg p$ (or q instead of $\neg q$). We note that for each of the three CTL operators, this sequence will be a witness for K', if the original sequence was a witness for K. Thus, $solve_{s,\phi}(T', A')$ holds as well.

It is easy to see that $\wedge$ and $\vee$ are positive monotonic in the same way, and $\neg$ is negative monotonic. Excluding negation, then, all the CTL operators needed to express formulas in ENF have positive Boolean monotonic $solve$ predicates, while negation alone has a negative Boolean monotonic $solve$ predicate.

Until now, we have considered the model checking algorithm to compute a predicate that returns TRUE iff the initial state of the Kripke structure satisfies the formula. This can be extended to a function $solve(\phi, K)$ that evaluates the truth value of ϕ for each state in the Kripke structure, and returns a bit vector representing a set of states, that for each state is 1 iff that state satisfies ϕ. The monotonicity properties above also hold for $solve(\phi, K)$, as every state in the bitset can be viewed as an initial state for which the operators are monotonic.

We introduce for each CTL operator op an evaluation function $solve_{op}(X, K)$ that evaluates the operator on a set of states X, instead of a subformula. This is a standard interpretation of CTL (and how CTL model checking is often implemented), and we refer to the literature for common ways to compute $solve_{op}$ for each operator. Our function $solve(\phi, K)$ takes the top-most operator op of ϕ: if it is an atomic proposition, it returns the set of states in which the atomic proposition holds, otherwise it solves its argument(s) recursively and then applies $solve_{op}$ on the returned set of states. One can think of the set X as defining the states in which a fresh atomic proposition holds, and of $solve_{op}(X, K)$ as computing the application of op on that atomic proposition.

Algorithm 1. solveApprox(ϕ, K_{over}, K_{under})

---

if ϕ *is an atomic proposition* **then**
  | **return** *set of states satisfying* ϕ *in* K_{over}

else if ϕ *is a unary operator op with argument* ψ **then**
  | **if** *op is* $\neg$ **then**   // `negative monotonic`
  | | $X :=$ solveApprox(ψ, K_{under}, K_{over})
  | | **return** $solve_{op}(X, K_{under})$
  | **else**   // `op` $\in$ {`EX`, `EG`}
  | | $X :=$ solveApprox(ψ, K_{over}, K_{under})
  | | **return** $solve_{op}(X, K_{over})$

else   // ϕ `is binary` $op \in$ {`EU`, $\wedge$, $\vee$} `with arguments` ψ_1, ψ_2
  | $X_1 :=$ solveApprox(ψ_1, K_{over}, K_{under})
  | $X_2 :=$ solveApprox(ψ_2, K_{over}, K_{under})
  | **return** $solve_{op}(X_1, X_2, K_{over})$

Algorithm 1, $solveApprox(\phi, K_{over}, K_{under})$ takes a CTL formula ϕ and two Kripke structures, K_{over} and K_{under}. It returns a bit vector, representing a set of states.[2] We will show in Lemma 2 that for appropriate values of K_{over} and K_{under}, $solveApprox$ computes a safe over-approximation of $solve(\phi, K)$ for a third Kripke structure, K: $solve(\phi, K) \subseteq solveApprox(\phi, K_{over}, K_{under})$. Further, as K_{under} and K_{over} converge, so do $solveApprox(\phi, K_{over}, K_{under})$ and $solve(\phi, K)$. If $K_{under} = K_{over} = K$, then $solveApprox(\phi, K_{over}, K_{under}) = solve(\phi, K)$. This follows directly from Lemma 2.

In order for the over-approximation property of $solveApprox$ given in the following lemma to hold, K_{over} (determined by some T_1, A_1), K_{under} (determined

---

[2] A similar algorithm for evaluating CTL formulas on 'partial Kripke structures', in the context of model checking, can be found in [6].

Example: Initially, the SAT solver's assignment $\mathcal{A}_{init} = \emptyset$ to transitions and state properties is empty, which determines K_{under} and K_{over} in the following way.

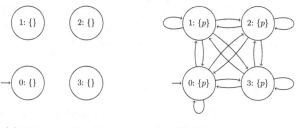

(a) K_{under} under $\mathcal{A}_{init}$ (b) K_{over} under $\mathcal{A}_{init}$

As the SAT solver makes assignments to theory atoms $trans(\ldots)$ and $sat(\ldots)$ (positive assignments affect K_{under}'s T_2, A_2, negative K_{over}'s T_1, A_1), both structures converge. Take for instance this partial assignment $\mathcal{A}_{ex}$:

$$\mathcal{A}_{ex} = sat(1, p) \wedge \neg sat(2, p) \wedge trans(0, 1) \wedge trans(1, 3) \wedge trans(3, 0) \wedge trans(2, 2)$$
$$\wedge \neg trans(0, 0) \wedge \neg trans(0, 2) \wedge \neg trans(0, 3) \wedge \neg trans(1, 0) \wedge \neg trans(1, 1)$$
$$\wedge \neg trans(2, 0) \wedge \neg trans(2, 1) \wedge \neg trans(2, 3) \wedge \neg trans(3, 1) \wedge \neg trans(3, 3)$$

The atoms $sat(0, p)$, $sat(3, p)$, $trans(1, 2)$, and $trans(3, 2)$ are unassigned by $\mathcal{A}_{ex}$. $\mathcal{A}_{ex}$ determines K_{under} and K_{over} in the following way:

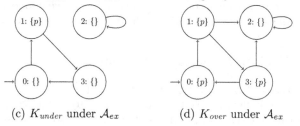

(c) K_{under} under $\mathcal{A}_{ex}$ (d) K_{over} under $\mathcal{A}_{ex}$

$solveApprox(\phi, K_{over}, K_{under})$ returns an over-approximation (resp. under-approx with K_{over} and K_{under} exchanged) of the set of states in which ϕ may hold in extensions of the partial assignment. Assume K_{over} and K_{under} are obtained from $\mathcal{A}_{ex}$ and $\phi = \texttt{EX}\ \neg p$:

$\qquad solveApprox(\texttt{EX}\ \neg p, K_{over}, K_{under})$

$\qquad = solve_{EX}(solveApprox(\neg p, K_{over}, K_{under}), K_{over})$

$\qquad = solve_{EX}(solve_{\neg}(solveApprox(p, K_{under}, K_{over}), K_{under}), K_{over})$

$\qquad = solve_{EX}(solve_{\neg}(\{1\}, K_{under}), K_{over})$

$\qquad = solve_{EX}(\{0, 2, 3\}, K_{over})$

$\qquad = \{1, 2, 3\}$

The initial state is not in the over-approximation of states, where $\texttt{EX}\ \neg p$ holds ($0 \notin solveApprox(\texttt{EX}\ \neg p, K_{over}, K_{under})$), therefore $\texttt{EX}\ \neg p$ does not hold in any Kripke structure obtained from a full extension of the partial assignment $\mathcal{A}_{ex}$.

Fig. 1. Example of a partial assignment $\mathcal{A}_{ex}$ determining to K_{under} and K_{over}, and the evaluation $solveApprox$ of a formula on K_{under} and K_{over}.

by some T_2, A_2) and K (determined by some T, A) must be Kripke structures with the same number of states, and K_{over} must have a superset, and K_{under} a subset, of the transitions and state properties of K: $T_2 \subseteq T \subseteq T_1$ and $A_2 \subseteq A \subseteq A_1$. To illustrate how this will be used in the context of SMT, Fig. 1 shows an example of how the SAT solver's partial assignment determines K_{over} and K_{under}, and how $solveApprox$ works on these structures.

Lemma 2. $solve(\phi, K) \subseteq solveApprox(\phi, K_{over}, K_{under})$ and $solve(\phi, K) \supseteq solveApprox(\phi, K_{under}, K_{over})$.

Proof. By induction over ϕ. If ϕ is an atomic proposition, then $solveApprox$ returns the set of states satisfying ϕ in K_{over}. $solve(\phi, K)$ will return the set of states satisfying ϕ in K. The first claim holds, since $A \subseteq A_1$.

If $\phi = op\ \psi$ with op a unary positive monotonic operator, $solve(\phi, K)$ is $solve_{op}(X, K)$ for $X = solve(\psi, K) \subseteq_{IH} solveApprox(\psi, K_{over}, K_{under}) = X'$. $solveApprox(\phi, K_{over}, K_{under})$ is $solve_{op}(X', K)$. The first claim holds, since $X \subseteq X'$ and $solve_{op}$ is positive monotonic. If op is unary negative monotonic, *i.e.* $\neg$, then $solve(\phi, K)$ is $solve_{op}(X, K)$ for $X = solve(\psi, K) \supseteq_{IH} solveApprox(\psi, K_{under}, K_{over}) = X'$. $solveApprox(\phi, K_{over}, K_{under})$ is $solve_{op}(X', K)$. The first claim holds, since $X \supseteq X'$ and $solve_{op}$ is negative monotonic.

The proof obligations for $solve(\phi, K) \supseteq solveApprox(\phi, K_{under}, K_{over})$ are left out here, as well as the proof obligations for positive monotonic binary operators. The proof for these proceeds similarly to the above cases.

3.2   CTL as a Boolean Monotonic Predicate

$solveApprox(\phi, K_{over}, K_{under})$ computes an over-approximation (*resp.*, with K_{over} and K_{under} exchanged, an under-approximation) of the set of states in which a CTL formula ϕ holds in Kripke structure K, so long as K_{over} and K_{under} are, as defined above, structures that are over-, and respectively under-approximating K. We construct a corresponding Boolean monotonic predicate $ModelApprox_{\phi,K}(T_1, A_1, T_2, A_2)$ which holds iff the initial state $s_0 \in solveApprox(\phi, K_{over}, K_{under})$.[3] Its monotonicity follows from the following lemma:

Lemma 3. $solveApprox(\phi, K_{over}, K_{under})$ is a function positive monotonic in K_{over} and negative monotonic in K_{under}.

Proof. By structural induction over ϕ. If ϕ is an atomic proposition, then $solveApprox$ returns the set of states satisfying ϕ in K_{over}. If a state or transition is added to K_{over} (call the resulting structure K_{over}'), then $solveApprox(\phi, K_{over}, K_{under}) \subseteq solveApprox(\phi, K_{over}', K_{under})$. If a state or transition is removed from K_{under} (resulting in K_{under}'), then $solveApprox(\phi, K_{over}, K_{under}) = solveApprox(\phi, K_{over}, K_{under}')$.

---

[3] If $T_2 \not\subseteq T_1$ or $A_2 \not\subseteq A_1$, $ModelApprox$ can be defined to evaluate in any arbitrary way that maintains monotonicity. As discussed below, we exclude this case in our implementation, by enforcing $T_1 = T_2$ and $A_1 = A_2$.

Assume $\phi = op\ \psi$ with op a unary positive monotonic operator. Then $solveApprox(\phi, K_{over}, K_{under})$ is the function composition of positive monotonic $solve_{op}$ and $solveApprox(\psi, K_{over}, K_{under})$, which is positive monotonic in K_{over} and negative monotonic in K_{under} by the induction hypothesis. The composed function is then also positive monotonic in K_{over} and negative in K_{under}.

Assume on the other hand that op is a unary negative monotonic operator, *i.e.* $\neg$. Then $solveApprox(\phi, K_{over}, K_{under})$ is the function composition of $solve_{\neg}$ and $solveApprox(\psi, K_{under}, K_{over})$, which is assumed by the induction hypothesis to be positive monotonic in K_{under}, and negative monotonic in K_{over}. Since $solve_{\neg}$ is negative monotonic in its first argument (and ignores its second argument), the composed function is positive monotonic in K_{over}, and negative in K_{under}.

The proof obligations for binary operators (all positive monotonic) are left out here. The proof for these proceeds similarly to the above cases.

Corollary 1. *$ModelApprox_{\phi,K}(T_1, A_1, T_2, A_2)$ is positive monotonic in T_1, A_1 and negative monotonic in T_2, A_2.*

Proof. By definition, $ModelApprox_{\phi,K}(T_1, A_1, T_2, A_2)$ holds if, and only if, $s_0 \in solveApprox(\phi, K_{over}, K_{under})$; therefore the monotonicity of $ModelApprox$ follows directly from the monotonicity of $solveApprox$ (Lemma 3).

We complete our theory of CTL model checking by forcing $T_1 = T_2$ and $A_1 = A_2$. As we proved above, $ModelApprox_{\phi,K}(T, A, T, A) = Model_{\phi,K}(T, A)$, and so in this way we recover the expected definition of CTL model checking in our theory solver. The equalities $T_1 = T_2$ and $A_1 = A_2$ could be enforced by adding a linear number of additional Boolean constraints to the SAT solver; in our implementation we found it more efficient to enforce this equality internally in the theory solver.

4   Implementation and Optimizations

Above, we showed how CTL model checking can be posed as a Boolean monotonic theory. We then built a lazy SMT theory solver, following the theory propagation techniques for Boolean monotonic theories described in [5]. We have also implemented some additional optimizations which greatly improve the performance of our CTL theory solver. One basic optimization that we implement is pure literal filtering (see, *e.g.*, [18]): For the case where $Model_{\phi,K}(T, A)$ is assigned TRUE (resp. FALSE), we only need to check whether $Model_{\phi,K}(T, A)$ is falsified (resp., made true) during theory propagation. In all of the instances we will examine in this paper, $Model_{\phi,K}(T, A)$ is assigned TRUE in the input formula, and so this optimization greatly simplifies theory propagation. We discuss several further improvements below:

In Sect. 4.1 we outline how our solver performs clause learning. In Sect. 4.2 we describe symmetry breaking constraints, which can greatly reduce the search space of the solver, and in Sect. 4.3 we show how several common types of CTL constraints can be cheaply converted into CNF, reducing the size of the formula the theory solver must handle. Finally, in Sect. 4.4, we discuss how in the common case of a CTL formula describing multiple communicating processes we can (optionally) add support for additional *structural constraints*, similarly to the approach described in [10]. These structural constraints allow our solver even greater scalability, at the cost of adding more states into the smallest solution that can be synthesized. Thus, if structural constraints are used, iteratively decreasing the bound may no longer yield a minimal structure.

4.1 Clause Learning

Supporting efficient clause learning (also called "justification set" or "conflict set" learning in the SMT literature) is a critically important function of lazy SMT theory solvers. Theory solvers can always return a naive conflict set consisting of the entire conflicting (partial) assignment, however, efficient theory solvers typically implement clause learning procedures which attempt to find smaller, or sometimes even minimal, conflict sets.

Unlike our theory propagation implementation, which operates on formulas in existential normal form, to perform clause learning we convert the CTL formula into *negation normal form* (NNF), pushing any negation operators down to the innermost terms of the formula. To obtain an adequate set, the formula may now also include universally quantified CTL operators and Weak Until. Each of these operators is handled separately.

Our procedure $learn(\phi, s)$ operates recursively on the NNF of the formula and returns a conflict set of literals, the disjunction of which yields a CNF clause which is learned by the SAT solver. The same conflict set is populated on every level of the recursion, *i.e.* the learned literals have an additive effect on the conflict clause. For instance, if the formula $\texttt{EX } \phi$ is in conflict with the partial assignment, we first consider the operator $\texttt{EX}$. Our clause learning strategy for $\texttt{EX}$ in the state s (in this case, the initial state) is to force the SAT solver to enable any disabled transitions from s, or to make ϕ true in any of the successor states. Literals for the latter are computed recursively via $learn(\phi, t)$ for every enabled transition (s, t). $learn(\phi, s)$ is defined as follows (for notation see Fig. 2):

- $learn(p, s)$ (resp. $learn(\neg p, s)$), where p is an atomic proposition. Add the literal $disableAPinState(p, s)$ (resp. $enableAPinState(p, s)$) to the conflict set.
- $learn(op\ \psi, s)$ (resp. $learn(\psi_1\ op\ \psi_2, s)$): Add the literals returned by the functions $learn_{op}(\psi, s)$ (resp. $learn_{op}(\psi_1, \psi_2, s)$) to the conflict set (see Fig. 2).

4.2 Symmetry Breaking

Due to the way we expose atomic propositions and transitions to the SAT solver with theory atoms, the SAT solver may end up exploring large numbers of isomorphic Kripke structures. We address this by enforcing extra symmetry-breaking constraints which prevent the solver from considering (some) redundant configurations of the Kripke structure. Symmetry reduction is especially helpful to prove instances UNSAT, which aids the search for suitable bounds.

Clause Learning functions $learn_{op}$

$learn_{EX}(\phi, s)$: Let N be the neighbors of s that do not satisfy ϕ. Let D be the set of disabled transitions from s. Add $enableTransitionSet(D)$ to the conflict set, and $learn(\phi, n)$ for each $n \in N$.

$learn_{AX}(\phi, s)$: Let n be a neighbor of s that does not satisfy ϕ. Add $disableTransition(s, n)$ to the conflict set, and $learn(\phi, n)$.

$learn_{EF}(\phi, s)$: Let R be all states reachable from s. Let D be the set of disabled transitions from reachable states R to unreachable states. Add $enableTransitionSet(D)$ to the conflict set, and add $learn(\phi, r)$ for each $r \in R$.

$learn_{AF}(\phi, s)$: Let R be a set of states satisfying $\neg\phi$ that form lasso from s. Let D be the set of transitions in the lasso. Add $disableTransitionSet(D)$ to the conflict set, and add $learn(\phi, r)$ for each $r \in R$.

$learn_{EG}(\phi, s)$: Let R be the the states reachable from s via a path on which all states satisfy ϕ. Let N be the set of successor states of R which do not satisfy ϕ. Let D be the set of disabled transitions leaving R. Add $enableTransitionSet(D)$ to the conflict set, and add $learn(\phi, n)$ for each $n \in N$.

$learn_{AG}(\phi, s)$: Find a path of transitions D from s to a state r that doesn't satisfy ϕ. Add $disableTransitionSet(D)$ to the conflict set, and add $learn(\phi, r)$.

$learn_{\wedge}(\phi, \psi, s)$: If ϕ does not hold in the over-approximation (but ψ does), add $learn(\phi, s)$. If ψ does not hold in the over-approximation (but ϕ does), add $learn(\psi, s)$. If both do not hold, then construct a temporary conflict set for each, and add the smaller set to the conflict.

$learn_{\vee}(\phi, \psi, s)$: Add $learn(\phi, s)$ and $learn(\psi, s)$ to the conflict.

$learn_{EW}(\phi, \psi, s)$: Let R be the states satisfying ϕ and reachable via ϕ-satisfying states from s. Let D be the set of disabled transitions from states in R. Let P be the set of successors of R that are not in R. Add D to the conflict set, add $learn(\psi, r)$ for each $r \in R$, and add $learn((\phi \vee \psi), p)$ for each $p \in P$.

$learn_{AW}(\phi, \psi, s)$: Find a path starting from s such that all except the last state satisfy ϕ, and no state satisfies ψ. Let D be the set of transitions on that path; add $disableTransitionSet(D)$ to the conflict set. Let R be the set of states on that path, except for the last state of the path, n. Add $learn(\phi, n)$ and $learn(\psi, r)$ for each $r \in R$ to the conflict set.

$learn_{EU}(\phi, \psi, s)$: Same as $learn_{EW}$, but D is restricted to transitions to states outside of R.

$learn_{AU}(\phi, \psi, s)$: If there exists a finite path starting from s such that all except the last states on the path satisfy ϕ, add $learn_{AW}(\phi, \psi, s)$ to the conflict set. Else, add $learn_{AF}(\psi, s)$ to the conflict set.

Notation: $enableAPinState(p, s)$ returns the literal that assigns property p to state s. $enableTransition(s, t)$ returns the literal for transition $s \rightarrow t$. $enableTransitionSet(D)$ returns $\{enableTransition(s,t) \mid (s, t) \in D\}$. $disableAPin-State, disableTransition, disableTransitionSet$ return corresponding negated literals. For existentially quantified CTL operators, transitions of K_{over} are used, for universally quantified CTL operators transitions of K_{under}. $solveApprox(\phi, K_{over}, K_{under})$ gives the set of states satisfying a subformula ϕ.
Notice that some functions (*e.g.*, $learn_{AG}$) are only correct if every state has an infinite path (**AG EX** TRUE), which is why we enforce this property in our solver.

Fig. 2. Clause learning functions returning sets of literals.

Let $label(s_i)$ be the binary representation of the atomic propositions of state s_i, and let $out(s_i)$ be the set of outgoing edges of state s_i. Let s_0 be the initial state. The following constraint enforces an order on the allowable assignments of state properties and transitions in the Kripke structure.

$$\forall i,j : [i < j \wedge i \neq 0 \wedge j \neq 0] \rightarrow$$
$$[label(s_i) \leq label(s_j) \wedge (label(s_i) = label(s_j) \rightarrow |out(s_i)| \leq |out(s_j)|)]$$

4.3   Preprocessing

Given a CTL specification ϕ, we identify certain common sub-expressions which can be cheaply converted directly into CNF, which is efficiently handled by the SAT solver at the core of MONOSAT. We do so if ϕ matches $\bigwedge_i \phi_i$, as is commonly the case when multiple properties are part of the specification. If ϕ_i is purely propositional, or of the form AG p with p purely propositional, we eliminate ϕ_i from the formula and convert ϕ_i into a logically equivalent CNF expression over the state property assignment atoms of the theory.[4] This requires a linear number of clauses in the number of states in K. We also convert formulas of the form AG ψ, with ψ containing only propositional logic and at most a single Next-operator (EX or AX). Both of these are very common sub-expressions in the CTL formulas that we have examined.

4.4   Wildcard Encoding for Concurrent Programs

As will be further explained later, the synthesis problem for synchronization skeletons assumes a given number of processes, which each have a local transition system. The state transitions in the full Kripke structure then represent the possible interleavings of executing the local transition system of each process. This local transition system is normally encoded into the CTL specification.

Both [3,10] explored strategies to take advantage of the case where the local transition systems of these processes are made explicit. [10] were able to greatly improve the scalability of their answer-set-programming based CTL synthesis procedure by deriving additional 'structural' constraints for such concurrent processes. As our approach is also constraint-based, we can (optionally) support similar structural constraints. In experiments below, we show that even though our approach already scales better than existing approaches without these additional structural constraints, we also benefit from such constraints.

Firstly, we can exclude any global states with state properties that are an illegal encoding of multiple processes. If the local state of each process is identified by a unique atomic proposition, then we can enforce that each global state must make true exactly one of the atomic propositions for each process. For every remaining combination of state property assignments, excluding those determined to be illegal above, we add a single state into the Kripke structure, with a

---

[4] Since AG p only specifies reachable states, the clause is for each state s a disjunction of p being satisfied in s, or s having no enabled incoming transitions. This changes the semantics of CTL for unreachable states, but not for reachable states.

pre-determined assignment of atomic propositions, such that only the transitions between these states are free for the SAT solver to assign. This is in contrast to the normal synthesis method, in which states are completely undetermined (but typically fewer are required).

Secondly, since we are interested in interleavings of concurrent programs, on each transition in the global Kripke structure we enforce that only a single process may change its local state, and it may change its local state only in a way that is consistent with the its local transition system.

The above two constraints greatly reduce the space of transitions in the global Kripke structure that are left free for the SAT solver to assign (and completely eliminate the space of atomic propositions to assign in each state). However these constraints make our procedure incomplete, since in general more than a single state with the same atomic propositions (but different behavior) need to be distinguished. To allow multiple states with equivalent atomic propositions, we also add a small number of 'wildcard' states into the Kripke structure, whose state properties and transitions (incoming and outgoing) are not set in advance. In the examples we consider in this paper, we have found that a small number of such wildcard states (between 3 and 20) are sufficient to allow for a Kripke structure that satisfies the CTL formula, while still greatly restricting the total space of Kripke structures that must be explored by the SAT solver.

We disable symmetry breaking when using the wildcard encoding, as the wildcard encoding is incompatible with the constraint in Sect. 4.2.

5 Experimental Results

There are few CTL synthesis implementations available for comparison. Indeed, the original CTL synthesis/model-checking paper [8] presents an implementation of CTL model checking, but the synthesis examples were simulated by hand. The only publicly available, unbounded CTL synthesis tool we could find is Prezza's open-source CTLSAT tool[5], which is a modern implementation of the classic tableau-based CTL synthesis algorithm [8].

We also compare to De Angelis et al.'s encoding of bounded CTL synthesis into ASP [10]. De Angelis et al. provide encodings[6] specific to the n-process mutual exclusion example, which exploit structural assumptions about the synthesized model (for example, that it is the composition of n identical processes). We label this encoding "ASP-structural" in the tables below. For ASP-structural, we have only the instances originally considered in [10].

To handle the general version of CTL synthesis (without added structural information), we also created ASP encodings using the methods from De Angelis et al.'s paper, but without problem-specific structural assumptions and optimizations. We label those results "ASP-generic". For both encodings, we use the

---

[5] https://github.com/nicolaprezza/CTLSAT
[6] http://www.sci.unich.it/~deangelis/papers/mutex_FI.tar.gz

latest version (4.5.4) of Clingo [13], and for each instance we report the best performance over the included Clasp configurations.[7]

We compare these tools to two versions of MONOSAT: MONOSAT-structural, which uses the wildcard optimization presented in Sect. 4.4, and MONOSAT-generic, without the wildcard optimization.

With the exception of CTLSAT, the tools we consider are bounded synthesis tools, which take as input both a CTL formula and a maximum number of states. For ASP-structural, the state bounds follow [10]. For the remaining tools, we selected the state bound manually, by repeatedly testing each tool with different bounds, and reporting for each tool the smallest bound for which it found a satisfying solution. In cases where a tool could not find any satisfying solution within our time or memory bounds, we report out-of-time or out-of-memory.

5.1 The Original Clarke-Emerson Mutex

The mutex problem assumes that there are n processes that run concurrently and on occasion access a single shared resource. Instead of synthesizing entire programs, the original Clarke-Emerson example [8] considers an abstraction of the programs called *synchronization skeletons*. In the instance of a mutex algorithm, it is assumed that each process is in one of three states: *non-critical section* (**NCS**), the *try section* (**TRY**) or the *critical section* (**CS**). A process starts in the non-critical section in which it remains until it requests to access the resource, and changes to the try section. When it finally enters the critical section it has access to the resource, and eventually loops back to the non-critical section. The synthesis problem is to find a global Kripke structure for the composition of the n processes, such that the specifications are met. Our first set of benchmarks are based on the Clarke and Emerson specification given in [8], that includes mutual exclusion and starvation freedom for all processes.

Results. Table 1 presents our results on the mutex formulation from [8]. Both versions of MONOSAT scale to much larger instances than the other approaches, finding solutions for 5 and 6 processes, respectively. CTLSAT, implementing the classical tableau approach, times out on all instances.[8] Only the -generic versions can guarantee minimal solutions, and MONOSAT-generic is able to prove minimal models for several cases.

As expected, structural constraints greatly improve efficiency for both ASP-structural and MONOSAT-structural relative to their generic counterparts.

---

[7] These are: "auto", "crafty", "frumpy", "handy", "jumpy", "trendy", and "tweety".

[8] Notably, CTLSAT times-out even when synthesizing the original 2-process mutex from [8], which Clarke and Emerson originally synthesized by hand. This may be because in that work, the local transition system was specified implicitly in the algorithm, instead of in the CTL specification as it is here.

Table 1. Results on the original Clarke-Emerson mutual exclusion example. Table entries are in the format *time(states)*, where *states* is the number of states in the synthesized model, and *time* is the run time in seconds. For ASP-structural, we only have the manually encoded instances provided by the authors. An asterisk indicates that the tool was able to prove minimality, by proving the instance is UNSAT at the next lower bound. TO denotes exceeding the 3 h timeout. MEM denotes exceeding 16 GB of RAM. All experiments were run on a 2.67 GHz Intel Xeon x5650 processor.

Approach	# of processes				
	2	3	4	5	6
CTLSAT	TO	TO	TO	TO	TO
ASP-generic	3.6 (7*)	1263.7 (14)	TO	MEM	MEM
ASP-structural	0.0 (12)	1.2 (36)	-	-	-
MONOSAT-generic	0.0 (7*)	1.4 (13*)	438.6 (23*)	1744.9 (42)	TO
MONOSAT-struct	0.2 (7)	0.5 (13)	4.5 (23)	166.7 (41)	1190.5 (75)

5.2 Mutex with Additional Properties

As noted in [14], the original Clarke-Emerson specification permits Kripke structures that are not *maximally parallel*, or even practically reasonable. For instance, our methods synthesize a structure in which one process being in NCS will block another process in TRY from getting the resource — the only transition such a global state has is to a state in which both processes are in the TRY section. In addition to the original formula, we present results for an augmented version in which we eliminate that solution[9] by introducing the "Non-Blocking" property, which states that a process may always remain in the NCS:

$$\text{AG } (\text{NCS}_i \to \text{EX NCS}_i) \tag{NB}$$

In addition, in the original paper there are structural properties implicit in the given local transition system, preventing jumping from NCS to CS, or from CS to TRY. We encode these properties into CTL as "No Jump" properties.

$$\text{AG } (\text{NCS}_i \to \text{AX } \neg\text{CS}_i) \quad \wedge \quad \text{AG } (\text{CS}_i \to \text{AX } \neg\text{TRY}_i) \tag{NJ}$$

We also consider two properties from [10]: Bounded Overtaking (BO), which guarantees that when a process is waiting for the critical section, each other process can only access the critical section at most once before the first process enters the critical section, and Maximal Reactivity (MR), which guarantees that if exactly one process is waiting for the critical section, then that process can enter the critical section in the next step.

---

[9] While the properties that we introduce in this paper mitigate some of the effects of underspecification, we have observed that the formulas of many instances in our benchmarks are not strong enough to guarantee a sensible solution. We are mainly interested in establishing benchmarks for synthesis performance, which is orthogonal to the task of finding suitable CTL specifications, which resolve these problems.

Results. We repeat our experimental procedure from Sect. 5.1, except with various combinations of additional properties. This provides a richer set of benchmarks, most of which are harder than the original.

Table 2 presents our results. As before, the -structural constraints greatly improve efficiency, but nevertheless, MONOSAT-generic outperforms ASP-structural. MONOSAT-generic is able to prove minimality on several benchmarks, and on one benchmark, MONOSAT-structural scales to 7 processes.

Table 2. Results on the mutual exclusion example with additional properties (described in Sect. 5.2). As with Table 1, entries are in the format *time(states)*. ORIG denotes the original mutual exclusion properties from Sect. 5.1. As before, although problem-specific structural constraints improve efficiency, MONOSAT-generic is comparably fast to ASP-structural on small instances, and scales to larger numbers of processes. MONOSAT-structural performs even better.

Approach	# of processes					
	2	3	4	5	6	7
Property: ORIG ∧ BO						
ASP-generic	3.4 (7*)	1442.0 (14)	TO/MEM	MEM	MEM	MEM
ASP-structural	0.0 (12)	2.3 (36)	-	-	-	-
MONOSAT-gen	0.0 (7*)	11.1 (13*)	438.3 (23*)	1286.6 (42)	TO	TO
MONOSAT-str	0.1 (7)	0.6 (13)	5.3 (23)	59.5 (41)	375.3 (75)	10739.5 (141)
Property: ORIG ∧ BO ∧ MR						
ASP-generic	10.1 (9*)	TO	MEM	MEM	MEM	MEM
ASP-structural	0.8 (10)	950.9 (27)	-	-	-	-
MONOSAT-gen	0.0 (9*)	6.0 (25*)	TO	TO	TO	TO
MONOSAT-str	0.1 (10)	8.7 (26)	TO	TO	TO	TO
Property: ORIG ∧ NB ∧ NJ						
ASP-generic	34.8 (9*)	TO	MEM	MEM	MEM	MEM
ASP-structural	0.1 (10)	7326.1 (27)	-	-	-	-
MONOSAT-gen	0.0 (9*)	1275.7 (22*)	TO	TO	TO	TO
MONOSAT-str	0.2 (10)	1.6 (26)	5314.7 (51)	TO	TO	TO
Property: ORIG ∧ NB ∧ NJ ∧ BO						
ASP-generic	15.4 (9*)	TO	MEM	MEM	MEM	MEM
ASP-structural	0.1 (10)	TO	-	-	-	-
MONOSAT-gen	0.0 (9*)	127.7 (22*)	TO	TO	TO	TO
MONOSAT-str	0.1 (10)	1.3 (24)	TO	TO	TO	TO
Property: ORIG ∧ NB ∧ NJ ∧ BO ∧ MR						
ASP-generic	10.7 (9*)	TO	MEM	MEM	MEM	MEM
ASP-structural	0.1 (10)	1917.6 (27)	-	-	-	-
MONOSAT-gen	0.0 (9*)	4.4 (25*)	TO	TO	TO	TO
MONOSAT-str	0.1 (10)	2.7 (26)	TO	TO	TO	TO

5.3   Readers-Writers

To provide even more benchmarks, we present instances of the related Readers-Writers problem [9]. Whereas the Mutex problem assumes that all processes require exclusive access to a resource, the Readers-Writers problem permits some simultaneous access. Two types of processes are distinguished: writers, which require exclusive access, and readers, which can share their access with other readers. This is a typical scenario for concurrent access to shared memory, in which write permissions and reading permissions are to be distinguished. The local states of each process are as in the Mutex instances.

We use Attie's [2] CTL specification. We note however that this specification allows for models which are not maximally parallel, and in particular disallows concurrent access by two readers. In addition to this original formula, we also consider one augmented with the Multiple Readers Eventually Critical (MREC) property. This ensures that there is a way for all readers, if they are in TRY, to simultaneously enter the critical section, if no writer requests the resource.

$$\text{AG} \left(\bigwedge_{w_i} \text{NCS}_{w_i} \rightarrow \left(\bigwedge_{r_i} \text{TRY}_{r_i} \rightarrow \text{EF} \bigwedge_{r_i} CS_{r_i} \right) \right) \tag{RW-MREC}$$

This property turns out not to be strong enough to enforce that concurrent access for readers must always be possible. We introduce the following property, which we call Multiple Readers Critical. It states that if a reader is in TRY, and all other readers are in CS, it is possible to enter the CS in a next state – as long as all writers are in NCS, since they have priority access over readers.

$$\text{AG} \left(\bigwedge_{w_i} \text{NCS}_{w_i} \rightarrow \left(\text{TRY}_{r_i} \bigwedge_{r_j \neq r_i} CS_{r_j} \rightarrow \text{EX} \bigwedge_{r_i} CS_{r_i} \right) \right) \tag{RW-MRC}$$

Using this property, we are able to synthesize a structure for two readers and a single writer, in which both readers can enter the critical section concurrently, independently of who enters it first, without blocking each other.

Results. We run benchmarks on problem instances of various numbers of readers and writers, and various combinations of the CTL properties. ASP-structural has identical process constraints, which make it unsuitable to solve an asymmetric problem such as Readers-Writers (we exclude it from these experiments). As with the Mutex problem, as CTLSAT is unable to solve even the simplest problem instances, we do not include benchmarks for the more complex instances.

Our experiments on each variation of the Readers-Writer problem are presented in Table 3. We observe that in general, Readers-Writers instances are easier to solve than Mutex instances with the same number of processes. At the same time, the additional properties introduced by us restrict the problem further, and make the instances harder to solve than the original Readers-Writers formulation. Taken together with the results from Tables 1 and 2, this comparison further strengthens our argument that MONOSAT-generic scales better than ASP-generic. The results also confirm that the structural MONOSAT solver making use of the wildcard encoding performs much better than MONOSAT-generic.

Table 3. Results on the readers-writers instances. Property (RW) is Attie's specification [2]. Data is presented as in Table 1, in the format *time(states)*.

Approach	# of processes (# of readers, # of writers)					
	2 (1, 1)	3 (2, 1)	4 (2, 2)	5 (3, 2)	6 (3, 3)	7 (4, 3)
Property: RW						
CTLSAT	TO	TO	TO	TO	TO	TO
ASP-generic	0.6 (5*)	9.5 (9*)	TO	MEM	MEM	MEM
MONOSAT-gen	0.0 (5*)	0.0 (9*)	2.8 (19*)	30.0 (35*)	5312.7 (74)	TO
MONOSAT-str	0.1 (5)	0.5 (9)	0.7 (19)	2.9 (35)	98.8 (74)	384.4 (142)
Property: RW ∧ NB ∧ NJ						
ASP-generic	6.8 (8*)	2865.5 (16)	MEM	MEM	MEM	MEM
MONOSAT-gen	0.0 (8*)	1.4 (16*)	110.4 (27*)	843.8 (46*)	TO	TO
MONOSAT-str	0.1 (9)	0.2 (16)	3.4 (27)	35.9 (54)	TO	TO
Property: RW ∧ NB ∧ NJ ∧ RW-MREC						
ASP-generic	2.4 (8*)	120.6 (22)	MEM	MEM	MEM	MEM
MONOSAT-gen	0.0 (8*)	238.4 (22*)	TO	TO	TO	TO
MONOSAT-str	0.1 (9)	0.25 (23)	5.3 (52)	159.1 (127)	TO	TO
Property: RW ∧ NB ∧ NJ ∧ RW-MRC						
ASP-generic	2.4 (8*)	TO	MEM	MEM	MEM	MEM
MONOSAT-gen	0.0 (8*)	1114.1 (22)	18.1 (27*)	251.6 (46*)	TO	TO
MONOSAT-str	0.1 (9)	0.2 (23)	2.5 (28)	28.0 (47)	TO	TO

6   Conclusion and Future Work

We have demonstrated a novel approach to CTL synthesis that greatly outperforms existing tools, with the ability to flexibly add additional constraints (e.g., about the structure of the desired solution), and without sacrificing generality (by e.g., assuming identical processes). In many cases, we are also able to compute a provably minimal satisfying Kripke structure.

Our approach is based on formulating CTL model checking in terms of monotonic theories, enabling use of the SAT Modulo Monotonic Theories (SMMT) approach to build an efficient, lazy SAT Modulo CTL solver. This success reinforces the claim that monotonic theories, and more generally the lazy SMT approach, are a performant and versatile basis for SMT solvers.

There are many directions for future work. Although we have not tested this yet, MONOSAT has support for optimization constraints, which might allow one to synthesize *maximally parallel solutions*, as described in [14]. At the implementation level, we have many ideas for improving performance and scalability. We have expended little effort to optimize the CTL model checker at the heart of the theory solver. With improved performance, more applications may be feasible. For example, we believe our solver is suitable for the *repair problem* [1], because we can easily specify constraints of the existing system, repair possibilities, and the specification of correctness. Another promising approach to scalability is to leverage techniques like Attie and Emerson's [3], which rely on synthesizing small 2-process Kripke structures and generalizing them to vast networks of similar processes; using our techniques in conjunction with theirs should allow much more realistic complexity in the pairwise synthesized programs. In a more theoretical direction, we have implemented preliminary support for fairness constraints. If this proves robust and scalable, it may open the door toward synthesis of more expressive temporal logics.

Acknowledgments. This work was supported in part by a grant from the Natural Sciences and Engineering Research Council of Canada. We also thank Javier Esparza for his encouragement and helpful advice.

References

1. Attie, P., Cherri, A., Dak Al Bab, K., Sakr, M., Saklawi, J.: Model and program repair via SAT solving. In: Formal Methods and Models for Codesign (MEMOCODE), pp. 148–157. ACM/IEEE (2015)
2. Attie, P.C.: Synthesis of large concurrent programs via pairwise composition. In: Baeten, J.C.M., Mauw, S. (eds.) CONCUR 1999. LNCS, vol. 1664, pp. 130–145. Springer, Heidelberg (1999)
3. Attie, P.C., Emerson, E.A.: Synthesis of concurrent systems with many similar processes. ACM Trans. Program. Lang. Sys. (TOPLAS) **20**(1), 51–115 (1998)
4. Attie, P.C., Emerson, E.A.: Synthesis of concurrent programs for an atomic read/write model of computation. ACM Trans. Program. Lang. Sys. (TOPLAS) **23**(2), 187–242 (2001)
5. Bayless, S., Bayless, N., Hoos, H.H., Hu, A.J.: SAT modulo monotonic theories. In: Twenty-Ninth AAAI Conference on Artificial Intelligence (2015)
6. Bruns, G., Godefroid, P.: Model checking partial state spaces with 3-valued temporal logics. In: Halbwachs, N., Peled, D.A. (eds.) CAV 1999. LNCS, vol. 1633, pp. 274–287. Springer, Heidelberg (1999)
7. Bustan, D., Grumberg, O.: Simulation-based minimization. ACM Trans. Comput. Logic **4**(2), 181–206 (2003)
8. Clarke, E., Emerson, E.: Design and synthesis of synchronization skeletons using branching time temporal logic. In: Kozen, D. (ed.) Logics of Programs. LNCS, vol. 131, pp. 52–71. Springer, Heidelberg (1982)
9. Courtois, P.J., Heymans, F., Parnas, D.L.: Concurrent control with readers and writers. Commun. ACM **14**(10), 667–668 (1971)
10. De Angelis, E., Pettorossi, A., Proietti, M.: Synthesizing concurrent programs using answer set programming. Fundamenta Informaticae **120**(3–4), 205–229 (2012)
11. de Moura, L., Bjørner, N.: Satisfiability modulo theories: an appetizer. In: Oliveira, M.V.M., Woodcock, J. (eds.) SBMF 2009. LNCS, vol. 5902, pp. 23–36. Springer, Heidelberg (2009)
12. Emerson, E.A., Halpern, J.Y.: Decision procedures and expressiveness in the temporal logic of branching time. In: Symposium on Theory of Computing, STOC 1982, pp. 169–180. ACM (1982)

13. Gebser, M., Kaufmann, B., Neumann, A., Schaub, T.: *clasp*: a conflict-driven answer set solver. In: Baral, C., Brewka, G., Schlipf, J. (eds.) LPNMR 2007. LNCS (LNAI), vol. 4483, pp. 260–265. Springer, Heidelberg (2007)
14. Heymans, S., Van Nieuwenborgh, D., Hadavandi, E.: Synthesis from temporal specifications using preferred answer set programming. In: Coppo, M., Lodi, E., Pinna, G.M. (eds.) ICTCS 2005. LNCS, vol. 3701, pp. 280–294. Springer, Heidelberg (2005)
15. Jacobs, S., Bloem, R.: Parameterized synthesis. In: Flanagan, C., König, B. (eds.) TACAS 2012. LNCS, vol. 7214, pp. 362–376. Springer, Heidelberg (2012)
16. Martin, A.: Adequate sets of temporal connectives in CTL. Electron. Notes Theor. Comput. Sci. **52**(1), 21–31 (2002). EXPRESS 2001, 8th International Workshop on Expressiveness in Concurrency (Satellite Event of CONCUR 2001)
17. Schewe, S., Finkbeiner, B.: Bounded synthesis. In: Namjoshi, K.S., Yoneda, T., Higashino, T., Okamura, Y. (eds.) ATVA 2007. LNCS, vol. 4762, pp. 474–488. Springer, Heidelberg (2007)
18. Sebastiani, R.: Lazy satisfiability modulo theories. J. Satisfiability Boolean Model. Comput. (JSAT) **3**, 141–224 (2007)

Synthesis of Self-Stabilising and Byzantine-Resilient Distributed Systems

Roderick Bloem[1], Nicolas Braud-Santoni[1], and Swen Jacobs[2(✉)]

[1] Graz University of Technology, Graz, Austria
{roderick.bloem,nicolas.braud-santoni}@iaik.tugraz.at
[2] Saarland University, Saarbrücken, Germany
jacobs@react.uni-saarland.de

Abstract. Fault-tolerant distributed algorithms play an increasingly important role in many applications, and their correct and efficient implementation is notoriously difficult. We present an automatic approach to synthesise provably correct fault-tolerant distributed algorithms from formal specifications in linear-time temporal logic. The supported system model covers synchronous reactive systems with finite local state, while the failure model includes strong self-stabilisation as well as Byzantine failures. The synthesis approach for a fixed-size network of processes is *complete* for realisable specifications, and can optimise the solution for small implementations and short stabilisation time. To solve the bounded synthesis problem with Byzantine failures more efficiently, we design an incremental, CEGIS-like loop. Finally, we define two classes of problems for which our synthesis algorithm obtains solutions that are not only correct in fixed-size networks, but in networks of arbitrary size.

1 Introduction

Distributed algorithms are hard to implement. While multi-core processors, communicating embedded devices, and distributed web services have become ubiquitous, it is very hard to correctly construct such systems because of the interplay between separate components and the possibility of uncontrollable faults.

While verification methods try to prove correctness of a system that has been implemented manually, the goal of *synthesis methods* is the automatic construction of systems that satisfy a given formal specification. The difference between these approaches is shown in Fig. 1, illustrating how synthesis can relieve the designer from tedious and error-prone manual implementation and bug-fixing. Despite these benefits, formal methods that guarantee correctness *a priori*, like synthesis, have hardly found their way into distributed system design. This is in contrast to *a posteriori* methods like *verification*, which are being studied very actively [35,45,46].

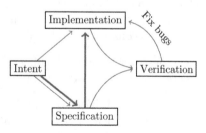

Fig. 1. Comparison of verification $(\longrightarrow)$ and synthesis $(\longrightarrow)$ workflows

© Springer International Publishing Switzerland 2016
S. Chaudhuri and A. Farzan (Eds.): CAV 2016, Part I, LNCS 9779, pp. 157–176, 2016.
DOI: 10.1007/978-3-319-41528-4_9

One reason for this is that the underlying computational problems in synthesis are even harder than in verification. However, research on synthesis has picked up again in recent years [1,8,24,36,52], pushed forward by advances in theorem proving [26,42] and model checking algorithms [10,40] that can be used as building blocks for efficient synthesis algorithms.

In particular, also the synthesis of *concurrent and distributed systems* has received more attention lately. However, research in this area is to a large extent still restricted to basic theoretical problems [23,24] or to simpler sub-problems, such as synthesis of synchronisation for existing programs [12,54].

Failure resilience is critical in this setting, for two reasons: firstly, it enables use in *safety-critical* applications with weaker assumptions on the environment and the component itself. Secondly, it is needed to ensure *scalability* in practice, since in large networks it is unrealistic to assume that all components work without failure. In this work, we consider two kinds of failures: *transient failures*, as exemplified by self-stabilising systems [16,53], where the whole system can be transported to an arbitrary state; and *permanent failures*, as exemplified by Byzantine failures [38], where some processes can deviate arbitrarily from the algorithm they should be executing.

Previous approaches for the synthesis of failure-resilient systems are either restricted in the systems that are considered [14], or in the kinds of failures that are supported [21].[1] For systems that support both self-stabilisation and Byzantine failures, the only result known to us is a problem-specific and semi-automatic approach by Dolev et al. [15], explained in the following.

Motivating Example [15]. Consider the problem of automatically constructing a distributed counter, ranging over m possible values. Processes in the system are arranged in a fully informed clique with synchronous timing, and should satisfy the following properties under self-stabilisation and Byzantine failures:

(a) *agreement*: at every turn, all processes output the *same* value;
(b) *increment*: the value is incremented in each step (mod m).

Since *increment* is an easy-to-implement local property, the main problem is *agreement* on the value. Dolev et al. [15] have recently shown a semi-automatic approach to obtain solutions for this problem. For a fixed number f of Byzantine nodes, they construct the distributed algorithm in two steps:

1. synthesis for a clique of sufficient size n;
2. extension to arbitrarily many processes.

The first step is based on a problem-specific encoding of the synthesis problem into a SAT problem. For a fixed number n of processes, the approach finds a solution – if one exists – by searching for implementations of increasing size and with increasing stabilisation time. The sufficient size of the clique is $n = 3 \cdot f + 1$, since this guarantees that (after stabilisation) the Byzantine nodes

---

[1] Related to this are also approaches for the synthesis of *robust* systems [6], essentially modelling failures in the environment of a single process.

cannot change the majority value [43]. Therefore, processes that are added to a correct system will be correct if they simply replicate the majority output of the existing processes.

The results of Dolev et al. [15] are impressive, since their solutions for the 2-counting problem extend to systems of arbitrary size, and have smaller state space and stabilisation time than any hand-crafted solution before. However, application of their approach to other problems requires significant effort for the development of a problem-specific encoding, and for proving its correctness.

In contrast, we introduce a general-purpose method for synthesis of failure-resilient systems that is fully automatic, can easily be proven correct, and is applicable to a wide range of problems. In particular, our preliminary implementation can replicate the results of Dolev et al. [15] and extend them to n-counting (with $n > 2$).

Contributions. In this paper, we propose a novel approach for the automatic synthesis of Byzantine-tolerant self-stabilising systems, in the form of distributed labelled transition systems. Our synthesis method takes as input a description of the network of processes and a specification in linear-time temporal logic, as well as a bound on the number of Byzantine processes in the network. It encodes the existence of a solution into a problem in satisfiability modulo theories (SMT), and synthesises correct implementations for all processes, if they exist.

We show that our method is correct and complete, and will terminate if a bound on the size of process implementations is given.

The first-order problems that result from our encoding critically need quantification over finite, but possibly large, sets. We provide a dedicated approach to solve those problems incrementally. On a prototype implementation of the approach, we show that this makes our examples tractable.

Finally, we give new results for extending our synthesis method from networks of fixed size to families of networks of unbounded size, based on the notion of *cutoffs* and the Parameterised Synthesis approach [30]. In particular, we define *colourless* specifications (or tasks) for non-terminating systems in cliques and similar network topologies, as well as a class of *local* specifications for networks with a fixed degree. For colourless specifications, we obtain cutoffs that depend on the number of Byzantine nodes, while for local specifications we obtain cutoffs that depend on the stabilisation time.

Structure. We introduce our system model and class of specifications in Sect. 2, and the basic synthesis approach in Sect. 3. We present the incremental approach for solving our synthesis problem in Sect. 4, the extension to parametric networks in Sect. 5, and experimental results in Sect. 6.

2   System and Failure Model, Specifications

We consider distributed systems that are defined by a fixed network of finite-state processes, in a *synchronous* composition: in every global step of the system, each process observes the outputs (possibly the complete state) of neighbouring components, and makes a transition. Our composition models atomic *snapshot*, the classical communication model for self-stabilising systems [13]. Furthermore, synchronous timing (possibly as an abstraction of the system behaviour) is a standard assumption when reasoning about consensus problems, as these problems are undecidable in asynchronous networks in the presence of faults [25,39,47]. To support asynchronous systems, one option is to use an abstraction to an effectively synchronous system, like for example in the model based on "communication rounds" by Dragoi et al. [18].

In the following, we formalise these notions for the case of fixed-size networks. We will consider networks of parametric size in Sect. 5.

2.1   System Model

Labelled Transition Systems. For given finite sets Σ of inputs and Υ of labels – or outputs – a Υ-*labelled Σ-transition system* (or short: a (Υ, Σ)-LTS) $\mathcal{T}$ is a tuple (T, T_0, τ, o) of a set T of states, a set $T_0 \subseteq T$ of initial states, a *transition function* $\tau : T \times \Sigma \rightarrow T$ and a *labelling (or output) function* $o : T \rightarrow \Upsilon$. $\mathcal{T}$ is called *finite* if T is finite.

We consider $\Upsilon = 2^O$ and $\Sigma = 2^I$, representing valuations of a set of Boolean output variables O (controlled by the system) and a set of Boolean input variables I (not controlled by the system).

Communication Graphs, Symmetry Constraints. A *communication graph* C is a tuple $(V, X, \mathcal{I}, \mathcal{O})$, where V is a finite set of nodes, X is a set of system variables, and $\mathcal{I} : V \rightarrow \mathcal{P}(X)$, $\mathcal{O} : V \rightarrow \mathcal{P}(X)$ assign sets of input and output variables to the nodes, with $\mathcal{O}(v) \cap \mathcal{O}(v') = \emptyset$ for all $v \neq v' \in V$. For a given v, we call $(\mathcal{I}(v), \mathcal{O}(v))$ the *interface* of v, and $(|\mathcal{I}(v)|, |\mathcal{O}(v)|)$ the *type* of the interface of v. If $\mathcal{I}(v) \cap \mathcal{O}(v') \neq \emptyset$, i.e., an output of v' is an input of v, then we say that v and v' are *neighbours* in C. Variables that are not assigned (by $\mathcal{O}$) as output variables to any of the nodes are *global input variables*, controlled by the environment. Denote this set of variables as $\mathcal{O}(env)$.

The communication graph may come with a *symmetry constraint*, given as a partitioning $V_1 \dot{\cup} \ldots \dot{\cup} V_m = V$ of the set of nodes. We assume that for every element V_i of the partition, nodes $v, v' \in V_i$ have the same type of interface, and that interfaces of all nodes have a fixed order that identifies corresponding in- and outputs of v and v'. The intended semantics is that nodes in the same element of the partition should have the same implementation modulo this correspondence.

Distributed Systems. An *implementation* of a node $v \in V$ in a communication graph C is a $(2^{\mathcal{O}(v)}, 2^{\mathcal{I}(v)})$-LTS. A *distributed system* is defined by a communication graph C and a finite family $(\mathcal{L}_v)_{v \in V}$ of implementations.

Let $C = (V, X, \mathcal{I}, \mathcal{O})$ be a communication graph with $V = \{v_1, \ldots, v_n\}$, and for every $v_i \in V$ let $\mathcal{L}_i = (L_i, L_{0,i}, \tau_i, o_i)$ be an implementation of v_i in C. The *composition* of $(\mathcal{L}_v)_{v \in V}$ in C is the $(2^X, 2^{\mathcal{O}(env)})$-LTS $\mathcal{G} = (G, G_0, \tau, o)$ with:

- $G = L_1 \times \ldots \times L_n$,
- $G_0 = L_{0,v_1} \times \ldots \times L_{0,v_n}$,
- $o(l_1, \ldots, l_n) = o_1(l_1) \cup \ldots \cup o_n(l_n)$, and

- $\tau((l_1, \ldots, l_n), e) = ((\tau_1(l_1, \sigma_1), \ldots, \tau_n(t_n, \sigma_n)))$, where $\sigma = o(l_1, \ldots, l_n) \cup e$ and σ_i is the restriction of σ to variables in $\mathcal{I}(v_i)$.

Note that this is essentially the same formalism as in Finkbeiner and Schewe's seminal paper [24], and in the following we re-use part of their work on encoding the synthesis problem for such systems into SMT.

2.2 Failure Model

We consider two kinds of failures: *transient failures* that are limited in *time*, but may affect the whole system, and *permanent failures* that are limited in their *locations*, i.e., only affect a subset of the processes. We model these failures as *self-stabilisation* and *Byzantine failures*, respectively. The conjunction of both kinds of failures is called *Byzantine tolerant self-stabilisation* [17].

Self-Stabilisation. Self-stabilisation is the strongest model for *transient failures*, introduced by Dijkstra [13,16,53]; it assumes that the system as a whole fails – once – and is put in an arbitrary state. When the failure is over, processes resume their execution from this state. In transition systems, it is thus easily modelled by making all global states of the system initial.

Since an arbitrary state of the system will in general not satisfy strict safety requirements, in self-stabilisation one usually requires that a specification will *eventually* be satisfied, i.e., after a (either fixed or unknown) *stabilisation time*.

Byzantine Failures. Byzantine failure is a model of *permanent failure* where some processes do not execute the protocol, but are under the control of a *Byzantine adversary*. Our assumptions on the adversary are:

- *non-adaptiveness*: the adversary picks the set of faulty nodes before the algorithm is run;
- *full information*: the adversary can read the global state of the system;
- *computational power*: the adversary has *unbounded* computational power.

In our setting, the *non-adaptiveness* does not remove any power from the adversary [11].[2] Therefore, it is equivalent to the *strong Byzantine adversary*, which subsumes most models of permanent failure. We will consider systems with a fixed upper bound f on the number of Byzantine failures.

2.3 Formal Specifications

We consider formal specifications in linear-time temporal logic (LTL), where the atomic propositions are the system variables. A formula that uses only the input and output variables of a tuple $\overline{v} = (v_1, \ldots, v_k)$ of nodes will sometimes be written $\varphi(\overline{v})$. We assume that the body of our specification is of the form

$$\forall \overline{v} \in V^k : \quad \varphi(\overline{v}),$$

for some $k \leq |V|$.

---

[2] Essentially, this is because our model is not probabilistic, and because the protocol must work for any choice of Byzantine nodes and any behaviour they can exhibit, which includes all possible behaviours of an adaptive adversary.

Example 1. Consider a fully connected network of a set of nodes V. Suppose every process $v \in V$ has a binary output variable c_v. In the 2-counting problem from Sect. 1, every node v has an output c_v, and the formal specification φ is the conjunction

$$\forall v \in V. \quad G\left(c_v = 0 \leftrightarrow X c_v = 1\right)$$
$$\wedge \forall v_1, v_2 \in V. \quad G\left(c_{v_1} = c_{v_2}\right),$$

stating that (for every node) the binary output should be flipped in every step, and (for all pairs of nodes) the output of two nodes should always be the same.

Fault-Tolerant Specifications. Since we consider systems that exhibit both self-stabilisation and Byzantine failures, we need to consider a special type of specifications:

- *self-stabilisation* implies that specifications φ with non-trivial safety requirements (like in Example 1) in general cannot be satisfied without explicitly allowing a stabilisation time. Therefore, we consider specifications φ that are either of the form $F\,\psi$ (if we allow an unspecified stabilisation time), or of the form $X^t\,\psi$ (if we require that the stabilisation time is bounded by t steps).
- *Byzantine failures* imply that the respective nodes can behave arbitrarily, and properties of the specification can not be expected to hold for them. Therefore, we require that for every choice of the Byzantine nodes, the specification holds only for tuples of *correct* nodes, i.e., where none of the nodes is Byzantine. Formally, this means that instead of the original specification $\forall \, \overline{v} \in V^k : \varphi(\overline{v})$ we consider the specification

$$\forall \, \overline{b} \in V^f, \overline{v} \in V^k : \left[\left(\bigwedge_{1 \leq i \leq k, 1 \leq j \leq f} v_i \neq b_j \right) \rightarrow \varphi(\overline{v}) \right]. \tag{1}$$

Example 2. Recall the second part of the 2-counting specification:

$$\forall v_1, v_2 \in V. \quad G\left(c_{v_1} = c_{v_2}\right).$$

For systems with one Byzantine node b in V, this property is modified to:

$$\forall b \in V. \, \forall v_1, v_2 \in V. \quad [(v_1 \neq b \wedge v_2 \neq b) \quad \rightarrow \quad G\left(c_{v_1} = c_{v_2}\right)].$$

3   Bounded Synthesis of Resilient Systems

Synthesising distributed systems is in general undecidable [23,44,48]—with or without failures—and only becomes decidable by bounding the size of the implementation. The *bounded synthesis* problem consists in constructing an implementation that satisfies a given temporal logic specification and a bound on the number of states.

Finkbeiner and Schewe [24] gave an algorithm for bounded synthesis based on an encoding into *satisfiability modulo theories (SMT)*. Inspired by their encoding, we describe in the following an algorithm for the bounded synthesis of distributed systems with Byzantine-tolerant self-stabilisation. The high-level structure of the approach is depicted in Fig. 2.

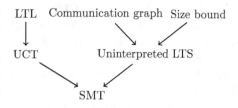

Fig. 2. The *bounded synthesis* approach

Input: Specification and Communication Graph. The input to our synthesis problem is a communication graph $C = (V, X, \mathcal{I}, \mathcal{O})$, possibly with a symmetry constraint $V_1 \dot\cup \ldots \dot\cup V_m = V$, and a (global) temporal specification φ over atomic propositions in X. In the following, let $O = \bigcup_{v \in V} \mathcal{O}(v)$ be the set of global output variables (controlled by the system), and $I = X \setminus O$ the set of global input variables (controlled by the environment) of C.

In the following we encode the existence of local implementations of the nodes in V such that the composition of these implementations in C satisfies φ.

Conversion of the Specification to an Automata. Using the approach of Kupferman and Vardi [37], the specification φ is translated into a *universal co-Büchi tree automaton (UCT)* $\mathcal{A}_\varphi = (Q, q_0, \delta, F)$, where Q is a finite set of states, $q_0 \in Q$ the initial state, $\delta : Q \times 2^O \to \mathcal{P}(Q \times 2^I)$ a transition relation, and $F \subseteq Q$ a set of rejecting states. A given UCT $\mathcal{A}$ *accepts* an $(2^O, 2^I)$-LTS $\mathcal{T}$ if no run in the parallel execution of $\mathcal{A}$ and $\mathcal{T}$ visits a rejecting state infinitely often. The UCT $\mathcal{A}_\varphi$ is constructed such that it accepts an LTS $\mathcal{T}$ if and only if $\mathcal{T} \models \varphi$.

As an optimisation, we use a Safra-less conversion to generalised Rabin automata [50] rather than converting to a co-Büchi automata, as the automatically-generated Rabin automata are smaller. However, co-Büchi and Rabin automata are known to be equally expressive.

Uninterpreted LTS Based on Size Bound and Communication Graph. Let s be a local size bound for implementations of nodes in C. Then, for each node $v_i \in \{v_1, \ldots, v_n\} = V$, we want to find a $(2^{\mathcal{O}(v_i)}, 2^{\mathcal{I}(v_i)})$-LTS $\mathcal{L}_i = (L_i, L_{0,i}, \tau_i, o_i)$, with:

- a set of (local) states L_i with $|L_i| = s$;
- a set of initial states $L_{0,i} \subseteq L_i$;
- a transition function $\tau_i : L_i \times 2^{\mathcal{I}(v_i)} \to L_i$;
- a labelling function $o : L_i \to 2^{\mathcal{O}(v_i)}$.

L_i can be considered a fixed set of elements, while the transition and labelling functions are to be synthesised. That is, in our SMT encoding they are considered as *uninterpreted* functions. If $v_i, v_j \in V_k$ for some V_k in the symmetry constraint, then we introduce just *one* uninterpreted function symbol that is used for both τ_i and τ_j, and similarly for o_i and o_j. This enforces the constraint that both nodes will have the same implementation. The choice of L_{0_i} is explained below.

Encoding of UCT and LTS into SMT Problem. To encode the synthesis problem, we follow the approach of Finkbeiner and Schewe [24]. Let $\mathcal{G} = (G, G_0, \tau, o)$ be the composition of the local implementations $\mathcal{L}_i$ in C. Then, we define an (uninterpreted) *annotation function* $\lambda : Q \times G \to \mathbb{Q} \cup \{\bot\}$ that maps states in the product automaton $\mathcal{A}_\varphi \times \mathcal{G}$ to either $\bot$ or a rational number. To ensure that $\mathcal{G}$ is accepted by $\mathcal{A}_\varphi$, we introduce constraints on λ such that λ tracks whether states in the product automaton $\mathcal{A}_\varphi \times \mathcal{G}$ are reachable, and bounds the number of visits to rejecting states in runs of $\mathcal{A}_\varphi \times \mathcal{G}$. In particular, we require that

$$\forall g_0 \in G_0 : \lambda(q_0, g_0) \neq \bot \tag{2}$$

$$\forall q, q' \in Q, g \in G, \sigma \in \Sigma : \lambda(q, g) \neq \bot \wedge (q', \sigma) \in \delta(q, o(g)) \wedge q' \notin F$$
$$\to \lambda(q', \tau(g, \sigma)) \geq \lambda(q, g) \tag{3}$$

$$\forall q, q' \in Q, g \in G, \sigma \in \Sigma : \lambda(q, g) \neq \bot \wedge (q', \sigma) \in \delta(q, o(g)) \wedge q' \in F$$
$$\to \lambda(q', \tau(g, \sigma)) > \lambda(q, g) \tag{4}$$

The conjunction (2) $\wedge$ (3) $\wedge$ (4), in the following denoted as SMT_φ, encodes the existence of an implementation that satisfies φ in a system *without failures*.

Encoding Self-Stabilisation. We encode self-stabilisation by considering all states of the system as initial states, i.e., $L_{0_i} = L_v$. Thus, a solution to our synthesis problem has to ensure that the specification φ is satisfied for *all* runs that begin in *any* of the states of the composed system. This corresponds directly to the definition of self-stabilisation introduced by Dijkstra [13].

Encoding Byzantine Failures. Byzantine nodes can behave arbitrarily, and the Byzantine adversary has information about the global state of the system [38]. Thus, the behaviour of Byzantine failures can be modelled by allowing them to give arbitrary outputs at any time, essentially re-assigning their outputs to outputs of the adversarial environment.

To encode this, we modify the constraints above such that Byzantine processes are observed with arbitrary output. In particular, if node v_i is Byzantine, then in (3) and (4) we replace each occurrence of a system variable $x \in \mathcal{O}(v_i)$ with a fresh variable x_b, and add a quantifier $\forall x_b \in \mathbb{B}$. For a given formula ψ and $\overline{x}(v) = \mathcal{O}(v)$, this substitution is denoted as $\forall \overline{x_b}(v) \in \mathbb{B}. \psi[\overline{x}(v) \mapsto \overline{x_b}(v)]$.

Example 3. Consider that the first component v_1 is Byzantine, let $\overline{x} = \mathcal{O}(v_1)$, $g = (l_1, \ldots, l_n)$ and $\sigma = (\sigma_1, \ldots, \sigma_n)$. Then, constraint (3) is modified to:

$$\forall \overline{x_b} \in \mathbb{B}, q, q' \in Q, g \in G, \sigma \in \Sigma :$$
$$\lambda(q, g) \neq \bot \wedge (q', \sigma[\overline{x} \mapsto \overline{x_b}]) \in \delta(q, o(g)) \wedge q' \notin F$$
$$\to \lambda(q', (\tau_1(l_1, \sigma_1[\overline{x} \mapsto \overline{x_b}]), \ldots, \tau_n(l_n, \sigma_n[\overline{x} \mapsto \overline{x_b}]))) \geq \lambda(q, g).$$

Finally, since the Byzantine adversary can choose a set of at most f Byzantine nodes, we have to quantify over all possible choices of the adversary. Since the satisfaction of the specification can depend on the choice of processes, we have an important change to the encoding: our quantification has to reflect that the correctness argument, and therefore the witness function λ, can depend on this choice, while the transition and labelling functions τ, o must not depend on this choice. This results in the following encoding:

$$\exists \tau, o. \ \forall \{b_1, \ldots, b_f\} \subseteq V. \ \exists \lambda.$$
$$\forall \overline{x_b}(b_1, \ldots, b_f) \in \mathbb{B}. \ \mathsf{SMT}_\varphi[\overline{x}(b_1, \ldots, b_f) \mapsto \overline{x_b}(b_1, \ldots, b_f)]. \quad (5)$$

Note that with this encoding, all neighbours of a Byzantine process observe the *same* outputs. It is straightforward to have different observed outputs for different neighbours in our encoding, at the cost of introducing one quantified variable for the observation of each neighbour.[3]

Furthermore, note that all quantification is over finite sets, so we can eliminate all quantifiers by Skolemising λ such that it is a function that depends on the choice of $\{b_1, \ldots, b_f\}$, and explicitly instantiating the universal quantifiers.

Correctness. For uninterpreted functions τ, o, λ, satisfiability of our encoding is equivalent to the existence of an LTS that satisfies the specification φ. Moreover, satisfying valuations of τ and o give us a solution to the synthesis problem, and the valuation of λ witnesses correctness of that solution.

Theorem 1 (Correctness for fixed bound). *The constraint system (5) is satisfiable if and only if the specification is finite-state realisable in a self-stabilising system with f Byzantine nodes in the given communication graph. A satisfying assignment of τ and o represents a solution to the synthesis problem.*

Up to the encoding of failures, our encoding is equivalent to that of Finkbeiner and Schewe, and correctness follows from Theorem 5 of [24]. Correctness of the encoding of self-stabilisation is straightforward, and correctness of the encoding of Byzantine failures follows from our elaborations above.

Increasing the Bound. By iterating bounded synthesis for increasing bounds, we obtain a semi-decision procedure for the synthesis problem.

Corollary 1 (General correctness and completeness). *A semi-procedure that iterates bounded synthesis of resilient systems for increasing bounds will eventually find a finite-state implementation of φ if it exists.*

Practical Applicability. Our encoding includes a large number of quantifiers, both universal and existential. Since we consider finite domains, they could all be explicitly instantiated, but experiments show that their full instantiation results in a combinatorial blowup that quickly makes the SMT formula intractable. For non-trivial examples, existing SMT solvers (such as Z3 and CVC3) were unable to solve the resulting problem instances.

---

[3] Also, note that *fail-stop failures* can be seen as a special case of Byzantine failures, and can be modelled in a similar way: instead of giving arbitrary outputs, the chosen nodes at some point move into a special *stop* state, from which they cannot recover.

Abstracting from the universal quantifiers inside the innermost existential quantifier (as these are treated rather efficiently by existing methods like incremental instantiation [29,41] or in some cases simply full instantiation) and the concrete meaning of the function symbols, our synthesis problem is of the form

$$\exists x.\, \forall y.\, \exists z.\, Q(x, y, z)$$

where $Q(x, y, z)$ is an SMT formula and x, y, z are from finite domains. In the following, we introduce a new, incremental algorithm that performs well for instances of this problem produced by our encoding.

4   Incremental Synthesis Algorithm

In this section, we introduce an algorithm that allows us to solve synthesis problems more efficiently than a direct application of an SMT solver on the full encoding of the previous section. To this end, we extend the approach of *Counter-Example-Guided Inductive Synthesis* (CEGIS) [52][51, Chapt. 4] to handle finite model extraction for first-order formulae with two quantifier alternations ($\exists\forall\exists$). Like CEGIS, our algorithm is only guaranteed to terminate when the universal quantification is over a finite domain.

4.1   Previous Work

Solar-Lezama et al. introduced CEGIS [51,52] in the context of template-based synthesis, but it is a general method for solving first-order problems of the form $\exists x.\, \forall y.\, Q(x, y)$. It is complete and terminating if y belongs to a finite domain Y. CEGIS performs *model extraction*, which is crucial when doing synthesis.

In the following, we will use x, y, z as first-order variables and $\hat{x}, \hat{y}, \hat{z}$ as concrete values for these variables. CEGIS proceeds by building a database of *counterexamples* $\hat{y}_i$ for any *candidate* $\hat{x}$ that it has encountered. In the worst case, CEGIS performs $O(|Y|)$ SMT queries until it reaches a conclusion; it is especially efficient if every $\hat{y}$ eliminates a large portion of the possible values for x.

The CEGIS algorithm is shown in Fig. 3. Formula $\phi(x)$ acts as the database of counterexamples. The algorithm uses two incremental SMT solvers. In Line 3, it extracts candidates for x that work for all counterexamples in the database. In Line 5 it uses a new variable y_{n_1} to extract a new counterexample that rejects at least the last candidate $\hat{x}$.

4.2   Extension to First-Order Model Extraction

The encoding of our synthesis problem is of the form

$$\exists x.\, \forall y.\, \exists z.\, Q(x, y, z). \tag{6}$$

In the specific case of our encoding, described earlier, x was called τ and ranges over uninterpreted functions over finite domains; y was called B and

Data: A first-order formula $\exists x.\, \forall y.\, Q(x, y)$
Result: **FALSE** or a value $\hat{x}$ such that $\forall y.\, Q(\hat{x}, y)$ holds

1   Initialise $\phi(x)$ to $\top$ and $n = 0$;
2   **while** *true* **do**
3   **if** $\phi(x)$ *is satisfiable* **then**
4   Extract a concrete value $\hat{x}$ for x from the model;
5   **if** $\neg Q(\hat{x}, y_{n+1})$ *is satisfiable* **then**
6   Extract a concrete value $\hat{y}_{n+1}$ for y_{n+1} from the model;
7               $\phi := \phi \wedge Q(x, \hat{y}_{n+1})$;
8               $n{+}{+}$;
9   **else**
10   **return** $\hat{x}$;
11   **end**
12   **else**
13   **return FALSE**;
14   **end**
15 **end**

Fig. 3. Original CEGIS algorithm, solving $\exists x.\, \forall y.\, Q(x, y)$

ranges over tuples of process identifiers from a finite domain and z was called λ and ranges over the rationals.

While we still keep a set of counterexamples $\hat{y}_i$, candidate generation is now a little more intricate: we look for one $\hat{x}$ and a $\hat{z}_i$ for every $\hat{y}_i$ in the database.

The algorithm is shown in Fig. 4. Here, $y_1 \ldots y_n$ is (still) the database of counterexamples. The candidate extraction is again in Line 3, but is more intricate: it now extracts a candidate $\hat{x}$ for x as well as a candidate $\hat{z}_i$ for each counterexample $\hat{y}_i$. In Line 5 we then look for a new counterexample $\hat{y}_{n+1}$ that shows that the formula is false for $\hat{x}$ and any of the $\hat{z}_i$.

Note that, again, we can use two incremental SMT solvers. In the outer satisfiability call (Line 3), we only add conjunctive constraints to ϕ. In the inner satisfiability call (Line 5), we add conjunctive constraints to $\bigwedge_{i=1}^{n} \neg Q(\hat{x}, y_{n+1}, \hat{z}_i)$ as long as $\hat{x}$ does not change, and we reset the formula if $\hat{x}$ does change.[4]

Correctness Argument. Let us assume the algorithm returns $\hat{x}$. At the point where it returns, it has concrete values $\hat{z}_1 \ldots \hat{z}_n$ such that there is no y that falsifies $Q(\hat{x}, y, \hat{z}_i)$ for all i. This means that for any y, there is a $\hat{z}_i$ such that $Q(\hat{x}, y, \hat{z}_i)$ is satisfied: we indeed exhibited a valid model for the formula.

Conversely, let us assume the algorithm returns **FALSE**: this means that the formula $\phi = \bigwedge_{i=1}^{n} Q(x, \hat{y}_i, z_i)$ is not satisfiable. Assuming our original formula

---

[4] In fact, in our prototype implementation we use a heuristic that avoids throwing away the formula by re-assigning the value of $\hat{x}$ in the formula whenever the outer SMT call returns a new value. Then, we do not throw away the formula at all, but risk that it grows unnecessarily large. In our experiments, this has shown favourable effects.

Data: A first-order formula $\exists x. \forall y. \exists z. Q(x, y, z)$
Result: **FALSE** or a value $\hat{x}$ such that $\forall y. \exists z. Q(\hat{x}, y, z)$ holds

```
1  Initialise φ(x, z₁, ..., zₙ) to ⊤ and n = 0;
2  while true do
3      if φ(x, z₁, ..., zₙ) is satisfiable then
4          Extract concrete values x̂, ẑ₁, ..., ẑₙ for x, z₁, ..., zₙ from the model;
5          if ⋀ⁿᵢ₌₁ ¬Q(x̂, yₙ₊₁, ẑᵢ) is satisfiable then
6              Extract a concrete value ŷₙ₊₁ for yₙ₊₁ from the model;
7              φ := φ ∧ Q(x, ŷₙ₊₁, zₙ₊₁);
8              n++;
9          else
10             return x̂;
11         end
12     else
13         return FALSE;
14     end
15 end
```

Fig. 4. Proposed algorithm, solving $\exists x. \forall y. \exists z. Q(x, y, z)$

was satisfiable, and given a model $x, z(\cdot)$ that satisfies it, then $x, z_i = z(\hat{y}_i)$ would be a model for ϕ: hence, our original formula is UNSAT.

Finally, termination of the algorithm follows from the fact that our domains are finite, which implies that every formula only has finitely many satisfying assignments, and every call to the inner SMT solver strengthens the formula ϕ such that at least one satisfying assignment is removed.

4.3   Related Work

Our work is close to Janota et al. [31] which extends CEGIS to decide QBF formulas with arbitrary quantifier alternation. Janota et al. propose a recursive algorithm which uses a number of nested SMT calls linear in the number of quantifier alternations, whereas we need only two. Moreover, since candidate values are changed by subsequent SMT calls more often, the algorithm cannot efficiently use incremental solving.

Another modification of CEGIS that is close to ours is that of Koksal et al. [34]. At a high level (i.e., the level we chose for our description in this section), their approach is very similar to ours. The differences between the algorithms are in the encoding of synthesis problems, as well as in the specialised verification and synthesis algorithms that are part of the description in Koksal et al. [34]. We chose a higher level of description for the CEGIS algorithm in order to increase its re-usability in different settings.

Finally, another approach for the synthesis of reactive systems that uses incremental refinement of candidate models is *lazy synthesis* [22]. The difference to our approach is that lazy synthesis is not based on CEGIS and a direct encoding of correctness into SAT or SMT, but instead uses LTL model checking and an encoding of error traces into SMT to obtain and refine candidate models. Lazy synthesis does not consider systems with Byzantine failures, but could probably be extended to our setting by extending the LTL model checking to all possible choices of Byzantine nodes and all possible actions taken by the Byzantine adversary. Whether this would be efficient is an open question.

5   Extension to Networks of Unbounded Size

The synthesis method we have introduced thus far is restricted to systems with a fixed number of components. However, correctness in networks of arbitrary size is needed for scalability, as it is unfeasible to synthesise a new solution whenever new processes are introduced into the system. In this section, we show how to obtain process implementations that are correct in systems of arbitrary size, based on the idea of *Parameterised Synthesis* [30]: by combining a general correctness argument for a specific class of systems and specifications, we can synthesise systems that will be correct in networks of unbounded size by synthesising a solution that (i) satisfies the specification and (ii) belongs to the class of systems for which the correctness argument holds.

Parameterised Systems. Let $\mathcal{C}$ be the set of all communication graphs. Then a parameterised communication graph is a function $\Gamma : \mathbb{N} \to \mathcal{C}$, where we assume that every $\Gamma(i)$ comes with a symmetry constraint that separates the nodes into a finite number of implementation classes (with identical interface types). A parameterised communication graph Γ is *of order k* if, for all $n \in \mathbb{N}$, the number of implementation classes in $\Gamma(n)$ is less or equal to k. Then, an *implementation* of a parameterised communication graph Γ of order k is a set of implementations $\{\mathcal{T}_1, \ldots, \mathcal{T}_k\}$ for its nodes, one for each implementation class.

Parameterised Specifications. In specifications of parameterised systems, the atomic propositions are the system variables, indexed by fixed component identifiers or identifier variables. An identifier variable i can be quantified *globally* in the form $\forall i.\varphi$, or *locally* in the form $\forall i : neighbour(x).\varphi$. In every given instance of the parameterised communication graph, this quantification is simply interpreted as a finite conjunction over all possible values for i.

Cutoffs for Parameterised Synthesis. A central notion of parameterised synthesis is the *cutoff*: an upper bound c on the number of nodes in a network that need to be considered, such that components that are correct in the network of size c are also correct in any network of a bigger size. Formally, $c \in \mathbb{N}$ is a cutoff for a set of specifications Φ and a class of systems S if, for every $\varphi \in \Phi$ and every $(\Gamma, \{\mathcal{T}_1, \ldots, \mathcal{T}_k\}) \in S$ (where Γ is of order k), it holds that

$$\forall n > c : \; (\{\mathcal{T}_1, \ldots, \mathcal{T}_k\}, \Gamma(c) \models \varphi \Leftrightarrow \{\mathcal{T}_1, \ldots, \mathcal{T}_k\}, \Gamma(n) \models \varphi).$$

Thus, a cutoff enables parameterised synthesis if and only if we can guarantee that our solution belongs to the system class S. In principle, this idea can directly be applied to failure-resilient systems, but existing cutoff results [2,3,7,19,20,27] usually do not take into account fault-tolerance.

Colourless Specifications. In distributed systems, there is a classical notion of (weakly) *colourless tasks* for terminating executions of a system. This includes many important properties of finite runs, such as consensus and k-set agreement. We extend this notion to infinite runs.

For a given global state $g = (l_1, \ldots, l_n)$ of a system $\mathcal{G}$, a *variant* of g is a state g' that can be obtained from g by changing the local state l_i of one process i to another local state $l_i' \in L_i$, such that $o_i(l_i') = o_j(l_j)$ for some $j \neq i$, or by a sequence of such changes.

Then, define a specification φ to be *colourless* if for every execution trace $o(g_0)o(g_1) \ldots o(g_n) \ldots$ that satisfies φ, and any variant g_n' of g_n, the partial trace $o(g_0)o(g_1) \ldots o(g_{n-1})o(g_n')$ can be extended to a trace that satisfies φ.

An example of a colourless specification is the m-counting specification from our motivating example. Note that colourlessness is a semantic property of a specification, and we do not supply a syntactic fragment of LTL that guarantees colourlessness.

Cutoffs for Colourless Specifications. We show how to extend an n-process system $\mathcal{G}$ satisfying a colourless specification φ into an $(n + k)$-process system, satisfying the same specification. We assume that the processes in $\mathcal{G}$ are fully connected (i.e., in a clique) and that state labels are unique, i.e., the output of a process is sufficient to conclude its current internal state. Based on these assumptions, we show how to synthesise a system that can be considered a larger clique, where the additional processes can have a different implementation.

The additional processes will have an implementation $\mathcal{L}'$ that is different from that of the original processes. $\mathcal{L}'$ reads the current input from the environment and the outputs of processes in the original clique, uses this information (which by assumption lets us conclude their current internal state) as well as knowledge about the original implementation $\mathcal{L}$ to anticipate their next transition, and moves to a state that has the same output as the majority of the next-states in the clique.

To ensure that this will result in a correct system even under up to f Byzantine nodes, we need to enforce an f-*majority property* in the original system: in every round, the output chosen by the largest number of correct nodes is picked by f more nodes than the second largest one.[5] Then, even if the computation of $\mathcal{L}'$ described above includes Byzantine nodes, its output will be equal to that of the majority of original implementations $\mathcal{L}$, and therefore the colourless specification will still be satisfied.

If we are synthesising the original system, the f-*majority property* can be directly encoded as an additional cardinality constraint over the outputs. This constraint preserves satisfiability of the synthesis constraints, even for a given state space.

To see this, assume that a given original system satisfies a colourless specification, but does not have the f-*majority property*. Then we can transform it into a system $\mathcal{G}'$ which simulates $\mathcal{G}$. At each step, processes in $\mathcal{G}'$ simulate $\mathcal{G}$ for one

---

[5] This is an extension of the argument for proving the exact number of Byzantine failures that can be survived while solving consensus problems [38].

step, and check whether f-majority is achieved. If it is not, then we can (partially) determinise the given system to obtain f-*majority*: for instance, nodes can be grouped by output value, and state and output value of some nodes can be replaced with ones from the largest group. The modified system still produces valid runs thanks to the specification being *colourless*.

Theorem 2. *If φ is a colourless specification, C is a fully informed clique and $(\mathcal{L}_v)_{v \in V}$ a set of implementations such that their composition $\mathcal{G}$ in C has the f-majority property and $\mathcal{G} \models \varphi$, then any extension of $\mathcal{G}$ with additional processes $\mathcal{L}'$ as described above will satisfy φ.*

Cutoffs for Local Specifications in Regular Networks. We can also obtain cutoffs for the setting that satisfies the following:

- the networks has a constant-degree – also called regular – where all nodes have the same interface and implementation,
- *local* specifications: specifications of the form $\forall i.\ \mathsf{X}^t\,\mathsf{G}\,\phi(i)$ (where $\phi(i)$ is a Boolean formula over the current state of processes in a maximal distance of r to a process i),
- a fixed number of Byzantine nodes f in a distance of r around any node, and
- a fixed stabilisation time t.

Theorem 3. *Let C be a constant-degree network with a given interface for all nodes, and such that all nodes have a maximal distance of $r + t$ from a central node v. If an implementation $\mathcal{L}$ satisfies a local specification $\varphi(v)$ in C, then $\mathcal{L}$ satisfies $\forall i.\ \varphi(i)$ in any C' with the same degree, the same interface, and a radius greater than $r + t$.*

The cutoff follows from the fact that our specifications only require that we enter the "legitimate states" specified by $\phi(i)$ within t steps, and never leave them afterwards, and within these t steps only information from nodes with this distance can enter the radius around i that $\phi(i)$ talks about. Because of full symmetry in these systems, it is sufficient to require $\varphi(v)$ instead of $\forall i.\ \varphi(i)$.

Specifications that can be expressed as purely first-order formulae can be rewritten as local specifications [9,49]. This suggests that local formulae are expressive enough to be of interest: for instance, consensus is local despite k-set agreement being non-local.[6]

6 Experimental Results

A preliminary implementation was written in OCaml, using Sickert's formally proven correct tool [50] to convert LTL specifications to automata, and de Moura and Bjørner's Z3 [42] as the backend SMT solver.

---

[6] It is not sufficient to prove that k-set agreement is not expressible in FO. However, k-set agreement – for any given $k \geq 2$ – can easily be proven non-local by contradiction.

Experiments were run on a number of computers equipped with 64GiB of memory and eight cores clocked at 2.6 GHz. Note that our solver is sequential and does not take advantage of multicore machines.

We were able to reproduce the results from Dolev *et al.* [15] regarding synchronous 2-counting with a single Byzantine adversary ($f = 1$). Each experiment – for a fixed set of parameters – took at most one hour. As in previous results [15], those solutions can be extended to any system of greater size while keeping the number f of failures, the stabilisation time t and the local state size s constants.

Moreover, we were able to synthesise a symmetric solution for 4-counting, for 4 processes with 5 states each, and stabilisation time 10. This improves on the solution suggested by Dolev et al. to simply duplicate a 2-counter to obtain a 4-counter, which would result in an implementation with 6 local states and a stabilisation time of at least 14 in this case. To our knowledge, this is the first instance of a solution to n-counting (with $n > 2$) ever synthesised. This result shows that our more general approach allows us to obtain even more efficient implementations than that of Dolev et al., without the need to manually devise a new encoding and argue about its correctness.

Class	processes (n)	local states (s)	Total states	Stabilisation time (t)
symmetric	4	3	12	7
	5	3	15	6
	6	3	18	3
	7	2	21	8
	8	2	16	4
general	4	4	16	5
	5	3	15	4
	6	2	12	6

Fig. 5. Synthesised algorithms for 2-counting with a single Byzantine failure

Attempts to replicate these results using directly a first-order model finder – such as CVC3 [5] – or existing extensions of CEGIS [31] resulted either in timeout (no result within 12h) or running out of memory.

Moreover, as mentioned in Sect. 3, we use a translation from LTL to Rabin automata [50]: we compared that approach to encoding universal co-Büchi automata obtained with ltl3ba [4] and observed a speedup from 25 % to 50 % depending on the instance.

7   Conclusion

We have presented a method to automatically synthesise distributed systems that are self-stabilising and resilient to Byzantine failures. We assume that the systems are specified in LTL. Our results apply to finite network graphs and extend to parameterised synthesis of processes on a graph of arbitrary size under reasonable conditions. The approach follows the basic idea of Bounded Synthesis. It constructs an SMT formula with two quantifier alternations that states that a fault-tolerant implementation of a given size exists, and it is complete if a bound on the size of the process implementation is given. We have presented a CEGIS-style decision procedure to decide such formulas that is far more efficient than existing approaches for the formulas we have encountered. Finally, we show that we can efficiently synthesise a small solution for the 2-counter problem.

In this work, we only consider the synthesis of basic building blocks of distributed systems, modelled as labelled transition systems. To obtain actual large-scale implementations, many additional layers of complexity need to be addressed, and in practice there will be a trade-off between formality and automation on the one hand, and scale or precision of the system model on the other hand, as for example demonstrated in recent work of Hawbitzel et al. [28].

In the near future, we plan to extend our approach to more general timing models and to study more general specifications for parameterised synthesis. In particular, we want to extend our approach to the system model of the PSync language of Dragoi et al. [18], which enables reasoning about asynchronous systems by introducing a notion of "communication rounds", and will make our approach applicable to a much larger class of problems. Furthermore, we will look into optimisations of the encoding, as described by Khalimov et al. [32,33] for parameterised synthesis of systems without fault-tolerance.

Acknowledgements. We thank Igor Konnov, Ulrich Schmid, Josef Widder, and the late Helmut Veith for interesting discussions on formal methods for distributed systems. We also thank the anonymous reviewers for their detailed and insightful comments.

This work was supported by the Austrian Science Fund (FWF) through projects LogiCS (W1255-N23), QUAINT (I774-N23) and RiSE (S11406-N23), and by the German Research Foundation (DFG) as part of the Transregional Collaborative Research Center AVACS (SFB/TR 14) and through project ASDPS (JA 2357/2-1).

References

1. Alur, R., Bodik, R., Juniwal, G., Martin, M.M., Raghothaman, M., Seshia, S., Singh, R., Solar-Lezama, A., Torlak, E., Udupa, A., et al.: Syntax-guided synthesis. In: Formal Methods in Computer-Aided Design (FMCAD), 2013, pp. 1–8. IEEE (2013)

2. Aminof, B., Jacobs, S., Khalimov, A., Rubin, S.: Parameterized model checking of token-passing systems. In: McMillan, K.L., Rival, X. (eds.) VMCAI 2014. LNCS, vol. 8318, pp. 262–281. Springer, Heidelberg (2014). http://doai.io/10.1007/978-3-642-54013-4_15

3. Außerlechner, S., Jacobs, S., Khalimov, A.: Tight cutoffs for guarded protocols with fairness. In: Jobstmann, B., et al. (eds.) VMCAI 2016. LNCS, vol. 9583, pp. 476–494. Springer, Heidelberg (2016). doi:10.1007/978-3-662-49122-5_23

4. Babiak, T., Křetínský, M., Řehák, V., Strejček, J.: LTL to Büchi automata translation: fast and more deterministic. In: Flanagan, C., König, B. (eds.) TACAS 2012. LNCS, vol. 7214, pp. 95–109. Springer, Heidelberg (2012). http://doai.io/10.1007/978-3-642-28756-5_8

5. Barrett, C.W., Tinelli, C.: CVC3. In: Damm, W., Hermanns, H. (eds.) CAV 2007. LNCS, vol. 4590, pp. 298–302. Springer, Heidelberg (2007)

6. Bloem, R., Chatterjee, K., Greimel, K., Henzinger, T., Hofferek, G., Jobstmann, B., Könighofer, B., Könighofer, R.: Synthesizing robust systems. Acta Informatica 51(3), 193–220 (2014). http://doai.io/10.1007/s00236-013-0191-5

7. Bloem, R., Jacobs, S., Khalimov, A., Konnov, I., Rubin, S., Veith, H., Widder, J.: Decidability of Parameterized Verification. Synthesis Lectures on Distributed Computing Theory. Morgan & Claypool Publishers, San Rafael (2015). http://doai.io/10.2200/S00658ED1V01Y201508DCT013

8. Bloem, R., Jobstmann, B., Piterman, N., Pnueli, A., Sa'ar, Y.: Synthesis of reactive(1) designs. J. Comput. Syst. Sci. 78(3), 911–938 (2012). http://doai.io/10.1016/j.jcss.2011.08.007

9. Bollig, B.: Logic for communicating automata with parameterized topology. In: CSL-LICS, pp. 18:1–18:10. ACM (2014)

10. Bradley, A.R.: SAT-based model checking without unrolling. In: Jhala, R., Schmidt, D. (eds.) VMCAI 2011. LNCS, vol. 6538, pp. 70–87. Springer, Heidelberg (2011). http://doai.io/10.1007/978-3-642-18275-4_7

11. Canetti, R., Damgrd, I., Dziembowski, S., Ishai, Y., Malkin, T.: On adaptive vs. non-adaptive security of multiparty protocols. In: Pfitzmann, B. (ed.) EUROCRYPT 2001. LNCS, vol. 2045, pp. 262–279. Springer, Heidelberg (2001)

12. Černý, P., Henzinger, T.A., Radhakrishna, A., Ryzhyk, L., Tarrach, T.: Efficient synthesis for concurrency by semantics-preserving transformations. In: Sharygina, N., Veith, H. (eds.) CAV 2013. LNCS, vol. 8044, pp. 951–967. Springer, Heidelberg (2013). http://doai.io/10.1007/978-3-642-39799-8_68

13. Dijkstra, E.W.: Self-stabilizing systems in spite of distributed control. Commun. ACM 17(11), 643–644 (1974)

14. Dimitrova, R., Finkbeiner, B.: Synthesis of fault-tolerant distributed systems. In: Liu, Z., Ravn, A.P. (eds.) ATVA 2009. LNCS, vol. 5799, pp. 321–336. Springer, Heidelberg (2009). http://doai.io/10.1007/978-3-642-04761-9_24

15. Dolev, D., Korhonen, J.H., Lenzen, C., Rybicki, J., Suomela, J.: Synchronous counting and computational algorithm design. In: Higashino, T., Katayama, Y., Masuzawa, T., Potop-Butucaru, M., Yamashita, M. (eds.) SSS 2013. LNCS, vol. 8255, pp. 237–250. Springer, Heidelberg (2013). http://doai.io/10.1007/978-3-319-03089-0_17

16. Dolev, S.: Self-Stabilization. MIT Press, Cambridge (2000)

17. Dolev, S., Welch, J.L.: Self-stabilizing clock synchronization in the presence of Byzantine faults. J. ACM (JACM) 51(5), 780–799 (2004)

18. Dragoi, C., Henzinger, T.A., Zufferey, D.: PSync: a partially synchronous language for fault-tolerant distributed algorithms. In: POPL, pp. 400–415. ACM (2016). http://doai.io/10.1145/2837614.2837650

19. Emerson, E.A., Namjoshi, K.S.: On reasoning about rings. Int. J. Found. Comput. Sci. 14(4), 527–550 (2003). http://doai.io/10.1142/S0129054103001881

20. Emerson, E., Kahlon, V.: Reducing model checking of the many to the few. In: McAllester, D. (ed.) Automated Deduction - CADE-17. LNCS, vol. 1831, pp. 236–254. Springer, Berlin Heidelberg (2000)

21. Faghih, F., Bonakdarpour, B.: SMT-based synthesis of distributed self-stabilizing systems. TAAS 10(3), 21 (2015). http://doai.io/10.1145/2767133

22. Finkbeiner, B., Jacobs, S.: Lazy synthesis. In: Kuncak, V., Rybalchenko, A. (eds.) VMCAI 2012. LNCS, vol. 7148, pp. 219–234. Springer, Heidelberg (2012)
23. Finkbeiner, B., Schewe, S.: Uniform distributed synthesis. In: (LICS 2005), pp. 321–330. IEEE Computer Society (2005). http://doai.io/10.1109/LICS.2005.53
24. Finkbeiner, B., Schewe, S.: Bounded synthesis. STTT **15**(5–6), 519–539 (2013). http://doai.io/10.1007/s10009-012-0228-z
25. Fischer, M.J., Lynch, N.A., Paterson, M.: Impossibility of distributed consensus with one faulty process. J. ACM **32**(2), 374–382 (1985). http://doai.io/10.1145/3149.214121
26. Ganzinger, H., Hagen, G., Nieuwenhuis, R., Oliveras, A., Tinelli, C.: DPLL(T): fast decision procedures. In: Alur, R., Peled, D.A. (eds.) CAV 2004. LNCS, vol. 3114, pp. 175–188. Springer, Heidelberg (2004). http://doai.io/10.1007/978-3-540-27813-9_14
27. German, S.M., Sistla, A.P.: Reasoning about systems with many processes. J. ACM **39**(3), 675–735 (1992)
28. Hawblitzel, C., Howell, J., Kapritsos, M., Lorch, J.R., Parno, B., Roberts, M.L., Setty, S.T.V., Zill, B.: Ironfleet: proving practical distributed systems correct. In: SOSP, pp. 1–17. ACM (2015)
29. Jacobs, S.: Incremental instance generation in local reasoning. In: Bouajjani, A., Maler, O. (eds.) CAV 2009. LNCS, vol. 5643, pp. 368–382. Springer, Heidelberg (2009)
30. Jacobs, S., Bloem, R.: Parameterized synthesis. Log. Methods Comput. Sci. **10**, 1–29 (2014). http://arxiv.org/abs/1401.3588
31. Janota, M., Klieber, W., Marques-Silva, J., Clarke, E.: Solving QBF with counterexample guided refinement. In: Cimatti, A., Sebastiani, R. (eds.) SAT 2012. LNCS, vol. 7317, pp. 114–128. Springer, Heidelberg (2012)
32. Khalimov, A., Jacobs, S., Bloem, R.: PARTY parameterized synthesis of token rings. In: Sharygina, N., Veith, H. (eds.) CAV 2013. LNCS, vol. 8044, pp. 928–933. Springer, Heidelberg (2013)
33. Khalimov, A., Jacobs, S., Bloem, R.: Towards efficient parameterized synthesis. In: Giacobazzi, R., Berdine, J., Mastroeni, I. (eds.) VMCAI 2013. LNCS, vol. 7737, pp. 108–127. Springer, Heidelberg (2013)
34. Köksal, A.S., Pu, Y., Srivastava, S., Bodík, R., Fisher, J., Piterman, N.: Synthesis of biological models from mutation experiments. In: POPL, pp. 469–482. ACM (2013)
35. Konnov, I., Veith, H., Widder, J.: SMT and POR beat counter abstraction: parameterized model checking of threshold-based distributed algorithms. In: Kroening, D., Păsăreanu, C.S. (eds.) CAV 2015. LNCS, vol. 9206, pp. 85–102. Springer, Heidelberg (2015). http://doai.io/10.1007/978-3-319-21690-4_6
36. Kuncak, V., Mayer, M., Piskac, R., Suter, P.: Functional synthesis for linear arithmetic and sets. STTT **15**(5–6), 455–474 (2013). http://doai.io/10.1007/s10009-011-0217-7
37. Kupferman, O., Vardi, M.Y.: Safraless decision procedures. In: FOCS 2005, pp. 531–542. IEEE Computer Society (2005). http://doai.io/10.1109/SFCS.2005.66
38. Lamport, L., Shostak, R., Pease, M.: The Byzantine generals problem. ACM Trans. Program. Lang. Syst. **4**(3), 382–401 (1982). http://doai.io/10.1145/357172.357176
39. Lamport, L.: Brief announcement: leaderless Byzantine paxos. In: Peleg, D. (ed.) Distributed Computing. LNCS, vol. 6950, pp. 141–142. Springer, Heidelberg (2011)
40. McMillan, K.L.: Applying SAT methods in unbounded symbolic model checking. In: Brinksma, E., Larsen, K.G. (eds.) CAV 2002. LNCS, vol. 2404, pp. 250–264. Springer, Heidelberg (2002). http://doai.io/10.1007/3-540-45657-0_19

41. de Moura, L., Bjørner, N.S.: Efficient e-matching for SMT solvers. In: Pfenning, F. (ed.) CADE 2007. LNCS (LNAI), vol. 4603, pp. 183–198. Springer, Heidelberg (2007)

42. de Moura, L., Bjørner, N.S.: Z3: an efficient SMT solver. In: Ramakrishnan, C.R., Rehof, J. (eds.) TACAS 2008. LNCS, vol. 4963, pp. 337–340. Springer, Heidelberg (2008). http://doai.io/10.1007/978-3-540-78800-3_24

43. Pease, M., Shostak, R., Lamport, L.: Reaching agreement in the presence of faults. J. ACM **27**(2), 228–234 (1980)

44. Pnueli, A., Rosner, R.: Distributed reactive systems are hard to synthesize. In: 2013 IEEE 54th Annual Symposium on Foundations of Computer Science 1990, vol. 2, pp. 746–757 (1990)

45. Qadir, J., Hasan, O.: Applying formal methods to networking: Theory, techniques and applications. CoRR abs/1311.4303 (2013). http://arxiv.org/abs/1311.4303

46. Saissi, H., Bokor, P., Muftuoglu, C.A., Suri, N., Serafini, M.: Efficient verification of distributed protocols using stateful model checking. In: SRDS, pp. 133–142. IEEE (2013). http://doai.io/10.1109/SRDS.2013.22

47. Saks, M.E., Zaharoglou, F.: Wait-free k-set agreement is impossible: the topology of public knowledge. SIAM J. Comput. **29**(5), 1449–1483 (2000). http://doai.io/10.1137/S0097539796307698

48. Schewe, S.: Distributed synthesis is simply undecidable. Inf. Process. Lett. **114**(4), 203–207 (2014). http://doai.io/10.1016/j.ipl.2013.11.012

49. Schwentick, T., Barthelmann, K.: Local norms forms for first-order logic with applications to games and automata. In: Meinel, C., Morvan, M. (eds.) STACS 1998. LNCS, vol. 1373, pp. 444–454. Springer, Heidelberg (1998)

50. Sickert, S.: Converting linear temporal logic to deterministic (generalised) rabin automata. Archive of Formal Proofs 2015 (2015)

51. Solar Lezama, A.: Program synthesis by sketching. Ph.D. thesis, EECS Department, University of California, Berkeley (2008). http://www.eecs.berkeley.edu/Pubs/TechRpts/2008/EECS-2008-177.html

52. Solar-Lezama, A., Tancau, L., Bodík, R., Seshia, S.A., Saraswat, V.A.: Combinatorial sketching for finite programs. In: ASPLOS 2006, pp. 404–415. ACM (2006). http://doai.io/10.1145/1168857.1168907

53. Tixeuil, S.: Self-stabilizing algorithms. In: Algorithms and Theory of Computation Handbook. Applied Algorithms and Data Structures, 2nd edn, pp. 26.1–26.45. Chapman & Hall/CRC, CRC Press, Taylor & Francis Group (2009)

54. Vechev, M., Yahav, E., Yorsh, G.: Inferring synchronization under limited observability. In: Kowalewski, S., Philippou, A. (eds.) TACAS 2009. LNCS, vol. 5505, pp. 139–154. Springer, Heidelberg (2009). http://doai.io/10.1007/978-3-642-00768-2_13

Constraint Solving I

A Decision Procedure for Sets, Binary Relations and Partial Functions

Maximiliano Cristiá[1,2]([⊠]) and Gianfranco Rossi[3]

[1] CIFASIS-UNR, Rosario, Argentina
cristia@cifasis-conicet.gov.ar
[2] LSIS-AMU, Marseille, France
[3] Università degli Studi di Parma, Parma, Italy
gianfranco.rossi@unipr.it

Abstract. In this paper we present a decision procedure for sets, binary relations and partial functions. The language accepted by the decision procedure includes untyped, hereditarily finite sets, where some of their elements can be variables, and basically all the classic set and relational operators used in formal languages such as B and Z. Partial functions are encoded as binary relations which in turn are just sets of ordered pairs. Sets are first-class entities in the language, thus they are not encoded in lower level theories. The decision procedure exploits set unification and set constraint solving as primitive features. The procedure is proved to be sound, complete and terminating. A Prolog implementation is presented.

1 Introduction

Set theory is a widely accepted formalism for software specification. Used as a modeling language (e.g. Z and B) it usually includes binary relations and partial functions seen as sets of ordered pairs[1]. On the other hand, formal verification tools, such as SMT solvers and theorem provers, support sets but usually by encoding them in other theories (e.g. arrays or predicate calculus). These encodings may lose or complicate specific semantic properties of set theory. Therefore, we think that a decision procedure for set theory (DPST) may complement these approaches if sets are first-class entities of the language.

The first step in defining a DPST is to precisely define the class of sets to be dealt with. Formal set theory traditionally focuses on sets as the only entities in the domain of discourse (*pure* sets). We extend this view by allowing arbitrary *non-set* entities as first-class citizens of the language (*hybrid* sets). In particular, our sets will allow ordered pairs as elements to accommodate binary relations. Furthermore, we restrict our attention to *unbounded finite sets*. Hence, sets can contain a finite number of elements, which can be either non-set elements—*flat sets*—or other finite sets—*nested sets*. This class of sets is commonly indicated as *hereditarily finite hybrid sets*.

---

[1] From now on, the term 'set' will always include binary relations and partial functions and the term 'binary relation' will include partial functions, unless stated differently.

© Springer International Publishing Switzerland 2016
S. Chaudhuri and A. Farzan (Eds.): CAV 2016, Part I, LNCS 9779, pp. 179–198, 2016.
DOI: 10.1007/978-3-319-41528-4_10

Another aspect of the sets to be considered is whether their elements can contain variables or not. For example, if x is a variable then $\{x\}$ is a set that actually represents as many different sets as values x can take. The DPST presented here works with sets whose elements can be either constant terms, variables or compound terms possibly containing variables. Furthermore, a part of any set can be left underspecified (i.e. this part can contain any number of elements).

The third issue to be considered is the family of operators of the language. Since we want a DPST for plain sets but also for binary relations and partial functions, then the supported operators include all the classic set operators (such as union, intersection, etc.) as well as widely used relational operators (such as domain, range, relational image, etc.).

Our DPST extends the decision procedure presented in [1]. This procedure is able to prove satisfiability of (quantifier-free) formulas of a constraint language over the universe of hereditarily finite sets. Here we consider the extension of this language, and its relevant decision procedure, to binary relations.

Whilst binary relations can be easily represented in the set constraint language of [1] as sets of pairs, there are basic operations on relations that cannot be expressed directly in this language, such as projection onto the domain/range of a relation and relational composition. Cristiá et al. [2] showed how these operations can be implemented as user-defined predicates by exploiting the full power, e.g. recursive definitions, of the general-purpose logic programming language where the set constraint language is embedded. When binary relations are completely specified this approach turns out to be quite satisfactory. On the other hand, when some elements of a relation or (part of) the relation itself are left unspecified—i.e., they are represented by variables—then this approach presents major flaws. For example, if the predicate $ran(R, A)$, which is intended to hold if A is the range of the binary relation R, is implemented through recursion on its first argument, then solving a goal such as $ran(R, \{1\})$, where R is a variable, will generate infinitely many distinct solutions $R = \{(x_1, 1)\}, R = \{(x_1, 1), (x_2, 1)\}, \ldots$, where x_i are variables. Given an unsatisfiable formula, such as $ran(R, \{1\}) \wedge ran(R, \{\})$, then the computation will loop forever.

Thus, support for binary relations must be added as new *primitive* features to the base language and its solver extended accordingly. An extension of the set constraint language of [1] to support partial functions is described in [3]. The resulting solver, however, is *incomplete*: if it returns *false* the input formula is surely unsatisfiable, whereas if it returns a formula in an irreducible form then we cannot conclude that the input formula is surely satisfiable. For example, the following formula (where $dom(R, A)$ holds if A is the domain of R and $A \parallel B$ holds if A and B are disjoint sets)[2]

$$ran(R, \{1\}) \wedge ran(S, \{1, 2\}) \wedge dom(R, A) \wedge dom(S, A) \wedge R \parallel S$$

is unsatisfiable with respect to the underlying interpretation structure, but the solver in [3] is not able to prove this fact.

---

[2] In the rest of the paper we will use $R, S, T, \ldots$ for relations; $f, g, h, \ldots$ for functions; $A, B, C, \ldots$ for sets; $t, u, v, w, x, y, z, \ldots$ for any other object.

In this paper we show how the proposal in [3] can be extended and substantively improved in order to: (i) support both *binary relations* and partial functions; (ii) provide a *complete* solver, rather than an incomplete one as in [3].

Dealing with binary relations exhibits some difficulties that are not present in the case of partial functions. For example, the predicate $dom(R, \{1\})$ has just one solution if R is a partial function—i.e. $R = \{(1, x)\}$, x variable—, whilst it has infinitely many solutions if R is just a binary relation. Similar difficulties arise for the composition of binary relations. Thus, enlarging our domain of discourse from partial functions to general binary relations requires a few non-trivial extensions. Completeness of the solver in [3] is strongly compromised by the presence in the final formula of irreducible predicates of the form $ran(R, \{\dots\})$ which make it difficult to check satisfiability of the formula. In this paper we prove that these predicates are expressible in terms of relational composition, hence they can be always eliminated. This result, along with the application of a procedure for removing all inequalities involving set variables borrowed from [1], allows the solver to generate irreducible formulas whose satisfiability is immediately apparent. The solver for the new language takes the form of a rewrite system acting on conjunctions of positive and negative primitive predicates. The rewrite rules reduce the syntactic complexity of these predicates and eliminate inequalities involving sets, until a fixpoint is reached. The generated formula can be either *false* or a disjunction of formulas in a simplified irreducible form, which is proved to be equisatisfiable with the original formula. The ability to prove that formulas in this form are surely satisfiable allows us to turn our solver into a DPST.

The proposed DPST is implemented in Prolog, as part of the $\{log\}$ tool (pronounced 'setlog') [4].

The paper is structured as follows. In Sect. 2, we present the main features of a set-based language extended to deal with binary relations. The DPST for this language is described in Sect. 3, by giving the rewrite rules for the solver. In Sect. 4 we show how our proposal can be further extended to incorporate partial functions as well. An empirical assessment of the implementation of the DPST, as part of the $\{log\}$ tool, is presented in Sect. 5. In Sect. 6 we compare our work with related proposals. The conclusions of this paper are in Sect. 7.

2   A Set-Based Language with Binary Relations

In this section we describe the syntax and (informal) semantics of our set-based language, called $\mathcal{L}_{\mathcal{BR}}$. For the sake of presentation, we consider first only the case of binary relations. Then, in Sect. 4, we add support also for partial functions.

Syntax of the language is defined primarily by giving the signature upon which terms and formulas of the language are built.

Definition 1 (Signature). *The signature $\Sigma_{\mathcal{BR}}$ of $\mathcal{L}_{\mathcal{BR}}$ is a quadruple $\langle \mathcal{F}, \Pi_C,$ $\Pi_U, \mathcal{V} \rangle$ where: $\mathcal{F}$ contains the constant $\{\}$, the binary function symbol $\{\cdot \mid \cdot\}$ and a set $\mathcal{F}'$ of user-defined constant and function symbols, including at least the binary function symbol $(\cdot, \cdot)$; Π_C is the set of primitive predicate symbols $\{=, \in, un, \|$*

, $set\} \cup \{dom, ran, comp, rel\}$; Π_U *is the set of* user-defined *predicate symbols, where* $\Pi_C \cap \Pi_U = \{\}$; $\mathcal{V}$ *is a denumerable set of variables.*

The $\Sigma_{\mathcal{BR}}$-*terms* are built using symbols in $\mathcal{F}$ and $\mathcal{V}$. The (uninterpreted) symbol $(\cdot, \cdot)$ is used to construct ordered pairs: (t, u), where t and u are $\Sigma_{\mathcal{BR}}$-terms, represents the pair with components t and u. $\{\}$ and $\{\cdot \mid \cdot\}$ are interpreted symbols, used to construct sets: $\{\}$ represents the empty set; $\{t \mid A\}$ represents the set composed of the elements of the set A plus the element t, i.e. $\{t\} \cup A$. Terms built using $\{\}$ and $\{\cdot \mid \cdot\}$ are called set terms.

Definition 2 (Set terms). *A set term is a* $\Sigma_{\mathcal{BR}}$-*term of the form* $\{\}$ *or* $\{t \mid A\}$ *where* t *is any term built over* $\mathcal{V} \cup \mathcal{F}$ *and* A *is a variable in* $\mathcal{V}$ *or a set term.*

We use the notation $\{t_1, t_2, \ldots, t_n \mid A\}$ as a shorthand for $\{t_1 \mid \{t_2 \mid \cdots \{t_n \mid A\} \cdots \}\}$ and the notation $\{t_1, t_2, \ldots, t_n\}$ as a shorthand for $\{t_1, t_2, \ldots, t_n \mid \{\}\}$. Observe that one can write terms representing sets which are nested at any level. Also, observe that the $\mathcal{L}_{\mathcal{BR}}$ language is in fact parametric with respect to a constraint domain based on the set of function symbols $\mathcal{F}'$ and the set of predicate symbols Π_U; this should allow us to easily accommodate for sets of elements of any type, e.g. sets of integers.

Example 1. The following terms are all set terms (assume that $1, 2, 3 \in \mathcal{F}'$): $\{1, 2\}$, denoting a set composed of two elements, 1 and 2; $\{x, \{\{\}, \{1\}\}, \{1, 2, 3\}\}$, denoting a set containing nested sets; $\{x, y \mid A\}$, where x, y and A are variables, denoting a *partially specified* set containing one or two elements, depending on whether x is equal to y or not, and a, possibly empty, unknown part A.

Binary relations are just sets of ordered pairs. Therefore, $\mathcal{L}_{\mathcal{BR}}$ does not introduce any special symbol to represent binary relations, since they can be conveniently represented as sets.

Definition 3 (Binary relations). *Let* $x_i, y_i, i = 1, \ldots, n$, *be* $\Sigma_{\mathcal{BR}}$-*terms. A set term* R *represents a* binary relation *if* R *has one of the following forms:* $\{\}$, *or* $\{(x_1, y_1), (x_2, y_2), \ldots, (x_n, y_n)\}$, *or* $\{(x_1, y_1), (x_2, y_2), \ldots, (x_n, y_n) \mid S\}$, *and* S *is either a variable or a set term representing a binary relation.*

Forcing a set R to represent a binary relation will be obtained at run-time by including the predicate $rel(R)$.

Definition 4 ($\mathcal{BR}$-constraints). *Let* t, u *be* $\Sigma_{\mathcal{BR}}$-*terms,* A, B, C *be variables or set terms,* R, S, T *be variables or set terms representing binary relations. A* $\mathcal{BR}$-*constraint is an atomic predicate of one of the following forms:* $t = u, t \in A, un(A, B, C), A \parallel B, set(t), dom(R, A), ran(R, A), comp(R, S, T), rel(A).$

When useful, we will refer to a $\mathcal{BR}$-constraint based on a predicate symbol p simply as a *p-constraint*. The interpretation of symbols in $\Sigma_{\mathcal{BR}}$ is given according to the *interpretation structure* $\mathcal{A}_{\mathcal{BR}} = \langle \mathcal{S}, (\cdot)^{\mathcal{S}} \rangle$, where $\mathcal{S}$ is the interpretation domain and $(\cdot)^{\mathcal{S}}$ is its associated interpretation function. In particular, the predicate symbols in Π_C are interpreted as in their intuitive meaning. Let $\bar{\alpha}$ denote the interpretation of the symbol α, i.e. $(\alpha)^{\mathcal{S}}$. Then: $\bar{t} =^{\mathcal{S}} \bar{u}$ (equality) iff $\bar{t}$ is identical to $\bar{u}$ in $\mathcal{S}$; $\bar{t} \in^{\mathcal{S}} \bar{A}$ (membership) iff there exists an element in $\bar{A}$ identical to $\bar{t}$ in $\mathcal{S}$; $un^{\mathcal{S}}(\bar{A}, \bar{B}, \bar{C})$ (union) iff $\bar{C} =^{\mathcal{S}} \bar{A} \cup \bar{B}$; $\bar{A} \parallel^{\mathcal{S}} \bar{B}$ (disjointness) iff $\bar{A} \cap \bar{B} =^{\mathcal{S}} \{\}$; $dom^{\mathcal{S}}(\bar{R}, \bar{A})$ (domain) iff $\bar{A} =^{\mathcal{S}} dom\,\bar{R}$; $ran^{\mathcal{S}}(\bar{R}, \bar{A})$ (range) iff $\bar{A} =^{\mathcal{S}} ran\,\bar{R}$; $comp^{\mathcal{S}}(\bar{R}, \bar{S}, \bar{T})$ (relational composition) iff $\bar{T} =^{\mathcal{S}} \bar{R} \,\mathring{,}\, \bar{S} =^{\mathcal{S}} \{(x,z) : \exists y((x,y) \in^{\mathcal{S}} \bar{R} \wedge (y,z) \in^{\mathcal{S}} \bar{S})\}$; $set^{\mathcal{S}}(\bar{t})$ iff $\bar{t}$ is a set; $rel^{\mathcal{S}}(\bar{t})$ iff $\bar{t}$ is a binary relation (notice that rel implies set).

Equality between sets is regulated by the standard *extensionality axiom*, which has been proved in [5] to be equivalent for hereditarily finite sets to the following equational axioms [1]: $(Ab)\{x \mid \{x \mid A\}\} = \{x \mid A\}$; $(C\ell)\{x \mid \{y \mid A\}\} = \{y \mid \{x \mid A\}\}$. Axiom (Ab) states that duplicates in a set do not matter (*Absorption property*). Axiom $(C\ell)$ states that the order of elements in a set is irrelevant (*Commutativity on the left*). These two properties capture the intuitive idea that, for instance, the set terms $\{1,2\}, \{2,1\}$, and $\{1,2,1\}$ all denote the same set $\{1,2\}$. Conversely, equality between non-sets is regulated by standard equality axioms. In particular, equality between ordered pairs (i.e. terms built using the function symbol $(\cdot, \cdot)$) calls into play standard (syntactic) unification.

The admissible formulas that our DPST can deal with are defined as follows.

Definition 5 ($\mathcal{L}_{\mathcal{BR}}$-formulas). *A $\mathcal{L}_{\mathcal{BR}}$-formula is a conjunction of $\mathcal{BR}$-constraints and negations of the $\mathcal{BR}$-constraints $=$ and $\in$ (denoted $\neq$ and $\notin$, respectively).*

Example 2. The following formula is an admissible $\mathcal{L}_{\mathcal{BR}}$-formula: $1 \in A \wedge 1 \notin B \wedge un(A, B, C) \wedge C = \{x\}$. Its informal interpretation is: the set C is the union between sets A and B; A must contain 1 and B must not; and C must be a singleton set. Note that all variables in a $\mathcal{L}_{\mathcal{BR}}$-formula are intended as implicitly existentially quantified.

A critical issue in the definition of $\mathcal{L}_{\mathcal{BR}}$ is how "rich" the set of primitive predicate symbols Π_C must be. Minimizing the number of predicate symbols in Π_C has the advantage of simplifying the language and possibly its implementation. On the other hand, there could be other basic set operators that cannot be expressed as $\mathcal{L}_{\mathcal{BR}}$-formulas if Π_C is too small. Dovier et al. [1] proved that $\{=, \in, un, \parallel, set\}$ is enough to define most other useful set-theoretical predicates, such as $\subseteq$, $diff$ and $inters$[3]. Here, we extend this result to binary relations by showing that the new extended collection of primitive predicates in $\Sigma_{\mathcal{BR}}$ is enough to define several relational operators widely used in formal notations such as B [6] and Z [7]. Among others, these notations define: domain anti-restriction as $A \lhd R = \{(x,y) : (x,y) \in R \wedge y \notin A\}$; relational image as $R[A] = \{y : \exists x((x,y) \in R \wedge x \in A)\}$; and overriding between $R, S \in X \leftrightarrow Y$ as $R \oplus S = (dom\,S \lhd R) \cup S$.

---

[3] $diff(A, B, C)$ holds iff $C = A \setminus B$; and $inters(A, B, C)$ holds iff $C = A \cap B$.

Theorem 1. *Predicates based on predicate symbols: dres (domain restriction, ◁), rres (range restriction, ▷), dares (domain anti-restriction, ◁̸), rares (range anti-restriction, ▷̸), rimg (relational image, · [·]) and oplus (overriding, ⊕) can be replaced by equivalent $\mathcal{L}_{\mathcal{BR}}$-formulas involving predicates based on $\subseteq, \|$, un, diff, dom, and ran, possibly adding new fresh variables.*

Proof (proofs of theorems in [8]). The following equivalences hold:

$$dres(A, R, S) \iff un(S, T, R) \land dom(S, B) \land B \subseteq A \land dom(T, C) \land A \parallel C$$
$$rres(A, R, S) \iff un(S, T, R) \land ran(S, B) \land B \subseteq A \land ran(T, C) \land A \parallel C$$
$$dares(A, R, S) \iff dres(A, R, T) \land diff(R, T, S)$$
$$rares(B, R, S) \iff rres(B, R, T) \land diff(R, T, S)$$
$$rimg(A, R, B) \iff dres(A, R, T) \land ran(T, B)$$
$$oplus(R, S, T) \iff dom(S, A) \land dares(A, R, Q) \land un(Q, S, T)$$

Thanks to Theorem 1, the language that our DPST can deal with is much richer than the language described in Definition 1. In fact, all the relational predicates mentioned in Theorem 1 can be easily made available by (automatically) replacing them with the corresponding equivalent $\mathcal{L}_{\mathcal{BR}}$-formulas, before calling the solver. On the other hand, the ability to express these predicates as $\mathcal{L}_{\mathcal{BR}}$-formulas allows us to not consider them in the definition of the DPST for our language and to focus our attention only on the $\mathcal{BR}$-constraints.

Remark 1. Selecting an adequate collection of primitive (as opposed to user-defined) predicates for dealing with binary relations is a non-trivial original result of this paper. It is worth noting, however, that the proposed collection is not the only possible choice. Proving that it is the minimal one, as well as comparing our choice with other possible choices, in terms of, e.g., expressive power, completeness, effectiveness, and efficiency, is out of the scope of the present work.

3   A Decision Procedure for Sets and Binary Relations

A DPST for a subset of the language $\mathcal{L}_{\mathcal{BR}}$ which includes only primitive predicates based on $=, \in, un, \|$, and *set* is proposed in [1]. In particular, the proposed procedure exploits *set unification* [9] to deal with equalities between set terms.

In this section we extend the DPST of [1] to $\mathcal{L}_{\mathcal{BR}}$ thus supporting binary relations; in Sect. 4 this language and the DPST are further extended to accommodate for partial functions.

3.1   The Solver

The global organization of the solver for $\mathcal{L}_{\mathcal{BR}}$, called $SAT_{\mathcal{BR}}$, is shown in Algorithm 1. $SAT_{\mathcal{BR}}$ uses three procedures: sort_infer, remove_neq and STEP.

sort_infer is used to automatically add the $\mathcal{BR}$-constraints based on *set* and *rel* to the input formula C to force variables to be sets or binary relations. The added constraints for a variable X are deduced from the form of the terms or constraints where X occurs. When X is expected to represent a binary relation, $rel(X)$ is automatically added. For example, if C contains $dom(R, A)$ then sort_infer(C) will add $rel(R) \land set(A)$ to C. The procedure remove_neq deals with the elimination of $\neq$-constraints involving set variables. Its motivation and definition will be made evident later in this section.

STEP applies specialized rewriting procedures to the current formula C and returns the modified formula. Each rewriting procedure applies a few non-deterministic rewrite rules—see next subsection—which reduce the syntactic complexity of the $\mathcal{BR}$-constraints of one kind. The execution of STEP is iterated until a fixpoint is reached—i.e., the formula cannot be simplified any further. Notice that STEP returns *false* whenever (at least) one of the procedures in it rewrites C to *false*. Moreover, STEP(*false*) returns *false*.

Algorithm 1. The $SAT_{\mathcal{BR}}$ solver. C is the input formula.

$C \leftarrow$ sort_infer(C);
repeat
    $C' \leftarrow C$;
    repeat
        $C'' \leftarrow C$;
        $C \leftarrow$ STEP(C);
    until $C = C''$;
    $C \leftarrow$ remove_neq(C)
until $C = C'$;
return C

When no rewrite rule applies to the considered $\mathcal{L}_{\mathcal{BR}}$-formula then the corresponding rewriting procedure terminates immediately and the formula remains unchanged. Since no other rewriting procedure deals with the same kind of $\mathcal{BR}$-constraints, the irreducible atomic formulas will be returned as part of the answer computed by $SAT_{\mathcal{BR}}$. The following definition precisely characterizes the form of the formulas returned by $SAT_{\mathcal{BR}}$.

Definition 6 (Solved form). *Let C be a $\mathcal{L}_{\mathcal{BR}}$-formula and let X and X_i be variables and t a term. A literal c of C is in* solved form *if it has one of the following forms:*

(i) *$X = t$ and neither t nor $C \setminus \{c\}$ contain X;*
(ii) *$X \neq t$ and X does not occur neither in t nor as an argument of any predicate $p(\cdots), p \in \{un, dom, ran, comp\}$, in C;*
(iii) *$t \notin X$ and X does not occur in t;*
(iv) *$un(X_1, X_2, X_3)$, where X_1 and X_2 are distinct variables, and for $i = 1, 2, 3$ there are no inequalities of the form $X_i \neq t$ in C;*
(v) *$X_1 \parallel X_2$, where X_1 and X_2 are distinct variables;*
(vi) *$dom(X_1, X_2)$, where X_1 and X_2 are distinct variables, and there are no inequalities of the form $X_i \neq t, i = 1, 2$, in C;*

(vii) $ran(X_1, X_2)$, *where X_1 and X_2 are distinct variables, and there are no inequalities of the form $X_i \neq t, i = 1, 2$, in C;*

(viii) $comp(X_1, t, X_2)$ *and* $comp(t, X_1, X_2)$, *where t is not the empty set, and there are no inequalities of the form $X_i \neq t, i = 1, 2$, in C;*

(ix) $set(X), rel(X)$.

A $\mathcal{L}_{\mathcal{BR}}$-*formula C is in solved form if it is* true *or if all its literals are simultaneously in solved form.*

The solved form literals allow trivial verification of satisfiability.

Theorem 2 (Satisfiability of solved form). *Any $\mathcal{L}_{\mathcal{BR}}$-formula in solved form is satisfiable w.r.t. the underlying interpretation structure $\mathcal{A}_{\mathcal{BR}}$.*

Proof (sketch; proofs of theorems in [8]*).* Basically, the proof of this theorem uses the fact that, given a $\mathcal{L}_{\mathcal{BR}}$-formula in solved form C, we are able to guarantee the existence of a successful assignment of values to all variables of C using pure sets only (in particular, the empty set for all set variables), with the only exception of the variables x occurring in terms of the form $x = t$ in C.

Notice that the result of Theorem 2 would no longer be true for predicates based on *dom, ran,* and *comp* if we allowed the presence of literals of the form $X_i \neq t$ in C. These literals are eliminated by remove_neq, which is explained in the next subsection.

Given a $\mathcal{L}_{\mathcal{BR}}$-formula C, $SAT_{\mathcal{BR}}$ non-deterministically transforms C to either *false* or to a finite collection of $\mathcal{L}_{\mathcal{BR}}$-formulas in *solved form*. According to Theorem 2 a $\mathcal{L}_{\mathcal{BR}}$-formula in solved form is always satisfiable. Moreover, as we will see in the next subsection, the disjunction of the formulas in solved form generated by $SAT_{\mathcal{BR}}$ preserves the set of solutions of the original formula C. We will come back to these results in the next subsection after having presented in more detail some of the rewrite rules used by $SAT_{\mathcal{BR}}$.

3.2   Rewriting Procedures

In what follows, we present some key rewrite rules of our DPST; the complete list is in [4]. The rewrite rules are given as $P \to \Phi$ where P is a $\mathcal{BR}$-constraint and Φ is a disjunction of $\mathcal{BR}$-constraints; if Φ has more than one disjunct then the rule is non-deterministic. $\mathcal{T}_{\mathcal{BR}}$ denotes the set of all $\Sigma_{\mathcal{BR}}$-terms; and $\mathcal{T}_{\mathcal{BR}}^{Set}$ the subset of set terms. Variable names n and N (possibly with sub and superscripts) are used to denote fresh variables. $A \not\equiv \{\}$ means that term A is not the term denoting the empty set; $\dot{x}$, for any name x, is a shorthand for $x \in \mathcal{V}$.

Figure 1 lists the rules for dealing with =-constraints, as presented in [1]. These rules implement a set unification algorithm which embeds the equational axioms (Ab) and $(C\ell)$ shown above. In particular, rules (6) and (7) handle equalities between two set terms.

If $x, y, t, t_i, u_i : \mathcal{T}_{\mathcal{BR}}$; $A, B : \mathcal{T}_{BR}^{Set} \cup \mathcal{V}$; $n, m \geq 0$, then:

$$\dot{x} = \dot{x} \rightarrow true \tag{1}$$

$$t = \dot{x} \rightarrow \dot{x} = t, \text{ if } t \notin \mathcal{V} \tag{2}$$

$$\dot{x} = \{t_0, \ldots, t_n \mid A\} \rightarrow false, \text{ if } \dot{x} \in vars(t_0, \ldots, t_n) \tag{3}$$

$$\begin{aligned} &\dot{x} = \{t_0, \ldots, t_n \mid \dot{x}\} \rightarrow \\ &\quad \dot{x} = \{t_0, \ldots, t_n \mid N\}, \text{ if } \dot{x} \notin vars(t_0, \ldots, t_n) \end{aligned} \tag{4}$$

$$\begin{aligned} &\dot{x} = t \rightarrow \text{substitute } t \text{ by } \dot{x} \text{ in the formula} \\ &\quad \text{if rules (3) and (4) do not apply} \end{aligned} \tag{5}$$

$$\begin{aligned} &\{x \mid A\} = \{y \mid B\} \rightarrow \\ &\quad x = y \wedge A = B \\ &\quad \vee\, x = y \wedge \{x \mid A\} = B \\ &\quad \vee\, x = y \wedge A = \{y \mid B\} \\ &\quad \vee\, A = \{y \mid N\} \wedge \{x \mid N\} = B, \text{ if rule (7) does not apply} \end{aligned} \tag{6}$$

$$\begin{aligned} &\{t_0, \ldots, t_m \mid \dot{x}\} = \{u_0, \ldots, u_n \mid \dot{x}\} \rightarrow \\ &\quad t_0 = u_j \wedge \{t_1, \ldots, t_m \mid \dot{x}\} = \{u_0, \ldots, u_{j-1}, u_{j+1}, \ldots, u_n \mid \dot{x}\} \\ &\quad \vee\, t_0 = u_j \wedge \{t_0, \ldots, t_m \mid X\} = \{u_0, \ldots, u_{j-1}, u_{j+1}, \ldots, u_n \mid \dot{x}\} \\ &\quad \vee\, t_0 = u_j \wedge \{t_1, \ldots, t_m \mid \dot{x}\} = \{u_0, \ldots, u_n \mid \dot{x}\} \\ &\quad \vee\, \dot{x} = \{t_0 \mid N\} \wedge \{t_1, \ldots, t_m \mid N\} = \{u_0, \ldots, u_n \mid N\} \end{aligned} \tag{7}$$

Fig. 1. Rewrite rules for equality

Figure 2 lists the rules dealing with the elimination of *ran*-constraints. Rule $(r\mathcal{V}^R)$ deals with the case in which the range of R is $\{x_1, \ldots, x_n \mid B\}, n > 1$. The result of repeatedly applying this rule is that R is rewritten as follows:

$$(B_1 \times \{x_1\} \cup \cdots \cup B_n \times \{x_n\}) \cup Q$$

where $B_1, \ldots, B_n$ are new fresh variables, and $\operatorname{ran} Q = B$. Rule (ro) deals with the case in which the range is a singleton set and removes the *ran*-constraint by replacing it with an equivalent conjunction of *comp* and $\neq$-constraints.

Figure 3 lists three of the six rules for *dom*-constraints. As can be seen they are symmetric to those of *ran*-constraints, as are also the rules not shown here. It is worth noting that the last two rules in Figs. 2 and 3 are crucial to prove satisfiability of the solved form (i.e. Theorem 2).

The rules in Fig. 4 deal with *comp*-constraints. In these rules, $un(A, B, C, D)$ is a shorthand for $un(A, B, N) \wedge un(N, C, D)$. Rules $(c\ \mathcal{V})$ and $(c\mathcal{V}^T)$ are based on the following equality:

If $R, A : \mathcal{T}_{\mathcal{BR}}^{Set} \cup \mathcal{V}$; $A \not\equiv \{\}$; $x, y : \mathcal{T}_{\mathcal{BR}}$ then:

$$ran(\dot{R}, \dot{R}) \rightarrow \dot{R} = \{\} \qquad\qquad (r\bot)$$

$$ran(R, \{\}) \rightarrow R = \{\} \qquad\qquad (r\{\})$$

$$ran(\{\}, A) \rightarrow A = \{\} \qquad\qquad (r\{\}^R)$$

$$ran(\{(x,y) \mid R\}, A) \rightarrow A = \{y \mid N_1\} \wedge ran(R, N_1) \qquad\qquad (r\mathcal{V})$$

$$ran(\dot{R}, \{y \mid B\}) \rightarrow un(N_1, N_2, \dot{R}) \wedge ran(N_1, \{y\}) \wedge ran(N_2, A) \qquad\qquad (r\mathcal{V}^R)$$

$$ran(\dot{R}, \{y\})\} \rightarrow comp(\dot{R}, \{(y,y)\}, \dot{R}) \wedge \dot{R} \neq \{\} \qquad\qquad (r\circ)$$

Fig. 2. Rewrite rules for *ran*-constraints

If $R, A, B : \mathcal{T}_{\mathcal{BR}}^{Set} \cup \mathcal{V}$; $B \not\equiv \{\}$; $x, y : \mathcal{T}_{\mathcal{BR}}$ then:

$$dom(\{(x,y) \mid R\}, A) \rightarrow A = \{x \mid N_1\} \wedge dom(R, N_1) \qquad\qquad (d\mathcal{V})$$

$$dom(\dot{R}, \{x \mid B\}) \rightarrow un(N_1, N_2, \dot{R}) \wedge dom(N_1, \{x\}) \wedge dom(N_2, B) \qquad\qquad (d\mathcal{V}^R)$$

$$dom(\dot{R}, \{x\})\} \rightarrow comp(\{(x,x)\}, \dot{R}, \dot{R}) \wedge \dot{R} \neq \{\} \qquad\qquad (d\circ)$$

Fig. 3. Rewrite rules for *dom*-constraints

$$(Q \cup R) \,\mathbin{\raise1pt\hbox{$\circ$}}\, (S \cup T) = (Q \,\mathbin{\raise1pt\hbox{$\circ$}}\, S) \cup (Q \,\mathbin{\raise1pt\hbox{$\circ$}}\, T) \cup (R \,\mathbin{\raise1pt\hbox{$\circ$}}\, S) \cup (R \,\mathbin{\raise1pt\hbox{$\circ$}}\, T)$$

Intuitively, this equality states that the composition of two "big" relations can be computed by computing the union of the composition of "smaller" relations.

Some of the rewrite rules for *dom* and *comp*-constraints are the extensions to binary relations of simpler rules presented in [3] that are correct only for partial functions (see Fig. 8). In particular, $\mathcal{BR}$-constraints of the form $dom(R, A)$, where R is a variable and A is a not-empty set, dealt with by rule $(d\mathcal{V}^R)$, can be easily rewritten to a finite conjunction of equalities when R represents a partial function. Conversely, this is no longer true if R represents a binary relation. In fact, if A is for instance the set $\{1\}$, R admits an infinite number of distinct solutions: $R = \{(1, y_1)\}, R = \{(1, y_1), (1, y_2)\} \wedge y_1 \neq y_2$, etc.

The remaining primitive constraint of $\mathcal{L}_{\mathcal{BR}}$ is *rel*. The rewrite rules for processing this constraint are listed in Fig. 5. As can be seen, they are straightforward. Rule $(\leftrightarrow \mathcal{V})$ states the obvious fact that the empty set is a binary relation; whereas rule $(\leftrightarrow \mathcal{V})$ recursively checks that each element in R is an ordered pair.

The $\mathcal{L}_{\mathcal{BR}}$-formula returned by repeatedly applying the rewrite rules (i.e., the result of executing the inner loop of Algorithm 1) is not necessarily a formula in

If $Q, R, S, T : \mathcal{T}_{BR}^{Set} \cup \mathcal{V}; \; t_i, u_i, x, z : \mathcal{T}_{BR}; \; h * k > 1$ then:

$$comp(\{\}, S, T) \rightarrow T = \{\} \qquad\qquad (cR\{\})$$

$$comp(R, \{\}, T) \rightarrow T = \{\} \qquad\qquad (cS\{\})$$

$$comp(R, S, \{\}) \rightarrow ran(R, N_1), dom(S, N_2), N_1 \parallel N_2 \qquad (cT\{\})$$

$$
\begin{aligned}
comp(R, S, \{(x, z) \mid Q\}) \rightarrow \\
R = \{(x, n) \mid N_1\} \wedge S = \{(n, z) \mid N_2\} \\
\wedge \, comp(\{(x, n)\}, N_2, N_3) \wedge comp(N_1, \{(n, z)\}, N_4) \\
\wedge \, comp(N_1, N_2, N_5) \wedge un(N_3, N_4, N_5, \{(x, z) \mid Q\})
\end{aligned}
\qquad (c\mathcal{V})
$$

$$
\begin{aligned}
comp(\{(x, u)\}, \{(t, z)\}, \dot{T}) \rightarrow \\
u = t \wedge \dot{T} = \{(x, z)\} \vee u \neq t \wedge \dot{T} = \{\}
\end{aligned}
\qquad (c11\mathcal{V}^T)
$$

$$
\begin{aligned}
comp(\{(x_1, t_1), \ldots (x_h, t_h) \mid R\}, \{(u_1, z_1), \ldots (u_h, z_k) \mid S\}, \dot{T}) \rightarrow \\
\bigwedge_{i=1}^{h} \bigwedge_{j=1}^{k} comp(\{(x_i, t_i)\}, \{(u_j, z_j)\}, N_{ij}) \\
\wedge \bigwedge_{i=1}^{h} comp(\{(x_i, t_i)\}, S, N_i^S) \\
\wedge \bigwedge_{j=1}^{k} comp(R, \{(u_j, z_j)\}, N_j^R) \\
\wedge \, comp(R, S, N^{RS}) \\
\wedge \, un(N_{11}, \ldots, N_{hk}, N_1^S, \ldots, N_h^S, N_1^R, \ldots, N_k^R, N^{RS}, \dot{T})
\end{aligned}
\qquad (c\mathcal{V}^T)
$$

Fig. 4. Rewrite rules for *comp*-constraints

If $R : \mathcal{T}_{BR}^{Set} \cup \mathcal{V}; \; t : \mathcal{T}_{BR}$ then:

$$rel(\{\}) \rightarrow true \qquad\qquad (\leftrightarrow\{\})$$

$$rel(\{t \mid R\}) \rightarrow t = (n_1, n_2) \wedge rel(R) \qquad (\leftrightarrow\mathcal{V})$$

Fig. 5. Rewrite rules for *rel*-constraints

solved form (see Definition 6). Hence, it is not guaranteed to be satisfiable. For example, the $\mathcal{L}_{\mathcal{BR}}$-formula

$$un(A, B, C) \wedge A \parallel C \wedge dom(R, A) \wedge R \neq \{\}$$

cannot be further rewritten by any of the rewrite rules considered above. Nevertheless, it is clearly unsatisfiable (the only solution for $un(A, B, C) \wedge A \parallel C$ is $A = \{\} \wedge C = \{\}$, whereas $A = \{\}$ is not a solution for $dom(R, A) \wedge R \neq \{\}$).

In order to guarantee that $SAT_{\mathcal{BR}}$ returns either *false* or $\mathcal{L}_{\mathcal{BR}}$-formulas in solved form, we still need to remove all inequalities of the form $X \neq t$, where X is a variable, occurring as an argument of $\mathcal{BR}$-constraints based on either $un, dom, ran,$ or $comp$. This is performed (see Algorithm 1) by executing the procedure remove_neq, which applies the rewrite rules described by the generic rule scheme of Fig. 6. Basically, these rules exploit extensionality to state that nonequal sets can be distinguished by asserting that a fresh element belongs to one but not to the other.

Let P be $p(X_1, \ldots, X_n)$, $p \in \{un, dom, ran, comp\}$, $n = 2, 3$; let X be X_i, $i = 1, 2, 3$; let t be a term

$$P \wedge X \neq t \rightarrow (P \wedge n \in X \wedge n \notin t) \vee (P \wedge n \in t \wedge n \notin X) \qquad (E\neq)$$

Fig. 6. Rule scheme for $\neq$-constraint elimination rules

As an example, the $\mathcal{L}_{\mathcal{BR}}$-formula $un(A, B, C) \wedge A \neq D$ is rewritten to either $un(A, B, C) \wedge n \in A \wedge n \notin D$ or $un(A, B, C) \wedge n \notin A \wedge n \in D$. Notice that, in the special case in which t is the empty set, the second disjunct of rule $(E\neq)$ is surely false, and the rule comes down to simply add the $\mathcal{BR}$-constraint $n \in X$ (i.e. $X = \{n \mid A\}$) to C. Thus, for example, given the $\mathcal{L}_{\mathcal{BR}}$-formula $comp(R, \{(y, y)\}, R) \wedge R \neq \{\}$, the application of rule $(E \neq)$ replaces $R \neq \{\}$ with $R = \{t \mid S\}$ which will lead to solve the $\mathcal{BR}$-constraint $comp(\{t \mid S\}, \{(y, y)\}, \{t \mid S\})$.

Termination of $SAT_{\mathcal{BR}}$ is stated by the following theorem.

Theorem 3 (Termination). *The $SAT_{\mathcal{BR}}$ procedure can be implemented in such a way it terminates for every input $\mathcal{L}_{\mathcal{BR}}$-formula C.*

Termination of $SAT_{\mathcal{BR}}$ and the finiteness of the number of non-deterministic choices generated during its computation guarantee the finiteness of the number of $\mathcal{L}_{\mathcal{BR}}$-formulas non-deterministically returned by $SAT_{\mathcal{BR}}$. Therefore, $SAT_{\mathcal{BR}}$ applied to a $\mathcal{L}_{\mathcal{BR}}$-formula C always terminates, returning either *false* or a (finite) collection of $\mathcal{L}_{\mathcal{BR}}$-formulas in solved form.

The following theorem ensures that the collection of $\mathcal{L}_{\mathcal{BR}}$-formulas in solved form generated by $SAT_{\mathcal{BR}}$ preserves the set of solutions of the input formula.

Theorem 4 (Equisatisfiability). *Let C be a $\mathcal{L}_{BR}$-formula and $C_1, C_2, \ldots, C_n$ be the collection of $\mathcal{L}_{BR}$-formulas in solved form returned by $SAT_{BR}(C)$. Then $C_1 \vee C_2 \vee \cdots \vee C_n$ is equisatisfiable to C, that is, every possible solution[4] of C is a solution of one of the $\mathcal{L}_{BR}$-formulas returned by $SAT_{BR}(C)$ and, vice versa, every solution of one of these formulas is a solution for C.*

Thanks to Theorems 2, 3 and 4 we can conclude that, given a $\mathcal{L}_{BR}$-formula C, C is satisfiable with respect to the intended interpretation structure if and only if there is a non-deterministic choice in $SAT_{BR}(C)$ that returns a $\mathcal{L}_{BR}$-formula in solved form—i.e. different from *false*. Hence, SAT_{BR} is a decision procedure for testing satisfiability of $\mathcal{L}_{BR}$-formulas.

4   A Decision Procedure for Partial Functions

A binary relation is a partial function if and only if no two ordered pairs share the same first component. Hence, the definition of a set term representing a binary relation (Definition 3) can be adapted to partial functions as follows:

Definition 7 (Partial functions). *Let $x_i, y_i, i = 1, \ldots, n$, be Σ_{BR}-terms. A set term f represents a partial function if f has one of the forms: $\{\}$, or $\{(x_1, y_1), (x_2, y_2), \ldots, (x_n, y_n)\}$, or $\{(x_1, y_1), (x_2, y_2), \ldots, (x_n, y_n) \mid g\}$, and g is either a variable or a set term representing a partial function, and the constraints $x_i \neq x_j, x_i \notin \text{dom}\, g$, hold for all $i, j = 1, \ldots, n, i \neq j$.*

The addition of partial functions is a substantive extension of the language $\mathcal{L}_{BR}$ since distinguishing the relations that are partial functions cannot be achieved without an additional primitive predicate. Thus we add the symbol *pfun* to Π_C, with the obvious meaning: *pfun(t)* holds iff t is a partial function (notice that *pfun* implies *rel*). Users should add a *pfun*-constraint for those sets they want to represent partial functions. The rewrite rules for *pfun*-constraints are listed in Fig. 7. As can be seen, rules $(\twoheadrightarrow \{\})$ and $(\twoheadrightarrow \mathcal{V})$ are similar to those of Fig. 5 for *rel*-constraints, but $(\twoheadrightarrow \mathcal{V})$ clearly imposes the notion of function.

If $f : \mathcal{T}_{BR}^{Set} \cup \mathcal{V}; t : \mathcal{T}_{BR}$ then:

$pfun(\{\}) \rightarrow true$ $\qquad\qquad\qquad\qquad\qquad\qquad\qquad (\twoheadrightarrow\{\})$

$pfun(\{t \mid f\}) \rightarrow t = (n_1, n_2) \wedge dom(f, N) \wedge n_1 \notin N \wedge pfun(f)$ $\qquad (\twoheadrightarrow\mathcal{V})$

Fig. 7. Rewrite rules for *pfun*-constraints

---

[4] More precisely, each solution of C expanded to the variables occurring in C_i but not in C, so to account for the possible fresh variables introduced into C_i.

The new language is called $\mathcal{L}_{\mathcal{PF}}$; the formulas that can be expressed in this language are the $\mathcal{L}_{\mathcal{BR}}$-formulas extended with *pfun* atoms. Given that partial functions are binary relations all the set and relational operators can be applied to them. In turn, function application (*apply*) and the identity function over a given set (*id*) can be replaced as we did in Theorem 1 due to:

Theorem 5. *The following equivalences hold:*

$$apply(f, x, y) \iff (x, y) \in f \wedge pfun(f)$$
$$id(A, f) \iff dom(f, A) \wedge ran(f, A) \wedge comp(f, f, f) \wedge pfun(f)$$

At the theoretical level, the same rewrite rules can be applied for relations and partial functions. From a practical point of view, however, it is convenient to introduce a few new rewrite rules which are specifically devoted to deal with partial functions. These rules are automatically applied in place of the corresponding ones for binary relations whenever the solver detects that the terms involved in the $\mathcal{BR}$-constraint at hand are constrained to be partial functions through *pfun*-constrains. The overall organization of the solver, however, remains unchanged (see Algorithm 1). All the rewrite rules specialized for partial functions can be found in [4]. As an example, rule (8) of Fig. 8 replaces $(d\mathcal{V}^R)$ and (do) of Fig. 3; and rule $(c\mathcal{V})$ replaces rule (9) of Fig. 4. It is evident that using the specialized rules allows the rewriting process to be sensibly simplified, hence, in general, to obtain better performance for the solver.

If $f, g, h, A : \mathcal{T}_{\mathcal{BR}}^{Set} \cup \mathcal{V}; x, z : \mathcal{T}_{\mathcal{BR}}$ then:

$$dom(\dot{f}, \{x \mid A\}) \wedge pfun(\dot{f}) \rightarrow \dot{f} = \{(x, n) \mid N\} \wedge dom(N, A) \wedge pfun(\dot{f}) \tag{8}$$

$$comp(f, g, \{(x, z) \mid h\}) \rightarrow$$
$$f = \{(x, n) \mid N_1\} \wedge g = \{(n, z) \mid N_2\} \wedge comp(N_1, g, h) \tag{9}$$

Fig. 8. Specialized rewrite rules for *dom* and *comp* dealing with partial functions

In contrast to [3], we assume here that the $\mathcal{BR}$-constraints of the form $ran(R, \{y \mid B\})$ are always eliminated by using rules $(r\mathcal{V}^R)$ and (ro), and that the $\neq$-constraint elimination rules (Fig. 6) are always applied. Thus, the definition of solved form formula is the same given for binary relations, except for the addition of the $\mathcal{BR}$-constraint $pfun(X)$, X variable. This is enough to guarantee that the result of Theorem 2 holds for partial functions as well. Moreover, since *pfun* is the only new predicate symbol, the termination of the decision procedure is not modified. Also the formulation of Theorem 4 remains unchanged. Thus the $SAT_{\mathcal{BR}}$ solver can be used as a decision procedure also for $\mathcal{L}_{\mathcal{PF}}$-formulas.

5   Empirical Assessment

This section presents the results of an empirical evaluation of the $SAT_{\mathcal{BR}}$ solver. $SAT_{\mathcal{BR}}$ is implemented in Prolog as part of $\{log\}$ version 4.9.1-20. The empirical evaluation consists in running $\{log\}$ on more than 2,400 formulas including sets, partial functions, binary relations and some of their operators. The objectives of this evaluation are: *(a)* to asses the efficiency and effectiveness of $\{log\}$ in solving set-based formulas; and *(b)* to compare these results with previous versions of $\{log\}$ to determine if the decision of including a decision procedure for binary relations and partial functions as part of its kernel was indeed good.

Around 2,000 of the $\mathcal{L}_{\mathcal{BR}}$-formulas to evaluate $\{log\}$ have been generated from 10 different Z specifications, some of which are formalizations of real requirements and, in general, they cover a wide range of applications—totalizing around 3,000 lines of Z code. We consider that they are a representative sample.

In relation to item *(a)* mentioned above, we want to know: *(i)* how many satisfiable and unsatisfiable formulas are found by $\{log\}$ in a reasonable time; and *(ii)* how long it takes to process all the formulas.

Experiments were performed on a 4 core Intel Core™ i5-2410M CPU at 2.30 GHz with 4 Gb of main memory, running Linux Ubuntu 12.04 (Precise Pangolin) 32-bit with kernel 3.2.0-95-generic-pae. $\{log\}$ 4.9.1-20 over SWI-Prolog 7.2.3 for i386 was used during the experiments. A 10 seconds timeout was set as the maximum time that $\{log\}$ can spend to give an answer for each goal (i.e. formula to be proved).

Table 1 displays the results of the experiments. The left-hand side of the table shows the results of running a previous version of $\{log\}$ (i.e. 4.8.2-2, which does not implement a decision procedure for $\mathcal{L}_{\mathcal{BR}}$), while the right-hand side shows the results with the current version. The meaning of the columns is as follows: GOALS, number of goals processed during the experiment; S, number of goals detected as satisfiable (in less than 10 s); U, number of goals detected as unsatisfiable (in less than 10 s); A, percentage of goals for which $\{log\}$ gives a meaningful answer; T, time spent by $\{log\}$ during the entire execution (in seconds).

As can be seen, $\{log\}$ 4.9.1-20 outperforms 4.8.2-2 in the number of goals for which $\{log\}$ gives a meaningful answer (either sat or unsat), although it performs faster for some experiments and slower for others. However, the total time spent by the new version in processing all the goals is lower (around 20 %) than the total time spent by the previous version. Note that 4.9.1-20 hits 100 % of right answers in all but three sets of goals while 4.8.2 does it only in 5.

As the formulas considered in these experiments seldom use binary relations, we have also developed a set of 300 formulas specially tailored to evaluate the rewrite rules for binary relations. In order to perform an evaluation as objective as possible, we took as base formulas the *standard partitions* proposed by the Test Template Framework (TTF) [10] for the relational operators of the Z notation. The standard partitions of the TTF are used in test case generation applications to generate test cases to exercise the implementation of the corresponding operators. Due to space limits, we can only show the net results of

Table 1. Summary of empirical assessment

Z Specification	Goals	4.8.2-2				4.9.1-20			
		S	U	A	T	S	U	A	T
SWPDC	196	99	26	64 %	1,402	99	45	73 %	711
Plavis	232	151	33	79 %	510	156	28	79 %	582
Scheduler	205	38	161	97 %	125	39	165	99 %	108
Security class	36	20	14	94 %	31	20	16	100 %	14
Bank (1)	100	25	75	100 %	28	25	75	100 %	44
Bank (3)	104	52	49	97 %	64	52	52	100 %	46
Lift	17	17	0	100 %	6	17	0	100 %	6
Launcher vehicle	1,206	23	1,183	100 %	370	23	1,183	100 %	558
Symbol table	27	11	16	100 %	9	11	16	100 %	9
Array of sensors	16	8	8	100 %	5	8	8	100 %	5
Totals	2,139	444	1,565		2,552	450	1,588		2,084
Binary relations	300					223	60	94 %	954

these experiments in the last row of Table 1. A comparison with version 4.8.2-2 is not possible as this version does not implement rules for binary relations. As can be seen, $\{log\}$ 4.9.1-20 solves 94 % of the goals that fire the rewrite rules for binary relations. A detailed description of these experiments and the related results can be downloaded from [4].

The experimental results show that completing the solver for binary relations and partial functions has been beneficial also from a practical point of view.

6   Discussion and Similar Approaches

The decidability issue for logic languages involving set operators and, possibly, relational operators, has been addressed both in the so-called *Computable Set Theory* (CST) field ([11] is a general survey), and in other more collateral fields such as Description Logics (see e.g. [12]). Work in CST has identified increasingly larger classes of computable formulas of suitable sub-theories of Zermelo-Fraenkel set theory for which satisfiability is decidable. It is of particular relevance to the DPST presented here, the work by Cantone et al. [13,14], where they demonstrate that there is a decision procedure for a language similar to $\mathcal{L}_{BR}$. Further extensions of the classes of computable formulas have been also considered, e.g. [15,16]. Hence, the decidability result presented in this paper is for the most part not new, although $\mathcal{L}_{BR}$ is not exactly the same language studied by other authors (e.g. the *comp*-constraint is not considered by others, at our knowledge). However, all the mentioned related works are mainly concerned with the decidability result in itself; no, or very little, concern is devoted to computing solutions and to providing an effective implementation of these results.

A number of proposals have been developed in the context of *constraint programming* that consider more restricted forms of set constraints but equipped with more efficient constraint solving techniques, e.g. [17–19]. However, the core language considered here [1] allows more general forms of sets to be dealt with: in particular, elements can be of any type, possibly other sets, and possibly unknown (e.g., $\{x, \{a, 1\}\}$). This has proved crucial to support the extensions described in this paper, where sets of pairs are naturally used to represent binary relations and partial functions.

Regarding the more specific problem of dealing with relations or partial functions, only very few works have addressed this problem in the context of constraint programming. For instance, the Conjunto language [18] provides relation variables where the domain and the range are limited to completely specified finite sets. Map variables where the domain and range of the mapping can be also finite set variables are introduced in CP(Map) [20]. All these proposals, however, do not consider the more general case of partially specified relations—where some elements of the domain or the range can be left unknown—which, on the contrary, are essential in our proposal. Moreover, the collection of primitive constraints on relation/map variables they provide is usually quite restricted.

The problem of deciding the satisfiability of formulas involving sets has also been approached by the formal verification community. Proof assistants [21–23] normally encode (typed) sets as predicates or as functions from a type onto the Boolean type. In this way, set operators are expressed in logical terms and thus a set formula becomes a quantified predicate. Theorem provers also support (total) functions, usually, as a primitive type [21,22]. In this context, functions are not expressed in terms of set theory. Theorems provers normally include extensive theorem libraries that are used by proving strategies.

Besides, SMT solvers provide support for sets by encoding them into other theories such as arrays or uninterpreted functions. As far as we know there is no SMT solver providing a decision procedure for sets, binary relations and partial functions where all of them are first-class entities. Kröning et al. [24] recognized the need of a solver for finite sets. This solver would be included in SMT solvers and would provide a SMT-LIB compatible interface. de Moura and Bjørner [25] show how some set operators can be defined over a very general theory of arrays. Proof assistants usually interact with SMT solvers. In particular, there are works showing how set theories supported by proof assistants can be encoded in different automated provers [26,27]. In some of these approaches, set formulas are flatten to the set membership level [26]. The Alloy analyzer [28] can find solutions to formulas involving binary relations but only if they are bound to finite domains. In fact, this tool transforms the formula into a SAT problem where all possible relations are represented. We believe that the approach presented here would be complementary to these other works since it takes full advantage of the semantics of sets, as described by a suitable set theory.

7 Conclusions

In this paper we have shown how to extend the decision procedure for hereditarily finite sets presented in [1] by adding to it binary relations and partial functions as first-class citizens of the language. Since binary relations and partial functions can be viewed as sets, all facilities for set manipulation offered in [1] are immediately available to manipulate relations and partial functions as well. We have added to the language a (limited) number of new primitive constraints, specifically devoted to deal with relations and partial functions and we have provided sound, complete and terminating rewriting procedures for them. We have also shown that basically all the classic set and relational operators widely used in formal notations such as B and Z are easily added to the base language by defining them as admissible formulas of the language itself. The resulting solver—implemented in Prolog—can be used as an effective decision procedure for sets, binary relations and partial functions.

Investigating the integration of our decision procedure into mainstream SMT solvers, such as CVC4, is a main goal of our future research. In this regard, the fact that $\mathcal{L}_{\mathcal{BR}}$ is parametric with respect to an arbitrary set of function and predicate symbols should allow us to easily combine our language with other existing theories. In particular, following the approach given in [29], we plan to extend our language and its relevant decision procedure to allow sets to be combined with integers in the presence of a cardinality operator, as proposed for instance in [30,31]. Another line of investigation is to extend the DPST as to allow for the definition of functions as intentional sets.

Acknowledgments. We would like to thank the reviewers, and specially the reviewer acting as our shepherd, for helping us to improve this paper. The work of M. Cristiá was partially supported by ANPCyT PICT 2014-2200.

References

1. Dovier, A., Piazza, C., Pontelli, E., Rossi, G.: Sets and constraint logic programming. ACM Trans. Program. Lang. Syst. **22**(5), 861–931 (2000)
2. Cristiá, M., Rossi, G., Frydman, C.: {*log*} as a test case generator for the test template framework. In: Hierons, R.M., Merayo, M.G., Bravetti, M. (eds.) SEFM 2013. LNCS, vol. 8137, pp. 229–243. Springer, Heidelberg (2013)
3. Cristiá, M., Rossi, G., Frydman, C.S.: Adding partial functions to constraint logic programming with sets. TPLP **15**(4–5), 651–665 (2015)
4. Rossi, G., Cristiá, M.: {*log*}. http://people.math.unipr.it/gianfranco.rossi/setlog. Home.html. Accessed 2016
5. Dovier, A., Policriti, A., Rossi, G.: A uniform axiomatic view of lists, multisets, and sets, and the relevant unification algorithms. Fundam. Inform. **36**(2–3), 201–234 (1998)
6. Abrial, J.R.: The B-Book: Assigning Programs to Meanings. Cambridge University Press, New York (1996)
7. Spivey, J.M.: The Z Notation: A Reference Manual. Prentice Hall International (UK) Ltd., Hertfordshire (1992)

8. Cristiá, M., Rossi, G.: Proofs for a decision procedure for binary relations. http://people.math.unipr.it/gianfranco.rossi/SETLOG/proofs.pdf. Accessed 2016

9. Dovier, A., Pontelli, E., Rossi, G.: Set unification. TPLP **6**(6), 645–701 (2006)

10. Stocks, P., Carrington, D.: A framework for specification-based testing. IEEE Trans. Softw. Eng. **22**(11), 777–793 (1996)

11. Cantone, D., Omodeo, E.G., Policriti, A.: Set Theory for Computing - From Decision Procedures to Declarative Programming with Sets. Monographs in Computer Science. Springer, New York (2001)

12. Calvanese, D., De Giacomo, G.: Expressive description logics. In: Baader, F., Calvanese, D., McGuinness, D.L., Nardi, D., Patel-Schneider, P.F. (eds.) The Description Logic Handbook: Theory, Implementation, and Applications, pp. 178–218. Cambridge University Press, Cambridge (2003)

13. Cantone, D., Schwartz, J.T.: Decision procedures for elementary sublanguages of set theory: XI. Multilevel syllogistic extended by some elementary map constructs. J. Autom. Reason. **7**(2), 231–256 (1991)

14. Zarba, C.G., Cantone, D., Schwartz, J.T.: A decision procedure for a sublanguage of set theory involving monotone, additive, and multiplicative functions, I: the two-level case. J. Autom. Reason. **33**(3–4), 251–269 (2004)

15. Cantone, D., Zarba, C.G., Cannata, R.R.: A tableau-based decision procedure for a fragment of set theory with iterated membership. J. Autom. Reason. **34**(1), 49–72 (2005)

16. Marnette, B., Kuncak, V., Rinard, M.: Polynomial constraints for sets with cardinality bounds. In: Seidl, H. (ed.) FOSSACS 2007. LNCS, vol. 4423, pp. 258–273. Springer, Heidelberg (2007)

17. Azevedo, F.: Cardinal: a finite sets constraint solver. Constraints **12**(1), 93–129 (2007)

18. Gervet, C.: Interval propagation to reason about sets: definition and implementation of a practical language. Constraints **1**(3), 191–244 (1997)

19. Hawkins, P., Lagoon, V., Stuckey, P.J.: Solving set constraint satisfaction problems using ROBDDs. J. Artif. Intell. Res. (JAIR) **24**, 109–156 (2005)

20. Deville, Y., Dooms, G., Zampelli, S., Dupont, P.: CP (graph+map) for approximate graph matching. In: 1st International Workshop on Constraint Programming Beyond Finite Integer Domains, pp. 31–47 (2005)

21. Coq Development Team: The Coq Proof Assistant Reference Manual, Version 8.4pl6. LogiCal Project, Palaiseau, France (2014)

22. Nipkow, T., Paulson, L.C., Wenzel, M.: Isabelle/HOL - A Proof Assistant for Higher-Order Logic. LNCS, vol. 2283. Springer, Heidelberg (2002)

23. Saaltink, M.: The Z/EVES system. In: Till, D., Bowen, J.P., Hinchey, M.G. (eds.) ZUM 1997. LNCS, vol. 1212, pp. 72–85. Springer, Heidelberg (1997)

24. Kröning, D., Rümmer, P., Weissenbacher, G.: A proposal for a theory of finite sets, lists, and maps for the SMT-Lib standard. In: Informal Proceedings of the 7th International Workshop on Satisfiability Modulo Theories at CADE 22 (2009)

25. de Moura, L.M., Bjørner, N.: Generalized, efficient array decision procedures. In: Proceedings of 9th International Conference on Formal Methods in Computer-Aided Design, FMCAD 2009, Austin, Texas, USA, 15–18 November 2009, pp. 45–52. IEEE (2009)

26. Déharbe, D., Fontaine, P., Guyot, Y., Voisin, L.: Integrating SMT solvers in Rodin. Sci. Comput. Program. **94**, 130–143 (2014)

27. Mentré, D., Marché, C., Filliâtre, J.-C., Asuka, M.: Discharging proof obligations from atelier B using multiple automated provers. In: Derrick, J., Fitzgerald, J., Gnesi, S., Khurshid, S., Leuschel, M., Reeves, S., Riccobene, E. (eds.) ABZ 2012. LNCS, vol. 7316, pp. 238–251. Springer, Heidelberg (2012)
28. Jackson, D.: Software Abstractions: Logic, Language, and Analysis. The MIT Press, Cambridge (2006)
29. Dal Palú, A., Dovier, A., Pontelli, E., Rossi, G.: Integrating finite domain constraints and CLP with sets. In: Proceedings of the 5th ACM SIGPLAN International Conference on Principles and Practice of Declaritive Programming, PPDP 2003, pp. 219–229. ACM, New York (2003)
30. Zarba, C.G.: Combining sets with cardinals. J. Autom. Reason. **34**(1), 1–29 (2005)
31. Yessenov, K., Piskac, R., Kuncak, V.: Collections, cardinalities, and relations. In: Barthe, G., Hermenegildo, M. (eds.) VMCAI 2010. LNCS, vol. 5944, pp. 380–395. Springer, Heidelberg (2010)

Precise and Complete Propagation Based Local Search for Satisfiability Modulo Theories

Aina Niemetz[(✉)], Mathias Preiner, and Armin Biere

Johannes Kepler University, Linz, Austria
aina.niemetz@jku.at

Abstract. Satisfiability Modulo Theories (SMT) is essential for many applications in computer-aided verification. A recent SMT solving approach based on stochastic local search for the theory of quantifier-free fixed-size bit-vectors proved to be quite effective on hard satisfiable instances, particularly in the context of symbolic execution. However, it still relies on brute-force randomization and restarts to achieve completeness. In this paper we simplify, extend, and formalize the propagation-based variant of this approach. We introduce a notion of essential inputs to lift the well-known concept of controlling inputs from the bit-level to the word-level, which allows to prune search. Guided by a formal completeness proof for our propagation-based variant we obtain a clean, simple and more precise algorithm, which yields a substantial gain in performance, as shown in our experimental evaluation.

1 Introduction

In many applications of hardware and software verification, such as (constrained random) test case generation [1–3] or white box fuzz testing [4], the vast majority of problems is satisfiable. Hence, for this kind of problems local search procedures for deciding satisfiability are useful even though they do not allow to determine unsatisfiability. They were further shown to be orthogonal to other approaches [5,6] and proved to be particularly beneficial in a portfolio setting [6].

Applications as above require bit-precise reasoning as provided by Satisfiability Modulo Theories (SMT) solvers for the theory of fixed-size bit-vectors. Current state-of-the-art SMT solvers [7–11] employ the so-called bit-blasting approach (e.g., [12]), where a given formula is eagerly translated to propositional logic (SAT) while heavily relying on rewriting techniques [13–21] to simplify the input during preprocessing.

Since the SAT Challenge 2012 [22], a new generation of (stochastic) local search (SLS) solvers with very simple architecture [23] achieved remarkable results not only in the random but also in the combinatorial tracks of recent SAT competitions [22,24,25]. In an attempt to reproduce these successful applications of SLS in SAT, in [5], Fröhlich et al. lifted SLS to SMT and proposed a

Supported by Austrian Science Fund (FWF) under NFN Grant S11408-N23 (RiSE).

S. Chaudhuri and A. Farzan (Eds.): CAV 2016, Part I, LNCS 9779, pp. 199–217, 2016.
DOI: 10.1007/978-3-319-41528-4_11

procedure to solve bit-vector formulas on the theory level (word-level) without bit-blasting. In contrast to previous attempts of utilizing SLS techniques in SMT by integrating a bit-level SLS solver in the SMT solver MathSAT [9], the SLS for SMT approach in [5] showed promising initial results. However, it does not fully exploit the word-level structure but rather simulates bit-level local search by focusing on single bit flips. As a consequence, in [6] we proposed a propagation-based extension of [5], which introduced an additional strategy to the original approach to propagate assignments from the outputs to the inputs. This significantly improves performance. We further showed that these techniques are beneficial in a sequential portfolio setting [26] in combination with bit-blasting.

Down propagation of assignments along a single path as in [6] utilizes inverse value computation. This process, however, can get stuck, in which case [6] falls back to either brute force randomization or SLS moves to achieve completeness, as does [5]. Further, inverse value computation as presented in [6] is, as we show in this paper, too restrictive for some operators. Actually, focusing on inverse values only is already too restrictive and may inadvertently prune the search.

In this paper, we simplify and extend the approach presented in [6]. Guided by a formal completeness proof, we present a precise and complete variant of the procedure proposed in [6]. In contrast to [6], our variant only uses propagation and neither relies on restarts nor SLS techniques to achieve completeness. We extend the concept of controlling inputs, used in [6] to determine propagation paths for bit-level operators, to the word-level by introducing the notion of essential inputs. This allows to further prune the search. To overcome the problem of too restrictive inverse value computation, we lift the ATPG [27] concept of "backtracing", which goes back to the PODEM algorithm [28], to the word-level and provide a formalization for both the bit-level and the word-level. Our experiments show that our techniques yield a substantial gain in performance.

Note that in contrast to backtracing in ATPG, our algorithm works with complete assignments. Existing algorithms for word-level ATPG [29,30] are based on branch-bound, use neither backtracing nor complete assignments, are further focused on HW models, and in general lack formal treatment. Other related work on structural bit-level solving from the AI community, e.g., [31–33], has not found actual applications yet, as far we know.

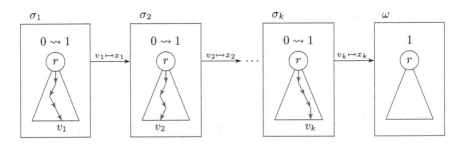

Fig. 1. Basic idea of our propagation-based (local search) strategy.

2 Overview

The propagation-based local search strategy presented in this paper follows the basic idea of the approach presented in [6] as illustrated in Fig. 1. It is applied to both Boolean formulas (bit-level) and quantifier-free fixed-size bit-vector formulas (word-level) and (in contrast to [6]) neither relies on restarts nor requires to fall back on SLS moves (as introduced in [5]) in order to achieve completeness but employs down propagation of assignments only.

Assume that formula ϕ is a directed acyclic graph (DAG) with root r, and σ_1 is a complete but non-satisfying initial assignment, i.e., $\sigma_1(r) = 0$. Our goal is to reach a satisfying assignment ω by changing the value of some primary inputs such that $\omega(r) = 1$. Therefore, we first force root r to assume its target value $\omega(r) = 1$ (denoted as $0 \rightsquigarrow 1$ in Fig. 1), and then propagate this information along a path towards the primary inputs. This process is also known as "backtracing" [28]. Recursively propagating the target value $\omega(r) = 1$ from the root to a primary input (e.g., v_1 in Fig. 1) yields a new assignment $x_i \neq \sigma_i(v_i)$ for a primary input v_i. We then move from assignment σ_i to assignment σ_{i+1} by updating σ_i on v_i to $\sigma_{i+1}(v_i) = x_i$ without changing the value of other primary inputs but recomputing consistent values for inner nodes. Figure 2 describes this strategy more precisely in pseudo code. On the bit-level, as in [6], during path propagation selection of controlling inputs is prioritized w.r.t. the current assignment σ, a well-known concept from ATPG. On the word-level, in contrast to [6], we introduce our new notion of essential inputs, which lifts the bit-level concept of controlling inputs to the word-level while trying to maximally reduce non-deterministic choices without sacrificing completeness.

```
1    function sat (r, σ)              // returns Boolean value B = {0,1}
2        while σ(r) ≠ 1               // while not satisfied
3            g = r, t = 1             // initialize path as root path
4            while ¬leaf(g)           // while current node is an operator
5                n = child(σ, t, g)   // select backtracing node
6                x = value(σ, t, g, n) // select backtracing value
7                g = n, t = x         // backtracing step (propagation)
8            if ¬constant(g)          // check if leaf is variable v = g
9                σ = update(σ, g, t)  // apply move to variable v = g
10       return 1                     // return with 1 (true) if satisfied
```

Fig. 2. The core sat procedure in pseudo-code.

As expected for local search, our propagation strategy is not able to determine unsatisfiability. When determining satisfiability, however, our strategy is complete in the sense that if there is a solution, then there exists a non-deterministic choice of moves according to the strategy that leads to a solution.

In the following, we first introduce and formalize our propagation-based approach on the bit-level and prove its completeness. We then lift it to the word-level, again prove its completeness, and show in our experimental evaluation that our techniques yield substantial performance improvements.

3   Bit-Level

In order to simplify the exposition we consider a fixed Boolean formula ϕ and restrict the set of Boolean operators to $\{\wedge, \neg\}$. We can interpret ϕ as a single-rooted And-Inverter-Graph (AIG) [34], where an AIG is a DAG represented as a 5-tuple (r, N, G, V, E). The set of nodes $N = G \cup V$ contains the single root node $r \in N$, and is further partitioned into a set of *gates* G and a set of *primary inputs* (or *variables*) V. We require that $V \neq \emptyset$ and assume that the Boolean *constants* $\mathbb{B} = \{0, 1\}$, i.e., *true* (1) and *false* (0), do not occur in N. This assumption is without loss of generality since every occurrence of *true* and *false* as input to a gate $g \in G$ can be eliminated through rewriting. The set of gates $G = A \cup I$ consists of a set of *and*-gates A and a set of *inverter*-gates I. We write $g = n \wedge m$ if $g \in A$, and $g = \neg n$ if $g \in I$, and refer to the children of a node $g \in G$ as *its* (gate) inputs (e.g., n or m). Let $E = E_A \cup E_I$ be the edge relation between nodes, with $E_A \colon A \to N^2$ and $E_I \colon I \to N$ describing edges from *and*- resp. *inverter*-gates to its input(s). We write $E(g) = (n, m)$ for $g = n \wedge m$ and $E(g) = n$ for $g = \neg n$ and further introduce the notation $g \to n$ for an edge between a gate g and one of its inputs n.

We define a *complete assignment* σ of the given fixed ϕ as a *complete* function $\sigma \colon N \to \mathbb{B}$, and a *partial assignment* α of ϕ as a *partial* function $\alpha \colon N \to \mathbb{B}$. We say that a complete assignment σ is *consistent* on a gate $g \in I$ with $g = \neg n$ iff $\sigma(g) = \neg \sigma(n)$, and consistent on a gate $g \in A$ with $g = n \wedge m$ iff $\sigma(g) = \sigma(n) \wedge \sigma(m)$. A complete assignment σ is *globally consistent* on ϕ (or just *consistent*) iff it is consistent on all gates $g \in G$. An assignment σ is *satisfying* if it is consistent (thus complete) and satisfies the root, i.e., $\sigma(r) = 1$. We use the letter ω to denote a satisfying assignment. A formula ϕ is satisfiable if it has a satisfying assignment. Let $\mathcal{C}$ be the set of *consistent* assignments, and let $\mathcal{W}$ with $\mathcal{W} \subseteq \mathcal{C}$ be the set of *satisfying* assignments of formula ϕ.

Given two consistent assignments σ and σ', we say that σ' is obtained from σ by *flipping* the (assignment of a) variable $v \in V$, written as $\sigma \xrightarrow{v} \sigma'$, iff $\sigma(v) = \neg \sigma'(v)$ and $\sigma(u) = \sigma'(u)$ for all $u \in V \setminus \{v\}$. We also refer to flipping a variable as a *move*. Note that $\sigma'(g)$ for gates $g \in G$ is defined implicitly due to consistency of σ' after fixing the values for the primary inputs V.

Given as a set of variables V that can be flipped non-deterministically, let $S \colon \mathcal{C} \to \mathbb{P}(\mathcal{M})$ be a (local search) *strategy* that maps a consistent assignment to a set of possible moves $\mathcal{M} = V$. The move $v \in V$ is *valid* under strategy S for a consistent assignment $\sigma \in \mathcal{C}$ if $v \in S(\sigma)$. Similarly, a sequence of moves $\mu = (v_1, \ldots, v_k) \in V^*$ of length $k = |\mu|$ with $v_1, \ldots, v_k \in V$ is *valid* under strategy S iff there exists a sequence of consistent assignments $(\sigma_1, \ldots, \sigma_{k+1}) \in \mathcal{C}^*$ such that $\sigma_i \xrightarrow{v_i} \sigma_{i+1}$ and $v_i \in S(\sigma_i)$ for $1 \leq i \leq k$. In this case σ_{k+1} can be *reached* from σ_1 under S (with k moves), also written $\sigma_1 \to^* \sigma_{k+1}$.

Definition 1. *If formula ϕ is satisfiable, then a strategy S is called* complete *iff for all consistent assignments $\sigma \in \mathcal{C}$ there exists a satisfying assignment $\omega \in \mathcal{W}$ such that ω can be reached from σ under S, i.e., $\sigma \to^* \omega$.*

Given a satisfiable assignment $\omega \in W$ and a consistent assignment $\sigma \in \mathcal{C}$, let $\Delta(\sigma, \omega) = \{v \in V \mid \sigma(v) \neq \omega(v)\}$. Thus $|\Delta(\sigma, \omega)|$ is the Hamming Distance between σ and ω on V. We say that a strategy S is (non-deterministically) *distance reducing*, if for all $\sigma \in \mathcal{C} \backslash W$ and $\omega \in W$ there exists a move $\sigma \xrightarrow{v} \sigma'$ valid under S which reduces the Hamming Distance, i.e., move v is in $\Delta(\sigma, \omega)$ thus $|\Delta(\sigma, \omega)| - |\Delta(\sigma', \omega)| = 1$. Obviously, any distance reducing strategy can reach a satisfying assignment (though not necessarily ω) within at most $|\Delta(\sigma, \omega)|$ moves. This first observation is the key argument in the completeness proofs for our propagation based strategies later on (both on the bit-level and word-level).

Proposition 2. *A distance reducing strategy is also complete.*

The ultimate goal of this paper is to define a strategy that maximally reduces non-deterministic choices without sacrificing completeness. In the algorithm shown in Fig. 2, selecting the backtracing node (line 5) and its value (line 6) constitute the only source of non-determinism. This non-determinism can be reduced by using the notion of controlling inputs from ATPG [27], which was already considered in [6], but only for Boolean expressions.

Definition 3 (Controlling Input). *Let $n \in N$ be an input of a gate $g \in G$, i.e., $g \to n$, and let σ be a complete assignment consistent on g. We say that input n is* controlling *under σ, if for all complete assignments σ' consistent on g with $\sigma(n) = \sigma'(n)$ we have $\sigma(g) = \sigma'(g)$.*

In other words, gate input n is controlling, if the assignment of g, i.e., its output value, remains unchanged as long as the assignment of n does not change. Given an assignment σ consistent on a gate $g \in G$, we denote a *target value* t for g as $\sigma(g) \rightsquigarrow t$. On the bit-level, t is *implicitly* given through σ as $t = \neg\sigma(g)$, i.e., t can not be reached as long as the controlling inputs of g remain unchanged. On the word-level, t may be any value $t \neq \sigma(g)$.

Example 4. Figure 3 shows all possible assignments σ consistent on a gate $g \in G$. At the outputs we denote current assignment $\sigma(g)$ and target value t as $\sigma(g) \rightsquigarrow t$ with $t = \neg\sigma(g)$, e.g., $0 \rightsquigarrow 1$. At the inputs we show their assignment under σ. All controlling inputs are indicated with an underline. Note that for $\sigma(g) = 1$, *and*-gate $g = n \wedge m$ has *no* controlling inputs.

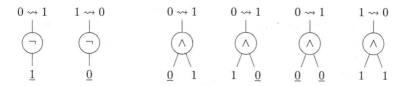

Fig. 3. An *inverter* and an *and*-gate and their controlling (underlined) inputs. Given output values indicate the transition from current to target value.

A sequence of nodes $\pi = (n_1, \ldots, n_k) \in N^+$ is a *path* of length $k = |\pi|$ iff $n_i \to n_{i+1}$ for $0 < i < k$, also written as $n_1 \to \ldots \to n_k$. A path π is *rooted* if $n_1 = r$, and (fully) *expanded* if $n_k \in V$. We call $n_k \in V$ the *leaf* of π in this case. As a restriction on ϕ, we require all paths to be acyclic, i.e., for all $n \in N$ there is no path $n \to^+ n$, and all nodes $n \in N$ to be reachable from the root, i.e., there exists a path $\pi = (r, \ldots, n)$. Note that as a consequence of representing ϕ as a DAG, any path in ϕ is acyclic. Given a path $\pi = (\ldots, g)$ with $g \in G$ and $g \to n$, we say that $\pi.n = (\ldots, g, n)$ is an *extension* of path π with node n.

Definition 5 (Path Selection). *Let* $\sigma \in C$ *be a (complete) consistent assignment, and let* $\pi = (\ldots, g)$ *be a path as above. Then* input n *can be selected w.r.t.* σ *to extend* π *to* $\pi.n$ *if* n *is controlling or if* g *has no controlling input.*

Path selection based on the notion of controlling inputs as introduced above exploits observability don't cares as defined in the context of ATPG [27]. Similarly, we adopt the ATPG idea of backtracing [27,28], as follows.

Definition 6 (Backtracing Step). *Let* $\sigma \in C$ *be a (complete) consistent assignment. Given a gate* $g \in G$ *with* $g \to n$, *a backtracing step w.r.t.* σ *selects input* n *of* g *w.r.t.* σ *as in Definition 5, and determines a backtracing value* x *for* n *as follows. If* $g = \neg n$, *then* $x = \sigma(g)$. *Else, if* $g = n \wedge m$, *then* $x = \neg\sigma(g)$.

As an important observation it turns out that performing a (bit-level) backtracing step always flips the value of the selected input under σ. For a selected input the backtracing value is therefore always unique. This can be checked easily by considering all possible scenarios shown in Fig. 3.

Proposition 7. *A backtracing step always yields as backtracing value* $x = \neg\sigma(n)$.

Example 8. Consider $g = n \wedge m$ and the assignment $\sigma = \{g \mapsto 0, n \mapsto 0, m \mapsto 1\}$ consistent on g as depicted in Fig. 3. Assume that $t = \neg\sigma(g) = 1$ is the target value of g, i.e., $\sigma(g) \rightsquigarrow t$ with $0 \rightsquigarrow 1$. We select n as the single controlling input of g (underlined), which yields backtracing value $x = \neg\sigma(n) = 1$ for n.

A *trace* $\tau = (\pi, \alpha)$ is a rooted path $\pi = (n_1, \ldots, n_k)$ labelled with a partial assignment α, where α is defined exactly on $\{n_1, \ldots, n_k\}$. A trace (π, α) is (fully) *expanded*, if π is a fully expanded path, i.e., node $n_k \in V$ is the *leaf* of π and τ.

Let $\sigma \in C\backslash W$ be a consistent but non-satisfying assignment. Then the notion of extension is lifted from paths to traces as follows. A trace $\tau' = (\pi', \alpha')$ *extends* $\tau = (\pi, \alpha)$ by a *propagation step* (or backtracing step) w.r.t. σ, denoted $\tau \to \tau'$, if $\pi' = \pi.n$ is an extension of $\pi = (\ldots, g)$ with $g \in G$, $\alpha'(m) = \alpha(m)$ for all nodes m in π, and $x = \alpha'(n)$ is the (unique) backtracing value of this backtracing step on g w.r.t. σ and target value $t = \neg\sigma(g)$. The *root trace* $\rho = ((r), \{r \mapsto 1\})$ is a trace that maps r to its target value $\omega(r) = 1$. A *propagation trace* τ w.r.t. σ is a (partial) trace that starts from the root trace ρ and is extended by propagation steps w.r.t. σ, i.e., $\rho \to^* \tau$. Note that α is redundant on the bit-level, given π and σ. We use the same notation on the word-level though, where α captures updates to σ along π, which (in contrast to the bit-level) are not uniquely defined.

Definition 9 (Propagation Strategy). *Given a non-satisfying but consistent assignment* $\sigma \in \mathcal{C}\backslash\mathcal{W}$, *the set of valid moves* $\mathcal{P}(\sigma)$ *for* σ *under propagation strategy* $\mathcal{P}$ *contains exactly the leafs of all expanded propagation traces w.r.t* σ.

In the following, we present and prove the main Lemma of this paper, which then immediately gives completeness of $\mathcal{P}$ in Theorem 11. It is further reused for proving completeness of the extension of $\mathcal{P}$ to the word-level in Theorem 26.

Lemma 10 (Propagation Lemma). *Given a non-satisfying but consistent assignment* $\sigma \in \mathcal{C}\backslash\mathcal{W}$, *then for any satisfying assignment* $w \in \mathcal{W}$, *used as oracle, there exists an expanded propagation trace* τ *w.r.t.* σ *with leaf* $v \in \Delta(\sigma, w)$.

Proof. The idea is to inductively extend the root trace ρ to traces $\tau = (\pi, \alpha)$ through propagation steps, i.e., $\rho \rightarrow^* \tau$, which all satisfy the (key) invariant

$$\alpha(n) = w(n) \neq \sigma(n) \quad \text{for all nodes } n \text{ in } \pi. \tag{1}$$

The root trace $\rho = ((r), \{r \mapsto w(r)\})$ obviously satisfies this invariant. Now, let $\tau = (\pi, \alpha)$ be a trace that satisfies the invariant but is *not fully expanded*, i.e., $\pi = (r, \dots, g)$ with $g \in G$ and $\alpha(g) = w(g) \neq \sigma(g)$. Since $\sigma(g) \neq w(g)$ it follows that g has at least one input n with $\sigma(n) \neq w(n)$. If g has no controlling input, then by Definition 5 it is allowed to select n as an input with $\sigma(n) \neq w(n)$. Otherwise, input n is selected as any controlling input. In both cases we select $x = w(n) \neq \sigma(n)$ as backtracing value using Proposition 7. Trace τ is now extended by n with backtracing value x to τ', i.e., $\tau \rightarrow \tau'$, which in turn concludes the inductive proof of Eq. (1). Any fully expanded propagation trace $\tau = (\pi, \alpha)$ with leaf $v \in V$, as generated above, also satisfies the invariant in Eq. (1). Thus, we have $\alpha(v) = w(v) \neq \sigma(v)$ with $v \in \Delta(\sigma, w)$. $\qquad\square$

In essence, given σ and w as above, our propagation strategy propagates target value $w(r)$ from root r towards the primary inputs, ultimately producing a fully expanded propagation trace τ. In case of non-deterministic choices for extending the trace we use w as an oracle to pick an input n with $\sigma(n) \neq w(n)$, which can be selected according to Definition 5. The oracle allows us to ensure that $v \in \Delta(\sigma, w)$ for leaf v of τ. Thus, using Lemma 10, our propagation strategy turns out to be distance reducing, and therefore, according to Proposition 2, complete. This important contribution of this paper serves in the following as a basis for lifting our approach from the bit-level to the word-level.

Theorem 11. *Under the assumptions of the previous Lemma 10 we also get* $v \in \mathcal{P}(\sigma)$. *Thus* $\mathcal{P}$ *is distance reducing and, as a consequence, complete.*

Our notion of completeness follows the traditional notion of non-deterministic computation of Turing machines. For the purpose of this paper, it is equivalent to the more established property of *probabilistically approximately complete* (PAC) [35], commonly used in the AI community to discuss completeness properties of local search algorithms. This holds as long as probabilistic choices are treated as non-deterministic choices, which actually also is the case in [35].

4   Word-Level

We only consider bit-vector expressions of *fixed* bit-width $w \in \mathbb{N}$, and denote a bit-vector expression n of width w as $n_{[w]}$. We will not explicitly state the bit-width of an expression if the context allows. We refer to the i-th bit of $n_{[w]}$ as $n[i]$ for $1 \leq i \leq w$, and further interpret $n[1]$ as the least significant bit (LSB) and $n[w]$ as the most significant bit (MSB). Similarly, we denote bit ranges over n from bit index j down to index i as $n[j:i]$. Note that for the sake of simplicity, bit indices start from 1 rather than 0. Further, in string representations of bit-vectors we interpret the bit at the far left index as the MSB.

To simplify the exposition and w.l.o.g. we consider a fixed single-rooted quantifier-free bit-vector formula ϕ with Boolean expressions interpreted as bit-vector expressions of bit-width one. The set of bit-vector operators is restricted to $\mathcal{O} = \{\&, \sim, =, <, \ll, \gg, +, \cdot, \div, \mathrm{mod}, \circ, [:], \text{if-then-else}\}$ and interpreted according to Table 1. The selection of operators in $\mathcal{O}$ is rather arbitrary but provides a good compromise between effective and efficient word-level rewriting and compact encodings for bit-blasting approaches. It is complete, though, in the sense that all operators defined in SMT-LIB [36] (in particular signed operators) can be modeled in a compact way. Note that our methods are not restricted to single-rootedness or this particular selection of operators, and can easily be lifted to the full set of operators in SMT-LIB as well as the multi-rooted case.

We interpret formula ϕ as a single-rooted DAG represented as an 8-tuple $(r, N, \kappa, O, F, V, B, E)$. The set of nodes $N = O \cup V \cup B$ contains the single root node $r \in N$ of bit-width one, and is further partitioned into a set of operator nodes O, a set of primary inputs (or bit-vector variables) V, and a set of bit-vector constants $B \subseteq \mathbb{B}^*$, which are denoted in either decimal or binary notation if the context allows. The bit-width of a node is given by $\kappa: N \to \mathbb{N}$, thus $\kappa(r) = 1$. Operator nodes are interpreted as bit-vector operators via $F: O \to \mathcal{O}$, which in turn determines their arity and input and output bit-widths as defined in Table 1. The edge relation between nodes is given as $E = E_1 \cup E_2 \cup E_3$, with $E_i: O \to N^i$ describing the set of edges from unary, binary, and ternary operator nodes to its input(s), respectively. We again use the notation $o \to n$ for an edge between an operator node o and one of its inputs n.

We only consider well-formed formulas, where the bit-widths of all operator nodes and their inputs conform to the conditions imposed via interpretation F as defined in Table 1. For instance, we denote a bit-vector addition node o with inputs n and m as $o = n + m$, where $o \in O$ of arity 2 with $F(o) = +$, and therefore $\kappa(o) = \kappa(n) = \kappa(m)$. In the following, if more convenient we will use the functional notation $o = \diamond(n_1, \ldots, n_k)$ for operator node $o \in O$ of arity k with inputs $n_1, \ldots, n_k$ and $F(o) = \diamond$, e.g., $+(n, m)$. Note that the semantics of all operators in $\mathcal{O}$ correspond to their SMT-LIB counterparts listed in Table 1, with three exceptions. Given a logical shift operation $n \ll m$ or $n \gg m$, w.l.o.g. and as implemented in our SMT solver Boolector [7], we restrict bit-width $\kappa(n)$ to $2^{\kappa(m)}$. Further, as implemented by Boolector and other state-of-the-art SMT solvers, e.g., Mathsat [9] Yices [10] and Z3 [11], we define an unsigned division by

Table 1. Considered bit-vector operators – bit-widths and indices $w, p, q, i, j \in \mathbb{N}$.

Operator	SMT-LIB	Output bit-width	Arity	1st	2nd	3rd	
$[j:i]$	extract	$j - i + 1$	1	w	–	–	extraction $(1 \leq i \leq j \leq w)$
$\sim$	bvnot	w	1	w	–	–	bit-wise negation
$\&$	bvand	w	2	w	w	–	bit-wise conjunction
$=$	=	1	2	w	w	–	equality
$<$	bvult	1	2	w	w	–	unsigned less than
$\ll$	bvshl	w	2	w	q	–	logical shift left $(w = 2^q)$
$\gg$	bvshr	w	2	w	q	–	logical shift right $(w = 2^q)$
$+$	bvadd	w	2	w	w	–	addition
$\cdot$	bvmul	w	2	w	w	–	multiplication
$\div$	bvudiv	w	2	w	w	–	unsigned division
mod	bvurem	w	2	w	w	–	unsigned remainder
$\circ$	concat	w	2	p	q	–	concatenation $(w = p + q)$
if-then-else	ite	w	3	1	w	w	conditional

zero to return the greatest possible value rather than introducing uninterpreted functions, i.e., $x \div 0 = \sim 0$. Similarly, $x \bmod 0 = x$.

A complete function $\sigma: N \rightarrow \mathbb{B}^*$ with $\sigma(n) \in \mathbb{B}^{\kappa(n)}$ of a given fixed ϕ is called a *complete assignment* of ϕ, and a partial function $\alpha: N \rightarrow \mathbb{B}^*$ with $\alpha(n) \in \mathbb{B}^{\kappa(n)}$ a *partial assignment*. Given an operator node $o \in O$ with $o = \diamond(n_1, \ldots, n_k)$ and $\diamond \in \mathcal{O}$, a complete assignment σ is *consistent* on o if $\sigma(o) = f(\sigma(n_1), \ldots, \sigma(n_k))$, where $f: \mathbb{B}^{\kappa(n_1)} \times \cdots \times \mathbb{B}^{\kappa(n_k)} \rightarrow \mathbb{B}^{\kappa(o)}$ is determined by the standard semantics of bit-vector operator $\diamond$ as defined in SMT-LIB [36] (with the exceptions discussed above). A complete assignment is (globally) *consistent* on ϕ (or just *consistent*), iff it is consistent on all bit-vector operator nodes $o \in O$ and $\sigma(b) = b$ for all bit-vector constants $b \in B$. A *satisfying* assignment ω is a complete and consistent assignment that satisfies the root, i.e., $\omega(r) = 1$. In the following, we will again use the letter $\mathcal{C}$ to denote the set of complete and consistent assignments, and the letter $\mathcal{W}$ with $\mathcal{W} \subseteq \mathcal{C}$ to denote the set of satisfying assignments of formula ϕ.

Given a bit-vector variable $v \in V$ with $\kappa(v) = w$, we adopt the notion of obtaining an assignment σ' from an assignment σ by assigning a new value x to v with $x \in \mathbb{B}^w$ where $x \neq \sigma(v)$, written as $\sigma \xrightarrow{v \mapsto x} \sigma'$, which we refer to as a *move*. Thus, the set of word-level moves is defined as $\mathcal{M} = \{(v, x) \mid v \in V, x \in \mathbb{B}^{\kappa(v)}\}$, and accordingly, a word-level strategy is defined as a function $S: C \mapsto \mathbb{P}(\mathcal{M})$ mapping a consistent assignment to a set of moves.

Our propagation strategy $\mathcal{P}$ is lifted from the bit-level to the word-level starting with our new notion of essential inputs for word-level operators, which lifts and extends the corresponding notion of controlling inputs.

Definition 12 (Essential Inputs). *Let $n \in N$ be an input of a bit-vector operator node $o \in O$, i.e., $o \rightarrow n$, and let σ be a complete assignment consistent* on o. *Further, let t be the* target value *of o, i.e., $\sigma(o) \rightsquigarrow t$, with $t \neq \sigma(o)$. We say that n is an* essential input *under σ w.r.t. target value t, if for all complete assignments σ' consistent on o with $\sigma(n) = \sigma'(n)$ we have $\sigma'(o) \neq t$.*

In other words, an operator node input n is essential w.r.t. target value t, if o can not assume t as long as the assignment of n does not change. As an example, consider the bit-vector operators and their essential inputs under some consistent assignment σ w.r.t. some target value t as in Fig. 4.

Example 13. Consider the bit-vector operators $\&$, $\ll$, $\cdot$, $\div$, mod, and $\circ$ of bit-width 2 in Fig. 4. For an operator node o, at the outputs we denote given assignment $\sigma(o)$ and target value t as $\sigma(o) \rightsquigarrow t$, e.g., $10 \rightsquigarrow 01$. At the inputs we show their assignment under σ. Essential inputs are indicated with an underline. Consider, e.g., operator node $o := n \mathbin{\&} m$ with $t = 01$ and $\sigma = \{o \mapsto 10,\ n \mapsto 10,\ m \mapsto 11\}$. Since $t \mathbin{\&} \sigma(n) \neq t$, it is not possible to find a value x for m such that $\sigma(n) \mathbin{\&} x = t$. Hence, input n is essential w.r.t. target value t. Input m, however, is obviously not essential since $t \mathbin{\&} \sigma(m) = t$.

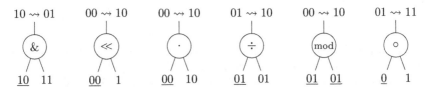

Fig. 4. Bit-vector operator nodes and examples for essential (underlined) inputs. Given output values indicate the transition from current to target value.

Note that AIGs can be represented by bit-vectors of bit-width one, which can be interpreted as Boolean expressions. In this sense, as in [6], the notion of controlling inputs can also be applied to word-level Boolean expressions.

Proposition 14. *When applied to bit-level or Boolean expressions, the notion of* essential inputs *exactly matches the notion of* controlling inputs.

Proof. For applying the notion of essential inputs to the bit-level, consider the operator set $\{\neg, \wedge\}$ for $o \in G$ with $o \to n$. Further, target value $t \neq \sigma(o)$ on the bit-level implies $t = \neg\sigma(o)$, which exactly matches the corresponding implicit definition of the target value of o on the bit-level. Now assume that input n is essential w.r.t. t. Then, if $\sigma(n) = \sigma'(n)$, by Definition 12 we have that $\sigma'(o) \neq t$, and therefore $\sigma'(o) = \neg t = \sigma(o)$. The other direction works in the same way. $\square$

The definition of a (rooted and expanded) *path* as a sequence of nodes $\pi = (n_1, \ldots, n_k) \in N^*$ is lifted from the bit-level to the word-level in the natural way. Corresponding restrictions and implications of Sect. 3 apply. The notions of *path selection* and *path extension* are lifted to the word-level as follows.

Definition 15 (Path Extension). *Given a path $\pi = (\ldots, o)$ with $o \in O$ and $o \rightarrow n$, we say that $\pi.n = (\ldots, o, n)$ is an extension of path π with node n.*

Definition 16 (Path Selection). *Given a (complete) consistent assignment $\sigma \in C$, a path $\pi = (\ldots, o)$ as in Definition 15 above, and $\sigma(o) \rightsquigarrow t$, i.e., $t \neq \sigma(o)$, then* input n *can be selected w.r.t. σ and t to extend π to $\pi.n$ if n is essential or if o has no essential input (in both cases essential under σ w.r.t. t).*

In contrast to the bit-level, where a *backtracing step* always flips the assigned value of a selected input (and the output), on the word-level we also have to select a *backtracing value*. We consider three variants of value selection under the following assumptions. Let t be the target value of an operator node $o \in O$, and let σ be a complete assignment such that $\sigma(o) \neq t$. Further, assume that input n with $o \rightarrow n$ is selected w.r.t. t and σ as in Definition 16 above.

Definition 17 (Random Value). *Any value x with $\kappa(x) = \kappa(n)$ is called a* random value *for n.*

Definition 18 (Consistent Value). *A* random value x *is a* consistent value *for n w.r.t. t, if there is a complete assignment σ' consistent on o with $\sigma'(n) = x$ and $\sigma'(o) = t$.*

In other words, a value is consistent for an input, if it allows to produce the target value after changing values of other inputs if necessary.

Example 19 (Consistent Value Computation). Consider operator node $o := n \cdot m$, and assume that input n is selected w.r.t. t and σ as in Definition 16. Let ctz be defined as the function *counting the number of trailing zeroes* of a given bit-vector, i.e., the number of consecutive 0-bits starting from the LSB, e.g., $ctz(0101) = 0$, $ctz(111100) = 2$. Then any random value x with $ctz(t) \geq ctz(x)$ is a consistent value for n, except that $t = 0$ if $x = 0$.

Restricting the notion of consistent values even further, however, may be beneficial in some cases. Consider the following motivating example from [6].

Example 20 (From [6]). Let $\phi := 274177_{[65]} \cdot v = 18446744073709551617_{[65]}$. Computing $x = 18446744073709551617_{[65]} \div 274177_{[65]} = 67280421310721_{[65]}$ immediately concludes with a satisfying assignment for ϕ.

The chances to select $x = 67280421310721$ if consistent values for the multiplication operator are chosen as in Example 19 are arbitrarily small. Hence, as in [6], we use the notion of *inverse values* which utilize the inverse of a given operator.

Definition 21 (Inverse Value). *A* consistent value x *is an* inverse value *for n w.r.t. t and σ, if there exists a complete assignment σ' consistent on o with $\sigma'(n) = x$, $\sigma'(o) = t$ and $\sigma'(m) = \sigma(m)$ for all m with $o \rightarrow m$ and $m \neq n$.*

In other words, we define an inverse value as a consistent value for an input n such that operator node o assumes target value t without changing the assignment of its other inputs.

Example 22 (Inverse Value Computation). Consider operator node $o := n \cdot m$ of bit-width w. Assume that input n is selected w.r.t. t and σ as in Definition 16. If $t = \sigma(m) = 0$, any x is an inverse value. However, this contradicts assumption $\sigma(o) \neq t$. If $t \neq 0$ and $\sigma(m) = 0$, or if $\sigma(m) \neq 0$ with $ctz(t) < ctz(\sigma(m))$, there exists no inverse value. Otherwise, $ctz(t) \geq ctz(\sigma(m))$ and $\sigma(m) \neq 0$. Let $y = m \gg ctz(\sigma(m))$, thus y is odd. We compute y^{-1} as its multiplicative inverse modulo 2^w via the Extended Euclidean algorithm (similar to word-level rewriting techniques that require solving for a variable, e.g. [14]) and determine x as $(t \gg ctz(\sigma(m))) \cdot y^{-1}$ except that all bits in $x[w : w - ctz(\sigma(m)) + 1]$ are set arbitrarily, with $w = \kappa(n)$.

In contrast to [6], we require inverse value computation for all operators in $\mathcal{O}$ to generate all possible inverse values. This holds for the rule for inverse computation for multiplication discussed in the example above, while it does not hold for the corresponding rule in [6]. The same applies for operators $\ll$, $\gg$, $\div$, and mod.

Definition 23 (Backtracing Step). *Let $\sigma \in \mathcal{C}$ be a (complete) consistent assignment. Given an operator node $o \in O$ with $o \rightarrow n$ and a target value $t \neq \sigma(o)$, then a* backtracing step *selects input n of o w.r.t. σ as in Definition 16 and selects a* backtracing value x *for n as a consistent (and optionally inverse) value w.r.t. σ and t, if such a value exists, and a* random value *otherwise.*

Note that it is not always possible to find an inverse value for n, e.g., $o := n \, \& \, m$ with $\sigma = \{o \mapsto 00, n \mapsto 00, m \mapsto 00\}$ and $t = 01$. Further, even for operators that allow to always produce inverse values, e.g., operator $+$, doing so may lead to inadvertently pruning the search space, see Example 24 below.

Example 24. Given $r := p_2 = 0_{[2]}$ with $p_2 := v + p_1$ and $p_1 := v + 2_{[2]}$ and a complete consistent assignment $\sigma_1 = \{v \mapsto 00, p_1 \mapsto 10, p_2 \mapsto 10, r \mapsto 0\}$, as shown in Fig. 5. Let $t = 1$ be the target value of root node r, i.e., we want to find a value for bit-vector variable v such that $p_2 = 00$. Assume that only inverse values are selected for $+$ operators during propagation. Propagating along the path indicated by blue arrows in Fig. 5 the move $v \mapsto 10 = \alpha_1(v)$ is generated, which yields assignment $\sigma_2 = \{v \mapsto 10, p_1 \mapsto 00, p_2 \mapsto 10, r \mapsto 0\}$. Selecting the other possible propagation path, the same move is produced. Thus, σ_2 is independent of which of the two paths is selected. Since $\sigma_2(r) \neq t$, target value t is again propagated down, which generates move $v \mapsto 00 = \alpha_2(v)$, again independently of which path is selected. With this, we move back to the initial assignment σ_1. Consequently, a satisfying assignment, e.g., $\omega(v) = 01$ or $\omega'(v) = 11$, can not be reached by only selecting inverse values. However, selecting a consistent but non-inverse value for p_1 generates move $v \mapsto 01 = \alpha'_1(v)$, which yields ω.

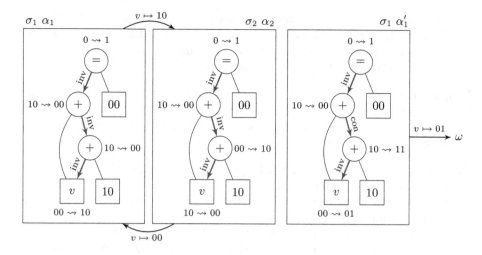

Fig. 5. Example illustrating the necessity of choosing between random and inverse values. The output values indicate the (desired) transition from current to target value. Other values indicate the transition from current value to the value yielded by down propagating the target output value. Thus a propagation based strategy without further randomization using only inverse values as in [6] is incomplete. (Color figure online)

As a consequence, when performing a backtracing step we in general select some consistent non-inverse value, if no inverse value exists, and otherwise non-deterministically choose between consistent (but not necessarily inverse) and inverse values. Since all operators in $\mathcal{O}$ are *surjective* (i.e., they can produce any target value) for our selected semantics (e.g., $\sim 0\bmod 0 = \sim 0$), it is not necessary to select inconsistent random values. For other sets of operators, however, this might be necessary. For the sake of completeness we therefore included the selection of random values in the formal definition of backtracing steps.

Note that on the bit-level, the backtracing value for a selected input is uniquely determined (see Proposition 7). Thus, the issue of value selection is specific to the word-level. Further, when interpreting AIGs as word-level expressions, the notion of backtracing steps on the bit-level as in Definition 6 exactly matches the word-level notion as in Definition 23 using Proposition 14.

The *word-level propagation strategy* $\mathcal{P}$ is defined in exactly the same way as for the bit-level (see Definition 9) except that the word-level notion of backtracing based on essential inputs and consistent value selection (Definition 23) replaces bit-level backtracing based on controlling inputs (Definition 6), and the set of valid moves $\mathcal{P}(\sigma)$ contains not only the leafs of all expanded propagation traces but also their updated assignments, i.e., $(v, \alpha(v))$ for a leaf v. Further important concepts defined on the bit-level in Sect. 3 can be extended naturally to the word-level. These concepts include (expanded) paths and traces, leafs, and trace extension. We omit formal definitions accordingly.

The completeness proof on the word-level is almost identical to the bit-level proof, except that the bit-level Proposition 7, which is substantial for the bit-level proof of Lemma 10, requires more attention due to the more sophisticated selection of backtracing values on the word-level.

Proposition 25. *Let* $\sigma \in \mathcal{C}$ *be a (complete) consistent assignment, and let* ω *be a satisfying assignment* $\omega \in \mathcal{W}$. *Given operator node* $o \in O$ *and target value* $t = \omega(o) \neq \sigma(o)$, *i.e.,* $\sigma(o) \rightsquigarrow t$. *Then there exists a backtracing step w.r.t.* σ *and* t, *which selects input* n *with* $o \rightarrow n$ *and backtracing value* $x = \omega(n) \neq \sigma(n)$.

Proof. First, assume o has an essential input w.r.t. σ. Then we select an arbitrary essential input n of o. Since target value $t = \omega(o) \neq \sigma(o)$, we get $\sigma(n) \neq \omega(n)$ by contraposition of Definition 12. Similarly, if o has no essential inputs, then we select n as an arbitrary input with $\sigma(n) \neq \omega(n)$, which has to exist since $\omega(o) \neq \sigma(o)$. In both cases, we can select $x = \omega(n) \neq \sigma(n)$ as backtracing value, which is consistent for o w.r.t. σ and t since ω is consistent. Picking a random value as backtracing value, which is the last case in Definition 23, can not occur under the given assumptions since, as already discussed, ω is consistent on o. □

With Proposition 25, the proof of the key Lemma 10 for completeness on the bit-level can be lifted to the word-level by replacing each occurrence of gate g with operator node o and the notion of "controlling" with "essential" input, and further using Proposition 25 instead of Proposition 7, as discussed above.

Theorem 26. *Theorem 11 and Lemma 10 also apply to the word-level setting, and thus, propagation strategy* $\mathcal{P}$ *is also complete for the word-level.*

As a side note, the problem of value selection during word-level backtracing and subsequent word-level propagation is similar to the problem of making a theory decision and propagating this decision in MCSat [37,38].

5   Experimental Evaluation

We implemented our approach within our SMT solver Boolector and consider two configurations PAIG and PW to be evaluated against [6] on the same set of benchmarks[1] (16436 total). Configuration PAIG works on AIGs obtained after bit-blasting by Boolector. Configuration PW works directly on the bit-vector formula, with inverse values prioritized over consistent values during backtracing with a probability of 99 to 1. As base case, we use the *best* configurations BB, BPROP and BB+BPROP of the version of Boolector used in [6], where BB is its bit-blasting engine and BPROP implements the propagation-based approach of [6]. As in [6], BB+BPROP serves as a "virtual" sequential portfolio, i.e., BPROP is run for a certain time limit as a preprocessing step prior to invoking BB. The best portfolio setting in [6] used random walks for recovery and is called BB+BPROP+FRW in [6]. We only compare against this best version, but call it

---

[1] All experimental data of this evaluation can be found at http://fmv.jku.at/cav16.

BB+BPROP. Corresponding to BB+BPROP, we introduce a "virtual" sequential portfolio configuration BB+PW, which combines BB and PW as above.

The benchmark set of [6] was compiled from all benchmarks with status sat and unknown in the QF_BV category of the SMT-LIB[2] benchmark library, where all benchmarks proved by BB to be unsatisfiable within a time limit of 1200 s where excluded. Further excluded where all benchmarks solved by Boolector via rewriting only as well as all benchmarks from the *Sage2* family that were not SMT-LIB v2 compliant due to the use of non-compliant operators.

Table 2. Numbers in parentheses indicate the number of instances solved by a configuration within the given time limit, but not solved by BB in 1200 s.

	BPROP	PAIG	PW	BB	BB+BPROP	BB+PW
time limit	10 sec	10 sec	10 sec	1200 sec	1200 sec	1200 sec
# solved	7539 (56)	6789 (14)	**8012** (67)	14806	14862	**14873**
total time	90462	99442	**86061**	2611840	2575700	**2562108**
time limit	1 sec	1 sec	1 sec	1200 sec	1200 sec	1200 sec
# solved	7268 (38)	6016 (2)	**7632** (60)	14806	14844	**14866**
total time	9544	11151	**9106**	2611840	2534471	**2513348**

All experiments were performed on a cluster with 30 nodes of 2.83 GHz Intel Core 2 Quad machines with 8 GB of memory using Ubuntu 14.04.3 LTS. Each run is limited to use 7 GB of main memory. In terms of run time we consider CPU time only and apply the same time limits as in [6], i.e., a limit of 1 and 10 s for the propagation-based approaches and a limit of 1200 s for the bit-blasting configuration and its combinations. In case of a time out or a memory out, the time limit is used as run time.

Table 2 summarizes the results, where the numbers given in parentheses indicate the number of uniquely solved instances solved by a configuration within the given time limit but not solved by BB within 1200 s.

For propagation-based configurations, the two considered time limits are 1 and 10 s for both scenarios, i.e., within and without a sequential portfolio setting. With a time limit of 10 s, our word-level configuration PW outperforms BPROP by 473 instances. Considering only instances solved within 1 s, PW solves 364 more instances than BPROP.

Combining BB with PW into BB+PW with a time limit of 10 s for the propagation-based configuration PW improves the overall performance by 67 instances and outperforms BB+BPROP by 11 instances. Restricting the time limit for PW to 1 second, BB+PW still improves performance by 60 instances, with an even larger gap of 22 instances compared to BB+BPROP.

In contrast to BPROP, PW utilizes our new word-level notion of essential inputs for path selection. Restricting PW to select paths as in [6], i.e., based

---

[2] http://www.smt-lib.org.

on controlling inputs of bit-level operators only, solves 118 instances less. This shows that the notion of essential inputs indeed allows to prune the search space. Restricting Pw to select inverse values only solves 41 instances less. Selecting consistent values only, on the other hand, performs even worse, with 1456 less solved instances. Prioritizing inverse values shows the best results.

Configuration Pw does not rely on restarts. Introducing restarts as employed in [5,6] does not improve performance and even solves 19 instances less. In case of multi-rooted DAGs, Pw randomly selects a yet unsatisfied root for path propagation, instead of selecting roots based on the heuristics suggested in [5] (and also employed in [6]). Introducing this heuristic in Pw, substantially decreases performance with 323 less solved instances. These observations are consistent with results obtained in SAT competitions by SAT solvers based on the Walk-SAT [39,40] architecture, such as [23]. In terms of Paig, neither restarts nor the root selection heuristic mentioned above have an impact on the number of solved instances or the run time of Paig.

We experimented using different seeds for the random number generator of Pw, where the number of solved instances with a time limit of 10 (1) seconds ranged from 8012 (7596) to 8054 (7649). With a time limit of 10 (1) seconds for Pw the number of solved instances of configuration Bb+Pw ranges from 14869 (14864) to 14874 (14869). Due to space constraints, a statistical analysis on randomization effects is left to future work.

Overall, our new propagation-based technique Pw significantly outperforms all other propagation-based configurations. Further, combined with a bit-blasting engine it considerably improves performance in terms of the number of solved instances, run time, and particularly w.r.t. instances solved within 1 second that Bb was not able to solve even within 1200 s. The number of these uniquely solved instances increased by a factor of 1.6 compared to previous work.

6   Conclusion

We extended and formalized a propagation-based local search procedure for SMT, instantiated for bit-vector logics. Guided by a completeness proof, we avoid brute-force randomization as in earlier work. This not only simplifies the whole approach dramatically, but also improves performance. We further formalized the notion of controlling inputs and backtracing from ATPG and extended it to the word-level, by introducing the new concept of essential inputs.

Our procedure was evaluated on bit-level as well as word-level problems, but can be applied to other than bit-vector logics as well, which is probably the most interesting future work. Extending our techniques by introducing strategies for conflict detection and resolution during backtracing as well as lemma generation in order to obtain an algorithm that is able to prove unsatisfiability and not just satisfiability is another intriguing direction for future work.

Finally we would like to thank Andreas Fröhlich for helpful comments, and Holger Hoos for fruitful discussions on the relation between non-deterministic completeness and the notion of probabilistically approximately complete (PAC).

References

1. Tillmann, N., Schulte, W.: Parameterized unit tests. In: Proceedings of ESEC/SIGSOFT FSE 2005, pp. 253–262. ACM (2005)
2. Yuan, J., Pixley, C., Aziz, A.: Constraint-Based Verification. Springer, Heidelberg (2006)
3. Naveh, Y., Rimon, M., Jaeger, I., Katz, Y., Vinov, M., Marcus, E., Shurek, G.: Constraint-based random stimuli generation for hardware verification. AI Mag. **28**(3), 13–30 (2007)
4. Godefroid, P., Levin, M.Y., Molnar, D.A.: Automated whitebox fuzz testing. In: Proceedings of NDSS 2008. The Internet Society (2008)
5. Fröhlich, A., Biere, A., Wintersteiger, C.M., Hamadi, Y.: Stochastic local search for satisfiability modulo theories. In: Proceedings of AAAI 2015, pp. 1136–1143. AAAI Press (2015)
6. Niemetz, A., Preiner, M., Biere, A., Fröhlich, A.: Improving local search for bit-vector logics in SMT with path propagation. In: Proceedings of DIFTS 2015, pp. 1–10 (2015)
7. Niemetz, A., Preiner, M., Biere, A.: Boolector 2.0. JSAT **9**, 53–58 (2015)
8. Barrett, C., Conway, C.L., Deters, M., Hadarean, L., Jovanović, D., King, T., Reynolds, A., Tinelli, C.: CVC4. In: Gopalakrishnan, G., Qadeer, S. (eds.) CAV 2011. LNCS, vol. 6806, pp. 171–177. Springer, Heidelberg (2011)
9. Cimatti, A., Griggio, A., Schaafsma, B.J., Sebastiani, R.: The MathSAT5 SMT solver. In: Piterman, N., Smolka, S.A. (eds.) TACAS 2013 (ETAPS 2013). LNCS, vol. 7795, pp. 93–107. Springer, Heidelberg (2013)
10. Dutertre, B.: Yices 2.2. In: Biere, A., Bloem, R. (eds.) CAV 2014. LNCS, vol. 8559, pp. 737–744. Springer, Heidelberg (2014)
11. de Moura, L., Bjørner, N.S.: Z3: an efficient SMT solver. In: Ramakrishnan, C.R., Rehof, J. (eds.) TACAS 2008. LNCS, vol. 4963, pp. 337–340. Springer, Heidelberg (2008)
12. Kroening, D., Strichman, O.: Decision Procedures - An Algorithmic Point of View. Texts in Theoretical Computer Science. An EATCS Series. Springer, Heidelberg (2008)
13. Ganesh, V.: Decision procedures for bit-vectors, arrays and integers. Ph.D. thesis, Stanford University (2007)
14. Ganesh, V., Dill, D.L.: A decision procedure for bit-vectors and arrays. In: Damm, W., Hermanns, H. (eds.) CAV 2007. LNCS, vol. 4590, pp. 519–531. Springer, Heidelberg (2007)
15. Bruttomesso, R.: RTL verification: from SAT to SMT(BV). Ph.D. thesis, University of Trento (2008)
16. Brummayer, R.: Efficient SMT solving for bit-vectors and the extensional theory of arrays. Ph.D. thesis, Johannes Kepler University Linz (2009)
17. Bruttomesso, R., Cimatti, A., Franzén, A., Griggio, A., Hanna, Z., Nadel, A., Palti, A., Sebastiani, R.: A lazy and layered *SMT*(BV) solver for hard industrial verification problems. In: Damm, W., Hermanns, H. (eds.) CAV 2007. LNCS, vol. 4590, pp. 547–560. Springer, Heidelberg (2007)
18. Franzen, A.: Efficient solving of the satisfiability modulo bit-vectors problem and some extensions to SMT. Ph.D. thesis, University of Trento (2010)
19. Hansen, T.A.: A constraint solver and its application to machine code test generation. Ph.D. thesis, University of Melbourne (2012)

20. Hadarean, L., Bansal, K., Jovanović, D., Barrett, C., Tinelli, C.: A tale of two solvers: eager and lazy approaches to bit-vectors. In: Biere, A., Bloem, R. (eds.) CAV 2014. LNCS, vol. 8559, pp. 680–695. Springer, Heidelberg (2014)
21. Bruttomesso, R., Pek, E., Sharygina, N., Tsitovich, A.: The OpenSMT solver. In: Esparza, J., Majumdar, R. (eds.) TACAS 2010. LNCS, vol. 6015, pp. 150–153. Springer, Heidelberg (2010)
22. Balint, A., Belov, A., Järvisalo, M., Sinz, C.: Overview and analysis of the SAT challenge 2012 solver competition. Artif. Intell. **223**(2015), 120–155 (2012)
23. Balint, A., Schöning, U.: Choosing probability distributions for stochastic local search and the role of make versus break. In: Cimatti, A., Sebastiani, R. (eds.) SAT 2012. LNCS, vol. 7317, pp. 16–29. Springer, Heidelberg (2012)
24. Balint, A., Belov, A., Heule, M.J.H., Järvisalo, M. (eds.): Proceedings of SAT Competition 2013. Volume B-2013-1 of Department of Computer Science Series of Publications B., University of Helsinki (2013)
25. Belov, A., Heule, M.J.H., Järvisalo, M. (eds.): Proceedings of SAT Competition 2014. Volume B-2014-2 of Department of Computer Science Series of Publications B., University of Helsinki (2014)
26. Xu, L., Hutter, F., Hoos, H.H., Leyton-Brown, K.: Satzilla: portfolio-based algorithm selection for SAT. J. Artif. Intell. Res. (JAIR) **32**, 565–606 (2008)
27. Kunz, W., Stoffel, D.: Reasoning in Boolean Networks: Logic Synthesis and Verification Using Testing Techniques. Kluwer Academic Publishers, Norwell (1997)
28. Goel, P.: An implicit enumeration algorithm to generate tests for combinational logic circuits. IEEE Trans. Comput. **30**(3), 215–222 (1981)
29. Huang, C., Cheng, K.: Assertion checking by combined word-level ATPG and modular arithmetic constraint-solving techniques. In: Proceedings of DAC 2000, pp. 118–123 (2000)
30. Iyer, M.A.: Race: a word-level atpg-based constraints solver system for smart random simulation. In: Proceedings of ITC 2003, pp. 299–308. IEEE Computer Society (2003)
31. Järvisalo, M., Junttila, T.A., Niemelä, I.: Unrestricted vs restricted cut in a tableau method for boolean circuits. Ann. Math. Artif. Intell. **44**(4), 373–399 (2005)
32. Drechsler, R., Junttila, T.A., Niemelä, I.: Non-clausal SAT and ATPG. In: Handbook of Satisfiability, vol. 185. Frontiers in Artificial Intelligence and Applications, pp. 655–693. IOS Press (2009)
33. Belov, A., Järvisalo, M., Stachniak, Z.: Depth-driven circuit-level stochastic local search for SAT. In: IJCAI, IJCAI/AAAI, pp. 504–509 (2011)
34. Kuehlmann, A., Paruthi, V., Krohm, F., Ganai, M.K.: Robust boolean reasoning for equivalence checking and functional property verification. IEEE Trans. Comput.-Aided Des. Integr. Circ. Syst. **21**(12), 1377–1394 (2002)
35. Hoos, H.H.: On the run-time behaviour of stochastic local search algorithms for SAT. In: Proceedings of AAAI/IAAI 1999, pp. 661–666. AAAI Press/The MIT Press (1999)
36. Barrett, C., Fontaine, P., Tinelli, C.: The SMT-LIB Standard: Version 2.5. Technical report, Department of Computer Science, The University of Iowa (2015). www.SMT-LIB.org
37. de Moura, L., Jovanović, D.: A model-constructing satisfiability calculus. In: Giacobazzi, R., Berdine, J., Mastroeni, I. (eds.) VMCAI 2013. LNCS, vol. 7737, pp. 1–12. Springer, Heidelberg (2013)

38. Jovanović, D., Barrett, C., de Moura, L.: The design and implementation of the model constructing satisfiability calculus. In: FMCAD, pp. 173–180. IEEE (2013)
39. Selman, B., Kautz, H.A., Cohen, B.: Noise strategies for improving local search. In: Proceedings of AAAI 1994, pp. 337–343. AAAI Press/The MIT Press (1994)
40. McAllester, D.A., Selman, B., Kautz, H.A.: Evidence for invariants in local search. In: Proceedings of AAAI/IAAI 1997, pp. 321–326. AAAI Press/The MIT Press (1997)

Progressive Reasoning
over Recursively-Defined Strings

Minh-Thai Trinh[✉], Duc-Hiep Chu, and Joxan Jaffar

National University of Singapore, Singapore, Singapore
{trinhmt,hiepcd,joxan}@comp.nus.edu.sg

Abstract. We consider the problem of reasoning over an expressive constraint language for unbounded strings. The difficulty comes from "recursively defined" functions such as **replace**, making state-of-the-art algorithms *non-terminating*. Our first contribution is a progressive search algorithm to not only *mitigate* the problem of non-terminating reasoning but also *guide* the search towards a "minimal solution" when the input formula is in fact satisfiable. We have implemented our method using the state-of-the-art Z3 framework. Importantly, we have enabled conflict clause learning for string theory so that our solver can be used effectively in the setting of program verification. Finally, our experimental evaluation shows leadership in a large benchmark suite, and a first deployment for another benchmark suite which requires reasoning about string formulas of a class that has not been solved before.

Keywords: String solving · Progressive search · Termination · Web security

1 Introduction

Web applications provide critical services over the Internet and handle sensitive data. Unfortunately, many of them are vulnerable to attacks by malicious users. According to the Open Web Application Security Project [16], the most serious web application vulnerabilities include: (#1) Injection flaws (such as SQL injection) and (#3) Cross Site Scripting (XSS) flaws. Both vulnerabilities involve string-manipulating operations and occur due to inadequate sanitisation and inappropriate use of input strings provided by users. Therefore, reasoning about *strings* is necessary to ensure the security of web applications [18,21].

In web applications, recursively defined string functions also play an important role. For example, the string function **replace** which is used frequently in sanitizers in order to prevent insecure user inputs, can be recursively defined as follows:

$$Y=\textbf{replace}(X,r,Z) \overset{def}{=} (X \notin /.^*r.^*/ \wedge Y=X) \vee$$
$$(X=X_1 \cdot X_2 \cdot X_3 \cdot X_4 \wedge X_2 \cdot X_3 \in /r/ \wedge \textbf{length}(X_3)=1 \wedge$$
$$X_1 \cdot X_2 \notin /.^*r.^*/ \wedge Y=X_1 \cdot Z \cdot Y_1 \wedge Y_1=\textbf{replace}(X_4,r,Z))$$

© Springer International Publishing Switzerland 2016
S. Chaudhuri and A. Farzan (Eds.): CAV 2016, Part I, LNCS 9779, pp. 218–240, 2016.
DOI: 10.1007/978-3-319-41528-4_12

The first disjunct corresponds to the base case where the input X does not contain any substring that matches the regular expression r. The resulting string Y will be the same as X. In the other disjunct, the first substring of X that matches r is $X_2 \cdot X_3$. So we replace this substring by Z and then make a recursive call for the remaining part X_4. (The greedy version, using as many characters as possible in the match against r, can be defined and treated in a similar manner.)

Unfortunately, reasoning about unbounded strings defined recursively is in general an *undecidable* problem. As a concrete example, string functions such as **replace** that are applied to any number of occurrences of a string (even limited to single-character strings) would make the satisfiability problem undecidable [6,7]. We must therefore be content with an *incomplete* solution.

Even so, we do not yet have an algorithm that is plausibly effective in practice. To generally handle recursive functions, a state-of-the-art technique [21] is "unfold-and-consume" which is to incrementally reduce recursive functions via splitting (and/or unfolding) process, until their subparts are bounded with constant strings/characters to be consumed. This technique has shown very promising results. However, because the main purpose of [21] is vulnerability detection, i.e., generating attack inputs for each satisfiable query, and that every query is invoked with a timeout limit, there was less emphasis on the detection of *unsatisfiable* queries. By contrast, in the setting of program verification, or in using verification technologies to speed up concolic testing [3,12], the problem of determining unsatisfiability becomes paramount. In short, we can no longer depend on a timeout, and must seek a *terminating* algorithm as far as possible.

The main contribution of this paper is an algorithm whose goal is to determine if a string formula is unsatisfiable, and if not, to be able to generate a solution for it. The key feature of our algorithm is a *pruning method* on the subproblems, in a way that is *directed*. More specifically, our algorithm aims to detect non-progressive scenarios (Sect. 4.2) with respect to a criterion of minimizing the "lexicographical length" of the returned solution, if a solution in fact exists. Informally, in the search process based on reduction rules, we can soundly prune a subproblem when the answer we seek can be found more efficiently *elsewhere*. If a subproblem is deemed non-progressive, it means if the original input formula is satisfiable, then another satisfiable solution of shorter "length" will be found. If, on the other hand, the input formula is unsatisfiable, then any pruning is obviously sound. A technical challenge we will overcome is that at the point of pruning, the satisfiability of the input formula is *unknown*.

An additional important feature of our algorithm is applicable only when the input formula is unsatisfiable. Here, we want to produce a set of *conflict clauses*, a generalization of the input formula, that is now known to be unsatisfiable (Sect. 5.2). The benefits of such learning is of course well-known. It is, for example, at the heart of the attractiveness of SMT solvers. However, the key technical challenge is, how conflict clause learning can work in tandem with the pruning of non-progressive formulas, because at the time of pruning, again, the unsatisfiability of the input formula is unknown.

Finally, we present an experimental evaluation with two case studies. First is on the well-known Kudzu benchmark [18] where we show that (a) our new algorithm surpasses four state-of-the-art solvers in its ability to detect unsatisfiable formulas or generate a model in satisfiable formulas (and in good running time), and (b) the number of unsatisfiable cores is very small, thus paving the way to accelerate the consideration of large collections of formulas. The second case study considers web applications used in the Jalangi framework [19], and shows how we can deal with the **replace** operation in string formulas. No other system has been demonstrated on this class of problems, and thus the purpose of our evaluation is simply to show that we are applicable.

2   Motivation

The common reason for non-termination in string solving is non-progression. For example, after applying some reduction steps, if the reduced problem is not easier to solve than the original one, then it may lead to non-terminating computations. To illustrate, let us first look at the JavaScript example in Fig. 1.

```
1   function json_decode(str) {
2       str = str.replace(/ip/g, "ip address");
3       str = str.replace(/dom/g, "domain");
4       return str;}
5   function json_show(str) {
6       var arr = JSON.parse(str);
7       var c = arr[0].content.split("&");
8       var s = c[0]+" "+c[1];
9       document.getElementById("info").innerHTML = s;}
10  res = json_decode(input);
11  json_show(res);
```

Fig. 1. A JavaScript example using **replace** operation

The program takes as its input a JSON [10] string. Here is an example of a string input:

$$[\{\text{``content''} : \text{``ip=1.1.1.1\&dom=nus.edu.sg''}\},$$
$$\{\text{``content''} : \text{``ip=0.0.0.0\&dom=google.com''}\}]$$

Specifically, we store the JSON data in an array. Each element of the array is an object. Inside an object, we declare a property with its name and its value (i.e., a {name : value} pair). To access the value, we simply refer to the name of the property we need (e.g., we use a[0].content to access the value of the first element of the array a). In Fig. 1, the program first decodes the input string by replacing all occurrences of "ip" with "ip address" and "dom" with "domain". Then it parses the decoded string into an array **arr**, and splits the value of the first element of this array into two parts using "&" delimiter. Finally, it shows the resulting string s in a web browser by updating the **innerHTML** attribute of the **info** element.

Now, suppose we want to detect XSS vulnerabilities in the program. We then need to determine the security sink and source of XSS attacks. Here, the security sink is `innerHTML`, while the corresponding source is an input JSON string (i.e. `input`). Next, against the sink, we define the specification for XSS attacks which is some (regular) grammar encoding a set of strings that would constitute an XSS attack. For simplicity, we choose: all the strings that contain `"<script"`. Lastly, in order to generate a test input that leads to an XSS attack, we will need to solve the formula:

$$\text{contains}(s,\texttt{"<script"}) \land \text{tmp}=\text{replace}(\text{input},\texttt{"ip"},\texttt{"ip address"})$$
$$\land\ \text{res}=\text{replace}(\text{tmp},\texttt{"dom"},\texttt{"domain"}) \land \text{arr}=\text{parse}(\text{res})\ \land$$
$$c=\text{split}(\text{arr}[0].\text{content},\texttt{"\&"}) \land s=c[0]\cdot\texttt{""}\cdot c[1]$$

to make it easier for presentation, we simplify the formula into:

$$\text{res}=\text{replace}(\text{input},\texttt{"ip"},\texttt{"ip address"})\ \land$$
$$\text{contains}(\text{res},\texttt{"<script"})$$

If we now perform some intuitive steps of "unfolding" the definition of **replace**, we will reduce the simplified formula into two disjuncts. Since the first one is unsatisfiable due to the conflict between $\text{res} \notin /.^* \texttt{"ip"} .^*/$ and $\text{contains}(\text{res},\texttt{"<script"})$, we proceed to find a solution in the second disjunct, that is

$$\text{input}=X_1\cdot\texttt{"ip"}\cdot\text{input}_1 \land X_1\cdot\texttt{"i"}\notin /.^* \texttt{"ip"} .^*/\ \land$$
$$\text{res}=X_1\cdot\texttt{"ip address"}\cdot\text{res}_1\ \land$$
$$\text{res}_1=\text{replace}(\text{input}_1,\texttt{"ip"},\texttt{"ip address"})\ \land$$
$$\text{contains}(\text{res},\texttt{"<script"})$$

After applying the unfolding step some $n-1$ times, we still have to find a solution in the following formula:

$$\text{input}=X_1\cdot\texttt{"ip"}\cdot\text{input}_1 \land X_1\cdot\texttt{"i"}\notin /.^* \texttt{"ip"} .^*/\ \land$$
$$\text{res}=X_1\cdot\texttt{"ip address"}\cdot\text{res}_1 \land \text{input}_1=X_2\cdot\texttt{"ip"}\cdot\text{input}_2\ \land$$
$$X_2\cdot\texttt{"i"}\notin /.^* \texttt{"ip"} .^*/ \land \text{res}_1=X_2\cdot\texttt{"ip address"}\cdot\text{res}_2 \land \ldots \land$$
$$\text{res}_n=\text{replace}(\text{input}_n,\texttt{"ip"},\texttt{"ip address"})\ \land$$
$$\text{contains}(\text{res},\texttt{"<script"})$$

Obviously, this will lead us to a non-terminating computation.

As a matter of fact, non-termination is common in string solving. In addition to the case of solving constraints on (JavaScript) recursive string operations (e.g. **replace**, **split**, **match**), we also have non-termination when handling membership predicates with unbounded Kleene-star regular expressions.

Example 1. Unbounded regular expressions:

$$X=Y\cdot Z\cdot T \land Y \in /\texttt{a}^*/ \land Z \in /\texttt{b}^*/ \land T \in /\texttt{c}^*/\ \land$$
$$\text{length}(Y)=\text{length}(Z) \land \text{length}(Z)=\text{length}(T) \land X=X_1\cdot\texttt{"d"}\cdot X_2$$

Since the first 6 constraints state that X can be any string in the context-sensitive language $\{\ a^n{\cdot}b^n{\cdot}c^n\ |\ n{\geq}0\ \}$, automata techniques and the alike which approximate strings using context free grammars, are not able to handle this example. Instead, to generally deal with unboundedness of regular expressions which are constructed by using Kleene-star operators, state-of-the-art techniques [21,23] represent the membership predicate $X{\in}$/a*/ as an equation between string variable X and **star**(a,N) function which can be defined recursively as below:

$$\texttt{X=star(a,N)} \stackrel{def}{=} \texttt{(X = "") } \vee \texttt{ (X=a{\cdot}star(a,M) } \wedge \texttt{ N=M+1)}$$

To facilitate the solving process, [21,23] will need to apply the definition of **star** functions to incrementally reduce them (according to the unfold-and-consume technique). However, they cannot handle Example 1 as they will go into an infinite loop of searching for a solution. We will discuss this example more in Sect. 4.

Finally, we note that the problem of non-terminating reasoning is not solely due to the recursive definitions we employ in this paper. For example, the non-termination problem also happens when we do splitting on unbounded string variables. Below is a well-known example.

Example 2. Overlapping variables:

$$\texttt{X } \cdot \texttt{ "a" = "b" } \cdot \texttt{ X}$$

The classic work [15] is able to solve the satisfiability problem of word equations (and not including recursively defined string operations). In this work, the big advance was to discover a termination criteria within the reasoning steps, and prominent amongst these was the "splitting" step. For the above example, such a step would split X in the left hand side to obtain a new formula X."a"="b".X $\wedge$ X="b".Y . This can then be simplified into Y."a"="b".Y $\wedge$ X="b".Y . Notice that the last formula is, in some sense, equally difficult to solve as the original one. The huge contribution of [15] was thus to provide a bound for the number of times such "non-progressive" steps that needs to be made. However, the elaboration of this bound is extremely complex and is not considered feasible for a direct implementation.

3   The Core Language

We introduce the core constraint language in Fig. 2. In our implementation, the string theory solver is a component of Z3 solver [9]. Though Z3 supports more primitive types, we only mention string type and integer type in Fig. 2.

Variables: We deal with two types of variables: V_{str} consists of string variables (X, Y, Z, T, and possibly with subscripts); and V_{int} consists of integer variables (M, N, P, and possibly with subscripts).

Constants: Correspondingly, we have two types of constants: string and integer constants. Let C_{str} be a subset of $\Sigma^\star$ for some finite alphabet Σ. Elements of

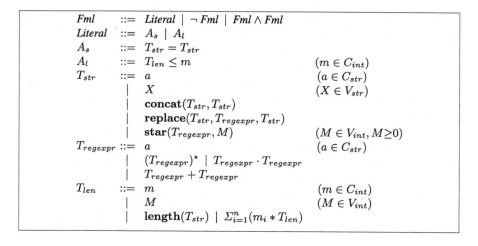

Fig. 2. The syntax of our core constraint language

C_{str} are referred to as string constants or constant strings. They are denoted by a, b, and possibly with subscripts. Elements of C_{int} are integers and denoted by m, n, and possibly with subscripts.

Terms: Terms may be string terms or length terms. A string T_{str} term (denoted D, E, and possibly with subscripts) is either an element of V_{str}, an element of C_{str}, or a function on terms. More specifically, we classify those functions into two groups: recursive and non-recursive functions. An example of recursive function is **replace**, while an example of non-recursive function is **concat**. The concatenation of string terms is denoted by **concat** or interchangeably by · operator. For simplicity, we do not discuss string operations such as **match**, **split**, **exec** which return an array of strings. We note, however, these operations are fully supported in our implementation.

A length term (T_{len}) is an element of V_{int}, an element of C_{int}, **length** function applied to a string term, a constant integer multiple of a length term, or their sum.

In addition, $T_{regexpr}$ represents regular expression terms. They are constructed from string constants by using operators such as concatenation (·), union (+), and Kleene star (⋆). However, regular expression terms are only used as parameters of functions such as **replace** and **star**.

Following [21], we use the **star** function in order to reduce a membership predicate involving Kleene star to a word equation. The **star** function takes two parameters as its input. The first parameter is a regular expression term while the second is a non-negative integer variable. For example, $X \in (r)^\star$ is modelled as $X = \mathbf{star}(r, N)$, where N is a *fresh* variable denoting the number of times that r is repeated.

Literals: They are either string equations (A_s) or length constraints (A_l).

Formulas: Formulas (denoted F, G, H, I, and possibly with subscripts) are defined inductively over literals by using operators such as conjunction (∧), and negation ($\neg$). Note that, each theory solver of Z3 considers only a conjunction of literals at a time. The disjunction will be handled by the Z3 core. We use $\text{Var}(F)$ to denote the set of all variables of F, including bound variables.

Define L to be the quantifier-free first-order two-sorted language over which the formulas described above are constructed. This logic can be considered as equality logic facilitated with recursive and non-recursive functions, along with length constraints.

As shown in [21], to sufficiently reason about web applications, string solvers need to support formulas of quantifier-free first-order logic over string equations, membership predicates, string operations and length constraints. Given a formula of that logic, similarly to other approaches such as [21,23], our top level algorithm will reduce membership predicates into string equations where Kleene star operations are represented as recursive **star** functions. After such reduction, the new formula can be represented in our core constraint language L in Fig. 2.

4   Algorithm

In Sect. 4.1, we first present the background and limitation of existing methods. In Sect. 4.2, we then present the foundations of our progressive algorithm, along with the formal statements about its soundness and semi-completeness. Implementation details are discussed later in Sect. 5.

4.1   Preliminaries

This paper builds on top of the string solver S3 [21]. Essentially, the S3 solver is a string theory plug-in built into the Z3 SMT solver [9], whose architecture is summarised as follows. Z3 core component consists of three modules: the congruence closure engine, a SAT solver-based DPLL layer, and several built-in theory solvers such as integer linear arithmetic, bit-vectors. The congruence closure engine can detect equivalent terms and then classify them into different equivalence classes which are shared among all theory solvers. Each theory solver can consult the Z3 core to detect equivalent terms if needed. In particular, the string theory solver has a bi-directional interaction with a built-in integer theory solver [21,23].

In the string theory solver, the search for a solution is driven by a set of *rules*.

Definition 1 (Derivation Rule). *Each rule is of the general form*

$$(RULE\text{-}NAME)\ \frac{F}{\bigvee_{i=1}^{m} G_i}$$

where F, G_i are conjunctions of literals[1], $F \equiv \bigvee_{i=1}^{m} G_i$, and $\text{Var}(F) \subseteq \text{Var}(G_i)$. $\qquad\square$

---

[1] As per Fig. 2.

An application of this rule transforms a formula at the top, F, into the formula at the bottom, which comprises a number (m) of *reducts* G_i.

Definition 2 (Derivation Tree). *A derivation tree for a formula F is obtained by applying a derivation rule R to F. If the rule produces the single reduct* false, *then the tree comprises the single node labelled with F. Otherwise, let the reducts of R be G_i, $1 \leq i \leq m$. Then the tree comprises a root node labelled with F and there are m child nodes, labelled with G_i, $1 \leq i \leq m$.* □

The concepts of descendant and ancestor nodes are defined in the usual way.

A derivation tree rooted at formula F is built using some search strategy. The search strategy used by Z3 is a form of Depth First Search. This importantly means that the process can be nonterminating even though there is a finite path leading to a satisfying assignment to the variables in F. In navigating the construction of the derivation tree, we backtrack when we encounter a `false` formula. If all the leaf nodes of a subtree rooted at F are `false`, we can decide that the formula F is unsatisfiable.

On the other hand, when we encounter a formula for which no derivation rules can be applied, we can in fact terminate and decide that F is satisfiable. To ensure the soundness of this step, we employ a standard procedure of instantiating steps which enumerates and thus performs a *brute-force* method. This method looks for satisfying assignments for all the string variables in the root nodes of a dependency graph for string variables — a string variable in a root node does not depend on the values of any string variables. Consequently, when we terminate and declare satisfiability, it also means that every string variable has been successfully grounded. This brute-force method is part of Z3-str, S3, Z3-str2, and is also adopted by this paper. We will henceforth assume this method tacitly, and not discuss it further.

Note that we control the branching order in navigating the derivation tree by dictating the order of the rules to be applied, as well as the order in which the reducts to be considered. In general, this order can affect significantly the overall performance of the algorithm. However, because of the way our progressive algorithm works, and in particular because of its pruning step (introduced later), the choice of order becomes much less important. For this reason, when we present our algorithm in detail below, we shall not impose any order on the application of derivation rules.

We next discuss the set of rules used by our solver. Then we will illustrate the application of rules and show an example of the derivation tree later in Example 3. The set of rules is described in two parts:

- one-reduct rules: in Figs. 3 and 4;
- multi-reduct rules: in Fig. 5.

We first describe the one-reduct rules in Fig. 3. These rules are to propagate length constraints, so that these constraints can be sent to integer theory solver. They are triggered by the encounter with a string constant, a string variable, a concatenation, and a string equation. In the figure, we use $\mathtt{Var}(F)$, $\mathtt{Constant}(F)$,

Concat(F), and Equality(F) to denote the set of variables, constants, concatenations, and equations of F respectively. Note that we need to mark them in those corresponding sets so that these rules are applied once for each constant, variable, concatenation, and equation.

$$\text{(L-CST)} \quad \frac{F}{F \wedge \mathbf{length}(a) = |a|} \quad a \in \mathtt{Constant}(F) \text{ and } |a| \text{ is the length of a string constant } a$$

$$\text{(L-VAR)} \quad \frac{F}{F \wedge \mathbf{length}(X) \geq 0} \quad X \in \mathtt{Var}(F)$$

$$\text{(L-CAT)} \quad \frac{F}{F \wedge \mathbf{length}(D \cdot E) = \mathbf{length}(D) + \mathbf{length}(E)} \quad D \cdot E \in \mathtt{Concat}(F)$$

$$\text{(L-EQL)} \quad \frac{F}{F \wedge \mathbf{length}(D) = \mathbf{length}(E)} \quad D = E \in \mathtt{Equality}(F)$$

Fig. 3. Length constraint propagation rules

We comment here that in a practical implementation, it is useful to have some more rules, for example, to deal with membership predicates and string operations. But for a more focused presentation, we shall not discuss them further.

$$\text{(CON)} \quad \frac{F \wedge D = E}{\mathtt{false}} \quad D, E \text{ are string terms and } D \neq E$$

$$\text{(SUB)} \quad \frac{F \wedge X = C}{F[X/C] \wedge X = C} \quad X \in \mathtt{Var}(F) \text{ and } C \text{ is (semi-)grounded}$$

$$\text{(SIM)} \quad \frac{F \wedge a \cdot D \cdot b = a \cdot E \cdot b}{F \wedge D = E} \quad D, E \text{ are string terms}$$

Fig. 4. Simplification rules for string constraints

Next, consider Fig. 4 which shows three basic simplification rules. First, the (CON) rule is to detect a contradiction in the string theory. Second, the (SUB) rule is to substitute all variables X in F with C, where C is either grounded or semi-grounded. A string is *grounded* if it is a constant string. It is called *semi-grounded* if it is either a **star** function, or a concatenation of which at least a component is either grounded or semi-grounded. For example, "a" is grounded, while "a" $\cdot Y_2$ is semi-grounded. Finally, the (SIM) rule is to eliminate matching constant strings on both sides of an equation. For each formula in the derivation tree, only one rule is applied at a time. For each application, only one literal is considered at a time. For example, in (SUB) rule, only $X = C$ is involved. The choice of which literal to be involved is decided by Z3.

We comment here that in our implementation, we do employ other specialized rules. For example, because the string theory solver also receives the information of length constraints from the integer theory solver, we can craft a more specialized instance of the (CON) rule of Fig. 4 where a variant side condition is that the lengths of D and E are different. Further, our implementation accommodates string operations such as **substring**, **indexOf**, with new simplification rules. Again, for presentation purposes, we shall not discuss these detailed rules further.

Finally, we present the remainder of our rules: multi-reduct rules, which we call *splitting* rules. Before proceeding, note that in the rules in Figs. 3 and 4, no disjunction is introduced. The disjunctions are only introduced in the splitting rules, which we will present in two parts: the unfolding (UNF) rules, and the variable-splitting (SPL) rules.

$$\text{(SPL-1)} \quad \frac{F \wedge D \cdot a = b \cdot E}{\bigvee_{i=1}^{min(|a|,|b|)} (F \wedge D = b_0^{|b|-i} \wedge E = a_i^{|a|}) \vee (F \wedge \exists X_1 : D = b \cdot X_1 \wedge X_1 \cdot a = E)}$$

$$\text{(SPL-2)} \quad \frac{F \wedge D_1 \cdot E_1 = a \cdot D_2}{\bigvee_{i=0}^{|a|-1} (F \wedge D_1 = a_0^i \wedge E_1 = a_i^{|a|} \cdot D_2) \vee (F \wedge \exists X_1 : D_1 = a \cdot X_1 \wedge X_1 \cdot E_1 = D_2)}$$

$$\text{(SPL-3)} \quad \frac{F \wedge D_1 \cdot E_1 = D_2 \cdot b}{\bigvee_{i=|b|}^{1} (F \wedge E_1 = b_i^{|b|} \wedge D_1 = D_2 \cdot b_0^i) \vee (F \wedge \exists X_1 : E_1 = X_1 \cdot b \wedge D_1 \cdot X_1 = D_2)}$$

$$\text{(UNF-}\star1) \quad \frac{F \wedge D_1 \cdot D_2 = \mathbf{star}(a, N) \cdot E_2}{(F \wedge D_1 \cdot D_2 = E_2) \vee (F \wedge \exists M : D_1 \cdot D_2 = a \cdot \mathbf{star}(a, M) \cdot E_2 \wedge N = M+1)}$$

$$\text{(UNF-}\star2) \quad \frac{F \wedge D_1 \cdot D_2 = E_1 \cdot \mathbf{star}(a, N)}{(F \wedge D_1 \cdot D_2 = E_1) \vee (F \wedge \exists M : D_1 \cdot D_2 = E_1 \cdot \mathbf{star}(a, M) \cdot a \wedge N = M+1)}$$

Fig. 5. Split rules and unfold rules for **star** functions

An *unfolding rule* applies the definition of a recursive function, replacing the head with the body that typically contains a number of disjuncts (cf. the `replace` function presented in Sect. 2). We describe such a rule using an unfolding rule *schema* (UNF) for a recursive function E as follows:

$$\text{(UNF)} \quad \frac{F \wedge D_1 \cdot D_2 = E \cdot D_3}{\bigvee (F \wedge D_1 \cdot D_2 = E_i \cdot D_3)} \quad E \text{ is defined as } \bigvee E_i$$

A *variable-splitting rule* is used to split a string variable into sub-variables. We shall describe such a rule using a variable-splitting rule schema (SPL) as follows:

$$\text{(SPL)} \; \frac{F \wedge D_1 \cdot D_2 = E_1 \cdot E_2}{(F \wedge D_1 = E_1 \wedge D_2 = E_2) \vee (F \wedge \exists Z : D_1 = E_1 \cdot Z \wedge Z \cdot D_2 = E_2 \wedge \mathbf{length}(Z) > 0)} \\ \vee (F \wedge \exists T : E_1 = D_1 \cdot T \wedge D_2 = T \cdot E_2 \wedge \mathbf{length}(T) > 0)$$

The specific instances of (SPL) and (UNF) rules used in this paper are listed in Fig. 5. There are 3 split rules to deal with string equations and 2 unfold rules for **star** functions. The notation a_i^j denotes the substring of a from bound i to j.

We now discuss the relationship between the splitting rules and the issue of non-termination. Intuitively, the aim of the splitting rules is to reduce/break the current formula into "sub-formulas", where the complexity is reduced. A problem arises when the rule reduces the current formula into sub-formulas, where the complexity is actually *not* reduced. In other words, even though we have reduced the formula, we are in fact not any closer in finding a satisfying solution nor in finding a proof for unsatisfiability. This is the main reason for non-termination.

Let us now illustrate, in more detail, the issue of non-termination. We use Example 3, a simplified version of Example 1. Here, non-termination comes from dealing with recursive function **star** which is used to represent Kleene star regular expressions. We note that both Examples 3 and 1 address the same non-progression problem in dealing with unbounded strings. Our purpose in choosing Example 3 to present is for simplicity.

Example 3. Recursive function **star**:

$$X = \mathbf{star}(\text{"}a\text{"}, N) \wedge X = Y_1 \cdot \text{"}b\text{"} \cdot Z$$

Figure 6 summarizes the main steps of solving Example 3. (For simplicity, we ignore existential variables.) Similarly to solving Example 1, here we also need to unfold the definition of **star**("a", N) function and normalize the formula to DNF. An application of the unfold rule (UNF-$\star$1) would result in a disjunction of two reducts:

$$X = \text{""} \wedge X = Y_1 \cdot \text{"}b\text{"} \cdot Z \quad \text{and}$$
$$X = \text{"}a\text{"} \cdot \mathbf{star}(\text{"}a\text{"}, M) \wedge N = M + 1 \wedge X = Y_1 \cdot \text{"}b\text{"} \cdot Z$$

The first reduct leads to a contradiction:

$$\text{(SUB)} \; \frac{X = \text{""} \wedge X = Y_1 \cdot \text{"}b\text{"} \cdot Z}{X = \text{""} \wedge \text{""} = Y_1 \cdot \text{"}b\text{"} \cdot Z}$$
$$\text{(CON)} \; \frac{}{\texttt{false}}$$

This contradiction appears in the tree depicted in Fig. 6, but is hidden in the part of the tree that was abbreviated away for brevity.

In the second reduct, by substituting X with $Y_1 \cdot \text{"}b\text{"} \cdot Z$, we introduce a new constraint $Y_1 \cdot \text{"}b\text{"} \cdot Z = \text{"}a\text{"} \cdot \mathbf{star}(\text{"}a\text{"}, M)$. Now the only way to proceed is to split Y_1 into two parts: "a" and Y_2 (for brevity, we omitted the base case where $Y_1 = \text{""}$). After substituting Y_1 with "a"$\cdot Y_2$ and simplifying the formula, we obtain a new constraint: $Y_2 \cdot \text{"}b\text{"} \cdot Z = \mathbf{star}(\text{"}a\text{"}, M)$. If we repeat this process of unfolding the definition of **star** function, clearly we will go into an infinite loop.

$$\text{(UNF-$\star$1)} \quad \frac{X = \mathbf{star}(\text{``}a\text{''}, N) \wedge X = Y_1 \cdot \text{``}b\text{''} \cdot Z}{}$$

$\vdots$

$$\text{(SUB)} \quad \frac{X = \text{``}a\text{''} \cdot \mathbf{star}(\text{``}a\text{''}, M) \wedge N = M+1 \wedge X = Y_1 \cdot \text{``}b\text{''} \cdot Z}{}$$

$$\text{(SPL-2)} \quad \frac{Y_1 \cdot \text{``}b\text{''} \cdot Z = \text{``}a\text{''} \cdot \mathbf{star}(\text{``}a\text{''}, M) \wedge N = M+1 \wedge X = Y_1 \cdot \text{``}b\text{''} \cdot Z}{}$$

$$\text{(SUB)} \quad \frac{Y_1 \cdot \text{``}b\text{''} \cdot Z = \text{``}a\text{''} \cdot \mathbf{star}(\text{``}a\text{''}, M) \wedge Y_1 = \text{``}a\text{''} \cdot Y_2 \wedge N = M+1 \wedge X = Y_1 \cdot \text{``}b\text{''} \cdot Z}{}$$

$$\text{(SIM)} \quad \frac{\text{``}a\text{''} \cdot Y_2 \cdot \text{``}b\text{''} \cdot Z = \text{``}a\text{''} \cdot \mathbf{star}(\text{``}a\text{''}, M) \wedge Y_1 = \text{``}a\text{''} \cdot Y_2 \wedge N = M+1 \wedge X = Y_1 \cdot \text{``}b\text{''} \cdot Z}{}$$

$$\text{(UNF-$\star$1)} \quad \frac{Y_2 \cdot \text{``}b\text{''} \cdot Z = \mathbf{star}(\text{``}a\text{''}, M) \wedge Y_1 = \text{``}a\text{''} \cdot Y_2 \wedge N = M+1 \wedge X = Y_1 \cdot \text{``}b\text{''} \cdot Z}{}$$

$\vdots$

$$\text{(SPL-2)} \quad \frac{\begin{array}{c} Y_2 \cdot \text{``}b\text{''} \cdot Z = \text{``}a\text{''} \cdot \mathbf{star}(\text{``}a\text{''}, P) \wedge \\ M = P+1 \wedge Y_1 = \text{``}a\text{''} \cdot Y_2 \wedge N = M+1 \wedge X = Y_1 \cdot \text{``}b\text{''} \cdot Z \end{array}}{}$$

$$\text{(SUB)} \quad \frac{\begin{array}{c} Y_2 \cdot \text{``}b\text{''} \cdot Z = \text{``}a\text{''} \cdot \mathbf{star}(\text{``}a\text{''}, P) \wedge Y_2 = \text{``}a\text{''} \cdot Y_3 \wedge \\ M = P+1 \wedge Y_1 = \text{``}a\text{''} \cdot Y_2 \wedge N = M+1 \wedge X = Y_1 \cdot \text{``}b\text{''} \cdot Z \end{array}}{}$$

$$\text{(SIM)} \quad \frac{\begin{array}{c} \text{``}a\text{''} \cdot Y_3 \cdot \text{``}b\text{''} \cdot Z = \text{``}a\text{''} \cdot \mathbf{star}(\text{``}a\text{''}, P) \wedge Y_2 = \text{``}a\text{''} \cdot Y_3 \wedge \\ M = P+1 \wedge Y_1 = \text{``}a\text{''} \cdot Y_2 \wedge N = M+1 \wedge X = Y_1 \cdot \text{``}b\text{''} \cdot Z \end{array}}{}$$

$$\text{(UNF-$\star$1)} \quad \frac{\begin{array}{c} Y_3 \cdot \text{``}b\text{''} \cdot Z = \mathbf{star}(\text{``}a\text{''}, P) \wedge Y_2 = \text{``}a\text{''} \cdot Y_3 \wedge \\ M = P+1 \wedge Y_1 = \text{``}a\text{''} \cdot Y_2 \wedge N = M+1 \wedge X = Y_1 \cdot \text{``}b\text{''} \cdot Z \end{array}}{}$$

$\vdots$

Fig. 6. Derivation tree for Example 3

4.2 Progressive Search Strategy

As mentioned earlier, the key idea to achieve progression is to prune away a subtree when we are sure that a shorter solution can be found elsewhere. We first need to define a measure to decide which solution is shorter. This measure is parameterized by a sequence of variables. We use σ, τ to denote sequences.

Definition 3 (Lexical Length of a Solution). *Given a formula F, let $\sigma = (x_1, x_2, \ldots, x_n)$ be a sequence of variables constructed from a non-empty subset of $\mathrm{Var}(F)$. For each solution α of F, i.e. α is an assignment $[x_1 = a_1, x_2 = a_2, \ldots, x_n = a_n, \ldots]$, the lexical length of α is defined as a n-tuple $(\mathbf{length}(a_1), \mathbf{length}(a_2), \ldots, \mathbf{length}(a_n))$. We use $\mathrm{Len}_\sigma(\alpha)$ to denote the lexical length of α w.r.t. the sequence σ.* □

We now use a lexical order to sort the solution set of a formula F based on the lexical length of each solution. If F has a solution then its minimum lexical length w.r.t. a sequence σ, denoted by $l(\sigma, F)$, is defined as the lexical length of a minimal solution of F. If F has no solution then its minimum lexical length is denoted by $\top$. We assume that $\forall \sigma, F : l(\sigma, F) \leq \top$. We now can compare two arbitrary formulas based on their minimum lexical length of solutions.

Definition 4 (Total Order for Formulas). *Given two formulas F and G and let σ be a sequence of variables constructed from a non-empty subset of the common variables of F and G, a total order $\preceq_\sigma$ is defined as follows:*

$$F \preceq_\sigma G \overset{def}{=} l(\sigma, F) \leq l(\sigma, G) \qquad \qquad \square$$

We define equality $=_\sigma$ and strict inequality $\prec_\sigma$ in the obvious way. We now outline three important properties[2] of $\prec_\sigma$:

- [Prop-1]: If $F \equiv (G \vee H)$ where $\mathtt{Var}(F) \subseteq \mathtt{Var}(H)$ and $\exists \sigma : F \prec_\sigma G$ then $F =_\sigma H$
- [Prop-2]: If $(G \vee H) \Rightarrow F$ and $\exists \sigma : F =_\sigma G$ then $F =_\sigma (G \vee H)$
- [Prop-3]: If $\exists \sigma : F =_\sigma G$ and τ is a prefix of σ then $F =_\tau G$

Among them, we want to direct the attention towards the third property. It is used to ensure the soundness of the proposed method later. It states that if two formulas F and G have the same minimum lexical length of solutions w.r.t. a sequence σ, then they also have the same minimum lexical length of solutions w.r.t. a sequence τ, where τ is a prefix of σ.

Input: $I : Fml$, τ : a sequence on $\mathtt{Var}(I)$
Output: SAT/UNSAT
$\langle 1 \rangle$ **if** SOLVE($I, \tau, \emptyset$) **return** SAT **else return** UNSAT

function SOLVE($H : Fml$, σ_I: a sequence, γ: a list of pairs of a formula and a sequence)
$\langle 2 \rangle$ **if** ($H \equiv$ false) **return false**
$\langle 3 \rangle$ **if** (there is no rule to apply) **return true**
$\langle 4 \rangle$ $\bigvee G_i \leftarrow$ APPLYRULE(H)   /* Apply a derivation rule */
$\langle 5 \rangle$ Let Υ be the set of all the reducts G_i
$\langle 6 \rangle$ **foreach** reduct $G \in \Upsilon$ **do**   /* Choose G by following Z3 heuristics */
$\langle 7 \rangle$ **if** (G contains a recursive term or a non-grounded concatenation)
$\langle 8 \rangle$ **if** ($\exists (F, \sigma) \in \gamma$ s.t. $F \prec_\sigma G$) **return false**   /* PRUNE !!! */
$\langle 9 \rangle$ Let σ_H be a sequence on $\mathtt{Var}(H)$ s.t. σ_I is a prefix of σ_H /* CONDITION 1 */
$\langle 10 \rangle$ $\gamma \leftarrow \gamma \cup \langle H, \sigma_H \rangle$
$\langle 11 \rangle$ **endif**
$\langle 12 \rangle$ **if** SOLVE(G, σ_I, γ) **return true**
$\langle 13 \rangle$ **if** (G contains a recursive term or a non-grounded concatenation)
$\langle 14 \rangle$ $\gamma \leftarrow \gamma \setminus \{H, \sigma_H\}$
$\langle 15 \rangle$ **endfor**
$\langle 16 \rangle$ **return false**
end function

Algorithm S3P. Progressive Search

Now we show how to prune a derivation subtree when we are sure that a solution with shorter lexical length can be found elsewhere. We do this by augmenting the strategy already described in Sect. 4.1 with a new step which enables us to prune the proof tree.

Definition 5 (Progressive Pruning). *Let there be a derivation tree rooted at an input formula I, and let τ be a sequence of all the variables of I. Let F be a formula labelling a node in the tree. A set of prunable subtrees of F is a set of its descendants G_i such that there exists a sequence σ constructed from all variables of F satisfying the two conditions:*

---

[2] All the proofs are in our technical report [22].

- τ *is a prefix of* σ *and*
- $F \prec_\sigma G$.

We then prune *derivation subtrees rooted at formulas* G_i.   □

The first condition ensures that a minimal solution of a formula F w.r.t. a sequence of all variables of F is also a minimal solution of F w.r.t. a sequence of all variables of the input formula I (according to [Prop-3]). Meanwhile, the second condition ensures that whenever we prune G, we still preserve a minimal solution of formula F w.r.t. a sequence of all of the variables of F.

We now present our algorithm as Algorithm S3P. Line 2 corresponds to the case when we find a contradiction. In Line 6, we iterate over the set of subformulas; the ordering between them is not important. (In fact, in our implementation, we simply follow the heuristics of Z3.) Line 8 represents the key feature of our algorithm; it implements our pruning step (by returning false). Line 9 prepares for the pruning of a descendant of the current formula H (by ensuring that the first condition of Definition 5 is met).

Theorem 1 (Soundness). *Given an input formula* I, *if Algorithm S3P*

- *returns SAT: then* I *is satisfiable;*
- *returns UNSAT: then* I *is unsatisfiable.*

□

We now consider the completeness of Algorithm S3P. Before we can formalize this property, we need to discuss the condition check in line 8. This check determines the lexical order between two formulas, and is by no means a primitive operation. In fact, we do not know if the check is, in general, decidable. Our completeness result below nevertheless assumes that we have a decision procedure for this check. Later, in Sect. 5.1, we present an implementation which, though not a decision procedure, is sound and practical. We follow this up in Sect. 6 with an experimental evaluation.

Theorem 2 (Semi-completeness). *Suppose the given input formula* I *is satisfiable. Then Algorithm S3P will return SAT, and produce a minimal solution w.r.t some sequence* τ *of all the variables of* I.   □

5 Implementation

We first show how to implement the pruning step of our search algorithm. Then we present the conflict clause learning for string theory, especially in the setting of Z3.

5.1   The Pruning Step

To implement the pruning step of the Algorithm S3P, we have to keep track of the set γ which contains pairs of the current formula H and some sequence σ_H of all of the variables of H. When backtracking, such pair will be removed from γ correspondingly. Let τ be the sequence of all of the variables of the input formula I. The sequence σ_H is constructed by concatenating the sequence τ with additional variables from $\mathbf{Var}(H)$. Specifically, $\sigma_H = \tau \ll \delta$ where $\mathbf{Var}(\delta) = \mathbf{Var}(H) \setminus \mathbf{Var}(\tau)$. For Example 3, after the first unfolding:

$$\tau \text{ is } (N, X, Y_1, Z) \text{ and } \gamma \text{ is } \{(X = \mathbf{star}(\text{``}a\text{''}, N) \wedge X = Y_1 \cdot \text{``}b\text{''} \cdot Z, \ \tau)\}.$$

We now show how to implement the condition check in line 8 of Algorithm S3P. Suppose the current formula is G, if

- we find a pair (F, σ) in γ and a substitution θ such that $G\theta \Rightarrow F$, and
- the substitution θ is a progressive substitution (as defined in Definition 6 below) w.r.t a sequence σ.

then the condition check is satisfied. Obviously, θ must not introduce new conflicts in $G\theta$, which prevents $G\theta$ from being `false` trivially.

Definition 6 (A Progressive Substitution). *Let G be a formula, and σ be a sequence of subset variables of G. A substitution θ is progressive w.r.t a sequence σ if for every solution α of G, there exists a solution β of $G\theta$ such that $\mathbf{Len}_\sigma(\beta) < \mathbf{Len}_\sigma(\alpha)$.*   □

For Example 3, in the second unfolding, the current formula is

$$G \equiv Y_2 \cdot \text{``}b\text{''} \cdot Z = \mathbf{star}(\text{``}a\text{''}, M) \wedge Y_1 = \text{``}a\text{''} \cdot Y_2 \wedge N = M + 1 \wedge X = Y_1 \cdot \text{``}b\text{''} \cdot Z$$

Obviously, there exists $F \equiv X = \mathbf{star}(\text{``}a\text{''}, N) \wedge X = Y_1 \cdot \text{``}b\text{''} \cdot Z$ and a substitution $\theta = [M/N, N/N+1, X/\text{``}a\text{''} \cdot X, Y_1/\text{``}a\text{''} \cdot Y_1, Y_2/Y_1, Z/Z]$, such that the implication check $G\theta \Rightarrow F$ succeeds. Furthermore, the substitution θ is progressive w.r.t the sequence τ, that is (N, X, Y_1, Z). This is because if $\mathbf{length}(N) = k$ in a solution α (if any) of G, we have $\mathbf{length}(M) = k - 1$. Then, we have $\mathbf{length}(N) = k - 1$ in the corresponding solution α' of $G\theta$. Because $\mathbf{Len}_\tau$ function returns a 4-tuple whose first element is $\mathbf{length}(N)$, θ is progressive. As a result, we can stop the second unfolding.

Lemma 1. *The implementation of the pruning step is sound*   □

5.2   Conflict Clause Learning

We present our conflict clause learning technique for string theory, with the focus on the case when non-progression is detected. Specifically, in the implementation of the pruning step, suppose there exists (F, σ) in γ and a substitution θ such that $G\theta \Rightarrow F$ and θ is progressive w.r.t σ. A corollary of Lemma 1 is that we have $F \prec_\sigma G$ (see the proof of Lemma 1 in [22]). Now, in addition to returning `false` as in line 8 of Algorithm S3P, we also mark $\widehat{G}$ as a possible conflict clause. We derive $\widehat{G}$ from G by removing all equations in solved form which is defined for both string and integer theories as below. If later we can not find any solution in solving F, then we can conclude F is unsatisfiable and produce a conflict clause $\widehat{G}$. The soundness of this learning is stated in Lemmas 2 and 3.

Definition 7 (String Solved Form). *A string equation is in solved form if it is in the form of* $X = f(Y_1, \ldots, Y_n, a_1, \ldots, a_m)$, *where* $X \in V_{str}$, $Y_1, \ldots, Y_n \in V_{str}$, $a_1, \ldots, a_n \in C_{str}$, $X \notin \{Y_1, \ldots, Y_n\}$, *and* f *is a non-recursive function.* □

For example, $X = \mathbf{concat}(Y, Z)$ is in solved form. $X = \mathbf{concat}(Y, \mathbf{concat}(Y_1, Y_2))$ can be rewritten into two formulas $X = \mathbf{concat}(Y, Z)$ and $Z = \mathbf{concat}(Y_1, Y_2)$, which are both in solved form. Similarly, we can define a solved form in integer theory:

Definition 8 (Integer Solved Form). *An equation is in solved form if it is in the form of* $M = g(N_1, .., N_n, p_1, \ldots, p_m)$, *where* $M \in V_{int}$, $V_1, .., V_n \in V_{int} \cup V_{str}$, $p_1, \ldots, p_m \in C_{int} \cup C_{str}$, $M \notin \{N_1, \ldots, N_n\}$, *and* g *is a function.* □

Now, suppose some formula G contains an equation $X = f(\cdots)$ in solved form, we are able to eliminate variable X by substituting X with $f(\cdots)$ in G. To obtain $\widehat{G}$, we need to remove all equations in solved form from G. The purpose of deriving $\widehat{G}$ is to obtain the core reason for pruning G, which helps us to extract a smaller unsatisfiable core for the input formula. For Example 3, G is $Y_2 \cdot \text{``}b\text{''} \cdot Z = \mathbf{star}(\text{``}a\text{''}, M) \wedge Y_1 = \text{``}a\text{''} \cdot Y_2 \wedge N = M + 1 \wedge X = Y_1 \cdot \text{``}b\text{''} \cdot Z$. So we have 3 equations $Y_1 = \text{``}a\text{''} \cdot Y_2$, $N = M + 1$, and $X = Y_1 \cdot \text{``}b\text{''} \cdot Z$ which are in solved form. Therefore, we mark $\widehat{G} \equiv Y_2 \cdot \text{``}b\text{''} \cdot Z = \mathbf{star}(\text{``}a\text{''}, M)$ as a possible conflict clause. Later, when we can decide the unsatisfiability of the input formula, based on the implication graph, we can trace back to extract an unsat core for the input formula. Specifically, it is $X = \mathbf{star}(\text{``}a\text{''}, N) \wedge X = Y_1 \cdot \text{``}b\text{''} \cdot Z$.

Lemma 2. *Suppose the pruning condition check is applied for specific formulas F and G. Then F can be written into the form $G \vee G_r$ and the following holds: if G_r is unsatisfiable, F is unsatisfiable.* □

Lemma 3. $\widehat{G}$ *is satisfiable iff G is satisfiable.* □

Now we present the detailed implementation of obtaining $\widehat{G}$ in Z3, given that Z3 manages theory terms via its congruence closure engine. First, we give an overview on how Z3 builds its equivalence classes. Given an equation, its two sides will be represented as two nodes in an equivalence class. For Example 3, since G is $Y_2 \cdot \text{``}b\text{''} \cdot Z = \mathbf{star}(\text{``}a\text{''}, M) \wedge Y_1 = \text{``}a\text{''} \cdot Y_2 \wedge N = M + 1 \wedge X = Y_1 \cdot \text{``}b\text{''} \cdot Z$, we have 4 equivalence classes as follows:

- X, $Y_1 \cdot \text{``}b\text{''} \cdot Z$
- $Y_2 \cdot \text{``}b\text{''} \cdot Z$,    $\mathbf{star}(\text{``}a\text{''}, M)$
- Y_1, $\text{``}a\text{''} \cdot Y_2$
- N, $M + 1$

Note that given a node e representing a term Q, we are able to access all nodes representing terms that take term Q as their parameters (e.g., for string term D and E, we can access the nodes representing $\mathbf{length}(D)$, $\mathbf{concat}(D, E)$). We call the later parent nodes of e.

There are three steps to remove an equation $V = f(\cdots)$ in solved form. First, we mark the node representing variable V. A node e is marked when:

- it represents a single variable V (V can be either a string variable or an integer variable),
- the size of its equivalence class is greater than 1,
- its parent nodes are not in the same equivalence class as e, and
- not all of remaining nodes in the equivalence class of e contain recursive functions.

Second, we substitute the value of all marked nodes in their parent nodes with the value of another node in the equivalence classes of the marked nodes. Finally, we need to traverse all unmarked nodes in the equivalence classes to create a conjunction of all equations. For Example 3, according to above conditions, nodes representing X, Y_1, and N will be marked in their corresponding equivalence classes. Then, we can traverse all unmarked nodes to obtain the formula $\widehat{G} \equiv Y_2 \cdot \text{``}b\text{''} \cdot Z = \mathbf{star}(\text{``}a\text{''}, M)$.

6   Evaluation

We implemented our algorithm into S3 [21] which itself was built on top of the Z3 framework [9]. Our solver is called S3P which stands for *Progressive S3*. To evaluate our solver, we conduct two case studies which involve practical benchmark constraints generated from testing JavaScript web applications. All experiments are run on a 3.2 GHz machine with 8GB memory.

In the first case study, we used a large and popular set of benchmark constraints generated using the Kudzu symbolic execution framework [18]. State-of-the-art string solvers are also evaluated using this benchmark suite, making it convenient for us to provide detailed comparisons on the applicability and efficiency of our new solver.

Note that the constraints in Kudzu's benchmarks have already been pre-processed and/or over-simplified. In particular, the string lengths have been bounded and recursive string function such as **replace** have been transformed to primitive operators so that the underlying solver of Kudzu [18] can handle. Because strong support for the **replace** function is critical for enhancing security analysis of web applications, we conduct a second case study, of a smaller scale, but with special focus on the **replace** function. The main purpose is to show that S3P is more applicable than existing solvers in such domain applications.

Kudzu Benchmarks: In this case study, we use the set of constraints which can be downloaded at: http://webblaze.cs.berkeley.edu/2010/kaluza. They were generated using Kudzu [18], a symbolic execution framework for JavaScript,

Table 1. Constraints generated by Kudzu

	Norn	CVC4	S3	Z3-str2	S3P
Sat	27068	33227	34961	34931	35270
Unsat	11561	11625	11799	11799	12014
Unk	0	0	0	524	0
Error	6187	0	0	0	0
TO (20s)	2468	2432	524	30	0
Time (s)	178960	50346	16547	6309	6972

Table 2. Usefulness of unsatisfiable cores for Kudzu framework

# unsat files		12014
S3P	Time	1129 s
S3P with unsat core	# unsat cores	59
	% skipped	99.5
	Time	11 s

when testing 18 subject applications consisting of popular AJAX applications. The generated constraints are of boolean, integer and string types. Integer constraints also include ones on length of string variables, while string constraints include string equations, membership predicates. To compare with other solvers, we choose to use the SMT-format version of Kaluza benchmark as provided in [14].

This case study consists of two parts. The first part is to evaluate our non-progression detection technique. Table 1 shows the result of solving Kudzu constraints by S3P, compared with 4 state-of-the-art solvers: Norn (v1.0), CVC4 (v1.4), S3 (v17092015), Z3-str2 (v1.0.0). While Norn is automata-based string solver, the others, including S3P, are word-based string solvers, in which string is treated as a basic type.

It can be seen that automata-based solvers such as Norn are not good at handling constraints generated from concolic testing of web applications. This is because such constraints are usually of multi-sorted theory, including both string constraints and integer constraints, such as those coming from the string lengths.

In fact, for the case of Kudzu constraints, all word-based string solvers dominate Norn. Not counting S3P, Z3-str2 is the solver that produces the best result. Z3-str2 also terminates on 524 benchmarks where Norn, CVC4 and S3 all time out. Specifically, Z3-str2 terminates with an Unknown answer if the input formula contains the so-called "overlapping variables" [23].

Compared with Z3-str2, S3P can in fact decide the satisfiability of these 524 benchmarks. S3P achieves this by employing the proposed technique for non-progression detection. Specifically,

- if an input formula is unsatisfiable, S3P is able to decide the unsatisfiability of that formula. For example, it can decide the unsatisfiability of 215 input formulas in those 524 benchmarks.
- otherwise, being able to effectively prune away non-progressive paths, S3P has a chance of finding solutions in other search branches. As such, the remaining of those 524 benchmarks are decided as satisfiable with the correct models.

In fact, for each of the 35270 benchmarks which S3P declares to be satisfiable, we conjoin the model generated by S3P with the original input formula and pass it to the other 4 solvers. As a result, all 4 solvers can now decide, with an answer confirming the satisfiability, even on those benchmarks they could not decide before. In other words, all models produced by S3P are cross-checked and all the solvers reach a consensus for every single case.

In the second part of this case study, we focus on benchmarks which are unsatisfiable, in order to demonstrate our conflict clause learning technique. More specifically, we will extract the unsatisfiable cores from those input constraints, and show the potential usefulness of the cores in a dynamic symbolic execution (DSE) framework (e.g. Kudzu). To do this, we compare the result of solving 12014 unsatisfiable formulas in Kudzu benchmarks by two versions of S3P. The first version (S3P) will solve each formula independently. In contrast, when deciding a formula as unsatisfiable, the second version will cache its unsat core. Subsequently, it will attempt to skip a formula if the formula is discharged by some cached unsat core. The result is summarized in Table 2. There are two important observations:

- By extracting and caching the unsatisfiable cores of 59 formulas, we can skip checking the satisfiability of the remaining formulas (99.5 %) (which in fact represent infeasible paths to the attack against the sink). Overall, we achieve the speedup of about 102x faster.
- Unsatisfiable cores are also useful for validating/debugging the result. By inspecting a much smaller number of constraints compared to the original ones, we are able to validate the final result. For example, we are able to confirm that all unsatisfiable answers are correct by inspecting them manually.

Jalangi Benchmarks: This second case study is to focus on the **replace** string function. As such, we collect constraints generated by testing web applications using the concolic tester in Jalangi framework [19], and do not make any preprocessing with those constraints. These applications are `annex`, `tenframe`, `calculator`, `go`, and `shopping`. Note that all of them are not vulnerable to XSS attacks.

Let us first present the set-up to collect this set of constraint benchmarks. For each web application, we choose a sink point, that is innerHTML. Then we symbolically execute paths from a source to the sink. These path constraints will be combined with attack specifications at the sink. The resulting formulas are sent to a constraint solver.

Table 3. Constraints generated by Jalangi

# benchmarks	# constraints	# **replace** operation	Time of S3P
48	624	96	143.7 s

Table 3 summarizes the statistics of those formulas, along with the running time of S3P. In 48 benchmarks, there are 624 constraints and 96 constraints are involved in **replace** operation. So the percentage of **replace** operation is about 15 %.

More importantly, **replace** operation appears in all benchmarks. The reason is that after a source point, a web application usually provides some sanitizing mechanism, for example, by replacing all "<" with "<" and ">" with ">". As such, the path constraints usually involve the **replace** function. For a concrete example, after symbolically executing the program, a DSE framework will combine the path constraints with the specifications for attacks, to create queries for the constraint solver. A specification for innerHTML sink can be all the strings that contain " < script". Then a simplified example of a common pattern is:

$$\text{input}_1 = \textbf{replace}(\text{input}, \text{``<''}, \text{``\<''}) \wedge \text{input}_2 = \textbf{replace}(\text{input}_1, \text{``>''}, \text{``\>''}) \ \wedge$$
$$\text{output} = \text{input}_2 \ \cdot \ \text{``</br>''} \ \wedge \ \textbf{contains}(\text{output}, \text{``<script''})$$

Given that Z3-str2, CVC4, and Norn *cannot* deal with **replace** operation, the only work which is comparable in term of the expressiveness as our solver, is S3. However, S3 *timeouts* for all of those formulas because it goes into infinite loops (similarly to what we have shown in Sect. 2). In contrast, S3P can decide the unsatisfiability of all benchmarks. Since S3P is the only solver that is applicable in those constraints (which are generated from testing web applications), we believe it will make a remarkable contribution to ensuring the security of web applications.

7   Related Work

There is a vast literature on the problem of string solving. Practical methods for solving string equations can loosely be divided into bounded and unbounded methods. Bounded methods (e.g., HAMPI [13], CFGAnalyzer [4, 11]) often assume fixed length string variables, then treat the problem as a normal constraint satisfaction problem (CSP). These methods can be quite efficient in finding satisfying assignments and often can express a wider range of constraints than the unbounded methods. However, as also identified in [18], there is still a big gap in order to apply them to constraints arising from the analysis of web applications.

To reason about feasibility of a symbolic execution path from high-level programs, of which string constraints are involved, one approach [6, 18] is to proceed by first enumerating concrete length values, before encoding strings into bit-vectors. In a similar manner, [17] addresses multiple types of constraints for Java PathFinder. Though this approach can handle many operators, it provides limited support for **replace**, requiring the result and arguments to be concrete. Furthermore, it does not handle regular expressions. In summary, all of them have similar limitations such as performance [21].

Unbounded methods are often built upon the theory of automata or regular languages. We will be brief and mention a few notable works. Java String Analyzer (JSA) [8] applies static analysis to model flow graphs of Java programs in order to capture dependencies among string variables. A finite automata is then derived to constrain possible string values. The work [20] used finite state machines (FSMs) for abstracting strings during symbolic execution of Java programs. They handle a few core methods in the `java.lang.String` class, and some other related classes. They partially integrate a numeric constraint solver. For instance, string operations which return integers, such as **indexOf**, trigger case-splits over all possible return values. A recent work [5] provides an automata-based technique for solving string constraints, and further, a method for counting the number of solutions to such constraints. A recent string solver Norn [1,2] is also based on automata techniques.

Using automata and/or regular language representations potentially enables the reasoning of infinite strings and regular expressions. However, most of existing approaches have difficulties in handling string operations related to integers such as **length**, let alone other high-level operations addressed in this paper. More importantly, to assist web application analysis, it is necessary to reason about both string and non-string behavior together. It is not clear how to adapt such techniques for the purpose, given that they do not provide native support for constraints of the type integer.

Most of recent work on string solving are based on unbounded methods with string as a primitive data type. Examples are Z3-str [24], CVC4 [14], S3 [21], Z3-str2 [23]. However, none of them addresses the non-termination issues in string solving as in this paper. Though in [23], the authors address non-termination in splitting overlapping string variables, they currently can not decide the satisfiability of such formulas. In contrast, we generalize common non-termination issues that appear in solving string constraints generated from reasoning about web applications. Along with that is a progressive algorithm which we believe is applicable to not just S3, but also other solvers in this family of word-based string solvers.

8   Conclusion

This paper presents a progressive algorithm for solving string constraints for the intended purpose of analyzing practical web applications. Its main feature is its ability to handle the termination problem when unfolding recursive definitions which define the constraints. This, together with another feature of conflict clause learning, were demonstrated to show usefulness in pruning the search space and new levels of results in Javascript benchmarks arising from web applications. Finally, because our algorithm deals with recursive definitions in a somewhat general manner, we believe it can be extended to support reasoning about unbounded data structures, for example heap-allocated data structures.

References

1. Abdulla, P.A., Atig, M.F., Chen, Y.-F., Holík, L., Rezine, A., Rümmer, P., Stenman, J.: String constraints for verification. In: Biere, A., Bloem, R. (eds.) CAV 2014. LNCS, vol. 8559, pp. 150–166. Springer, Heidelberg (2014)
2. Abdulla, P.A., Atig, M.F., Chen, Y.-F., Holík, L., Rezine, A., Rümmer, P., Stenman, J.: Norn: an SMT solver for string constraints. In: Kroening, D., Păsăreanu, C.S. (eds.) CAV 2015. LNCS, vol. 9206, pp. 462–469. Springer, Heidelberg (2015)
3. Avgerinos, T., Rebert, A., Cha, S.K., Brumley, D.: Enhancing symbolic execution with veritesting. In: ICSE, pp. 1083–1094. ACM (2014)
4. Axelsson, R., Heljanko, K., Lange, M.: Analyzing context-free grammars using an incremental SAT solver. In: Aceto, L., Damgård, I., Goldberg, L.A., Halldórsson, M.M., Ingólfsdóttir, A., Walukiewicz, I. (eds.) ICALP 2008, Part II. LNCS, vol. 5126, pp. 410–422. Springer, Heidelberg (2008)
5. Aydin, A., Bang, L., Bultan, T.: Automata-based model counting for string constraints. In: Kroening, D., Păsăreanu, C.S. (eds.) CAV 2015. LNCS, vol. 9206, pp. 255–272. Springer, Heidelberg (2015)
6. Bjørner, N., Tillmann, N., Voronkov, A.: Path feasibility analysis for string-manipulating programs. In: Kowalewski, S., Philippou, A. (eds.) TACAS 2009. LNCS, vol. 5505, pp. 307–321. Springer, Heidelberg (2009)
7. Buchi, J.R., Senger, S.: Definability in the existential theory of concatenation and undecidable extensions of this theory. In: Mathematical Logic Quarterly, pp. 337–342 (1988)
8. Christensen, A.S., Møller, A., Schwartzbach, M.I.: Precise analysis of string expressions. In: SAS, pp. 1–18 (2003)
9. de Moura, L., Bjørner, N.S.: Z3: an efficient SMT solver. In: Ramakrishnan, C.R., Rehof, J. (eds.) TACAS 2008. LNCS, vol. 4963, pp. 337–340. Springer, Heidelberg (2008)
10. ECMA-404. Javascript object notation. http://www.json.org/
11. He, J., Flener, P., Pearson, J., Zhang, W.: Solving string constraints: the case for constraint programming. In: CP, pp. 381–397 (2013)
12. Jaffar, J., Murali, V., Navas, J.A.: Boosting concolic testing via interpolation. In: FSE, pp. 48–58. ACM (2013)
13. Kiezun, A., Ganesh, V., Guo, P.J., Hooimeijer, P., Ernst, M.D.: Hampi: a solver for string constraints. In: ISSTA, pp. 105–116. ACM (2009)
14. Liang, T., Reynolds, A., Tinelli, C., Barrett, C., Deters, M.: A DPLL(T) theory solver for a theory of strings and regular expressions. In: Biere, A., Bloem, R. (eds.) CAV 2014. LNCS, vol. 8559, pp. 646–662. Springer, Heidelberg (2014)
15. Makanin, G.S.: The problem of solvability of equations in a free semigroup. Math. USSR-Sbornik **32**(2), 129 (1977)
16. OWASP. Top ten project, May 2013. http://www.owasp.org/
17. Redelinghuys, G., Visser, W., Geldenhuys, J.: Symbolic execution of programs with strings. In: SAICSIT, pp. 139–148. ACM (2012)
18. Saxena, P., Akhawe, D., Hanna, S., Mao, F., McCamant, S., Song, D.: A symbolic execution framework for javascript. In: SP, pp. 513–528 (2010)
19. Sen, K., Kalasapur, S., Brutch, T., Gibbs, S.: Jalangi: a selective record-replay and dynamic analysis framework for javascript. In: FSE, pp. 488–498 (2013)
20. Shannon, D., Ghosh, I., Rajan, S., Khurshid, S.: Efficient symbolic execution of strings for validating web applications. In: DEFECTS, pp. 22–26 (2009)

21. Trinh, M.-T., Chu, D.-H., Jaffar, J.: S3: a symbolic string solver for vulnerability detection in webapplications. In: ACM-CCS, pp. 1232–1243. ACM (2014)
22. Trinh, M.-T., Chu, D.-H., Jaffar, J.: Progressive reasoning over recursively-defined strings. Technical report (2016). http://www.comp.nus.edu.sg/~trinhmt/progressive/
23. Zheng, Y., Ganesh, V., Subramanian, S., Tripp, O., Dolby, J., Zhang, X.: Effective search-space pruning for solvers of string equations, regular expressions and length constraints. In: Kroening, D., Păsăreanu, C.S. (eds.) CAV 2015. LNCS, vol. 9206, pp. 235–254. Springer, Heidelberg (2015)
24. Zheng, Y., Zhang, X., Ganesh, V.: Z3-str: a z3-based string solver for web application analysis. In: ESEC/FSE, pp. 114–124 (2013)

String Analysis via Automata Manipulation with Logic Circuit Representation

Hung-En Wang[1], Tzung-Lin Tsai[1], Chun-Han Lin[2], Fang Yu[2], and Jie-Hong R. Jiang[1($\boxtimes$)]

[1] Graduate Institute of Electronics Engineering,
National Taiwan University, Taipei, Taiwan
jhjiang@ntu.edu.tw
[2] Department of Management Information Systems,
National Chengchi University, Taipei, Taiwan

Abstract. Many severe security vulnerabilities in web applications can be attributed to string manipulation mistakes, which can often be avoided through formal string analysis. String analysis tools are indispensable and under active development. Prior string analysis methods are primarily automata-based or satisfiability-based. The two approaches exhibit distinct strengths and weaknesses. Specifically, existing automata-based methods have difficulty in generating counterexamples at system inputs to witness vulnerability, whereas satisfiability-based methods are inadequate to produce filters amenable for firmware or hardware implementation for real-time screening of malicious inputs to a system under protection. In this paper, we propose a new string analysis method based on a scalable logic circuit representation for (nondeterministic) finite automata to support various string and automata manipulation operations. It enables both counterexample generation and filter synthesis in string constraint solving. By using the new data structure, automata with large state spaces and/or alphabet sizes can be efficiently represented. Empirical studies on a large set of open source web applications and well-known attack patterns demonstrate the unique benefits of our method compared to prior string analysis tools.

1 Introduction

Analyzing string manipulating code is of great importance because string manipulation is ubiquitous in modern software systems, such as web applications and database services. String analysis aims to determine the set of assignments to the string variables in string expressions that may arise from program execution or other sources. It can be applied, e.g., to identify security vulnerabilities by checking if a security sensitive function can receive an input string that contains an exploit [24,29,32], to identify behaviors of JavaScript code that use the `eval` function by computing the string values that can reach the `eval` function [15], to identify html generation errors by computing the html code generated by web applications [20], to identify the set of queries that are sent to back-end database

© Springer International Publishing Switzerland 2016
S. Chaudhuri and A. Farzan (Eds.): CAV 2016, Part I, LNCS 9779, pp. 241–260, 2016.
DOI: 10.1007/978-3-319-41528-4_13

by analyzing the code that generates the SQL queries [12], and to patch input validation and sanitization functions by automatically synthesizing repairs [31].

Prior string analysis methods are mainly automata-based or satisfiability-based. For automata-based approaches, explicit state-graph represented finite automata [8,13], MTBDD represented finite automata [2,32], and Boolean algebra represented symbolic finite automata [10,27,28] have been proposed. By characterizing a set of strings as a language, these methods are not restricted to particular bounds on string lengths. They can be used to synthesize filters or sanitizers [31] to screen out malicious string inputs to systems under protection, but have difficulty in generating counterexamples at system inputs to witness vulnerability. For satisfiability-based approaches, bit-vector based bounded checking [4,18,19,23] and satisfiability modulo theories (SMT) based constraint solving [1,3,26,34] have been proposed. They may answer a certain set of string queries with length constraints not doable for automata-based methods. By searching a solution to a given set of string constraints, they can generate counterexamples to witness vulnerability, but cannot support the synthesis of string filters amenable for firmware or hardware implementation for real-time screening of malicious inputs to a system under protection.

In this paper, we intend to support string analysis of acyclic constraints with both counterexample generation and filter synthesis capabilities. To achieve this goal, we develop a nondeterministic finite automata (NFA) manipulation engine with logic circuit representation. In particular, we adopt the and-inverter graph (AIG) [21], which have been widely adopted in logic synthesis for industrial applications in electronic design automation (EDA) in recent years, as the underlying data structure. Thereby automata manipulations can be performed implicitly using logic circuits while determinization is largely avoided. Our method is scalable to automata with large alphabet sizes in contrast to BDD-based automata representation. We further extend our method to represent symbolic finite automata [10], which may have infinite (or very large) alphabets [25]. Our method enables the generation of counterexamples for backtracking attack input strings to a vulnerable application and the synthesis of filters amenable for firmware or hardware implementation to avoid exploits of vulnerabilities in real time. The proposed method is implemented as a new string analysis tool, named SLOG. We conduct comprehensive experimental study on over 20000 string constraints generated from real web applications to compare state-of-the-art tools, including JSA [8], STRANGER [30], Z3-STR2 [34], CVC4 [3], and NORN [1]. Experiments suggest the performance advantage of SLOG in contrast to other string solvers with counterexample generation capabilities. Moreover, the scalability of SLOG is shown for automata with large alphabets in contrast to BDD-based methods of automata representation.

2   Preliminaries

A *finite automaton* A is a five-tuple (Q, Σ, I, T, O), where Q is a finite state set, Σ is an alphabet, $I \subseteq Q$ is a set of initial states, $T \subseteq \Sigma \times Q \times Q$ is a state transition relation, and $O \subseteq Q$ is a set of accepting states. In the sequel, we shall instead represent the initial states, transition relation, and accepting states in terms of characteristic functions $I : Q \rightarrow \mathbb{B}$, $T : \Sigma \times Q \times Q \rightarrow \mathbb{B}$, and $O : Q \rightarrow \mathbb{B}$, respectively. (A characteristic function χ represents a (Boolean encoded) set S by having $\chi(e) = 1$ (TRUE) if $e \in S$ and $\chi(e) = 0$ (FALSE) if $e \notin S$.) A finite automaton can be either a deterministic finite automaton (DFA) or a nondeterministic finite automaton (NFA) depending on the determinicity of its state transition. In the sequel, we refer $\boldsymbol{x}$, $\boldsymbol{s}$ and $\boldsymbol{s}'$ to the input, current-state and next-state variables in the Boolean domain, and relate the valuations of variables $\boldsymbol{x}$, denoted $[\![\boldsymbol{x}]\!]$, and the valuations of variables $\boldsymbol{s}$, denoted $[\![\boldsymbol{s}]\!]$, to the alphabet Σ and state set Q, respectively. A *trace* of an automaton is a state-input alternating sequence $q_1, \sigma_1, q_2, \sigma_2, \ldots, q_\ell$, which satisfies $T(\sigma_i, q_i, q_{i+1})$ for $i = 1, \ldots, \ell - 1$.

A (finite) *string* $\sigma_1, \ldots, \sigma_n$, for $n \geq 0$ (an *empty string*, denoted ϵ, when $n = 0$), over alphabet Σ is accepted by an automaton if there exist states $q_1, \ldots, q_{n+1}$ such that $I(q_1) = 1$ (for q_1 being an initial state), $O(q_{n+1}) = 1$ (for q_{n+1} being an accepting state), and the sequence $q_1, \sigma_1, q_2, \sigma_2, \ldots, q_{n+1}$ forms a trace. The set of strings accepted by an automaton A is called the *(regular) language* accepted by A, denoted as $\mathcal{L}(A)$.

Because a finite automaton $A = (Q, \Sigma, I, T, O)$ can be fully described by the characteristic functions of I, T, and O, with Boolean encoding on Q and Σ the automaton A can be represented as a logic circuit, denoted $\mathcal{C}(A)$, that realizes these characteristic functions. In the sequel, we shall not distinguish between characteristic functions I, T, O and their circuit representations. In this work, we show how various string and automata manipulations can be achieved under the logic circuit representation of (nondeterministic) finite automata. For practical implementation, we exploit the *and-inverter graph (AIG)* [21] as the underlying data structure for scalable logic circuit representation and manipulation. An AIG is a directed acyclic graph $G(V, E)$, where each vertex $v \in V$ is either a primary input node without any fanin or a function node representing a two-input AND gate, and each edge $(u, v) \in E$ denotes a complemented or uncomplemented connection from vertex u to v. Due to its simplicity, the AIG has been efficiently implemented as a Boolean reasoning engine widely used in various logic synthesis and formal verification tasks in industrial very-large-scale integration (VLSI) designs.

In the sequel, we assume a finite automaton can be nondeterministic and may even take ϵ-transitions. To represent an ϵ-transition under the circuit representation, we reserve a symbol "ϵ" as an addendum to Σ with a special handling. Given a state transition relation T, we denote its equivalent variant with an ϵ self-transition inserted for each state as T^ϵ. That is, $T^\epsilon(\boldsymbol{x}, \boldsymbol{s}, \boldsymbol{s}')$ represents $T(\boldsymbol{x}, \boldsymbol{s}, \boldsymbol{s}') \vee ((\boldsymbol{s} = \boldsymbol{s}') \wedge (\boldsymbol{x} = \epsilon))$.

Given a web application and an attack pattern (specified as a regular expression) we can first extract *dependency graphs* for security sensitive functions, called the *sinks*, from the web application using static program analysis techniques [14,17]. Each extracted dependency graph shows how the input values flow to a sink, including all the string operations performed on the input values before they reach the sink. A dependency graph is vulnerable if its sink node accepts an attack string (with respect to a given attack pattern). From the dependency graph, we can generate string constraint formulas and check whether the intersection of the sink node's language and the attack pattern is empty. If it is empty, then the web application is not vulnerable. Otherwise, a counterexample witnessing the vulnerability is to be computed.

3   String and Automata Operations

We show that string/language operations, including *intersection, union, concatenation, deletion, replacement,* and *emptiness checking,* can be achieved under logic circuit representation. We omit other less used operations, including reversion, prefix, suffix, and substring, due to space limitation.

In the following exposition we assume an automaton A (or A_i) is represented as a circuit of its characteristic functions $T(x, s, s')$, $I(s)$, and $O(s)$ (or $T_i(x, s_i, s_i')$, $I_i(s_i)$, and $O_i(s_i)$ for $i = 1, 2, 3$). Also we assume without loss of generality that $|s_1| = m$ and $|s_2| = n$ for automata A_1 and A_2, respectively, with $m \leq n$ in our following discussion unless otherwise said.

3.1   Intersection

Given two automata A_1 and A_2, the automaton $A_{\text{INT}} = \text{INT}(A_1, A_2)$ that accepts language $\mathcal{L}(A_{\text{INT}}) = \mathcal{L}(A_1) \cap \mathcal{L}(A_2)$ is the product machine with the characteristic functions $T_{\text{INT}}, I_{\text{INT}}, O_{\text{INT}}$ constructed by first augmenting the transition relations T_1 and T_2 to T_1^ϵ and T_2^ϵ, respectively, by inserting an ϵ self-transition for each state, and second conjuncting the resultant characteristic functions of A_1 and A_2. Accordingly, we have

$$\frac{(T_1, I_1, O_1) \qquad (T_2, I_2, O_2)}{(T_{\text{INT}}, I_{\text{INT}}, O_{\text{INT}})} \text{ INT}$$

with

$$T_{\text{INT}}(x, s, s') = T_1^\epsilon(x, s_1, s_1') \wedge T_2^\epsilon(x, s_2, s_2'),$$
$$I_{\text{INT}}(s) = I_1(s_1) \wedge I_2(s_2),$$
$$O_{\text{INT}}(s) = O_1(s_1) \wedge O_2(s_2),$$

for $s = (s_1, s_2)$. The corresponding circuit construction is illustrated in Fig. 1(a). The constructed circuit is of size $O(|\mathcal{C}(A_1)| + |\mathcal{C}(A_2)|)$ and has $(|s_1| + |s_2|)$ state variables.

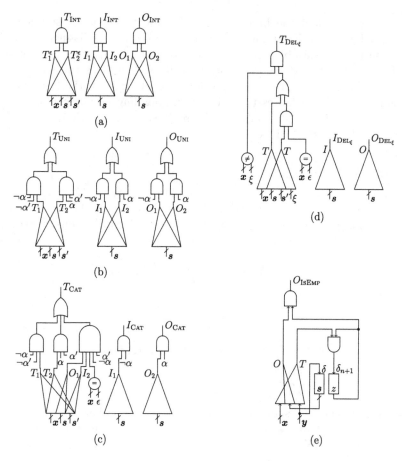

Fig. 1. Circuit construction of (a) INT, (b) UNI, (c) CAT, (d) DEL$_\xi$, and (e) ISEMP operations.

3.2   Union

Given two automata A_1 and A_2, the automaton $A_{\mathrm{UNI}} = \mathrm{UNI}(A_1, A_2)$ that accepts language $\mathcal{L}(A_{\mathrm{UNI}}) = \mathcal{L}(A_1) \cup \mathcal{L}(A_2)$ can be constructed by disjointly unioning the two with state variables being merged and states being distinguished by an auxiliary variable α, similar to the multiplexed machine in [16], as follows.

$$\frac{(T_1, I_1, O_1) \qquad (T_2, I_2, O_2)}{(T_{\mathrm{UNI}}, I_{\mathrm{UNI}}, O_{\mathrm{UNI}})} \ \mathrm{UNI}$$

with

$$T_{\mathrm{UNI}}(\boldsymbol{x}, \boldsymbol{s}, \boldsymbol{s}') = (\neg\alpha \wedge \neg\alpha' \wedge T_1(\boldsymbol{x}, \langle \boldsymbol{s}_2 \rangle_m, \langle \boldsymbol{s}'_2 \rangle_m)) \vee (\alpha \wedge \alpha' \wedge T_2(\boldsymbol{x}, \boldsymbol{s}_2, \boldsymbol{s}'_2)),$$
$$I_{\mathrm{UNI}}(\boldsymbol{s}) = (\neg\alpha \wedge I_1(\langle \boldsymbol{s}_2 \rangle_m)) \vee (\alpha \wedge I_2(\boldsymbol{s}_2)),$$
$$O_{\mathrm{UNI}}(\boldsymbol{s}) = (\neg\alpha \wedge O_1(\langle \boldsymbol{s}_2 \rangle_m)) \vee (\alpha \wedge O_2(\boldsymbol{s}_2)),$$

where $s = (s_2, \alpha)$ and the bracket "$\langle s_2 \rangle_m$" indicates taking a subset of the first m variables of s_2. Essentially the state variables s of A_1 is merged into s_2 so that the first m variables of s_2 are shared by both A_1 and A_2. Moreover, the α bit signifies the states of A_1 by $\alpha = 0$, and signifies the states of A_2 by $\alpha = 1$. That is, a state $q \in [\![s]\!]$ belongs to A_1 if its variable α valuates to 0, and to A_2 if α valuates to 1. The corresponding circuit construction is illustrated in Fig. 1(b). The constructed circuit is of size $O(|\mathcal{C}(A_1)| + |\mathcal{C}(A_2)|)$ and has $(\max\{|s_1|, |s_2|\} + 1)$ state variables.

3.3 Concatenation

Given two automata A_1 and A_2, the automaton $A_{\mathrm{CAT}} = \mathrm{CAT}(A_1, A_2)$ that accepts language $\mathcal{L}(A_{\mathrm{CAT}}) = (\mathcal{L}(A_1).\mathcal{L}(A_2))$, which contains the set of concatenated strings $\sigma_1.\sigma_2$ for $\sigma_1 \in \mathcal{L}(A_1)$ and $\sigma_2 \in \mathcal{L}(A_2)$, can be constructed, in a way similar to UNI, as follows.

$$\frac{(T_1, I_1, O_1) \qquad (T_2, I_2, O_2)}{(T_{\mathrm{CAT}}, I_{\mathrm{CAT}}, O_{\mathrm{CAT}})} \; \mathrm{CAT}$$

with

$$T_{\mathrm{CAT}}(x, s, s') = (\neg\alpha \wedge \neg\alpha' \wedge T_1(x, \langle s_2 \rangle_m, \langle s_2' \rangle_m)) \vee (\alpha \wedge \alpha' \wedge T_2(x, s_2, s_2')) \vee$$
$$((x = \epsilon) \wedge \neg\alpha \wedge \alpha' \wedge O_1(\langle s_2 \rangle_m) \wedge I_2(s_2')),$$
$$I_{\mathrm{CAT}}(s) = \neg\alpha \wedge I_1(\langle s_2 \rangle_m),$$
$$O_{\mathrm{CAT}}(s) = \alpha \wedge O_2(s_2),$$

for $s = (s_2, \alpha)$. The corresponding circuit construction is illustrated in Fig. 1(c). The constructed circuit is of size $O(|\mathcal{C}(A_1)| + |\mathcal{C}(A_2)|)$ and has $(\max\{|s_1|, |s_2|\} + 1)$ state variables.

3.4 Deletion

Given an automaton A, the automaton $A_{\mathrm{DEL}_\xi} = \mathrm{DEL}(A, \xi)$ for $\xi \in \Sigma$ that accepts the strings of $\sigma \in \mathcal{L}(A)$ but with each appearance of symbol "ξ" in σ being removed can be constructed as follows.

$$\frac{(T, I, O)}{(T_{\mathrm{DEL}_\xi}, I_{\mathrm{DEL}_\xi}, O_{\mathrm{DEL}_\xi})} \; \mathrm{DEL}_\xi$$

with

$$T_{\mathrm{DEL}_\xi}(x, s, s') = (T(x, s, s') \vee ((x = \epsilon) \wedge T(\xi, s, s'))) \wedge (x \neq \xi),$$
$$I_{\mathrm{DEL}_\xi}(s) = I(s),$$
$$O_{\mathrm{DEL}_\xi}(s) = O(s),$$

(The deletion operation is a special case of the replacement operation by replacing an alphabet symbol with ϵ.) The corresponding circuit construction is illustrated in Fig. 1(d). The constructed circuit is of size $O(|\mathcal{C}(A)|)$ and has $|s|$ state variables.

3.5   Replacement

Given three automata A_1, A_2, A_3, we study how to construct the automata $A_{\text{REP}} = \text{REP}(A_1, A_2, A_3)$ that accepts the language $\{(\sigma_1.\tau_1.\sigma_2.\tau_2 \ldots) \in \Sigma^* \mid (\sigma_1.\rho_1.\sigma_2.\rho_2 \ldots) \in \mathcal{L}(A_1), \sigma_i \notin (\Sigma^*.\mathcal{L}(A_2).\Sigma^*), \rho_i \in \mathcal{L}(A_2)$ and $\tau_i \in \mathcal{L}(A_3)$ for all $i\}$, that is, replacing $\mathcal{L}(A_2)$ with $\mathcal{L}(A_3)$ in $\mathcal{L}(A_1)$. Based upon [32], we construct the automata A_{REP} as follows.

$$\frac{(T_1, I_1, O_1) \qquad (T_2, I_2, O_2) \qquad (T_3, I_3, O_3)}{(T_{\text{REP}}, I_{\text{REP}}, O_{\text{REP}})} \; \text{REP}$$

First, we build automaton $A_1^{\lhd\rhd}$, which parenthesizes any substrings of a string in $\mathcal{L}(A_1)$ by two fresh new symbols "$\lhd$" and "$\rhd$". It yields from A_1 the automaton $A_1^{\lhd\rhd}$ with

$$T_1^{\lhd\rhd} = ((\alpha = \alpha') \wedge (\boldsymbol{x} \neq \lhd) \wedge (\boldsymbol{x} \neq \rhd) \wedge T_1(\boldsymbol{x}, \boldsymbol{s}_1, \boldsymbol{s}_1')) \vee$$
$$((\boldsymbol{s}_1 = \boldsymbol{s}_1') \wedge ((\neg\alpha \wedge \alpha' \wedge (\boldsymbol{x} = \lhd)) \vee (\alpha \wedge \neg\alpha' \wedge (\boldsymbol{x} = \rhd)))),$$
$$I_1^{\lhd\rhd} = \neg\alpha \wedge I_1(\boldsymbol{s}_1),$$
$$O_1^{\lhd\rhd} = \neg\alpha \wedge O_1(\boldsymbol{s}_1).$$

The above construction makes two copies of the state space distinguished by variable α. When the input symbol is not equal to $\lhd$ or $\rhd$, the state transition is the same as A_1. When the input symbol equals $\lhd$ (resp. $\lhd$), the state in the $\alpha = 0$ (resp. $\alpha = 1$) space transitions to its counterpart in the $\alpha = 1$ (resp. $\alpha = 0$) space.

Second, we build automaton A_4, which is the automaton that accepts the strings $\{(\sigma_1.\lhd.\rho_1.\rhd.\sigma_2.\lhd.\rho_2.\rhd \ldots) \in \Sigma^* \mid \sigma_i \in \overline{\Sigma^*.\mathcal{L}(A_2).\Sigma^*}$ and $\rho_i \in \mathcal{L}(A_2)\}$. Let A_h be the automaton that accepts the language $\Sigma^*.\mathcal{L}(A_2).\Sigma^*$ with characteristic functions $T_h(\boldsymbol{x}, \boldsymbol{s}_h, \boldsymbol{s}_h')$, $I_h(\boldsymbol{s}_h)$, $O_h(\boldsymbol{s}_h)$. Notice that constructing the automaton A_h requires complementing an NFA and is of exponential cost. Fortunately in most applications the automaton A_2 is known *a priori* and thus can be precomputed. Given A_2 and A_h, assuming without loss of generality $|\boldsymbol{s}_h| = n \geq |\boldsymbol{s}_2| = m$, automata A_4 can be derived as follows.

$$T_4 = (\neg\beta \wedge \neg\beta' \wedge (\boldsymbol{x} \neq \lhd) \wedge (\boldsymbol{x} \neq \rhd) \wedge T_h(\boldsymbol{x}, \boldsymbol{s}_h, \boldsymbol{s}_h')) \vee$$
$$(\beta \wedge \beta' \wedge (\boldsymbol{x} \neq \lhd) \wedge (\boldsymbol{x} \neq \rhd) \wedge T_2(\boldsymbol{x}, \langle \boldsymbol{s}_h \rangle_m, \langle \boldsymbol{s}_h' \rangle_m)) \vee$$
$$(\neg\beta \wedge \beta' \wedge (\boldsymbol{x} = \lhd) \wedge O_h(\boldsymbol{s}_h) \wedge I_2(\langle \boldsymbol{s}_h' \rangle_m)) \vee$$
$$(\beta \wedge \neg\beta' \wedge (\boldsymbol{x} = \rhd) \wedge O_2(\langle \boldsymbol{s}_h \rangle_m) \wedge I_h(\boldsymbol{s}_h')),$$
$$I_4 = \neg\beta \wedge I_h(\boldsymbol{s}_h),$$
$$O_4 = \neg\beta \wedge (O_h(\boldsymbol{s}_h) \vee I_h(\boldsymbol{s}_h)).$$

Third, let $A_5 = \text{INT}(A_1^{\lhd\rhd}, A_4)$ with characteristic functions $T_5(\boldsymbol{x}, \boldsymbol{s}_5, \boldsymbol{s}_5')$, $I_5(\boldsymbol{s}_5)$, $O_5(\boldsymbol{s}_5)$, where $\boldsymbol{s}_5 = (\boldsymbol{s}_1, \alpha, \boldsymbol{s}_4)$ with $\boldsymbol{s}_4 = (\boldsymbol{s}_h, \beta)$. Hence A_5 accepts the strings in $\mathcal{L}(A_1)$ with all the substrings in $\mathcal{L}(A_2)$ being marked. Then, in

$\mathcal{L}(A_5)$ instead of replacing substrings $\lhd\mathcal{L}(A_2)\rhd$ with strings in $\mathcal{L}(A_3)$, we replace $\lhd$ with $\mathcal{L}(A_3)$, $\rhd$ with ϵ, and $\mathcal{L}(A_2)$ with ϵ. We obtain

$$
\begin{aligned}
T_{\text{REP}}(\boldsymbol{x}, \boldsymbol{s}, \boldsymbol{s}') = \ & (\neg\alpha \wedge \neg\alpha' \wedge T_5(\boldsymbol{x}, \boldsymbol{s}_5, \boldsymbol{s}_5') \wedge \neg\gamma \wedge \neg\gamma' \wedge I_3(\boldsymbol{s}_3) \wedge I_3(\boldsymbol{s}_3')) \vee \\
& (\neg\alpha \wedge \neg\alpha' \wedge (\boldsymbol{s}_5 = \boldsymbol{s}_5') \wedge (\boldsymbol{x} = \epsilon) \wedge \neg\gamma \wedge \gamma' \wedge I_3(\boldsymbol{s}_3) \wedge I_3(\boldsymbol{s}_3')) \vee \\
& (\neg\alpha \wedge \neg\alpha' \wedge (\boldsymbol{s}_5 = \boldsymbol{s}_5') \wedge \gamma \wedge \gamma' \wedge T_3(\boldsymbol{x}, \boldsymbol{s}_3, \boldsymbol{s}_3')) \vee \\
& (\neg\alpha \wedge \alpha' \wedge T_5(\lhd, \boldsymbol{s}_5, \boldsymbol{s}_5') \wedge (\boldsymbol{x} = \epsilon) \wedge \gamma \wedge \neg\gamma' \wedge I_3(\boldsymbol{s}_3') \wedge O_3(\boldsymbol{s}_3)) \vee \\
& (\alpha \wedge \alpha' \wedge \exists \boldsymbol{y}.[T_5(\boldsymbol{y}, \boldsymbol{s}_5, \boldsymbol{s}_5')] \wedge (\boldsymbol{x} = \epsilon) \wedge \neg\gamma \wedge \neg\gamma' \wedge I_3(\boldsymbol{s}_3) \wedge I_3(\boldsymbol{s}_3')) \vee \\
& (\alpha \wedge \neg\alpha' \wedge T_5(\rhd, \boldsymbol{s}_5, \boldsymbol{s}_5') \wedge (\boldsymbol{x} = \epsilon) \wedge \neg\gamma \wedge \neg\gamma' \wedge I_3(\boldsymbol{s}_3) \wedge I_3(\boldsymbol{s}_3')), \\
I_{\text{REP}}(\boldsymbol{s}) = \ & \neg\gamma \wedge I_5(\boldsymbol{s}_5) \wedge I_3(\boldsymbol{s}_3), \\
O_{\text{REP}}(\boldsymbol{s}) = \ & \neg\gamma \wedge O_5(\boldsymbol{s}_5) \wedge I_3(\boldsymbol{s}_3),
\end{aligned}
$$

for $\boldsymbol{s} = (\boldsymbol{s}_5, \boldsymbol{s}_3, \gamma)$.

The constructed circuit is of size $O(|\mathcal{C}(A_1)| + |\mathcal{C}(A_2)| + |\mathcal{C}(A_h)| + |\mathcal{C}(A_3)|)$ and has $|\boldsymbol{x}|$ quantified internal variables.

3.6   Emptiness Checking

One important query, $\text{IsEMP}(A)$, about an automaton A is asking whether the language $\mathcal{L}(A)$ is empty. We employ property directed reachability (PDR) [11], an implementation of the state-of-the-art model checking algorithm IC3 [5] in the Berkeley ABC system [6], to test whether an accepting state is reachable from an initial state in A. Note that PDR only accepts a sequential circuit specified in transition functions, rather than a transition relation, as input; furthermore, it assumes the given circuit shall have a single initial state. Unfortunately because our automata are nondeterministic in general, their nondeterministic transitions can only be specified using transition relations and they may have multiple initial states.

To overcome the above mismatch between transition relation and transition function, we devise a mechanism converting $(T(\boldsymbol{x}, \boldsymbol{s}, \boldsymbol{s}'), I(\boldsymbol{s}), O(\boldsymbol{s}))$ representation of NFA A into a form acceptable by PDR as follows. To handle the single initial state restriction, let A_ϵ be the automaton accepting only the ϵ string, which is composed of a single initial accepting state without any transition. We modify A by $\text{CAT}(A_\epsilon, A)$ to enforce a single initial state. Moreover, to convert a transition relation to a set of transition functions, we introduce n new input variables $\boldsymbol{y}$ for $n = |\boldsymbol{s}|$ and a new state variable z with initial value 1, and construct a new sequential circuit with

- the output function: $O_{\text{IsEMP}} = (O(\boldsymbol{s}) \wedge z)$, and
- the next-state functions: $\delta_i = (y_i)$ for state variables s_i, $i = 1, \ldots, n$, and $\delta_{n+1} = (T(\boldsymbol{x}, \boldsymbol{s}, \boldsymbol{y}) \wedge z)$ for the state variable z.

Fig. 1(e) shows the corresponding circuit construction, where the rectangular boxes denote state-holding elements. With these conversions, PDR can be directly applied on the constructed new circuit. The constructed circuit is of size $O(\mathcal{C}(A))$ and has $(|\boldsymbol{s}| + 1)$ state variables and $(|\boldsymbol{x}| + |\boldsymbol{y}|)$ input variables. The complexity of checking language emptiness is PSPACE-complete in the circuit size of the underlying automaton.

4   Counterexample Generation

The automata manipulation flow specified in a dependency graph often ends with an ISEMP query asking whether a vulnerability exists for the application under verification. If the answer to ISEMP is negative, it is desirable to generate a counterexample witnessing the vulnerability. Such a counterexample should be expressed in terms of the inputs to the application. However since the counterexample to the ISEMP query is a trace demonstrating the reachability from an initial state to an accepting state in the final automaton, it does not directly correspond to the counterexample at the inputs. By counterexample generation, we compute counterexample traces at the inputs of a dependency graph that together induce a specific counterexample trace at the sink node. Prior automata-based methods cannot easily generate such counterexamples because the output automaton resulted from an automata operation does not contain information about its input automata whereas our circuit construction preserves such information through the introduced auxiliary variables.

Below we show how to backtrack from the negative answer to ISEMP to extract the input counterexamples. The backtrack process traverses the dependency graph in a reverse topological order and deduces the upstream counterexamples according to the corresponding operations in the following. Notice that an automata circuit iteratively constructed by our method may contain internally quantified variables. These variables are treated as free variables in PDR computation without explicit quantifier elimination, and their corresponding assignments are determined by PDR and returned along with the trace information.

Intersection. Let $(p_1, q_1), (\sigma_1, \rho_1, \varrho_1), (p_2, q_2), (\sigma_2, \rho_2, \varrho_2), \ldots, (p_\ell, q_\ell)$ be the counterexample trace of automaton $A_{\text{INT}} = \text{INT}(A_1, A_2)$, where $p_i \in [\![s_1]\!], q_i \in [\![s_2]\!], \sigma_i \in \Sigma, \rho_i \in \Sigma^k, \varrho_i \in \Sigma^l$, for some $k, l \geq 0$ and (s_1, s_2) being the state variables of A_{INT} as constructed in Sect. 3.1. Let the values $\rho_i \in \Sigma^k$ and $\varrho_i \in \Sigma^l$ correspond to the assignments to the internally quantified variables of A_1 and A_2, respectively. Then the counterexample traces of A_1 and A_2 can be extracted backward by the following rule.

$$\frac{A_1\colon (p_1, (\sigma_1, \rho_1), \ldots, p_\ell) \qquad A_2\colon (q_1, (\sigma_1, \varrho_1), \ldots, q_\ell)}{A_{\text{INT}}\colon ((p_1, q_1), (\sigma_1, \rho_1, \varrho_1), \ldots, (p_\ell, q_\ell))} \text{ INTCEX}$$

Union. Let $(q_1, c), (\sigma_1, \rho_1), (q_2, c), (\sigma_2, \rho_2), \ldots, (q_\ell, c)$ be the counterexample trace of automaton $A_{\text{UNI}} = \text{UNI}(A_1, A_2)$, where $q_i \in [\![s_2]\!], c \in [\![\alpha]\!], \sigma_i \in \Sigma$, and $\rho_i \in \Sigma^k$, for some $k \geq 0$ and s_2 being the state variables of A_{UNI} as constructed in Sect. 3.2. Let the values $\rho_i \in \Sigma^k$ correspond to the assignments to the internally quantified variables of A_1 or A_2. The the counterexample traces of A_1 and A_2 can be extracted backward by the following rules.

$$\frac{A_1: (q_1, (\sigma_1, \rho_1), \ldots, q_\ell) \qquad A_2: (\bot)}{A_{\text{UNI}}: ((q_1, c), (\sigma_1, \rho_1), \ldots, (q_\ell, c))} \text{ UNiCEX, } c = 0$$

$$\frac{A_1: (\bot) \qquad A_2: (q_1, (\sigma_1, \rho_1), \ldots, q_\ell)}{A_{\text{UNI}}: ((q_1, c), (\sigma_1, \rho_1), \ldots, (q_\ell, c))} \text{ UNiCEX, } c = 1$$

Concatenation. Let $(q_1, c_1), (\sigma_1, \rho_1), (q_2, c_2), (\sigma_2, \rho_2), \ldots, (q_\ell, c_\ell)$ be the counterexample trace of automaton $A_{\text{CAT}} = \text{CAT}(A_1, A_2)$, where $q_i \in [\![s_2]\!]$, $c_i \in [\![\alpha]\!]$, $\sigma_i \in \Sigma$, and $\rho_i \in \Sigma^{k_i}$, for some $k_i \geq 0$ and (s_2, α) being the state variables of A_{CAT} as constructed in Sect. 3.3. Let the values $\rho_i \in \Sigma^{k_i}$ correspond to the assignments to the internally quantified variables of A_1 or A_2. Then the counterexample traces of A_1 and A_2 can be extracted backward by the following rule.

$$\frac{A_1: (q_1, z_1, \ldots, q_i) \qquad A_2: (q_{i+1}, z_{i+1}, \ldots, q_n)}{A_{\text{CAT}}: (p_1, z_1 \ldots, p_i, z_i, p_{i+1}, z_{i+1}, \ldots, p_\ell)} \text{ CATCEX}$$

where each $p_j = (q_j, 0)$ for all $j \leq i$, $p_j = (q_j, 1)$ for all $j \geq i+1$, and $z_j = (\sigma_j, \rho_j)$ for all $j \neq i$, and $z_i = (\epsilon, \rho_i)$.

Replacement. Let $(p_1, c_1, q_1, r_1, d_1), (\sigma_1, \rho_1, \varrho_1), \ldots, (p_{n_1}, c_{n_1}, q_{n_1},$ $r_{n_1}, d_{n_1}), (\sigma_{n_1}, \rho_{n_1}, \varrho_{n_1}), (p_{n_1+1}, c_{n_1+1}, q_{n_1+1}, r_{n_1+1}, d_{n_1+1}), (\sigma_{n_1+1}, \rho_{n_1+1},$ $\varrho_{n_1+1}), \ldots, (p_{n_2}, c_{n_2}, q_{n_2}, r_{n_2}, d_{n_2}), (\sigma_{n_2}, \rho_{n_2}, \varrho_{n_2}), (p_{n_2+1}, c_{n_2+1}, q_{n_2+1},$ $r_{n_2+1}, d_{n_2+1}), (\sigma_{n_2+1}, \rho_{n_2+1}, \varrho_{n_2+1}), \ldots, (p_\ell, c_\ell, q_\ell, r_\ell, d_\ell)$ be the counterexample trace of automaton $A_{\text{REP}} = \text{REP}(A_1, A_2, A_3)$, where $p_i \in [\![s_1]\!]$, $c_i \in [\![\alpha]\!]$, $q_i \in [\![s_4]\!]$, $r_i \in [\![s_3]\!]$, $d_i \in [\![\gamma]\!]$, $\sigma_i, \varrho_i \in \Sigma$, and $\rho_i \in \Sigma^k$, for some $k \geq 0$ and $(s_1, \alpha, s_4, s_3, \gamma)$ being the state variables of A_{REP} as constructed in Sect. 3.5. The trace must have the following form: Consider $(p_{n_i+1}, c_{n_i+1}, q_{n_i+1}, r_{n_i+1}, d_{n_i+1}), (\sigma_{n_i+1}, \rho_{n_i+1}, \varrho_{n_i+1}), \ldots, (p_{n_{i+1}}, c_{n_{i+1}}, q_{n_{i+1}},$ $r_{n_{i+1}}, d_{n_{i+1}})$. (Notice the subtle subscript difference between $n_i + 1$ and n_{i+1}.) For $i = 3m$, we have $c_j = 0$, $d_j = 0$ for $n_i + 1 \leq j \leq n_{i+1}$, and $\sigma_{n_i+1}\sigma_{n_i+2}\cdots\sigma_{n_{i+1}-1} \notin \Sigma^*.\mathcal{L}(A_2).\Sigma^*$. For $i = 3m+1$, we have $c_j = 0, d_j = 1$ for $n_i + 1 \leq j \leq n_{i+1}$, and $\sigma_{n_i+1}\sigma_{n_i+2}\cdots\sigma_{n_{i+1}-1} \in \mathcal{L}(A_3)$. For $i = 3m + 2$, we have $c_j = 1, d_j = 0, \sigma_j = \epsilon$ for $n_i + 1 \leq j \leq n_{i+1}$, and $\varrho_{n_i+1}\varrho_{n_i+2}\cdots\varrho_{n_{i+1}-1} \in \mathcal{L}(A_2)$. Also $\sigma_{n_i} = \epsilon$ for all i.

Let the values $\rho_i \in \Sigma^k$ and $\varrho_i \in \Sigma$ correspond to the assignments to the internally quantified variables of A_1 and to the assignments to the internally quantified variables added in the construction of A_{REP}, respectively. Then the counterexample trace of A_1 can be extracted backward by the following rule.

$$\frac{A_1:((\omega_1^\dagger)^-, (\omega_3^\ddagger)^-, (\omega_4^\dagger)^-, (\omega_6^\ddagger)^-, \ldots, (\omega_\ell^\dagger))}{A_{\text{REP}}:(\omega_1, z_1, \omega_2, z_2, \omega_3, z_3, \omega_4, z_4, \omega_5, z_5, \omega_6, z_6, \ldots, \omega_\ell)} \text{ REPCEX}$$

where each ω_i denote the trace $(p_{n_{i-1}+1}, c_{n_{i-1}+1}, q_{n_{i-1}+1}, r_{n_{i-1}+1}, d_{n_{i-1}+1}),$ $(\sigma_{n_{i-1}+1}, \rho_{n_{i-1}+1}, \varrho_{n_{i-1}+1}), \ldots, (p_{n_i}, c_{n_i}, q_{n_i}, r_{n_i}, d_{n_i})$, each z_i denote

$(\epsilon, \rho_{n_i}, \varrho_{n_i})$, each $\omega_i\dagger$ denote the trace $p_{n_{i-1}+1}$, $(\sigma_{n_{i-1}+1}, \rho_{n_{i-1}+1})$, $p_{n_{i-1}+2}$, $(\sigma_{n_{i-1}+2}, \rho_{n_{i-1}+2})$, ..., p_{n_i}, and each $\omega_i^{\ddagger}$ denote the trace $p_{n_{i-1}+1}$, $(\varrho_{n_{i-1}+1}, \rho_{n_{i-1}+1})$, $p_{n_{i-1}+2}$, $(\varrho_{n_{i-1}+2}, \rho_{n_{i-1}+2})$, ..., p_{n_i}. Also, for a trace $\omega = p_1, \sigma_1, \ldots, p_i, \sigma_i, p_{i+1}$, we denote its tail-removed subtrace $p_1, \sigma_1, \ldots, p_i, \sigma_i$ as ω^-.

5 Filter Generation

In addition to counterexample generation, one may further generate filters (also called vulnerability signatures in [31]) to block malicious input strings from the considered web application. By computing filters backward in the dependency graph, the filters for the input strings to an application can be obtained. The derived filters in our circuit representations are amenable for further hardware or firmware implementation to support a high-speed and low-power way of filtering malicious inputs from a web application. Notice that our circuit representation characterizes NFA in general, and further determinization may be needed for firmware or hardware implementation of filters. Although automata determinization can be costly, it is doable. Below we study how filter generation can be done under the proposed circuit representation.

First of all, the filter for the sink node of the dependency graph is available, assuming that sensitive strings to the underlying string manipulating program are known *a priori*. Moreover, consider an operator OP on a given set of input automata $A_1, \ldots, A_k$ yielding $A = \text{OP}(A_1, \ldots, A_k)$. Let B be an automaton with its language $\mathcal{L}(B) \subseteq \mathcal{L}(A)$ containing all illegal strings in $\mathcal{L}(A)$. We intend to construct the filter automaton B_i for some $i = 1, \ldots, k$ of concern such that $\mathcal{L}(B_i) \subseteq \mathcal{L}(A_i)$ and any $\sigma \in \mathcal{L}(A_i)$ satisfies $(\mathcal{L}(\text{OP}(A_1, \ldots, A_{i-1}, A_\sigma, A_{i+1}, \ldots, A_k)) \cap \mathcal{L}(B)) = \emptyset$ if and only if $\sigma \notin \mathcal{L}(B_i)$, where A_σ denotes the automaton that accepts exactly the string σ. Note that $\mathcal{L}(B_i)$ satisfying the above condition is a minimal filter provided that the relation among the inputs of an automata operation is ignored. Since the above condition guarantees that for each string in B_i, there exists a set of strings in other A_j's, $j \neq i$, such that some string in B is generated after apply OP on this set of strings of B_i and A_j's. Under the ignorance of the relation among the inputs of OP, a string should be kept in the language of filter automaton B_i as long as it may possibly result in a string in B through OP. The different OP cases are detailed in the following.

Intersection. Given the filter automaton B for the automaton $A = \text{INT}(A_1, A_2)$, the filter B can be directly applied as a filter for A_1 as well as A_2.

Union. Given the filter automaton B for $A = \text{UNI}(A_1, A_2)$, observe that every string in $\mathcal{L}(B)$ is in $\mathcal{L}(A_1)$ or in $\mathcal{L}(A_2)$. Hence automata $B_1 = \text{INT}(A_1, B)$ and $B_2 = \text{INT}(A_2, B)$ form legitimate filters for A_1 and A_2, respectively.

Concatenation. Given the filter automaton B for $A = \text{CAT}(A_1, A_2)$, to generate the corresponding filters B_1 and B_2 for A_1 and A_2, respectively, we first construct $B^\dagger = \text{INT}(A, B)$. Clearly, $\mathcal{L}(B^\dagger)$ equals $\mathcal{L}(B)$ because $\mathcal{L}(B) \subseteq \mathcal{L}(A)$. By the circuit construction of A, the auxiliary state variable α distinguishes between the substrings from $\mathcal{L}(A_1)$ and the substrings from $\mathcal{L}(A_2)$. As this information may not be seen in B, the purpose of this intersection is to identify the separation points between the two substring sources. Let B_1 be a copy of $B^\dagger$ but with the input symbol on every transition between states of $\alpha = 1$ being replaced with ϵ. Consider a trace $(q_1, c_1), \sigma_1, \ldots, (q_i, c_i), \epsilon, (q_{i+1}, c_{i+1}), \epsilon, \ldots, (q_\ell, c_\ell)$ accepted by B_1, where $(q_j, c_j) \in [\![s]\!]$ for s being the state variables of B_1, and $c_j \in [\![\alpha]\!]$ with $c_j = 0$ for $j \leq i$ and $c_j = 1$ for $j \geq i+1$. By the construction of B_1, there should be a trace $(q_1, c_1), \sigma_1, \ldots, (q_i, c_i), \epsilon, (q_{i+1}, c_{i+1}), \sigma_{i+1}, \ldots, (q_\ell, c_\ell)$ accepted by $B^\dagger$. The existence of such a trace ensures $\sigma_1 \sigma_2 \ldots \sigma_{i-1} \in \mathcal{L}(A_1)$, $\sigma_{i+1} \sigma_{i+2} \ldots \sigma_{\ell-1} \in \mathcal{L}(A_2)$, and $\sigma_1 \sigma_2 \ldots \sigma_{\ell-1} \in \mathcal{L}(B)$. The above trace accepted by $B^\dagger$ also ensures for each string, $\boldsymbol{\sigma} \in \mathcal{L}(B_1)$ if and only if there exists another string $\boldsymbol{\rho}$ in A_2 such that $\boldsymbol{\sigma}.\boldsymbol{\rho} \in \mathcal{L}(B)$. So B_1 forms a legitimate filter for A_1. Similarly, let B_2 be a copy of $B^\dagger$ but with the input symbol on every transition between states of $\alpha = 0$ being replaced with ϵ. Then B_2 forms a legitimate filter for A_2.

Replacement. Given the filter automaton B for $A = \text{REP}(A_1, A_2, A_3)$, to generate the filter B_1 for automaton A_1, each string in $\mathcal{L}(B)$ has the form $\boldsymbol{\sigma}_1 \boldsymbol{\tau}_1 \boldsymbol{\sigma}_2 \boldsymbol{\tau}_2 \ldots \boldsymbol{\sigma}_\ell$, where $\boldsymbol{\sigma}_i \in \overline{\Sigma^*.\mathcal{L}(A_2).\Sigma^*}$ and $\boldsymbol{\tau}_i \in \mathcal{L}(A_3)$ for $i = 1, \ldots, \ell$. We recognize each $\boldsymbol{\tau}_i$ and replace it with some string $\boldsymbol{\rho}_i \in \mathcal{L}(A_2)$. We then remove from the resultant language those strings not in A_1 by intersecting it with A_1. Therefore, B_1 can be constructed as follows.

First, similar to the construction of $A_1^{\triangleleft\triangleright}$ in Sect. 3.5, we build automaton $B^{\triangleleft\triangleright}$, which parenthesizes any substrings of a string in $\mathcal{L}(A_1)$. Second, similar to the construction of A_4 in Sect. 3.5, we build automaton B_4, which accepts the strings $\{(\boldsymbol{\sigma}_1. \triangleleft .\boldsymbol{\tau}_1. \triangleright .\boldsymbol{\sigma}_2. \triangleleft .\boldsymbol{\tau}_2. \triangleright \ldots) \in \Sigma^* \mid \boldsymbol{\sigma}_i \in \overline{\Sigma^*.\mathcal{L}(A_2).\Sigma^*} \text{ and } \boldsymbol{\tau}_i \in \mathcal{L}(A_3)\}$. Third, let $B_5 = \text{INT}(B^{\triangleleft\triangleright}, B_4)$. Hence $\mathcal{L}(B_5) = \{(\boldsymbol{\sigma}_1. \triangleleft .\boldsymbol{\tau}_1. \triangleright .\boldsymbol{\sigma}_2. \triangleleft .\boldsymbol{\tau}_2. \triangleright \ldots) \in \Sigma^* \mid (\boldsymbol{\sigma}_1.\boldsymbol{\tau}_1.\boldsymbol{\sigma}_2.\boldsymbol{\tau}_2 \ldots) \in \mathcal{L}(B) \text{ and } \boldsymbol{\sigma}_i \in \overline{\Sigma^*.\mathcal{L}(A_2).\Sigma^*} \text{ and } \boldsymbol{\tau}_i \in \mathcal{L}(A_3)\}$. Then, in $\mathcal{L}(B_5)$ instead of replacing substrings $\triangleleft\mathcal{L}(A_3)\triangleright$ with strings in $\mathcal{L}(A_2)$, we replace $\triangleleft$ with $\mathcal{L}(A_2)$, $\triangleright$ with ϵ, and $\mathcal{L}(A_3)$ with ϵ. Let the resultant automaton be $B_1^\dagger$. Finally, $B_1 = \text{INT}(B_1^\dagger, A_1)$ forms a legitimate filter for A_1.

The fact that B_1 is a legitimate filter for A_1 can be shown as follows. Consider a string $\boldsymbol{\sigma} = \boldsymbol{\sigma}_1.\boldsymbol{\rho}_1.\boldsymbol{\sigma}_2.\boldsymbol{\rho}_2 \ldots \notin \mathcal{L}(B_1)$, where $\boldsymbol{\sigma}_i \notin \Sigma^*.\mathcal{L}(A_2).\Sigma^*$ and $\boldsymbol{\rho}_i \in \mathcal{L}(A_2)$. Also consider another string $\boldsymbol{\sigma}_1.\boldsymbol{\tau}_1.\boldsymbol{\sigma}_2.\boldsymbol{\tau}_2 \ldots$ obtained from replacing each $\boldsymbol{\rho}_i$ with $\boldsymbol{\tau}_i \in \mathcal{L}(A_3)$. If $\boldsymbol{\sigma}_1.\boldsymbol{\tau}_1.\boldsymbol{\sigma}_2.\boldsymbol{\tau}_2 \ldots \in \mathcal{L}(B)$, then we have $\boldsymbol{\sigma}_1. \triangleleft .\boldsymbol{\tau}_1. \triangleright .\boldsymbol{\sigma}_2. \triangleleft .\boldsymbol{\tau}_2. \triangleright \ldots \in \mathcal{L}(B^{\triangleleft\triangleright})$. It is easy to see that $\boldsymbol{\sigma}_1. \triangleleft .\boldsymbol{\tau}_1. \triangleright .\boldsymbol{\sigma}_2. \triangleleft .\boldsymbol{\tau}_2. \triangleright \ldots \in \mathcal{L}(B_5)$. Finally, for each $\triangleleft.\boldsymbol{\tau}_i.\triangleright$, replacing $\triangleleft$ with $\boldsymbol{\rho}_i$, replacing $\boldsymbol{\tau}_i$ with ϵ, and replacing $\triangleright$ with ϵ yield $\boldsymbol{\sigma}_1.\boldsymbol{\rho}_1.\boldsymbol{\sigma}_2.\boldsymbol{\rho}_2 \ldots \in \mathcal{L}(B_1)$, which contradicts to the assumption $\boldsymbol{\sigma}_1.\boldsymbol{\rho}_1.\boldsymbol{\sigma}_2.\boldsymbol{\rho}_2 \ldots \notin \mathcal{L}(B_1)$. So we have $\mathcal{L}(\text{REP}(A_{\boldsymbol{\sigma}}, A_2, A_3)) \cap \mathcal{L}(B) = \emptyset$ for any string $\boldsymbol{\sigma} \notin \mathcal{L}(B_1)$. Similarly, consider string $\boldsymbol{\sigma} = \boldsymbol{\sigma}_1.\boldsymbol{\rho}_1.\boldsymbol{\sigma}_2.\boldsymbol{\rho}_2 \ldots \in \mathcal{L}(B_1)$, where $\boldsymbol{\sigma}_i \notin \Sigma^*.\mathcal{L}(A_2).\Sigma^*$ and

$\rho_i \in \mathcal{L}(A_2)$. Then it is in $\mathcal{L}(B_1^\dagger)$. By the construction of $B_1^\dagger$, there should be another string $\sigma_1. \triangleleft .\tau_1. \triangleright .\sigma_2. \triangleleft .\tau_2. \triangleright \ldots \in \mathcal{L}(B_5)$, where $\tau_i \in \mathcal{L}(A_3)$. We have $\sigma_1. \triangleleft .\tau_1. \triangleright .\sigma_2. \triangleleft .\tau_2. \triangleright \ldots \in \mathcal{L}(B^{\triangleleft\triangleright})$, and hence $\sigma_1.\tau_1.\sigma_2.\tau_2 \ldots \in \mathcal{L}(B)$. It is easy to see that $\sigma_1.\tau_1.\sigma_2.\tau_2 \ldots \in \mathcal{L}(\text{REP}(A_\sigma, A_2, A_3))$, which means $\mathcal{L}(\text{REP}(A_\sigma, A_2, A_3)) \cap \mathcal{L}(B) \neq \emptyset$. Consequently B_1 characterizes the desired language.

6 Extension to Symbolic Finite Automata

Symbolic finite automata (SFA) [26] extend conventional finite automata by allowing transition conditions to be specified in terms of predicates over a Boolean algebra with a potentially infinite domain. Formally, an SFA A is a 5-tuple $(Q, \mathcal{D}, I, \Delta, O)$, where Q is a finite set of states, $\mathcal{D}$ is the designated domain, $I \subseteq Q$ is the set of initial states (here we allow multiple initial states in contrast to the standard single-initial-state assumption of SFA), $\Delta : Q \times \Psi \times Q$ is the move relation for Ψ being the set of all quantifier-free formulas with at most one free variable, say χ, over a Boolean algebra of domain $\mathcal{D}$, $O \subseteq Q$ is the set of accepting states. We assume ϵ transitions are allowed and properly encoded in Δ in an SFA. Since $\mathcal{D}$ may not be bounded, a predicate logic formula over variable χ cannot be represented with logic circuits. We separate predicates from the logic circuit representation of SFA by abstracting each formula ψ appearing in Δ with its designated propositional variable x_ψ. Let $[\![\psi]\!]$ be extended to denote the set of solution values of χ satisfying ψ. Then the move relation of an SFA can be expressed with a transition relation

$$T(\boldsymbol{x}, \boldsymbol{s}, \boldsymbol{s}') = \bigvee_{(p,\psi,q) \in \Delta} (x_\psi \wedge (\boldsymbol{s} = p) \wedge (\boldsymbol{s}' = q))$$

and a predicate relation

$$P(\boldsymbol{x}, \chi) = \bigwedge_{(p,\psi,q) \in \Delta} (x_\psi \leftrightarrow (\chi \in [\![\psi]\!])).$$

Therefore we can represent an SFA A with four characteristic functions I, O, T, and P.

With the above construction, our circuit constructions of Sect. 3 naturally extend to SFA except that the predicate relation has to be additionally handled as follows. For SFA $A_{\text{INT}} = \text{INT}(A_1, A_2)$, the predicate relation

$$P_{\text{INT}}(\boldsymbol{x}, \chi) = P_1(\boldsymbol{x}_1, \chi) \wedge P_2(\boldsymbol{x}_2, \chi) \wedge (x_{\chi=\epsilon} \leftrightarrow \chi = \epsilon),$$

for $\boldsymbol{x} = (\boldsymbol{x}_1, \boldsymbol{x}_2, x_{\chi=\epsilon})$.

For SFA $A_{\text{UNI}} = \text{UNI}(A_1, A_2)$, the predicate relation

$$P_{\text{UNI}}(\boldsymbol{x}, \chi) = P_1(\boldsymbol{x}_1, \chi) \wedge P_2(\boldsymbol{x}_2, \chi),$$

for $\boldsymbol{x} = (\boldsymbol{x}_1, \boldsymbol{x}_2)$.

For SFA $A_{\text{CAT}} = \text{CAT}(A_1, A_2)$, the predicate relation

$$P_{\text{CAT}}(\boldsymbol{x}, \chi) = P_1(\boldsymbol{x}_1, \chi) \wedge P_2(\boldsymbol{x}_2, \chi) \wedge (x_{\chi=\epsilon} \leftrightarrow \chi = \epsilon),$$

for $\boldsymbol{x} = (\boldsymbol{x}_1, \boldsymbol{x}_2, x_{\chi=\epsilon})$.

For SFA $A_{\text{REP}} = \text{REP}(A_1, A_2, A_3)$, we construct the predicate relation for A_{REP} as follows. The predicate relation of SFA $A_1^{\triangleleft\triangleright}$ is first obtained from A_1 by

$$P_1^{\triangleleft\triangleright}(\boldsymbol{x}_1^{\triangleleft\triangleright}, \chi) = P_1(\boldsymbol{x}_1) \wedge (x_{\chi=\triangleleft} \leftrightarrow (\chi = \triangleleft)) \wedge (x_{\chi=\triangleright} \leftrightarrow (\chi = \triangleright)) \wedge$$
$$(x_{\chi\neq\triangleleft} \leftrightarrow (\chi \neq \triangleleft)) \wedge (x_{\chi\neq\triangleright} \leftrightarrow (\chi \neq \triangleright))),$$

for $\boldsymbol{x}_1^{\triangleleft\triangleright} = (\boldsymbol{x}_1, x_{\chi=\triangleleft}, x_{\chi=\triangleright}, x_{\chi\neq\triangleleft}, x_{\chi\neq\triangleright})$. Then the predicate relation of A_4 is constructed from those of A_2 and A_h by

$$P_4(\boldsymbol{x}_4, \chi) = P_2(\boldsymbol{x}_2, \chi) \wedge P_h(\boldsymbol{x}_h, \chi) \wedge (x_{\chi=\triangleleft} \leftrightarrow \chi = \triangleleft) \wedge (x_{\chi=\triangleright} \leftrightarrow \chi = \triangleright) \wedge$$
$$(x_{\chi\neq\triangleleft} \leftrightarrow \chi \neq \triangleleft) \wedge (x_{\chi\neq\triangleright} \leftrightarrow \chi \neq \triangleright),$$

for $\boldsymbol{x}_4 = (\boldsymbol{x}_2, \boldsymbol{x}_h, x_{\chi=\triangleleft}, x_{\chi=\triangleright}, x_{\chi\neq\triangleleft}, x_{\chi\neq\triangleright})$. Then the predicate relation of A_5 is obtained by

$$P_5(\boldsymbol{x}_5, \chi) = P_1^{\triangleleft\triangleright}(\boldsymbol{x}_1^{\triangleleft\triangleright}, \chi) \wedge P_4(\boldsymbol{x}_4, \chi) \wedge (x_{\chi=\epsilon} \leftrightarrow \chi = \epsilon),$$

for $\boldsymbol{x}_5 = (\boldsymbol{x}_1^{\triangleleft\triangleright}, \boldsymbol{x}_4, x_{\chi=\epsilon})$. Finally, the transition and predicate relations of SFA A_{REP} can be obtained by

$$\begin{aligned}
T_{\text{REP}}(\boldsymbol{x}, \boldsymbol{s}, \boldsymbol{s}') = &(\neg\alpha \wedge \neg\alpha' \wedge T_5(\boldsymbol{x}_5, s_5, s_5') \wedge \neg\gamma \wedge \neg\gamma' \wedge I_3(s_3) \wedge I_3(s_3')) \vee \\
&(\neg\alpha \wedge \neg\alpha' \wedge (s_5 = s_5') \wedge (x_{\chi=\epsilon}) \wedge \neg\gamma \wedge \gamma' \wedge I_3(s_3) \wedge I_3(s_3')) \vee \\
&(\neg\alpha \wedge \neg\alpha' \wedge (s_5 = s_5') \wedge \gamma \wedge \gamma' \wedge T_3(\boldsymbol{x}_3, s_3, s_3')) \vee \\
&(\neg\alpha \wedge \alpha' \wedge T_5(\boldsymbol{x}_5, s_5, s_5')|_{\Delta[\chi/\triangleleft]} \wedge \gamma \wedge \neg\gamma' \wedge O_3(s_3) \wedge I_3(s_3') \wedge (x_{\chi=\epsilon})) \vee \\
&(\alpha \wedge \alpha' \wedge T_5(\boldsymbol{y}, s_5, s_5') \wedge (x_{\chi=\epsilon}) \wedge \neg\gamma \wedge \neg\gamma' \wedge I_3(s_3) \wedge I_3(s_3')) \vee \\
&(\alpha \wedge \neg\alpha' \wedge T_5(\boldsymbol{x}_5, s_5, s_5')|_{\Delta[\chi/\triangleright]} \wedge \neg\gamma \wedge \neg\gamma' \wedge I_3(s_3) \wedge I_3(s_3') \wedge (x_{\chi=\epsilon})),
\end{aligned}$$

$$P_{\text{REP}}(\boldsymbol{x}, \chi, \boldsymbol{y}, \chi^\dagger) = P_5(\boldsymbol{x}_5, \chi) \wedge P_3(\boldsymbol{x}_3, \chi) \wedge P_5(\boldsymbol{y}, \chi^\dagger),$$

where $\boldsymbol{x} = (\boldsymbol{x}_5, \boldsymbol{x}_3)$, $\boldsymbol{y}$ is a set of newly introduced propositional variables for $|\boldsymbol{x}|$, $\chi^\dagger$ is a newly introduced variable for χ serving for existential quantifications, and $T|_{\Delta[\chi/a]}$ denotes transition relation T is obtained under the modified move relation Δ in which variable χ is substituted with symbol a. (Here we avoid existentially quantifying out $\boldsymbol{y}$ and $\chi^\dagger$ by treating them as free variables.)

For emptiness checking of an SFA, we can treat the SFA as an infinite state transition system by considering $(\chi, \boldsymbol{x}, \boldsymbol{s})$ as the state variables. Let the transition relation be the conjunction of T and P, and let I and O be the initial and accepting state conditions, respectively, of the infinite state transition system. Then the model checking method [9], effectively PDR modulo theories, can be applied for reachability analysis.

7   Experimental Evaluation

Our tool, named SLOG, was implemented in the C language under the Berkeley logic synthesis and verification system ABC [6]. The experiments were conducted on a machine with Intel Xeon(R) 8-core CPU and 16 GB memory under the Ubuntu 12.04 LCS operating system.

We compared SLOG against other modern constraint solvers: CVC4 [3], NORN [1], Z3-STR2 [34], and string analysis tools: JSA [8] and STRANGER [30]. For the experiments, 20386 string analysis instances were generated from real web applications via STRANGER [30]. The web applications includes MOODLE, PHP-FUSION, etc., and these instances are tested for vulnerabilities such as SQL-injection, cross-site scripting (XSS), etc. Each instance corresponds to an acyclic dependency graph of a sink node in the program that consists of union, concatenation, and replacement operations. For each instance, we generated the string constraint that checks whether the dependency graph is vulnerable with respect to an attack pattern. String constraints were generated in the SMT-lib format for CVC4, NORN, and Z3-STR2, and in the Java-program format for JSA.

The statistics of the benchmark instances are as follows. There are 85919 concatenation operations in total distributed in 18898 instances, 510 string replacement operations in 255 instances, and 25160 union operations in 5109 instances. All of these 20386 instances have membership checking at the end to determine whether an attack string can reach the sink node. All the solvers except for NORN, which does not support the replacement operation, provide full support on these string operations. Timeout limits 300 and 9000 s were set for small and large instances, respectively. An instance with fewer (resp. no fewer) than 100 concatenation operations is classified as small (resp. large).

The results of the solvers on the total 20386 instances are shown in Table 1, where #SAT, #UNS, #TO, #FL, and #Run denote the numbers of solved SAT, solved UNSAT, timeout, failed (with unexpected termination), and checked instances, respectively. The total runtimes for SAT and UNSAT instances are also shown in the table. Solvers SLOG, STRANGER, CVC4, JSA and Z3-STR2 checked all 20386 instances (runs) with successful rate 100%, 100%, 93.12%, 99.98%, 77.60%, respectively; NORN checked 20131 instances with the successful rate 82.17% without running the 255 instances with replacement operations.

Table 1. Statistics of solver performance

Solver	#SAT (time (s))	#UNS (time (s))	#TO	#FL	#Run
SLOG	8684 (65915)	11663 (72195)	39	0	20386
STRANGER	8723 (10309)	11663 (1069)	0	0	20386
CVC4	7503 (8217)	11480 (1139)	1136	267	20386
JSA	8719 (7141)	11663 (8708)	0	4	20386
Z3-STR2	4285 (249437)	11535 (921325)	2728	1838	20386
NORN	6306 (16586)	10236 (17383)	3344	245	20131

To evaluate solver performance on instances of different sizes, we classify the 20386 instances into three groups: the replacement-free small ones (with fewer than 100 concatenations and without replacement operations), the replacement-free large ones (with no fewer than 100 concatenations and without replacement operations), and the ones with replacement operations. By the classification, there are 20091 replacement-free small instances, 40 replacement-free large instances, and 255 instances with replacement operations. Note that the replacement-free large instances also have a large number of union operations.

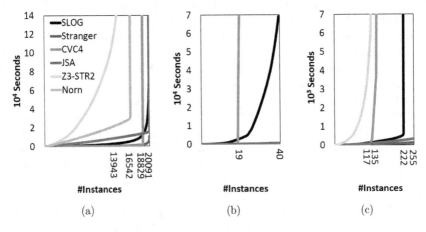

Fig. 2. Accumulated solving time for (a) replacement-free small instances, (b) replacement-free large instances, and (c) instances with replacement operations.

For the replacement-free small instances (under a 300-s timeout limit), the performances of solvers are shown in Fig. 2(a), where the x-axis is indexed by the number of solved instances, which are sorted by their runtimes in an ascending order for each solver, and the y-axis is indexed by the accumulated runtime in seconds. As shown in Fig. 2(a), SLOG successfully solves 20054 cases in 137670 seconds (with 37 timeout cases), outperforming Z3-STR2 (13943 cases in 1399712 s), CVC4 (18829 cases in 5555 s) and NORN (16542 cases in 33969 s). In contrast, STRANGER (20091 cases in 10590 s) and JSA (20087 cases in 15336 s) outperform SLOG on almost all the cases. For the replacement-free large instances (under a 9000-s timeout limit), both Z3-STR2 and NORN failed to solve any due to timeout. As seen from Fig. 2(b), SLOG solved most of the large cases (with an average of 1750 s per case), while CVC4 solved fewer than half of the instances (19 out of 40) but took less time on solvable instances. STRANGER and JSA outperform SLOG and other SMT-based solvers, being able to solve all the 40 cases with less time. For the instances with replacement operations (under a 300-s timeout limit), all solvers are applicable except for NORN. Figure 2(c) shows that the relative performances of the solvers are similar to those in the other two instance groups. The reason that STRANGER outperforms SLOG might be explained by the fact that the emptiness checking of a sink automaton in STRANGER is of constant time complexity (due to the canonicity of state-minimized DFA), while that in SLOG requires reachability analysis. Therefore as long as STRANGER succeeds in building the sink automaton, it is likely to outperform SLOG.

With the auxiliary variables and other information embedded in the circuit construction, SLOG can generate counterexamples. We applied SLOG to find witnesses of all 8684 vulnerable instances. It took 524 s in total to generate counterexamples for all 8684 instances, only a small fraction of the total constraint solving time 65915 s. The high efficiency of counterexample generation in SLOG can be attributed to the fact that the assignments to the internally quantified variables in our circuit construction are already computed by PDR. There is no need to re-derive them in generating counterexample traces by the rules of Sect. 4 (Table 2).

Table 2. SLOG performance on counterexample generation

Group	#SAT	SolveTime (s)	CexGenTime (s)
Small	8426	60664	481
Large	22	4236	18
Replacement	236	1015	25

In summary, SLOG performed the best among the solvers with counterexample generation capability, including CVC4, Z3-STR2 and NORN. In fact, a significant portion of runtime spent by SLOG is on running PDR for language emptiness checking. Although STRANGER and JSA performed better than SLOG in runtime, both are incapable of finding as a witness the values of input nodes to a specific attack string in the sink node.

To justify that our circuit-based method can be more scalable than BDD-based methods for representing automata with large alphabets, consider the automata over alphabet $\Sigma \times \Sigma$ with $|\Sigma| = 2^n$ accepting the language $(a, a)^*$ for $a \in \Sigma$. The automata have a linear $O(n)$ AIG representation ($4n + 1$ gates), but have an exponential $O(2^n)$ BDD representation (e.g., 46 BDD nodes for $n = 4$, 766 nodes for $n = 8$, and 196606 nodes for $n = 16$) in MONA [7], which is used by STRANGER. Although a good BDD variable ordering exists to reduce the BDD growth rate to linear in this example, a good BDD variable ordering can be hard to find and even may not exist in general. In addition, because SLOG represents NFA instead of DFA, it may avoid costly subset construction and can be more compact than (DFA-based) STRANGER.

8   Discussions

While SLOG demonstrates its ability on string constraint solving and counterexample generation by taking advantage of circuit-based NFA representation, it should be noted that the compared string analysis tools have varied focuses and expressiveness of specifying (non)string constraints. CVC4 [3] is a SMT-based solver that supports many-sorted first-order logic. NORN [1] is another SMT-based string constraint solver that employs Craig interpolation to handle word equations over (unbounded length) string variables, constraints of string length, and regular language membership constraints. Z3-STR2 [34] is a string theory plug-in built upon SMT solver Z3 [22]. These string solvers address string constraints with lengths and can generate witness for satisfying constraints. In the experimental evaluation, we did not consider length constraints when generating dependency graphs. String constraints with lengths are not currently supported by SLOG. The circuit-based representation could be extended to model arithmetic automata for automata-based string-length constraint solving [2,33]. JSA is an explicit automata tool for analyzing the flow of strings and string operations in Java programs. STRANGER is an MTBDD-based automata library for symbolic string analysis, which can be used to solve string constraints and compute pre- and post-images of string manipulation operations. JSA employes grammatical string analysis with regular language approximation and incorporates finite state transducers to support language-based replacement operations, while STRANGER can conduct forward and backward reachability analysis of string manipulation programs along with DFA constructions for language operations. In the evaluation, we did not conduct analysis on cyclic dependency graphs that can be analyzed with JSA and STRANGER. Conducting fixpoint computation on cyclic dependency graphs may require efficient complement operation in our circuit-based NFA representation that is not currently supported by SLOG.

9   Conclusions

We have presented a circuit-based NFA manipulation package for string analysis. Compared to BDD-based methods of automata representation, our circuit-based representation is scalable to automata with large alphabets. Our method avoids costly determinization whenever possible. It supports both counterexample generation and filter synthesis. In addition, extension to symbolic finite automata has been shown. Experiments have shown the unique benefits of our method. For future work, it would be interesting to explore the usage of SLOG as a string analysis engine in SMT solvers.

Acknowledgments. This work was supported in part by the Ministry of Science and Technology of Taiwan under grants MOST 104-2628-E-002-013-MY3, 104-2218-E-001-002, and 103-2221-E-004-006-MY3.

References

1. Abdulla, P.A., Atig, M.F., Chen, Y.-F., Holík, L., Rezine, A., Rümmer, P., Stenman, J.: Norn: an SMT solver for string constraints. In: Kroening, D., Păsăreanu, C.S. (eds.) CAV 2015. LNCS, vol. 9206, pp. 462–469. Springer, Heidelberg (2015)

2. Aydin, A., Bang, L., Bultan, T.: Automata-based model counting for string constraints. In: Kroening, D., Păsăreanu, C.S. (eds.) CAV 2015. LNCS, vol. 9206, pp. 255–272. Springer, Heidelberg (2015)

3. Barrett, C., Conway, C.L., Deters, M., Hadarean, L., Jovanović, D., King, T., Reynolds, A., Tinelli, C.: CVC4. In: Gopalakrishnan, G., Qadeer, S. (eds.) CAV 2011. LNCS, vol. 6806, pp. 171–177. Springer, Heidelberg (2011)

4. Bjørner, N., Tillmann, N., Voronkov, A.: Path feasibility analysis for string-manipulating programs. In: Kowalewski, S., Philippou, A. (eds.) TACAS 2009. LNCS, vol. 5505, pp. 307–321. Springer, Heidelberg (2009)

5. Bradley, A.R.: SAT-based model checking without unrolling. In: Jhala, R., Schmidt, D. (eds.) VMCAI 2011. LNCS, vol. 6538, pp. 70–87. Springer, Heidelberg (2011)

6. Brayton, R., Mishchenko, A.: ABC: an academic industrial-strength verification tool. In: Touili, T., Cook, B., Jackson, P. (eds.) CAV 2010. LNCS, vol. 6174, pp. 24–40. Springer, Heidelberg (2010)

7. BRICS: The MONA project. http://www.brics.dk/mona/

8. Christensen, A.S., Møller, A., Schwartzbach, M.I.: Precise analysis of string expressions. In: Cousot, R. (ed.) SAS 2003. LNCS, vol. 2694, pp. 1–18. Springer, Heidelberg (2003)

9. Cimatti, A., Griggio, A., Mover, S., Tonetta, S.: IC3 modulo theories via implicit predicate abstraction. In: Ábrahám, E., Havelund, K. (eds.) TACAS 2014 (ETAPS). LNCS, vol. 8413, pp. 46–61. Springer, Heidelberg (2014)

10. D'Antoni, L., Veanes, M.: Extended symbolic finite automata and transducers. Formal Meth. Syst. Des. **47**(1), 93–119 (2015)

11. Een, N., Mishchenko, A., Brayton, R.: Efficient implementation of property directed reachability. In: FMCAD, pp. 125–134 (2011)

12. Gould, C., Su, Z., Devanbu, P.: Static checking of dynamically generated queries in database applications. In: ICSE, pp. 645–654 (2004)

13. Hooimeijer, P., Weimer, W.: StrSolve: solving string constraints lazily. Autom. Softw. Eng. **19**(4), 531–559 (2012)

14. Huang, Y.W., Yu, F., Hang, C., Tsai, C.H., Lee, D.T., Kuo, S.Y.: Securing web application code by static analysis and runtime protection. In: WWW, pp. 40–52 (2004)

15. Jensen, S.H., Jonsson, P.A., Møller, A.: Remedying the eval that men do. In: ISSTA, pp. 34–44 (2012)

16. Jiang, J.H.R., Brayton, R.K.: On the verification of sequential equivalence. IEEE Trans. Comp. Aid. Des. Int. Circ. Syst. **22**(6), 686–697 (2003)

17. Jovanovic, N., Krügel, C., Kirda, E.: Pixy: a static analysis tool for detecting web application vulnerabilities. In: S&P, pp. 258–263 (2006)

18. Kiezun, A., Ganesh, V., Guo, P.J., Hooimeijer, P., Ernst, M.D.: HAMPI: a solver for string constraints. In: ISSTA, pp. 105–116 (2009)

19. Li, G., Ghosh, I.: PASS: string solving with parameterized array and interval automaton. In: Bertacco, V., Legay, A. (eds.) HVC 2013. LNCS, vol. 8244, pp. 15–31. Springer, Heidelberg (2013)

20. Minamide, Y.: Static approximation of dynamically generated web pages. In: WWW, pp. 432–441 (2005)

21. Mishchenko, A., Chatterjee, S., Jiang, J.H.R., Brayton, R.: FRAIGs: a unifying representation for logic synthesis and verification. In: ERL Technical report, UC Berkeley (2005)

22. de Moura, L., Bjørner, N.S.: Z3: an efficient SMT solver. In: Ramakrishnan, C.R., Rehof, J. (eds.) TACAS 2008. LNCS, vol. 4963, pp. 337–340. Springer, Heidelberg (2008)
23. Saxena, P., Akhawe, D., Hanna, S., Mao, F., McCamant, S., Song, D.: A symbolic execution framework for javascript. In: S&P, pp. 513–528 (2010)
24. Su, Z., Wassermann, G.: The essence of command injection attacks in web applications. In: POPL, pp. 372–382 (2006)
25. Veanes, M.: Applications of symbolic finite automata. In: Konstantinidis, S. (ed.) CIAA 2013. LNCS, vol. 7982, pp. 16–23. Springer, Heidelberg (2013)
26. Veanes, M., de Halleux, P., Tillmann, N.: Rex: symbolic regular expression explorer. In: ICST, pp. 498–507 (2010)
27. Veanes, M., Hooimeijer, P., Livshits, B., Molnar, D., Bjørner, N.: Symbolic finite state transducers: algorithms and applications. In: POPL, pp. 137–150 (2012)
28. Veanes, M., Mytkowicz, T., Molnar, D., Livshits, B.: Data-parallel string-manipulating programs. In: POPL, pp. 139–152 (2015)
29. Wassermann, G., Su, Z.: Sound and precise analysis of web applications for injection vulnerabilities. In: PLDI, pp. 32–41 (2007)
30. Yu, F., Alkhalaf, M., Bultan, T.: STRANGER: an automata-based string analysis tool for PHP. In: Esparza, J., Majumdar, R. (eds.) TACAS 2010. LNCS, vol. 6015, pp. 154–157. Springer, Heidelberg (2010)
31. Yu, F., Alkhalaf, M., Bultan, T.: Patching vulnerabilities with sanitization synthesis. In: ICSE, pp. 251–260 (2011)
32. Yu, F., Alkhalaf, M., Bultan, T., Ibarra, O.H.: Automata-based symbolic string analysis for vulnerability detection. Formal Meth. Syst. Des. **44**(1), 44–70 (2014)
33. Yu, F., Bultan, T., Ibarra, O.H.: Symbolic string verification: combining string analysis and size analysis. In: Kowalewski, S., Philippou, A. (eds.) TACAS 2009. LNCS, vol. 5505, pp. 322–336. Springer, Heidelberg (2009)
34. Zheng, Y., Ganesh, V., Subramanian, S., Tripp, O., Dolby, J., Zhang, X.: Effective search-space pruning for solvers of string equations, regular expressions and length constraints. In: Kroening, D., Păsăreanu, C.S. (eds.) CAV 2015. LNCS, vol. 9206, pp. 235–254. Springer, Heidelberg (2015)

RAHFT: A Tool for Verifying Horn Clauses Using Abstract Interpretation and Finite Tree Automata

Bishoksan Kafle[1]([✉]), John P. Gallagher[1,2], and José F. Morales[2]

[1] Roskilde University, Roskilde, Denmark
{kafle,jpg}@ruc.dk
[2] IMDEA Software Institute, Madrid, Spain
josef.morales@imdea.org

Abstract. We present RAHFT (Refinement of Abstraction in Horn clauses using Finite Tree automata), an *abstraction refinement* tool for verifying safety properties of programs expressed as Horn clauses. The paper describes the architecture, strength and weakness, implementation and usage aspects of the tool. RAHFT loosely combines three powerful techniques for program verification: (i) program specialisation, (ii) abstract interpretation, and (iii) trace abstraction refinement in a non-trivial way, with the aim of exploiting their strengths and mitigating their weaknesses through the complementary techniques. It is interfaced with an abstract domain, a tool for manipulating finite tree automata and various solvers for reasoning about constraints. Its modular design and customizable components allows for experimenting with new verification techniques and tools developed for Horn clauses.

1 Constrained Horn Clause Verification and Our Approach

A constrained Horn clause (CHC) is a first order predicate logic formula usually written in the form $p(X) \leftarrow \phi, p_1(X_1), \ldots, p_k(X_k)$ $(k \geq 0)$ using Constraint Logic Programming (CLP) syntax, where ϕ is a first order logic formula (constraint) with respect to some background theory, X_i, X are (possibly empty) tuples of distinct variables, and $p_1, \ldots, p_k, p$ are predicate symbols. There is a distinguished predicate symbol *false* which is interpreted as FALSE. Clauses with *false* head are called *integrity constraints*. A set of CHCs is called a (CLP) program.

An interpretation of a set of CHCs P is a set of *constrained facts* of the form $A \leftarrow \phi$ where A is an atom and ϕ is a formula with respect to some background

B. Kafle—Funded by the EU FP7 project 318337, *ENTRA*.

J.P. Gallagher—Funded by the EU FP7 project 611004, coordination and support action ICT-Energy.

J.F. Morales—Work partially funded by Comunidad de Madrid project S2013/ICE-2731 N-Greens Software, MINECO Projects TIN2012-39391-C04-03 (StrongSoft) and TIN2015-67522-C3-1-R (TRACES), and EU FP7-ICT-2013.3.4 project 610686 POLCA.

© Springer International Publishing Switzerland 2016
S. Chaudhuri and A. Farzan (Eds.): CAV 2016, Part I, LNCS 9779, pp. 261–268, 2016.
DOI: 10.1007/978-3-319-41528-4_14

theory. An interpretation that satisfies each clause is called a *model* (a *solution* in some works [6,34]). In Horn clause verification, *integrity constraints* represent the safety properties to be verified; other clauses represent the program's behaviours. The CHC verification problem is to check whether there exists a model of P.

Several verification tools have been developed for CHCs, including SeaHorn [24], QARMC [21], VeriMap [16], Convex polyhedral analyser [31], TRACER [29], ELDARICA [27], and Trace abstraction refinement tool [37]. They exploit either Formulation I or Formulation II for Horn clause verification.

Formulation I (deductive): P has a model if and only if $P \not\vdash false$ (*false* is not derivable from P). In CLP terminology, $P \vdash A$ if and only if the query $\leftarrow A$ succeeds in P. In this formulation it is sufficient to show that the query $\leftarrow false$ fails finitely or infinitely. Formulation I forms the basis of the tools described in [25,37]. As the *minimal model* of P contains exactly the set of atoms that succeed [28], we have another formulation of the CHC verification problem [20].

Formulation II (model-based): P has a model if and only if $false \notin M[\![P]\!]$, where $M[\![P]\!]$ is the minimal model of P. In Formulation II it is sufficient to find a model $M' \supseteq M[\![P]\!]$, where $false \notin M'$. It forms the basis of tools based on *abstract interpretation, interpolation* or *predicate abstraction* [21,24,31].

The program in Fig. 1(a) is a simple but challenging problem for many verification tools. $1(X, Y) \equiv X \geq Y \land Y \geq 0$ is a model of the program, whose solution requires the discovery of the invariants $X \geq Y$ and $Y \geq 0$. For example neither QARMC [21] nor SeaHorn [24] (using only the PDR engine [7]) terminates on this program. However, SeaHorn (with PDR and the abstract interpreter IKOS [8]) solves it. RAHFT solves it with the pre-processing step alone.

RAHFT exploits both of the above formulations using techniques based on *abstract interpretation* over the domain of convex polyhedra, *trace abstraction-refinement* using finite tree automata (FTAs) and *program specialisation* using *constraint specialisation* [30]. The motivations behind this combination are: (i) to benefit from a powerful and scalable technique such as *abstract interpretation* [13] for verifying properties of programs, (ii) to refine *abstract interpretation* through automata theoretic operations which offers the advantages of simplicity and generality [31] and (iii) to construct highly parametric and configurable verification tools through *program transformation* [16].

2   RAHFT Architecture and Interface

Figure 1(b) gives an overview of RAHFT. It compiles to a standalone command line utility that accepts a set of CHCs as input. It consists of two modules namely, *Abstraction* (green box) and *Refinement* (red box). RAHFT takes a file containing a set of CHCs P as input and returns *safe* or *unsafe* respectively if P has or does not have a model.

2.1   Abstraction

The *Abstraction* module takes a set of CHCs P as input and returns *safe*, *unsafe* or a trace representing the abstract derivation of *false* together with the set of all

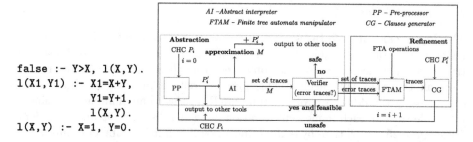

```
false :- Y>X, l(X,Y).
l(X1,Y1) :- X1=X+Y,
            Y1=Y+1,
            l(X,Y).
l(X,Y) :- X=1, Y=0.
```

Fig. 1. (a) Example program; (b) the architecture of Rahft. (Color figure online)

derivations (traces) (both represented as FTAs) used while applying *abstraction interpretation* to P. It consists of the following components:

Pre-processor (PP): Pre-processing is a model-preserving source-to-source program transformation of Horn clauses. In principle, any such transformation can be used as a pre-processor, but we use *constraint specialisation* [30]. The specialisation consists of strengthening the constraints in the clauses using *abstract interpretation* [13] and *query-answer transformation* [3,17] of the original program. The specialisation is independent of the *abstract domain* and the background theory underlying the clauses and does not unfold the clauses at all. This has been proven to be an effective transformation [30] for verifying Horn clauses [15] and as a pre-processor to other Horn clause verification tools such as [21].

Abstract Interpreter (AI): The AI implements a fixed point algorithm over the domain of *convex polyhedra* [12] based on *abstract interpretation* [13]. It constructs an over-approximation M of the *minimal model* of a program P, where M contains at most one *constrained fact* $p(X) \leftarrow \phi$ for each predicate p. The constraint ϕ is a conjunction of linear inequalities, representing a convex polyhedron. The set of traces used during abstract interpretation of P can be captured by an FTA, say $\mathcal{A}_P$, using M as shown in [32]. An FTA is a mathematical model capable of capturing tree structured computations (Horn clauses derivations) (see [31] for the correspondence between a program and an FTA).

The approximation M and the pre-processed clauses can be used by other Horn clause tools, for example [21]. These tools can strengthen M (which may contain some useful invariants) incrementally to construct a model of P rather than starting from a coarse abstraction ($p(X) \leftarrow true$ for each predicate p of P).

Verifier: The verifier receives M and $\mathcal{A}_P$ and checks the *safety* of the clauses based on some simple condition. The clauses are safe if there is no constrained fact for *false* in M (M is called *safe inductive invariant* or a *model* of P) or there are no error traces rooted at *false*. Otherwise we do not know whether the clauses are unsafe or whether the approximation was too imprecise. In this case, the verifier picks a trace, say $t \in \mathcal{A}_P$, representing the abstract derivation of *false* (if any) from the set of traces. If t is feasible (while simulating in P), then P is unsafe and t is a *counterexample*, otherwise we refine P.

2.2   Refinement

The *Refinement* module takes as input a program P and two FTAs (i) recognising the set of all possible traces of P; and (ii) recognising a set of infeasible traces. A difference automaton is computed from these automata which recognises all traces except the infeasible ones. A refined program is obtained as output using the difference automaton and P. Rather than eliminating a single infeasible trace in each refinement iteration, we generalise it using an *interpolant automaton* [25, 32, 37] thereby eliminating a possibly infinite number of infeasible traces. The refinement offers the advantages of simplicity and generality which is independent of the abstract domain and background theory underlying the clauses. The *Refinement* module consists of following components:

Finite tree automata manipulator (FTAM): FTAM takes as input two FTAs and outputs their difference automaton. The FTA difference construction needs *determinisation*; we built upon an optimised determinisation algorithm by Gallagher, Ajspur and Kafle [19] which scales well in practice, generating transitions of the determinised automaton in a very compact form called *product form*.

Clause generator (CG): Given a set of clauses P, and an automaton recognising an over-approximation of all feasible traces of P, CG produces a set of clauses which is equisatisfiable to P. For this purpose, we exploit a correspondence between the traces using the clauses and the language of FTAs to generate a new set of clauses.

The refinement offers two advantages: (i) the refinement is manifested in the clauses generated – we do not need to keep track of the previous refinements; and (ii) the original predicates get split in refined clauses which help improve the precision of analysis [20].

2.3   Implementation

RAHFT is implemented in Ciao [26] and is available from https://github.com/bishoksan/RAHFT. It consists of a collection of reusable Prolog modules which rely on state-of-the-art specialised external libraries written in C and C++ for handling constraints. We use the Yices SMT solver [18] and the Parma Polyhedra Library [2] for handling the constraints and the FTA library [19] for manipulating FTAs. The construction of an *interpolant tree automaton* uses an algorithm presented in [36] for computing an interpolant of two formulas. The code consists of over 7,000 lines of Ciao Prolog code split over 42 modules, interfaced to the above-mentioned external libraries. The implementation of iterative fixpoint algorithms is inspired by the approach to the abstract interpretation of logic programs described by Codish and Søndergaard [10]. Data structures for manipulating Horn clauses are based on terms and the internal Prolog database, reusing the optimizations of the underlying machine (e.g., clause indexing) rather than reimplementing them in our tool. The glue code that ties together the general purpose Prolog engine and the specialised solvers written in C and C++ is generated via the Ciao foreign interface [26].

2.4   Strength and Weakness

RAHFT is a verification tool for *safety* properties of programs expressed as Horn clauses; it can be used as a *back end* solver by different *front end* tools outputting in CLP form. It handles clauses whose underlying theory is *linear arithmetic*; other theories are not supported currently. It accepts input in CLP form.

Since different components of RAHFT are loosely coupled, the tool can be reconfigured (with a very little effort) to produce verification tools solely based on (i) program transformation as in iterated specialisation approach [15] by iterating the pre-processing component, (ii) abstract interpretation, only with the AI component, (iii) trace abstraction refinement [25,37] by iterating the FTAM component, and (iv) a sensible combination thereof – all followed by a lightweight verifier which checks the *safety* of the clauses based on some condition. Since our tool uses both *state abstraction* and *trace abstraction*, it allows application of a wide range of tools and techniques.

We have evaluated RAHFT on software verification benchmarks from a variety of sources [4,5,22,23,27,29] and the results show that it compares favourably (in time and the number of instances solved) with the other state-of-the-art Horn clause verification tools (see [30–32] for the details).

Convex polyhedra is an expensive abstract domain and is a potential bottleneck for verification of large code bases. Instead, we can use cheaper domains supported by the Parma Polyhedra Library such as *octagons* or *intervals* at the cost of precision. RAHFT is also limited by the *hard-coded* limits of the libraries and the Prolog implementation used (e.g. *arity* limit of the predicates), which may be too restrictive for some verification problems and we intend to improve this by some suitable data representation. We are aware of some examples from SV-COMP if not many which cross this limit.

We can leverage state-of-the-art interpolating SMT solvers [9,33] for the *tree interpolant* generation which can be used for constructing an *interpolant tree automaton*; our current implementation does not scale well. Furthermore we aim to handle more advanced data structures such as arrays, maps and sets, requiring more expressive theories than linear arithmetic. One way to achieve this is by composing abstract domains as described in [11,14]; we are also aware of the support for the reduced product of domains in the PPL library.

RAHFT is able to generate a *model* (*a counterexample*) if it proves the *safety* (*unsafety*) a program. We need bookkeeping to generate these witnesses with respect to the original program; and sometimes it becomes rather challenging because of the use of external libraries, tools or the transformations applied.

3   Future Work

Future work will involve making RAHFT a more flexible tool so that the user can configure other parameters such as abstract domains and pre-processors. We are also planning for a detailed performance measurement of the tool to detect bottlenecks; and work on language-based optimisations to minimize them. Generation of a *model* or a *counterexample* with respect to the original program, handling clauses with richer background theories (arrays, uninterpreted functions) is on our to-do list. In addition, we are extending RAHFT to consider Horn clauses in SMT-LIB format [1], though several Horn clause verification tools use standard CLP notation [16,21,31].

References

1. SMT-LIB format. http://smtlib.cs.uiowa.edu. Accessed 5 May 2016
2. Bagnara, R., Hill, P.M., Zaffanella, E.: The Parma Polyhedra Library: toward a complete set of numerical abstractions for the analysis and verification of hardware and software systems. SCP **72**(1–2), 3–21 (2008)
3. Bancilhon, F., Maier, D., Sagiv, Y., Ullman, J.: Magic sets and other strange ways to implement logic programs. In: Proceedings of the 5th ACM SIGMOD-SIGACT Symposium on Principles of Database Systems (1986)
4. Beyer, D.: Second competition on software verification - (summary of SV-COMP 2013). In: Piterman and Smolka [35], pp. 594–609
5. Beyer, D.: Software verification and verifiable witnesses. In: Baier, C., Tinelli, C. (eds.) TACAS 2015. LNCS, vol. 9035, pp. 401–416. Springer, Heidelberg (2015)
6. Bjørner, N., McMillan, K., Rybalchenko, A.: On solving universally quantified Horn clauses. In: Logozzo, F., Fähndrich, M. (eds.) Static Analysis. LNCS, vol. 7935, pp. 105–125. Springer, Heidelberg (2013)
7. Bradley, A.R., Manna, Z.: Property-directed incremental invariant generation. Formal Asp. Comput. **20**(4–5), 379–405 (2008)
8. Brat, G., Navas, J.A., Shi, N., Venet, A.: IKOS: a framework for static analysis based on abstract interpretation. In: Giannakopoulou, D., Salaün, G. (eds.) SEFM 2014. LNCS, vol. 8702, pp. 271–277. Springer, Heidelberg (2014)
9. Cimatti, A., Griggio, A., Schaafsma, B.J., Sebastiani, R.: The MathSAT5 SMT solver. In: Piterman and Smolka [35], pp. 93–107
10. Codish, M., Søndergaard, H.: Meta-circular abstract interpretation in prolog. In: Mogensen, T.Æ., Schmidt, D.A., Sudborough, I.H. (eds.) The Essence of Computation. LNCS, vol. 2566, pp. 109–134. Springer, Heidelberg (2002)
11. Cortesi, A., Costantini, G., Ferrara, P.: A survey on product operators in abstract interpretation. In: Banerjee, A., Danvy, O., Doh, K., Hatcliff, J. (eds.) Semantics, Abstract Interpretation, and Reasoning About Programs. EPTCS, vol. 129, pp. 325–336 (2013)
12. Cousot, P., Halbwachs, N.: Automatic discovery of linear restraints among variables of a program. In: Proceedings of the 5th Annual ACM Symposium on Principles of Programming Languages, pp. 84–96 (1978)
13. Cousot, P., Cousot, R.: Abstract interpretation: a unified lattice model for static analysis of programs by construction or approximation of fixpoints. In: Graham, R.M., Harrison, M.A., Sethi, R. (eds.) POPL, pp. 238–252. ACM (1977)
14. Cousot, P., Cousot, R., Mauborgne, L.: The reduced product of abstract domains and the combination of decision procedures. In: Hofmann, M. (ed.) FOSSACS 2011. LNCS, vol. 6604, pp. 456–472. Springer, Heidelberg (2011)
15. De Angelis, E., Fioravanti, F., Pettorossi, A., Proietti, M.: Program verification via iterated specialization. SCP **95**, 149–175 (2014)
16. De Angelis, E., Fioravanti, F., Pettorossi, A., Proietti, M.: VeriMAP: a tool for verifying programs through transformations. In: Ábrahám, E., Havelund, K. (eds.) TACAS 2014 (ETAPS). LNCS, vol. 8413, pp. 568–574. Springer, Heidelberg (2014)

17. Debray, S., Ramakrishnan, R.: Abstract interpretation of logic programs using magic transformations. J. Logic Program. **18**, 149–176 (1994)
18. Dutertre, B.: Yices 2.2. In: Biere, A., Bloem, R. (eds.) CAV 2014. LNCS, vol. 8559, pp. 737–744. Springer, Heidelberg (2014)
19. Gallagher, J.P., Ajspur, M., Kafle, B.: An optimised algorithm for determinisation and completion of finite tree automata. CoRR, abs/1511.03595 (2015)
20. Gallagher, J.P., Kafle, B.: Analysis and transformation tools for constrained Horn clause verification. TPLP **14**(4–5 (additional materials in online edition)), 90–101 (2014)
21. Grebenshchikov, S., Lopes, N.P., Popeea, C., Rybalchenko, A.: Synthesizing software verifiers from proof rules. In: Vitek, J., Lin, H., Tip, F. (eds.) PLDI, pp. 405–416. ACM (2012)
22. Gulavani, B.S., Chakraborty, S., Nori, A.V., Rajamani, S.K.: Automatically refining abstract interpretations. In: Ramakrishnan, C.R., Rehof, J. (eds.) TACAS 2008. LNCS, vol. 4963, pp. 443–458. Springer, Heidelberg (2008)
23. Gupta, A., Rybalchenko, A.: InvGen: an efficient invariant generator. In: Bouajjani, A., Maler, O. (eds.) CAV 2009. LNCS, vol. 5643, pp. 634–640. Springer, Heidelberg (2009)
24. Gurfinkel, A., Kahsai, T., Komuravelli, A., Navas, J.A.: The SeaHorn verification framework. In: Kroening, D., Păsăreanu, C.S. (eds.) CAV 2015. LNCS, vol. 9206, pp. 343–361. Springer, Heidelberg (2015)
25. Heizmann, M., Hoenicke, J., Podelski, A.: Refinement of trace abstraction. In: Palsberg, J., Su, Z. (eds.) SAS 2009. LNCS, vol. 5673, pp. 69–85. Springer, Heidelberg (2009)
26. Hermenegildo, M.V., Bueno, F., Carro, M., López-García, P., Mera, E., Morales, J.F., Puebla, G.: An overview of Ciao and its design philosophy. TPLP **12**(1–2), 219–252 (2012)
27. Hojjat, H., Konečný, F., Garnier, F., Iosif, R., Kuncak, V., Rümmer, P.: A verification toolkit for numerical transition systems - tool paper. In: Giannakopoulou, D., Méry, D. (eds.) FM 2012. LNCS, vol. 7436, pp. 247–251. Springer, Heidelberg (2012)
28. Jaffar, J., Maher, M.: Constraint logic programming: a survey. J. Logic Program. **1920**, 503–581 (1994)
29. Jaffar, J., Murali, V., Navas, J.A., Santosa, A.E.: TRACER: a symbolic execution tool for verification. In: Madhusudan, P., Seshia, S.A. (eds.) CAV 2012. LNCS, vol. 7358, pp. 758–766. Springer, Heidelberg (2012)
30. Kafle, B., Gallagher, J.P.: Constraint specialisation in Horn clause verification. In: Asai, K., Sagonas, K. (eds.) Proceedings Workshop on PEPM, PEPM, Mumbai, India, 15–17 January 2015, pp. 85–90. ACM (2015)
31. Kafle, B., Gallagher, J.P.: Horn clause verification with convex polyhedral abstraction and tree automata-based refinement. Comput. Lang. Syst. Struct. (2015, In press). http://www.sciencedirect.com/science/article/pii/S1477842415000822, doi:10.1016/j.cl.2015.11.001
32. Kafle, B., Gallagher, J.P.: Interpolant tree automata and their application in Horn clause verification. CoRR, abs/1601.06521 (2016)
33. McMillan, K.L.: Interpolants from Z3 proofs. In: Bjesse, P., Slobodová, A. (eds.) FMCAD 2011, Austin, TX, USA, 30 October–02 November 2011, pp. 19–27. FMCAD Inc. (2011)
34. McMillan, K.L., Rybalchenko, A.: Solving constrained Horn clauses using interpolation. Technical report, Microsoft Research (2013)

35. Piterman, N., Smolka, S.A. (eds.): TACAS 2013 (ETAPS 2013). LNCS, vol. 7795. Springer, Heidelberg (2013)
36. Rybalchenko, A., Sofronie-Stokkermans, V.: Constraint solving for interpolation. J. Symb. Comput. **45**(11), 1212–1233 (2010)
37. Wang, W., Jiao, L.: Trace abstraction refinement for solving Horn clauses. Technical report ISCAS-SKLCS-15-19, SCAS-SKLCS, December 2015. http://lcs.ios.ac.cn/wangwf/TechReportISCAS-SKLCS-15-19.pdf

Model Checking I

Infinite-State Liveness-to-Safety via Implicit Abstraction and Well-Founded Relations

Jakub Daniel[1,2(✉)], Alessandro Cimatti[1], Alberto Griggio[1], Stefano Tonetta[1], and Sergio Mover[3]

[1] Fondazione Bruno Kessler, Trento, Italy
{cimatti,griggio,tonettas}@fbk.eu
[2] Charles University in Prague, Faculty of Mathematics and Physics, Department of Distributed and Dependable Systems, Prague, Czech Republic
daniel@d3s.mff.cuni.cz
[3] University of Colorado Boulder, Boulder, USA
sergio.mover@colorado.edu

Abstract. We present a fully-symbolic LTL model checking approach for infinite-state transition systems. We extend *liveness-to-safety*, a prominent approach in the finite-state case, by means of *implicit abstraction*, to effectively prove the absence of abstract fair loops without explicitly constructing the abstract state space. We increase the effectiveness of the approach by integrating termination techniques based on *well-founded relations* derived from ranking functions. The idea is to prove that any existing abstract fair loop is covered by a given set of well-founded relations. Within this framework, k-liveness is integrated as a generic ranking function. The algorithm iterates by attempting to remove spurious abstract fair loops: either it finds new predicates, to avoid spurious abstract prefixes, or it introduces new well-founded relations, based on the analysis of the abstract lasso. The implementation fully leverages the efficiency and incrementality of the underlying safety checker IC3IA. The proposed approach outperforms other temporal checkers on a wide class of benchmarks.

1 Introduction

Model checking of liveness properties is a fundamental verification problem. In finite-state model checking, the most prominent approaches are liveness-to-safety (L2S) [6] and k-liveness [18], that reduce the problem to one or more safety checks. Their success is motivated by the possibility to leverage the progress of SAT-based invariant checking techniques, such as interpolation-based model checking [34] and IC3 [10].

The verification of liveness properties for *infinite-state* systems has been primarily tackled in the setting of analysis of imperative program [21,23,24,30,39,40], or other specific classes [2,8,15,25,32]. However, in many practical cases the model

---

J. Daniel—Partially supported by the Grant Agency of the Czech Republic project 14-11384S.

S. Chaudhuri and A. Farzan (Eds.): CAV 2016, Part I, LNCS 9779, pp. 271–291, 2016.
DOI: 10.1007/978-3-319-41528-4_15

is described as a symbolic transition system (e.g. [12,35]), or it is compiled into a symbolic transition system from a higher level language (e.g. networks of timed and hybrid automata [16,43], architecture description language [4,7,9]).

In this paper we present a new approach for LTL model checking of infinite-state transition systems, which we call L2SIA-WFR. The approach relies on two ingredients. First, we extend *liveness-to-safety* by means of *implicit abstraction* [44]. Implicit abstraction is a form of predicate abstraction that does not require the explicit construction of the abstract transition system, and is able to deal with a large number of predicates. In this setting, implicit abstraction is key to checking the existence of abstract fair loops efficiently, given a set of predicates. Second, we integrate termination techniques based on *well-founded relations* [23]. Specifically, the technique tries to prove that any existing abstract fair loop is covered by a given set of well-founded relations. At the top level, the algorithm iterates trying to remove spurious abstract fair loops while maintaining a set of predicates and a set of well-founded relations. New predicates are added if they expose the spuriousness of the abstract path at hand by showing that its abstract prefixes can not be concretized. The set of well-founded relations is extended as a result of the analysis of the abstract lasso, guided by the construction of a ranking function. Within this framework, we also integrate k-liveness, that infers the validity of the property by proving that no path can fulfill the fairness condition more than a given number of times. As such, k-liveness is seen as a generic well-founded relation.

We implemented L2SIA-WFR on top of IC3IA, a model checking engine for safety properties that extends IC3 to the infinite-state case with the use of implicit abstraction at its core [14]. We exploit the fact that the L2SIA-WFR algorithm is highly incremental with respect to the refinement iterations to tighten the integration with IC3IA.

We carried out an experimental evaluation using liveness property benchmarks for transition systems and for imperative programs. To compare various temporal checkers, we translate transition systems to programs, and programs to transition systems. The results highlight a positive interaction between implicit abstraction and well-founded relations. Overall, L2SIA-WFR outperforms the competitor temporal checkers, not only on the benchmarks for transition systems, but also on the ones for imperative programs.

The paper is structured as follows. In Sect. 2 we discuss the related work. In Sect. 3 we present some background. In Sect. 4 we discuss the L2SIA-WFR approach, and in Sect. 5 we discuss the experimental results. In Sect. 6 we draw some conclusions, and outline directions for future work.

2   Related Work

The most prominent approaches to symbolic LTL model checking are based on SAT techniques and typically lift naturally to the infinite-state case using SMT solvers. k-liveness [18] remains a sound technique in the infinite-state case, although not complete since even if there is no fair path, the fairness can be visited an unbounded number of times. In this paper, we embed k-liveness as a special case of well-founded relation based on counting the occurrences of fairness along a path.

Liveness-to-safety was extended to infinite-state systems in [42] for a number of classes of infinite-state systems, namely, (ω-)regular model checking, pushdown systems, and timed automata. However, the approach is in general not sound for infinite-state transition systems, where a liveness property can be violated even if there is no lasso-shaped counterexample. In fact, in this paper, we are applying liveness-to-safety on the abstract state space, which is finite.

Predicate abstraction [28] is a general technique for model checking infinite-state systems. Once the abstract transition relation is computed, any algorithm for finite-state systems can be applied. However, on one side, the computation of the abstract state space typically blows up with few dozens of predicates, and on the other side, a finite number of predicates is not sufficient to prove the property (for example, when there are loops with counters that are not initialized). In this paper, we consider implicit abstraction to tackle the first problem and well-founded relations for the second.

The counterexample-based refinement we propose is very similar to the one presented in [3]: in both approaches, if an abstract counterexample contains a spurious prefix, new predicates are added to the abstraction, while new ranking functions are discovered in case the lasso is spurious. Our approach is completely different regarding the method used to prove the property: in [3] a ranking abstraction is used to add a monitor of a ranking function and a strong fairness on its decreasing/increasing and then conventional (i.e. "explicit") predicate abstraction is used to prove the modified liveness property; our approach is instead based on reachability analysis and a novel combination of liveness-to-safety, implicit abstraction, and well-founded relations, all tightly integrated within an efficient IC3-based algorithm.

Our algorithm presents some similarities also with the work of [24], where the abstraction is based on the control-flow graph and is refined by removing paths obtained from spurious counterexamples by generalizing infeasible prefixes or termination arguments on loops. Both techniques start from the observation that it is typically easier to refute spurious counterexamples that are due to an infeasible (and bounded) execution prefix than to synthesize a termination argument showing the infeasibility of an infinite path. However, the two approaches differ in the way this observation is turned into an actual procedure. In particular, the approach of [24] is specialised for imperative programs with an explicit control-flow graph, and is based on the construction and manipulation of Büchi automata. Our approach, instead, works on fully-symbolic transition systems, and is based on implicit predicate abstraction.

Another kind of abstraction, targeting liveness properties, is transition predicate abstraction [40]. It extends the classical predicate abstraction by annotating abstract states with abstract transitions. It builds on transition invariants [39] to reduce liveness to fair termination. The technique proves that abstract transitions are well-founded to determine termination. To prove the liveness property, the technique determines whether all fair states are terminating. Our approach differs because it uses predicate abstraction (and well-known refinement techniques) and symbolic liveness model checking techniques such as liveness-to-safety and k-liveness.

Other techniques such as [11,23,39] focus on the specific problem of termination, which is reduced to a binary reachability using disjunctively well-founded invariants. They have also been extended to address temporal properties as in [21,22].

There are several other approaches to the verification of special classes of infinite-state systems such as (ω-)regular model checking [8], push-down systems [25], timed and hybrid automata [15]. The current paper focuses on the verification of generic symbolic transition systems. Specialization of the proposed methods for the above classes is left to future work.

3   Background

Transition Systems. Our setting is standard first order logic. We use the standard notions of theory, satisfiability, validity, logical consequence. We denote formulas with $\phi, \varphi, \psi, I, T$, variables with x, y, and sets of variables with X, Y, $\overline{X}$, $\widehat{X}$. A literal is an atomic formula or its negation. Given a formula φ and the set of its atoms A, an implicant is a conjunction of literals over A that implies φ. In this paper, we shall deal with *linear arithmetic* formulas, that is, Boolean combinations of propositional variables and linear inequalities. A *transition system* S is a tuple $\langle X, I, T \rangle$ where X is a set of (state) variables, $I(X)$ is a formula representing the initial states, and $T(X, X')$ is a formula representing the transitions. Given a formula ϕ over variables X, we denote with ϕ' [$\phi^{\langle n \rangle}$, respectively] the formula obtained by replacing each $x \in X$ with x' [x with n primes] in ϕ. A *state* of S is an assignment to the variables X. A [finite] *path* of S is an infinite sequence $s_0, s_1, \ldots$ [resp., finite sequence $s_0, s_1, \ldots, s_k$] of states such that $s_0 \models I$ and, for all $i \geq 0$ [resp., $0 \leq i < k$], $s_i, s'_{i+1} \models T$. Given two transitions systems $S_1 = \langle X_1, I_1, T_1 \rangle$ and $S_2 = \langle X_2, I_2, T_2 \rangle$, we denote with $S_1 \times S_2$ the synchronous product $\langle X_1 \cup X_2, I_1 \wedge I_2, T_1 \wedge T_2 \rangle$. A predicate is a formula over state variables. Given a set P of predicates and a path $\pi \overset{\text{def}}{=} s_0, s_1, \ldots$ of a transition system, we call the *abstraction of π wrt. P*, denoted $[\widehat{\pi}]_P$, the sequence of sets of states $[\widehat{s_0}]_P, [\widehat{s_1}]_P, \ldots$ obtained by evaluating the predicates in P in the states of π. Given a predicate ϕ, the invariant model checking problem, denoted with $S \models_{inv} \phi$, is the problem to check if, for all finite paths $s_0, s_1, \ldots, s_k$ of S, for all i, $0 \leq i \leq k$, $s_i \models \phi$.

Linear-Time Temporal Logic Verification Using Symbolic Automata-Based Techniques. We use the standard notions of Linear-time Temporal Logic (LTL) formulas and their semantics wrt. infinite paths of a symbolic transition system, as can be found e.g. in [37]. We denote temporal operators in boldface (e.g. **F** for **F**inally, **G** for **G**lobally, **X** for ne**X**t, **U** for **U**ntil).

Given a transition system $S \stackrel{\text{def}}{=} \langle X, I, T \rangle$ and an LTL formula ϕ over X, we focus on the model checking problem of finding if, for all infinite paths π of S, ϕ is true in π. We denote this with $S \models \phi$. The automata-based approach [45] to LTL model checking consists of building a transition system $S_{\neg \phi}$ with a fairness condition $f_{\neg \phi}$, such that $S \models \phi$ iff $S \times S_{\neg \phi} \models \mathbf{FG} \neg f_{\neg \phi}$. Showing that $S \not\models \phi$ amounts to find a counterexample in the form of a fair path, i.e., a path that visits the $f_{\neg \phi}$ infinitely many times. In finite-state systems, if ϕ does not hold, there is always a counterexample in lasso-shaped form, i.e., formed by a prefix (or stem) and a loop. In the following, without loss of generality, we assume that the automata-based transformation has been applied to the LTL model checking problem, and consider a problem in the form $S \models \mathbf{FG} \neg f_{\neg \phi}$, where ϕ is a formula whose atoms are either propositional variables or linear arithmetic (in)equalities. When clear from the context, we also drop the subscript $\cdot_{\neg \phi}$, and simply use $\mathbf{FG} \neg f$.

Liveness to Safety (L2S). The *liveness to safety reduction* (L2S) [6] is a technique for reducing an LTL model checking problem on a finite-state transition system to an invariant model checking problem. The idea is to encode as an invariant property the absence of a lasso-shaped path violating the property $\mathbf{FG} \neg f$. This is achieved by transforming the original transition system S to the transition system S_{L2S}, introducing a set $\overline{X}$ of variables containing a copy $\overline{x}$ for each state variable x of the original system, plus additional variables *seen*, *triggered* and *loop*. Let $S \stackrel{\text{def}}{=} \langle X, I, T \rangle$. L2S transforms the transition system in $S_{\text{L2S}} \stackrel{\text{def}}{=} \langle X \cup X_{\text{L2S}}, I_{\text{L2S}}, T_{\text{L2S}} \rangle$ so that $S \models \mathbf{FG} \neg f$ if and only if $S_{\text{L2S}} \models \neg bad_{\text{L2S}}$, where:

$$X_{\text{L2S}} \stackrel{\text{def}}{=} \{seen, triggered, loop\} \cup \overline{X}$$
$$I_{\text{L2S}} \stackrel{\text{def}}{=} I \wedge \neg seen \wedge \neg triggered \wedge \neg loop$$
$$T_{\text{L2S}} \stackrel{\text{def}}{=} T \wedge \left[\bigwedge_X \overline{x} \leftrightarrow \overline{x}' \right] \wedge \left[seen' \leftrightarrow (seen \vee \bigwedge_X (x \leftrightarrow \overline{x})) \right]$$
$$\wedge \left[triggered' \leftrightarrow (triggered \vee (f \wedge seen')) \right]$$
$$\wedge \left[loop' \leftrightarrow (triggered' \wedge \bigwedge_X (x' \leftrightarrow \overline{x}')) \right]$$
$$bad_{\text{L2S}} \stackrel{\text{def}}{=} loop$$

The variables $\overline{X}$ are used to non-deterministically guess a state of the system from which a reachable fair loop starts. The additional variables are used to remember that the guessed state was seen once and that the signal f was true at least once afterwards.

Termination via Disjunctive Well-Founded Transition Invariants. If S is a transition system with reachable states R and transition relation T, a relation ρ over the states of S is said to be a *transition invariant* if it contains the transitive closure of T restricted to the states in R (i.e. $T^+ \cap (R \times R) \subseteq \rho$) [39]. A binary relation $\rho \subseteq Q \times Q$ is *well-founded* if every non-empty subset $U \subseteq Q$

has a minimal element wrt. ρ, i.e. there is $m \in U$ such that no $u \in U$ satisfies $\rho(u, m)$. A relation is said to be *disjunctively well-founded* if it is a finite union of well-founded relations. Termination of a program can be reduced to finding a (disjunctively) well-founded transition invariant for it. The technique of [23] reduces the problem of finding a disjunctively well-founded transition invariant to the verification of invariant properties. It works on imperative programs with an explicit representation of the control-flow graph (although in principle it can be applied also in a fully-symbolic setting). A given set of well-founded relations W is conjectured to be a transition invariant for the program. This condition is encoded as an invariant property, and checked with an off-the-shelf invariant-checking engine. In case of failure, the encoding is refined in a counterexample-guided manner by adding new well-founded relations to W, obtained by synthesizing ranking functions for potentially non-terminating lasso-shaped paths in the control-flow graph.

IC3 with Implicit Abstraction. IC3 [10] is a SAT-based algorithm for the verification of invariant properties of transition systems. It incrementally builds an inductive invariant for the property by discovering relatively-inductive formulas obtained by generalization while disproving candidate counterexamples. A a novel approach to lift IC3 to the SMT case has been recently presented in [14]. The technique is able to deal with infinite-state systems by means of a tight integration with *predicate abstraction* [28]. The approach leverages *Implicit Abstraction* [44] to express abstract transitions without computing explicitly the abstract system, and is fully incremental with respect to the addition of new predicates. The main idea of IC3 with Implicit Abstraction (IC3IA) is that of replacing the *relative induction* check of IC3, which is the central operation of the algorithm, with an *abstract* version, defined using implicit abstraction. Given a transition system $S = \langle X, I, T \rangle$, a formula $\varphi(X)$ representing a set of states, and an overapproximation $F(X)$ of states of S reachable in up to k steps, a relative induction query determines whether φ is inductive relative to F, by checking if the formula $\varphi(X) \wedge F(X) \wedge T(X, X') \wedge \neg\varphi(X')$ is unsatisfiable. Given a set of state predicates $P = \{p_i(X)\}_i$, and assuming that both F and φ are Boolean combinations of predicates from P, the corresponding abstract query is the check for unsatisfiability of the following SMT formula:

$$\varphi(X) \wedge F(X) \wedge T(Y, Y') \wedge \bigwedge_{p_i \in P} [(p_i(X) \leftrightarrow p_i(Y)) \wedge (p_i(X') \leftrightarrow p_i(Y'))] \wedge \neg\varphi(X')$$

where Y, Y' are sets of fresh variables. Using the above, IC3 can be generalized from SAT to SMT with very little effort, at the cost of introducing spurious error paths. When this happens, the abstraction can be refined in a counterexample-guided manner, using standard techniques for extracting new predicates (e.g. interpolation). The loop continues until either a real counterexample is found (and so the property does not hold), no more counterexamples are found (and so the abstraction is precise enough to conclude that the property holds), or resources (e.g. time or memory) are exhausted. We refer the reader to [14] for more details about IC3IA.

4   Liveness-to-Safety for Infinite-State Systems

Top-Level Algorithm. We reduce the problem of checking an LTL property $\mathbf{FG}\neg f$ on a transition system S to a sequence of invariant checking problems $S_0 \models_{inv} \phi_0$, $S_1 \models_{inv} \phi_1$, ... For each j, S_j and ϕ_j are the result of an encoding operation dependent on given sets of *state predicates* P and *well-founded relations* W: $S_j, \phi_j :=$ ENCODE(S, f, P, W). ENCODE ensures that if $S_j \models_{inv} \phi_j$, then $S \models \mathbf{FG}\neg f$, in which case the iteration terminates. If $S_j \not\models_{inv} \phi_j$, we analyze a (finite) counterexample trace π in S_j to determine whether it corresponds to an (infinite) counterexample for $\mathbf{FG}\neg f$ in S. If so, then we conclude that the property doesn't hold. Otherwise, if we can conclude that π doesn't correspond to any real counterexample in S, we try to extract new predicates P' and/or well-founded relations W' to produce a refined encoding: $S_{j+1}, \phi_{j+1} :=$ ENCODE$(S, f, P \cup P', W \cup W')$, where $P', W' :=$ REFINE(S_j, π, P, W). If we can neither confirm nor refute the existence of real counterexamples, we abort the execution, returning "unknown". We might also diverge and/or exhaust resources in various intermediate steps (e.g. in checking $S_j \models \phi_j$ or during refinement). In the following, we describe in detail our encoding and refinement procedures. We begin in Sect. 4.1 with a simplified version that only uses predicates from P, i.e. $W = \emptyset$. We then describe how to extend the encoding to exploit also well-founded relations in Sect. 4.2.

4.1   Liveness-to-Safety with Implicit Abstraction

Our first contribution is an extension of the L2S reduction described above to the infinite-state case. We first note that the original L2S transformation is not sound for infinite-state systems. This is because L2S produces a transition system that reaches the error condition if and only if there exists a lasso-shaped path. While for finite-state systems it is enough to consider lasso-shaped counterexamples, this is not true in the infinite-state case. Consider the transition system $S = \langle \{x\}, x = 0, x' = x + 1 \rangle$, with x integer, and the property $\phi \stackrel{\text{def}}{=} \mathbf{FG}(x < 5)$. Clearly, ϕ does not hold in S. Suppose to apply the L2S transformation to S as described in the previous Section, obtaining the transition system S_{L2S}. Since in S there are no lasso-shaped paths, in S_{L2S} there are no paths such that the value of $\overline{x}$ (the copy of the variable x introduced in S_{L2S}) is equal to x. Thus, S_{L2S} is safe even if $S \not\models \phi$.

We overcome this problem by incorporating implicit abstraction in the L2S encoding. Intuitively, the idea is to search for a sufficiently precise predicate abstraction of the original system, if there is one, that does not admit a path visiting the fairness condition an infinite number of times. This exploits the fact that predicate abstraction preserves the validity of universal properties [19] (therefore, if a property $\mathbf{FG}\neg f$ holds in the abstract system, then it holds also in the concrete one).

In fact, we do not need to compute the full predicate abstraction of the system S. Instead, we characterize abstract paths directly in the property, by reducing the LTL model checking problem on $\mathbf{FG}\neg f$ to proving the absence of paths with an *abstract fair loop*. Given a set of predicates $P = \{p_i(X)\}_i$, the encoding consists of storing only the truth assignments to the predicates non-deterministically, and detecting a loop if the system visits again the same abstract state, with the fairness signal f satisfied at least once in the loop. More specifically, from a system $S = \langle X, I, T \rangle$, a property $\mathbf{FG}\neg f$, and a set of predicates P, our abstract L2S transformation (αL2S) produces a system $S_{\alpha L2S} = \langle X \cup X_{\alpha L2S}, I_{\alpha L2S}, T_{\alpha L2S} \rangle$ and an invariant property $\neg bad_{\alpha L2S}$ as follows:

$$X_{\alpha L2S} \stackrel{\text{def}}{=} \{seen, triggered, loop\} \cup \{c_{p_i} \mid p_i \in P\}$$
$$I_{\alpha L2S} \stackrel{\text{def}}{=} I \wedge \neg seen \wedge \neg triggered \wedge \neg loop$$
$$T_{\alpha L2S} \stackrel{\text{def}}{=} T \wedge \left[\bigwedge_{p_i \in P} c_{p_i} \leftrightarrow c'_{p_i} \right] \wedge \left[seen' \leftrightarrow (seen \vee \bigwedge_{p_i \in P} (p_i \leftrightarrow c_{p_i})) \right]$$
$$\wedge \left[triggered' \leftrightarrow (triggered \vee (f \wedge seen')) \right]$$
$$\wedge \left[loop' \leftrightarrow (triggered' \wedge \bigwedge_{p_i \in P} (p'_i \leftrightarrow c'_{p_i})) \right]$$
$$bad_{\alpha L2S} \stackrel{\text{def}}{=} loop$$

where $X_{\alpha L2S}$ is a set of fresh Boolean variables.

Theorem 1 (αL2S soundness). *Let $S = \langle X, I, T \rangle$ be a transition system, P a set of predicates over X, and ψ an LTL property $\mathbf{FG}\neg f$. Let the system $S_{\alpha L2S}$ and invariant property $\neg bad_{\alpha L2S}$ be the results of applying αL2S to S and ψ. Then $S_{\alpha L2S} \models_{inv} \neg bad_{\alpha L2S}$ only if $S \models \psi$.*

Proof. First, we observe that all initial states I are represented in $I_{\alpha L2S}$, and that if we take any state s of S and any successor s' of s under T then there exist corresponding states $s_{\alpha L2S}$ and $s'_{\alpha L2S}$ related by $T_{\alpha L2S}$. This can be seen by noticing that the extra constraints added to T to obtain $T_{\alpha L2S}$ do not restrict the values of the original variables of the system. Therefore, we can lift the correspondence relation to paths, and conclude that every path π of S corresponds to at least one path of $S_{\alpha L2S}$.

Suppose now by contradiction that $S_{\alpha L2S} \models_{inv} \neg bad_{\alpha L2S}$, but $S \not\models \mathbf{FG}\neg f$. Then, there exists an infinite path $\pi \stackrel{\text{def}}{=} s_0, s_1, \ldots$ of S in which f holds infinitely-often. Let $\hat{\pi} \stackrel{\text{def}}{=} \hat{s}_0, \hat{s}_1, \ldots$ be a path in $S_{\alpha L2S}$ corresponding to π, and let $[\hat{\pi}]_P \stackrel{\text{def}}{=} [\hat{s}_0]_P, [\hat{s}_1]_P, \ldots$ be its abstraction wrt. P. Since P is finite, so is the number of different states in $[\hat{\pi}]_P$. Let i be a position in $[\hat{\pi}]_P$ such that all different abstract states occur at least once in $[\hat{s}_0]_P, \ldots, [\hat{s}_i]_P$. Let $j > i$ be a position in π such that $s_j \models f$. Since π is infinite and f holds infinitely-often, j must exist. Then, $[\hat{s}_j]_P$ must be equal to one of the states in $[\hat{s}_0]_P, \ldots, [\hat{s}_i]_P$, and therefore $\hat{s}_0, \ldots, \hat{s}_j$ is a counterexample for $\neg bad_{\alpha L2S}$ in $S_{\alpha L2S}$, which contradicts our initial assumption. $\qed$

Counterexamples and Refinement. If $\neg bad_{\alpha L2S}$ holds in $S_{\alpha L2S}$, then $S \models \mathbf{FG}\neg f$. The converse, however, is not true. A counterexample path leading to $bad_{\alpha L2S}$ in $S_{\alpha L2S}$ might correspond to a real counterexample in S, but it might also be due to an insufficient precision of the abstraction induced by the predicates P. We deal with this case using the following counterexample-guided refinement step. A violation of the property $bad_{\alpha L2S}$ in $S_{\alpha L2S}$ implies that the counterexample path forms a lasso in the abstract state space induced by the predicates P. We first search for a concrete lasso witnessing a real violation of the LTL property, using standard bounded model checking. If this fails, we try to prove that the abstract lasso is infeasible. We check an increasing number of finite unrollings of the lasso, and, upon infeasibility, we extract new predicates from sequence interpolants, similarly to popular refinement strategies used for invariant properties (e.g. [31]). More specifically, let $\pi \stackrel{\text{def}}{=} s_0, \ldots, s_l, \ldots, s_{l+k}$ be a finite path in $S_{\alpha L2S}$ such that $s_{l+k} \models bad_{\alpha L2S}$, $s_{l-1} \models \neg seen$ and $s_l \models seen$. Let $[\widehat{\pi}]_P$ be the abstraction of π wrt. P. We search for the smallest integer $i \geq 0$ such that the formula

$$\underbrace{I \wedge \left[\widehat{s_0}\right]_P \wedge T \wedge \ldots \wedge \left[\widehat{s_{l-1}}\right]_P^{\langle l-1 \rangle} \wedge T^{\langle l-1 \rangle}}_{\phi_0 \qquad\qquad\qquad \phi_{l-1}} \wedge \bigwedge_{j=0}^{i} \underbrace{\left[\left[\widehat{s_l}\right]_P^{\langle l+j\cdot k \rangle} \wedge T^{\langle l+1+j\cdot k \rangle}\right.}_{\phi_{l+1+j\cdot k}} \wedge \ldots$$
$$\ldots \wedge \underbrace{\left[\widehat{s_{l+k-1}}\right]_P^{\langle l+k-1+j\cdot k \rangle} \wedge T^{\langle l+k-1+j\cdot k \rangle}}_{\phi_{l+k-1+j\cdot k}} \left.\right] \wedge \underbrace{\left[\widehat{s_{l+k}}\right]_P^{\langle l+k+i\cdot k \rangle}}_{\phi_n} \tag{1}$$

is unsatisfiable. If i exists, we then use an interpolating SMT solver to produce a sequence interpolant $\iota_1, \ldots, \iota_{n-1}$ for $\phi_0, \ldots, \phi_n$, and extract the set P^{ι} of all the atomic predicates in $\iota_1, \ldots, \iota_{n-1}$, to be added to the set of predicates used at the next iteration.

4.2   Extending Liveness-to-Safety with Well-Founded Relations

The abstract L2S transformation described above is inherently limited in the kind of properties it can prove. This is not only due to the potential divergence of the refinement loop, which is a possibility shared by all approaches based on predicate abstraction applied to undecidable problems, but also to the fact that a single refinement operation may not terminate. If the abstract counterexample that is being simulated can be concretized only with paths that are not in a lasso-shaped form, then (1) will always be satisfiable. However, refinement might not terminate even if the abstract path cannot be concretized. This happens in all cases in which there is no feasible concrete path that executes the abstract loop an infinite number of times, but all finite unrollings of the loop are instead concretizable. As an example, consider the system $S \stackrel{\text{def}}{=} \langle \{x_1, x_2\}, (x_1 = 0) \wedge (x_2 \geq 0), (x_2' = x_2) \wedge (x_1' = x_1 + 1) \rangle$ with x_1, x_2 integers, the property $\psi \stackrel{\text{def}}{=} \mathbf{FG}(x_1 > x_2)$, and the predicates $P \stackrel{\text{def}}{=} \{(x_1 \leq x_2), (0 \leq x_2), (x_1 = 0)\}$. The property holds, but $\alpha L2S$ will not be able to prove it. In fact, $\alpha L2S$ admits an abstract path with a self loop on the abstract state $\langle (x_1 \leq x_2), (0 \leq x_2), \neg(x_1 = 0) \rangle$. In this case, the unrolling of the abstract loop will not terminate: any finite path of S in which the abstract loop is unrolled i times is feasible, e.g. by starting from the initial state $\langle x_1 = 0, x_2 = i + 1\rangle$.

We address the problem of abstract counterexamples whose finite prefixes are all feasible by extending our encoding to incorporate well-founded relations. The intuitive idea is to prove that such abstract counterexamples are spurious and to block them by finding suitable termination arguments in the form of (disjunctively) well-founded transition invariants. The extended αL2S reduction with well-founded relations, denoted with αL2S$_\downarrow$, takes as input a transition system $S \overset{\text{def}}{=} \langle X, I, T\rangle$, an LTL property $\mathbf{FG}\neg f$, a set P of state predicates, and a set W of well-founded binary relations. The encoding extends αL2S producing a transition system $S_{\alpha\text{L2S}_\downarrow} \overset{\text{def}}{=} \langle X_{\alpha\text{L2S}_\downarrow}, I_{\alpha\text{L2S}_\downarrow}, T_{\alpha\text{L2S}_\downarrow}\rangle$ and an invariant property $\neg bad_{\alpha\text{L2S}_\downarrow}$ defined as:

$$X_{\alpha\text{L2S}_\downarrow} \overset{\text{def}}{=} X \cup X_{\alpha\text{L2S}} \cup \{x_0, \overline{x} \mid x \in X\} \cup \{r, s, w\}$$

$$I_{\alpha\text{L2S}_\downarrow} \overset{\text{def}}{=} I_{\alpha\text{L2S}} \wedge \bigwedge_{x \in X}(x_0 = x) \wedge r \wedge \neg s \wedge w$$

$$T_{\alpha\text{L2S}_\downarrow} \overset{\text{def}}{=} T_{\alpha\text{L2S}} \wedge \bigwedge_{x \in X}(x_0' = x_0) \wedge \left[w' \leftrightarrow (w \wedge (f \to r))\right] \wedge T_{mem} \wedge T_{check}$$

$$T_{mem} \overset{\text{def}}{=} \left[(s \leftrightarrow s') \wedge \bigwedge_{x \in X}(\overline{x}' = \overline{x})\right]$$
$$\qquad\quad \vee \left[(seen \wedge \neg s \wedge s' \wedge f) \wedge \bigwedge_{x \in X}(\overline{x}' = x)\right]$$

$$T_{check} \overset{\text{def}}{=} r' \leftrightarrow \left[r \wedge \left((s' \wedge f') \to \bigvee W'\right)\right]$$

$$bad_{\alpha\text{L2S}_\downarrow} \overset{\text{def}}{=} (loop \wedge \neg w)$$

where r, s, and w are additional auxiliary Boolean variables, and for every variable $x \in X$, two fresh variables x_0 and $\overline{x}$ are introduced, representing the initial value of x and a stored value of x at some previous occurrence of f respectively.

Intuitively, we weaken the invariant $\neg bad_{\alpha\text{L2S}}$ of Sect. 4.1 by allowing abstract loops with the fairness f to occur as long as w holds. The variable w initially holds and can change its phase at most once, when the current valuation of X and the stored valuation of $\overline{X}$ do not satisfy any of the relations in W. In the subformula T_{check}, the variable r captures the truth value of this test and the variable s ensures the test is carried out only when the valuation of $\overline{X}$ captures some previous valuation of X stored non-deterministically by the subformula T_{mem}.

Theorem 2 (Soundness). *Assuming a fixed finite collection W of well-founded relations, if $S_{\alpha\text{L2S}_\downarrow} \models_{inv} \neg bad_{\alpha\text{L2S}_\downarrow}$ then $S \models \mathbf{FG}\neg f$.*

In order to prove the Theorem, we need the following lemma.

Lemma 1. *For any infinite suffix π_+ of a path π satisfying $\mathbf{GF}f$ and any finite set W of well-founded relations there is a pair of states π_{+1} and π_{+2} satisfying f such that (π_{+1}, π_{+2}) is not in any relation in W.*

Proof. Let π_f denote the transitive closure of π_+ restricted to states where f holds, i.e. an infinite graph over nodes corresponding to those states of π_+ that satisfy f and edges connecting nodes π_{f_i} and π_{f_j} when the latter is reachable from the former. Because all the states lie on a single straight path, the graph is complete. And suppose all edges (π_{f_i}, π_{f_j}) are covered by W. By Ramsey's theorem [41] there exists a complete infinite subgraph π_{W_k} of π_f whose edges are all covered by $W_k \in W$ for some k. The subgraph π_{W_k} forms an infinite chain in the set of states in the ordering imposed by the path π_+. This is in conflict with the fact that all the relations in W are well-founded and thus do not admit infinite chains. □

We can now prove Theorem 2.

Proof (Theorem 2). First, with an argument analogous to that used for proving Theorem 1, we can conclude that every path π of S corresponds to at least one path of $S_{\alpha L2S_\downarrow}$.

Let us assume (by contradiction) $S_{\alpha L2S_\downarrow}$ is safe and $S \not\models \mathbf{FG}\neg f$, then there exists a path $\pi \overset{\text{def}}{=} s_0, s_1, \ldots$ of S where f appears infinitely often (the witness to violation of the property $\mathbf{FG}\neg f$). Let $\widehat{\pi} \overset{\text{def}}{=} \widehat{s_0}, \widehat{s_1}, \ldots$ be a path in $S_{\alpha L2S_\downarrow}$ corresponding to π and let $[\widehat{\pi}]_P$ be its abstraction wrt. P. Let $[\widehat{s_k}]_P$ be the first step where all the distinct abstract states occurring on $[\widehat{\pi}]_P$ were visited at least once. By Lemma 1 there are s_{i_2} and s_{i_3} such that $k < i_2 < i_3$ and (s_{i_2}, s_{i_3}) are not in any relation in W. But $[\widehat{s_{i_3}}]_P$ must be equal to some state $[\widehat{s_{i_1}}]_P$ for $i_1 \leq k$. Thanks to T_{mem}, $\overline{X}$ stores the valuation of X at $\widehat{s_{i_2}}$ and preserves it for the rest of the path. There exists a valuation of the variables $\{c_{p_i} \mid p_i \in P\}$ and an induced partitioning $\langle \widehat{s_0}, \ldots, \widehat{s_{i_1}}, \ldots, \widehat{s_{i_2}}, \ldots, \widehat{s_{i_3}}, \ldots \rangle$ of path $\widehat{\pi}$ such that the predicates $p_i \in P$ assume the values of the corresponding c_{p_i} at $\widehat{s_{i_1}}$ and $\widehat{s_{i_3}}$, and $f \in \widehat{s_{i_1}}, \widehat{s_{i_2}}, \widehat{s_{i_3}}$, and (s_{i_2}, s_{i_3}) is not in any relation in W. The variables *seen*, *triggered*, and s become satisfied after $\widehat{s_{i_1}}$ and the literals *loop*, $\neg w$, and $\neg r$ become satisfied at $\widehat{s_{i_3}}$. Therefore, there exists some positive integer n such that

$$I_{\alpha L2S_\downarrow} \wedge T_{\alpha L2S_\downarrow} \wedge \ldots \wedge T_{\alpha L2S_\downarrow}^{\langle n-1 \rangle} \wedge bad_{\alpha L2S_\downarrow}^{\langle n \rangle}$$

is satisfiable and thus $\widehat{\pi}$ violates the invariant property $\neg bad_{\alpha L2S_\downarrow}$ in finite number of steps, which contradicts our initial assumptions. We conclude that if $S_{\alpha L2S_\downarrow}$ satisfies the invariant property $\neg bad_{\alpha L2S_\downarrow}$ then $S \models \mathbf{FG}\neg f$. □

Counterexamples and Refinement. In order to refine the extended encoding in case of spurious counterexamples, we modify the procedure described in Sect. 4.1 as follows. We first check if the set of predicates P can be refined by blocking a finite unrolling of the abstract loop (or if a real lasso-shaped counterexample can be found). We set an upper bound on the maximum number of unrollings of the abstract loop. If this bound is reached, we try to prove that no infinite unrolling of the loop exists by finding a suitable termination argument based on ranking functions. A violation of $\neg bad_{\alpha L2S_\downarrow}$ implies that the abstract counterexample path $[\widehat{\pi}]_P \overset{\text{def}}{=}$ $[\widehat{s_0}]_P, \ldots, [\widehat{s_l}]_P, \ldots, [\widehat{s_j}]_P, \ldots, [\widehat{s_k}]_P, \ldots, [\widehat{s_{l+n}}]_P$ forms a lasso in the space of the predicates P, with stem $[\widehat{\pi_{stem}}]_P \overset{\text{def}}{=} [\widehat{s_0}]_P, \ldots, [\widehat{s_{l-1}}]_P$ and loop $[\widehat{\pi_{loop}}]_P \overset{\text{def}}{=}$ $[\widehat{s_l}]_P, \ldots, [\widehat{s_{l+n}}]_P$. Within the loop there are two distinct steps $[\widehat{s_j}]_P$ and $[\widehat{s_k}]_P$

that both satisfy f but $([\widehat{s_j}]_P, [\widehat{s_k}]_P)$ is not in any relation in W. Let φ_{stem} and φ_{loop} be defined as:

$$\varphi_{stem} \stackrel{\text{def}}{=} \bigwedge_{i=0}^{l-1}([\widehat{s_i}]_P^{\langle i \rangle} \wedge T^{\langle i \rangle}) \wedge [\widehat{s_l}]_P^l \qquad \varphi_{loop} \stackrel{\text{def}}{=} \bigwedge_{i=l+1}^{l+n}(T^{\langle i-1 \rangle} \wedge [\widehat{s_i}]_P^{\langle i \rangle})$$

where T is the transition relation of the original system S. If T doesn't contain disjunctions, then several off-the-shelf techniques for ranking function synthesis (e.g. [30,38]) can be used for constructing a termination argument for the simple lasso represented by $\varphi_{stem} \wedge \varphi_{loop}$. However, in general T does contain disjunctions. In this case, we can enumerate the simple lassos symbolically represented by $\varphi_{stem} \wedge \varphi_{loop}$ (i.e. lassos without disjunctions), and attempt to build a termination argument for each of them. We do this using the algorithm presented in [36], a technique for enumerating an overapproximation of the prime implicants of a formula by exploiting SMT solving under assumptions. Each implicant of $\varphi_{stem} \wedge \varphi_{loop}$ corresponds to a simple lasso, for which we try to build a termination argument with the technique of [30]. In case of success, we use the ranking function $r(X)$ and its lower bound b produced by [30] to generate a well-founded relation. If this relation was not in the set W already, we add it to W, add its atomic predicates to P, stop the enumeration of simple lassos, and refine the encoding, proceeding to checking the new invariant property on the refined system.[1] Otherwise, we continue with the enumeration, until we either eventually find some new information that allows us to refine our encoding, or we fail to build a termination argument for all the simple lassos represented by the abstract counterexample. In the latter case, the algorithm is aborted, and "unknown" is returned.

k-Liveness as a Well-Founded Relation. Generally, infinite-state systems admit counterexamples that are not lasso-shaped. But we analyze infeasibility of a strict subset of all possible infinite unrollings of the abstract lasso. Consequently, the refinement may fail to produce new abstraction predicates or well-founded relations as well as fail to find a concrete counterexample. However, we may use k-liveness to recover from such situations in hope to make further progress. By extending the transition system with an auxiliary integer variable k representing a counter of occurrences of f, and the necessary updates of k, the refinement may always discover a new well-founded relation $\rho(\overline{X}, X) \stackrel{\text{def}}{=} \overline{k} < k \le n$ where $\overline{k} \in \overline{X}$ is introduced by the reduction αL2S$_\downarrow$ and n is an arbitrary positive integer. We usually let n be the number of occurrences of f in the current counterexample. By adding these free relations we allow the procedure to progress by blocking all short spurious counterexamples as w holds for the first n steps of the re-encoded system. Notice that this is sound.

---

[1] An alternative heuristic could be to not stop the enumeration, and instead generate well-founded relations covering all simple lassos represented by the abstract counterexample. We use a conservative/lazy heuristic, that tries to avoid the potentially-expensive exhaustive enumeration of implicants as much as possible.

4.3 Implementation Within IC3IA

In principle, the technique described in the previous Sections can be implemented on top of any off-the-shelf invariant verification algorithm. In practice, however, we exploit the features of the IC3IA algorithm of [14] to obtain an efficient implementation, in which our liveness-to-safety encoding is tightly integrated in the incremental IC3-based invariant checking procedure and its interpolation-based abstraction refinement.

First, we observe that the interpolation-based refinement of the αL2S encoding (see Sect. 4.1) is very similar to the refinement procedure already implemented in IC3IA, making it possible to reuse most of the code. More importantly, our technique can be integrated in IC3IA in a highly incremental manner. In particular, there is no need of restarting from scratch the IC3 search at every refinement iteration; rather, all the relatively-inductive formulas discovered by IC3IA in the process of constructing an inductive invariant can be retained across refinements. This is possible because: (a) our encoding only monotonically adds constraints to the original transition system, and (b) the new safety property obtained after the $i+1$-th refinement step is weaker than the previous ones; in particular, if IC3 has concluded that no state can violate the property corresponding to the i-th refinement in k steps or less, then this is true also for the $i+1$-th property. Therefore, all the invariants on which IC3 relies for its correctness are preserved by our refinement procedure, thus allowing it to continue the search without resetting its internal state.

5 Experimental Evaluation

We have implemented L2SIA-WFR as an extension of the IC3IA algorithm described in [14]. The MATHSAT SMT solver [17] is used for solving SMT queries, computing interpolants, and synthesizing ranking functions (using the technique of [30]). The LTL extension to IC3IA consists of about 1500 lines of C++ code. In the evaluation, in addition to L2SIA-WFR, we consider L2SIA, i.e. the variant where well-founded relations are disabled. The source code of the implementation is available at https://es-static.fbk.eu/people/griggio/ic3ia/.

Tools Used. We compare our implementation with the following state-of-the-art tools for temporal property verification of infinite-state systems:

HSF [29], a solver for Horn-like clauses that also supports proving well-foundedness of a given relation, using transition invariants. In order to check an LTL property φ, we apply the technique described in [39]: we encode the input transition system and a (symbolic representation of a) Büchi automaton for $\neg\varphi$ as Horn-like clauses, and ask HSF to find a (disjunctively) well-founded transition invariant showing that the accepting states of the automaton cannot be visited infinitely often. We use the LTL2BA tool of [26] to generate the Büchi automaton.

T2-CTL* [21], an extension to the T2 termination prover for imperative programs supporting CTL* temporal properties. LTL properties can be verified by

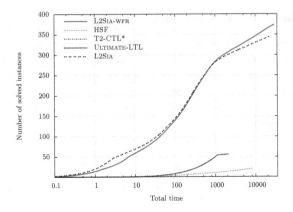

Tool	# Solved	Safe	Unsafe	$\Delta_{\text{L2Sia-wfr}}$	Gained	Lost	Cumulative time (sec)
L2Sia-wfr	374	341	33	–	–	–	29438
L2Sia	344	320	24	-30	1	31	22144
Ultimate-LTL	56	56	0	-318	0	318	2113
HSF	21	21	0	-353	0	353	8116
T2-CTL*	0	0	0	-374	0	374	0

Fig. 1. Experimental results on symbolic transition systems

simply checking the equivalent CTL* specification.[2] T2-CTL* works by recursively computing preconditions of subformulas of the input property (starting from the leaves), and checking whether the precondition of the topmost formula is satisfied by the initial states of the program. Path subformulas are approximated in ACTL, the program is partially determinized using prophecy variables to reduce the imprecision of the approximation. Formula preconditions are then computed via CTL model checking. We remark that T2-CTL* is more general than L2Sia-wfr, being able to handle arbitrary CTL* properties. This fact should be considered when interpreting the experimental results presented.

Ultimate-LTL [24], a tool for the verification of LTL properties of sequential C programs. Ultimate-LTL works by enumerating the fair paths of the input program (i.e. paths visiting the accepting condition of a Büchi automaton for $\neg\varphi$ infinitely often) and trying to prove each of them unfeasible (either by refuting a finite prefix of the path, or by finding a suitable termination argument for it). If a fair path is determined to be feasible, the property is shown not to hold. Otherwise, if the fair path is successfully refuted, it is generalized and then subtracted from the input program: if the result is empty, then the property is shown to hold. Otherwise, an unknown result is reported.

---

[2] T2 supports also verification of CTL properties under fairness constraints [20], which could in principle be used for verifying LTL properties. Here we use the CTL* mode as suggested by the tool authors.

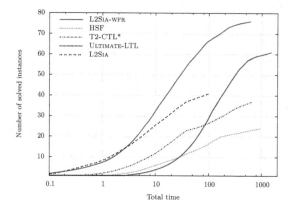

Tool	# Solved	Safe	Unsafe	$\Delta_{\text{L2Sia-wfr}}$	Gained	Lost	Cumulative time (sec)
L2Sia-wfr	76	54	22	–	–	–	618
Ultimate-LTL	61	44	17	-15	2	17	1512
L2Sia	41	26	15	-35	0	35	104
T2-CTL*	36	36	0	-40	2	42	663
HSF	24	24	0	-52	0	52	951

Fig. 2. Experimental results on imperative programs.

Benchmark Sets. Our benchmark set consists of 835 LTL verification problems, grouped in three different subsets:

Symbolic Transition Systems. The first set consists of a collection of symbolic transition systems: BIP models from [7], and systems derived from standard examples in the real-time domain (e.g. [1,5,27]) in which the variables have been converted to integers, in order to be able to use all the tools mentioned above. The LTL properties have been manually generated, in order to capture standard liveness requirements on the considered domains. The set consists of 556 instances, 66 of which are unsafe. For tools working with imperative programs (T2-CTL*, Ultimate-LTL), we encode a system $S = \langle X, I, T \rangle$ as shown in the box on the right, where nondet is a function that returns a non-deterministic value. We then translate an LTL property $\mathbf{FG}\neg f$ into $\mathbf{FG}(ok \rightarrow \neg f)$.[3]

```
ok := false
∀xᵢ∈X xᵢ := nondet()
ok := true
if ¬I(X)
    ok := false
while ok
    ok := false
    ∀xᵢ∈X oldxᵢ := xᵢ
    ∀xᵢ∈X xᵢ := nondet()
    ok := true
    if ¬T(oldX, X)
        ok := false
```

Imperative-style Programs. This set consists of 86 imperative-style programs collected from three different sources:

---

[3] The encoding shown is a slightly simplified one. In practice, we have experimented with several variations, and picked for each tool the encoding giving the best results.

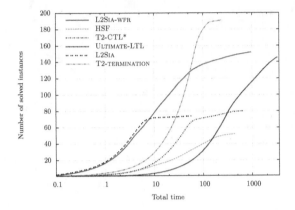

	Tool	# Solved	Safe	Unsafe	$\Delta_{\text{L2Sia-wfr}}$	Gained	Lost	Cumulative time (sec)
	L2Sia-wfr	152	82	70	–	–	–	956
	Ultimate-LTL	146	85	61	-6	15	21	3311
	T2-CTL*	80	80	0	-72	6	78	638
	L2Sia	74	18	56	-78	1	79	57
	HSF	52	52	0	-100	1	101	442
	T2-termination	191	89	102	+39	40	1	235

Fig. 3. Experimental results on T2 termination benchmarks.

(i) 17 simple hand-crafted imperative programs with LTL properties that were specifically written to make approaches based on αL2S fail. The instances are all safe.

(ii) the 41 C programs belonging to the "coolant" and "decision-predicates" groups of benchmark instances used in [24]. The programs have been translated to transition systems using the C front-end of the KRATOS [13] software model checker.[4]

(iii) the 28 instances of the "cav13-ctl-examples" in the source distribution of T2, in which the LTL properties have been obtained by simply removing the path quantifiers from the corresponding CTL properties in the original files.

T2 Termination Benchmarks. The last set we considered consists of the 193 instances of the "testsuite" group in the source distribution of T2. These are termination problems that have been encoded into LTL by checking that a distinguished "sink" location is eventually reached. For this group of benchmarks, in addition to the tools described above, we compare also with the specialised procedure for termination checking in T2 [11] (called T2-TERMINATION in the following).

Results. We ran our experimental evaluation on a cluster of machines with 2.67 GHz Xeon X5650 CPUs and 96 GB of RAM, running Scientific Linux 6.7. We used a timeout of 1200 s and a memory limit of 6 GB.

---

[4] The benchmark set from [24] contains also a third group of instances ("rers2012"), which could however not be handled by the C front-end of KRATOS.

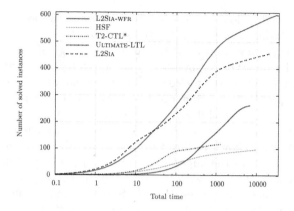

Tool	# Solved	Safe	Unsafe	$\Delta_{\text{L2Sia-wfr}}$	Gained	Lost	Cumulative time (sec)
L2Sia-wfr	602	477	125	–	–	–	31012
L2Sia	459	364	95	-143	2	145	22304
Ultimate-LTL	263	185	78	-339	17	356	6936
T2-CTL*	116	116	0	-486	8	494	1300
HSF	97	97	0	-505	1	506	9509

Fig. 4. Experimental results on all benchmarks.

As a preliminary remark, we analyze the number of predicates used. For the verification of the benchmarks, L2Sia-wfr discovered up to 85 predicates for the $\alpha\text{L2S}_\downarrow$ encoding and up to 278 predicates for checking the sequence of invariant properties with IC3ia, with an average of 20 predicates for $\alpha\text{L2S}_\downarrow$ and 45 predicates for IC3ia (with median values of 14 and 34 respectively). These numbers do not include Boolean state variables in the system, that are always tracked precisely. We conclude that Implicit Abstraction is a key enabler for the proposed approach: an eager computation of the abstract transition system, based for example on AllSMT [33], is typically unable to deal with such high numbers of predicates.

The results of the evaluation are summarized in Figs. 1, 2, 3 and 4. The plots show, for each tool, the number of solved instances (y-axis) in the given total execution time (x-axis), not including timeouts/unknowns. More information is provided in the tables under the plots, where for each tool we show the number of solved instances (distinguishing also between safe and unsafe ones), the difference in number of solved instances wrt. L2Sia-wfr, the number of instances gained (i.e. solved by the given tool but not by L2Sia-wfr) and lost, and the total execution time taken on solved instances. From the results, we can make the following observations:

(i) L2Sia-wfr significantly outperforms all the other tools on symbolic transition systems (Fig. 1). Most of the instances are solved without the need of any ranking function, relying exclusively on abstract L2S. However, as can be seen from the comparison with L2Sia, the integration of ranking functions gives a non-negligible benefit, allowing to solve 31 instances that were out of reach before, and only losing one. It is also interesting to observe that this is beneficial not only for proving properties, but also for finding counterexamples. We attribute the performance of L2Sia-wfr to its tight integration with the engine based on IC3 with Implicit Abstraction [14], that can handle very efficiently the symbolic encodings of these benchmarks. In contrast, and as expected, tools that are optimized to exploit control-flow graphs of programs (T2-CTL*, Ultimate-LTL) perform very poorly when such information is not available.

(ii) Interestingly, as shown in Fig. 2 L2Sia-wfr is the best performing tool also on the benchmarks of the imperative programs group, for which a control-flow graph is available. The gap with the other tools in this case is much smaller, and there are a number of instances which L2Sia-wfr cannot solve but some of the other tools can. However, L2Sia-wfr is still the most effective tool overall, both for safe and for unsafe instances.[5] For this set of benchmarks, the integration of ranking functions is crucial for performance.

(iii) The results on termination benchmarks (Fig. 3) show that there is still a significant gap between tools supporting arbitrary LTL properties and specialised procedures for termination such as T2-TERMINATION, for which almost all these instances are very easy. Also in this case, however, L2Sia-wfr is very competitive with other tools of similar expressiveness (HSF and Ultimate-LTL).

(iv) Overall (Fig. 4), L2Sia-wfr performs very well across all the categories of benchmarks we have considered, comparing very favorably with the state of the art. We think that this demonstrates the generality and potential of our approach.

6   Conclusions

In this paper we presented a novel algorithm, called L2Sia-wfr, to check liveness properties on infinite state transition systems. The algorithm combines liveness-to-safety with implicit abstraction and well-founded relations. The implementation demonstrates substantial advantages in performance over other temporal checkers for infinite-state systems.

In the future, we will explore techniques for non-termination to find counterexamples that are not lasso-shaped, thus extending the effectiveness of the algorithm in the case of property violation. Furthermore, we will investigate domain-specific techniques for the analysis of real-time/hybrid systems, such as the integration with k-zeno [15], and the extension of the class of well-founded relations over the reals. Finally, we will evaluate the application of L2Sia-wfr to temporal satisfiability of first-order temporal logic.

---

[5] To the best of our understanding, HSF can only prove that an LTL property holds, but it is not able to find counterexamples. In principle, T2-CTL* instead should also be able to find counterexamples; however, even after asking its authors, we haven't been able to find a reliable way to distinguish an "unsafe" answer from an "unknown" one.

References

1. Alur, R., Dang, T., Ivancic, F.: Counterexample-guided predicate abstraction of hybrid systems. Theor. Comput. Sci. **354**(2), 250–271 (2006)
2. Alur, R., Dill, D.L.: A theory of timed automata. Theor. Comput. Sci. **126**(2), 183–235 (1994)
3. Balaban, I., Pnueli, A., Zuck, L.D.: Ranking abstraction as companion to predicate abstraction. In: Wang, F. (ed.) FORTE 2005. LNCS, vol. 3731, pp. 1–12. Springer, Heidelberg (2005)
4. Basu, A., Bozga, M., Sifakis, J.: Modeling heterogeneous real-time components in BIP. In: SEFM, pp. 3–12. IEEE Computer Society (2006)
5. Bengtsson, J., Larsen, K.G., Larsson, F., Pettersson, P., Yi, W.: Uppaal - a tool suite for automatic verification of real-time systems. In: Hybrid Systems, pp. 232–243 (1995)
6. Biere, A., Artho, C., Schuppan, V.: Liveness checking as safety checking. Electr. Notes Theor. Comput. Sci. **66**(2), 160–177 (2002)
7. Bliudze, S., Cimatti, A., Jaber, M., Mover, S., Roveri, M., Saab, W., Wang, Q.: Formal verification of infinite-state BIP models. In: Finkbeiner, B., et al. (eds.) ATVA 2015. LNCS, vol. 9364, pp. 326–343. Springer, Heidelberg (2015). doi:10. 1007/978-3-319-24953-7_25
8. Bouajjani, A., Legay, A., Wolper, P.: Handling liveness properties in (ω-)regular model checking. Electr. Notes Theor. Comput. Sci. **138**(3), 101–115 (2005)
9. Bozzano, M., Cimatti, A., Lisagor, O., Mattarei, C., Mover, S., Roveri, M., Tonetta, S.: Safety assessment of AltaRica models via symbolic model checking. Sci. Comput. Program. **98**, 464–483 (2015)
10. Bradley, A.R.: SAT-based model checking without unrolling. In: Jhala, R., Schmidt, D. (eds.) VMCAI 2011. LNCS, vol. 6538, pp. 70–87. Springer, Heidelberg (2011)
11. Brockschmidt, M., Cook, B., Fuhs, C.: Better termination proving through cooperation. In: Sharygina, N., Veith, H. (eds.) CAV 2013. LNCS, vol. 8044, pp. 413–429. Springer, Heidelberg (2013)
12. Cavada, R., Cimatti, A., Dorigatti, M., Griggio, A., Mariotti, A., Micheli, A., Mover, S., Roveri, M., Tonetta, S.: The NUXMV symbolic model checker. In: Biere, A., Bloem, R. (eds.) CAV 2014. LNCS, vol. 8559, pp. 334–342. Springer, Heidelberg (2014)
13. Cimatti, A., Griggio, A., Micheli, A., Narasamdya, I., Roveri, M.: KRATOS – a software model checker for systemC. In: Gopalakrishnan, G., Qadeer, S. (eds.) CAV 2011. LNCS, vol. 6806, pp. 310–316. Springer, Heidelberg (2011)
14. Cimatti, A., Griggio, A., Mover, S., Tonetta, S.: IC3 modulo theories via implicit predicate abstraction. In: Ábrahám, E., Havelund, K. (eds.) TACAS 2014 (ETAPS). LNCS, vol. 8413, pp. 46–61. Springer, Heidelberg (2014)
15. Cimatti, A., Griggio, A., Mover, S., Tonetta, S.: Verifying LTL properties of hybrid systems with K-LIVENESS. In: Biere, A., Bloem, R. (eds.) CAV 2014. LNCS, vol. 8559, pp. 424–440. Springer, Heidelberg (2014)
16. Cimatti, A., Griggio, A., Mover, S., Tonetta, S.: HYCOMP: an SMT-based model checker for hybrid systems. In: Baier, C., Tinelli, C. (eds.) TACAS 2015. LNCS, vol. 9035, pp. 52–67. Springer, Heidelberg (2015)
17. Cimatti, A., Griggio, A., Schaafsma, B.J., Sebastiani, R.: The mathSAT5 SMT solver. In: Piterman, N., Smolka, S.A. (eds.) TACAS 2013 (ETAPS 2013). LNCS, vol. 7795, pp. 93–107. Springer, Heidelberg (2013)

18. Claessen, K., Sörensson, N.: A liveness checking algorithm that counts. In: FMCAD, pp. 52–59. IEEE (2012)

19. Clarke, E.M., Grumberg, O., Jha, S., Lu, Y., Veith, H.: Counterexample-guided abstraction refinement for symbolic model checking. J. ACM **50**(5), 752–794 (2003)

20. Cook, B., Khlaaf, H., Piterman, N.: Fairness for infinite-state systems. In: Baier, C., Tinelli, C. (eds.) TACAS 2015. LNCS, vol. 9035, pp. 384–398. Springer, Heidelberg (2015)

21. Cook, B., Khlaaf, H., Piterman, N.: On automation of CTL* verification for infinite-state systems. In: Kroening, D., Păsăreanu, C.S. (eds.) CAV 2015. LNCS, vol. 9206, pp. 13–29. Springer, Heidelberg (2015)

22. Cook, B., Koskinen, E., Vardi, M.: Temporal property verification as a program analysis task. In: Gopalakrishnan, G., Qadeer, S. (eds.) CAV 2011. LNCS, vol. 6806, pp. 333–348. Springer, Heidelberg (2011)

23. Cook, B., Podelski, A., Rybalchenko, A.: Termination proofs for systems code. In: PLDI, pp. 415–426 (2006)

24. Dietsch, D., Heizmann, M., Langenfeld, V., Podelski, A.: Fairness modulo theory: a new approach to LTL software model checking. In: Kroening, D., Păsăreanu, C.S. (eds.) CAV 2015. LNCS, vol. 9206, pp. 49–66. Springer, Heidelberg (2015)

25. Esparza, J., Hansel, D., Rossmanith, P., Schwoon, S.: Efficient algorithms for model checking pushdown systems. In: Emerson, E.A., Sistla, A.P. (eds.) CAV 2000. LNCS, vol. 1855, pp. 232–247. Springer, Heidelberg (2000)

26. Gastin, P., Oddoux, D.: Fast LTL to Büchi automata translation. In: Berry, G., Comon, H., Finkel, A. (eds.) Computer Aided Verification. LNCS, vol. 2102, pp. 53–65. Springer, Heidelberg (2001)

27. Ghilardi, S., Ranise, S.: MCMT: a model checker modulo theories. In: Giesl, J., Hähnle, R. (eds.) IJCAR 2010. LNCS, vol. 6173, pp. 22–29. Springer, Heidelberg (2010)

28. Graf, S., Saïdi, H.: Construction of abstract state graphs with PVS. In: Grumberg, O. (ed.) CAV 1997. LNCS, vol. 1254, pp. 72–83. Springer, Heidelberg (1997)

29. Grebenshchikov, S., Lopes, N.P., Popeea, C., Rybalchenko, A.: Synthesizing software verifiers from proof rules. In: PLDI, pp. 405–416. ACM (2012)

30. Heizmann, M., Hoenicke, J., Leike, J., Podelski, A.: Linear ranking for linear lasso programs. In: Van Hung, D., Ogawa, M. (eds.) ATVA 2013. LNCS, vol. 8172, pp. 365–380. Springer, Heidelberg (2013)

31. Henzinger, T., Jhala, R., Majumdar, R., McMillan, K.: Abstractions from proofs. In: POPL, pp. 232–244 (2004)

32. Henzinger, T., Kopke, P., Puri, A., Varaiya, P.: What's decidable about hybrid automata? In: STOC, pp. 373–382 (1995)

33. Lahiri, S.K., Nieuwenhuis, R., Oliveras, A.: SMT techniques for fast predicate abstraction. In: Ball, T., Jones, R.B. (eds.) CAV 2006. LNCS, vol. 4144, pp. 424–437. Springer, Heidelberg (2006)

34. McMillan, K.L.: Interpolation and SAT-based model checking. In: Hunt Jr., W.A., Somenzi, F. (eds.) CAV 2003. LNCS, vol. 2725, pp. 1–13. Springer, Heidelberg (2003)

35. de Moura, L., Owre, S., Rueß, H., Rushby, J., Shankar, N., Sorea, M., Tiwari, A.: SAL 2. In: Alur, R., Peled, D.A. (eds.) CAV 2004. LNCS, vol. 3114, pp. 496–500. Springer, Heidelberg (2004)

36. Niemetz, A., Preiner, M., Biere, A.: Turbo-charging lemmas on demand with don't care reasoning. In: FMCAD, pp. 179–186. IEEE (2014)

37. Pnueli, A.: The temporal logic of programs. In: FOCS, pp. 46–57 (1977)

38. Podelski, A., Rybalchenko, A.: A complete method for the synthesis of linear ranking functions. In: Steffen, B., Levi, G. (eds.) VMCAI 2004. LNCS, vol. 2937, pp. 239–251. Springer, Heidelberg (2004)
39. Podelski, A., Rybalchenko, A.: Transition invariants. In: LICS, pp. 32–41. IEEE Computer Society (2004)
40. Podelski, A., Rybalchenko, A.: Transition predicate abstraction and fair termination. ACM Trans. Program. Lang. Syst. 29(3) (2007)
41. Ramsey, F.P.: On a problem in formal logic. Proc. Lond. Math. Soc. 3(30), 264–286 (1930)
42. Schuppan, V., Biere, A.: Liveness checking as safety checking for infinite state spaces. Electron. Notes Theor. Comput. Sci. 149(1), 79–96 (2006)
43. Tiwari, A.: HybridSAL relational abstracter. In: Madhusudan, P., Seshia, S.A. (eds.) CAV 2012. LNCS, vol. 7358, pp. 725–731. Springer, Heidelberg (2012)
44. Tonetta, S.: Abstract model checking without computing the abstraction. In: Cavalcanti, A., Dams, D.R. (eds.) FM 2009. LNCS, vol. 5850, pp. 89–105. Springer, Heidelberg (2009)
45. Vardi, M.: An Automata-theoretic approach to linear temporal logic. In: Banff Higher Order Workshop, pp. 238–266 (1995)

Proving Parameterized Systems Safe by Generalizing Clausal Proofs of Small Instances

Michael Dooley and Fabio Somenzi[✉]

Department of Electrical, Computer and Energy Engineering,
University of Colorado Boulder,
Boulder, CO 80309, USA
{michael.dooley,fabio}@colorado.edu

Abstract. We describe an approach to proving safety properties of parameterized reactive systems. Clausal inductive proofs for small instances are generalized to quantified formulae, which are then checked against the whole family of systems. Clausal proofs are generated at the bit-level by the IC3 algorithm. The clauses are partitioned into blocks, each of which is represented by a quantified implication formula, whose antecedent is a conjunction of modular linear arithmetic constraints.

Each quantified formula approximates the set of clauses it represents; good approximations are computed through a process of proof saturation, and through the computation of convex hulls. Candidate proofs are conjunctions of quantified lemmas. For systems with a small-model bound, the proof can often be shown valid for all values of the parameter. When the candidate proof cannot be shown valid, it can still be used to bootstrap finite proofs to permit verification at larger values of the parameter.

While the method is incomplete, it produces non-trivial invariants for a suite of benchmarks including hardware circuits and protocols.

1 Introduction

Parameterized families of systems are often encountered among hardware and software designs. Design libraries often contain arbiters, queues, interfaces, which can be instantiated in different sizes. Verification of such components benefits from the ability to produce a proof valid for all their instances. Moreover, techniques that can prove properties for the entire family of systems can often save time even when compared to verifying just one instance, if it is sufficiently large. However, the undecidability of the problem in its general form [2] and even in rather restricted classes of systems [11,21] means that incomplete methods are often applied to the discovery of parameterized proofs.

We present one such incomplete method called FORHULL-N, which learns a parameterized proof by generalizing inductive invariants for instances of the system. The inspiration for this approach comes from the ability of IC3 [8] to often produce inductive invariants in clausal form with a high degree of regularity. From these clausal proofs, our generalization procedure often extracts parameterized proofs that are even more regular and simple.

S. Chaudhuri and A. Farzan (Eds.): CAV 2016, Part I, LNCS 9779, pp. 292–309, 2016.
DOI: 10.1007/978-3-319-41528-4_16

The rest of this paper is organized as follows. In Sect. 2 we give an overview of the proposed technique, while Sect. 3 reviews related work. Section 4 is devoted to a description of the algorithm. We describe experimental results in Sect. 5, and conclude in Sect. 6.

2 Overview

We present a technique for the verification of invariants on parameterized systems, in which instance proofs are generated for potentially small values of the parameter; from these we attempt to construct and verify a parameterized proof.

Instance proofs are comprised of instance lemmas; for us these proofs are conjunctions of clauses produced by bit-level model checking.[1] We partition the set of instance proofs into classes of clauses, based on which literals appear, in what number, and in what polarity. For each class a universally quantified lemma is constructed, and their conjunction composes a candidate universally quantified proof. In many cases we can guarantee that this candidate proof holds for all values of the parameter. For systems that enjoy a small-model property, a candidate proof may be verified by showing it holds up to a prescribed value of the parameter [20]. In other cases, it may be possible to use an SMT solver to close the proof. Even in cases where the candidate proof cannot be verified, it may still be used to bootstrap the verification process for large parameter values.

For each class of instance clauses we construct a candidate universally quantified lemma with the form:

$$\forall N, \boldsymbol{i}. \ \text{constraint}(N, \boldsymbol{i}) \rightarrow \text{template}(\boldsymbol{i}). \tag{1}$$

A template is a clause in FOL, from which instance lemmas are obtained by substitution of the index variables $\boldsymbol{i}$. The simplest form of lemma is a clause whose literals are Boolean variables and Boolean array references. For example:

Instance Lemma:	$a \vee b_2 \vee c_3$	
Template:	$a \vee b_i \vee c_j$	$i, j \in \boldsymbol{i}.$ (2)

Figure. 1 shows the steps by which the parameterized lemma $\forall N, i. (0 \leq i < N) \rightarrow (b_i \rightarrow (a = i))$ may be recovered from instance clauses.

Since we infer from bit-level instance proofs, the main requirement for the systems handled by FORHULL-N is that their instances be finite-state. Our method seeks to find a proof composed of parameterized lemmas, and can only succeed if one exists. We make the further assumption that if parameterized lemmas exist, they will be witnessed in the instance proofs. While the existence of a parameterized proof often belies symmetry of the system, no explicit symmetry information or preliminary analysis is needed. The instance lemmas in Fig. 1 have been reconstructed from the instance clauses above them and the knowledge that a, for $N = 4$, is a three-bit integer variable.

---

[1] As mentioned in the Introduction, we mostly use IC3, which in our experience produces invariants better suited to our purpose than BDD-based reachability analysis.

Instance clauses ($N = 4$): $\{\neg b_0 \vee \neg a_0, \ \neg b_0 \vee \neg a_1, \ \neg b_0 \vee \neg a_2,$

$\neg b_2 \vee \neg a_0, \ \neg b_2 \vee a_1, \ \neg b_2 \vee \neg a_2\}$

Instance lemmas: $b_0 \rightarrow (a = 0), \quad b_2 \rightarrow (a = 2)$

Template: $b_i \rightarrow (a = j)$

Index tuples: $(0, 0, 4), \ (2, 2, 4)$

Saturated index tuples: $(0, 0, 4), \ (1, 1, 4), \ (2, 2, 4), \ (3, 3, 4)$

Candidate lemma: $\forall \, N, i, j \, . \, (0 \leq i < N \ \wedge \ i = j) \rightarrow (b_i \rightarrow (a = j))$

Fig. 1. Deriving a quantified integer lemma

In general not all index assignments for a template correspond to valid instance lemmas. We therefore restrict the index values by a constraint as in (1). The constraint is a Boolean formula over predicates in modular linear arithmetic. It is inferred by associating to each instance lemma a tuple of integer values and treating each tuple as a point in a multi-dimensional space. The desired constraint is a combination of hulls of convex sets of such point. In this way we transform a logic problem into one of computational geometry.

The success of generalization depends on including as many valid instance lemmas as possible. Therefore we try to *saturate* the set of points by testing whether nearby points correspond to invariants. For example, to produce the candidate lemma in Fig. 1 the index tuples $(1, 1, 4)$ and $(3, 3, 4)$ must first be found through saturation.

Once a candidate proof is constructed, we attempt to verify whether it holds for all values of the parameter. When the small-model property of [20] applies, this can be done by showing that the candidate proof holds up to the computed bound. In these cases *invisible invariants* and related techniques could also be used. We will demonstrate that our technique is in general more expressive.

When a small-model bound is not available or is impractical, it may be possible to use an SMT solver to check that the parameterized proof is an inductive invariant. However, the quantifier instantiation heuristics used by SMT solvers often fail [13]. In these cases, breaking up the proof into simpler obligations may allow the solver to succeed. It is also possible to provide quantifier instantiations manually. In some cases, this may produce proof obligations that are entirely propositional.

All else failing, the candidate proof can be used to generate finite strengthenings for arbitrary values of the parameter. In cases where the candidate proof is correct, these instantiated proofs are immediately inductive. Even if the instantiated strengthening is not inductive, assuming it during verification may be cheaper than verifying the invariant from scratch. In Sect. 5 we show a case where verification can continue to much higher values of the parameter using the candidate proof than without it.

3   Related Work

The general problem of parameterized verification is known to be undecidable [2]. There are therefore two approaches: devising techniques for decidable fragments of the domain, such as the restricted topologies [1,11,14], and incomplete methods, of which our technique is one. Early approaches were not fully automated, and required induction over the parameterized structure [7,17,22].

In the technique presented in [9], parameterized lemmas are approximations of backward-reachable states obtained by iterated symbolic pre-image computation. Small instances are used to establish forward reachability information, so as to refine their parameterized invariants. In contrast, we extract lemmas directly from instance proofs that are arbitrary inductive invariants.

Pnueli, Zuck and others pioneered the use of small-model theorems for parameterized systems in their work on invisible invariants [3,20]. Symmetry is assumed in order to construct a candidate parameterized invariant from a projection of the reachable states. Properties are proven for Bounded Data Systems for which the small-model theorem applies. The approach was extended to support distributed topologies in [5]. Auxiliary assertions were generalized to include Boolean combinations of ∀-assertions in [4].

If the property or its strengthening relies on arithmetic or modular reasoning the small-model theorem does not apply. In [12] the authors defined the so-called *modest model theorem*, which applies to a larger class of systems than the theorem in [20], but unfortunately often produces impractically large bounds.

Whereas techniques derived from invisible invariants produce strengthenings by assuming symmetry, our technique derives lemmas which are constrained by index relations which are custom-learned from instance proofs. The advantage of the invisible invariant approach is that obtaining a strengthening by existentially projecting a BDD for the reachable states is often very fast, especially when a split invariant may be computed [19].

There is significant overlap between our work and that related to the generation of universally quantified invariants. The work in [6] produces invariants in the form of universally quantified Horn clauses. An SMT solver is used with heuristic instantiation, but unlike our own work it requires the program to be decorated with symbolic invariants. Similarly, [18] requires the determination of a set of useful predicates.

The language used in [15], unlike ours, permits statements about reachability. Candidate proofs are also checked using SMT directly, and so do not share our requirement for finite instantiability. However, a significantly different generalization technique is used, whose effectiveness will have to be established through experimentation.

4   Description of Algorithm

We are concerned with families of systems indexed by a parameter N that takes positive integer values. A system is a pair (I, T), where $I(x, N)$ is a predicate describing the initial states and $T(x, x', N)$ is the transition relation. The x variables encode the current state, while the x' variables encode the next state. We assume that for each value of N, (I, T) is a finite state model.

We want to prove that $M = (I, T)$ satisfies the parameterized safety property P for all $N \geq 1$, where $P(x, N)$ describes a parameterized set of "good" states. Our approach is outlined in Algorithm 1. It proceeds by invoking IC3 on finite model instances for selected values of the parameter. If an instance proof is obtained, it is used to improve the quantified lemmas composing a candidate proof. If the candidate proof is found to hold for all $N \geq 1$, the process terminates successfully (at Line 26).

Algorithm 1. Model check parameterized safety property

```
 1: function FORHULL-N (M, P)
 2:     // Takes parameterized model M and parameterized safety property P.
 3:     // Attempt to produce quantified proof from proofs for small values of N.
 4:     // Returns True if P is proven an invariant of M (∀N ≥ 1).
 5:     n = 1
 6:     Store = {
 7:         // Knowledge store for prover data.
 8:         t2instances : templates × P(instances) = {},
 9:         t2lemma : templates × lemmas = {},
10:     }
11:     while True do
12:         S = ⋀ Store.t2lemma[t] for t ∈ ACTIVETEMPLATES(Store)
13:         result, proof, cex = IC3(INSTANTIATE(M, S ∧ P, n))
14:         if result == sat then
15:             R = RESPONSIBLETEMPLATE(Store, P, cex)
16:             if R == P then
17:                 return False
18:             else
19:                 Store.t2lemma = Store.t2lemma \ {R}
20:                 continue
21:         converged = len(proof) == 0
22:         if converged then
23:             S = ⋀ Store.t2lemma[t] for t ∈ ACTIVETEMPLATES(Store)
24:             result = TESTQUANTIFIEDPROOF(M, S ∧ P, n)
25:             if result == success then
26:                 return True
27:         else
28:             UPDATESTORE(Store, proof, n)
29:         n = CHOOSENEXTN(result, Store, n, converged)
```

As the algorithm progresses it accumulates knowledge in the data structure Store, which contains two maps from templates to related data. For each template, t2instances associates a set of index tuples from all values of N already examined, describing lemma instances known to be invariants. For templates that

---

Algorithm 2. Modify and generalize data in Store

1: **function** UPDATESTORE(Store, proof, n)
2:     // Modify store to integrate information in instance proof.
3:     // Relies on templatized proof (templates $\times \mathcal{P}$).
4:     // Lemmas are generalized for templates with added instance tuples.
5:     tproof = TEMPLATIZEPROOF(proof, n)
6:     **for** t $\in$ tproof **do**
7:         instances = tproof[t]
8:         **if** t $\notin$ Store.t2instances **then**
9:             Store.t2instances[t] = {}
10:         Store.t2instances[t] = Store.t2instances[t] $\bigcup$ instances
11:         result, lemma = GENERALIZELEMMA(t, Store.t2instances[t])
12:         **if** result == success **then**
13:             Store.t2lemma[t] = lemma
14:         **else**
15:             Store.t2lemma = Store.t2lemma $\setminus \{t\}$

---

generalize, t2lemma associates a quantified formula. The function ACTIVETEM-PLATES returns the set of templates in the domain of t2lemma. The generalized strengthening S on Line 12 is the conjunction of the formulae in the co-domain of t2lemma. To weaken the strengthening, an element from the domain of t2lemma is removed on Line 19. Initially the relations in Store are empty.

The function INSTANTIATE takes two quantified formulae, which describe a parameterized model and a safety property, and an integer value n. It returns the finite model produced when instantiating the input formulae with $N = n$.

Each model instance is checked by IC3, producing either a proof or a counterexample. If the strengthened property $S \wedge P$ passes, IC3 produces a proof, which is then used by UPDATESTORE to modify and generalize the information in Store. The function of UPDATESTORE is detailed in Algorithm 2. If the proof is empty, it means that the instantiation of $P \wedge S$ is an inductive formula, and we say that the generalized proof has *converged*.

If the proof at $N = n$ has converged, TESTQUANTIFIEDPROOF checks whether it can be verified. If it succeeds, the generalized proof is a valid inductive strengthening for all positive values of the parameter. Therefore P is an invariant, and FORHULL-N returns True.

If the generalized proof has not converged, or the attempt to verify it fails, the next parameter value is determined by CHOOSENEXTN. If the generalized proof has converged, all instance proofs at the same value n will be empty, so the value must change to make progress. Otherwise it may be wise to retry at the same value some number of times, or until converged. The set of instance tuples in t2instances grows monotonically, and as a rule, additional lemma instances improve the chance that generalization succeeds. The intuition behind this criterion is to learn as much as possible on smaller models before continuing, while allowing progress to be made if a proof for a higher value of N would be helpful or necessary.

If instead, on Line 13, IC3 returns sat, either P fails for a given N or S is too strong. Based on the result of RESPONSIBLETEMPLATE, FORHULL-N either returns failure or weakens S by removing the identified template. The function RESPONSIBLETEMPLATE is described in Algorithm 3 in Sect. 4.3.

4.1 Example: Busy Ring Arbiter

As a running example we introduce the Busy Ring arbiter, a distributed speed-independent circuit with a parameterized number of agents [16]. Each agent is composed of a client and an arbiter cell as shown in Fig. 2.

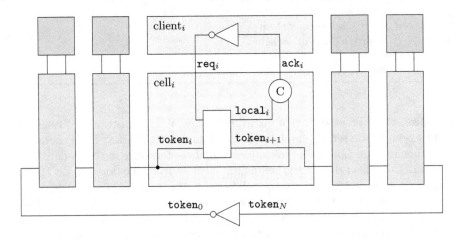

Fig. 2. Busy Ring arbiter

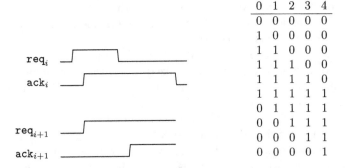

	0	1	2	3	4
	0	0	0	0	0
	1	0	0	0	0
	1	1	0	0	0
	1	1	1	0	0
	1	1	1	1	0
	1	1	1	1	1
	0	1	1	1	1
	0	0	1	1	1
	0	0	0	1	1
	0	0	0	0	1

Fig. 3. Busy Ring: four-phase RTZ signaling

Fig. 4. Busy Ring: N=4 reachable states for token

The arbiter cell consists of a mutex circuit and a C-element. The client is abstracted by an inverter with bounded, non-deterministic delay. Cell and client communicate by four-phase return-to-zero (RTZ) signaling. (See Fig. 3.) Since a client lowers the request line after leaving the critical section, mutual exclusion is expressed by:

$$\forall N, i, j\,.(0 \le i < j < N) \rightarrow \neg(\mathsf{req}_i \wedge \mathsf{ack}_i \wedge \mathsf{req}_j \wedge \mathsf{ack}_j). \tag{3}$$

Algorithm 1 produces a parameterized inductive strengthening of this property comprised of the following lemmas:

$$\forall N, i\,.(0 \le i < N) \rightarrow (\neg\mathsf{local}_i \vee \neg\mathsf{token}_{i+1}) \tag{4}$$

$$\forall N, i\,.(0 \le i < N) \rightarrow (\neg\mathsf{ack}_i \vee \mathsf{local}_i \vee \neg\mathsf{req}_i) \tag{5}$$

$$\forall N, i\,.(0 \le i < N) \rightarrow (\mathsf{ack}_i \vee \neg\mathsf{local}_i \vee \mathsf{req}_i) \tag{6}$$

$$\forall N, i, j, k\,.(0 \le i < j < k < N) \rightarrow (\mathsf{token}_i \vee \neg\mathsf{token}_j \vee \mathsf{token}_k) \tag{7}$$

$$\forall N, i, j, k\,.(0 \le i < j < k < N) \rightarrow (\neg\mathsf{token}_i \vee \mathsf{token}_j \vee \neg\mathsf{token}_k) \tag{8}$$

$$\forall N, i\,.(0 < i < N) \rightarrow (\neg\mathsf{ack}_i \vee \neg\mathsf{req}_i \vee \mathsf{token}_i) \tag{9}$$

Lemmas (4)–(6) describe the behavior of an agent in isolation. Lemmas (7) and (8) characterize the token. Each row of Fig. 4 shows one of its possible values for $N = 4$. Lemma (9) states a condition on the critical section.

4.2   Templatization

The first step that UPDATESTORE takes in constructing a parameterized lemma is to partition the latest instance proof into classes keyed on templates. Templates are FOL formulae, as seen in the consequent of (1), and are produced from instance lemmas by replacing concrete index values with variables to be quantified. In the simplest case, as in (2), the instance clause contains only Boolean and Boolean-array variables, and so the template has the form of a propositional clause as well. Prior to variable substitution the instance lemma must be put in a canonical form, since the relations in Store are keyed on them. For clausal lemmas we order the set of literals lexicographically by variable name and then by index. The ordering by index is important for lemmas that contain repeated literals: lemmas such as (7) and (8) only emerge when the indices are ordered. For clauses that contain FOL predicates, additional consideration must be taken when deciding how to regularize templates as in the case of Fig. 1.

As an example the lemma given by (4) can be expressed as:

$$\forall N, i, j\,.(0 \le i < N \wedge j = i + 1) \rightarrow (\neg\mathsf{local}_i \vee \neg\mathsf{token}_j). \tag{10}$$

This lemma characterizes the mutex circuit. IC3 finds all instances of this lemma, which for $N{=}3$ are:

$$\{\neg\mathsf{local}_0 \vee \neg\mathsf{token}_1, \quad \neg\mathsf{local}_1 \vee \neg\mathsf{token}_2, \quad \neg\mathsf{local}_2 \vee \neg\mathsf{token}_3\}.$$

Each instance can be produced by the template $\neg\mathsf{local}_i \vee \neg\mathsf{token}_j$, and so they all belong to the same class. The index values form a set of *instance tuples*, which are stored in Store.t2instances by UPDATESTORE so that:

$$\{(0, 1, 3), (1, 2, 3), (2, 3, 3)\} \subseteq \texttt{Store.t2instances}[(\neg\mathsf{local}_i \vee \neg\mathsf{token}_j)].$$

The last entry of each tuple is the value of the parameter at which the instance was found. The other entries are the index values for that instance.

4.3 Proof Generalization

The association of instance lemmas to index tuples described in Sect. 4.2 allows UPDATESTORE to treat lemma instances as points in a multidimensional space. Proof generalization infers a pattern in these points, and it is responsible for producing the antecedent in (1). The generalization process takes place within the call to GENERALIZELEMMA on Line 11 of Algorithm 2.

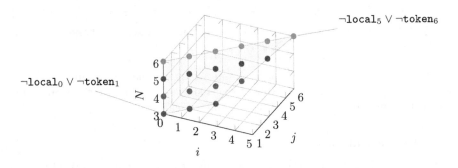

Fig. 5. Busy Ring mutex polytope

Figure 5 plots the index tuples corresponding to the lemma instances of the template $\neg local_i \vee \neg token_j$ from instance proofs for $N \in \{3, 4, 5, 6\}$. The shaded polytope is the convex hull of these instance points, described by a set of linear inequalities, like the following:

$$\{i \geq 0, \quad i = j - 1, \quad i < N, \quad N \geq 3, \quad N \leq 6\}.$$

In this polytope all lattice points correspond to invariants of model instances.

If there are sufficiently many instance points at the highest parameter value, then there is guaranteed to be a facet that restricts N to have a constant upper bound. If such a facet exists, generalization is done by simply removing the corresponding inequalities. If no such facet exists then generalization fails, and the template is skipped. After generalization the constraint describes an unbounded polytope, in this case:

$$\text{constraint} = (0 \leq i < N) \wedge (j = i + 1) \wedge (3 \leq N).$$

Since the coefficients in the linear constraints describing the convex hulls are rational, arbitrary precision arithmetic is used to avoid rounding errors.

Instance Saturation. In most cases the instance proofs do not contain all instances of a template. Part of the reason is that the IC3 proofs are made irredundant by dropping clauses and literals, in order to reduce the number of templates represented in each instance proof. The flip side of this reduction is that oftentimes not all instances of a template are included because they are not necessary. The problem is that the resulting subset of a template's instances often produce polytopes that do not generalize. Take for example the instances of Lemma (7) plotted in Fig. 6. The polytope in Fig. 6(a) is obtained from only those instance lemmas found directly by IC3. The irregularity of the polytope makes it difficult to generalize. In contrast, in Fig. 6(b) many points have been added which correspond to additional invariant instances of the same template.

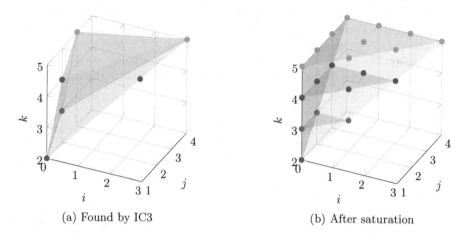

(a) Found by IC3   (b) After saturation

Fig. 6. Instance points for Busy Ring Lemma (7) $2 \leq N \leq 5$

In these plots the parameterized dimension N is omitted, therefore the plots are 3-dimensional projections onto the axes i, j, and k. The instances for $2 \leq N \leq 5$ are plotted simultaneously. Each group of points, denoted by different coloring, represents lemma instances that were first found at a particular value of the parameter. At $N = 5$ all points represent instance lemmas. Likewise at $N = 4$ all points except those where $k = 5$ describe instance lemmas.

Saturation starts with the polytope in Fig. 6(a). At this point IC3 has identified some lemma instances, and we can begin to guess at what is missing. One heuristic is to proceed with a neighbor-based exploration, starting with the points already known to be invariants. Neighbors are those points in which the coordinate value of each dimension differs by at most 1; specifically, these are the lattice points whose distance has a max norm equal to 1. The distance is computed modulo the length of each dimension, so as to discover parameterized lemmas that require modular arithmetic.

To check whether an instance is an invariant, we model check

$$\text{INSTANTIATE}(M, \text{instance} \wedge S \wedge P, n),$$

where n is the last index of the point. If IC3 returns a counterexample the neighbor point is remembered as a non-invariant point. If the instance is proved an invariant, the point is added to the set of instance points and its neighbors are in turn visited. If the invariance proof is non-empty, we additionally extract any instances belonging to existing templates. This harvesting is not essential, but is intended to accelerate saturation.

After saturation a new convex hull is constructed. Through repeated satisfiability queries any unvisited lattice points in the polytope are tested for invariance. At the end of this procedure the status of all lattice points in the hull is known. If there are no known non-invariants inside the hull, generalization successfully proceeds with the saturated polytope.

For most models, saturation is very important to producing lemmas that generalize. In some cases this can expand constraints for which a small-model bound does not apply to one where it does. For example, saturation may strengthen a lemma by changing the neighbor-based constraints $(0 \leq i < N-1) \wedge (j = i+1)$, to the constraints $(0 \leq i < j < N)$. The latter does not make use of addition; hence it can appear in the inductive assertion to be checked by the small model theorem of [3].

Polytope Boolean Combination. If, however, the final saturated convex hull contains instance points corresponding to non-invariants, we attempt to carve out the "bad" points by intersecting with additional, potentially unbounded, convex hulls. This procedure may fail when attempting to carve too few instance points to compute a convex hull. If it fails we attempt to generalize with a disjunction of polytopes. Instance points are heuristically grouped by the ordering of their indices, e.g., for two dimensions, points are classified according to whether $i < j$ or $j \leq i$, and each group is generalized separately. This allows certain non-convex properties to be found, such as mutual exclusion between neighbors around a ring:

$$(\forall N, i \,.(1 \leq i < N) \rightarrow (\neg \textbf{token}_i \vee \neg \textbf{token}_{i-1})) \; \wedge$$
$$(\forall N, i \,.(i = N - 1) \rightarrow (\neg \textbf{token}_0 \vee \neg \textbf{token}_i)).$$

While permitting Boolean combinations of polytopes substantially increases the generality of FORHULL-N, the proofs we currently find do not require these combinations.

Dimensionality Reduction. Saturation can be an expensive procedure. If the points from the instance proofs satisfy simple relations, we want to use those relations to guide saturation. This guidance improves speed, as the instances that are avoided are unlikely to be necessary for the proof.

Take as an example the Busy Ring mutex lemma expressed in (10). Instance points for $3 \leq N \leq 6$ are plotted in Fig. 5. The constraint in (10) contains the simple linear relation $j = i + 1$, which is satisfied by all known instance points. If this relationship can be inferred before saturation, many unnecessary instance lemmas need not be checked for invariance.

The procedure takes as input a matrix, where each row is a point. In a first pass we examine single columns and pairs of columns to identify easy relationships (e.g., $i = 3$, $i < j$, or $i = j + 2$). In a second pass we analyze the null space of the point matrix, augmented with a constant column, to find remaining affine relations of the form $v = \sum_t w_t \cdot v_t + c$, such as $i = j + 2 \cdot k + 1$.

In the case that the relation is functional the dimensionality can be reduced, which has the benefit of avoiding degeneracy in the convex hull computation. However, care must be taken when including lemmas with functional constraints, since the inclusion of linear arithmetic may preclude the application of a small-model bound.

Proof Refinement. A candidate generalized proof may produce an instantiation that leads to IC3 finding a counterexample trace. This can never happen at the same value of the parameter at which the candidate proof was derived, but may at a different value. If this happens the candidate proof may be too strong, and so we first try to refine it through weakening until all counterexamples have been removed.

One possibility is that we learned a mistaken lemma. For example, in the classic dining philosophers it is possible to learn the incorrect lemma $\forall i, j, N . (0 \leq i < j < N) \rightarrow (\neg eating_i \vee \neg eating_j)$ for $N \leq 3$ when only $\forall i, N . (0 \leq i < N) \rightarrow (\neg eating_i \vee \neg eating_{i+1})$ holds in general.

Algorithm 3. Identify reason for proof failure

```
1: function RESPONSIBLETEMPLATE(Store, P, cex)
2:     // Candidate proof failed because it is too strong.
3:     // Identifies template responsible for counterexample trace.
4:     s = cex[-1]    // last state
5:     for t in Store.t2instances do
6:         tinsts = Store.t2instances[t]
7:         if s ⊭ ⋀ SUBSTITUTE(t, i, inst) for inst ∈ tinsts then
8:             return t
9:     // If no template identified, counterexample due to P.
10:    assert s ⊭ INSTANTIATE(P)
11:    return P
```

If a counterexample is found, RESPONSIBLETEMPLATE determines how it may be removed, as described in Algorithm 3. Let s be the last state of the counterexample trace. We try to identify a template which has some instance not modeled by s. Template instances are obtained by the function SUBSTITUTE, which replaces the variables to be quantified in a template with the values from an index tuple. If a template is identified it is returned, to be removed from Store.t2lemma, thereby eliminating one impediment to inductiveness. Note that the removed template still remains in Store.t2instances; so if new instances are discovered a lemma for the template may be reintroduced.

If no such template is found, it must be that a real counterexample to the property has been discovered, and the program terminates on Algorithm 1, Line 17. After dropping a template the generalized proof is retried at the same value of N, effectively preventing progress until all counterexamples are dealt with. Note that it may be that s violates more than one template, but removing one at a time is sufficient to guarantee that each counterexample is removed, and that the refinement process terminates.

4.4   Testing Candidate Proofs

Once a generalized proof has converged, it is a candidate for being a valid proof $\forall N \geq 1$. One way to prove validity of the candidate proof relies on the small-model theorem of [3,20]. If the theorem applies with bound N_0, and we prove validity for instances $1 \leq N \leq N_0$, the candidate proof is valid for all N.

However, the small-model theorem of [3,20] does not support strengthenings that include addition. In these cases the more general modest-model theorem [12] may apply, which unfortunately usually predicts bounds much higher than is practical.

Another possibility for closing the proof is to use an SMT solver to discharge the obligations of the inductive proof. The consecution query is:

$$\forall N . P \wedge S \wedge T \rightarrow (P' \wedge S') \qquad (11)$$

SMT solver heuristic instantiation of quantifiers is sufficient in some cases for closing the proof. To further aid the solver, (11) is decomposed so that instead of providing the $P' \wedge S'$ in the consequent, each parameterized lemma is proven separately.

Even when the candidate proof cannot be shown to be valid, it may still be useful in bootstrapping the proof of large instances, as seen in Fig. 7 of Sect. 5.

4.5   Discussion

A converged proof is guaranteed to be an inductive invariant for all values of N that FORHULL-N has considered up to that point. However, it does not need to be either stronger or weaker than the instance proofs from which it was derived. On the one hand, each parameterized lemma in the proof, when instantiated for a given value of N, produces all template instances in the instance proof. On the other hand, templates that are not sufficiently represented in the instance proofs, or that produced counterexamples, do not contribute to the parameterized proof. This ability of FORHULL-N to both strengthen and weaken instance proofs allows it to produce simple invariants that have a good chance to generalize.

The generalization procedure as described can only learn lemmas that depend on a fixed number of literals and whose constraints are Boolean combinations of integer linear constraints. While lemmas that do not fit those restrictions are occasionally encountered, the approach we have described strikes a reasonable balance between simplicity and power.

When no small-model theorem applies, or the small-model bound is large, FORHULL-N may use the Z3 SMT solver [10] to verify candidate proofs. While we have observed simple models in which this leads to success at very small values of N, it is often the case that the SMT solver is unable to instantiate quantifiers to close the proof [13].

5 Experimental Results

Our method is implemented by a prototype model checker, written mostly in Python. Parameterized models are described in an intermediate language embedded in Python, and can be compiled either into finite AIGER models, or quantified SMT descriptions. Finite proofs are carried out by the IC3 implementation in the model checker IImc, which returns irredundant proofs on demand. SMT obligations are discharged by Z3 [10] using the Z3Py interface. Convex hulls are computed using the Qhull package, included in Octave, using the Python interface Oct2Py.

Results were obtained for a suite of benchmarks, and are reported in Table 1. Experiments were conducted on identical machines with quad-core 2.80 GHz Intel CPUs and 9 GB of memory.

Each model was verified for one or more safety properties, whose number is listed in column $p\#$. For each property three trials were done. The data reported are the average over all properties and trials. For models with multiple verified properties, a hyphenated range of values across all properties is supplied.

Benchmark models are divided into two categories. The first group of models represents hardware circuits and includes examples of synchronous and asynchronous arbiters. The second group is a collection of different protocols.

The column *lemmas* reports the number of parameterized lemmas included in the final candidate proof. Next, *convergeN* reports the smallest parameter value at which the candidate proof holds that is greater than the parameter values instantiated to derive it. The value in *validN* gives the parameter value at which the candidate proof was proven to hold for all N. The column *boundN* reports the computed small-model bound given the model, property, and candidate proof at the end of the run.

Some models require specific validation or generalization heuristics to produce the reported results as noted at the foot of the table. These are: (1) proof validation by an SMT solver (as opposed to a small-model bound), (2) lemmas involving modular reasoning, and (3) lemmas encoding integer facts.

An asterisk in any cell denotes that no such value was available; for instance, if a small-model property does not apply an asterisk appears in column *boundN*. In the cases where *convergeN* has a value, but *validN* has an asterisk, the converged candidate proof could not be verified. When *convergeN* has an asterisk as well, it means that the process did not converge on a candidate proof, up to the bound explored. If *convergeN* has an asterisk, but *validN* does not, it indicates that the property was immediately inductive and no strengthening was necessary.

Table 1. Benchmark results

model	p#	lemmas	convergeN	validN	boundN	runtime	iimctime	checktime
tokens[1]	1	1	5	5	*	8.2	0.1	0.1
databus	1	12	3	3	1	13.2	0.6	0.6
databus_init	1	20	3	3	1	19.6	1.9	0.7
mcmillan_arb[1]	1	1	5	5	*	10.5	0.1	0.7
sync_ring[2]	9	0–28	4–8	*–*	*–*	17.5–147.9	0.2–84.3	1.3–4.6
busy_ring	1	6	4	4	3	12.0	0.8	0.6
dme[2]	3	0–70	7–*	*–*	*–*	50.9–787.4	0.7–640.0	3.6–9.4
german	5	17–30	3–3	3–3	3–3	24.0–32.1	1.9–5.8	2.0–2.3
szymanski	1	9	5	5	5	29.3	2.9	2.1
semaphore[3]	1	2	4	4	4	9.0	0.2	0.3
semaphore2	2	3–4	5–5	5–5	5–5	11.3–11.4	1.0–1.0	0.7–0.8
wheel[3]	1	2	5	5	4	11.4	0.7	0.5
central_book	3	0–0	3–3	3–3	2–3	7.0–7.2	0.0–0.0	0.3–0.3
philosophers	2	0–0	2–2	2–2	1–2	6.8–6.8	0.0–0.0	0.1–0.1
eisenberg	1	4	4	4	4	13.9	0.3	1.7
burns	1	2	4	4	4	10.0	0.2	0.6
dijkstra_me	1	2	4	5	5	12.3	0.3	1.0

Heuristics: [1]SMT validation.   [2] Modular reasoning.   [3] Integer reasoning.

Additionally three times are provided: *runtime* reflecting the total time until validation, or giving up, *iimctime* providing the elapsed time spent proving finite models, and *checktime* the time spent verifying the proof (doing final instantiation/finite model check).

It is interesting that the table contains only averaged values, yet also contains integer values for all the columns but the times. This is a consequence of the apparent stability of the proof process. When verifying a particular property and model across multiple trials, only the time metrics vary slightly; the number of lemmas and N values are identical across the trials. While randomness in proving finite instances can lead to variation in the candidate proofs, this result highlights the success of regularizing the proof.

When a small-model bound is not available we try to close the proof using the SMT solver Z3 [10]. In Table 1, the safety properties for model *philosophers* are inductive invariants and therefore are easily proved for many values of N. However, using Z3 we were able to prove the properties for all N in negligible time using the proof derived at $N = 4$.

Table 1 shows that FORHULL-N is able to prove most benchmarks safe for all parameter values. The exceptions are the properties of *sync_ring* and *dme*. The models *tokens* and *mcmillan_arb* are synchronous circuits for which a small-model bound does not apply, but their proofs were validated using Z3.

Note that for *sync_ring* and *dme* Table 1 provides a value for *convergeN* but none for *boundN*. In these cases the small-model property does not apply due to the candidate proof including modular reasoning. Applying the modest model theorem results in a bound that is prohibitively large. Therefore, even if a generalized proof is obtained, we are currently unable to verify it. However, the candidate proof may still be useful in verifying finite models for larger values of the parameter.

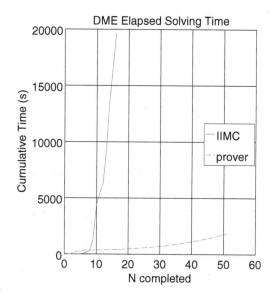

Fig. 7. Verifying instances of *dme* with increasing N, cumulative elapsed time.

Figure 7 shows the cumulative elapsed time spent verifying mutual exclusion on finite instances of *dme* of increasing size. The solid blue curve shows the time spent solving each model using IImc, the largest reported size is $N = 16$. The dashed red curve shows the result of applying our method, which bootstraps each IImc query with the corresponding instantiation of the candidate proof. For *DME* property 0, at $N = 6$ the candidate proof converges. Subsequently, for all N shown, the property conjoined with the strengthening is immediately inductive. Also note that for low values of N our method takes more time than model checking directly, due to the initial cost of constructing the generalized proof.

6   Conclusions and Future Work

We have presented FORHULL-N, a procedure for parameterized verification. While applicable to a large class of systems, FORHULL-N currently works best when a small-model bound is available to verify the parameterized proof on a small finite instance. To extend the reach of FORHULL-N, work is underway on exploiting the structure of the parameterized model to derive hints for quantifier instantiation in the SMT solver. While "closing the proof" is obviously desirable, we have shown that parameterized proofs may also be used to bootstrap proofs of large instances of the system. The bootstrapping is particularly effective when a parameterized proof has converged, because then it is likely to be an inductive invariant. More general lemma structures (e.g., clauses whose number of literals depends on the parameter) and improved handling of lemmas involving integer-valued variables will let FORHULL-N find converged proofs for a larger set of systems.

Acknowledgments. The authors thank Aaron Bradley, who suggested the extraction of templates from IC3 proofs and discussed parameterized verification with them. This research was supported in part by the Semiconductor Research Corporation under contract GRC 2220 and by NSF grant 1549478.

References

1. Abdulla, P.A., Haziza, F., Holík, L.: All for the price of few. In: Giacobazzi, R., Berdine, J., Mastroeni, I. (eds.) VMCAI 2013. LNCS, vol. 7737, pp. 476–495. Springer, Heidelberg (2013)
2. Apt, K., Kozen, D.: Limits for automatic verification of finite-state concurrent systems. Inf. Process. Lett. **22**(6), 307–309 (1986)
3. Arons, T., Pnueli, A., Ruah, S., Xu, J., Zuck, L.D.: Parameterized verification with automatically computed inductive assertions. In: Berry, G., Comon, H., Finkel, A. (eds.) CAV 2001. LNCS, vol. 2102, pp. 221–234. Springer, Heidelberg (2001)
4. Balaban, I., Fang, Y., Pnueli, A., Zuck, L.D.: IIV: an invisible invariant verifier. In: Etessami, K., Rajamani, S.K. (eds.) CAV 2005. LNCS, vol. 3576, pp. 408–412. Springer, Heidelberg (2005)
5. Balaban, I., Pnueli, A., Zuck, L.D.: Invisible safety of distributed protocols. In: Bugliesi, M., Preneel, B., Sassone, V., Wegener, I. (eds.) ICALP 2006. LNCS, vol. 4052, pp. 528–539. Springer, Heidelberg (2006)
6. Bjørner, N., McMillan, K., Rybalchenko, A.: On solving universally quantified horn clauses. In: Logozzo, F., Fähndrich, M. (eds.) Static Analysis. LNCS, vol. 7935, pp. 105–125. Springer, Heidelberg (2013)
7. Bouajjani, A., Jonsson, B., Nilsson, M., Touili, T.: Regular model checking. In: Emerson, E.A., Sistla, A.P. (eds.) CAV 2000. LNCS, vol. 1855, pp. 403–418. Springer, Heidelberg (2000)
8. Bradley, A.R.: SAT-based model checking without unrolling. In: Jhala, R., Schmidt, D. (eds.) VMCAI 2011. LNCS, vol. 6538, pp. 70–87. Springer, Heidelberg (2011)
9. Conchon, S., Goel, A., Krstic, S., Mebsout, A., Zaïdi, F.: Invariants for finite instances and beyond. In: Formal Methods in Computer-Aided Design, Portland, OR, pp. 61–68, October 2013
10. de Moura, L., Bjørner, N.S.: Z3: an efficient SMT solver. In: Ramakrishnan, C.R., Rehof, J. (eds.) TACAS 2008. LNCS, vol. 4963, pp. 337–340. Springer, Heidelberg (2008)
11. Emerson, E.A., Namjoshi, K.: Reasoning about rings. In: Principles of Programming Languages, San Francisco, California, pp. 85–94 (1995)
12. Fang, Y., Piterman, N., Pnueli, A., Zuck, L.D.: Liveness with incomprehensible ranking. In: Jensen, K., Podelski, A. (eds.) TACAS 2004. LNCS, vol. 2988, pp. 482–496. Springer, Heidelberg (2004)

13. Ge, Y., de Moura, L.: Complete instantiation for quantified formulas in satisfiabiliby modulo theories. In: Bouajjani, A., Maler, O. (eds.) CAV 2009. LNCS, vol. 5643, pp. 306–320. Springer, Heidelberg (2009)
14. Kaiser, A., Kroening, D., Wahl, T.: Dynamic cutoff detection in parameterized concurrent programs. In: Touili, T., Cook, B., Jackson, P. (eds.) CAV 2010. LNCS, vol. 6174, pp. 645–659. Springer, Heidelberg (2010)
15. Karbyshev, A., Bjørner, N., Itzhaky, S., Rinetzky, N., Shoham, S.: Property-directed inference of universal invariants or proving their absence. In: Kroening, D., Păsăreanu, C.S. (eds.) CAV 2015. LNCS, vol. 9206, pp. 583–602. Springer, Heidelberg (2015)
16. Kinniment, D.: Synchronization and Arbitration in Digital Systems. Wiley, Hoboken (2007)
17. Kurshan, R.P., McMillan, K.L.: A structural induction theorem for processes. In: Proceedings of the Eighth Annual ACM Symposium on Principles of Distributed Computing, Edmonton, Alberta, Canada, pp. 239–247, August 1989
18. Lahiri, S.K., Bryant, R.E.: Indexed predicate discovery for unbounded system verification. In: Alur, R., Peled, D.A. (eds.) CAV 2004. LNCS, vol. 3114, pp. 135–147. Springer, Heidelberg (2004)
19. Namjoshi, K.S.: Symmetry and completeness in the analysis of parameterized systems. In: Cook, B., Podelski, A. (eds.) VMCAI 2007. LNCS, vol. 4349, pp. 299–313. Springer, Heidelberg (2007)
20. Pnueli, A., Ruah, S., Zuck, L.D.: Automatic deductive verification with invisible invariants. In: Margaria, T., Yi, W. (eds.) TACAS 2001. LNCS, vol. 2031, pp. 82–97. Springer, Heidelberg (2001)
21. Suzuki, I.: Proving properties of a ring of finite-state machines. Inf. Process. Lett. 28(4), 213–214 (1988)
22. Wolper, P., Lovinfosse, V.: Verifying properties of large sets of processes with network invariants. In: Sifakis, J. (ed.) Automatic Verification Methods for Finite State Systems. LNCS, vol. 407, pp. 68–80. Springer, Heidelberg (1990)

Learning-Based Assume-Guarantee Regression Verification

Fei He[1,2,3]([✉]), Shu Mao[1,2,3], and Bow-Yaw Wang[4]

[1] Tsinghua National Laboratory for Information Science and Technology
(TNList), Beijing, China
hefei@tsinghua.edu.cn
[2] School of Software, Tsinghua University, Beijing, China
[3] Key Laboratory for Information System Security, Ministry of Education,
Beijing, China
[4] Academia Sinica, Taipei, Taiwan

Abstract. Due to enormous resource consumption, model checking each revision of evolving systems repeatedly is impractical. To reduce cost in checking every revision, contextual assumptions are reused from assume-guarantee reasoning. However, contextual assumptions are not always reusable. We propose a fine-grained learning technique to maximize the reuse of contextual assumptions. Based on fine-grained learning, we develop a regressional assume-guarantee verification approach for evolving systems. We have implemented a prototype of our approach and conducted extensive experiments (with 1018 verification tasks). The results suggest promising outlooks for our incremental technique.

1 Introduction

Software systems evolve throughout their life cycles. In order to add new features, many revisions are released over time. Since errors may be introduced with new releases, each revision needs to be formally verified. Formal verification however is still very time-consuming. Verifying every revision of an evolving system is impractical. A more effective technique to ensure correctness of evolving software systems is desired.

Model checking is a formal verification technique [4,17]. In model checking, lots of internal information is computed during a verification run. Note that two consecutive revisions share many behaviors. When a revision is verified, internal information from model checking may still be useful to verifying the next revision. Regression verification expands this idea by reusing internal information to speed up the verification of later revisions [3,6,7,10,22,27–29]. Various internal information has been proposed for reuse, including state space graphs [22,29], constraint solving results [28], function summaries [3,25], and abstract precisions [6].

This work was supported in part by the Chinese National 973 Plan (2010CB328003) and the NSF of China (61272001, 91218302).

S. Chaudhuri and A. Farzan (Eds.): CAV 2016, Part I, LNCS 9779, pp. 310–328, 2016.
DOI: 10.1007/978-3-319-41528-4_17

Assume-guarantee reasoning [18] is a compositional technique to improve the scalability of model checking. In the compositional technique, contextual assumptions decompose verification tasks by summarizing component behaviors. Depending on compositional proof rules, contextual assumptions are required to fulfill different criteria for sound verification. Although they used to be constructed manually, contextual assumptions can be generated automatically by machine learning algorithms [13,14,18,21].

Like internal information from model checking, contextual assumptions for the current revision may be reused for the next revision as well. Since contextual assumptions contains the most important information for verifying the current revision, they may immediately conclude the verification of the next revision. Contextual assumptions may be more suitable for regression verification. Compared to internal information from model checking, contextual assumptions are external information. They can be stored and reused without modifying model checking algorithms. In [26], contextual assumptions are exploited in regression verification. When the component summarized by contextual assumptions is not changed, the contextual assumptions are reused and modified to verify revised composed systems. If a system evolves into a new version, components may all be revised. Contextual assumptions thus can not be reused in regression verification. This can be a severe limitation.

Recall that system models are often represented by logic formulas in symbolic verification algorithms. A component may be represented by several logic formulas. Moreover, such logic formulas are further decomposed into more subformulas to attain the best performance. When a system with few components is updated, it is unlikely that all subformulas are revised. The chance of information reuse can be greatly improved if systems are decomposed into finer constituents. In our fine-grained learning framework, an instance of the learning algorithm [8,19,23] is deployed for each logic subformulas. When all instances infer their conjectures, a contextual assumption can be built from these conjectures and sent for assume-guarantee reasoning. We call this the *fine-grained learning-based verification*.

Using our fine-grained technique, we improve regression verification by *incremental assume-guarantee reasoning*. The word *incremental* means the previously-computed results are reused in later verification runs. Given a new revision of the system model represented as a number of logical formulas. We compare the previous revision and the new revision for each subformula. If they remain the same, the inferred conjecture in the previous verification for this subformula can be safely reused. Otherwise the conjecture is re-constructed. Since two revisions have similar behaviors, many of their subformulas remain unchanged. Previously inferred conjectures is likely to be reused.

We have implemented a prototype on top of NuSMV. We performed extensive experiments (with 1018 verification tasks) to evaluate the efficiency of our technique. Experimental results are very promising. If properties are satisfied before and after revisions, our new technique is about four times faster than conventional assume-guarantee reasoning. A similar speedup is also observed for unsatisfied properties before and after revisions. If properties are satisfied before but unsatisfied after revisions, incremental assume-guarantee reasoning also outperforms but less significantly. Overall, we report more than three times speedup on more than a thousand verification tasks.

The remainder of this paper is organized as follows. Section 2 introduces necessary background. Section 3 explains our motivation. Fine-grained learning is discussed in Sect. 4. Our regression verification framework is presented in Sect. 5. Experimental results are reported in Sect. 6. Related work are discussed in Sect. 7. Finally Sect. 8 concludes this paper.

2   Background

Let $\mathbb{B}$ be the Boolean domain and X a finite set of Boolean *variables*. A *valuation* $s : X \rightarrow \mathbb{B}$ of X is a mapping from X to $\mathbb{B}$. A *predicate* $\phi(X)$ over X maps a valuation of X to $\mathbb{B}$. We may write ϕ if its variables are clear from the context.

Definition 1. *A transition system* $M = (X, \Lambda, \Gamma)$ *consists of a finite set of variables* X, *an initial condition* Λ *over* X, *and a transition relation* Γ *which is a predicate over* X *and* $X' = \{x' : x \in X\}$.

Definition 2. *Let* $M_i = \langle X_i, \Lambda_i, \Gamma_i \rangle$ *be transition systems for* $i = 0, 1$ *(*X_i*'s are not necessarily disjoint), the composition* $M_0 \| M_1 = \langle X, \Lambda, \Gamma \rangle$ *is a transition system where* $X = X_0 \cup X_1$, $\Lambda(X) = \Lambda_0(X_0) \wedge \Lambda_1(X_1)$, *and* $\Gamma(X) = \Gamma_0(X_0) \wedge \Gamma_1(X_1)$.

Let $M = (X, \Lambda, \Gamma)$ be a transition system. A *state* s of M is a valuation over X. A *trace* σ of M is a sequence of states $s_0, s_1, \cdots, s_n$, such that s_0 is an initial state, and there is a transition from s_i to s_{i+1} for $i = 0, \ldots, n - 1$. For any predicate ϕ, a sequence σ of states $s_0, s_1, \ldots, s_n$ *satisfies* ϕ (written $\sigma \models \phi$) if $s_i \models \phi$ for $i = 0, \ldots, n$. We say M *satisfies* ϕ (written $M \models \phi$) if $\sigma \models \phi$ for all traces of M. Given a transition system M and a predicate ϕ, the *invariant checking* problem is to decide whether M satisfies ϕ.

2.1   Learning-Based Assume-Guarantee Verification

Assume-guarantee reasoning aims to mitigate the state explosion problem by divide-and-conquer strategy. It uses assumptions to summarize components. Since details of components can be ignored in assumptions, the compositional technique can be more effective than monolithic verification.

Definition 3. *Let* $M_i = \langle X, \Lambda_i, \Gamma_i \rangle$ *be transition systems for* $i = 0, 1$, M_1 *simulates* M_0 *(written* $M_0 \preceq M_1$*) if* $\Lambda_0 \Rightarrow \Lambda_1$ *and* $\Gamma_0 \Rightarrow \Gamma_1$.

Note that the above simulation relation is defined over first-order representation of models. Informally, $M_0 \preceq M_1$ if M_1 simulates all behaviors of M_0.

Theorem 1 [14]. *Let $M_i = \langle X_i, \Lambda_i, \Gamma_i \rangle$ be transition systems for $i = 0, 1$, $X = X_0 \cup X_1$, and $\phi(X)$ a predicate, the following assume-guarantee reasoning rule is sound and invertible:*

$$\frac{M_0 \preceq A \qquad A \| M_1 \models \phi}{M_0 \| M_1 \models \phi} \tag{1}$$

A rule is *sound* if its conclusion holds when its premises are fulfilled. A rule is *invertible* if its premises can be fulfilled when its conclusion holds. In the proof rule (1), the transition system A is called a *contextual assumption* (for short, *assumption*) of M_0. A contextual assumption is *valid* if it either satisfies both premises of above rule, or is able to reveal a counterexample to $M_0 \| M_1 \models \phi$.

Active learning algorithms have been deployed to automatically learn the assumptions for compositional verification [1,13,14,18,20,21]. Let U be an *unknown* predicate. A learning algorithm infers a Boolean formula characterizing U by making queries. It assumes a teacher who knows the target predicate U and answers the following two types of queries:

- On a *membership query* $MQ(s)$ with a valuation s, the teacher answers *YES* if $U(s)$ holds, and *NO* otherwise.
- On a *equivalence query* $EQ(H)$ with a *hypothesis* Boolean formula H, the teacher answers *YES* if H is semantically equal to U. Otherwise, she returns a valuation t on which H and U evaluate to different Boolean values as a counterexample.

Figure 1 shows the learning-based verification framework [13,14,21]. In the framework, a mechanical teacher is designed to answer queries from the learner. For simplicity of illustration, the mechanical teacher in the figure is divided into two parts, each answering one type of queries. Let $M_0 = \langle X_0, \Lambda_0, \Gamma_0 \rangle$ be a transition system. The mechanical teacher knows Λ_0 and Γ_0, and guides *Learner* to infer an assumption $A = \langle X_0, \Lambda_A, \Gamma_A \rangle$ fulfilling the premises of the proof rule (1). Two learning algorithms are instantiated: one for the initial condition Λ_A, the other for the transition relation Γ_A. For instance, consider the learning algorithm for Γ_A. For a membership query $MQ_\Gamma(s,t)$ from *Learner$_\Gamma$*, the mechanical teacher checks if $\langle s, t \rangle$ satisfies Γ_0. If so, the mechanical teacher answers *YES*. Otherwise, she answers *NO*. Conceptually, the mechanical teacher uses Γ_0 as the target predicate. In the worst case, the mechanical teacher infers Γ_0 as Γ_A.

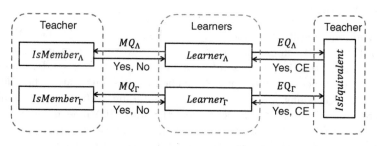

Fig. 1. The learning-based verification framework

The equivalence queries of the two learning algorithms need be synchronized. Let $\overline{\Lambda}_A$ and $\overline{\Gamma}_A$ be the current purported representations of Λ_A and Γ_A, respectively, the mechanical teacher first constructs $\overline{A} = \langle X_0, \overline{\Lambda}_A, \overline{\Gamma}_A \rangle$, then it checks if the purported conjecture of $\overline{A}$ satisfies both premises of the assume-guarantee reasoning rule. If it does, the verification terminates and returns "safe". Otherwise, the premises checker returns a counterexample. The teacher then proceeds to check whether this counterexample is real or not. If it is a real counterexample, the verification algorithm terminates and reports "unsafe". Otherwise, the teacher returns this counterexample to *Learner*. *Learner* will use this counterexample to refine its purported formulas. This process repeats until a valid assumption is inferred.

2.2   Regression Verification

Computer systems evolve during their life time. Since the current version of a system has different behaviors from its previous versions, properties must be re-verified against the current version. In regression verification, we consider the invariant checking problem on two versions of a system. We would like to exploit any information from the previous verification in the current verification.

Definition 4. *Let $M = (X, \Lambda, \Gamma)$ and $M' = (X, \Lambda', \Gamma')$ be transition systems and $\phi(X)$ a specification. The* regression verification *problem is to check whether $M' \models \phi$ after the verification of $M \models \phi$.*

Note that Definition 4 does not assume whether the previous version M satisfies the property ϕ or not. We would like to re-use any information from the previous verification regardless of whether $M \models \phi$ holds or not.

3   Motivation

Let M_0 and M_1 be two components of a system, and A^* a valid contextual assumption. To perform regression verification on updated components M_0' and M_1', a natural idea is to reuse the contextual assumption A^*. However, it is shown in [26] that A^* as a whole can only be reused if $M_0' = M_0$ and M_1' simulates M_1. This can be a severe limitation.

3.1   An Example

Consider an email system composed of two clients c_i ($i = 0, 1$). The client c_i is shown in Fig. 2(a). Each c_i is associated with a data variable msg_i, whose value being true indicates that c_i is sending a message. When c_i sends a message, c_{1-i} will be informed and vice versa. The client c_i has four states: the idle state ("idle"), the receiving state ("recv"), the outgoing state ("otgo"), and the sent state ("sent"). Initially, c_i is at the idle state. If a message arrives (that is, $msg_{1-i} = \text{true}$), c_i transits to the receiving state recv. Otherwise, it non-deterministically transits to the outgoing state otgo and sets msg_i to true, or

Variable: msg_i;
Input: msg_{1-i};

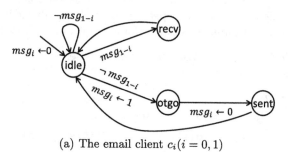

(a) The email client $c_i (i = 0, 1)$

Variable: msg_i;
Input: $msg_{1-i}, turn$;

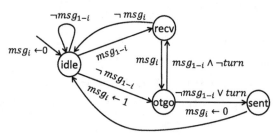

(b) The updated email client $c'_i (i = 0, 1)$

Fig. 2. The email client

remains at the idle state `idle`. After the message is sent, the client transits to its `sent` state. Denote M_{c_i} the model of c_i.

The requirement ϕ_{es} is that all sent emails are well received. Formally, $\phi_{es} := (state_0 = sent) \leftrightarrow (state_1 = recv)$. Apparently, ϕ_{es} is not satisfied by the model. Assume that both clients transit from their `idle` states to their `otgo` states simultaneously, representing both are going to send a message. The only next state for both of them is the `sent` state, which means that both clients have sent their messages, but none of them was well received.

The original model needs be revised to satisfy the requirement. Let $c'_i (i = 0, 1)$ be the updated client, shown in Fig. 2(b). In the new model, sending out a message is granted for a client if another client does not require sending at the same time. If both clients simultaneously want to send their messages, a new variable, called "$turn$", is introduced to assign priority to one of them.

Let us consider the regression verification of $M_{c'_0} \| M_{c'_1}$. Apparently, $M_{c'_0} \neq M_{c_0}$ and $M_{c'_1} \neq M_{c_1}$. According to [26], the contextual assumptions inferred in the verification of $M_{c_0} \| M_{c_1}$ cannot be reused in the verification of $M_{c'_0} \| M_{c'_1}$. However, if we take a look at the symbolic representations of these two revisions of the system, many commonalities can be identified.

Denote $M_{c_i} = \langle X_{c_i}, \Lambda_{c_i}, \Gamma_{c_i} \rangle$ for $i = 0, 1$, where X_{c_i} is a set including a state variable $state_i \in \{\text{idle}, \text{recv}, \text{otgo}, \text{sent}\}$ and a data variable msg_i. The model M_{c_i} can be specified in a way that specifies for each variable x its initial values $init(x)$ and its next-state values $next(x)$. (for example, in NuSMV language [16]):

$$init(state_i) := \text{idle}, init(msg_i) := \text{false},$$
$$next(state_i) :=$$
$$\quad case$$
$$\qquad (state_i = \text{idle}) \wedge msg_{1-i} : \text{recv};$$
$$\qquad (state_i = \text{idle}) \wedge \neg msg_{1-i} : \{\text{idle}, \text{otgo}\};$$
$$\qquad (state_i = \text{otgo}) : \text{sent};$$
$$\qquad (state_i = \text{recv}) : \text{idle};$$
$$\qquad (state_i = \text{sent}) : \text{idle};$$
$$\quad esac$$
$$next(msg_i) :=$$
$$\quad case$$
$$\qquad (state_i = \text{idle}) \wedge (next(state_i) = \text{otgo}) : \text{true};$$
$$\qquad (state_i = \text{otgo}) \wedge (next(state_i) = \text{sent}) : \text{false};$$
$$\qquad \text{true} : msg_i;$$
$$\quad esac$$

The "$case \ldots esac$" expression in above formulas returns the first expression on the right hand side of "$:$", such that the corresponding condition on the left hand side evaluates to true [16]. For short, we write λ_x for the logic formula $x = init(x)$ and γ_x for the formula $x' = tran(x)$. Then Λ_{c_i} and Γ_{c_i} can be represented as:

$$\Lambda_{c_i} = \lambda_{state_i} \wedge \lambda_{msg_i}, \qquad\qquad \Gamma_{c_i} = \gamma_{state_i} \wedge \gamma_{msg_i}.$$

The formulas $init(state_i)$, $init(msg_i)$ and $next(msg_i)$ in the new model are identical to those in the old model. The only difference lies in the formula $next(state_i)$, which in the new model is:

$$next(state_i) :=$$
$$\quad case$$
$$\qquad (state_i = \text{idle}) \wedge msg_{1-i} : \text{recv};$$
$$\qquad (state_i = \text{idle}) \wedge \neg msg_{1-i} : \{\text{idle}, \text{otgo}\};$$
$$\qquad (state_i = \text{otgo}) \wedge msg_{1-i} \wedge \neg turn : \text{recv};$$
$$\qquad (state_i = \text{otgo}) \wedge (\neg msg_{1-i} \vee turn) : \text{sent};$$
$$\qquad (state_i = \text{recv}) \wedge msg_i : \text{otgo};$$
$$\qquad (state_i = \text{recv}) \wedge \neg msg_i : \text{idle};$$
$$\qquad (state_i = \text{sent}) : \text{idle};$$
$$\quad esac$$

3.2 Our Solutions

To take full advantage of commonalities between revisions, we propose to learn the contextual assumptions in a fine-grained fashion. Recall that M_{c_i} in the email system is represented using four predicate formulas, i.e., λ_{state_i}, γ_{state_i}, λ_{msg_i} and γ_{msg_i}. Instead of inferring the contextual assumption as a whole model [26], we suggest to learn it as these four formulas. Note that the former three formulas are identical in the updated model, the inferred conjectures for these three formulas can be safely reused. In this way, the chance of assumption reuse is improved.

We intend to learn the contextual assumptions also in a symbolic fashion. In [26], the contextual assumptions are represented as deterministic finite automata (DFA's). However, the DFA is not a compact representation of a model. A Boolean formula representable by a BDD having n nodes may need mn nodes even in its most compact DFA representation [23], where m is the number of variables in the formula. Learning models via their DFA representations is thus not an efficient approach. We utilize the learning technique in [21] to learn the BDD representation of contextual assumptions. The benefits are multiple folds. Firstly, the symbolic representation of a model is more compact. Recording and reusing the contextual assumption in its symbolic representation is thus more memory-efficient. Secondly, symbolic assumptions can be better adapted to the symbolic model checking. Finally, with the symbolic representations, the equivalence checking of models can be performed in a much more efficient way.

4 Fine-Grained Learning Technique

In this section, we propose a fine-grained learning technique for assume-guarantee verification. Let $M_U = \langle X, \Lambda, \Gamma \rangle$ be the *unknown* target model. Its initial condition Λ and transition relation Γ can oftentimes be represented as a set of logical formulas. Instead of inferring M_U as a DFA, or as two big logical formulas (i.e. Λ and Γ), we propose to infer it as a set of small logical formulas. Fine-grained learning technique will give us more chances to reuse the inferred results.

Without loss of generality, we assume Λ and Γ are decomposed into n predicate formulas: $\varphi_1, \varphi_2, \cdots, \varphi_n$. Define *templates* to be constructed inductively by logical operators and subscripted square parentheses ($[\bullet]_k$). Let ζ_Λ and ζ_Γ be two templates. With ζ_Λ and ζ_Γ, we can construct a contextual assumption from the purported formulas. For example, consider the templates $\zeta_\Lambda[\bullet]_1[\bullet]_2 = [\bullet]_1 \wedge [\bullet]_2$ and $\zeta_\Gamma[\bullet]_1[\bullet]_2 = [\bullet]_1 \wedge [\bullet]_2$ in the email system. Suppose $\overline{\lambda}_{state_0}$, $\overline{\lambda}_{msg_0}$, $\overline{\gamma}_{state_0}$ and $\overline{\gamma}_{msg_0}$ are the current purported formulas. The initial condition and transition relation of the contextual assumption can be constructed as $\zeta_\Lambda[\overline{\lambda}_{state_0}]_1[\overline{\lambda}_{msg_0}]_2 = \overline{\lambda}_{state_0} \wedge \overline{\lambda}_{msg_0}$, and $\zeta_\Gamma[\overline{\gamma}_{state_0}]_1[\overline{\gamma}_{msg_0}]_2 = \overline{\gamma}_{state_0} \wedge \overline{\gamma}_{msg_0}$, respectively.

The fine-grained learning model is shown in Fig. 3. For each subformula φ_i ($1 \leq i \leq n$), one instance of the learning algorithm is deployed. All learners make membership and equivalence queries to a mechanical teacher. Similar to the learning-based framework in Sect. 2.1, equivalence queries need be

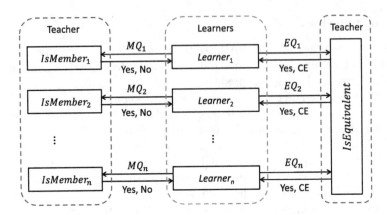

Fig. 3. The fine-grained learning framework

synchronized. When all learners get a conjecture, the mechanical teacher constructs a contextual assumption (using ζ_Λ and ζ_Γ). If the constructed assumption fulfills both premises of the assume-guarantee reasoning rule (1), the verification is finished. Otherwise, the mechanical teacher helps the learners refine their conjectures by providing counterexamples.

Note that our fine-grained technique is not limited to the NuSMV language, and the target model is not necessary to be decomposed by variables (as in the email system example). To see an example, consider the ELTS (extended labelled transition systems with variables) model that is usually specified by transitions. Let k be the number of transitions in an ELTS model. Encoding each transition as a logical formula, the transition relation of the ELTS model is the disjunction of all transition formulas, and the template $\zeta_\Gamma = [\bullet]_1 \vee [\bullet]_2 \vee \cdots \vee [\bullet]_k$. Generally, we follow the syntactic structure to decompose the symbolic representation of the target model.

5   Assume-Guarantee Regression Verification

In this section, we discuss the data structures of contextual assumptions, propose our regression verification framework, and finally prove the correctness of our technique.

5.1   Data Structures of Contextual Assumptions

Our framework employs Nakamura's algorithm [23] to infer the BDD representation of contextual assumptions. Nakamura's algorithm is an instance of the active learning algorithm. Its basic procedure follows that discussed in Sect. 2.1. When we say assumption reusing, we actually mean reusing the data structure of the learning algorithm. We thus discuss in the following the data structures used in Nakamura's algorithm.

Let D be the target (*reduced* and *ordered*) BDD with m variables. A BDD is a directed acyclic graph with one root node and two sink nodes. Each sink node is labeled with 0 or 1, and each non-sink node is labeled with a variable. A BDD can be regarded as a DFA. For any node of D, an *access string* u is a string that leads the BDD from its initial node to that node. Each node of D can be represented by its access string. In the following, we abuse the notation of u (and v) to represent both a node and its access string. For any two distinct nodes u and v, a *distinguishing string* w is a string such that uw reaches the terminal 1 and vw reach the terminal 0, or vice versa. Denote $nodes(D)$ the set of strings $a_1 a_2 \cdots a_k$ such that $k = m$ or the assignment of $x_1 \leftarrow a_1, x_2 \leftarrow a_2, \cdots, x_k \leftarrow a_k$ leads to a node labeled x_{k+1} in D. Let v be a string of length m, denote $D(v)$ the sink label that v reaches in D.

Two data structures are maintained in the BDD learning algorithm: a BDD with access strings (for short, BDDAS) S, and a set $T = \{T_1, T_2, \cdots, T_m\}$ of classification trees. A *BDDAS* is different from an ordinary BDD mainly in the following points: it may have a dummy root node; each of its nodes has an access string; each of its edges is labeled with a binary string. Denote $nodes_i^S(S)$ the set of access strings possessed by the non-dummy nodes in S whose length is i. Let $nodes^S(S) = \bigcup_{i=0}^m nodes_i^S(S)$. Let v be a string of length m, denote $S(v)$ the sink label that v reaches in S.

A *classification tree* T_i $(1 \leq i \leq m)$ decides which node in S a given string of length i will reach. It is composed of internal nodes and leaf nodes. Each internal node is labeled with a distinguishing string of length $m - i$, and each leaf node is labeled with either a special symbol μ, or an access string of length i that is possessed by a node of S. Any string α of length i is classified by T_i into one of its leaf nodes. Denote $T_i(\alpha)$ the leaf label into which α is classified. A string classified into a leaf node labeled with μ means that this string cannot reach any node in the corresponding OBDDAS.

A BDD can be obtained from a BDDAS. The obtained BDD is sent to the teacher for equivalence checking. If it passes the equivalence checking, we are done. Otherwise, a string is returned by the teacher as a counterexample. With this counterexample, the learner updates its BDDAS and classification trees. During the updating, the teacher's answers to membership queries are stored in classification trees. After updating, the cardinality of S (i.e. the number of nodes in S) increases by one. The target BDD is restored when the cardinality of S equals the number of nodes in the target BDD [23].

5.2   Regression Verification Framework

Our assume-guarantee regression verification algorithm is depicted in Algorithm 1. Before the new round of verification starts, an initialization step is performed, which attempts to reuse the contextual assumption inferred in the previous round of verification.

Let M_0 and M_1 be two components of a system. Recall that M_0 is the learning target. Assume M_0 is represented as n logical formulas: $\varphi_1, \varphi_2, \cdots, \varphi_n$. Let φ_i' $(1 \leq i \leq n)$ be the updated form of φ_i in M_0'. In the regression verification, the algorithm checks for each i $(1 \leq i \leq n)$ if φ'_i is equivalent to φ_i. If it is, the data structures (the BDDAS and classification trees) of the previous learner $Learner_{\varphi_i}$ is restored and used to initialize $Learner_{\varphi'_i}$. Otherwise, $Learner_{\varphi'_i}$ starts with empty data structures.

---

1 **for** $1 \leq i \leq m$ **do**
2   **if** $\varphi'_i \equiv \varphi_i$ **then**
3 | $Learner_{\varphi'_i} \leftarrow Learner_{\varphi_i}$
4   **else**
5 | Initialize $Learner_{\varphi'_i}$ with empty data structures
6   **end**
7 **end**
8 Use the technique in Sect. 4 to verify $M'_0 \| M'_1 \models \phi$;

Algorithm 1. *IncrementalAG(M'_0, M'_1, ϕ)*

5.3 Correctness

We prove the correctness of our assume-guarantee regression verification framework in this subsection.

Let α_1, α_2 be two binary strings, we use $|\alpha_1|$ to denote the length of α_1, $pre(\alpha_1, i)$ the prefix string of α_1 with length i, and $\alpha_1 \cdot \alpha_2$ the concatenation of α_1 and α_2.

Definition 5. *A BDDAS S and a set $T = \{T_1, \cdots, T_m\}$ of classification trees are said valid for the target BDD D, if the following conditions are satisfied [23]:*

1. *$nodes^S(S) \subseteq nodes(D)$;*
2. *$\forall v \in nodes^S_{\equiv}(S)$, $S(v) = D(v)$;*
3. *$\forall v_1, v_2 \in nodes^S(S)$, if v_1 and v_2 lead to the same node in D, there must be $v_1 = v_2$;*
4. *$\forall v \in nodes^S(S)$, $T_{|v|}(v) = v$;*
5. *for any binary string α of length $i(1 \leq i \leq m)$, $\alpha \notin nodes(D) \Rightarrow T_i(\alpha) = \mu$;*
6. *for any edge in S that is from u to v and labeled with l,*
   - *$T_{|v|}(u \cdot l) = v$, and*
   - *$|u| < \forall j < |v|$, $T_j(u \cdot pre(l, j - |u|)) = \mu$.*

Lemma 1 [23]. *The Nakamura's learning algorithm terminates with a correct result starting from any BDDAS S and classification trees T_i for $i = 1, \cdots, m$ that are valid for the target BDD D.*

Theorem 2. *Given two BDD's D_1 and D_2, if $D_1 \equiv D_2$, the BDDAS S and classification trees T_i for $i = 1, \cdots, m$ generated by the learner of D_1 are valid for D_2.*

Recall that in our verification framwork, only results of equivalent formulas are reused. Theorem 2 is thus applicable. The correctness of our assume-guarantee regression verification framework (Algorithm 1) follows from Lemma 1 and Theorem 2.

Theorem 3 (Correctness). *The assume-guarantee regression verification algorithm (Algorithm 1) always terminates with a correct result.*

Note that our regression verification framework is not limited to Nakamura's algorithm [23]. Conceptually, any active learning algorithm can apply, such as the L^* algorithm for regular languages [2]. However, to be better suited for the fine-grained learning technique, an implicit learning algorithm is preferred. Alternatively, one can also use the CDNF learning algorithm [8] that infers Boolean functions.

6   Evaluation

A prototype of our regressional assume-guarantee verification technique was implemented on top of NuSMV 2.4.3 [16]. We have performed extensive experiments (in total, 1018 verification tasks from 108 revisions of 7 examples) to evaluate the efficiency of our technique. All experiments were conducted on a machine with 3.06 GHz CPU and 2G RAM, running the Ubuntu 12.04 operation system.

A verification task is specified by a base model, an update to the base model, and a specification. It consists of two rounds of verifications. The contextual assumption inferred in the first round of verification (on the base model) can be optionally reused in the second round of verification (on the updated model). We compare the performance of the second round of verification with and without assumption reuse. The maximal run time is set to 3 h.

The experiments are performed on seven examples, where *Gigamax* models a cache coherence protocol for the Gigamax multiprocess, *MSI* models a cache coherence protocol for consistence ensuring between processors and main memory, *Guidance* models the Shuttle Digital Autopilot engines out (3E/O) contingency guidance requirements, *SyncArb* models a synchronous bus arbiter, *Philo* models the dining philosophers problem [12], *Phone* models a simple phone system with four terminals [24], and *Lift* models the lift system in [5]. The former four examples are obtained from the NuSMV website[1], while the latter two are obtained from literatures. Each example model contains a number of interacting components. Our tool selects one component as M_0 and the composition of others as M_1.

We consider different degrees of changing a model: small changes (using mutations) and significant changes (with significant difference in the functionalities).

Two performance metrics are used in our experiments: (a) the run time (*Time*) for each verification run; (b) the number of membership queries ($|MQ|$)

---

[1] http://nusmv.fbk.eu/examples/examples.html.

and the number of equivalence queries ($|EQ|$) raised in each verification run. Recall that answering learners' queries is the most costly operation in the learning-based verification framework, these two metrics are related to each other.

6.1   Results for Small Changes

Model changes are often small. We realized a program to randomly produce a number of mutations to a model either by introducing new variables or by changing the initial condition or transition relation of an existing variable.

This experiment was performed on five examples: *Gigamax, MSI, Guidance, SyncArb* and *Philo*. Results are shown in the upper part of Table 1. The columns $|Update|$, $|Spec.|$ and $|Task|$ list for each example the numbers of updates, specifications, and verification tasks, respectively. The following two column show the performance of the regression verification with and without assumption reuse respectively. All performance results (including the number of membership queries $|MQ|$, the number of equivalence queries $|EQ|$, and the run time) are given in average values over all tasks per example. The last column compares these two approaches. More experiment details of the highlighted example *SyncArb* will be discussed in Sect. 6.3. The experiment analysis is deferred to the next subsection. We will combine other examples' results and give a combined analysis.

6.2   Results for Significant Changes

During the evolution of a system, new features can be added to improve the original design. This kind of updates involves significant changes to the original model.

The second experiment was performed on two examples: *Phone* and *Lift*. These two examples were obtained from the software product-line engineering community [5,24]. For each example, there are a base model and a set of features. Each feature is considered as a significant change to the base model. Results of this experiment are shown in the bottom part of Table 1. The last *Total* row gives the average of respective values over all examples, including the examples mentioned in the former experiment and those in this experiment.

From Table 1, we observe an impressive improvement of our incremental approach with assumption reuse. Depending on examples, the average speed up of assumption reuse is between 1.26 to 3.79. Over all examples (with 1018 verification tasks in total), the average speed up is 3.47. We also find that the number of queries made by the incremental approach is greatly reduced compared to those without reuse. Over all examples, the average number of membership queries $|MQ|$ is reduced by a ratio of 2.89, and the average number of equivalence queries $|EQ|$ is reduced by a ratio of 3.44. Recall that answering learners' queries is the most costly operation in the learning-based assume-guarantee verification, these results conforms to those about run time.

Table 1. Results for all examples: time in seconds

Example	|Update|	|Spec.|	|Task|	*with* Reuse			*without* Reuse			*without/with*		
				|MQ|	|EQ|	Time	|MQ|	|EQ|	Time	|MQ|	|EQ|	Time
Gigamax	35	6	210	657	12	58.41	2962	69	221.57	4.51	5.66	3.79
MSI	23	14	322	196	6	2.78	2695	97	5.99	13.74	16.26	2.15
Guidance	19	15	285	188	12	53.99	1197	82	199.15	6.37	6.76	3.69
SyncArb	10	2	19	1151	62	23.49	5336	425	81.22	4.64	6.85	3.46
Philo	7	1	7	4848	207	57.50	5834	245	72.37	1.20	1.18	1.26
Phone	7	17	119	9176	85	25.38	25917	328	51.66	2.82	3.86	2.04
Lift	7	8	56	40855	783	11.32	100455	1864	21.06	2.46	2.38	1.86
Total			1018	3625	63	32.47	10494	218	112.56	2.89	3.44	3.47

There is no significant difference for the performance improvement of our incremental approach between the examples with small changes and others with significant changes. This observation supports that our incremental approach is applicable to both degrees of model changes.

6.3   Results for a Single Example

Detailed results for *SyncArb* example are shown in Table 2. The *Sat.* column shows a pair of Boolean values ("T" for true, "F" for false), representing the satisfiability of the specification on the base model and the updated model, respectively. The term "**max**" in the last column denotes a divided-by-zero value. The bottom two rows report the sum and the average of the respective values over all verification tasks.

With assumption reuse, the numbers of membership queries $|MQ|$ and the number of equivalence queries $|EQ|$ are 0's in 15 out of 19 tasks. In other words, the reused assumptions immediately conclude the second round of verification in these tasks. This observation further witnesses the usability of assumption reuse to regression verification.

6.4   Impact of the Satisfiability Results to the Performance

Recall that when models change, the previously established (or falsified) specifications may become unsatisfied (or satisfied). We test in this experiment the impact of the satisifiability results to the efficiency of our incremental approach.

We group verification tasks of each example by their satisfiability results. In total, there are four types of groups: both true (denoted as (T, T)), true on the base model and false on the updated model (denoted as (T, F)), false on the base model and true on the updated model (denoted as (F, T)), and both false (denoted as (F, F)). Results are shown in Table 3, where $|Task|$ column lists the number of verification tasks in each group. Empty groups (with $|Task| = 0$) are omitted from the table.

We got very interesting findings from these results. The last column of Table 3 shows that the regression verification is most likely to be improved by the assumption reuse if the specification was previously satisfied. There are two

Table 2. Results for *SyncArb*: time in seconds

Spec.	Update	Sat.	*with* Reuse			*without* Reuse			*without/with*		
			$|MQ|$	$|EQ|$	Time	$|MQ|$	$|EQ|$	Time	$|MQ|$	$|EQ|$	Time
1	1	(T, F)	17	1	22.10	6561	551	81.24	385.94	551.00	3.68
	2	(T, F)	10083	584	85.45	14312	974	167.75	1.42	1.67	1.96
	4	(T, T)	0	0	10.80	6525	550	108.21	max	max	10.02
	5	(T, F)	7152	358	28.86	17017	1030	531.28	2.38	2.88	18.41
	6	(T, F)	0	0	184.56	6525	550	243.95	max	max	1.32
	7	(T, T)	0	0	5.77	6521	550	85.47	max	max	14.81
	8	(T, T)	0	0	7.79	6525	550	85.84	max	max	11.02
	9	(T, T)	0	0	8.43	6510	550	91.17	max	max	10.82
	10	(T, F)	4618	236	64.83	10693	746	114.12	2.32	3.16	1.76
2	1	(F, F)	0	0	2.64	1972	200	3.28	max	max	1.24
	2	(F, F)	0	0	2.99	1978	200	3.58	max	max	1.20
	3	(F, F)	0	0	2.47	1964	200	3.07	max	max	1.24
	4	(F, F)	0	0	2.85	1974	200	3.61	max	max	1.27
	5	(F, F)	0	0	2.74	1964	200	3.38	max	max	1.23
	6	(F, F)	0	0	2.71	1974	200	3.41	max	max	1.26
	7	(F, F)	0	0	2.74	1974	200	3.35	max	max	1.22
	8	(F, F)	0	0	2.73	1974	200	3.42	max	max	1.25
	9	(F, F)	0	0	3.05	1980	200	3.62	max	max	1.19
	10	(F, F)	0	0	2.76	2440	230	3.36	max	max	1.21
Sum			21870	1179	446.28	101383	8081	1543.11	4.64	6.85	3.46
Average			1151	62	23.49	5336	425	81.22	4.64	6.85	3.46

(F, T) groups (*Gigamax, Phone*) and two (F, F) groups (*Guidance, Philo*) on which the assumption reuse leads to notably performance degeneration. In contrast, the performance of the regression verification is always improved (or nearly improved) by assumption reuse in all (T, T) and (T, F) groups. We speculate the reasons as follows. Recall the assume-guarantee reasoning rule (1). If the specification is satisfied by the system, we need to find a contextual assumption to prove both premises in the rule. In contrast, if the specification is dissatisfied by the system, we need only an assumption that reveals a counterexample to the specification. Finding a counterexample is always much easier than proving the correctness. From the viewpoint of reuse, the assumption revealing a counterexample is certainly less useful than the one proving the correctness of the model.

The *Total* row in Table 3 gives that the average speedup of the incremental technique over all examples for (T, T), (T, F), (F, T) and (F, F) groups are 4.12, 1.75, 0.59, and 4.29, respectively. It further shows that the incremental technique tends to gets the best performance when the staisfiability of the specification are the same on both models. This phenomenon is also reasonable. Given that many behaviors are shared between these two models, the previously found proof (or counterexample) is very likely to be a valid proof (or a valid counterexample) for the updated model.

Table 3. Results grouped by the satisfiability results on the base and the updated models: time in seconds

Model	Sat.	|Task|	*with* Reuse			*without* Reuse			*without*/*with*		
			|MQ|	|EQ|	Time	|MQ|	|EQ|	Time	|MQ|	|EQ|	Time
Gigamax	(T, T)	139	0	0	37.12	0	0	55.47	-	-	1.49
	(T, F)	1	474	31	0.06	474	31	0.08	1.00	1.00	1.36
	(F, T)	23	447	10	60.41	1702	40	26.61	3.81	4.05	0.44
	(F, F)	47	2706	49	121.60	12392	286	812.92	4.58	5.89	6.69
MSI	(T, T)	180	77	2	4.88	3648	124	10.14	47.54	56.12	2.08
	(T, F)	4	56	5	0.04	216	18	0.07	3.89	4.00	1.51
	(F, T)	1	2808	83	4.97	4369	169	15.99	1.56	2.04	3.22
	(F, F)	137	338	10	0.09	1502	64	0.64	4.44	6.14	7.41
Guidance	(T, T)	211	0	0	27.86	968	66	211.70	max	max	7.60
	(T, F)	34	1425	93	176.80	2559	172	299.43	1.80	1.86	1.69
	(F, F)	40	127	7	87.47	1250	88	47.71	9.85	11.76	0.55
SyncArb	(T, T)	4	0	0	8.20	6520	550	92.67	max	max	11.31
	(T, F)	5	4374	236	77.16	11022	770	227.67	2.52	3.27	2.95
	(F, F)	10	0	0	2.77	2019	203	3.41	max	max	1.23
Philo	(T, T)	1	0	0	152.92	0	0	212.77	-	-	1.39
	(T, F)	5	6666	282	38.09	6666	282	57.24	1.00	1.00	1.50
	(F, F)	1	608	40	59.15	7511	300	7.58	12.35	7.50	0.13
Phone	(T, T)	77	11141	96	35.57	30783	367	76.63	2.76	3.82	2.15
	(F, T)	4	15747	159	62.96	20361	252	41.11	1.29	1.58	0.65
	(F, F)	38	4502	55	0.78	16643	257	2.17	3.70	4.69	2.77
Lift	(T, T)	10	497	8	0.37	185932	3229	51.60	374.41	419.35	138.71
	(T, F)	2	172319	3195	44.94	175354	3288	44.31	1.02	1.03	0.99
	(F, T)	3	444478	8530	152.80	451580	8780	149.01	1.02	1.03	0.98
	(F, F)	41	14752	287	2.00	50262	955	3.11	3.41	3.32	1.56
Total	(T, T)	623	1407	13	23.83	8213	159	98.24	5.84	12.57	4.12
	(T, F)	51	8804	239	130.93	10343	349	229.30	1.17	1.46	1.75
	(F, T)	31	45468	856	67.89	47732	918	39.99	1.05	1.07	0.59
	(F, F)	314	3042	57	30.03	11335	245	128.84	3.73	4.30	4.29
		1018	3621	63	32.44	10484	218	112.45	2.89	3.44	3.47

7   Related Work

The first technique on learning-based assume-guarantee reasoning was proposed in [18], where the L^* algorithm [2] was adopted to learn the DFA representation of contextual assumptions. The L^*-based assume-guarantee reasoning was further optimized in different directions by many researchers, including [1,11,15,30]. An implicit learning framework for assume-guarantee reasoning was proposed in [14], where contextual assumptions are inferred in their symbolic representations. Both the BDD learning algorithm [23] and *CDNF* learning algorithm [8] have been adapted to this framework. Moreover, the techinque in [21] improves the implicit learning framework by a progressive witness analysis algorithm. In [20], the learning-based assume-guarantee reasoning was fruther applied to probabilistic model checking. Our technique contributes in assume-guarantee reasoning by providing a new fine-grained learning technique.

Regression verification was investigated mainly in two directions, the equivalence analysis, and the reuse of previously computed results. In the latter direction, a variety of information have been proposed for reuse in regression verification. In [22,29], the state-space graphs are recorded for reuse in latter verification runs. In [28], the intermediate results of a constraint solver are stored and reused. In [7], the abstraction precision used for performing predicate abstraction on previous program is reused. Note that the precision reuse technique is orthogonal to ours. Our technique contributes in this area by integrating regression verification and automated assume-guarantee reasoning.

The most relevant work to ours are [9,26]. They used the idea of assumption reuse to solve the dynamic component substitutability problem. Their technique requires $M_0' = M_0$ and M_1' simulates M_1. This is surely a severe limitation. We removed this limitation by fine-grained learning technique. With our technique, the assume-guarantee regression verification is enabled.

8   Conclusions and Future Work

We presented in this paper a learning-based assume-guarantee regression verification technique. With this technique, contextual assumptions of the previous round of verification can be efficiently reused in the current verification. Correctness of this techniques is established. Experimental results (with 1018 verification tasks) show significant improvements of our technique.

Currently, we implemented a prototype of our technique on top of NuSMV. We are considering to extend this technique to a component-based modeling language that allows hierarchical components and sophisticated interactions. We are also planning to integrate our technique with predicate abstraction, and then apply it to program verification.

References

1. Alur, R., Madhusudan, P., Nam, W.: Symbolic compositional verification by learning assumptions. In: Etessami, K., Rajamani, S.K. (eds.) CAV 2005. LNCS, vol. 3576, pp. 548–562. Springer, Heidelberg (2005)
2. Angluin, D.: Learning regular sets from queries and counterexamples. Inf. Comput. **75**(2), 87–106 (1987)
3. Backes, J., Person, S., Rungta, N., Tkachuk, O.: Regression verification using impact summaries. In: Bartocci, E., Ramakrishnan, C.R. (eds.) SPIN 2013. LNCS, vol. 7976, pp. 99–116. Springer, Heidelberg (2013)
4. Baier, C., Katoen, J.P.: Principles of Model Checking. MIT Press, Cambridge (2008)
5. Berry, M.: Proving properties of the lift system. Master's thesis, School of Computer Science, University of Birmingham, vol. 199, issue 6 (1996)
6. Beyer, D., Löwe, S., Novikov, E., Stahlbauer, A., Wendler, P.: Precision reuse for efficient regression verification. In: Proceedings of the 2013 9th Joint Meeting on Foundations of Software Engineering, pp. 389–399. ACM (2013)

7. Beyer, D., Wendler, P.: Reuse of verification results. In: Bartocci, E., Ramakrishnan, C.R. (eds.) SPIN 2013. LNCS, vol. 7976, pp. 1–17. Springer, Heidelberg (2013)
8. Bshouty, N.H.: Exact learning Boolean function via the monotone theory. Inf. Comput. 123(1), 146–153 (1995)
9. Chaki, S., Clarke, E., Sharygina, N., Sinha, N.: Verification of evolving software via component substitutability analysis. Formal Methods Syst. Des. 32(3), 235–266 (2008)
10. Chaki, S., Gurfinkel, A., Strichman, O.: Regression verification for multi-threaded programs. In: Kuncak, V., Rybalchenko, A. (eds.) VMCAI 2012. LNCS, vol. 7148, pp. 119–135. Springer, Heidelberg (2012)
11. Chaki, S., Strichman, O.: Optimized L^*-based assume-guarantee reasoning. In: Grumberg, O., Huth, M. (eds.) TACAS 2007. LNCS, vol. 4424, pp. 276–291. Springer, Heidelberg (2007)
12. Chaum, D.: The dining cryptographers problem: unconditional sender and recipient untraceability. J. Cryptol. 1(1), 65–75 (1988)
13. Chen, Y.-F., Clarke, E.M., Farzan, A., He, F., Tsai, M.-H., Tsay, Y.-K., Wang, B.-Y., Zhu, L.: Comparing learning algorithms in automated assume-guarantee reasoning. In: Margaria, T., Steffen, B. (eds.) ISoLA 2010, Part I. LNCS, vol. 6415, pp. 643–657. Springer, Heidelberg (2010)
14. Chen, Y.-F., Clarke, E.M., Farzan, A., Tsai, M.-H., Tsay, Y.-K., Wang, B.-Y.: Automated assume-guarantee reasoning through implicit learning. In: Touili, T., Cook, B., Jackson, P. (eds.) CAV 2010. LNCS, vol. 6174, pp. 511–526. Springer, Heidelberg (2010)
15. Chen, Y.-F., Farzan, A., Clarke, E.M., Tsay, Y.-K., Wang, B.-Y.: Learning minimal separating DFA's for compositional verification. In: Kowalewski, S., Philippou, A. (eds.) TACAS 2009. LNCS, vol. 5505, pp. 31–45. Springer, Heidelberg (2009)
16. Cimatti, A., Clarke, E., Giunchiglia, E., Giunchiglia, F., Pistore, M., Roveri, M., Sebastiani, R., Tacchella, A.: NuSMV 2: an opensource tool for symbolic model checking. In: Brinksma, E., Larsen, K.G. (eds.) CAV 2002. LNCS, vol. 2404, pp. 359–364. Springer, Heidelberg (2002)
17. Clarke, E.M., Grumberg, O., Peled, D.: Model Checking. MIT Press, Cambridge (1999)
18. Cobleigh, J.M., Giannakopoulou, D., Păsăreanu, C.S.: Learning assumptions for compositional verification. In: Garavel, H., Hatcliff, J. (eds.) TACAS 2003. LNCS, vol. 2619, pp. 331–346. Springer, Heidelberg (2003)
19. Gavaldà, R., Guijarro, D.: Learning ordered binary decision diagrams. In: Zeugmann, T., Shinohara, T., Jantke, K.P. (eds.) ALT 1995. LNCS, vol. 997, pp. 228–238. Springer, Heidelberg (1995)
20. He, F., Gao, X., Wang, B.Y., Zhang, L.: Leveraging weighted automata in compositional reasoning about concurrent probabilistic systems. In: Proceedings of the 42nd Annual ACM SIGPLAN-SIGACT Symposium on Principles of Programming Languages, pp. 503–514. ACM (2015)
21. He, F., Wang, B.Y., Yin, L., Zhu, L.: Symbolic assume-guarantee reasoning through BDD learning. In: ICSE, pp. 1071–1082. ACM (2014)
22. Lauterburg, S., Sobeih, A., Marinov, D., Viswanathan, M.: Incremental state-space exploration for programs with dynamically allocated data. In: Proceedings of the 30th International Conference on Software Engineering, pp. 291–300. ACM (2008)
23. Nakamura, A.: An efficient query learning algorithm for ordered binary decision diagrams. Inf. Comput. 201(2), 178–198 (2005)

24. Plath, M., Ryan, M.: Feature integration using a feature construct. Sci. Comput. Program. **41**(1), 53–84 (2001)
25. Sery, O., Fedyukovich, G., Sharygina, N.: Incremental upgrade checking by means of interpolation-based function summaries. In: Formal Methods in Computer-Aided Design (FMCAD), pp. 114–121. IEEE (2012)
26. Sharygina, N., Chaki, S., Clarke, E., Sinha, N.: Dynamic component substitutability analysis. In: Fitzgerald, J.S., Hayes, I.J., Tarlecki, A. (eds.) FM 2005. LNCS, vol. 3582, pp. 512–528. Springer, Heidelberg (2005)
27. Strichman, O., Godlin, B.: Regression verification - a practical way to verify programs. In: Meyer, B., Woodcock, J. (eds.) VSTTE 2005. LNCS, vol. 4171, pp. 496–501. Springer, Heidelberg (2008)
28. Visser, W., Geldenhuys, J., Dwyer, M.B.: Green: reducing, reusing and recycling constraints in program analysis. In: Proceedings of the ACM SIGSOFT 20th International Symposium on the Foundations of Software Engineering, p. 58. ACM (2012)
29. Yang, G., Dwyer, M.B., Rothermel, G.: Regression model checking. In: IEEE International Conference on Software Maintenance, ICSM 2009, pp. 115–124. IEEE (2009)
30. Zhu, H., He, F., Hung, W.N., Song, X., Gu, M.: Data mining based decomposition for assume-guarantee reasoning. In: FMCAD, pp. 116–119. IEEE (2009)

Automated Circular Assume-Guarantee Reasoning with N-way Decomposition and Alphabet Refinement

Karam Abd Elkader[1]([✉]), Orna Grumberg[1],
Corina S. Păsăreanu[2], and Sharon Shoham[3]

[1] Technion – Israel Institute of Technology,
Haifa, Israel
skaramt@gmail.com
[2] CMU/NASA Ames Research Center,
Mountain View, USA
[3] Tel Aviv University, Tel Aviv, Israel

Abstract. In this work we develop an *automated* circular reasoning framework that is applicable to systems decomposed into *multiple* components. Our framework uses a family of circular assume-guarantee rules for which we give conditions for soundness and completeness. The assumptions used in the rules are initially approximate and their alphabets are automatically refined based on the counterexamples obtained from model checking the rule premises. A key feature of the framework is that the compositional rules that are used change *dynamically* with each iteration of the alphabet refinement, to only use assumptions that are relevant for the current alphabet, resulting in a smaller number of assumptions and smaller state spaces to analyze for each premise. Our preliminary evaluation of the proposed approach shows promising results compared to 2-way and monolithic verification.

1 Introduction

We present an automated assume-guarantee style compositional approach to address the state explosion problem in model checking. Model checking [7] is a well-known technique for automatically checking that software systems satisfy desired properties. Despite its many successes, the technique suffers from the *state explosion problem*, which refers to the worst-case exponential growth of a program's state space with the number of variables and concurrent components. Compositional techniques have shown promise in addressing this problem, by breaking-up the global verification of a system into the local, more manageable, verification of the system's individual components. The environment for each component, consisting of the other components, is replaced by a "small" *assumption*, making each verification task easier. This is often referred to as *assume-guarantee* reasoning [21,24].

Significant progress has been made on automating compositional reasoning using learning and abstraction-refinement techniques [2–6,8,23]. Most of this

© Springer International Publishing Switzerland 2016
S. Chaudhuri and A. Farzan (Eds.): CAV 2016, Part I, LNCS 9779, pp. 329–351, 2016.
DOI: 10.1007/978-3-319-41528-4_18

work has been done in the context of applying a simple compositional assume-guarantee rule, where components of a system are checked using assumptions and properties which are related in an *acyclic* manner.

Another important category of assume-guarantee rules involves *circular reasoning* and uses inductive arguments over time to ensure soundness [1,15,18,19,21]. Circular rules have often been found to be more effective than non-circular rules [13,14,18–20,25]. However, their applicability has been hindered by the manual effort involved in defining assumptions, while automation remained a challenge due to the more involved inductive reasoning and the mutual dependency between assumptions.

Recent work [10] proposed an automated compositional technique for *circular reasoning* which has shown better scalability results compared with an established learning-based method which implements acyclic reasoning [8]. This circular technique is only applicable to a system decomposed into two components (or two subsystems), thus limiting its applicability in practice. Further, the constructed assumptions are defined over the full interface alphabet of the components, thus causing a blowup in the sizes of the assumptions (and the verification tasks) that is in many cases unnecessary.

We propose an automated circular assume-guarantee technique for reasoning about systems decomposed into an arbitrary (but fixed) number of components. We consider a synchronous composition, where components synchronize on the common alphabet (shared actions), and interleave on the remaining actions. We give a *generic n*-component circular rule which can be instantiated into a number of circular rules that can be used for verification. The rule checks that a system composed of M_1, M_2 .. M_n satisfies safety property P based on assumptions g_i ($1 \leq i \leq n$). The first n premises of the rule have the form $M_i \models G_i \triangleright g_i$ and the last premise is $G_n \models P$ (to be formally defined later). The first n premises verify, for each g_i, that it is a correct "guarantee" of M_i, based on a set G_i of "assumptions" representing the guarantees of other components. The last premise ensures that P holds under the assumptions.

We further devise an algorithm that automates the process of building the assumptions g_i based on SAT solving. The algorithm works for any rule that can be derived from the generic rule. The assumption generation algorithm can be viewed as a two layered counterexample-guided search, where the outer layer searches for appropriate assumption alphabets, and the inner layer searches for appropriate assumptions, given a set of alphabets for each of the assumptions.

In the inner layer, the search for assumptions with fixed alphabets is performed similarly to [10]. The algorithm starts with approximate assumptions for all components, and attempts to apply the rule. When the application fails, i.e., at least one of the premises of the rule does not hold, the algorithm uses the counterexamples obtained from checking the failed premises to accumulate *joint* constraints on behaviors (traces) that should or should not be exhibited by the assumptions. These constraints reflect dependencies between assumptions of different components – which is essential for exploiting the circularity of the rule. A SAT solver is then used to determine how to update the assumptions while satisfying all the constraints.

The inner search may return a set of minimal assumptions over the given alphabets that satisfy the rule premises. In this case, we conclude that the property holds and the overall algorithm terminates. Alternatively, the inner search may return a counterexample in the form of a trace of the system over the partial alphabet that violates the property. Since the alphabet is partial, the counterexample is *abstract*: it might turn out to be infeasible (spurious) when considering the full alphabet (which adds synchronization constraints). Feasibility of the abstract counterexample is checked by the outer layer.

The outer layer employs an iterative refinement over the alphabets of the assumptions. It starts with only a subset of the interface alphabet of the components which is sufficient to guarantee soundness of the proof rule and it adds actions to it only as needed. Actions to be added are discovered by analysis of counterexamples obtained from the inner layer. The analysis attempts to extend the counterexample to a trace over the full system alphabet. If the counterexample is successfully extended (indicating a real error in the system), the overall algorithm terminates. Otherwise, new actions are added to the alphabet and a new iteration of the inner search begins. Intuitively these new actions are sufficient for preventing the same counterexample to appear in future iterations. Finally, either a concrete counterexample is found, or the property is verified via a successful application of the rule.

A key feature of our approach is the interplay between the two layers of the search, which manifests itself in two ways. First, the abstraction of the alphabet gives rise to *simplifications* of the assume-guarantee rule. We show that any rule can be simplified based on the inter-dependency induced by the assumption alphabets. Namely, in each premise $M_i \models G_i \triangleright g_i$, assumptions in G_i that contain no common actions with either g_i or with other assumptions in G_i that share actions with g_i can be safely eliminated from G_i, since they do not affect the outcome of checking the premise. The last premise gets simplified as well and the resulting rule becomes easier to check than the original rule. As the alphabets change with each iteration of alphabet refinement, so do the dependencies between assumptions. This leads to different simplifications of the assume-guarantee rule in different iterations. Hence, even though the algorithm searches assumptions for a *fixed* rule, the rules used by the inner search change dynamically between different "outer" iterations.

The second interaction point between the two layers is in the constraints on the assumptions accumulated by the assumption generation algorithm. In each alphabet refinement step, some of these constraints are refined as well according to the new alphabet and are re-used by the inner layer. This makes the search for assumptions *incremental*, resulting in better running time and faster convergence.

Our preliminary evaluation shows that circular compositional reasoning with n-way decomposition, alphabet refinement and dynamic rule simplification can significantly outperform both 2-way compositional and monolithic verification.

Related Work. While the literature on assume-guarantee reasoning is vast, for space reason, we only discuss here some closely related work. Previous work has proposed learning and abstraction-refinement techniques for automating the generation of assumptions [2–6,8,12,23]. This work has been done in the context of applying simple compositional rules, where there is no circular dependency between assumptions and no inductive reasoning involved. Our automatic alphabet refinement uses the heuristics from previous work [11] which were developed for non-circular reasoning. Note however that unlike [11] our approach is *incremental*, i.e. it *re-uses* the results across refinement iterations. Further we employ rule simplification based on the current alphabet which is new. N-way decompositions were handled in e.g. [23] by a recursive application of a non-circular rule. Unlike our approach, that work is sensitive to the order in which the components are analyzed and is not incremental. Our search for minimal assumptions using SAT with an increasing bound is inspired by [12]. However there, a single (separating) assumption is generated while we generate multiple mutually dependent assumptions.

Circular rules have been studied extensively [1,15,18,19,21], however not for full automation as we do here. The approach in [10] addresses assumption generation for 2-way circular reasoning, shown to perform better than non-circular reasoning. We improve on it by providing N-way compositional reasoning and incremental alphabet refinement. An interesting result [22] makes the connection between circular and non-circular rules, using complex (auxiliary) assumptions that use induction over time. Recent work [16] addresses synthesizing circular compositional proofs based on logical abduction. A key difference is that they refer to a decomposition of a sequential program, while we consider concurrent systems. Similar to [16], the approach in [20] also employs a circular compositional approach and uses different abstractions to discharge proof subgoals.

2   Preliminaries

We use Labeled Transition Systems (LTSs) to model the behavior of communicating components in a concurrent system. We briefly present here LTSs and semantics of their operators following the presentation in [10]. Let Act be a set of actions and let $\tau \notin Act$ denote a special "local" action.

Definition 1. *A* Labeled Transition System *(LTS)* M *is a quadruple* $(Q, \mathcal{A}, \delta, q_0)$ *where* Q *is a finite set of states,* $\mathcal{A} \subseteq Act$ *denotes the alphabet of* M, $\delta \subseteq Q \times (\mathcal{A} \cup \{\tau\}) \times Q$ *is a transition relation, and* $q_0 \in Q$ *is the initial state.*

Throughout the paper we use αM to denote the alphabet of an LTS M.

Paths and Traces. A *trace* σ is a sequence of actions, not including τ. We use σ_i to denote the prefix of σ of length i. A *path* in an LTS M is a sequence $p = q_0, a_0, q_1, a_1 \cdots, a_{n-1}, q_n$ of alternating states and actions of M, such that for every $k \in \{0, \ldots, n-1\}$ we have $(q_k, a_k, q_{k+1}) \in \delta$. The *trace* of p is the sequence of actions along p, obtained by removing from $a_0 \cdots a_{n-1}$ all occurrences of τ. The set of traces obtained from all the paths in M forms the *language* of M, denoted $L(M)$. Note that $L(M)$ is prefix-closed.

An LTS $M = (Q, \alpha M, \delta, q_0)$ is *deterministic* (denoted as DLTS) if it contains no τ transitions and no transitions $(q, a, q'), (q, a, q'') \in \delta$ such that $q' \neq q''$. Any LTS can be converted to a deterministic LTS that recognizes the same language.

Projections. For $\Sigma \subseteq Act$, projection $\sigma{\downarrow}_\Sigma$ is the trace obtained by removing from σ all actions $a \notin \Sigma$. $M{\downarrow}_\Sigma$ is defined as the LTS over alphabet Σ obtained by renaming to τ all the actions that are not in Σ. Note that $L(M{\downarrow}_\Sigma) = \{\sigma{\downarrow}_\Sigma \mid \sigma \in L(M)\}$.

Parallel Composition. Let $M_1 = (Q_1, \alpha M_1, \delta_1, q_{0_1})$ and $M_2 = (Q_2, \alpha M_2, \delta_2, q_{0_2})$ be two LTSs. Then $M_1 \| M_2$ is an LTS $M = (Q, \alpha M, \delta, q_0)$, where $Q = Q_1 \times Q_2$, $q_0 = (q_{0_1}, q_{0_2})$, $\alpha M = \alpha M_1 \cup \alpha M_2$, and δ is defined as follows where $a \in \alpha M \cup \{\tau\}$:

- if $(q_1, a, q_1') \in \delta_1$ for $a \notin \alpha M_2$, then $((q_1, q_2), a, (q_1', q_2)) \in \delta$ for every $q_2 \in Q_2$,
- if $(q_2, a, q_2') \in \delta_2$ for $a \notin \alpha M_1$, then $((q_1, q_2), a, (q_1, q_2')) \in \delta$ for every $q_1 \in Q_1$,
- if $(q_1, a, q_1') \in \delta_1$ and $(q_2, a, q_2') \in \delta_2$ for $a \neq \tau$, then $((q_1, q_2), a, (q_1', q_2')) \in \delta$.

Lemma 1 [8]. *For every $t \in (\alpha M_1 \cup \ldots \cup \alpha M_n)^*$, $t \in L(M_1 \| \ldots \| M_n)$ if and only if $t{\downarrow}_{\alpha M_i} \in L(M_i)$ for every $1 \leq i \leq n$.*

We define the interface alphabet of a component (with respect to the rest of the system) as follows.

Definition 2 (Interface Alphabet). *For $1 \leq i \leq n$, the interface alphabet of M_i w.r.t. $M_1 \| M_2 \| \cdots \| M_n$, denoted αJ_i, is: $\alpha J_i = \alpha M_i \cap \left(\bigcup\{\alpha M_j \mid 1 \leq j \leq n, j \neq i\}\right)$.*

Intuitively, the interface alphabet of M_i contains all the actions that are common between M_i and its environment.

Safety Properties. A *safety property* is specified as an LTS P. An LTS M over $\alpha M \supseteq \alpha P$ satisfies P, denoted $M \models P$, if for every $\sigma \in L(M)$, $\sigma{\downarrow}_{\alpha P} \in L(P)$. A trace $\sigma \in \alpha M^*$ is a *counterexample* for $M \models P$ if $\sigma \in L(M)$ but $\sigma{\downarrow}_{\alpha P} \notin L(P)$.

To check $M \models P$, the LTS of P is transformed into a deterministic LTS, which is completed with a special "error state" π by adding transitions from every state q in the deterministic LTS to π for all the missing outgoing actions of q; the resulting LTS is called an *error LTS*, denoted by P_{err}. Checking $M \models P$ reduces to checking that π is not reachable in $M \| P_{err}$.

Assume-Guarantee Formulas. In the circular assume-guarantee reasoning paradigm a formula has the form $M \models A \triangleright P$, where M, A and P are LTSs. Intuitively M stands for a component, A for an assumption about M's environment (i.e. the rest of the components in the system), and P for a property that is "guaranteed" by the component.

Definition 3. *Let M, A and P be LTSs such that $\alpha P \subseteq \alpha M$. Then $M \models A \triangleright P$ holds if for every $k \geq 1$ and for every $\sigma \in (\alpha M \cup \alpha A)^*$ of length k such that $\sigma{\downarrow}_{\alpha M} \in L(M)$, if $\sigma_{k-1}{\downarrow}_{\alpha A} \in L(A)$ then $\sigma{\downarrow}_{\alpha P} \in L(P)$.*

Checking $M \models A \rhd P$ is done by building the LTS $M \| A \| P_{err}$ and labeling its states with (parameterized) propositions err_a, where $a \in \alpha P$. (s_M, s_A, s_P) is labeled by err_a if s_M has an outgoing transition in M labeled by a, but the corresponding transition (labelled by a) leads to π in P_{err}. We then check if a state labeled by err_a is reachable or not in $M \| A \| P_{err}$ [10].

Notations. For LTSs M and P and a finite nonempty set $G = \{g_1, \dots, g_k\}$ of LTSs, we use $G \models P$ as a shorthand for $g_1 \| \cdots \| g_n \models P$, and $M \models G \rhd P$ as a shorthand for $M \models g_1 \| \cdots \| g_k \rhd P$. Moreover, if $G = \emptyset$, then $M \models G \rhd P$ denotes $M \models P$. Given a set S of LTSs, we denote by αS their alphabet union, i.e. $\alpha S = \bigcup_{M \in S} \alpha M$.

3   Circular Reasoning with N-way Decomposition

In this section we introduce the family of circular assume-guarantee rules that form the basis of our technique for proving that a system composed of a finite number of components $M_1 \| M_2 \dots \| M_n$ (n is fixed) satisfies a safety property P. We use a set of n auxiliary properties $G = \{g_1, g_2 \dots g_n\}$. Components and properties are described by Labeled Transition Systems (LTSs) such that $\alpha P \subseteq \bigcup_{i=1}^{n} \alpha M_i$; further, g_i is the "guarantee" property for M_i, specified as an LTS over alphabet $\alpha g_i \subseteq \alpha M_i$.

Instead of using a particular assume-guarantee rule, we propose to use a generic rule that defines multiple assume-guarantee rules, all following the same general pattern:

$$
\begin{array}{ll}
\text{(Premise 1)} & M_1 \models G_1 \rhd g_1 \\
\text{(Premise 2)} & M_2 \models G_2 \rhd g_2 \\
\quad \cdots & \\
\text{(Premise n)} & M_n \models G_n \rhd g_n \\
\text{(Premise n+1)} & G_{n+1} \models P \\
\hline
& M_1 \| M_2 \| \cdots \| M_n \models P
\end{array}
$$

In each premise i, G_i represents the set of left-hand side assumptions to be used in the premise and is defined such that $G_i \subseteq G - \{g_i\}$ for $i < n+1$, i.e. the "guarantees" of the other components are used as "assumptions" when checking M_i. Furthermore $G_{n+1} = G$, i.e. all the assumptions are used in the last premise. There are many rules that can be derived from the above pattern. For example, one rule can be derived by requiring the *maximal* number of assumptions for each premise, i.e. each G_i contains all the assumptions except g_i (we use this rule in our experiments). Another rule can be derived by requiring on the contrary a minimal number of assumptions to be used in each premise. For instance, G_i may contain only the assumptions that share actions with g_i. In fact sets $G_1, ..$ G_n can be chosen arbitrarily (possibly guided by domain knowledge), as long as each G_i is a subset of $G - \{g_i\}$.

As an example, for $n = 2$, the instantiation $G_1 = \{g_2\}, G_2 = \{g_1\}$ and $G_3 = \{g_1, g_2\}$ gives rule **CIRC-AG** from [10].

One can use such rules to check the system in a *compositional* way: instead of checking $M_1 \| M_2 \ldots \| M_n$ directly, which may be too expensive, we can check each premise separately, which is potentially much cheaper. However coming up manually with assumptions g_1, g_2, .. g_n that are sufficient for proving or disproving the property, and at the same time are small enough to enable efficient verification is very difficult. The goal of our work is to derive the assumptions automatically. Furthermore we aim to *simplify* the rule to eliminate unnecessary assumptions and premises, to enable efficient verification.

Soundness and Completeness. We first argue the soundness and completeness of *any* rule that can be obtained from the general rule. Let $CIRC - AG_N$ denote a rule derived from the general rule, i.e. we fix the assumption sets G_1, G_2, ..., G_n, G_{n+1} such that $G_i \subseteq G - \{g_i\}$ for $i < n + 1$ and $G_{n+1} = G$.

Similarly to the 2-component rule used in [10] we need additional conditions on the assumption alphabets to ensure soundness and completeness. Soundness is ensured by requiring $\alpha g_i \supseteq \alpha M_i \cap \alpha P$ for every $1 \le i \le n$. Completeness is ensured by considering assumptions over alphabets that include the interface alphabets of the components, i.e. we require $\alpha g_i \supseteq (\alpha M_i \cap \alpha P) \cup \alpha J_i$ for every $1 \le i \le n$ (we say that this is the *completeness condition*). We use $\alpha_F(g_i)$ to denote $(\alpha M_i \cap \alpha P) \cup \alpha J_i$, i.e. the alphabet *sufficient for completeness*.

Theorem 1. *Rule CIRC-AG$_N$ is sound if $\alpha g_i \supseteq \alpha M_i \cap \alpha P$ for every $1 \le i \le n$. It is complete if $\alpha g_i \supseteq (\alpha M_i \cap \alpha P) \cup \alpha J_i$ for every $1 \le i \le n$.*

Intuitively, premises $1, \ldots, n$ prove in a compositional and inductive manner that every trace in the language of $M_1 \| M_2 \| \cdots \| M_n$ is also included in the language of $g_1 \| g_2 \| \cdots \| g_n$ while the last premise ensures that every trace in the language of $g_1 \| g_2 \| \cdots \| g_n$ is also in the language of P. Completeness stems from the fact that $M_1, M_2, \ldots, M_n$ (restricted to appropriate alphabets) can be used for $g_1, g_2, \ldots, g_n$ in a successful application of the rule.

Note that we can remove the completeness condition on the alphabets to obtain rules that are sound but not necessarily complete. These rules would still be useful in practice since the alphabet assumptions are smaller, and therefore the assumptions necessary for the proof may be smaller as well and easier to check. Furthermore, this would give us more opportunities to simplify the rules by removing the assumptions that become irrelevant for the proof, due to the smaller alphabets used. This simplification is described in the next section.

4   Alphabet-Based Simplification

At the heart of our automated approach is a method for simplifying the assume-guarantee rules as dictated by the assumption alphabets. Specifically, when we apply our technique, we fix an n-way rule, and an initial alphabet for each assumption. The alphabets induce a simplification of the rule which makes the

Algorithm 1 . Main algorithm for checking $M_1 \| M_2 \| \ldots \| M_n \models P$ using CIRC-AG$_N$

1: **procedure** ACR
2:    Initialize: $\mathcal{A} = \alpha P$, $C = \emptyset$, $k = n$, $IncTr = \emptyset$
3:    $\alpha g_i \triangleq \mathcal{A} \cap \alpha M_i$, $\forall 1 \leq i \leq n$ // Initially $\alpha g_i = \alpha P \cap \alpha M_i$
4:    **while** (true) **do**
5:       **repeat**
6:          $(g_1, g_2, \ldots, g_n) = $GENASSMP$(C, k, \mathcal{A})$
7:          $(C', Result, IncTr') = $APPLYAG$(g_1, g_2, \ldots, g_n)$ using S(CIRC-AG$_N$)
8:          $C = C \cup C'$, $k = \sum_{i=1}^{n} |g_i|$, $IncTr = IncTr \cup IncTr'$
9:       **until** ($Result \neq$ "continue")
10:       **if** ($Result ==$"false"(σ)) **then**   // σ is a cex for $M_1 \downarrow_{\alpha g_1} \| \ldots \| M_n \downarrow_{\alpha g_n} \models P$
11:          $(\mathcal{A}, C, k, Result) = $ALPHAREFINE$(\sigma, \mathcal{A}, IncTr)$
12:          **if** ($Result ==$ "false") **then return** "false"   // else continue to next iteration
13:       **else return** "true"

---

rule easier to check (premises become simpler, and some premises become redundant). When the alphabets are refined, the simplification of the rule changes accordingly. Hence, essentially, the rule changes dynamically during the compositional verification.

We describe here this rule simplification. Let CIRC-AG$_N$ be an assume-guarantee rule. Suppose that we fix the alphabets over which the assumptions are defined, such that the rule is sound. These alphabets induce a natural simplification of the rule as follows. We define assumptions of G_i that *directly affect* g_i as the assumptions that have common actions with M_i. This provides the basis of an inductive definition, as other assumptions in G_i *indirectly affect* g_i if they have common actions with an assumption in G_i that (directly or indirectly) affects g_i.

The dependency between assumptions can be computed statically, by building, for each premise i, a graph where vertices are the assumptions in $G_i \cup \{g_i\}$, and edges are common actions between them (except that edges of g_i represent common actions with M_i). The assumptions which are not connected to g_i can be safely eliminated from G_i since they cannot influence the outcome of checking the premise.

We also define the set of assumptions from $G_{n+1} = \{g_1, \ldots, g_n\}$ that affect P (directly or indirectly) in a similar way. All the assumptions that do not share actions with P (directly or indirectly) can be eliminated from the last premise. Furthermore the removed assumptions become redundant and their premises are removed altogether.

For a premise i, let $S(G_i)$ denote the set of assumptions used in the premise after simplification. The following lemma states that each simplified premise is equivalent to the original one.

Lemma 2. $M_i \models S(G_i) \rhd g_i$ iff $M_i \models G_i \rhd g_i$ for $i \leq n$. $S(G_{n+1}) \models P$ iff $G_{n+1} \models P$.

It follows that we can use the simplified rule instead of the original rule, to obtain the same results.

Example 1. Consider the (last) premise of a rule that has the form $g_1\|g_2\|g_3 \models P$ with $\alpha g_1 = \{a, b\}$, $\alpha g_2 = \{b\}$, $\alpha g_3 = \{c\}$ and $\alpha P = \{a, b\}$. Since assumption g_3 contains neither actions that participate in the parallel composition with g_1 and g_2 nor actions that appear in the property, we can safely remove it resulting in a simplified premise $g_1\|g_2 \models P$ which is cheaper to check and results in faster convergence of our algorithms, as explained later in the paper.

If, on the other hand, we consider the same rule with increased alphabets $\alpha g_1 = \{a, b, d\}$ and $\alpha g_3 = \{c, d\}$, then simplification will leave the last premise unchanged.

Thus, for a given rule, and by varying the assumption alphabets, we can obtain a family of sound rules using alphabet-based simplifications. If the alphabets satisfy the completeness condition, the rules are complete as well.

5   Automated Circular Reasoning

In this section we provide an overview of our Automated Circular Reasoning (ACR) algorithm for the compositional verification of a system composed of $M_1, \ldots, M_n$ with respect to property P, where n is fixed. The pseudocode of the algorithm appears in Algorithm 1. ACR can be used with any rule that can be derived from the general pattern described in Sect. 3. Let CIRC-AG_N be such a rule. The assumptions to be used in the rule are derived automatically using a two layered approach which combines *iterative assumption generation* (the inner layer) with *automatic refinement over the assumption alphabets* (the outer layer). The two layers are closely intertwined.

The algorithm maintains in $\mathcal{A}$ the current assumption alphabet, where $\alpha g_i = \mathcal{A} \cap \alpha M_i$, for $1 \leq i \leq n$. In the following, we use $\mathcal{A}$ and $\alpha g_1, \ldots, \alpha g_n$ interchangeably, as the former determines the latter. In addition, the algorithm maintains a set of constraints C on the desired assumptions and a bound k, which is the sum of the number of states in each assumption. The algorithm also maintains a set $IncTr$ of *incremental traces*, whose role will become clear in the sequel.

Initially, we allow for each assumption to have a single state, hence $k = n$ for n assumptions. The assumption alphabets over which the assumptions are derived are initialized as follows: $\mathcal{A} = \alpha P$, which means that $\alpha g_i = \alpha P \cap \alpha M_i$ for each $1 \leq i \leq n$. These are the minimal sets needed to guarantee soundness. The sets C and $IncTr$ are both initialized to the empty set.

Iterative Assumption Generation. The inner layer of the algorithm builds assumptions over alphabets $\alpha g_1, \ldots, \alpha g_n$ iteratively (in the "repeat ... until" loop, lines 5–9) based on the collected constraints C and the bound k (procedure GENASSMP). For the current assumptions $g_1, \ldots, g_n$, the framework runs model checking to check the premises of the (simplified) assume-guarantee rule (see procedure APPLYAG). The result returned by APPLYAG is either "true", "continue" or "false" (together with a counterexample σ): "true" indicates that all the premises of the rule hold, so ACR finishes returning that the property holds (since the rule is sound); "continue" means that the analysis was inconclusive. Hence the inner loop continues its execution, with a new set of constraints C' that is added to C, resulting in a refinement of the assumptions in the next iteration. The third case ("false") requires further analysis to determine if the counterexample obtained for $M_1\downarrow_{\alpha g_1}\|\ldots\|M_n\downarrow_{\alpha g_n} \models P$ is real or if the assumption alphabets need to be refined. This is explained in more detail below.

Alphabet Refinement. To reduce the complexity of the verification task, we use alphabet refinement over the assumption alphabets. This is the role of the outer layer of our algorithm (in the "while" loop, lines 4–13). Our motivation is that even though completeness of the rule is only guaranteed for the "full" assumption alphabets (i.e. $\alpha_F(g_i)$), there may be smaller alphabets that are enough to prove or disprove the property, and at the same time enable more efficient verification. We aim to discover them iteratively starting with the minimal alphabets that guarantee soundness and only enlarging them as needed.

As long as only subsets of the alphabets are used for the assumptions, counterexamples that are found by the inner loop for $M_1\downarrow_{\alpha g_1}\|\ldots\|M_n\downarrow_{\alpha g_n} \models P$ might not indicate a real error in $M_1\|\ldots\|M_n$, i.e. the counterexamples may be "spurious". Procedure ALPHAREFINE performs a counterexample analysis to determine if a counterexample is real or not. In the former case, ACR terminates and reports an error. In the latter case ALPHAREFINE uses heuristics to add actions to $\mathcal{A}$ (and accordingly to αg_i) that are guaranteed to avoid producing the same counterexample in subsequent iterations. ALPHAREFINE returns "continue" with a new alphabet $\mathcal{A}$, and ACR executes a new iteration.

A key novelty of our approach is that the assume-guarantee rules change dynamically during alphabet refinement. With each update to $\mathcal{A}$, rule CIRC-AG_N is simplified according to the procedure described in Sect. 4 and procedure APPLYAG applies the simplified rule (denoted $S(\text{CIRC-AG}_N)$). As the algorithm progresses, the assumption alphabets change resulting in new simplifications applied to the rule.

When alphabet refinement takes place, we need to restart the construction of assumptions (in the inner loop) with a new set of assumptions that are built over the new alphabets. We have optimized this step by re-using some of the constraints from the previous iteration. The set $IncTr$ keeps track of the traces used to derive the constraints. The refined constraints are used to initialize the g_i's in the new iteration. Our *incremental* approach avoids getting and re-analyzing traces that were already removed at previous iterations. Thus, it reduces the number of iterations and improves runtime.

Theorem 2. *(Correctness and Termination) The framework implemented by* ACR *terminates and returns true if* $M_1\|M_2..\|M_n \models P$ *and false otherwise.*

Partial correctness holds since ACR returns true if and only if all premises of CIRC-AG_N hold, in which case correctness follows from the soundness of the rule. Further, if ACR returns false, then this corresponds to σ being a counterexample in $M_1\downarrow_{\alpha_F(g_1)}\|..M_n\downarrow_{\alpha_F(g_n)}$ (see ALPHAREFINE) which corresponds to a real counterexample (Lemma 7).

As for termination, ACR executes a new iteration of the inner loop if the assumptions need to be refined (but the alphabet stays the same). For a given $\mathcal{A}$, there can only be finitely many iterations before "true" or "false" is obtained from APPLYAG. This is shown similarly to [10]. A "true" result makes ACR terminate, while a "false" result might lead to an alphabet refinement step (if the counterexample does not extend to all actions). The result of refinement is that more interface actions are added to $\mathcal{A}$, and a new iteration of the outer loop is executed. In the worst case, all interface actions are added (if no conclusive reply is obtained before) in which case no more spurious counterexamples can be obtained and the algorithm is guaranteed to terminate.

6   Iterative Construction of Assumptions over a Given Alphabet

In this section we describe in detail the inner layer of ACR, which searches for assumptions over a given alphabet. As we explain next, this can be understood as a search for assumptions for an *abstract system*, where the abstraction is defined by the alphabet.

Recall that $\mathcal{A} = \alpha g_1 \cup .. \cup \alpha g_n$. The assumption alphabets induce a natural abstraction over the system by projecting each component M_i to the alphabet αg_i, i.e. $M_1{\downarrow}_{\alpha g_1} \| M_2{\downarrow}_{\alpha g_2} \| .. M_n{\downarrow}_{\alpha g_n}$. This is an abstraction since $M_i{\downarrow}_{\alpha g_i} = M_i{\downarrow}_{\mathcal{A}}$ for every $1 \leq i \leq n$, and $L(M_1 \| M_2 \| .. M_n){\downarrow}_{\mathcal{A}} \subseteq L(M_1{\downarrow}_{\mathcal{A}} \| M_2{\downarrow}_{\mathcal{A}} \| .. M_n{\downarrow}_{\mathcal{A}})$ [8].

Further, note that since $\alpha G_i, \alpha g_i \subseteq \mathcal{A}$, premises of the form $M_i \models G_i \triangleright g_i$ are equivalent to $M_i{\downarrow}_{\mathcal{A}} \models G_i \triangleright g_i$. Intuitively this means that applying CIRC-AG$_N$ with the alphabets restricted to $\mathcal{A}$ can be interpreted as a compositional analysis of the abstracted system $M_1{\downarrow}_{\alpha g_1} \| M_2{\downarrow}_{\alpha g_2} \| .. M_n{\downarrow}_{\alpha g_n}$, which may be smaller and therefore easier to analyze (i.e. may require smaller assumptions to be used in the rule). Furthermore note that the rule is complete for this abstraction, since the alphabets of the abstract components $M_i{\downarrow}_{\alpha g_i}$ are equal to the assumption alphabets, ensuring that the alphabets satisfy the completeness condition in the abstraction.

6.1   Assumption Generation in GENASSMP

Given a set of constraints C, a lower bound k on the total number of states in $\sum_{i=1}^{n} |g_i|$, and an alphabet sequence $\mathcal{A}$, GENASSMP computes assumptions $g_1, g_2, \cdots, g_n$ over $\mathcal{A}$ that satisfy C. Assumptions are built as deterministic LTSs. The implementation of GENASSMP is a natural generalization of previous work [10] where it was used to generate two assumptions. Roughly speaking, for each value of k starting from the given k, GENASSMP creates a SAT instance $SatEnc_k(C)$ that encodes the structure of the desired DLTSs $g_1, g_2, \cdots, g_n$ (e.g., deterministic and prefix closed) with $\sum_{i=1}^{n} |g_i| \leq k$, as well as the requirement that they satisfy the constraints in C. GENASSMP then searches for a satisfying assignment and transforms the satisfying assignment into DLTSs $g_1, g_2, \cdots, g_n$ that satisfy all the constraints in C. The bound k is increased only when $SatEnc_k(C)$ is unsatisfiable, hence minimal DLTSs that satisfy C are obtained.

The key difference in our encoding compared to [10] is the need to handle disjunctive constraints with up to n disjuncts (as opposed to 2 in [10]). While in [10] each disjunctive constraint with 2 disjuncts is handled with a single "selector" variable, we use $\log n$ selector variables to encode a disjunctive constraint with n disjuncts.

6.2 APPLYAG **Algorithm**

Given assumptions $g_1, g_2, \ldots, g_n$, APPLYAG (see Algorithm 2) applies assume-guarantee reasoning with the current circular rule simplified under the current alphabets. This is done by model checking all premises of the rule (the order does not matter).[1] If all the premises are satisfied, then, since the rule is sound, it follows that $M_1\|M_2\| \cdots \|M_n \models P$ holds (and the result "true" is returned to the user). Otherwise, at least one of the premises does not hold and a counterexample trace is found.

APPLYAG performs an analysis of the counterexample trace as described below. The counterexample analysis is performed with respect to the projections $M_i\downarrow_{\alpha g_i}$.

The counterexample analysis may conclude that "$M_1\downarrow_{\alpha g_1}\| \cdots \|M_n\downarrow_{\alpha g_n} \not\models P$", indicating an error in the abstract system induced by the current alphabet, in which case "false" is returned. Recall, however, that due to the abstraction this is not necessarily an error in $M_1\| \ldots \|M_n$. If the analyzed trace does not correspond to an error in the abstract system, we conclude that the counterexample is a result of imprecise assumptions. We then compute a set of new constraints C on the assumptions in order to avoid getting the same counterexample in subsequent iterations and return "continue".

Similar to [10] we use constraints to gather information about traces over the current alphabet that need or need not be in the languages of the assumptions. The constraints are of the form: $+(\sigma, i)$ – meaning that σ should be in $L(g_i)$, $-(\sigma, i)$ – meaning that σ should not be in $L(g_i)$, or boolean combinations of them, where $\sigma \in \alpha g_i^*$.

The check for an error in the abstract system or for new constraints is performed by APPLYAG directly (if last premise failed) or by UPDATECONSTRAINT (if other premises failed). Essentially the counterexample indicates an error if it corresponds to a trace in each $M_i\downarrow_{\alpha g_i}$ and furthermore it violates the property. Since all assumptions whose alphabet affects P (directly or indirectly) are in $S(G_{n+1})$, it suffices to check membership in $M_i\downarrow_{\alpha g_i}$ for every $g_i \in S(G_{n+1})$ when searching for an error. The formal justification is provided by the following lemma:

Lemma 3. Let $S(G_{n+1}) = \{g_{i_1}, \ldots, g_{i_k}\}$. Then $M_1\downarrow_{\alpha g_1}\| \cdots \|M_n\downarrow_{\alpha g_n} \models P$ if and only if $M_{i_i}\downarrow_{\alpha g_{i_1}}\| \cdots \|M_{i_k}\downarrow_{\alpha g_{i_k}} \models P$.

---

[1] The check of the premise i is performed over the full alphabet of M_i in order to maintain the set $IncTr$ which enables our incremental approach for alphabet refinement, as explained in Sect. 7. In addition, it helps in detecting errors.

Algorithm 2 . Applying $S(\text{CIRC-AG}_N)$ with $g_1, g_2, \ldots g_n$, and constraint updating.

1: **procedure** APPLYAG($g_1, g_2, \ldots, g_n$)
2:    **for** $i \in I_A$ **do**
3:       **if** $M_i \not\models S(G_i) \rhd g_i$ **then**
4:          Let $\sigma_i a_i$ be a counterexample for $M_i \not\models S(G_i) \rhd g_i$
5:          **return** UPDATECONSTRAINTS($i, \sigma_i a_i$)
6:    **if** $S(G_{n+1}) \not\models P$ **then**
7:       Let σ be a counterexample
8:       **if** ($\bigwedge\limits_{g_i \in S(G_{n+1})} (\sigma{\downarrow}_{\alpha g_i} \in L(M_i{\downarrow}_{\alpha g_i}))$ **then**
9:          **return** ($\emptyset$, "false", $\emptyset$)   // " $M_1{\downarrow}_{\alpha g_1} \| M_2{\downarrow}_{\alpha g_2} \| \ldots \| M_n{\downarrow}_{\alpha g_n} \not\models P$ "
10:      **else**   // Remove σ from one of $g_j \in S(G_{n+1})$
11:          $C = \{ \bigvee\limits_{g_i \in S(G_{n+1})} -(\sigma{\downarrow}_{\alpha g_i}, i) \}$
12:         **return** (C, "continue", $\emptyset$)
13:   **return** ($\emptyset$, "true", $\emptyset$)   // " $M_1 \| M_2 \| \cdots \| M_n \models P$ "

For a counterexample obtained for the last premise the checks are done at line 8 in APPLYAG. If one of these checks fails, a new constraint is added to make sure that the same trace will not be in $g_1 \| \cdots \| g_n$ in the next iterations (see line 11 in APPLYAG). However a similar check in UPDATECONSTRAINT is more involved, and is described in the next subsection.

6.3   Assumption Refinement in UPDATECONSTRAINTS

UPDATECONSTRAINT (Algorithm 3) gets a counterexample σa for one of the inductive premises i where $1 \leq i \leq n$ and checks whether the trace corresponds to an error (in the abstract system). If it does, then "false" is returned. Otherwise, the counterexample analysis continues in order to decide which constraint(s) need to be added to the set of constraints C in order to refine the assumptions and avoid getting the same counterexample in subsequent iterations.

Trace Extension. The counterexample of premise i is over the alphabet $\alpha M_i \cup \alpha S(G_i)$. However, in order to determine whether the trace corresponds to an error and if not to determine which constraints to add, UPDATECONSTRAINT needs to check membership of (projections) of this trace in other components as well as in P . The first step taken by UPDATECONSTRAINTS therefore calls EXTENDTRACE to extend the counterexample trace to a trace over the alphabet $\mathcal{A}$ such that its projection to $\alpha M_i \cup \alpha S(G_i)$ remains unchanged. The algorithm works correctly with any such extension, including the one that keeps the trace unchanged. However, more sophisticated extension schemes can contribute to a faster convergence of the algorithm.

Specifically, our implementation of EXTENDTRACE, presented in Algorithm 4, employs a greedy extension algorithm that considers the LTSs whose alphabet is (potentially) uncovered in an arbitrary order, and iteratively extends the trace by simulating it on these LTSs one by one in that order. Whenever the simulation

---

Algorithm 3. Computation of constraints based on a counterexample for $M_i \models S(G_i) \triangleright g_i$. We use $\sigma \downarrow \in L(B)$ as a shorthand for $\sigma \downarrow_{\alpha B} \in L(B)$.

1: // σa is a counterexample for $M_i \models S(G_i) \triangleright g_i$, i.e. $\sigma a \downarrow \in L(M_i), \sigma \downarrow \in L(g_j)$ for every $g_j \in S(G_i), \sigma a \downarrow \notin L(g_i)$.

2: **procedure** UPDATECONSTRAINTS$(i, \sigma a)$

3:     $\sigma a = $ EXTENDTRACE$(\sigma a, (\alpha S(G_i) \cup \alpha M_i), \{M_j \downarrow_{\alpha g_j} | \ g_j \notin (S(G_i) \cup \{g_i\})\} \cup \{P\})$

4:     **if** ($\bigwedge\limits_{g_j \in S(G_{n+1}), j \neq i} (\sigma a \downarrow \in L(M_j \downarrow_{\alpha g_j}))$ and $\sigma a \downarrow \notin L(P)$) **then**

5:         // $\sigma a \downarrow \in L(M_1 \downarrow_{\alpha g_1} \| \cdots \| M_n \downarrow_{\alpha g_n})$ and $\sigma a \downarrow \notin L(P)$

6:         **return** $(\emptyset, $ "false"$, \emptyset)$ // "$M_1 \downarrow_{\alpha g_1} \| M_2 \downarrow_{\alpha g_2} \| \ldots \| M_n \downarrow_{\alpha g_n} \not\models P$"

7:     // Optimized constraints

8:     **for each** $G \in T(g_i)$ **do**   // G is a closed set

9:         **if** ($\bigwedge\limits_{g_j \in G, j \neq i} (\sigma a \downarrow \in L(M_j \downarrow_{\alpha g_j}))$ **then**

10:         // Add σa to all assumptions in G based on Lemma 4(1).

11:         // Adding σa to $g_i \in G$ prevents getting σa as a cex to premise i in the future.

12:         $C = \bigcup\limits_{g_j \in G} \{+(\sigma a \downarrow_{\alpha g_j}, j)\}$

13:         **return** $(C, $ "continue"$, \emptyset)$

14:         **if** ($\bigwedge\limits_{g_j \in G, j \neq i} (\sigma \downarrow \in L(M_j \downarrow_{\alpha g_j}))$ **then**

15:         // Add σ to all assumptions in G based on Lemma 4(1).

16:         // Since $S(G_i) \subseteq G$, we cannot remove σ from $S(G_i)$, hence add σa to g_i.

17:         $C = \bigcup\limits_{g_j \in G} \{+(\sigma \downarrow_{\alpha g_j}, j)\} \cup \{+(\sigma a \downarrow_{\alpha g_i}, i)\}$

18:         **return** $(C, $ "continue"$, \emptyset)$

19:     **if** $\sigma a \downarrow \notin L(P)$ and $\sigma \downarrow \in L(P)$ **then**

20:         // Remove σ from $S(G_i)$ or (add σa to g_i and remove it from $S(G_{n+1}) \setminus \{g_i\}$).

21:         // In the latter case, the removal of σa from $S(G_{n+1}) \setminus \{g_i\}$ is due to Lemma 4(2).

22:         $C = \{(\bigvee\limits_{g_j \in S(G_i)} (-(\sigma \downarrow_{\alpha g_j}, j))) \vee$

23:                 $(+(\sigma a \downarrow_{\alpha g_i}, i) \wedge (\bigvee\limits_{g_j \in S(G_{n+1}) \setminus \{g_i\}} (-(\sigma a \downarrow_{\alpha g_j}, j))))\}$

24:         $IncTr = \{(\sigma a, i, 22)\}$

25:         **return** $(C, $ "continue"$, IncTr)$

26:     **if** $\sigma a \downarrow \notin L(P)$ and $\sigma \downarrow \notin L(P)$ **then**

27:         // Removal of σ from $S(G_{n+1}) \setminus (S(G_i) \cup \{g_i\})$ in line 30 is due to Lemma 4(2).

28:         // Since LTSs are prefix-closed, the latter implies removal of σa from $S(G_{n+1}) \setminus \{g_i\}$.

29:         $C = \{(\bigvee\limits_{g_j \in S(G_i)} (-(\sigma \downarrow_{\alpha g_j}, j))) \vee$

30:                 $(+(\sigma a \downarrow_{\alpha g_i}, i) \wedge (\bigvee\limits_{g_j \in S(G_{n+1}) \setminus (S(G_i) \cup \{g_i\})} (-(\sigma \downarrow_{\alpha g_j}, j))))\}$

31:         $IncTr = \{(\sigma a, i, 29)\}$

32:         **return** $(C, $ "continue"$, IncTr)$

33:     // Default constraint

34:     $C = \{(\bigvee\limits_{g_j \in S(G_i)} (-(\sigma a \downarrow_{\alpha g_j}, j)) \vee +(\sigma a \downarrow_{\alpha g_i}, i))\}$

35:     $IncTr = \{(\sigma a, i, 34)\}$

36:     **return** $(C, $ "continue"$, IncTr)$

Algorithm 4. Get trace σ over alphabet Σ and extend it to be over the alphabet of all assumptions

---

1: **procedure** EXTENDTRACE($\sigma, \Sigma, N_1, N_2, \cdots N_k$)
2:     **for** $i = 1, \ldots, k$ **do**
3:         **if** $(L(LTS(\sigma)\|N_i) \neq \emptyset)$ **then**
4:             σ = trace in $LTS(\sigma)\|N_i$
5:             $\Sigma = \Sigma \cup \alpha N_i$
6:     **return** σ over the alphabet $\Sigma \cup \bigcup_{i=1}^{n} \alpha N_i$

---

succeeds, the trace and its alphabet are extended accordingly. When it fails, the trace remains unchanged. Upon termination, the alphabet of the trace is extended to include the full alphabet, even if the simulation on some of the LTSs failed. The distinguishing feature of Algorithm 4 compared to other extensions (e.g., random extensions) is the fact that it tries to find an extension of the trace that is in the language of the LTSs that it gets as input. It therefore increases the chances of successful checks in UPDATECONSTRAINTS.

The analysis and computation of constraints are performed on the extended trace.

Default Constraints. If the (extended) counterexample trace corresponds to an error in the abstract system (line 4), then UPDATECONSTRAINTS returns "false". Otherwise, it computes a new set of constraints. The added constraints are a crucial ingredient as they guide the search for assumptions. They should be strong enough to eliminate the already seen counterexamples and allow progress and convergence of the algorithm, but should not over-constrain the assumptions, in order not to exclude viable assumptions.

Recall that the ith inductive premise in the simplified rule is of the form $M_i \models S(G_i) \triangleright g_i$, and a counterexample for it is a trace σa such that $\sigma a{\downarrow} \in L(M_i), \sigma{\downarrow} \in L(g_j)$ for every $g_j \in S(G_i)$ and $\sigma a{\downarrow} \notin L(g_i)$. The default constraint to eliminate such a counterexample σa is the constraint $+(\sigma a{\downarrow}_{\alpha g_i}, i) \vee \bigvee_{j \in S(G_i)} -(\sigma{\downarrow}_{\alpha g_j}, j)$ stating that the counterexample should be added to g_i or its prefix should be removed from $S(G_i)$ (i.e., from at least one of the assumptions in $S(G_i)$). Such a constraint is added in line 34. This specific constraint is also *incremental,* and the corresponding trace is therefore also added to $IncTr$, along with an identifier of the premise by which it was added and the line number in which the constraint was computed, in order to allow its re-use after alphabet refinement.

Optimized Constraints. A key aspect in the assumptions refinement is our ability to add stronger constraints, without over-constraining the assumptions. This helps the overall algorithm converge faster since a stronger constraint removes more irrelevant assumptions from the assumption space at once. Furthermore, stronger constraints are easier for GENASSMP to solve, thus the overall run-time of the algorithm is reduced.

We come up with several properties of useful assumptions (i.e., assumptions that can be successfully used in the rule) which enable the addition of stronger constraints in several cases. These properties are nontrivial extensions of the properties observed in [10] for the 2-component case.

For example, from the simplified rule we extract *closed sets* of assumptions. A set G of assumptions is *closed* if $g_i \in G$ implies that $S(G_i) \subseteq G$. We show that:

Lemma 4. *Let $g_1, \ldots, g_n$ be LTS assumptions over alphabets $\alpha g_1, \ldots, \alpha g_n$ successfully used in $CIRC\text{-}AG_N$, and let $S(\cdot)$ denote the simplification of $CIRC\text{-}AG_N$ with respect to the alphabets $\alpha g_1, \ldots, \alpha g_n$. Then*

1. *if $\{g_{i_1}, ..g_{i_m}\}$ is a closed set, then $M_{i_1} \| M_{i_2} \| \cdots \| M_{i_m} \models g_{i_1} \| g_{i_2} \| \cdots \| g_{i_m}$, and*
2. *forall $1 \leq i \leq n$, if $\{g_{i_1}, ..g_{i_m}\} = S(G_{n+1}) \setminus \{g_i\}$, then $M_i \| g_{i_1} \| g_{i_2} \cdots \| g_{i_m} \models P$.*

We carefully select closed sets and scenarios in which it is beneficial to use observation (1) for generation of constraints. Namely, we consider closed sets which are the *closures* of some assumption, defined as follows.

Definition 4 (Closure). *The closure of g_k, denoted $Cl(g_k)$, is the smallest set of assumptions G such that $S(G_k) \subseteq G$ and for every $g_j \in G$ it holds that $S(G_j) \subseteq G$ as well.*

The oset $Cl(g_k)$ includes all the assumptions in premise k (after simplification), and for each of them includes all the assumptions in their premises etc. Note that $Cl(g_k)$ is defined based on the simplified rule, and is a closed set. For every assumption g_i, we define the set of closures that it is part of, denoted $T(g_i)$:

Definition 5. *For every $1 \leq i \leq n$, $T(g_i) = \{Cl(g_k) \mid g_i \in Cl(g_k), 1 \leq k \leq n\}$.*

When UPDATECONSTRAINTS (Algorithm 3) analyzes a counterexample σa for premise i of (the simplified) CIRC-AG$_N$, it considers all the closures $G = \{g_{i_1}, ..g_{i_m}\}$ in $T(g_i)$ and checks whether $\sigma a {\downarrow}_{\alpha g_j} \in L(M_j {\downarrow}_{\alpha g_j})$ for every $g_j \in G$. If so, we add a constraint $+(\sigma a {\downarrow}_{\alpha g_j}, j)$ for every j such that $g_j \in G$ (see line 12) in order to ensure that (the projection of) σa is in $g_{i_1} \| \cdots \| g_{i_m}$, as follows from Lemma 4(1). Since $g_i \in G$, the added constraints imply $+(\sigma a {\downarrow}_{\alpha g_i}, i) \vee \bigvee_{j \in S(G_i)} -(\sigma {\downarrow}_{\alpha g_j}, j)$, thus they suffice to eliminate the counterexample and avoid the need for a disjunctive constraint.

Similar reasoning is performed in line 17 using σ. However, in this case, the added constraints $+(\sigma {\downarrow}_{\alpha g_j}, j)$ for every j such that $g_j \in G$ refer to σ and do *not* imply $+(\sigma a {\downarrow}_{\alpha g_i}, i) \vee \bigvee_{j \in S(G_i)} -(\sigma {\downarrow}_{\alpha g_j}, j)$. Still, the fact that $g_i \in G$ and G is a closed set, ensures that $S(G_i) \subseteq G$, and hence $\bigvee_{j \in S(G_i)} -(\sigma {\downarrow}_{\alpha g_j}, j)$ cannot hold. Therefore, the disjunctive constraint is strengthened into $+(\sigma a {\downarrow}_{\alpha g_i}, i)$, again avoiding the disjunction (see line 17).

Similarly, we use observation (2) to strengthen the $+(\sigma a\downarrow_{\alpha g_i}, i)$ disjunct of the default constraint by adding specialized constraints of the form $\bigvee_{g_j \in S(G_{n+1}) \setminus \{g_i\}} (-(\sigma a\downarrow_{\alpha g_j}, j))$ in the case where $\sigma a\downarrow_{\alpha P} \notin L(P)$ (line 22), with an additional strengthening in line 29 for the case where also $\sigma\downarrow_{\alpha P} \notin L(P)$. These specialized constraints are also incremental, hence the corresponding traces are added to $IncTr$.

Progress and Termination of Assumption Refinement. The assumption refinement continues until the assumptions satisfy all premises of the rule, or an error is found (in the abstract system). The progress of the assumption refinement is guaranteed by the following lemmas.

Lemma 5. *Let σ be a counterexample of premise i of CIRC-AG$_N$ and let C be the updated set of constraints. Then any LTSs $g'_1, g'_2, \cdots, g'_n$ that satisfy the set of constraints C will no longer exhibit σ as a counterexample for premise i of CIRC-AG$_N$.*

We conclude that any sequence of LTSs $g'_1, g'_2, \ldots, g'_n$ that satisfies C is different from every previous sequence of LTSs considered by the algorithm.

The following lemma states that the added constraints do not over-constrain the assumptions. It ensures that the "desired" assumptions that enable to verify (1) or falsify (2) the property are always within reach.

Lemma 6. *Let $g_1, \ldots, g_n$ be LTSs over $\alpha g_1, \ldots, \alpha g_n$ s.t. one of the following holds:*

1. *$g_1, \ldots, g_n$ satisfy all premises of CIRC-AG$_N$, or*
2. *$g_i = M_i\downarrow_{\alpha g_i}$ for every $1 \leq i \leq n$.*

Then $(g_1, \ldots, g_n)$ satisfy every set of constraints C produced by ACR.

Due to the above lemmas, along with the completeness of the rule with respect to the abstraction $M_1\downarrow_{\alpha g_1} \| M_2\downarrow_{\alpha g_2} \| .. M_n\downarrow_{\alpha g_n}$, the iterative construction of the assumptions over $\mathcal{A}$ (lines 5–9 of Algorithm 1) is guaranteed to terminate returning either minimal assumptions over $\mathcal{A}$ that satisfy the rule premises or a counterexample for the abstract system. This is shown similarly to [10].

7   Alphabet Refinement

This section describes the outer layer of ACR, which iteratively searches for an appropriate alphabet for the assumptions. Each iteration defines a different alphabet $\mathcal{A}$ which restricts the alphabet of the assumptions. Initially $\mathcal{A} = \alpha P$, and therefore $\alpha g_i = \alpha P \cap \alpha M_i$. As long as $\mathcal{A}$ is a strict subset of $\alpha P \cup \bigcup_{i=1}^n \alpha J_i$ (which means that αg_i is a strict subset of $(\alpha M_i \cap \alpha P) \cup \alpha J_i$), completeness is not guaranteed with respect to $M_1\| \cdots \|M_n$. This also means that a counterexample obtained by the inner layer might be spurious. Hence, when an abstract

---

Algorithm 5. Alphabet Refinement

1: **procedure** ALPHAREFINE$(\sigma, \mathcal{A}, IncTr)$
2:    **if** $(\alpha g_i = \alpha_F(g_i)$ for every $1 \le i \le n)$ **then**
3:        **return** (-,-,-,"false")
4:    **for** $1 \le i \le n$ **do**
5:        let σ_i be a trace in $L(LTS(\sigma\downarrow_{\alpha g_i})\|M_i\downarrow_{\alpha_F(g_i)})$
6:    **if** (MATCH$(\sigma_1, \sigma_2, \cdots, \sigma_n))$ **then**
7:        **return** (-,-,-,"false")
8:    // INCALPHA decides which new interface letters to add based on heuristics from 11.
9:    $\mathcal{A} = \mathcal{A} \cup$ INCALPHA$(\sigma_1, \sigma_2, \cdots, \sigma_n)$
10:    $k = n, C = \emptyset$
11:    **for** each $(\sigma, i, type) \in IncTr$ **do** // Update constraints based on incremental traces
12:        $C = C \cup RC(\sigma, i, type, \mathcal{A})$
13:    **return** $(\mathcal{A}, C, k,$"continue")

---

counterexample for $M_1\downarrow_{\alpha g_1}\| \cdots \|M_n\downarrow_{\alpha g_n} \models P$ is obtained, ALPHAREFINE (Algorithm 5) is called to check if the counterexample can be extended to a real counterexample. If it can not, ALPHAREFINE performs automatic alphabet refinement using heuristics similar to previous work [11] developed for non-circular assume-guarantee reasoning. Note however that a key difference from previous work is that our alphabet refinement enables dynamic simplification of the rule used for verification. Furthermore we improve upon [11] by providing a procedure for *re-using* the results across refinement iterations.

In essence, a counterexample σ is real if $\sigma\downarrow_{\alpha_F(g_i)} \in L(M_i\downarrow_{\alpha_F(g_i)})$ and $\sigma\downarrow_{\alpha P} \notin L(P)$. This is stated by the following lemma, extending the 2-component case [10].

Lemma 7. *If $\sigma\downarrow_{\alpha_F(g_i)} \in L(M_i\downarrow_{\alpha_F(g_i)})$ (for $i = 1..n$) and $\sigma\downarrow_{\alpha P} \notin L(P)$ then $M_1\|M_2\|..M_n \not\models P$. Moreover, σ can be extended into a full counterexample for $M_1\|M_2\|..M_n \models P$.*

ALPHAREFINE first checks if $\alpha g_i = \alpha_F(g_i)$, where $\alpha_F(g_i)$ is the alphabet sufficient for completeness. If this is not the case, and also if we do not manage to extend the counterexample to this alphabet, ALPHAREFINE chooses heuristically new interface actions to be added to the alphabet $\mathcal{A}$ (and to αg_i accordingly). The heuristic uses backward refinement shown to work well in previous studies. The counterexample σ is projected on all the components one by one with the full alphabet of completeness. We then perform a backward analysis for every two traces: the traces are scanned backward, from the end of each trace to the beginning looking for the first action where the two traces disagree. The alphabet $\mathcal{A}$ is refined by adding all these actions. The refined alphabet is used in the next iteration of ACR. Procedure MATCH simply checks that all counterexamples agree on common alphabets.

Once the alphabet changes, the set of constraints C maintained by the algorithm is no longer suitable and has to be emptied. A novel aspect of our approach is that we identify certain constraints that can be refined and moved to the new iteration (as described below).

7.1   Incremental Alphabet Refinement

Recall that constraints are computed based on counterexamples to premises of the form $M_i \models S(G_i) \triangleright g_i$. These are traces over $\alpha M_i \cup \alpha S(G_i)$. While $\alpha S(G_i)$ changes as the alphabet increases, αM_i does not. A naive incremental approach would therefore keep all these traces, and would regenerate constraints based on them by the same counterexample analysis, but with the refined alphabet of the assumptions. However, our goal is to avoid the overhead in analyzing the counterexamples again.

Ideally, we would like to simply derive the same constraints by projecting the counterexample traces on the new alphabet without any further checks. However, this might introduce incorrect constraints that would over-constrain the assumptions. The reason is that the correctness of an existing constraint relies on checks such as $\sigma a\downarrow_{\alpha g_j} \in L(M_j\downarrow_{\alpha g_j})$ performed with respect to the previous alphabet. The same checks might return different outcomes when conducted with the refined alphabet, in which case the correctness of the (refined) constraint is not guaranteed.

The key challenge to address when trying to re-use constraints is therefore to make sure that the same checks are valid after alphabet refinement. To that end, we identify a subset of the constraints for which this is the case. These are constraints whose correctness relies on checks over $\sigma\downarrow_{\alpha P}$, and checks such as $\sigma\downarrow_{\alpha g_j} \notin L(M_j\downarrow_{\alpha g_j})$, but no checks such as $\sigma\downarrow_{\alpha g_j} \in L(M_j\downarrow_{\alpha g_j})$. The justification for the re-use of such constraints stems from (i) the fact that αP is always a subset of $\mathcal{A}$, and hence checks over it remain unchanged, and (ii) the following lemma:

Lemma 8. *If $\sigma\downarrow_{\alpha g_j} \notin L(M_j\downarrow_{\alpha g_j})$ then $\sigma\downarrow_{\alpha g_j'} \notin L(M_j\downarrow_{\alpha g_j'})$ for any $\alpha g_j' \supseteq \alpha g_j$.*

For example, the constraints created in line 34 in Algorithm 3 are incremental. In order to re-use these constraints, we define an operator, RC (for *Refined Constraints*) which receives the full trace over $\alpha M_i \cup \alpha S(G_i)$ and an identifier of the constraints in the form of a pair of the premise index and the line in the algorithm in which the constraint was generated, referred to as the *type* of the constraint.

The RC operator then re-constructs the corresponding constraints by conducting projections according to the current alphabet, without re-performing any of the checks. For example, $RC(\sigma, i, 34, \mathcal{A}) = \{(\bigvee_{g_j \in S(G_i)} (-(\sigma\downarrow_{\alpha g_j}, j)) \vee$
$+(\sigma a\downarrow_{\alpha g_i}, i))\}$.

Table 1. Results of comparison of 2-way compositional verification with and without alphabet refinement (2W-AR and 2W), n-way compositional verification with and without alphabet refinement (NW-AR and NW) and monolithic verification (Mon).

Case	2W [T]	2W+AR [T]	$|g_1|$	$|g_2|$	NW [T]	NW+AR [T]	$|g_{max}|$	$|g_{min}|$	Mon [T]	$|Sys\|P_{err}|$
GasSt 3	26	2.187	3	3	40.053	17.434	3	1	0.01	1280
GasSt 4	48	6.87	3	3	72.135	22.274	3	1	0.008	10466
GasSt 5	309	27	3	3	127.802	21.008	3	1	0.09	80368
ClServ 9	248	25.5	10	2	6.08	3.297	2	2	0.09	14335
ClServ 10	815.6	69	11	2	7	5	2	2	0.026	34303
ClServ 11	–	307.6	12	2	11.883	6.675	2	2	0.063	80895
ClServ 12	–	–	–	–	15.617	8.213	2	2	0.31	188415
MER 6 4	–	–	–	–	132.958	9.422	3	2	33.931	5246875
MER 7 4	–	–	–	–	769.61	23.894	3	2	–	–
MER 8 4	–	–	–	–	1611.072	54.568	3	2	–	–
MER 4 5	–	–	–	–	43.4	3.6	3	2	0.235	159192
MER 5 5	–	–	–	–	91.5	5.9	3	2	6.5	2057616
MER 6 5	–	–	–	–	200	11	3	2	500	23685696
MER 7 5	–	–	–	–	1470.85	30.38	3	2	–	–
MER 8 5	–	–	–	–	–	89.278	3	2	–	–

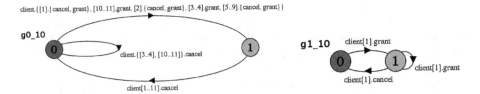

Fig. 1. Assumptions generated for: server (left) and a client (right) for client-server (11 clients) using n-way compositional verification with alphabet refinement

8   Evaluation

We implemented our approach in the LTSA (Labelled Transition System Analyser) tool [17]. We use MiniSAT [9] for SAT solving. As an optimization we made ACR return (at each iteration) k counterexamples for the $n + 1$ premises where, k is $n \times \sum_{i=0}^{n} |g_i|$.

We evaluated our approach on the following examples [10,23]: Gas Station (3 to 5 customers), Client Server (9 to 12 clients), and a NASA rover model: MER (4 to 8 users competing for 4–5 resources). Experiments were performed on a MacBook Pro with a 2.3 GHz Intel Core i7 CPU and with 16 GB RAM running OS X 10.9.4 and a Suns JDK version 7. We compared n-way verification using ACR with both 2-way ACR and monolithic verification.

Table 1 summarizes our results. We report the run time for: 2W (2-way ACR without alphabet refinement), 2W+AR (2-way ACR with alphabet refinement), NW (n-way ACR without alphabet refinement), NW+AR (n-way ACR with alphabet refinement); $|g_1|$ and $|g_2|$ are the assumption sizes produced by 2W, $|g_{max}|$ and $|g_{min}|$ are the sizes of the largest and smallest assumptions produced by NW. For 2W, each system was decomposed into two sub-systems, according to some "best decomposition" obtained before [10,23]. Mon is the run time of the monolithic classical algorithm and $|Sys\|P_{err}|$ is the number of states for the verification task, where Sys is the system $M_1\|M_1..\|M_n$. We put a limit of 1800 s for each experiment; "–" indicates that the time for that case exceeds this limit.

The results show that NW is better than 2W, and generates smaller assumptions. For example, Fig. 1 illustrates the small assumptions generated for the client-server example. Note that computing the "best" 2–way decomposition is expensive (its cost is not reported here). In contrast NW simply uses the natural decomposition of the system into its multiple components. Our results also show that alphabet refinement with rule simplification always improves circular reasoning, both in terms of analysis time and assumption sizes. Furthermore Mon performs better for small systems, but as the systems get larger n-way compositional verification significantly outperforms it. These lead to cases such as MER where, for large parameter values, Mon runs out of resources while NW+AR succeeds in under 2 min.

9   Conclusion and Future Work

We presented an automatic technique for the compositional analysis of systems decomposed into n components. The technique uses iterative assumption generation with incremental alphabet refinement and dynamic rule simplification. Preliminary results show its promise in practice. In the future we plan to check the rule premises in parallel to speed-up our approach. Further we plan to explore abstraction-refinement and learning as alternatives to our SAT-based assumption discovery.

Acknowledgments. We thank the reviewers for their detailed and helpful comments. This work was funded in part by the National Science Foundation (NSF Grant No. CSF-1329278) and the Binational Science Foundation (BSF Grant No. 2012259). Shoham was supported by the European Research Council under the European Union's Seventh Framework Program (FP7/2007–2013)/ERC grant agreement no. [321174-VSSC].

References

1. Alur, R., Henzinger, T.A.: Reactive modules. Formal Methods Syst. Des. **15**(1), 7–48 (1999)
2. Alur, R., Madhusudan, P., Nam, W.: Symbolic compositional verification by learning assumptions. In: Etessami, K., Rajamani, S.K. (eds.) CAV 2005. LNCS, vol. 3576, pp. 548–562. Springer, Heidelberg (2005)
3. Gheorghiu Bobaru, M., Păsăreanu, C.S., Giannakopoulou, D.: Automated assume-guarantee reasoning by abstraction refinement. In: Gupta, A., Malik, S. (eds.) CAV 2008. LNCS, vol. 5123, pp. 135–148. Springer, Heidelberg (2008)
4. Chaki, S., Clarke, E., Sinha, N., Thati, P.: Automated assume-guarantee reasoning for simulation conformance. In: Etessami, K., Rajamani, S.K. (eds.) CAV 2005. LNCS, vol. 3576, pp. 534–547. Springer, Heidelberg (2005)

5. Chen, Y.-F., Clarke, E.M., Farzan, A., Tsai, M.-H., Tsay, Y.-K., Wang, B.-Y.: Automated assume-guarantee reasoning through implicit learning. In: Touili, T., Cook, B., Jackson, P. (eds.) CAV 2010. LNCS, vol. 6174, pp. 511–526. Springer, Heidelberg (2010)
6. Chen, Y.-F., Farzan, A., Clarke, E.M., Tsay, Y.-K., Wang, B.-Y.: Learning minimal separating DFA's for compositional verification. In: Kowalewski, S., Philippou, A. (eds.) TACAS 2009. LNCS, vol. 5505, pp. 31–45. Springer, Heidelberg (2009)
7. Clarke, E., Grumberg, O., Peled, D.: Model Checking. MIT Press, Cambridge (1999)
8. Cobleigh, J.M., Giannakopoulou, D., Păsăreanu, C.S.: Learning assumptions for compositional verification. In: Garavel, H., Hatcliff, J. (eds.) TACAS 2003. LNCS, vol. 2619, pp. 331–346. Springer, Heidelberg (2003)
9. Een, N., Sörensson, N.: The minisat. http://minisat.se
10. Elkader, K.A., Grumberg, O., Păsăreanu, C.S., Shoham, S.: Automated circular assume-guarantee reasoning. In: Bjørner, N., de Boer, F. (eds.) FM 2015. LNCS, vol. 9109, pp. 23–39. Springer, Heidelberg (2015)
11. Gheorghiu, M.D., Giannakopoulou, D., Păsăreanu, C.S.: Refining interface alphabets for compositional verification. In: Grumberg, O., Huth, M. (eds.) TACAS 2007. LNCS, vol. 4424, pp. 292–307. Springer, Heidelberg (2007)
12. Gupta, A., McMillan, K.L., Fu, Z.: Automated assumption generation for compositional verification. Formal Methods Syst. Des. **32**(3), 285–301 (2008)
13. Henzinger, T.A., Liu, X., Qadeer, S., Rajamani, S.K.: Formal specification and verification of a dataflow processor array. In: ICCAD, pp. 494–499 (1999)
14. Henzinger, T.A., Qadeer, S., Rajamani, S.K.: You assume, we guarantee: methodology and case studies. In: Hu, A.J., Vardi, M.Y. (eds.) CAV 1998. LNCS, vol. 1427, pp. 440–451. Springer, Heidelberg (1998)
15. Henzinger, T.A., Qadeer, S., Rajamani, S.K., Taşıran, S.: An assume-guarantee rule for checking simulation. In: Gopalakrishnan, G.C., Windley, P. (eds.) FMCAD 1998. LNCS, vol. 1522, pp. 421–431. Springer, Heidelberg (1998)
16. Li, B., Dillig, I., Dillig, T., McMillan, K., Sagiv, M.: Synthesis of circular compositional program proofs via abduction. In: Piterman, N., Smolka, S.A. (eds.) TACAS 2013. LNCS, vol. 7795, pp. 370–384. Springer, Heidelberg (2013)
17. Magee, J., Kramer, J.: Concurrency: State Models and Java Programs. Wiley, New York (1999)
18. McMillan, K.L.: Verification of an implementation of Tomasulo's algorithm by compositional model checking. In: Hu, A.J., Vardi, M.Y. (eds.) CAV 1998. LNCS, vol. 1427, pp. 110–121. Springer, Heidelberg (1998)
19. McMillan, K.L.: Circular compositional reasoning about liveness. In: Pierre, L., Kropf, T. (eds.) CHARME 1999. LNCS, vol. 1703, pp. 342–346. Springer, Heidelberg (1999)
20. McMillan, K.L.: Verification of infinite state systems by compositional model checking. In: Pierre, L., Kropf, T. (eds.) CHARME 1999. LNCS, vol. 1703, pp. 219–237. Springer, Heidelberg (1999)
21. Misra, J., Chandy, K.M.: Proofs of networks of processes. IEEE Trans. Softw. Eng. **7**(4), 417–426 (1981)
22. Namjoshi, K.S., Trefler, R.J.: On the completeness of compositional reasoning. In: Allen Emerson, E., Sistla, A.P. (eds.) CAV 2000. LNCS, vol. 1855, pp. 139–153. Springer, Heidelberg (2000)

23. Pasareanu, C.S., Giannakopoulou, D., Bobaru, M.G., Cobleigh, J.M., Barringer, H.: Learning to divide and conquer: applying the L* algorithm to automate assume-guarantee reasoning. Formal Methods Syst. Des. **32**(3), 175–205 (2008)
24. Pnueli, A.: In transition from global to modular temporal reasoning about programs. In: Logics and Models of Concurrent Systems. NATO ASI Series (1985)
25. Rushby, J.: Formal verification of mcmillan's compositional assume-guarantee rule. CSL Technical report, SRI (2001)

JayHorn: A Framework for Verifying Java programs

Temesghen Kahsai[1], Philipp Rümmer[2], Huascar Sanchez[3],
and Martin Schäf[3]([✉])

[1] Nasa Ames / CMU, Moffett Field, USA
[2] Uppsala University, Uppsala, Sweden
[3] SRI International, Menlo Park, USA
martin.schaef@sri.com

Abstract. Building a competitive program verifiers is becoming cheaper. On the front-end side, openly available compiler infrastructure and optimization frameworks take care of hairy problems such as alias analysis, and break down the subtleties of modern languages into a handful of simple instructions that need to be handled. On the back-end side, theorem provers start providing full-fledged model checking algorithms, such as PDR, that take care looping control-flow.

In this spirit, we developed JayHorn, a verification framework for Java with the goal of having as few moving parts as possible. Most steps of the translation from Java into logic are implemented as bytecode transformations, with the implication that their soundness can be tested easily. From the transformed bytecode, we generate a set of constrained Horn clauses that are verified using state-of-the-art Horn solvers. We report on our implementation experience and evaluate JayHorn on benchmarks.

1   Introduction

Building a software model checking tool has always been a strenuous endeavor. Established tools, such as CBMC [11] or Java Pathfinder [9] have amassed countless man-hours of engineering and testing. However, over the recent years, this task has become a lot simpler with the increasing availability of off-the-shelf front-ends such as LLVM [13], Wala [1], or Soot [20], and verification back-ends such as Z3 [5], Corral [12], or Eldarica [18].

With the increasing availability of such tools, the task of building a software model checker becomes just a matter of picking a front-end and a back-end and writing the glue code to connect them. Recent verification competitions have shown that this approach is feasible in practice. Tools like SMACK [17] or SeaHorn [8] which use LLVM as a front-end and off-the-shelf verification backends have been able to outperform established tools in many categories.

Motivated by these developments, we have implemented JayHorn, a software model checking tool for Java. JayHorn uses the Java optimization framework Soot as a front-end, generates a set of constrained Horn clauses (CHCs) to encode the verification condition. The Horn clauses are then sent to a Horn engine. For the construction of JayHorn we made the following design decisions:

© Springer International Publishing Switzerland 2016
S. Chaudhuri and A. Farzan (Eds.): CAV 2016, Part I, LNCS 9779, pp. 352–358, 2016.
DOI: 10.1007/978-3-319-41528-4_19

1. Perform as much of the translation work as possible in Soot: Translation of exception handling, de-virtualization, and control-flow simplification are implemented as bytecode transformation. These steps do not alter a programs behavior which allows us to use Randoop [16] to test their correctness.
2. Keep the glue code that generates verification conditions small, modular, and extensible: by performing many steps as bytecode transformation, the step of generating verification conditions becomes relatively simple and is implemented in a few hundred lines of Java code. The implementation is modular and extensible to allow, for example, different encoding of memory or numeric types.
3. Keep the back-end exchangeable: Horn solvers are constantly improving and new tools are being released frequently. To ensure that JayHorn builds on the most efficient back-end, we made it modular and replaceable. Currently, JayHorn supports Z3 and Eldarica as back-ends but can be easily extended to support other tools.

Roadmap. In Sect. 2 we discuss the architecture of JayHorn in more detail and address issues such as soundness and limitations. In Sect. 3 we evaluate JayHorn on a set of benchmarks. Then we conclude and discuss our next steps.

2   Architecture of JayHorn

In the following, we discuss architecture, soundness, and limitations of JayHorn. The big picture is outlined in Fig. 1. In it's default configuration, JayHorn takes Java bytecode as input and checks if any Java **assert** can be violated.

JayHorn accepts any input that is accepted by Soot. That is, Java class files, Jar archives, or Android apk's. For code that is not annotated with **assert**

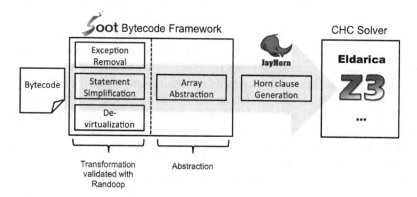

Fig. 1. Architectural overview of JayHorn. The tool takes Java bytecode as input. It then uses Soot to perform a set of transformations that do not alter the input/output behavior of the program, followed by an abstraction step to simplify arrays. The transformed bytecode is passed to JayHorn's glue code that constructs a system of CHCs which are passed into a Horn engine to check the safety of the input program.

statements, JayHorn also provides an option to guard possible NullPointer-Exceptions, ArrayIndexOutOfBoundsExceptions, and ClassCastExceptions with assertions (note that this affects soundness because developers may catch these exceptions on purpose even though it is not good practice).

Soot converts the given input into the Jimple intermediate format, which is a three-address code version of the Java bytecode. The benefit of operating on Jimple is that we only have to handle 15 different operations instead of over 200 as in the case of raw bytecode.

Program Transformation. We use the Soot infrastructure to apply (and implement) a set of bytecode transformations to simplify the input program. First, we eliminate exception handling and make all implicit exceptional control-flow explicit. To that end, we introduce a global variable (i.e., a public class with one public static field) to hold the last thrown exception. A thrown exception is then transformed into an assignment to this variable followed by a return (for primitive types we return a minimal values, for all other types we return null). After each method call, we first check if this exception variable has been set and, if so, ignore the return value and move control to the exceptional successor of the call statement. At the end of each entry point (e.g., main), we check if the exception variable has been set and throw the exception if necessary. This transformation does not alter the input/output behavior of the transformed program.

In the next step, we simplify the input program further by replacing switch statements by if statements and by removing unreachable code. In this step, we also add a public field dyntype to each class that carries the dynamic type of an object and set this field every time an object is created with new. For example, a Jimple statement A a :=new B(); would be followed an assignment a.dyntype = B.getClass();. Like the previous step, this step does not change the behavior of the input program.

Then, we de-virtualize the input program. That is, any call to a virtual method is replaced by a distinction of cases over the dyntype of the base of that call and calls to the corresponding methods. The de-virtualize can significantly increase the size of a program but Soot's built-in alias analysis' (and de-virtualization) can be used to reduce the number of cases that need to be distinguished.

Note that, up to this point, JayHorn has significantly simplified the program by removing exceptional flow, virtual method calls, and some statements that are syntactic sugar, without altering the behavior of the input program. Hence, we can test the correctness (or soundness) of these steps by comparing input/output behavior of the original and transformed code. Since this step is crucial for the soundness of the overall system, we employ Randoop [16] to automate this test. We also allow the user to generate these tests for a given input program to increase confidence.

Array Abstraction. On the simplified input program, JayHorn performs one abstraction step to eliminate arrays. Like the previous steps, this step is implemented as a bytecode transformation in Soot and can easily be replaced or modified if requirements change. Arrays in Java are objects, however, there are a few subtleties that makes it harder to handle them. For example, access to the `length` field of an array is not a regular field access but a special bytecode instruction. To simplify the generation of CHCs in the next step we transform arrays into real objects. To that end, we generate a new class for each array type used in the input program. The class extends Object and has a public field `length` and a field `elType` containing the type of the array elements. For each element of the array, we generate a private field of appropriate type. For reading and writing, the array class provides a `get` and `put` method with a distinction of cases over the used index. We can bound the number of fields that are generated for the array. If the used index exceeds this number, we return a dedicated constant that is later translated into an uninterpreted symbol. This step allows us to treat arrays like any other object, however, if we bound the number of fields, it introduces abstraction. Since this step is still a bytecode transformation we can again use Randoop to check how it affects our precision.

Generating Horn Clauses. The transformed program only contains primitive types and Objects, and a small set of statements, which simplifies the translation to CHCs; the entire translation takes less than 600 lines of Java code which keeps the risk of introducing bugs and thus unsoundess low. Our encoding as CHCs is inspired by the concept of refinement types [6,21], and uses uninterpreted predicates to represent:

- for each method `m`, pre-conditions `pre_m` and post-conditions `post_m` talking about parameters and result;
- for each control location `l`, invariants `loc_l` talking about local variables that are in scope;
- for each class `C`, instance invariants `inv_C` talking about the dynamic type and fields of objects.

The translation of programs to clauses then proceeds method by method, mapping each instruction to one clause. Accesses to heap and object fields are replaced by `unpack` instructions that apply invariants `inv_C` to determine the possible values of fields, and `pack` instructions that assert instance invariants after write accesses. Method calls are mapped to clauses that assert the precondition `pre_m` of the called method, and clauses that exploit the method postcondition `post_m` to determine possible results and effects of the call.

Soundness and Completeness. JayHorn is implemented in the spirit of soundiness [14]. Our analysis does not have a fully sound handling of the following features: JNI, implicit method invocations, integer overflow, reflection API, `invokedynamic`, code generation at runtime, dynamic loading, different class loaders, and key native methods We have determined that the unsoundness in our handling of these features has no effect the validity of our experimental evaluation. To the best of our knowledge, our analysis has a sound handling of all language features other than those listed above.[1]

---

[1] Generated using the Soundiness Statement Generator from http://soundiness.org.

Further, JayHorn over-approximates variables of type `double`, `float`, and `long` and may over-approximate array usage (as discussed above). Other than that, completeness mostly depends on the selected back-end.

3   Evaluation

We demonstrate the current capabilities and limitations of JayHorn on a set of examples. Table 1 show the results of our evaluation. We JayHorn with Eldarica and Z3 as a back-end to three sets of single threaded benchmark problems: CBMC-java tests, which are simple examples involving a variety of Java constructs provided by the authors of CBMC; MinePump, a product line provided by the authors of CPAChecker, and a Java version of the recursive benchmarks from SVCOMP 2015. For each benchmark problem we record if a tool produces the correct answer (✓), the wrong answer (✗), or times out (TO).

Table 1. Evaluation of JayHorn on three sets of benchmarks with Z3 and Eldarica back-end. For each benchmark problem we record how often JayHorn is able to find the correct answer (✓), how often it fails to prove a correct program (✗) and how often the execution times out after 60 s (TO).

Benchmark	# Problems	JayHorn + Z3			JayHorn + Eldarica		
		✓	✗	TO	✓	✗	TO
CBMC-Java tests	44	26	12	6	33	8	3
MinePump	64	36	0	28	39	25	0
SVCOMP Recursive	23	7	2	14	14	2	7

The experiments show that JayHorn is currently able to handle a range of examples even though some language features are not fully implemented. The cases where JayHorn fails to produce the expected result (✗) are all cases where an assertion holds but the tool is not able to show it (i.e., JayHorn is sound on these benchmarks). The wrong results are caused by our current encoding of integers as mathematical integers, the abstraction of float and double numbers are arbitrary values, and the missing implementation of bit operations. The experiments also show the importance of a modular translation: JayHorn performs significantly better with Eldarica than Z3 which can largely be attributed to our encoding of programs in CHC. A different encoding might lead to the opposite result.

We tried to compare JayHorn with Java Pathfinder (JPF) as a baseline but due to different approaches, no comparison was possible. On the MinePump benchmarks, JPF is significantly faster than JayHorn. On the other two benchmarks, however, JPF failed since those initialize variables with random number and as JPF is an explicit state model checker, it fails to enumerate those states.

4   Related Work

Fully automated program analysis is a very active research area with many high quality tools (e.g., [2,4,8–11,15,17,19]). The work on JayHorn is primarily inspired by the success of SMACK [17] and SeaHorn [8] in the previous verification competitions.

Currently, not many tools of this kind are available for comparison that target Java. AProVE [7] and Ultimate [10] competed on termination analysis for Java programs. During the writing of this paper, the authors of Ultimate, CBMC, and CPAChecker [3] were actively working on tools for Java (and we would like to thank them for their test cases and examples) but none of them was available for a direct comparison with JayHorn. We will make JayHorn and our test cases and benchmarks publicly available to contribute to this development with the hope of having a verification competition for Java in the near future.

5   Conclusion

We have presented a new software verification framework for Java in the spirit of SeaHorn and Smack. JayHorn is continuously evolving. It's current status does not yet have any of the amenities needed in industrial practice, such as built-in specification for common libraries. However, it performs well on a set of well known verification problems and we are eager to compete with other tools. In the future, we plan to extend JayHorn to also handle termination.

The main contribution of JayHorn is its modular design. The front-end phase of JayHorn significantly simplifies the input program without changing its behavior which makes it easy to develop new analysis tools on top of this front-end. Further, JayHorn can connect to different tools that accept Horn clauses as input which can serve as an interesting benchmark.

Acknowledgement. This work is funded in parts by AFRL contract No. FA8750-15-C-0010, NSF Award No. 1422705, and the Swedish Research Council.

References

1. T.J. Watson library for analysis (wala). http://wala.sf.net
2. Beyer, D., Henzinger, T.A., Jhala, R., Majumdar, R.: The software model checker blast: applications to software engineering. Int. J. Softw. Tools Technol. Transf. **9**(5), 505–525 (2007)
3. Beyer, D., Keremoglu, M.E.: CPACHECKER: a tool for configurable software verification. In: Gopalakrishnan, G., Qadeer, S. (eds.) CAV 2011. LNCS, vol. 6806, pp. 184–190. Springer, Heidelberg (2011)
4. Cordeiro, L., Fischer, B., Marques-Silva, J.: SMT-based bounded model checking for embedded Ansi-C software. In: ASE, Washington, DC, USA, pp. 137–148. IEEE Computer Society (2009)

5. de Moura, L., Bjørner, N.S.: Z3: an efficient SMT solver. In: Ramakrishnan, C.R., Rehof, J. (eds.) TACAS 2008. LNCS, vol. 4963, pp. 337–340. Springer, Heidelberg (2008)

6. Freeman, T., Pfenning, F.: Refinement types for ML. In: Proceedings of the ACM SIGPLAN 1991 Conference on Programming Language Design and Implementation, PLDI 1991, New York, NY, USA, pp. 268–277. ACM (1991)

7. Giesl, J., et al.: Proving termination of programs automatically with AProVE. In: Demri, S., Kapur, D., Weidenbach, C. (eds.) IJCAR 2014. LNCS, vol. 8562, pp. 184–191. Springer, Heidelberg (2014)

8. Gurfinkel, A., Kahsai, T., Komuravelli, A., Navas, J.A.: The seahorn verification framework. In: Kroening, D., Păsăreanu, C.S. (eds.) CAV 2015. LNCS, vol. 9206, pp. 343–361. Springer, Heidelberg (2015)

9. Havelund, K., Pressburger, T.: Model checking Java programs using Java pathfinder. Int. J. Softw. Tools Technol. Transf. **2**(4), 366–381 (2000)

10. Heizmann, M., Dietsch, D., Leike, J., Musa, B., Podelski, A.: ULTIMATE AUTOMIZER with array interpolation. In: Baier, C., Tinelli, C. (eds.) TACAS 2015. LNCS, vol. 9035, pp. 454–456. Springer, Berlin (2015)

11. Kroening, D., Tautschnig, M.: CBMC – C bounded model checker. In: Ábrahám, E., Havelund, K. (eds.) TACAS 2014 (ETAPS). LNCS, vol. 8413, pp. 389–391. Springer, Heidelberg (2014)

12. Lal, A., Qadeer, S., Lahiri, S.K.: A solver for reachability modulo theories. In: Madhusudan, P., Seshia, S.A. (eds.) CAV 2012. LNCS, vol. 7358, pp. 427–443. Springer, Heidelberg (2012)

13. Lattner, C., Adve, V.: LLVM: a compilation framework for lifelong program analysis and transformation. In: CGO, Washington, DC, USA, p. 75. IEEE Computer Society (2004)

14. Livshits, B., Sridharan, M., Smaragdakis, Y., Lhoták, O., Amaral, J.N., Chang, B.-Y.E., Guyer, S.Z., Khedker, U.P., Møller, A., Vardoulakis, D.: In defense of soundiness: aamanifesto. Commun. ACM **58**(2), 44–46 (2015)

15. Nutz, A., Dietsch, D., Mohamed, M.M., Podelski, A.: ULTIMATE KOJAK with memory safety checks. In: Baier, C., Tinelli, C. (eds.) TACAS 2015. LNCS, vol. 9035, pp. 458–460. Springer, Heidelberg (2015)

16. Pacheco, C., Ernst, M.D.: Randoop: feedback-directed random testing for Java. In: OOPSLA, New York, NY, USA, pp. 815–816. ACM (2007)

17. Rakamarić, Z., Emmi, M.: SMACK: decoupling source language details from verifier implementations. In: Biere, A., Bloem, R. (eds.) CAV 2014. LNCS, vol. 8559, pp. 106–113. Springer, Heidelberg (2014)

18. Rümmer, P., Hojjat, H., Kuncak, V.: Disjunctive interpolants for Horn-clause verification. In: Sharygina, N., Veith, H. (eds.) CAV 2013. LNCS, vol. 8044, pp. 347–363. Springer, Heidelberg (2013)

19. Spoto, F.: The nullness analyser of Julia. In: LPAR, pp. 405–424 (2010)

20. Vallée-Rai, R., Hendren, L., Sundaresan, V., Lam, P., Gagnon, E., Co, P.: Soot - a Java optimization framework. In: CASCON (1999)

21. Vazou, N., Rondon, P.M., Jhala, R.: Abstract refinement types. In: Felleisen, M., Gardner, P. (eds.) ESOP 2013. LNCS, vol. 7792, pp. 209–228. Springer, Heidelberg (2013)

Program Analysis

Trigger Selection Strategies to Stabilize Program Verifiers

K.R.M. Leino[1]([⊠]) and Clément Pit-Claudel[2]

[1] Microsoft Research, Redmond, USA
leino@microsoft.com
[2] MIT CSAIL, Cambridge, USA
cpitcla@mit.edu

Abstract. SMT-based program verifiers often suffer from the so-called butterfly effect, in which minor modifications to the program source cause significant instabilities in verification times, which in turn may lead to spurious verification failures and a degraded user experience. This paper identifies matching loops (ill-behaved quantifiers causing an SMT solver to repeatedly instantiate a small set of quantified formulas) as a significant contributor to these instabilities, and describes some techniques to detect and prevent them. At their core, the contributed techniques move the trigger selection logic away from the SMT solver and into the high-level verifier: this move allows authors of verifiers to annotate, rewrite, and analyze user-written quantifiers to improve the solver's performance, using information that is easily available at the source level but would be hard to extract from the heavily encoded terms that the solver works with. The paper demonstrates three core techniques (quantifier splitting, trigger sharing, and matching loop detection) by extending the Dafny verifier with its own trigger selection routine, and demonstrates significant predictability and performance gains on both Dafny's test suite and large verification efforts using Dafny.

1 Introduction

Automated program verifiers like Frama-C [18], AutoProof [26], VeriFast [16], SPARK 2014 [14], and Dafny [19] provide usable environments in which to write provably correct programs. By employing efficient (semi-)decision procedures (found in satisfiability-modulo-theories (SMT) solvers [3,4,9,11]) and aggressive caching [5,21], these verifiers provide users with generally responsive feedback, and by shielding the user from all direct interaction with the decision procedures, the program verifiers offer a gentle learning curve. While SMT solvers are often pretty darn fast, their efficiency ultimately involves various heuristics, which leads to a problem in SMT-based program verifiers: we call it the butterfly effect.

The *butterfly effect* describes the phenomenon that a minor modification in one part of the program source causes changes in the outcome of the verification in other, unchanged and unrelated parts of the program. When this

---

* Authors are listed alphabetically.

© Springer International Publishing Switzerland 2016
S. Chaudhuri and A. Farzan (Eds.): CAV 2016, Part I, LNCS 9779, pp. 361–381, 2016.
DOI: 10.1007/978-3-319-41528-4_20

change in outcome causes the verifier to hit a time limit or other resource limit, previously succeeding verifications turn into spurious verification failures. The butterfly effect thus leads to verification instability, user frustration, and overall a degraded user experience.

By profiling the behavior of an SMT solver (Z3 in the context of the Dafny program verifier), we have found many spurious verification failures to contain *matching loops*—ill-behaved quantifiers causing the SMT solver to repeatedly instantiate a small set of quantified formulas [11]. Such matching loops are bad news, but with some luck, the heuristic proof search in the SMT solver may happen to find a proof without falling into the trap of the matching loop. Evidently, such "luck" occurs often enough that when an unrelated change in the program source tickles the heuristics differently, latent matching loops are perceived as verification instability, whereas the real culprit was the presence of the matching loop in the first place.

In this paper, we contribute strategies for making quantifiers better behaved. The major part of the novelty of our strategies lies in a willingness to rewrite user-defined quantifiers. Our technique automatically selects *matching triggers*, which give a way to control how the SMT solver processes quantifiers. Because our technique finds candidate matching triggers *before* it rewrites quantifiers, we achieve better trigger selection than if the user had rewritten the quantifiers manually. Part of our strategies is also to select the triggers at the program-source level, rather than at the level of formulas in the SMT input. This is a good idea, because it lets our technique avoid some liberal triggers that consist only of functions added during the generation of verification conditions. Moreover, source-level trigger selection gives a clear way to explain to users which triggers were selected and how matching loops were averted, a simple but important feature for which we have received praise from users. We have implemented our strategies in the Dafny program verifier. Our paper also contributes experimental data that shows that our strategies significantly improve both predictability and performance of the verifier.

2   Background

In this section, we give the necessary background on how matching triggers are used by the SMT solver to handle quantifiers and on the architecture of the program verifier.

2.1   Matching Triggers

We assume the SMT solver deals with quantifiers along the lines proposed by Nelson [24], which has been implemented, for example, in Simplify [11] and Z3 [8,9]. The idea can be described as follows.

At any time during its proof search, the state of the SMT solver includes the set of formulas from which it is attempting to discharge the proof goal. These formulas are represented by various cooperating decision procedures. The decision procedure for uninterpreted functions is of special importance, as it not only keeps tracks of equivalence classes of terms (typically in a data structure called an *E-graph* [12, 25]), but also serves as a mediator between the theories. When an existentially quantified formula is equated with **true**, it is Skolemized and the resulting formula is equated with **true** in the E-graph. When a universally quantified formula is equated with **true**, the strategy of the SMT solver is to instantiate the quantifier and equate the resulting formulas with **true**.

Logically, it is sound to instantiate a universal quantifier with anything at all. However, arbitrary instantiations are not likely to help the proof search. To make more informed instantiation decisions, the SMT solver relies on *matching patterns*, also known as *matching triggers* or just *triggers*. Given some triggers for a quantifier, the SMT solver looks for terms in the E-graph that match any of the triggers and then instantiates the quantifier accordingly. The process is a bit like in term rewriting, except that the new instantiations are added to the E-graph, rather than somehow replacing the matching terms.

Let us illustrate with an example. A possible trigger for the quantifier

```
forall x: int · f(x) = 3 * g(x) + 5
```

is f(x), meaning that the presence of any term f(E) in the E-graph gives rise to the instantiation x := E (yielding the formula f(E) = 3 * g(E) + 5). From now on, we will surround the terms of a trigger with curly braces. In this example, we may choose to understand the trigger as saying "wherever there is an interest in f, instantiate the quantifier". Another possible trigger is {g(x)}, which would have the effect of producing information about g in terms of f. It is possible to associate both triggers with the quantifier, which says to instantiate the quantifier if either an f term or a g term is found in the E-graph: {f(x)} {g(x)}. Yet another possibility is to use the trigger {f(x), g(x)}, which says to instantiate the quantifier only with those terms that appear in the E-graph as arguments to both f and g.

Here is more subtle example. The quantifier

```
forall x: int · 0 < x ⟹ f(x) = f(x-1) + f(g(x))
```

may tempt us to consider any of {f(x)}, {f(x-1)}, or {f(g(x))} as candidate triggers. However, {f(x)} is problematic. If the E-graph contains a term f(E), then the instantiation x := E will produce a term f(E-1), which gives rise to another possible instantiation, x := E-1. This is known as a *matching loop* [11] and should be avoided. The fact that the term f(E-1) in the instantiation is guarded by the antecedent 0 < E does not help, because E may be term whose distance from 0 cannot be determined from the proof context.

Candidate trigger {f(x-1)} is also problematic, but for another (or rather, additional) reason: it contains the symbol -, which is interpreted by the decision procedure for arithmetic. When a symbol is interpreted, one cannot rely on it appearing in this form in the E-graph. For example, the E-graph may contain a term f(y+2) but this may still not cause the instantiation x := y+3, because the term y+3, let alone the equality y+2 = (y+3)-1, may be unknown to the E-graph.

Candidate {f(g(x))} does not suffer from the problems we just described. It is rather discriminating—it will cause an instantiation x := E only if the E-graph contains a term that applies f to a term in the equivalence class where g is applied to E. Of course, depending on the application, this is possibly too discriminating to give rise to the instantiations that are needed to reach the proof goal.

Triggers can be specified as part of the SMT-LIB 2 input to the SMT solver. In effect, this provides a way to program the SMT solver [22]. If the input does not specify a trigger for a quantifier, the SMT solver attempts to select triggers from the terms in the quantifier's body. As we argue in this paper, leaving trigger selection to the SMT solver can contribute to verification instabilities. Instead, we show a strategy for selecting triggers at a level closer to the problem domain. A formal semantics of triggers, as well as ways to define decision procedures using quantifiers and triggers, has been studied by Dross et al. [13].

2.2 Architecture of the Program Verifier

The verification conditions generated for a Dafny program contain quantifiers from three major sources. One source is the axiomatization of standard Dafny operators and types, like the axiomatization of finite sequences. These quantifiers have hand-written triggers. A second source is the encoding of constructs defined in the Dafny program, like user-defined recursive functions. The triggers for these quantifiers come from hand-crafted schemas (see, e.g., [1]). The third form is user-written quantifiers. Previously, these were translated into SMT input without any attempts at computing triggers. Consequently, it had been left to the SMT solver to select triggers. To better understand why this can cause problems, let us say a few words about the architecture of the verifier and about what we will call parasitic terms.

The architecture of the Dafny verifier is the standard one of translating the source language into an *intermediate verification language* (Dafny uses Boogie [2,20]) and then generating (using the Boogie tool) verification conditions from it. Each of these two steps does a translation into more coarse-grained types and more concrete encodings.

For example, consider the Dafny expression

```
forall x · 0 ≤ x < a.Length ⟹ a[x] = 31
```

where a denotes a reference to an integer array. In the translation of this expression into Boogie, the heap dereference is made explicit and the offset into the array is computed from the integer x. Here is (a slight simplification of) the Boogie encoding:

```
forall x: int ·  0 ≤ x ∧ x < _System.array.Length(a) ⟹
               Unbox(read($Heap, a, IndexField(x))) = 31
```

As one can glean from this expression, the logical encoding of Dafny uniformly stores array elements as being of a type Box, so the read from the heap is followed by an `Unbox` operation. Furthermore, when Boogie translates this expression into SMT input, the formula becomes:

```
forall x: int ·  0 ≤ x ∧ x < _System.array.Length(a) ⟹
    U_2_int(Unbox(intType, MapType1Select($Heap, a, IndexField(x)))) = 31
```

Here, we see yet another translation between types, where most of Boogie's types are collected into a type called `U` and the formula includes a mapping from `U` to `int` [20].

As can be seen in this example, what at the level of Dafny seems like a good trigger—the term `a[x]`, which would express "whenever there is an interest in an element of `a`, instantiate the quantifier"—is not easily identifiable in the SMT formula. In fact, at the SMT level, the term `IndexField(x)` may look like a good trigger, but that is quite a liberal trigger and is likely to lead to far too many irrelevant instantiations. We call the terms involving these additional functions *parasitic*. In other words, parasitic terms are terms introduced by Dafny's translation solely for encoding purposes; examples include `Box`, `Unbox`, and `IndexField`.

The Dafny front-end and verifier already infer from the given program various pieces of information, like omitted types and rank functions for termination. Dafny IDEs make this information available as hover text. In line with this tradition of informing users about inferred elements, our attitude is that Dafny users should not need to write triggers themselves, but may need to understand triggers in order to diagnose poor verification performance. It would thus be nice to communicate selected triggers to the user. Unfortunately, triggers selected in the SMT solver are difficult to obtain, and their inclusion of parasitic terms would not make sense to the Dafny user. Moreover, in many cases, translating back from a trigger picked by the SMT solver to a Dafny expression is hard: the translation from Dafny to the SMT solver's language is not a bijection.

These two aspects (avoiding parasitic terms and informing the user about trigger selections) lead us quite naturally to argue that it makes sense to select triggers at the source level rather than leaving this task to the SMT solver. From the use of good triggers, one can hope for better behaved instantiations and thus more stable verification. Moreover, information from the trigger-selection process can more easily be explained to the user through hover text. Of course, selecting triggers at the source level would be easy to accomplish by applying the SMT solver's algorithms to the nodes of a different abstract syntax tree (AST). However, our strategy goes beyond merely selecting triggers at the source level, as we explain in the next section.

3   Trigger Selection

When tasked with adding triggers to a quantifier, our code proceeds in a series of small steps. At a high level, it first walks down the AST of the body of the quantifier, collecting terms that could be part of a trigger. Then, it enumerates subsets of these terms, thus generating a large collection of trigger candidates (each candidate trigger is a set of terms). It then rejects candidates that fail to mention all quantified variables, and filters the set of candidates to remove redundancy and improve the performance of the SMT solver. Finally, it uses heuristics to select relevant triggers, attempting to predict and prevent matching loops, and issuing warnings if matching loops seem unavoidable.

Each individual step is detailed below. Though previous literature has not given them extensive treatment, and in particular not with a focus on efficiency of implementation, some of these steps have appeared in one form or another in previous work. Apart from a rigorous description, our contribution lies beyond these steps: in addition to annotating single quantifiers, we introduce two new techniques, quantifier splitting and trigger sharing. These techniques are the key to preserving as much expressiveness as possible despite matching loop suppression. We describe them in detail at the end of this section.

3.1 Annotating the AST

Our extension first annotates subterms of each quantifier's body by labeling some of them as trigger heads, and others as trigger killers. *Trigger killers* are terms that are not permitted to appear in triggers: typically, these have forms that do not reduce to uninterpreted functions, such as arithmetic operations (`a + b`) or logical connectives (`a ⟹ b`). Conversely, *Trigger heads* are terms that may appear in triggers, such as applied functions (`P(x)`), array accesses (`a[x]`), member accesses (`this.someField`), or set membership tests (`a in S`). More precisely, trigger heads are nodes of the AST of a quantifier's body whose children include at least one of the quantified variables, and do not include trigger killers. After annotating each subterm, our code collects all trigger heads, and attaches them to the quantifier.

As an example, in `forall x · x in S ⟺ f(x) > f(x+1)`, our prototype annotates `x in S` and `f(x)` as trigger heads, and `x+1` and `f(x) > f(x+1)` (and thus all of their ancestors, like `f(x+1)` and the whole body of the quantifier) as trigger killers.

This phase takes time linear in the cumulative size of the ASTs all quantifiers in the source program, which is bounded by the size of the source program itself.

3.2 Generating Candidates

After collecting terms suitable for inclusion in a trigger, our code generates candidate triggers by enumerating combinations of these suitable terms. Since the powerset of all collected terms can quickly grow large, this enumeration is restricted by ensuring that each generated candidate has two properties: *adequacy* as a trigger (each candidate mentions all variables, as required by the SMT solver), and *parsimony* (removing a term from any candidate causes it to become inadequate). This parsimony property is highly desirable: since it puts more constraints on quantifier instantiations, any non-parsimonious candidate matches less often than its parsimonious counterparts.

As an example of the effect of the parsimony requirement, consider a collection of three suitable terms `P(x, y)`, `Q(y, z)`, and `R(x, z)`. From this collection, our code constructs three candidate triggers: {P(x, y), Q(y, z)}, {P(x, y), R(x, z)}, and {Q(y, z), R(x, z)}. {P(x, y), Q(y, z), R(x, z)} is eliminated because it is redundant (we call a candidate trigger *redundant* when it is strictly more specific than another candidate trigger; this happens when any match against the more specific trigger induces a match against the less specific one).

The parsimony requirement is particularly useful when the body of a quantifier mentions many predicates (in the extreme case of forall x · P1(x) ... Pn(x), it allows our code to generate only n candidates, instead of the naïve 2^n), but implementing it efficiently is non-trivial. Indeed, it is not enough to check as subsets are enumerated that each added term mentions a previously unmentioned variable: the addition of a new term can make a previous term redundant, as for example when adding R(x, y, z) to a candidate containing P(x) and Q(y). To track parsimony efficiently, our code keeps track of ownership relations between terms and variables. When recursively constructing subsets of a given set of terms, our code first ensures that the newly added term does mention a previously unmentioned variable; if so, the term is added, and it gains ownership of all variables that it mentions. After this operation, if any term is left without ownership of any variable, the whole subset is marked as redundant, and that branch of the subset generation recursion is cut. For performance, as it recursively constructs subsets, our code equips each partially constructed set of terms with two hashmaps: one hashmap from each term to the set of variables owned by that term, and the other hashmap from each variable to its (single) owner, if any. By incrementally constructing these hashsets of variables owned by each term and hashmaps associating each variable to its owner term, our code can efficiently (in time linear in the number of quantified variables in the context) determine whether adding a term to a partially constructed set makes it redundant (with regard to variables mentioned)[1].

Continuing on the previous example forall x · x in S ⟺ f(x) > f(x+1), our code generates only two triggers: {f(x)} and {x in S}. The candidate trigger {f(x), x in S} is redundant, and thus our code excludes it.

Without the parsimony requirement, this step would have for each quantifier a worst-case time complexity exponential in the number of previously collected trigger heads. Thanks to that requirement, however, this step has complexity $k · n · n_1 · ... · n_k$ where k is the number of quantified variables and $n = \sum_i n_i$ is the number of trigger heads in the quantifier's body (each n_i counts how many of these terms mention the ith quantified variable). This yields an upper bound of $k · n^{k+1}$; in practice, this upper bound is seldom reached: each trigger head often mentions a single quantified variable.

3.3 Picking Triggers and Preventing Matching Loops

In its last phase, our code uses a (necessarily incomplete) heuristic to evaluate whether each candidate trigger may cause a matching loop. Roughly, this

---

[1] Curious readers are directed to the CopyWithAdd method of the SetOfTerms class implemented in the Triggers/TriggerUtils.cs part of our implementation.

heuristic flags a trigger as potentially looping if instantiating the quantifier may lead to a ground term that again matches the trigger.

In more details, our code proceeds as follows for each candidate:

1. For each term t of the candidate, our code collects all terms of the quantifier's body that match the term t. For example, it may pick f(x+1), f(if a then b else c), and f(0) for the candidate term f(x) (a match occurs with a term t' when t' can be unified with t; that is, when there exists an instantiation of the variables of t that yields t').

2. For each matching term, our code decides whether the match should be deemed a false positive, and if so removes it. False positives are terms that
   – are equal to the trigger (a term f(x) does not cause loops if the trigger is f(x)),
   – also appear in the trigger (a term f(g(x)) does not cause loops if the trigger is {f(y), f(g(x))}, despite being a match for f(y)),
   – differ from the trigger only by variables (a term f(y, x) is not deemed to cause a loop if the trigger is f(x, y); indeed, forall x,y · f(x, y) = f(y, x) is a quantifier that harmlessly can use either term as a trigger), or
   – differ by terms that do not contain bound variables (a term f(0) does not cause loops if the trigger is f(x)).

3. If any terms are left that could cause loops, our code marks the trigger as risky, recording the terms with which it may loop, and excludes it from the pool of candidate triggers.

With matching loops mostly eliminated, our code then proceeds to pick triggers: it analyzes the set of generated trigger candidates, ordering them according to a trigger specificity relation (wherein a trigger is less specific than another one if every match of the latter is also a match of the former), and excluding all non-minimal candidates. Indeed, just like non-parsimonious candidates, non-minimal candidates are redundant.

Note that, crucially, this selection phase happens after the matching loop suppression phase. As an example of minimality, and of the importance of this ordering, consider a collection of two terms f(x) and f(f(x)). In this case, our minimality heuristic would retain only one trigger, {f(x)}. But since its matching loop detection logic preemptively removes {f(x)} from the candidate pool, {f(f(x))} is selected instead, indeed preventing a matching loop.

This phase has, for each quantifier, a time complexity bounded by $k \cdot n^2$, where k is the number of candidates, and n the size of the body of the quantifier (the quadratic factor is obtained by bounding the cost of comparing two terms for equality by the size of the quantifier's entire body).

3.4   Splitting Quantifiers and Sharing Triggers

The strategy presented above suffers from one crucial weakness: in practice, users tend to collect related conditions under a single quantifiers. Thus, expressions of the form `forall x · P(x) ∧ (Q(x) ⟹ P(x+1))` are quite common. The algorithm presented above finds `{P(x)}` and `{Q(x)}` as reasonable trigger candidates, but proceeds to eliminate `{P(x)}` from the candidates pool, noticing its potential to loop with `{P(x+1)}`. Unfortunately, this means that with the naïvely auto-generated trigger `{Q(x)}`, this quantifier is not enough to prove a proposition such as `P(0)`, which should follow trivially.

To offset this over-specificity, our code implements *quantifier splitting*, a Dafny-to-Dafny rewriting technique that splits user-written quantifiers to reduce the chances of large quantifier bodies causing self-loops. For the example above, it thus produces two quantifiers, not one, and proceeds to annotate them separately. `forall x · P(x)` gets a trigger `{P(x)}`, and `forall x · Q(x) ⟹ P(x+1)` gets a trigger `{Q(x)}`.

Exactly how to perform trigger splitting is an interesting design concern: on one extreme, one could simply split the body of the quantifier around conjunctions.

On the other extreme, one could rewrite the body into conjunctive normal form before splitting. The former approach is too weak: it fails to split quantifier bodies in the common case where a collection of properties is predicated by a common condition, such as `forall i · 0 ≤ i < |a| ⟹ (... ∧ ... ∧ ...)`. The latter approach correctly handles this pattern, producing three predicated quantifiers, but can introduce exponential increases in formula size. Our approach is therefore a compromise between these two extremes, where only one level of normalization is allowed, around ⟹.

This properly handles the example above, without leading to significant increases in formula size. It is also in line with Dafny's predicated quantifier notation: the example above can be written `forall i | 0 ≤ i < |a| · ... ∧ ... ∧ ...`, which gets split into three quantifiers of the same shape `forall i | 0 ≤ i < |a| · ...`.

Splitting a quantifier before performing matching loop detection, however, is still not enough to recover its original expressiveness: after splitting the example above into `forall x · P(x)` and `forall x · Q(x) ⟹ P(x+1)`, and assigning `{P(x)}` as the trigger for the first split quantifier and `{Q(x)}` for the second, adding a term `Q(n)` to the collection of ground terms of the SMT solver does not immediately entail learning `P(n)` (it did for the original quantifier with `{Q(x)}` as the trigger). To recover more of the lost expressiveness, our code enriches the pool of terms to be considered for trigger elaboration at the beginning of the trigger generation process by sharing candidates between all quantifiers that derive from the same split quantifier. This strategy, which we call *trigger sharing*, yields two triggers for the first split quantifier `forall x · P(x)`, namely `{P(x)}` and `{Q(x)}`. The second quantifier still only gets one trigger, since `{P(x)}` would loop with `P(x+1)`. Interestingly, this strategy leads to quantifiers whose triggers are composed of terms that do not necessarily appear in the quantifier's body; an otherwise uncommon, but not undesirable, situation: in a sense, the shared trigger captures insight gathered from the programmer about weak connections between relatively independent propositions.

This phase has a time complexity linear in the size of each quantifier.

4   Evaluation

Our new trigger selection strategy brings three main benefits:

- **Verification is more predictable:** adding auto-generated triggers to split quantifiers significantly reduce verification instabilities. We demonstrate this effect on Dafny's test suite by comparing the standard deviations of test running times across multiple runs with different seeds, with and without Dafny-generated triggers.
- **Verification is faster:** Dafny-generated triggers prevent certain matching loops from occurring, improving verification times. We demonstrate this effect on a large verification effort from the IronFleet project [15].
- **Debugging is easier:** Dafny-generated triggers are built from terms found in the bodies of user-written quantifiers, allowing Dafny to print detailed warnings and error messages. We discuss our experience using these messages as a debugging aid while adjusting examples that relied on promiscuous trigger instantiations to verify, and while verifying new programs.

We discuss these three aspects in the following subsections, before presenting experimental results supporting these conclusions.

4.1   Improved Predictability

Measuring the impact of Dafny-level trigger generation on predictability is particularly difficult. Indeed, triggers selected at the Dafny level are often much more specific triggers than those which the SMT solver would have picked from encoded terms. This is mostly desirable, but it still causes a number of problems: certain examples for which the SMT solver was lucky and could find a proof of thanks to absurdly liberal triggers stop working; other examples that (again, due to luck) had a short proof using promiscuous triggers take much longer to verify. In most cases, the problems are easily fixable: tightening the proof by adding a few assertions is often enough to drive the solver down the right proof path, without using unreasonable triggers. To ensure fairness, our experiments separate the contribution of these modifications to improvements in verification performance or stability; yet we still view these added annotations as net gains: it is preferable to invest slightly more work in ensuring that a verification is stable than to rely on luck and liberal trigger choices.

Looking more closely at instabilities, we see two ways in which unpredictable performance manifests itself: one derives from variations in solver behavior due to choices of random seeds, and the other derives from the specific way in which the verification problem is stated by the user. Ideally, we wish our verification tool to be robust to both.

In the first case, we expect a robustly annotated collection of quantifiers to be agnostic to the random choices that inform the solver's behavior, and thus verification times to be mostly independent from the choice of random seed used by the solver, or from the version of the solver used. We call this static predictability, or robustness to prover changes.

In the second case, we expect equivalent formulations of verification conditions to lead to roughly similar verification performance, and equal verification results. In particular, we do not expect users to adjust their writing to minimize unpredictable verification performance, or to make insignificant source changes to finding "the" right formulation that causes Dafny to succeed (unfortunately, the current verification process encourages users to do precisely this: since triggers are hard to debug, it is often simpler to experiment with various formulations of the problem, until one is found that does not seem to send the prover into a loop). We call this dynamic predictability, or robustness to source changes.

4.2 Improved Verification Speeds

Beyond the improved predictability, Dafny-generated triggers offer a significant performance boost in large verification projects. Analysis of traces produced by the SMT solver shows that in many cases, lax triggers are the cause of numerous useless instantiations, slowing down the proof search process. By ensuring that we never pick generic, uninformative triggers, we can perceptibly reduce the verification times of many complex developments.

4.3 Easier Debugging and Interaction

Beyond performance and predictability, Dafny-generated triggers provide a meaningful improvement in user experience:

- Triggers are Dafny terms, and can therefore easily be displayed to the user, in the form of informative tooltips in Dafny IDEs. In contrast, triggers collected by the SMT solver are parts of Dafny's and Boogie's combined encodings, and thus hardly meaningful to the user.
- Quantifier splitting happens at the Dafny level, and therefore is also amenable to presentation to the user, in the form of subtle mouseover messages.
- Potential matching loops can be detected early, and reported to the user. Instead of being an arcane part of SMT performance debugging, triggers become a discreet part of the usual verification landscape, which the user is reminded of only when it may start causing issues.
- Common patterns introducing matching loop (such as `forall x · a[x] ≤ a[x+1]`, or `forall x · f(x) = f(f(x))`) can be the object of specific advice, beyond the "potential matching loop" warnings. Our implementation does not offer such specialized advice, but it would be a reasonable extension of our current efforts.

In practice, we have received very enthusiastic feedback from users of the new system, and praise for the integrated, single-language experience that triggers at the Dafny level allow.

4.4   Experimental Results

We evaluate the impact of Dafny-generated triggers on Dafny programming through three experiments:[2]

- In the first one, we run most of the Dafny test suite (about 350 test files of varying complexity and running times) with varying random seeds, and measure per-test completion times and standard deviations across ten runs. We run the original Dafny code on the original test suite, followed by our own version of Dafny with and without triggers, on a version of the test suite updated to verify successfully with Dafny-generated triggers. Running these three tests allows us to evaluate performance and static predictability gains derived both from adding triggers to user-written quantifiers, and from editing the test suite to correct the warnings issued by our trigger-generating code.
- In the second experiment, we use our implementation to process a large code base after enabling Dafny-generated triggers, and show significantly improved verification times.
- In the third, informal experiment, we fully verify a version of the classic Union-Find algorithm, and discuss how auto-triggers improve the verification experience as the code and its proofs are being written. Contrary to our performance and static predictability tests, this experiment shows the dynamic predictability benefits of using Dafny-generated triggers throughout the process of developing and verifying new code.

Performance and Stability Evaluation Across Multiple Runs of the Test Suite.
Most of Dafny's test suite (perhaps 70 %) is unaffected by the addition of Dafny-generated triggers: verification is and remains stable, with newly added triggers often slightly reducing variance across multiple runs, and performance remaining mostly unchanged. This is expected (and fortunate!), for two reasons: first, most of the test suite is made up of small programs, whose complexity is too low to cause significant verification issues. In that case, more precise triggers can help direct the search faster, but not by very much. Second, we expect matching loops to be relatively uncommon (especially given that the more complex examples in Dafny's test suite were written by experts). Figure 1 shows a high-level summary of these results, by comparing the distribution of standard deviations of verification times across the entire updated test suite, with and without Dafny-level triggers. In general, the addition of triggers slightly improves stability, diminishing variance across the entire test suite.

Beyond this general improvement in stability, measuring performance and instabilities across prover runs for the remaining 30 % of the test suite shows

---

[2] All experiments in this section were run on two cores of an Intel Core i7-4810MQ CPU (2.80 GHz), on a machine equipped with 32 GB of RAM and running Z3 version 4.4.1.

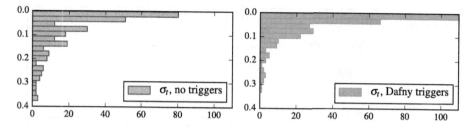

Fig. 1. Histogram of standard deviations of verification times in seconds across five runs of Dafny's entire test suite, with and without Dafny-generated triggers. The right figure shows that using Dafny-generated triggers yields a marked shift towards lower deviations (i.e. towards the top of the figure). (Color figure online)

many interesting patterns. Figure 2 shows detailed measurements for a few such examples. To produce it, we repeatedly ran Dafny in three distinct configurations:

- With Dafny-generated triggers, on a copy of the test suite modified to work with these new triggers (these modifications are described at the end of this section)
- Without Dafny-generated triggers, on the same modified test-suite
- Without Dafny-generated triggers, on the original test suite

In all three cases we ran Dafny 10 times, passing a new random seed to Z3's arithmetic, SMT and SAT modules on each run[3].

Figure 2 shows the performance and predictability consequences of automatically selecting triggers for a corpus of six example programs taken from Dafny's test suite. These programs are a mix of algorithms and submissions to various verification competitions, with about 100 to 300 lines of Dafny code each.

We conclude this section with a quick review of the changes that adapting the Dafny test suite to use our trigger generation strategy required. With automatically generated triggers, but no loop detection nor quantifier splitting, about 55 tests (out of 350) initially failed to verify. Adding matching loop detection fixed about 10. Adding quantifier splitting with trigger sharing fixed 10 more. For the remaining 35 tests, the causes were distributed as follows:

- About 10 tests were using explicitly recursive constructs, where matching loops were expected, and needed no changes beyond silencing warnings
- About 10 tests were implicitly relying on excessively liberal triggering to prove complex correspondences between expressions involving sequences (looking at a Z3 trace for the offending quantifier would show that Z3 was picking a very unspecific term to trigger on, and triggering a lot). Adding stricter triggering annotations caused these sequence equivalences to become unprovable; it was easy to fix these issues by adding extra annotations.

---

[3] The seeds used were 32901, 52510, 15712, 371, 65410, 21223, 38836, 27584, 7013, and 11502.

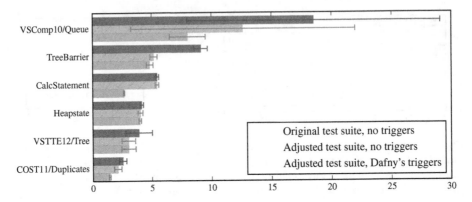

Fig. 2. Verification times in seconds for six example programs taken from Dafny's test suite, running the original Dafny on its test suite, our own version of Dafny with trigger generation turned off on an updated copy of the test suite, and our own version of Dafny with trigger generation turned on that same copy of the test suite. Error bars show the standard deviation of verification times across ten runs with distinct random seeds. (Color figure online)

- About 5 tests had unnecessary matching loops, which can be fixed by rephrasing quantifiers, thus acting upon the warning issued by our implementation.
- The rest had various issues, where specific properties were not being proved due to stricter triggering. In most cases, adding extra assertions was enough to lead Z3 to a proof, in a much more principled way that the haphazard matching that was occurring in the original Dafny.

Performance Results on Large Verification Efforts.

Focusing on verification performance, our second experiment pitted our implementation against the original Dafny to check the proofs of the implementation layer of IronFleet's IronRSL, a Paxos-based replicated-state-machine library. The focus of our attention was thus a collection of 48 source files totaling 13916 lines of Dafny source code. Figure 3 compares the running times of each of the 48 files with and without Dafny-generated triggers, sorted by descending relative improvement. Across the full corpus, our implementation achieves an overall speedup factor of 1.6, reducing the total running time from 1 hour and 4 min to 39 min. The average speedup across the test suite is 1.15, and the average speedup on tests that the change significantly affects (>20 % speedup or slowdown) is 1.45. These results are even more encouraging that these programs were written by experienced Dafny hackers.

Experience Report on Verifying a Simple Algorithm with and Without Dafny-Generated Triggers.

As a final experiment, we informally assessed the dynamic robustness of our new implementation. We verified a number of small programs using Dafny with auto-

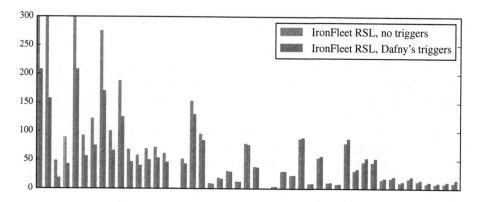

Fig. 3. Verification times in seconds for the 48 programs composing the implementation layer of IronRSL, with trigger generation at the Dafny level turned on and off. The experiment shows a significant speedup across the entire library, with programs that suffer from the change being only slowed down by a small proportion. (Color figure online)

generated triggers, including a Union-Find implementation. As we worked on it, we did not notice significant differences: everything was running smoothly, and Dafny was not reporting specific warnings about our quantifiers. Switching to a different environment, however, revealed how much Dafny-level triggers were doing for us: at multiple points we tried to verify the program without these auto-selected triggers; in most cases, verification simply timed out.

In total, it took about 10 h to write 330 lines of verified Dafny code. The program includes 25 universal quantifiers; checking its proofs takes 18 s with Dafny-generated triggers, and 31 s without. Most of the performance difference results from Z3 exploring fruitless paths due to overly permissive triggers.

Figure 4 shows an example of a quantifier annotation, displayed as an in-editor mouseover tooltip.

```
method Main() {
   assume ∀ x · P(x) ∧ (Q(x)⟹P(x+1));
}
       For expression "Q(x) ==> P(x + 1)":
          Selected triggers: {Q(x)}
          Rejected triggers: {P(x)} (may loop with "P(x + 1)")

       For expression "P(x)":
          Selected triggers:
             {Q(x)}, {P(x)}
```

Fig. 4. Emacs' *dafny-mode* (part of the *boogie-friends* package) showing a trigger-related message. Our code has correctly split the quantifier, adding two triggers ({P(x)} and {Q(x)}) to the first half, and a single one ({Q(x)}) to the second half, thus avoiding a matching loop. This type of information was useful for our Union-Find experiment.

5 Related Work

The idea of using matching triggers to instantiate quantifiers in SMT solvers stems from Nelson's PhD thesis [24] and they were first implemented in the SMT solver Simplify [11]. When a quantifier is not given an explicit trigger, Simplify attempts to select one. It first looks for single, minimal terms that can be used as triggers, and selects all of these, except ones that would give rise to a matching loop for the quantifier according to a simple heuristic. If no such triggers exist, then Simplify attempts to find a trigger with multiple terms. It only picks one multiple-term trigger in order to avoid having to consider exponentially many. In contrast, we may consider polynomially many. This gives us extra flexibility in trigger choices.

Z3 has a similar trigger-selection mechanism, but due to its more efficient matching technique [8], it does not make a hard distinction between single-term triggers and multiple-term triggers. On the downside, Z3 does not check for matching loops.

SMT solvers CVC4 [3] and Alt-Ergo [4] also support quantifiers and triggers. We have tried running Dafny with CVC4 version 1.4, which supports SMT-LIBv2 input. Unfortunately, this version of CVC4 fails to verify most of Dafny's test suite, except in tiny examples where the verification conditions do not involve any significant quantifiers. Some preliminary experiments with the upcoming version 1.5 show promise of being a viable alternative to Z3 for Dafny.

The program verifier VCC [7] also computes its own triggers for user-written quantifiers, rather than leaving this to the SMT solver. The selection criteria is aware of the VCC style of specifications and gives priority to certain terms, for example those that mention the special "ownership" field \owns or user-defined functions. The quantifiers are not rewritten for the purpose of finding better triggers, but some form of loop prevention is used.

There have been other attempts to rewrite verification conditions in order to make them perform better with SMT solvers. Böhme and Moskal measured the performance impact of different heap encodings [6]. In the context of Viper [23], Uri Juhasz has implemented Boogie-to-Boogie transformations that summarize in join nodes information common to all branches, which can reduce the need for case splits in the SMT solver and thus increase performance [17].

6 Future Work

While our work addresses the most prevalent source of verification instability we have found, there are other sources.

One other source that involves quantifiers involves a quantifier that many users write: expressing with a quantifier that an array is sorted

```
forall i · 0 ≤ i < a.Length - 1 ⟹ a[i] ≤ a[i+1]
```

For this quantifier, our technique reports that it cannot find a valid trigger without introducing a possible matching loop. This provides a noticeable improvement over Dafny's previous behavior of silently accepting the quantifier, because it calls to the user's attention the fact that the quantifier may cause problems for the verifier. We could, however, go one step further and rewrite the quantifier:

```
forall i,j · 0 ≤ i < a.Length - 1 ∧ j == i+1 ⟹ a[i] ≤ a[j]
```

The trigger {a[i], a[j]} for this quantifier has the nice property that the instantiations it causes do not introduce any more array-dereference terms. We would like to introduce automatic rewrites of this form, but have not yet implemented them.[4]

Such automatic rewrites of problematic quantifiers could be investigated systematically, and could be distributed as an auto-fix IDE feature: in cases where obtaining a confirmation from the user before doing a rewrite is desirable, we would display a tooltip offering the rewrite. Such an investigation would make for good future work.

Another source of verification instability is the use of non-linear arithmetic. To keep such issues manageable, the Ironclad Apps project chose to mostly turn off Z3's support of non-linear arithmetic and instead rely on manually crafted lemmas about the needed properties. Providing better automated and stable support for non-linear arithmetic remains fertile research ground.

Finally, we would like to comment on the fact that we have implemented our matching-loop detection inside Dafny on a per-quantifier basis. Our infrastructure has the basic building blocks for doing the matching-loop detection given a larger collection of quantifiers. Within Dafny, a possible extension of our work would be to look for possible matching loops within some cluster of declarations, for example among all loop invariants that a user has supplied for a loop; a significant difficulty would be to deal with the exponential number of combinations that arise from matching sequences involving triggers composed of multiple terms in multiple quantifiers.

Outside Dafny, matching-loop detection could do well at the Boogie or Z3 level. This would allow non-Dafny tools to benefit from this functionality. One could also imagine an automatic postmortem analysis of an SMT-solver run to detect loops that caused bad performance. Trying to prove the absence of matching loops in a given verification condition would be wonderful. This seems related to termination issues in rewriting systems (see, e.g., [10]), but we are unaware of any work that specifically addresses this problem for triggers where congruence closure is involved.

7   Conclusion

We have presented effective strategies for selecting matching triggers for quantifiers that make the proof search of SMT solvers better behaved, thus improving

---

[4] For this particular property, the quantifier `forall i,j · 0 ≤ i < j < a.Length ⟹ a[i] ≤ a[j]` is often even better, because it makes it more readily usable without having to appeal to transitivity of ≤ and induction.

the experience of users of automated program verifiers. Our implementation of these techniques in the Dafny program verifier demonstrates significant improvements in verification stability, verification performance, and proof elaboration and debugging experiences. We have received extremely positive feedback from early users of our implementation, on large verification efforts. By rewriting some quantifiers, our technique is able to select suitable triggers for quantifiers that otherwise would be ill-behaved or rejected for fear of matching loops. By applying our technique at the level of source expressions, we avoid triggering on parasitic terms introduced in the translation to first-order formulas, and obtain better-behaved triggers that we can directly report to users, thereby giving them meaningful feedback about the automatic trigger selection process.

We have tightened up a major source of verification instability. While other sources remain, we argue that our strategies are ready to be used in program verifiers and look forward to further stability improvements.

Acknowledgments. We are grateful to Chris Hawblitzel and Bryan Parno for productive discussions and feedback during the development of the auto-generated triggers and for help in setting up the IronFleets experiments, to Michał Moskal for his help in understanding how VCC generates triggers, and to Claire Dross and the anonymous reviewers for their comments on drafts of this paper. We also thank Andrew Reynolds for discussions about quantifiers and Dafny support in CVC4, Jay Lorch for his help testing the Dafny mode for Emacs, and Daan Leijen for typesetting assistance in Madoko. A special thanks goes to Jonathan Protzenko for connecting us authors and thus kickstarting this collaboration.

A   Pseudo-Code for the Main Algorithm

This annex offers high-level pseudo-code for the main algorithm introduced in this paper; it simplifies the types of many of the relevant functions for clarity, and glosses over most performance optimizations discussed in the body of the paper.

```
def AnnotateAndSplit(quantifier):
  AnnotateSubtree(quantifier.body, quantifier.variables)
  candidates = TriggerCandidates(quantifier)
  for split_q in SplitQuantifier(quantifier):
    safe_candidates = RemoveLoops(candidates, split_q)
    split_q.triggers = PickTriggers(safe_candidates)

def AnnotateSubtree(node, variables):
  for c in node.children:
    AnnotateSubtree(c, variables)
  if (node.type in KILLER_TYPES or
      any(c.annot == TriggerKiller for c in node.children)):
    node.annot = TriggerKiller
  elif any(node.mentions(v) or any(c.mentions(v) for c in node.children)
```

```
            for v in variables):
      node.annot = TriggerHead


def TriggerCandidates(quantifier):
  for subset in Subsets(quantifier.trigger_heads):
    # Adequacy: All quantified variables are mentionned
    if is_adequate(subset, quantifier.variables):
      # Parsimony: No term can be removed without breaking adequacy
      if not is_redundant(subset):
        yield TriggerCandidate(subset)


def SplitQuantifier(quantifier):
  if quantifier.type == ForallNode:
    if quantifier.body.type == AndNode:
      for c in quantifier.body.children:
        yield ForallNode(c, quantifier.variables)
    else: yield quantifier
    # (... Similar case of existential quantifiers omitted)


def RemoveLoops(candidates, split_quantifier):
  for candidate in candidates:
    matches = []
    for term in candidate.terms:
      for desc in split_quantifier.descendants:
        if desc.can_unify_with(term, split_quantifier.variables):
          if not FalsePositive(desc, term, candidate):
            matches.append(desc)
    if not any(matches): yield candidate


def FalsePositive(desc, term, candidate):
  return (desc == term or desc in candidate.terms or
          all(is_var(t) or is_const(t) for t in term.disjoint_union(desc)))


def PickTriggers(candidates):
  for candidate in candidates:
    if not any(candidate.more_specific_than(other) for other in candidates):
      yield candidate
```

References

1. Amin, N., Leino, K.R.M., Rompf, T.: Computing with an SMT solver. In: Seidl, M., Tillmann, N. (eds.) TAP 2014. LNCS, vol. 8570, pp. 20–35. Springer, Heidelberg (2014)
2. Barnett, M., Chang, B.-Y.E., DeLine, R., Jacobs, B., M. Leino, K.R.: Boogie: a modular reusable verifier for object-oriented programs. In: de Boer, F.S., Bonsangue, M.M., Graf, S., de Roever, W.-P. (eds.) FMCO 2005. LNCS, vol. 4111, pp. 364–387. Springer, Heidelberg (2006)

3. Barrett, C., Conway, C.L., Deters, M., Hadarean, L., Jovanović, D., King, T., Reynolds, A., Tinelli, C.: CVC4. In: Gopalakrishnan, G., Qadeer, S. (eds.) CAV 2011. LNCS, vol. 6806, pp. 171–177. Springer, Heidelberg (2011)

4. Bobot, F., Conchon, S., Contejean, É., Lescuyer, S.: Implementing polymorphism in SMT solvers. In: Barrett, C., de Moura, L., (eds.) SMT 2008: 6th International Workshop on Satisfiability Modulo Theories, pp. 1–5 (2008)

5. Bobot, F., Filliâtre, J.-C., Marché, C., Melquiond, G., Paskevich, A.: Preserving user proofs across specification changes. In: Cohen, E., Rybalchenko, A. (eds.) VSTTE 2013. LNCS, vol. 8164, pp. 191–201. Springer, Heidelberg (2014)

6. Böhme, S., Moskal, M.: Heaps and data structures: a challenge for automated provers. In: Bjørner, N., Sofronie-Stokkermans, V. (eds.) CADE 2011. LNCS, vol. 6803, pp. 177–191. Springer, Heidelberg (2011)

7. Cohen, E., Dahlweid, M., Hillebrand, M., Leinenbach, D., Moskal, M., Santen, T., Schulte, W., Tobies, S.: VCC: a practical system for verifying concurrent C. In: Berghofer, S., Nipkow, T., Urban, C., Wenzel, M. (eds.) TPHOLs 2009. LNCS, vol. 5674, pp. 23–42. Springer, Heidelberg (2009)

8. de Moura, L., Bjørner, N.S.: Efficient E-Matching for SMT solvers. In: Pfenning, F. (ed.) CADE 2007. LNCS (LNAI), vol. 4603, pp. 183–198. Springer, Heidelberg (2007)

9. de Moura, L., Bjørner, N.S.: Z3: an efficient SMT solver. In: Ramakrishnan, C.R., Rehof, J. (eds.) TACAS 2008. LNCS, vol. 4963, pp. 337–340. Springer, Heidelberg (2008)

10. Dershowitz, N.: Termination of rewriting. J. Symbolic Comput. 3(1/2), 69–116 (1987)

11. Detlefs, D., Nelson, G., James, B.: Saxe.: simplify: a theorem prover for program checking. J. ACM 52(3), 365–473 (2005)

12. Downey, P.J., Sethi, R., Tarjan, R.E.: Variations on the common subexpression problem. J. ACM 27(4), 758–771 (1980)

13. Dross, C., Conchon, S., Kanig, J., Paskevich, A.: Reasoning with triggers. In: Fontaine, P., Goel, A., (eds.) 10th International Workshop on Satisfiability Modulo Theories, SMT 2012, vol. 20 of EPiC, pp. 22–31. EasyChair, June–July 2013

14. Dross, C., Efstathopoulos, P., Lesens, D., Mentré, D., Moy, Y.: Rail, space, security: three case studies for SPARK 2014. In: 7th Europen Congress on Embedded Real Time Software and Systems (ERTS² 2014) 2014

15. Hawblitzel, C., Howell, J., Kapritsos, M., Lorch, J.R., Parno, B., Roberts, M.L., Setty, S., Zill, B.: IronFleet: proving practical distributed systems correct. In: Proceedings of the ACM Symposium on Operating Systems Principles (SOSP), ACM October 2015

16. Jacobs, B., Piessens, F.: The VeriFast program verifier. Technical report CW-520, Department of Computer Science, Katholieke Universiteit Leuven August 2008

17. Juhasz, U.: Boogie-to-Boogie transformations to speed up SMT solving. Personal communication (2015)

18. Kirchner, F., Kosmatov, N., Prevosto, V., Signoles, J., Yakobowski, B.: Frama-C: a software analysis perspective. Form. Aspects Comput. 27(3), 573–609 (2015)

19. Leino, K.R.M.: Dafny: an automatic program verifier for functional correctness. In: Clarke, E.M., Voronkov, A. (eds.) LPAR-16 2010. LNCS, vol. 6355, pp. 348–370. Springer, Heidelberg (2010)

20. Leino, K.R.M., Rümmer, P.: A polymorphic intermediate verification language: design and logical encoding. In: Esparza, J., Majumdar, R. (eds.) TACAS 2010. LNCS, vol. 6015, pp. 312–327. Springer, Heidelberg (2010)

21. Leino, K.R.M., Wüstholz, V.: Fine-grained caching of verification results. In: Kroening, D., Păsăreanu, C.S. (eds.) CAV 2015. LNCS, vol. 9206, pp. 380–397. Springer, Heidelberg (2015)

22. Moskal, M.: Programming with triggers. In: Dutertre, B., Strichman, O., (eds.) SMT 2009, 7th International Workshop on Satisfiability Modulo Theories, August 2009

23. Müller, P., Schwerhoff, M., Summers, A.J.: Viper: a verification infrastructure for permission-based reasoning. In: Jobstmann, B., et al. (eds.) VMCAI 2016. LNCS, vol. 9583, pp. 41–62. Springer, Heidelberg (2016). doi:10.1007/978-3-662-49122-5_2

24. Charles Gregory Nelson: Techniques for program verification. Technical report CSL-81-10, Xerox PARC, The author's PhD thesis June 1981

25. Nelson, G., Oppen, D.C.: Simplification by cooperating decision procedures. ACM Trans. Program. Lang. Syst. 1(2), 245–257 (1979)

26. Tschannen, J., Furia, C.A., Nordio, M., Polikarpova, N.: AutoProof: auto-active functional verification of object-oriented programs. In: Baier, C., Tinelli, C. (eds.) TACAS 2015. LNCS, vol. 9035, pp. 566–580. Springer, Heidelberg (2015)

Satisfiability Modulo Heap-Based Programs

Quang Loc Le[1(✉)], Jun Sun[1], and Wei-Ngan Chin[2]

[1] Singapore University of Technology and Design,
Singapore, Singapore
lequangloc@gmail.com
[2] National University of Singapore,
Singapore, Singapore

Abstract. In this work, we present a semi-decision procedure for a fragment of separation logic with user-defined predicates and Presburger arithmetic. To check the satisfiability of a formula, our procedure iteratively unfolds the formula and examines the derived disjuncts. In each iteration, it searches for a proof of either satisfiability or unsatisfiability. Our procedure is further enhanced with automatically inferred invariants as well as detection of cyclic proof. We also identify a syntactically restricted fragment of the logic for which our procedure is terminating and thus complete. This decidable fragment is relatively expressive as it can capture a range of sophisticated data structures with non-trivial pure properties, such as size, sortedness and near-balanced. We have implemented the proposed solver and a new system for verifying heap-based programs. We have evaluated our system on benchmark programs from a software verification competition.

Keywords: Decision procedures · Satisfiability · Separation logic · Inductive predicates · Cyclic proofs

1 Introduction

Satisfiability solvers, particularly those based on Satisfiability Modulo Theory (SMT) technology [3,19], have made tremendous practical advances in the last decade to the point where they are now widely used in tools for applications as diverse as bug finding [27], program analyses [4] to automated verification [2]. However, current SMT solvers are based primarily on first-order logic, and do not yet cater to the needs of resource-oriented logics, such as separation logic [26,40]. Separation logic has recently established a solid reputation for reasoning about programs that manipulate heap-based data structures. One of its strengths is the ability to concisely and locally describe program states that hold in separate regions of heap memory. In particular, a spatial conjunction (i.e., $\kappa_1*\kappa_2$) asserts that a given heap can be decomposed into two disjoint regions and the formulas, κ_1 and κ_2, hold respectively and separately in the two memory regions. In this work, we investigate the problem of verifying heap-manipulating programs in the

© Springer International Publishing Switzerland 2016
S. Chaudhuri and A. Farzan (Eds.): CAV 2016, Part I, LNCS 9779, pp. 382–404, 2016.
DOI: 10.1007/978-3-319-41528-4_21

framework of SMT. We reduce this problem to solving verification conditions representing precise program semantics [9,10,22,44].

Developing an SMT solver supporting separation logic with inductive predicates and Presburger arithmetic is challenging as the satisfiability problem for this fragment is undecidable [30,31]. We focus on an expressive fragment which consists of spatial predicates expressing empty heap assertion (emp), points-to assertion $(x \mapsto c(\bar{v}))$, and inductive predicate assertions $(P(\bar{v}))$. Moreover, it may include pure constraints on data values and capture desired properties of structural heaps (such as size, height, sortedness and even near-balanced tree properties). We thus face the challenge of handling recursive predicates with pure properties, that are inherently infinite. Furthermore, we would like to support both satisfiability (SAT) and unsatisfiability (UNSAT) checks.

There have been a number of preliminary attempts in this direction. For instance, early proposals *fixed* the set of shape predicates that may be used, for example, to linked lists (in SeLoger [17,23], and SLLB [34]) or trees (GRIT [36]). There are few approaches supporting user-defined predicates [14,25,39]. Brotherston *et al.* recently made an important contribution by introducing SLSAT, a decision procedure for a fragment of separation logic with arbitrary *shape-only* inductive predicates [12]. However, SLSAT is limited to the shape domain, whereas shape predicates extended with pure properties are often required for automated verification of functional correctness.

In this paper, we start by proposing a new procedure, called S2SAT, which combines under-approximation and over-approximation for simultaneously checking SAT and UNSAT properties for a sound and complete theory augmented with inductive predicates. S2SAT takes a set of user-defined predicates and a logic formula as inputs. It iteratively constructs *an unfolding tree* by unfolding the formula in a breadth-first, flow- and context-sensitive manner until either a symbolic model, or a proof of unsatisfiability or a fixpoint (e.g., a cyclic proof) is identified. In each iteration, it searches over the leaves of the tree (the disjunction of which is equivalent to the input formula) to check whether there is a satisfiable leaf (which proves satisfiability) or whether all leaves are unsatisfiable. In particular, to prove SAT, it considers *base disjuncts* which are derived from base-case branches of the predicates. These disjuncts are under-approximations of the input formula and critical for satisfiability. Disjuncts which have no inductive predicates are precisely decided. To prove UNSAT, S2SAT over-approximates the leaves prior to prove UNSAT. Our procedure systematically enumerates all disjuncts derived from a given inductive formula, so it is terminating for SAT. However, it may not be terminating for UNSAT with those undecidable augmented logic. To facilitate termination, we propose an approach for fixpoint computation. This fixpoint computation is useful for domains with finite model semantics i.e., collecting semantics for a given formula of such domains is finite. In other words, the input formula is unsatisfiable when the unfolding goes on forever without uncovering any models. We have implemented one instantiation of the fixpoint detection for inductive proving based on cyclic proof [13] s.t. the soundness of the cyclic proof guarantees the well-foundedness of all reasoning.

```
struct node {int val; node next;}    8  node ll(int i){
1 int main(int n){                    9    if(i==0) return null;
2  if(n<0) return 0;                 10    else return new node(i,ll(i−1)); }
3  node x=ll(n);
4  int r=test(x);                    11 int test(node p){
5  if(!r) ERROR();                   12   if(p==null) return 1;
6  return 1;                         13   else {if(p->val<0) return 0;
7 }                                  14        else return test(p->next); }}
```

Fig. 1. Motivating example.

To explicitly handle heap-manipulating programs, we propose a separation logic instantiation of S2SAT, called S2SAT$_{SL}$. Our base theory is a combination of the aforementioned separation logic predicates except inductive predicates. We show that our decision procedure for this base theory is sound and complete. S2SAT$_{SL}$ over-approximates formulas with soundly inferred predicate invariants. In addition, we describe some syntax restrictions such that S2SAT$_{SL}$ is always able to construct a cyclic proof for a restricted formula so that our procedure is terminating and complete.

To summarize, we make the following technical contributions in this work.

- We introduce cyclic proof into a satisfiability procedure for a base theory augmented with inductive predicates (refer to Sect. 3).
- We propose a satisfiability procedure for separation logic with user-defined predicates and Presburger arithmetic (Sect. 4).
- We prove that S2SAT$_{SL}$ is: (i) sound for SAT and UNSAT; (ii) and terminating (i.e., proposing a new decision procedure) for restricted fragments (Sect. 5).
- We present a mechanism to automatically derive sound (over-approximated) invariants for user-defined predicates (Sect. 6).
- We have implemented the satisfiability solver S2SAT$_{SL}$ and the new verification system, called S2$_{td}$. We evaluated S2SAT$_{SL}$ and S2$_{td}$ with benchmarks from recent competitions. The experimental results show that our system is expressive, robust and efficient (Sect. 7).

Proofs of Lemmas and Theorems presented in this paper are available in the companion technical report [30].

2 Illustrative Example

We illustrate how our approach works with the example shown in Fig. 1. Our verification system proves that this program is memory safe and function ERROR() (line 5) is never called. Our system uses symbolic execution in [6,14] and large-block encoding [8] to provide a semantic encoding of verification conditions. For safety, one of the generated verification conditions is: $\Delta_0 \equiv ll(n,x)_0^0 * test(x,r_1)_0^1 \wedge n \geq 0 \wedge r_1 = 0$. If Δ_0 is unsatisfiable, function ERROR() is never called. In Δ_0, ll and test are Interprocedural Control Flow Graph (ICFG) of the functions ll and $test$. Our system eludes these ICFGs as inductive predicates. For each predicate, a parameter res is appended at the end to model the return value of the function; for instance, the variables x (in ll) and r_1 (in $test$) of Δ_0 are the actual parameters corresponding to res. Each inductive predicate instance is also labeled with a subscript for the unfolding number and a superscript for the sequence number, which are used to control the unfolding in a breadth-first and flow-sensitive manner.

To discharge Δ_0, S2SAT$_{SL}$ iteratively derives a series of unfolding trees $\mathcal{T}_i$. An unfolding tree is a tree such that each node is labeled with an unfolded disjunct, corresponding to a path condition in the program. We say that a leaf of $\mathcal{T}_i$ is closed if it is unsatisfiable; otherwise it is open. During each iteration, S2SAT$_{SL}$ either proves SAT by identifying a satisfiable leaf of $\mathcal{T}_i$ which contains no user-defined predicate instances or proves UNSAT by showing that an over-approximation of all leaves is unsatisfiable. Initially, $\mathcal{T}_0$ contains only one node Δ_0. As Δ_0 contains inductive predicates, it is not considered for proving SAT. S2SAT$_{SL}$ then over-approximates Δ_0 to a first-order logic formula by substituting each predicate instance with its corresponding sound invariants in order to prove UNSAT. We assume that ll (resp. $test$) is annotated with invariant $i{\geq}0$ (resp. $0{\leq}res{\leq}1$). Hence, the over-approximation of Δ_0 is computed as: $\pi_0{\equiv}n{\geq}0{\wedge}0{\leq}r_1{\leq}1{\wedge}n{\geq}0{\wedge}r_1{=}0$. Formula π_0 is then passed to an SMT solver, such as Z3 [19], for unsatisfiable checking. As expected, π_0 is not unsatisfiable.

Next, S2SAT$_{SL}$ selects an open leaf for unfolding to derive $\mathcal{T}_1$. A leaf is selected in a breadth-first manner; furthermore a predicate instance of the selected leaf is selected for unfolding if its sequence number is the smallest. With Δ_0, the ll instance is selected. As so, $\mathcal{T}_1$ has two open leaves corresponding to two derived disjuncts:

$$\Delta_{11}{\equiv}test(x,r_1)_0^1{\wedge}n{\geq}0{\wedge}r_1{=}0{\wedge}n{=}0{\wedge}x{=}\texttt{null}$$
$$\Delta_{12}{\equiv}x{\mapsto}node(n,r_2){*}ll(n_1,r_2)_1^0{*}test(x,r_1)_0^1{\wedge}n{\geq}0{\wedge}r_1{=}0{\wedge}n{\neq}0{\wedge}n_1{=}n{-}1$$

Since Δ_{11} and Δ_{12} include predicate instances, they are not considered for SAT. To prove UNSAT, S2SAT$_{SL}$ computes their over-approximated invariants:

$$\pi_{11}{\equiv}0{\leq}r_1{\leq}1{\wedge}n{\geq}0{\wedge}r_1{=}0{\wedge}n{=}0{\wedge}x{=}\texttt{null}$$
$$\pi_{12}{\equiv}x{\neq}\texttt{null}{\wedge}n_1{\geq}0{\wedge}0{\leq}r_1{\leq}1{\wedge}n{\geq}0{\wedge}r_1{=}0{\wedge}n{\neq}0{\wedge}n_1{=}n{-}1$$

As neither π_{11} nor π_{12} is unsatisfiable, S2SAT$_{SL}$ selects $test$ of Δ_{11} for unfolding to construct $\mathcal{T}_2$. For efficiency, unfolding is performed in a context-sensitive manner. A branch is infeasible (and pruned in advance) if its invariant is inconsistent with the (over-approximated) context. For instance, the invariant of the $then$ branch at line 12 of $test$ is $inv_{test_o}{\equiv}p{=}\texttt{null}{\wedge}res{=}1$. As inv_{test_o} (after proper renaming) is inconsistent with π_{11}, this branch is infeasible. Similarly, both $else$ branches of $test$ are infeasible. For $\mathcal{T}_3$,

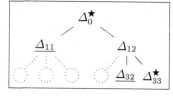

Fig. 2. Unfolding tree $\mathcal{T}_3$.

the remaining leaf Δ_{12} is selected for unfolding. As the test's unfolding number is smaller than 11's, test is selected. After the then branch is identified as infeasible and pruned, $\mathcal{T}_3$ is left with two open leaves as shown in Fig. 2, where infeasible leaves are dotted-lined. Δ_{32} and Δ_{33} are as below.

$$\Delta_{32} \equiv x \mapsto node(n,r_2)*ll(n_1,r_2)_1^0 \wedge \underline{n \geq 0} \wedge r_1 = 0 \wedge n \neq 0 \wedge n_1 = n-1 \wedge x \neq \mathtt{null} \wedge \underline{n < 0} \wedge r_1 = 0$$
$$\Delta_{33} \equiv x \mapsto node(n,r_2)*ll(n_1,r_2)_1^0 *test(r_2,r_1)_1^1 \wedge n \geq 0 \wedge r_1 = 0 \wedge n \neq 0 \wedge n_1 = n-1$$
$$\wedge x \neq \mathtt{null} \wedge n \geq 0$$

As Δ_{32} and Δ_{33} include inductive predicate instances, SAT checking is not applicable. For UNSAT checking, S2SAT$_{\mathrm{SL}}$ proves that Δ_{32} is unsatisfiable (its unsatisfiable cores are underlined as above); and shows that Δ_{33} can be linked back to Δ_0 (i.e., subsumed by Δ_0). The latter is shown based on some weakening and substitution principles (see Sect. 4.2). In particular: (i) Substituting Δ_{33} with $\theta = [n_2/n, x_1/x, n/n_1, x/r_2]$ such that predicate instances in the substituted formula, i.e., Δ_{33_a}, and Δ_0 are identical; as such, Δ_{33_a} is computed as below.

$$\Delta_{33_a} \equiv x_1 \mapsto node(n_2,x)*ll(n,x)_1^0 *test(x,r_1)_1^1 \wedge n_2 \geq 0 \wedge r_1 = 0 \wedge n_2 \neq 0 \wedge n = n_2-1$$
$$\wedge x_1 \neq \mathtt{null} \wedge n_2 \geq 0$$

(ii) subtracting identical inductive predicates between Δ_{33_a} and Δ_0; (iii) weakening the remainder of Δ_{33_a} (i.e., $x_1 \mapsto node(n_2,x)$ is eliminated); (iv) checking validity of the implication between pure of the remainder of Δ_{33_a} with the pure part of the remainder of Δ_0, i.e., $n_2 \geq 0 \wedge r_1 = 0 \wedge n_2 \neq 0 \wedge n = n_2 - 1 \wedge x_1 \neq \mathtt{null} \wedge n_2 \geq 0 \implies n \geq 0 \wedge r_1 = 0$. The back-link between Δ_{33} and Δ_0 establishes a cyclic proof which then proves Δ_0 is unsatisfiable.

Algorithm 1. S2SAT Procedure.

```
    input  : λ^ind
    output: SAT or UNSAT
1   i←0; T_0←{λ^ind} ;                                    /* initialize */
2   while true do
3   │   (is_sat,T_i) ← UA_test(T_i) ;                     /* check SAT */
4   │   if is_sat then return SAT ;                       /* SAT */
5   │   else
6   │   │   T_i←OA_test(T_i) ;                            /* prune UNSAT */
7   │   │   T_i←link_back(T_i) ;                          /* detect fixpoint */
8   │   │   if is_closed(T_i) then return UNSAT;          /* UNSAT */
9   │   │   else
10  │   │   │   λ^ind_i←choose_bfs(T_i) ;                 /* choose an open leaf */
11  │   │   │   i←i+1 ;
12  │   │   │   T_i←unfold(λ^ind_i);
13  │   │   end
14  │   end
15  end
```

---

3 S2SAT Algorithm

In this section, we present S2SAT, a procedure for checking satisfiability of formula with inductive predicates. We start by defining our target formulas. Let $\mathcal{L}$ be a *base theory* (logic) with the following properties: (i) $\mathcal{L}$ is closed under propositional combination and supports boolean variables; (ii) there exists a complete decision procedure for $\mathcal{L}$. Let $\mathcal{L}^{ind}$ be the extension of $\mathcal{L}$ with inductive predicate instances defined in a system with a set of predicates $\mathcal{P}=\{P_1, ..., P_k\}$. Each predicate may be annotated with a *sound* invariant. We use λ to denote a formula in $\mathcal{L}$ and λ^{ind} to denote a formula in the extended theory. Semantically, $\lambda^{ind} \equiv \bigvee_{i=0}^{n} \lambda_i$, $n \geq 0$.

S2SAT is presented in Algorithm 1. S2SAT takes a formula λ^{ind} as input, systematically enumerates disjuncts λ_i and can produce two possible outcomes if it terminates: SAT with a satisfiable formula λ_i or UNSAT with a proof. We remark that non-termination is classified as UNKNOWN.

S2SAT maintains a set of open leaves of the unfolding tree $\mathcal{T}_i$ that is derived from λ^{ind}. In each iteration, S2SAT selects and unfolds an open leaf so as either to include more reachable base formulas (with the hope to produce a SAT answer), or to refine inductive formulas (with the hope to produce an UNSAT answer). Specially, in each iteration, S2SAT checks whether the formula is SAT at line 3; whether it is UNSAT at line 6; whether a fixpoint can be established at line 7. Function UA_test searches for a satisfiable *base* disjunct (i.e., is_sat is set to true). Simultaneously, it marks all unsatisfiable base disjuncts *closed*. Next, function OA_test uses predicate invariants to over-approximate open leaves of $\mathcal{T}_i$, and marks those with an *unsatisfiable* over-approximation closed. After that, function link_back attempts to link remaining open leaves back to interior nodes so as to form a fixpoint (i.e., a (partial) pre-proof for induction proving). The leaves which have been linked back are also marked as closed. Whenever all leaves are closed, S2SAT decides λ^{ind} as UNSAT (line 8). Otherwise, the choose_bfs (line 10) chooses an *open* leave in breadth-first manner for unfolding.

Procedure link_back takes the unfolding tree $\mathcal{T}_i$ as input and checks whether each open leaf $\lambda^{ind^{bud}} \in \mathcal{T}_i$ matches with one interior node $\lambda^{ind^{comp}}$ in $\mathcal{T}_i$ via a *matching function* f_{fix}. f_{fix} is based on weakening and substitution principles [13]. Intuitively, f_{fix} detects the case of (i) the unfolding goes forever if we keep unfolding $\lambda^{ind^{bud}}$; and (ii) $\lambda^{ind^{bud}}$ has no model when $\lambda^{ind^{comp}}$ has no model. If $f_{fix}(\lambda^{ind^{bud}}, \Delta^{comp})$=true, Δ^{bud} is marked closed.

Our procedure systematically enumerates all disjuncts derived from a given inductive formula, so it is terminating for SAT. However, it may not be terminating for UNSAT with those undecidable augmented logic. In the next paragraph, we discuss the soundness of the algorithm.

Soundness. When S2SAT terminates, there are the following three cases.

- (case A) S2SAT produces SAT with a base satisfiable λ^{ind}_i;

- (case B) S2SAT produces UNSAT with a proof that all leaves of $\mathcal{T}_i$ are unsatisfiable;
- (case C) S2SAT produces UNSAT with a fixpoint: a proof that some leaves of $\mathcal{T}_i$ are unsatisfiable and the remaining leaves are linked back.

Under the assumption that $\mathcal{L}$ is both sound and complete, case A can be shown to be sound straightforwardly. Soundness of case B immediately follows the soundness of OA_test. In the following, we describe the cyclic proof instantiation of link_back for fixpoint detection and prove the soundness of case C.

We use CYCLIC to denote the cyclic proof for entailment procedure adapted from [13]. The following definitions are adapted from their analogues of CYCLIC.

Definition 1 (Pre-Proof). *A pre-proof derived for a formula λ^{ind} is a pair $(\mathcal{T}_i, \mathcal{L})$ where $\mathcal{T}_i$ is an unfolding tree whose root labelled by λ^{ind} and $\mathcal{L}$ is a back-link function assigning every open leaf $\lambda^{ind}{}_l$ of $\mathcal{T}_i$ to an interior node $\lambda^{ind}{}_c = \mathcal{L}(\lambda^{ind}{}_l)$ such that there exists some substitution θ i.e., $\lambda^{ind}{}_c = \lambda^{ind}{}_l[\theta]$. $\lambda^{ind}{}_l$ is referred as a bud and $\lambda^{ind}{}_c$ is referred as its companion.*

A *path* in a pre-proof is a sequence of nodes $(\lambda^{ind}{}_i)_{i \geq 0}$.

Definition 2 (Trace). *Let $(\lambda^{ind}{}_i)_{i \geq 0}$ be a path in a pre-proof $\mathcal{PP}$. A trace following $(\lambda^{ind}{}_i)_{i \geq 0}$ is a sequence $(\alpha_i)_{i \geq 0}$ such that, for all $i \geq 0$, α_i is a predicate instance $P(\bar{t})$ in the formula $\lambda^{ind}{}_i$, and either:*

1. *α_{i+1} is the subformula according to $P(\bar{t})$ occurrence in $\lambda^{ind}{}_{i+1}$, or*
2. *$\lambda^{ind}{}_i[\bar{t}/\bar{v}]$ where $\lambda^{ind}{}_i$ is branches of inductive predicate $P(\bar{v})$. i is a progressing point of the trace.*

To ensure that pre-proofs correspond to sound proofs, a global *soundness condition* must be imposed on such pre-proofs as follows.

Definition 3 (Cyclic Proof). *A pre-proof is a cyclic proof if, for every infinite path $(\lambda^{ind}{}_i)_{i \geq 0}$, there is a tail of the path $p = (\lambda^{ind}{}_i)_{i \geq n}$ such that there is an infinitely progressing trace following p.*

Theorem 1 (Soundness). *If there is a cyclic proof of $\lambda^{ind}{}_0$, $\lambda^{ind}{}_0$ is UNSAT.*

Proof. We reduce our cyclic proof problem for satisfiability to the cyclic proof problem for entailment check, i.e., $\lambda^{ind}{}_0 \vdash \mathtt{false}$ of CYCLIC. Assume there is a cyclic proof $\mathcal{PP}$ of $\lambda^{ind}{}_0$. From $\mathcal{PP}$ we construct the pre-proof $\mathcal{PP}_\vdash$ for the sequent $\lambda^{ind}{}_0 \vdash \mathtt{false}$ as follows. For each node $(\lambda^{ind}{}_i)_{i \geq 0}$ in $\mathcal{PP}$, we replace the formula $\lambda^{ind}{}_i$ by the sequent $\lambda^{ind}{}_i \vdash \mathtt{false}$. Since $\mathcal{PP}$ is a cyclic proof, it follows that for every infinite path $(\lambda^{ind}{}_i)_{i \geq 0}$, there is a tail of the path, $p = (\lambda^{ind}{}_i)_{i \geq n}$, such that there is an infinitely progressing trace following p (Definition 3). Since formulas in [13] are only traced through the LHS of the sequent and not its RHS, it is implied that for every infinite path $(\lambda^{ind}{}_i \vdash \mathtt{false})_{i \geq 0}$, there is a tail of the path, $p = (\lambda^{ind}{}_i \vdash \mathtt{false})_{i \geq n}$, such that there is an infinitely progressing trace following p. Thus, $\mathcal{PP}_\vdash$ is a cyclic proof (Definition 3 of [13]). As such $\lambda^{ind}{}_0 \models \mathtt{false}$ (Theorem 6 of [13]). In other words, $\lambda^{ind}{}_0$ is UNSAT. $\square$

To sum up, to implement a sound cyclic proof system besides the matching function, a global *soundness condition* must be established on pre-proofs to guarantee well-foundedness of all reasoning.

4   Separation Logic Instantiation of S2SAT

In this section, to explicitly handle heap-manipulating programs, we propose a separation logic instantiation of S2SAT, called S2SAT$_{SL}$. We start by presenting SLPA, a fragment of separation logic with inductive predicates and arithmetic.

4.1   A Fragment of Separation Logic

Syntax. The syntax of SLPA formulas is presented in Fig. 3. We use $\bar{x}$ to denote a sequence (e.g., $\bar{v}$ for sequence of variables), and x_i to denote the ith element. Whenever possible, we discard f_i of the points-to predicate and use its short form as $x \mapsto c(v_i)$. Note that $v_1 \neq v_2$ and $v \neq \texttt{null}$ are short forms for $\neg(v_1 = v_2)$ and $\neg(v = \texttt{null})$, respectively. All free variables are implicitly universally quantified at the outermost level. To express different scenarios for shape predicates, the fragment supports disjunction Φ over formulas. Each predicate instance is of the form $P(\bar{v})_u^o$ where o and u are labels used for context- and flow- sensitive unfolding. In particular, o captures the sequence number and u is the number of unfolding. For simplicity, we occasionally omit these two numbers if there is no ambiguity. A formula Δ is a *base formula* if it does not have any user-defined predicate instances. Otherwise, Δ is an *inductive formula*.

User-Defined Predicate. A user-defined predicate P is of the following general form

$$\texttt{pred } P(\bar{t}) \equiv \bigvee_{i=1}^{n} (\exists \bar{w}_i \cdot \Delta_i \mid \pi_i^b) \quad \overline{inv}: \pi;$$

Formula	$\Phi ::= \Delta \mid \Phi_1 \vee \Phi_2 \qquad \Delta ::= \exists \bar{v} \cdot (\kappa \wedge \pi)$
Spatial formula	$\kappa ::= \texttt{emp} \mid x \mapsto c(f_i{:}v_i) \mid P(\bar{v})_u^o \mid \kappa_1 * \kappa_2$
Pure formula	$\pi ::= \pi_1 \wedge \pi_2 \mid b \mid \alpha \mid \phi$
Ptr (Dis)Equality	$\alpha ::= v_1 = v_2 \mid v = \texttt{null} \mid v_1 \neq v_2 \mid v \neq \texttt{null} \mid \alpha_1 \wedge \alpha_2$
Presburger arith.	$\phi ::= i \mid \exists v \cdot \phi \mid \neg \phi \mid \phi_1 \wedge \phi_2 \mid \phi_1 \vee \phi_2$
Boolean formula	$b ::= \texttt{true} \mid \texttt{false} \mid v \mid b_1 = b_2$
Linear arithmetic	$i ::= a_1 = a_2 \mid a_1 \leq a_2$
	$a ::= k^{\text{int}} \mid v \mid k^{\text{int}} \times a \mid a_1 + a_2 \mid -a \mid max(a_1, a_2) \mid min(a_1, a_2)$
$P \in \mathcal{P} \quad c \in Node \quad f_i \in Fields \quad v, v_i, x, y, \textbf{res}, \textbf{res}' \in Var \quad \bar{v} \equiv v_1, \dots, v_n$	

Fig. 3. Syntax.

where P is predicate name; $\bar{t}$ is a set of formal parameters; and $\exists \bar{w}_i \cdot \Delta_i$ ($i \in 1...n$) is a branch. Each branch is optionally annotated with a sound invariant π_i^b which is a pure formula that over-approximates the branch. π is an optionally sound *predicate invariant*. It must be a superset of all possible models of the predicate P via a pure constraint on stack. The default invariant of each inductive predicate is true. For efficiency, we infer more precise invariants automatically (see Sect. 6). Inductive branches may be recursive. We assume that the recursion is direct, i.e., a recursive branch of predicate P includes at least one predicate instance P. In each branch, we require that variables which are not formal parameters must be existentially quantified i.e., $\forall i \in 1...n \cdot FV(\Delta_i) = \bar{t}$ and $\bar{w}_i \cap \bar{t} = \emptyset$ where $FV(\Delta)$ are all free variables in the formula Δ.

In the following, we apply SLPA to model two data structures: sorted lists (sortll) without an annotated invariant and AVL trees (avl) with annotated-invariant.

$$\text{pred sortll}(\text{root},n,m) \equiv \text{root} \mapsto node(m, \text{null}) \wedge n{=}1$$
$$\vee \ \exists \ q,n_1,m_1 \cdot \text{root} \mapsto node(m,q) * \text{sortll}(q,n_1,m_1) \wedge n{=}n_1{+}1 \wedge m{\leq}m_1$$

$$\text{struct } c_2 \ \{ \ c_2 \text{ left}; \ c_2 \text{ right}; \} \ // \textit{ data structure declaration}$$
$$\text{pred avl}(\text{root},n,h) \equiv \text{emp} \wedge \text{root}{=}\text{null} \wedge n{=}0 \wedge h{=}0 \ | \ \text{root}{=}\text{null} \wedge n{=}0 \wedge h{=}0$$
$$\vee \ \exists \ l,r,n_1,n_2,h_1,h_2 \cdot \text{root} \mapsto c_2(l,r) * \text{avl}(l,n_1,h_1) * \text{avl}(r,n_2,h_2) \wedge$$
$$n{=}n_1{+}n_2{+}1 \wedge h{=}\max(h_1,h_2){+}1 \wedge -1{\leq}h_1{-}h_2{\leq}1 \ | \ \text{root}{\neq}\text{null} \wedge n{>}0 \wedge h{>}0$$
$$\overline{inv}: n{\geq}0 \wedge h{\geq}0$$

Semantics. In the following, we discuss the semantics of SLPA. Concrete heap models assume a fixed finite collection *Node*, a fixed finite collection *Fields*, a disjoint set *Loc* of locations (heap addresses), a set of non-address values *Val*, such that null $\in$ *Val* and *Val* $\cap$ *Loc* $= \emptyset$. Further, we define:

$$Heaps \stackrel{\text{def}}{=} Loc \rightharpoonup_{fin} (Node \rightarrow Fields \rightarrow Val \cup Loc)$$
$$Stacks \stackrel{\text{def}}{=} Var \rightarrow Val \cup Loc$$

The semantics is given by a forcing relation: $s,h \models \Phi$ that forces the stack s and heap h to satisfy the constraint Φ where $h \in Heaps$, $s \in Stacks$, and Φ is a formula.

The semantics is presented in Fig. 4. $dom(f)$ is the domain of function f; $h_1 \# h_2$ denotes that heaps h_1 and h_2 are disjoint, i.e., $dom(h_1) \cap dom(h_2) = \emptyset$; and $h_1 \cdot h_2$ denotes the union of two disjoint heaps. Inductive predicates are interpreted using the least model semantics [42]. Semantics of pure formulas depend on stack valuations; it is straightforward and omitted in Fig. 4, for simplicity.

4.2   Implementation of Separation Logic Instantiation

In the following, we describe how S2SAT$_{SL}$ is realized. In particular, we show how the functions UA_test, OA_test, unfold, and link_back are implemented.

$$
\begin{array}{lll}
s,h \models \texttt{emp} & \text{iff} & h=\emptyset \\
s,h \models v{\mapsto}c(f_i : v_i) & \text{iff} & l=s(v), \mathrm{dom}(h)=\{l \to r\} \text{ and } r(c, f_i)=s(v_i) \\
s,h \models \texttt{p}(\bar{v}) & \text{iff} & (s(\bar{v}),h) \in [\![\texttt{p}(\bar{v})]\!] \\
s,h \models \kappa_1 * \kappa_2 & \text{iff} & \exists h_1, h_2 \cdot h_1 \# h_2 \text{ and } h=h_1 \cdot h_2 \text{ and} \\
& & s,h_1 \models \kappa_1 \text{ and } s,h_2 \models \kappa_2 \\
s,h \models \texttt{true} & \text{iff} & \text{always} \\
s,h \models \texttt{false} & \text{iff} & \text{never} \\
s,h \models \exists v_1,...,v_n \cdot (\kappa \wedge \pi) & \text{iff} & \exists \alpha_1 ... \alpha_n \cdot s(v_1 \mapsto \alpha_1 * ... * v_n \mapsto \alpha_n), h \models \kappa \\
& & \text{and } s(v_1 \mapsto \alpha_1 * ... * v_n \mapsto \alpha_n) \models \pi \\
s,h \models \Phi_1 \vee \Phi_2 & \text{iff} & s,h \models \Phi_1 \text{ or } s,h \models \Phi_2
\end{array}
$$

Fig. 4. Semantics.

Deciding Separation Logic Formula. Given an SLPA formula, the functions UA_test and OA_test in S2SAT$_{SL}$ work similarly, by reducing the formula to a first-order formula systematically and deciding the first-order formula. In the following, we define a function called eXPure, which transforms a separation logic formula into a first-order formula. eXPure is defined over the symbolic heap as follows:

$$
\begin{aligned}
&\texttt{eXPure}(\exists \bar{w} \cdot x_1 {\mapsto} c_1(\bar{v}_1) * ... * x_n {\mapsto} c_n(\bar{v}_n) * \texttt{P}_1(\bar{t}_1) * ... * \texttt{P}_\texttt{m}(\bar{t}_m) \wedge \pi) \equiv \\
&\exists \bar{w} \cdot \bigwedge \{x_i {\neq} \texttt{null} \mid i {\in} 1...n\} \wedge \bigwedge \{x_i {\neq} x_j \mid i,j {\in} 1...n \text{ and } i {\neq} j\} \wedge \\
&\bigwedge \{\texttt{inv}(\mathcal{P}, \texttt{P}_j, \bar{t}_j) \mid j \in 1...m\} \wedge \\
&\pi
\end{aligned}
$$

where the reduction at the first line (after $\equiv$) is for points-to predicates, and the second line is for user-defined predicates. The auxiliary function $\texttt{inv}(\mathcal{P}, \texttt{P}, \bar{v})$ returns the invariant of the predicate P with a proper renaming.

Next, the auxiliary procedure $\texttt{sat}_\texttt{p}(\exists \bar{w} \cdot \pi)$ takes a quantified first-order formula as input. It preprocesses the formula and then invokes an SMT solver to solve it. The preprocessing consists of two steps. First, the existential quantifiers $\bar{w}$ are eliminated through a projection $\Pi(\pi, \bar{w})$. Second, remaining existential quantifiers are skolemized and null is substituted by special number (i.e., zero). The preprocessed formulas are of the form of linear arithmetic with free function symbols. These formulas may contain existential ($\exists$) and universal ($\forall$) quantifiers but no $\exists \forall$ alternation. Hence, they are naively supported by SMT solvers.

Deriving Unfolding Tree. Next, we describe how function unfold works in S2SAT$_{SL}$. Given a formula, unfold selects one predicate instance for unfolding as follows.

$$
\frac{\pi_c \equiv \texttt{eXPure}(\kappa * \texttt{P}(\bar{v}) \wedge \pi) \qquad \Gamma_i = \texttt{unfoldP}(\texttt{P}(\bar{v})_u^o, \pi_c)}{\texttt{unfold}(\exists \bar{w}_0 \cdot \kappa * \texttt{P}(\bar{v})_u^o \wedge \pi) \rightsquigarrow \{\exists \bar{w}_0 \cdot \kappa * \Delta_i \wedge \pi \mid \Delta_i \in \Gamma_i\}}
$$

Predicate instances in κ are sorted by a pair of unfolding number and ordering number where the former has higher priority. The instance $\texttt{P}(\bar{v})_u^o$ is selected if u is the smallest number of unfoldings and o is the smallest number among instances which have the same unfolding number u. The procedure unfold outputs a set of disjuncts which are combined from branches of the predicate P with the remainder $\kappa \wedge \pi$. At the middle, the predicate instance is unfolded by the procedure unfoldP. This auxiliary procedure $\texttt{unfoldP}(\texttt{P}(\bar{t})_u^o, \pi_c)$ unfolds the user-defined predicate P with actual parameter $\bar{t}$ under the context π_c. It outputs branches of the predicate P that are not inconsistent with the context. It is formalized as follows.

$$
\frac{
\pi_c^P \equiv \Pi(\pi_c, \bar{v}) \quad (\bigvee_{i=1}^{m}(\exists \bar{w}_i \cdot \kappa_i \wedge \pi_i \mid \pi_i^b), \bar{t}) = \texttt{lookup}(\mathcal{P}, \texttt{P}) \quad \bar{w}_i' = \textit{fresh}(\bar{w}_i)
}{
\texttt{unfoldP}(\texttt{P}(\bar{v})_u^o, \pi_c) \rightsquigarrow \{\exists \bar{w}_i' \cdot [\rho_i]\kappa_i \wedge [\rho_i]\pi_i \wedge \pi_{eq} \mid \texttt{sat}_{\mathbf{p}}(\pi_c^P \wedge [\rho_i]\pi_i^b \wedge \pi_{eq}) \neq \texttt{unsat}, i \in 1...m\}
}
$$
$$
(\bar{v}', \pi_{eq}) = \texttt{freshEQ}(\bar{v}) \quad \rho_p = [\bar{v}'/\bar{t}] \quad \rho_i^{\exists} = [\bar{w}_i'/\bar{w}_i] \quad \rho_i = \rho_p \circ \rho_i^{\exists}
$$

In the first line, the procedure looks up the definition of P and refreshes the existential quantifiers (using the function $\textit{fresh}(...)$). In the second line, formal parameters are substituted by the corresponding actual arguments. Finally, the substituted definition is combined and pruned as shown in the RHS of $\rightsquigarrow$. Function $\texttt{freshEQ}(\bar{v})$ above refreshes the sequence of variables $\bar{v}$ and produces the equality constraints π_{eq} between the old and new ones, i.e. $\pi_{eq} \equiv \bigwedge v_i = v_i'$. Let $\texttt{Q}(\bar{t})^{o_l}$ denote a predicate instance of the derived κ_i, its unfolding number is set to u+1 if its corresponding branch Δ_i is recursive. Otherwise, it is u. Its sequence number is set to $o_l + o$.

The branch invariant is used as a *necessary condition* to unfold a branch. The formalism underlying the pruning process is as follows: given a context Δ_c with its over-approximation π_c and a branch Δ_i with its over-approximation π_i^b, if $\pi_c \wedge \pi_i^b$ is unsatisfiable, so is $\Delta_c * \Delta_i$. Similar to the specialization calculus [15], our unfolding mechanism also prunes infeasible disjuncts while unfolding user-defined predicates. However, the specialization calculus performs exhaustive pruning with multiple unfolding that may be highly costly and redundant compared with our one-step unfolding.

Detecting Cyclic Proof. In the following, we implement the *matching function* $\texttt{f}_{\texttt{cyclic}}$, an instantiation of $\texttt{f}_{\texttt{fix}}$, to form a cyclic proof for fixpoint detection. $\texttt{f}_{\texttt{cyclic}}$ checks whether there exists a *well-founded* ordering relation R between Δ^{comp} and Δ^{bud} so as to form an *infinite* path following the path between these two nodes. If Δ^{bud} matches with Δ^{comp}, Δ^{bud} is marked as closed. For global infinitary soundness, $\texttt{f}_{\texttt{cyclic}}$ only considers those Δ^{bud} and Δ^{comp} of the restricted form as: $\Delta^{comp} \equiv \Delta_{b_1} * \texttt{P}_1(\bar{t}_1)_m^0 * ... * \texttt{P}_i(\bar{t}_i)_m^i$, and $\Delta^{bud} \equiv \Delta_{b_2} * \texttt{P}_1(\bar{t}_1')_n^0 * ... * \texttt{P}_k(\bar{t}_k')_n^k$, where $k \geq i$, $n > m$, Δ_{b_1} and Δ_{b_2} are base formulas.

Like [13], $\texttt{f}_{\texttt{cyclic}}$ is implemented using the weakening and substitution principle. In particular, it looks for a substitution θ s.t. $\Delta^{bud}\theta \implies \Delta^{comp}$. $\texttt{f}_{\texttt{cyclic}}(\Delta^{bud}, \Delta^{comp})$ is formalized as the procedure $\Delta^{bud} \vdash_{lb} \Delta^{comp}$ whose rules are presented in Fig. 5. These rules are applied as follows.

- First, existential variables are refreshed ([**EX-L**], [**EX-R**] rules).

$$\frac{\bar{w}'{=}\textit{fresh }\bar{w} \quad \Delta_1[\bar{w}'/\bar{w}] \vdash_{lb} \Delta_2}{\exists \bar{w}{\cdot}\Delta_1 \vdash_{lb} \Delta_2} \text{[EX--L]} \quad \frac{\bar{w}'{=}\textit{fresh }\bar{w} \quad \Delta_1 \vdash_{lb} \Delta_2[\bar{w}'/\bar{w}]}{\Delta_1 \vdash_{lb} \exists \bar{w}{\cdot}\Delta_2} \text{[EX--R]} \quad \frac{\pi_1 \implies \pi_2}{\pi_1 \vdash_{lb} \pi_2} \text{[PURE]}$$

$$\frac{s{\in}\bar{v} \quad t{\in}\bar{w} \quad \exists R{\cdots}R(s,t) \quad t'{=}\textit{fresh }t \quad (\kappa_1{*}\mathrm{P}(\bar{v}){\wedge}\pi_1)[t'/t; t/s] \vdash_{lb} \kappa_2{*}\mathrm{P}(\bar{w}){\wedge}\pi_2}{\kappa_1{*}\mathrm{P}(\bar{v}){\wedge}\pi_1 \vdash_{lb} \kappa_2{*}\mathrm{P}(\bar{w}){\wedge}\pi_2} \text{[SUBST]}$$

$$\frac{(\kappa_1{\wedge}\pi_1)[\bar{v}/\bar{w}] \vdash_{lb} \kappa_2{\wedge}\pi_2}{\kappa_1{*}\mathrm{P}(\bar{v}){\wedge}\pi_1 \vdash_{lb} \kappa_2{*}\mathrm{P}(\bar{w}){\wedge}\pi_2} \text{[PRED--MATCH]} \quad \frac{\mathrm{P}(\bar{w}){\not\in}\kappa_2 \quad \bar{v}{\cap}FV(\kappa_1{\wedge}\pi_1){=}\emptyset \quad \kappa_1{\wedge}\pi_1 \vdash_{lb} \kappa_2{\wedge}\pi_2}{\kappa_1{*}\mathrm{P}(\bar{v}){\wedge}\pi_1 \vdash_{lb} \kappa_2{\wedge}\pi_2} \text{[PRED--WEAKEN]}$$

$$\frac{(\kappa_1{\wedge}\pi_1){\wedge}[\bar{v}_1/\bar{v}_2] \vdash_{lb} \kappa_2{\wedge}\pi_2}{\kappa_1{*}v{\mapsto}c(\bar{v}_1){\wedge}\pi_1 \vdash_{lb} \kappa_2{*}v{\mapsto}c(\bar{v}_2){\wedge}\pi_2} \text{[PTO--MATCH]} \quad \frac{v{\mapsto}c(\bar{w}){\not\in}\kappa_1 \quad (\kappa_1{\wedge}\pi_1)[\bar{v}_1/\bar{v}_2] \vdash_{lb} \kappa_2{\wedge}\pi_2}{\kappa_1{*}v{\mapsto}c(v_1){\wedge}\pi_1 \vdash_{lb} \kappa_2{*}v{\mapsto}c(v_2){\wedge}\pi_2} \text{[PTO--WEAKEN]}$$

Fig. 5. Rules for back-link.

- Second, *inductive* variables in Δ^{bud} are substituted ([SUBST] rule). This substitution is based on well-ordering relations R. Let $\mathrm{P}(t)_m^k$ be a predicate instance in Δ^{comp} and its corresponding subformula in Δ^{bud} be $R(s,t)$, then s, t are inductive variables. Two examples of well-founded relations R are structural induction for pointer types where $R(s,t)$ iff s is a subterm of t and natural number induction on integers where $R(s,t)$ iff $0{<}s{<}t$.
- Third, heaps are exhaustively matched ([PRED--MATCH] and [PTO--MATCH] rules) and weakened ([PRED--WEAKEN] and [PTO--WEAKEN] rules). Soundness of these rules directly follows from the frame rule [26,40].
- Last, back-link is decided via the implication between pure formulas ([PURE] rule).

5   Soundness and Termination of S2SAT$_{SL}$

In the following, we establish the correctness of S2SAT$_{SL}$.

5.1   Soundness

We show that (i) S2SAT$_{SL}$ is sound and complete for base formulas; and (ii) the functions UA_test, OA_test and link_back in S2SAT$_{SL}$ are sound. These two tasks rely on soundness and completeness of the function eXPure over base formulas, soundness of eXPure over inductive formulas, and soundness of the function f$_{cyclic}$.

Lemma 1 (Equiv-Satisfiable   Reduction). *Let* $\Delta{\equiv}\exists \bar{w}{\cdot}x_1{\mapsto}c_1(\bar{v}_1){*}...$ $*x_n{\mapsto}c_n(\bar{v}_n){\wedge}\alpha{\wedge}\phi$ *be a base formula.* Δ *is satisfiable iff* eXPure(Δ) *is satisfiable.*

The proof is based on structural induction on Δ.

Lemma 2 (Over-Approximated Reduction). *Given a formula Δ such that the invariants of user-defined predicates appearing in Δ are sound, then*

$$\forall s, h \cdot s, h \models \Delta \implies s \models \text{eXPure}(\Delta)$$

In the following lemma, we consider the case $\Gamma = \{\}$ at line 8 of Algorithm 1.

Lemma 3. *Given a formula Δ_0 and the* matching function f_{cyclic} *as presented in the previous section, Δ_0 is UNSAT if $\Gamma = \{\}$ (line 8).*

To prove this Lemma, in [30] we show that there is a "trace manifold" which implies the global infinitary soundness (see [11], ch. 7) when a bud is linked back.

Theorem 2 (Soundness). *Given a formula Δ and a set of user-defined predicates $\mathcal{P}$,*

- *Δ is satisfiable if S2SAT$_{\text{SL}}$ returns SAT.*
- *if S2SAT$_{\text{SL}}$ terminates and returns UNSAT, Δ is unsatisfiable.*

While the soundness of SAT queries follows Lemma 1, the soundness of UNSAT queries follows Lemmas 2 and 3. As satisfiability for SLPA is undecidable [30, 31], there is no guarantee that S2SAT$_{\text{SL}}$ terminates on all inputs. In the next subsection, we show that S2SAT$_{\text{SL}}$ terminates for satisfiable formulas in SLPA and with certain restrictions on the fragment, S2SAT$_{\text{SL}}$ always terminates.

5.2 Termination

Termination for SAT. In this paragraph, we show that S2SAT$_{\text{SL}}$ always terminates when it decides a satisfiable formula. Given a satisfiable formula

$$\Delta \equiv \exists \bar{w} \cdot x_1 \mapsto c_1(\bar{v}_1) * \ldots * x_n \mapsto c_n(\bar{v}_n) * P_0(\bar{t}_0)_0^0 * \ldots * P_n(\bar{t}_n)_0^n \wedge \pi$$

There exists a satisfiable base formula Δ_k such as:

$$\Delta_k \equiv x_1 \mapsto c_1(\bar{v}_1) * \ldots * x_n \mapsto c_n(\bar{v}_n) * \Delta_{k_0}^{P_0} * \ldots * \Delta_{k_n}^{P_n} \wedge \pi$$

where Δ_k^P ($k \geq 0$) denotes a base formula derived by unfolding the predicate P k times and then substituting all predicate instances P by P's base branch. Let k_m be the maximal number among $k_0, \ldots, k_n$. The breadth-first unfolding manner in the algorithm S2SAT ensures that S2SAT$_{\text{SL}}$ identifies Δ_k before it encounters the following leaf:

$$y_1 \mapsto c_1(\bar{t}_1) * \ldots * y_i \mapsto c_i(\bar{t}_i) * P_0(\bar{t}_0)_{\bar{k}_m+1} * \ldots * P_j(\bar{t}_j)_{\bar{k}_m+1} \wedge \pi$$

We remark that the soundness of cyclic proof ensures that our link_back function only considers *infinitely* many unfolding traces. Thus, it never links *finite* many unfolding traces, i.e., traces connecting the root to satisfiable base leaves, like Δ_k.

Decidable Fragment. In the following, we describe universal SLPA_{ind}, a fragment of SLPA, for which we prove that S2SAT_{SL} always terminates. Compared to SLPA, universal SLPA_{ind} restricts the set of inductive predicates $\mathcal{P}$ as well as the inputs of S2SAT_{SL}.

Definition 4 (SLPA_{ind}). *An inductive predicate* $\text{pred } P(\bar{t}) \equiv \Phi$ *is well-founded* SLPA_{ind} *if it has one induction case with* N *occurrences of* P, *and it has the shape as follows.*

$$\Phi \equiv \Phi_0 \vee \exists \bar{w} \cdot x_1 \mapsto c_1(\bar{v}_1) * \ldots * x_n \mapsto c_n(\bar{v}_n) * P(\bar{w}_1) * \ldots * P(\bar{w}_N) \wedge \pi$$

where Φ_0 *is disjunction of base formulas and the two following restrictions.*

1. $\forall n \in 1 \ldots N$ $\bar{w}_n \subseteq \bar{w} \cup \{\text{null}\}$ *and* $\bar{w}_n$ *do not appear in the equalities of* π,
2. *if* t_i *is a numerical parameter and there exists a well-ordering relation* R *such that* $R(s, t_i, w_{1_i}, \ldots, w_{m_i})$ $(1 \le m \le N)$ *is a subformula of* π, *the following conditions hold.*
   - t_i *is constrained separately (i.e., there does not exist* $j \neq i$ *and a subformula* ϕ *of* π *such that* $\{t_i, t_j\} \subseteq FV(\phi)$ *or* $\{t_i, w_{n_j}\} \subseteq FV(\phi)$ *or* $\{w_{m_j}, w_{n_j}\} \subseteq FV(\phi)$ $\forall m, n \in 1 \ldots N$, *and*
   - $\forall n \in 1 \ldots N$, $\pi \implies t_i > w_{n_i}$ *or* $\pi \implies t_i < w_{n_i}$.
   - *if* $t_i \in FV(\Phi_0)$ *then* $\Phi_0 \implies t_i = k$, *for some integer* k
   t_i *is denoted as* inductive *parameters.*

Restriction 1 guarantees that f_{cyclic} can soundly weaken the heap by discarding irrelevant points-to predicates and $N-1$ occurrences of P (when $N \ge 2$) while it links back. Restriction 2 implies that $t_i > w_i \ge k_1$ or $t_i < w_i \le k_2$ for some integer k_1, k_2. This ensures that leaf nodes of unfolding trees of an unsatisfiable input must be UNSAT or linked back.

The above SLPA_{ind} fragment is expressive enough to describe a range of data structures, e.g. sorted lists sortll, lists/trees with size properties, or even AVL trees avl.

Definition 5 (Universal SLPA_{ind}). *Given a separation logic formula*

$$\Delta_0 \equiv x_1 \mapsto c_1(\bar{v}_1) * \ldots * x_n \mapsto c_n(\bar{v}_n) * P_1(\bar{t}_1) * \ldots * P_n(\bar{t}_n) \wedge \phi_0$$

Δ_0 *is universal* SLPA_{ind} *if all predicates* $P_1, \ldots, P_n$ *are well-founded* SLPA_{ind}, *and if all* $\bar{x}$ *of free, arithmetical, inductive variables, with* $\bar{x} \subseteq (\bar{t}_1 \cup \ldots \cup \bar{t}_n)$, ϕ_0 *is a conjunction of* $\phi_{0,i}$ *where* $\phi_{0,i}$ *is either of the following form: (i)* true; *or (ii)* $x_i \ge k_1$ *for some integer* k_1; *or (iii)* $x_i \le k_2$ *for some integer* k_2.

Theorem 3 (Termination). S2SAT_{SL} *terminates for universal* SLPA_{ind} *formulas.*

6 Sound Invariant Inference

In order to perform fully automatic verification without user-provided invariants, S2SAT$_{SL}$ supports automatic invariant inference. In this section, we describe invariant inference from user-defined predicates and predicate branches. While the former is used for over-approximation, the latter is used for context-sensitive predicate unfolding. To infer invariants for a set of user-defined predicates, we first build a dependency graph among the predicates. After that, we process each group of mutual dependent predicates following a bottom-up manner. For simplicity, we present the inference for one directly recursive predicate. The inference for a group of mutual inductive predicates is similar.

Inferring Predicate Invariant. Our invariant inference is based on the principle of second-order abduction [28,45]. Given the predicate P defined by m branches as $P(\bar{t}) \equiv \bigvee_{i=1}^{m} \Delta_i$, we assume a sound invariant of P as an unknown (second-order) variable $I(\bar{t})$. After that we prove the lemma $P(\bar{v}) \vdash I(\bar{v})$ via induction; and simultaneously generate a set of pure relational assumptions using second-order abduction. The steps to prove the above lemma and generate a set of m relational assumptions over I are as follows.

1. Unfold LHS of the lemma to generate a set of m subgoals i.e. $\Delta_i[\bar{v}/\bar{t}] \vdash I(\bar{v})$ where $i \in 1...m$. The original lemma is taken as the induction hypothesis.
2. For each subgoal i, over-approximate its LHS to a pure formula π_i and form an assumption relation $\pi_i \implies I(\bar{v})$. There are two cases to compute π_i.
   - if Δ_i is a base formula, then $\pi_i \equiv \mathsf{eXPure}(\Delta_i)$.
   - if Δ_i includes k instances P such that $\Delta_i \equiv \Delta_{rest_i} * P(\bar{v}_1) * ... * P(\bar{v}_k)$, then we compute $\pi_{i_0} \equiv \mathsf{eXPure}(\Delta_{rest_i})$, $\pi_{i_j} \equiv I(\bar{v}_j)$, for all $j \in 1...k$, and $\pi_i \equiv \bigwedge_{j=1}^{k} \pi_{i_k}$.
3. Our system applies a least fixed point analysis to the set of gathered relational assumptions. We use the analyzer LFP presented in [45] to compute these invariants.

We illustrate this procedure to infer an invariant for sortll. First, our system introduces an unknown relation $I(\mathtt{root},n,m)$. Second, it generates the below relational constraints.

$$\mathtt{root} \neq \mathtt{null} \wedge n = 1 \implies I(\mathtt{root},n,m)$$
$$\mathtt{root} \neq \mathtt{null} \wedge I(Q,N_1,M_1) \wedge n = N_1 + 1 \wedge m \leq M_1 \implies I(\mathtt{root},n,m)$$

Finally, it analyzes these two constraints and produces the following result:

$$I(\mathtt{root},n,m) \equiv \mathtt{root} \neq \mathtt{null} \wedge n \geq 1$$

Lemma 4 (Sound Invariant Inference). *Given a predicate* $P(\bar{t}) \equiv \Phi$, *and* $\mathcal{R}$ *be a set of relational assumptions generated by the steps above. If* $\mathcal{R}$ *has a solution, i.e.,* $I(\bar{v}) \equiv \pi$, *then we have* $\forall s, h \cdot s, h \models P(\bar{v})$, $s \models \pi$.

Proof Sketch: Soundness of Lemma 2 implies that for all $i \in 1...m$, π_i is an over-approximated abstraction of Δ_i. As such, the soundness of this lemma immediately follows from the soundness of second-order abduction [28,45]. □

Table 1. Exponential time and space satisfiability checks.

Succ-circuit (1–20)						Succ-rec (1–20)					
n	SLSAT	S2SAT$_{\text{SL}}$	n	SLSAT	S2SAT$_{\text{SL}}$	n	SLSAT	S2SAT$_{\text{SL}}$	n	SLSAT	S2SAT$_{\text{SL}}$
1	1 ms	21 ms	11	SO	37.46 s	1	0 ms	25 ms	11	1796.4 s	410.92 s
2	2 ms	23 ms	12	SO	170.53 s	2	1 ms	30 ms	12	TO	TO
3	27 ms	30 ms	13	SO	988.29 s	3	4 ms	33 ms	13	TO	TO
4	867 ms	34 ms	14	SO	TO	4	21 ms	39 ms	14	X	TO
5	30 s	0.05 s	15	SO	TO	5	134 ms	52 ms	15	X	TO
6	30 s	0.09 s	16	SO	TO	6	830 ms	76 ms	16	X	TO
7	SO	0.20 s	17	SO	TO	7	5.0 s	0.21 s	17	X	TO
8	SO	0.61 s	18	SO	TO	8	29.5 s	0.87 s	18	X	TO
9	SO	2.21 s	19	SO	TO	9	167.8 s	4.83 s	19	X	TO
10	SO	8.49 s	20	SO	TO	10	1065 s	45.28 s	20	X	TO

Inferring Branch Invariant. Given a predicate P defined by m branches as $P(\bar{t}) \equiv \bigvee_{i=1}^{m}(\exists \bar{w}_i \cdot \Delta_i)$ $\overline{inv}$: π, we compute invariants for each branch of P as $\Pi(\texttt{eXPure}(\Delta_i), \bar{w}_i)$ $\forall$ $i=1...m$. For example, with the invariant inferred for the predicate *sortll* as above, our system computes its branch invariants π_1^b for the base branch and π_2^b for the inductive branch as below.

$$\pi_1^b \equiv \Pi(\texttt{eXPure}(\texttt{root}\mapsto node(m, \texttt{null}) \wedge \texttt{n=1}), \{\}) \equiv \texttt{root}\neq\texttt{null} \wedge \texttt{n=1}$$
$$\pi_2^b \equiv \Pi(\texttt{eXPure}(\texttt{root}\mapsto node(m, q) * \texttt{sortll}(q, n_1, m_1) \wedge \texttt{n}=n_1+1 \wedge m \leq m_1),$$
$$\{q, n_1, m_1\}) \equiv \texttt{root}\neq\texttt{null} \wedge n \geq 1$$

Soundness of eXPure implies that the branch invariant over-approximates its branch.

7 Implementation and Evaluation

We have implemented the proposed solver S2SAT$_{\text{SL}}$ and a new interprocedural (top-down) program verification tool, called S2$_{\text{td}}$, which uses S2SAT$_{\text{SL}}$. We make use of Omega Calculator [38] to eliminate existential quantifiers, Z3 [19] as a back-end SMT solver, and FixCalc [37] to find closure form in inferring invariants for user-defined predicates.

In the following, we evaluate S2SAT$_{\text{SL}}$ and S2$_{\text{td}}$'s robustness and efficiency on a set of benchmarks from the software verification competition SV-COMP [7]. We also present an evaluation of S2SAT$_{\text{SL}}$ in compositional (modular) program verification with the HIP/S2 system [14,28] for a range of data structures.

7.1 Robustness and Efficiency

In [12], Brotherston *et al.* introduced a new and challenging set of satisfiability benchmarks discussed in Proposition 5.13 of [12]. In this Proposition, Brotherston *et al.* stated that there exists a family of predicates of size $O(n)$ and that SLSAT runs in $\Omega(2^n)$ time and space regardless of search strategies. Since SLSAT relies on bottom-up and *context-insensitive* fixed point computation, it has to explore all possible models before answering a query. Their approach is designed for computing invariants of shape predicates rather than satisfiability checks. In contrast, S2SAT$_{SL}$ performs top-down and *context-sensitive* searches, as it is dedicated for satisfiability solving. Moreover, it prunes infeasible disjuncts, significantly reduces the search space, and provides better support for model discovery.

We conducted an experiment on comparing SLSAT's and S2SAT$_{SL}$'s performance on this set of benchmarks. The results are shown in Table 1. The size n of `succ−circuit∗` (`succ−rec∗`) benchmarks expresses the breadth (depth, resp.) of dependency. This set of benchmarks is a part of the User-Defined Predicate Satisfiability (UDB_sat) suite of SL-COMP 2014 [41]. The output is either a definite answer (sat, unsat) with running time (in milliseconds (ms), or seconds (s)), or an error. In particular, SO denotes stack overflow; TO denotes timeout (i.e., tools run longer than 1800 s); and X denotes a fatal error. The experimental results show that S2SAT$_{SL}$ is much more robust and also more efficient than SLSAT. While S2SAT$_{SL}$ successfully solved 24 (out of 40) benchmarks, SLSAT was capable of handling 17 benchmarks. Furthermore, on 17 benchmarks that SLSAT discharged successfully, S2SAT$_{SL}$ outperforms SLSAT, i.e., about 6.75 (3126 s/462 s) times faster. As shown in the table, S2SAT$_{SL}$ ran with neither stack overflow nor fatal errors over all these challenging benchmarks.

Table 2. Experimental results on complex data structures.

Data structure (pure props)	#Query	#UNSAT	#SAT	Time
Singly llist (size)	666	75	591	1.25
Even llist (size)	139	125	14	2.40
Sorted llist (size, sorted)	217	21	196	0.91
Doubly llist (size)	452	50	402	2.07
Complete tree (size, minheight)	387	33	354	143.98
Heap trees (size, maxelem)	467	67	400	13.87
AVL (height, size, near-balanced)	881	64	817	84.82
BST (height, size, sorted)	341	34	307	2.28
RBT (size, height, color)	1741	217	1524	65.54
rose-tree	55	6	49	0.34
TLL	128	13	115	0.24
Bubble (size, sorted)	300	20	280	1.09
Quick sort (size, sorted)	225	29	196	2.33

7.2 Modular Verification with S2SAT$_{SL}$

In this subsection, we evaluate S2SAT$_{SL}$ in the context of modular program verification. S2SAT$_{SL}$ solver is integrated into the HIP/S2 [14,28,29] system to prune infeasible program paths in symbolic execution. Furthermore, S2SAT$_{SL}$ is also used by the entailment procedure SLEEK to discharge verification conditions (VC) generated. In particular, when SLEEK deduces a VC to the following form: $\Delta \vdash \mathsf{emp} \wedge \pi_r$, the error calculus in SLEEK [29] invokes S2SAT$_{SL}$ to discharge the following queries: Δ and $\Delta \wedge \neg \pi_r$ for safety and $\Delta \wedge \pi_r$ for *must* errors. In experiments, we have extracted those VCs generated while HIP/S2 verified heap-manipulating programs.

We have evaluated S2SAT$_{SL}$ deciding the VCs discussed above. The experimental results are described in Table 2. Each line shows a test on one program. The first column lists data structures and their pure properties. rose-trees are trees with nodes that are allowed to have a variable number of children, stored as doubly-linked lists. TLL is a binary tree whose nodes point to their parents and all leaf nodes are linked as a singly-linked list. #Query is the number of satisfiability queries sent to S2SAT$_{SL}$ for each data structure. The next two columns report the outputs from S2SAT$_{SL}$. The last column shows the time (in seconds) taken by the S2SAT$_{SL}$ solver. In this experiment, S2SAT$_{SL}$ terminated on all queries. Furthermore it exactly decided all SAT and UNSAT queries. These experimental results affirm the correctness of our algorithm S2SAT$_{SL}$. They also show that S2SAT$_{SL}$ is expressive, effective, and can be integrated into program verification systems for discharging satisfiability problems of separation logic formulas.

7.3 Recursive Program Verification with S2SAT$_{SL}$

We have evaluated and compared our verification system S2$_{td}$ with state-of-the-art verification tools on a set of SV-COMP benchmarks[1]. The results are presented in Table 3. There are 102 recursive/loop programs taken from *Recursive* and *HeapReach* sub-categories

Table 3. Experimental results on recursive programs.

Tool	#s√	#e√	#unk	#s✗	#e✗	Points	Mins
ESBMC [18]	38	40	21	0	3	20	53
UAutomizer [24]	17	23	62	0	0	57	23
SeaHorn [22]	48	45	5	4	0	77	26
CBMC [16]	33	39	29	1	0	89	90
Smack-corral [1]	33	37	28	0	0	103	105
S2$_{td}$	41	45	16	0	0	127	25

in the benchmark; timeout is set to 180 s. In each program, there is at least one user-supplied assertion to model safety properties. The first column identities the subset of verification systems which competed in both the above sub-categories. The next three columns count the instances of correct safe (s√), correct error (e√) and unknown (e.g., timeout). The next two columns capture the number of false positives (s✗) and false negatives (e✗). We rank these tools based on their points. Following the SV-COMP competition, we gave +2 for one s√, +1 for one

---

[1] http://sv-comp.sosy-lab.org/2016/.

e√, 0 for unk, −16 for one s✗, and −32 for one e✗. The last column expresses the total time in minutes. The results show that the proposed verification approach is promising; indeed, our system is effective and efficient: it produces the best correctness with *zero* false answers within the nearly-shortest time.

8   Related Work

Close to our work is the SeaHorn verification system [22]. While SeaHorn relies on Z3-PDR to handle inductive predicates on non-heap domains, it is unclear (to us) how SeaHorn supports induction reasoning for heap-based programs (which is one contribution of our present work).

Our S2SAT satisfiability procedure is based on unfolding which is similar to the algorithm in the Leon system [43,44]. Leon, a verifier for functional programs, adds an unfolding mechanism for inductive predicates into complete theories. However, Leon only supports classic logic and not structural logic (i.e., separation logic). Neither does Leon support inductive reasoning. Furthermore, our system infers sound invariants for inductive predicates to facilitate over-approximation.

Our work is related to work on developing satisfiability solvers in separation logic. In the following, we summarize the development in this area. Smallfoot [5] has the first implemented decision procedure for a fragment of separation logic. This solver was originally customized to work with spatial formulas over list segments. Based on a fixed equality (disequality) constraint branches of the list segment, the proposals presented by [17,32] further enhanced decision procedure for this fragment with equality reasoning. They provided normalization rules with a graph technique [17] and a superposition calculus [32] to infer (dis)equality constraints on pointers and used these constraints to prune infeasible branches of predicate instances during unfolding. Although these proposals can decide the formula of that fragment in polynomial time, it is not easy to extend them to a fragment with general inductive predicates (i.e., the fragment SLPA). Decision procedures in [33–36] support decidable fragments of separation logic with inter-reachable data structures using SMT. Our proposal extends these procedures to those fragments with general inductively-defined predicates. Indeed, our decidable fragment can include more complex data structures, such as AVL trees.

S2SAT$_{SL}$ is closely related to the satisfiability solvers [12,25] which are capable of handling separation logic formulas with general user-defined predicates. Decision procedures [12,25] are able to handle predicates without pure properties. The former described a decidable fragment of user-defined predicates with bounded tree width. The problem of deciding separation logic formulas is then reduced to monadic second-order logic over graphs. The latter, SLSAT, decides formulas with user-defined predicates via a equi-satisfiable fixed point calculation. The main disadvantage of SLSAT is that it is currently restricted to the domain of pointer equality and disequality, so that it cannot be used to support predicates with pure properties from infinite abstract domains.

Using over-approximation in decision procedures is not new. For example, D'Silva *et al.* have recently made use of abstract domains inside satisfiability solvers [20,21]. In separation logic, satisfiability procedures in HIP/SLEEK [14] and Dryad [39] decide formulas via a sound reduction that over-approximates predicate instances. HIP/SLEEK and Dryad are capable of proving the validity of a wide range of expressive formulas with arbitrary predicates. However, expressivity comes with cost; as these procedures are incomplete, and they do not address the satisfiability problem. We believe that S2SAT can be integrated into these systems to improve upon these two shortcomings.

9 Conclusion and Future Work

We have presented a satisfiability procedure for an expressive fragment of separation logic. Given a formula, our procedure examines both under-approximation (so as to prove SAT) and over-approximation (so as to prove UNSAT). Our procedure was strengthened with invariant generation and cyclic proof detection. We have also implemented a solver and a new verification system for heap-manipulating programs. We have evaluated them on a range of competition problems with either complex heap usage patterns or exponential complexity of time and space.

For future work, we might investigate S2SAT-based decision procedures for other complete theories (i.e., Presburger, string, bag/set) augmented with inductive predicates. We would also study a more general decidable fragment of separation logic by relaxing the restrictions for termination. Finally, we would like to improve $S2_{td}$ for array, string and pointer arithmetic reasoning as well as witness generation for erroneous programs.

Acknowledgements. We wish to thank Christopher M. Poskitt for his helpful comments on the manuscript. Quang Loc and Jun Sun are partially supported by NRF grant RGNRF1501 and Wei-Ngan by NRF grant NRF2014NCR-NCR001-040.

References

1. Haran, A., Carter, M., Emmi, M., Lal, A., Qadeer, S., Rakamarić, Z.: SMACK+corral: a modular verifier. In: Baier, C., Tinelli, C. (eds.) TACAS 2015. LNCS, vol. 9035, pp. 451–454. Springer, Heidelberg (2015)
2. Barnett, M., Chang, B.-Y.E., DeLine, R., Jacobs, B., M. Leino, K.R.: Boogie: a modular reusable verifier for object-oriented programs. In: de Boer, F.S., Bonsangue, M.M., Graf, S., de Roever, W.-P. (eds.) FMCO 2005. LNCS, vol. 4111, pp. 364–387. Springer, Heidelberg (2006)
3. Barrett, C., Conway, C.L., Deters, M., Hadarean, L., Jovanović, D., King, T., Reynolds, A., Tinelli, C.: CVC4. In: Gopalakrishnan, G., Qadeer, S. (eds.) CAV 2011. LNCS, vol. 6806, pp. 171–177. Springer, Heidelberg (2011)
4. Beckman, N.E., Nori, A.V., Rajamani, S.K., Simmons, R.J.: Proofs from tests. In: ISSTA, pp. 3–14. ACM, New York (2008)
5. Berdine, J., Calcagno, C., W.O'Hearn, P.: A decidable fragment of separation logic. In: Lodaya, K., Mahajan, M. (eds.) FSTTCS 2004. LNCS, vol. 3328, pp. 97–109. Springer, Heidelberg (2004)

6. Berdine, J., Calcagno, C., O'Hearn, P.W.: Symbolic execution with separation logic. In: Yi, K. (ed.) APLAS 2005. LNCS, vol. 3780, pp. 52–68. Springer, Heidelberg (2005)

7. Beyer, D.: Reliable and reproducible competition results with benchexec and witnesses (report on SV-COMP 2016). In: Chechik, M., Raskin, J.-F. (eds.) TACAS 2016. LNCS, vol. 9636, pp. 887–904. Springer, Heidelberg (2016). doi:10.1007/978-3-662-49674-9_55

8. Beyer, D., Cimatti, A., Griggio, A., Keremoglu, M.E., Sebastiani, R.: Software model checking via large-block encoding. In: Proceedings of 9th International Conference on Formal Methods in Computer-Aided Design, FMCAD 2009, pp. 25–32 (2009)

9. Bjørner, N., Gurfinkel, A., McMillan, K., Rybalchenko, A.: Horn clause solvers for program verification. In: Blass, A., Dershowitz, N., Finkbeiner, B., Schulte, W., Beklemishev, L.D., Beklemishev, L.D. (eds.) Gurevich Festschrift II 2015. LNCS, vol. 9300, pp. 24–51. Springer, Heidelberg (2015). doi:10.1007/978-3-319-23534-9_2

10. Bjørner, N., McMillan, K.L., Rybalchenko, A.: Program verification as satisfiability modulo theories. In: SMT, pp. 3–11 (2012)

11. Brotherston. J.: Sequent calculus proof systems for inductive definitions. Ph.D. thesis, University of Edinburgh, November 2006

12. Brotherston, J., Fuhs, C., Pérez, J.A.N., Gorogiannis, N.: A decision procedure for satisfiability in separation logic with inductive predicates. In: CSL-LICS 2014, pp. 25:1–25:10. ACM, New York (2014)

13. Brotherston, J., Gorogiannis, N., Petersen, R.L.: A generic cyclic theorem prover. In: Jhala, R., Igarashi, A. (eds.) APLAS 2012. LNCS, vol. 7705, pp. 350–367. Springer, Heidelberg (2012)

14. Chin, W., David, C., Nguyen, H., Qin, S.: Automated verification of shape, size and bag properties via user-defined predicates in separation logic. SCP **77**(9), 1006–1036 (2012)

15. Chin, W.-N., Gherghina, C., Voicu, R., Le, Q.L., Craciun, F., Qin, S.: A specialization calculus for pruning disjunctive predicates to support verification. In: Gopalakrishnan, G., Qadeer, S. (eds.) CAV 2011. LNCS, vol. 6806, pp. 293–309. Springer, Heidelberg (2011)

16. Clarke, E., Kroning, D., Lerda, F.: A tool for checking ANSI-C programs. In: Jensen, K., Podelski, A. (eds.) TACAS 2004. LNCS, vol. 2988, pp. 168–176. Springer, Heidelberg (2004)

17. Cook, B., Haase, C., Ouaknine, J., Parkinson, M., Worrell, J.: Tractable reasoning in a fragment of separation logic. In: Katoen, J.-P., König, B. (eds.) CONCUR 2011. LNCS, vol. 6901, pp. 235–249. Springer, Heidelberg (2011)

18. Cordeiro, L., Fischer, B.: Verifying multi-threaded software using smt-based context-bounded model checking. In: Proceedings of the 33rd International Conference on Software Engineering, ICSE 2011, pp. 331–340. ACM, New York (2011)

19. de Moura, L., Bjørner, N.S.: Z3: an efficient SMT solver. In: Ramakrishnan, C.R., Rehof, J. (eds.) TACAS 2008. LNCS, vol. 4963, pp. 337–340. Springer, Heidelberg (2008)

20. D'Silva, V., Haller, L., Kroening, D.: Satisfiability solvers are static analysers. In: Miné, A., Schmidt, D. (eds.) SAS 2012. LNCS, vol. 7460, pp. 317–333. Springer, Heidelberg (2012)

21. D'Silva, V., Haller, L., Kroening, D.: Abstract satisfaction. In: Proceedings of the 41st ACM SIGPLAN-SIGACT Symposium on Principles of Programming Languages, POPL 2014, pp. 139–150. ACM, New York (2014)

22. Gurfinkel, A., Kahsai, T., Komuravelli, A., Navas, J.A.: The seahorn verification framework. In: Kroening, D., Păsăreanu, C.S. (eds.) CAV 2015. LNCS, vol. 9206, pp. 343–361. Springer, Heidelberg (2015)

23. Haase, C., Ishtiaq, S., Ouaknine, J., Parkinson, M.J.: SeLoger: a tool for graph-based reasoning in separation logic. In: Sharygina, N., Veith, H. (eds.) CAV 2013. LNCS, vol. 8044, pp. 790–795. Springer, Heidelberg (2013)

24. Heizmann, M., Hoenicke, J., Podelski, A.: Software model checking for people who love automata. In: Sharygina, N., Veith, H. (eds.) CAV 2013. LNCS, vol. 8044, pp. 36–52. Springer, Heidelberg (2013)

25. Iosif, R., Rogalewicz, A., Simacek, J.: The tree width of separation logic with recursive definitions. In: Bonacina, M.P. (ed.) CADE 2013. LNCS, vol. 7898, pp. 21–38. Springer, Heidelberg (2013)

26. Ishtiaq, S., O'Hearn, P.: BI as an assertion language for mutable data structures. In: ACM POPL, pp. 14–26, London, January 2001

27. Jose, M., Majumdar, R.: Cause clue clauses: error localization using maximum satisfiability. In: PLDI, pp. 437–446. ACM, New York (2011)

28. Le, Q.L., Gherghina, C., Qin, S., Chin, W.-N.: Shape analysis via second-order bi-abduction. In: Biere, A., Bloem, R. (eds.) CAV 2014. LNCS, vol. 8559, pp. 52–68. Springer, Heidelberg (2014)

29. Le, Q.L., Sharma, A., Craciun, F., Chin, W.-N.: Towards complete specifications with an error calculus. In: Brat, G., Rungta, N., Venet, A. (eds.) NFM 2013. LNCS, vol. 7871, pp. 291–306. Springer, Heidelberg (2013)

30. Le, Q.L., Sun, J., Chin, W.-N.: Satisfiability modula heap-based programs. Technical report (2016). http://loc.bitbucket.org/papers/satsl-cav16.pdf

31. Makoto, T., Le, Q.L., Chin, W.-N.: Presburger arithmetic and separation logic with inductive definitions. Technical report, May 2016

32. Navarro Pérez, J.A., Rybalchenko, A.: Separation logic + superposition calculus = heap theorem prover. In: Proceedings of the 32nd ACM SIGPLAN Conference on Programming Language Design and Implementation (PLDI), pp. 556–566 (2011)

33. Navarro Pérez, J.A., Rybalchenko, A.: Separation logic modulo theories. In: Shan, C. (ed.) APLAS 2013. LNCS, vol. 8301, pp. 90–106. Springer, Heidelberg (2013)

34. Piskac, R., Wies, T., Zufferey, D.: Automating separation logic using SMT. In: Sharygina, N., Veith, H. (eds.) CAV 2013. LNCS, vol. 8044, pp. 773–789. Springer, Heidelberg (2013)

35. Piskac, R., Wies, T., Zufferey, D.: Automating separation logic with trees and data. In: Biere, A., Bloem, R. (eds.) CAV 2014. LNCS, vol. 8559, pp. 711–728. Springer, Heidelberg (2014)

36. Piskac, R., Wies, T., Zufferey, D., Piskac, R., Wies, T., Zufferey, D.: Automating separation logic with trees and data. In: Biere, A., Bloem, R. (eds.) CAV 2014. LNCS, vol. 8559, pp. 711–728. Springer, Heidelberg (2014)

37. Popeea, C., Chin, W.-N.: Inferring disjunctive postconditions. In: Okada, M., Satoh, I. (eds.) ASIAN 2006. LNCS, vol. 4435, pp. 331–345. Springer, Heidelberg (2008)

38. Pugh, W.: The omega test: a fast practical integer programming algorithm for dependence analysis. Commun. ACM 8, 102–114 (1992)

39. Qiu, X., Garg, P., Ştefănescu, A., Madhusudan, P.: Natural proofs for structure, data, and separation. In: PLDI, pp. 231–242. ACM, New York (2013)

40. Reynolds, J., Logic, S.: A logic for shared mutable data structures. In: Proceedings of the 17th Annual IEEE Symposium on Logic in Computer Science, pp. 55–74 (2002)

41. Sighireanu, M., Cok, D.R.: Report on SL-COMP 2014. In: JSAT (2016)
42. Sims, É.-J.: Extending separation logic with fixpoints and postponed substitution. Theor. Comput. Sci. **351**(2), 258–275 (2006)
43. Suter, P., Dotta, M., Kuncak, V.: Decision procedures for algebraic data types with abstractions. In: Proceedings of the 37th Annual ACM SIGPLAN-SIGACT Symposium on Principles of Programming Languages, POPL 2010, pp. 199–210. ACM, New York (2010)
44. Suter, P., Köksal, A.S., Kuncak, V.: Satisfiability modulo recursive programs. In: Yahav, E. (ed.) Static Analysis. LNCS, vol. 6887, pp. 298–315. Springer, Heidelberg (2011)
45. Trinh, M.-T., Le, Q.L., David, C., Chin, W.-N.: Bi-abduction with pure properties for specification inference. In: Shan, C. (ed.) APLAS 2013. LNCS, vol. 8301, pp. 107–123. Springer, Heidelberg (2013)

Automatic Verification of Iterated Separating Conjunctions Using Symbolic Execution

Peter Müller(✉), Malte Schwerhoff(✉),
and Alexander J. Summers(✉)

Department of Computer Science, ETH Zurich,
Zurich, Switzerland
{peter.mueller,malte.schwerhoff,
alexander.summers}@inf.ethz.ch

Abstract. In permission logics such as separation logic, the iterated separating conjunction is a quantifier denoting access permission to an unbounded set of heap locations. In contrast to recursive predicates, iterated separating conjunctions do not prescribe a structure on the locations they range over, and so do not restrict how to traverse and modify these locations. This flexibility is important for the verification of random-access data structures such as arrays and data structures that can be traversed in multiple ways such as graphs. Despite its usefulness, no automatic program verifier natively supports iterated separating conjunctions; they are especially difficult to incorporate into symbolic execution engines, the prevalent technique for building verifiers for these logics.

In this paper, we present the first symbolic execution technique to support general iterated separating conjunctions. We propose a novel representation of symbolic heaps and flexible support for logical specifications that quantify over heap locations. Our technique exhibits predictable and fast performance despite employing quantifiers at the SMT level, by carefully controlling quantifier instantiations. It is compatible with other features of permission logics such as fractional permissions, recursive predicates, and abstraction functions. Our technique is implemented as an extension of the Viper verification infrastructure.

1 Introduction

Permission logics such as separation logic [18] and implicit dynamic frames [19] associate an access permission with each memory location in order to reason about shared mutable state. Dynamic heap data structures require specifications to denote access permissions to a statically-unknown set of locations. Such specifications are typically expressed in existing tools using recursive predicates [15], which work well so long as the traversal of the data structure matches the definition of the predicate. However, access patterns that do not follow the predicate structure (*e.g.*, traversing a doubly-linked list from the end) or that follow no specific order (*e.g.*, random access into an array) are difficult to handle in existing program verifiers, requiring programmers to provide substantial manual

S. Chaudhuri and A. Farzan (Eds.): CAV 2016, Part I, LNCS 9779, pp. 405–425, 2016.
DOI: 10.1007/978-3-319-41528-4_22

proof steps (for instance, as ghost code) to bridge the mismatch between the program's access pattern and the imposed predicate structure.

Iterated separating conjunction [18] (hereafter, ISC) is an alternative way to denote properties of a set of heap locations, which has for instance been used in by-hand proofs to denote locations of arrays [18], cyclic data structures [3,23], the objects stored in linked lists [7], and graph algorithms [23]. Unlike recursive predicates, an ISC does not prescribe any particular traversal order.

Despite its usefulness and inclusion in early presentations of separation logic, no existing program verifier supports general ISCs directly. Among the tools based on symbolic execution, Smallfoot [2] does not support ISC; VeriFast [22] and jStar [7] allow programmers to encode some forms of ISC via abstract predicates that can be manipulated by auxiliary operations and lemmas (in VeriFast) or tailored rewrite rules (in jStar). For arrays, this encoding is partially supported by libraries. However, in the general case, programmers need to provide the extra machinery, which significantly increases the necessary manual effort.

Among the verifiers based on verification condition generation, Chalice [12] supports only a restricted form of ISC (ranging over all objects stored in a sequence), and VeriCool uses an encoding that leads to unreliable behaviour of the SMT solver [21, p. 46]. The GRASShopper tool [16] does not provide built-in or general support for ISC, but some ingredients of the technique we present (particularly, the technical usage of inverse functions) have been employed there to specify particular random access to data structures (*e.g.*, arrays). The Dafny verifier [10] can be used to write similar set and quantifier-based specifications, but does not support permission-based reasoning or concurrency.

In this paper, we present the first symbolic execution technique that directly supports general forms of ISC. Our technique is compatible with other features of permission logics: it supports fractional permissions [5], such that a heap location may be ranged over by several ISCs, and allows ISC to occur in predicate bodies and in preconditions of abstraction functions [8].

This combination of features allows one to specify and verify challenging examples such as graph-marking algorithms that so far were beyond the scope of automated verifiers based on permission logics.

Our main technical contributions are: (1) a novel representation of the partial heaps that are denoted by an ISC, along with algorithms to manipulate this representation; (2) a technique to preserve across heap changes (to frame) the values of expressions that depend on the unbounded set of heap locations denoted by ISCs; (3) an SMT encoding that carefully controls quantifier instantiations; (4) an implementation of our approach in the Viper verification infrastructure [14]. Our implementation and several interesting examples are available online [1].

Outline. In the next section, we explain the main technical challenges our work addresses, and illustrate them with a simple motivating example. Our design for a symbolic heap that can represent permissions described by ISCs is presented in Sect. 3. We explain the symbolic evaluation of expressions and framing with respect to this heap representation in Sect. 4. In Sect. 5, we discuss how we control quantifier instantiations. Section 6 presents an evaluation of our implementation. We conclude in Sect. 7.

2   Technical Challenges

Permission logics ensure that a heap location is accessed only when the corresponding permission is held. Dedicated assertions denote the permission to a heap location $e.f$, written as $e.f \mapsto$ _ in separation logic and as the *accessibility predicate* **acc**$(e.f)$ in implicit dynamic frames; we use the latter in this paper. These logics include a *separating conjunction* $*$, expressing that the permissions denoted by the two conjuncts must be disjoint. For instance, an assertion **acc**$(x.f) * $ **acc**$(y.f)$ implies the disequality $x \neq y$. Many permission logics allow permissions to be split into fractions, and to re-assemble fractions into a full permission. In these logics, any non-zero permission allows read access to a location, whereas write access requires the full permission. When appropriate permissions are held, assertions may also constrain the value of a heap location (for instance, $x.f > 3$); assertions that do not contain accessibility predicates are called *pure*. We use the terms *pure assertion* and *expression* synonymously.

Verification of many program constructs can be modelled by two basic operations. *Inhaling* an assertion A adds the permissions denoted by A to the current state and assumes the pure assertions in A. *Exhaling* an assertion A checks that the current state satisfies the pure assertions in A; it also checks that the state contains the permissions denoted by A and removes them. As soon as permission to a heap location is no longer held, information about its value cannot be retained. Inhale and exhale can be seen as the permission-aware analogues of assume and assert statements [12]; they are sometimes called produce and consume [20]. Using these operations, a method call (for example) can be encoded by exhaling the method precondition and then inhaling its postcondition.

Building a verification tool for a permission logic requires effective solutions to the following *technical challenges*:

1. How to model the program state, including permissions and values?
2. How to check for a permission in a state?
3. How to add and remove permissions to and from a state?
4. How to evaluate (heap-dependent) expressions in a state?
5. When to preserve (frame) an expression's value across heap changes?

In the remainder of this section, we summarize how existing verifiers solve these challenges for logics without ISC and then explain how providing support for ISC complicates these challenges.

2.1   Smallfoot-Style Symbolic Execution

Smallfoot [2] introduced a symbolic execution technique that has become the state-of-the-art way of building verifiers for permission logics. It provides simple and efficient solutions to the technical challenges above: (1) A symbolic state consists of a set of heap chunks, and a set of path conditions. A *heap chunk* has the form $o.f \mapsto [v, p]$, mimicking separation logic's points-to predicates. It records a receiver value o, a field name f, a *location value* v representing the value stored in location $o.f$, and a permission amount p. A permission amount is a value between 0 and 1 (inclusive); intermediate values can be used to support fractional permissions. Here, o, v, and p are (immutable) symbolic values. *Path conditions* are boolean constraints on the symbolic values collected while verifying a program path such as the branch conditions on that path. Path conditions may constrain heap values and may be quantified. An SMT solver is used to answer queries about the path conditions, for instance, equality of symbolic values. (2) Checking for permission to a heap location entails iterating through the heap chunks and finding those with matching receiver-field pairs. (3) Removing permissions is modelled by subtracting permissions from the corresponding chunk(s), and adding a permission is modelled by adding a heap chunk (with a fresh symbolic location value) that provides the added permission amount. (4) Evaluating a heap lookup $e.f$ yields the location value of the chunk for $e.f$ (and is not permitted if no such chunk exists). (5) Framing the value of such expressions happens implicitly so long as the same heap chunk provides non-zero permission to the location. When a chunk no longer provides any permission, it gets removed and its location value becomes inaccessible.

In order to specify unbounded heap structures, the Smallfoot approach has been extended to handle user-defined recursive predicates. In successor tools such as VeriFast [22], jStar [7], and Viper [14], heap chunks may also represent predicate instances. Smallfoot-style symbolic execution has also been extended to support heap-dependent pure functions in the assertion language [20]. For example, the operations of a list class may be specified in terms of an `itemAt` function. Such functions include a precondition that requires permission to all locations read by the function body; this information is used to frame function applications.

These extensions increase the expressiveness of permission logics significantly, but are not sufficient to simply specify and automatically reason about important data structures such as arrays and graphs: this requires support for ISCs.

2.2   Iterated Separating Conjunction

Figure 1 illustrates the usage of ISCs: method `Replace` replaces all occurrences of integer `from` by integer `to` in the segment of array `a` between `left` and `right`. The recursive calls to smaller array segments are performed concurrently using parallel composition ‖. The second precondition requires access permissions for all elements in the array segment, and the first postcondition returns these permissions to the caller; both are expressed using ISC. The second postcondition specifies the functional behaviour of the method using an **old**-expression to refer to the prestate of a method; this pure assertion needs heap-dependent expressions under a quantifier.

```
method Replace(a: Int[], left: Int, right: Int, from: Int, to: Int)
  requires 0 <= left < right <= a.length
  requires forall i: Int :: left <= i < right ==> acc(a[i])
  ensures  forall i: Int :: left <= i < right ==> acc(a[i])
  ensures  forall i: Int :: left <= i < right ==>
                 (old(a[i]) == from ? a[i] == to : a[i] == old(a[i]))
{
  if (right - left <= 1) {
    if(a[left] == from) { a[left] := to }
  } else {
    var mid := left + (right - left) / 2
    Replace(a, left, mid, from, to) || Replace(a, mid, right, from, to)
  }
}
```

Fig. 1. A parallel replace operation on array segments. The second precondition and the first postcondition denote access permissions to the elements of the array. The **forall** quantifier in these conditions denotes an ISC: the body of the quantifier includes accessibility predicates (of the form **acc(a[i])**). The second postcondition uses a regular (pure) quantifier to specify the functional behaviour of the method. Here, **old** expressions let the postcondition refer to values in the prestate; the access permissions for these expressions come from the second precondition.

Verifying the example entails splitting the symbolic state described by the ISC in the precondition in order to exhale the preconditions of the recursive calls, and to re-combine the states resulting from inhaling the postconditions of these calls after the parallel composition, in order to prove the callee's postcondition.

Providing support for ISCs complicates each of the five technical challenges discussed above:

1. Heap chunks must be generalised to denote permission to an unbounded number of locations simultaneously, and encode a symbolic value per location (for instance, to represent the values of each array location in Fig. 1).
2. Exhaling an ISC requires checking permission for an unbounded number of heap locations; these could be spread across multiple heap chunks, as in the case of exhaling the postcondition of Replace.
3. Removing permissions from a generalised chunk may affect only some of the locations to which it provides permission. For example, when exhaling the precondition of the first recursive call to Replace, the permissions required for the second call must be retained in the symbolic state.
4. Evaluating heap-dependent expressions under quantifiers may rely on symbolic values from multiple heap chunks. For example, proving the second postcondition of Replace requires information from both recursive calls.
5. Framing in existing Smallfoot-style verifiers requires that heap-dependent expressions depend only on a bounded number of symbolic values (which can include representations of predicate instances [20]). However, this requirement is too strong for pure quantifiers over heap locations and for functions whose preconditions use ISCs to require access to an unbounded set of locations (see for instance the client in the online version of our running example [1]).

Our technique is the first to provide automatic solutions to these challenging problems. Section 3 tackles the first 3 problems; Sect. 4 tackles the remaining 2.

3   Treatment of Permissions

We consider the following canonical form of source-level assertion for denoting an ISC: **forall** $x : T :: c(x) \Rightarrow$ **acc**$(e(x).f, p(x))$, in which $c(x)$ is a boolean expression, $e(x)$ a reference-typed expression, and $p(x)$ an expression denoting a permission amount. More complex assertions can be desugared into this canonical form, for instance, iterating over the conjunction of two accessibility predicates can be encoded by repeating the quantification over each conjunct. For simplicity, we do not consider nested ISCs, but an extension is possible. Our canonical form is sufficient to directly model quantifying over all receivers in a set (useful for graph examples) or over integer indices into an array, as shown in Fig. 1.

The permission expression $p(x)$ may be a complex expression including conditionals, and need not evaluate to the same value for each instantiation of x. This enables us to model complex access patterns such as requiring non-zero permission to every nth slot of an array, which is for instance important for the verification of GPU programs [4]. ISCs are complemented by unrestricted pure quantifiers over potentially heap-dependent expressions, which are essential for specifying functional properties.

In this section, we present the first key ingredient of our symbolic execution technique: a representation for ISCs as part of the verifier's symbolic state along with algorithms to manipulate this representation.

3.1   Symbolic Heap Representation

As explained in Sect. 2.1, Smallfoot-style heap chunks $o.f \mapsto [v, p]$ consist of a receiver value o, a field name f, a location value v and a permission amount p. A naïve generalisation of this representation would be to make o, v, and p functions of the bound variable of an ISC. However, such a representation has severe drawbacks. Checking whether a heap chunk provides permission to a location $y.f$ (challenge 2 above) amounts to the existential query $\exists x.o(x) = y$; SMT solvers provide poor support for such existential queries. In the presence of fractional permissions, determining *how much* permission such a heap chunk provides is worse still, requiring to calculate the sum of *all* $p(x_i)$ such that x_i satisfies the existential query.

Our design avoids these difficulties with a simple restriction: we require the receiver expressions $e(x)$ in an ISC to be *injective* in x, for all values of x to which the ISC provides permission. Under this restriction, we can soundly assume that the mapping between the bound variable x and receiver expression $e(x)$ is *invertible* for such values, by some function e^{-1}. We can then represent an ISC over receivers $r = e(x)$ directly, essentially by replacing x by $e^{-1}(r)$ throughout.

Our resulting design is to use *quantified chunks* of the form $r.f \mapsto [v(r), p(r)]$, in which r (which is implicitly bound in such a chunk) plays the role of a quantified (reference-typed) receiver. Such a quantified chunk represents $p(r)$ permission to all locations $r.f$; $p(r)$ may be any expression denoting a permission amount. The *domain* of a quantified chunk is the set of field locations $r'.f$ for which $p(r') > 0$. The *values* of these locations are modelled by the function v, which we call a *value map* and explain in Sect. 4. A *symbolic heap* is a set of quantified chunks; a *symbolic state* is a symbolic heap plus a set of path conditions, as usual.

Under our injectivity restriction, we represent a source-level assertion of the form **forall** $x : T :: c(x) \Rightarrow$ **acc**$(e(x).f, p(x))$ using a quantified chunk of the form $r.f \mapsto [v(r), (\underline{c}(e^{-1}(r)) ~?~ \underline{p}(e^{-1}(r)) : 0)]$ for a suitable value map v and inverse function e^{-1}. Whenever necessary to avoid ambiguity, we use underlined expressions to denote the results of symbolically evaluating corresponding source-level expressions; with the exception of heap-dependent expressions (see Sect. 4.1), this evaluation is orthogonal to the contributions of this paper.

Our injectivity restriction does not limit the data structures that can be handled by our technique, provided specifications are expressed appropriately. The restriction applies to memory *locations*, not to the *values* stored in the locations. Many examples such as ISCs ranging over array indices or elements of a set naturally satisfy the restriction. Ranges that may contain duplicates (for instance, the fields of all objects stored in an array) can be encoded by mapping them to a set (thereby ignoring multiplicities) or by using complex permission expressions p that reflect multiplicities appropriately.

3.2   Inhaling and Exhaling Permissions

Using the symbolic heap design explained above, we define the operations for inhaling and exhaling ISCs in Fig. 2. The **inhale** operation takes a symbolic heap h_0, path conditions π_0, and an ISC, and returns an updated heap and path conditions. Following the encoding described in the previous subsection, the operation introduces a (fresh) inverse function e^{-1}, which is constrained as the partial inverse of the (evaluated) receiver expression $\underline{e}(x)$ by adding the constraints INV-1 and INV-2 to the path conditions. We will discuss controlling the instantiation of these quantifiers (and others introduced by our technique) in Sect. 5. The fresh value map v models the (thus far unknown) values of the heap locations in the domain of the new quantified chunk, which is added to the symbolic heap h_0.

To encode our example (Fig. 1) in a tool without native array support, we model the array slots as a set of ghost objects, each with a field **val** (representing the slot's value). That is, an array location $a[i]$ is modelled by the location A(i).val, where A is an injective function mapping indices to these ghost objects. Full details of the encoding of the running example are given online [1, Example **Parallel Array Replace**]. Following Fig. 2, inhaling the second precondition (at the start of checking the method body) entails introducing an inverse function a^{-1} mapping array locations back to corresponding indices, and then adding a

---

inhale(h_0, π_0, **forall** $x\colon T :: c(x) \Rightarrow \mathbf{acc}(e(x).f, p(x))) \rightsquigarrow$
Let y be a fresh symbolic constant of type T
/* Symbolically evaluate source-level expressions   */
var $(\pi_1, \underline{c}(y)) := \mathsf{eval}(h_0, \pi_0, c(y))$
var $(\pi_2, \underline{e}(y)) := \mathsf{eval}(h_0, \pi_1 \cup \{\underline{c}(y)\}, e(y))$
var $(\pi_3, \underline{p}(y)) := \mathsf{eval}(h_0, \pi_2, p(y))$
var $\pi_4 := \pi_3 \setminus \{\underline{c}(y)\}$

/* Introduce inverse function   */
Let e^{-1} be a fresh function of type $T \to Ref$
var $\pi_5 := \pi_4 \cup \{\forall r\colon Ref \cdot \underline{c}(e^{-1}(r)) \Rightarrow \underline{e}(e^{-1}(r)) = r\}$ /* (Inv-1) */
var $\pi_6 := \pi_5 \cup \{\forall x\colon T \cdot \underline{c}(x) \Rightarrow e^{-1}(\underline{e}(x)) = x\}$ /* (Inv-2) */

Let v be a fresh value map
var $h_1 := h_0 \cup \{r.f \to [v(r), \underline{c}(e^{-1}(r)) ? \underline{p}(e^{-1}(r)) : 0]\}$
return (h_1, π_6)

exhale(h_0, π_0, **forall** $x\colon T :: c(x) \Rightarrow \mathbf{acc}(e(x).f, p(x))) \rightsquigarrow$
Let y be a fresh symbolic constant of type T
/* Symbolically evaluate source-level expressions   */
var $(\pi_1, \underline{c}(y)) := \mathsf{eval}(h_0, \pi_0, c(y))$
var $(\pi_2, \underline{e}(y)) := \mathsf{eval}(h_0, \pi_1 \cup \{\underline{c}(y)\}, e(y))$
var $(\pi_3, \underline{p}(y)) := \mathsf{eval}(h_0, \pi_2, p(y))$
var $\pi_4 := \pi_3 \setminus \{\underline{c}(y)\}$

/* Check injectivity of receiver expression   */
Let y_1, y_2 be fresh symbolic constants of type T
check $\pi_4 \models \underline{c}(y_1) \wedge \underline{c}(y_2) \wedge \underline{e}(y_1) = \underline{e}(y_2) \Rightarrow y_1 = y_2$

/* Introduce inverse function   */
Let e^{-1} be a fresh inverse function of type $T \to Ref$
var $\pi_5 := \pi_4 \cup \{\forall r\colon Ref \cdot \underline{c}(e^{-1}(r)) \Rightarrow \underline{e}(e^{-1}(r)) = r\}$ /* (Inv-1) */
var $\pi_6 := \pi_5 \cup \{\forall x\colon T \cdot \underline{c}(x) \Rightarrow e^{-1}(\underline{e}(x)) = x\}$ /* (Inv-2) */

/* Remove permissions   */
var $h_1 := \mathsf{remove}(h_0, \pi_6, f, (\lambda r \cdot \underline{c}(e^{-1}(r)) ? \underline{p}(e^{-1}(r)) : 0))$
return (h_1, π_6)

Fig. 2. Symbolic execution rules for inhaling and exhaling ISCs. The **check** instruction submits a query to the SMT solver. If the proof obligation does not hold, it aborts with a verification failure. The Eval function evaluates an expression in a symbolic state and yields updated path conditions and the resulting symbolic expression, see Sect. 4. In both rules, the constraint $\underline{c}(y)$ is temporarily added to the path conditions used during the evaluation of $e(y)$ and $p(y)$; these expressions may be well-formed only under this additional constraint.

quantified chunk $r.\mathsf{val} \mapsto [v(r), (\underline{\mathsf{left}} \leq \underline{a}^{-1}(r) < \underline{\mathsf{right}} ? 1 : 0)]$. Correspondingly, at the program point after the two recursive calls, the symbolic heap will contain two quantified chunks: one for each array segment.

The **exhale** operation is initially similar to **inhale**, one difference being that the injectivity of the receiver expression is checked before defining the inverse function. Removing permissions is more complex than adding permissions because it may involve updates to many existing quantified chunks in the symbolic state. This operation is delegated to the auxiliary operation **remove**, shown in Fig. 3.

The injectivity check performed by **exhale** guarantees that the introduced inverse functions exist and satisfy the constraints added to the path conditions, which is required for soundness. We assume here that each **inhale** operation has a corresponding **exhale**; for instance, inhaling a method precondition at the beginning of a method body corresponds to exhaling the precondition at the call site. Therefore, the check performed by **exhale** also covers the inverse functions introduced in corresponding **inhale** operations.

---

def remove(h_0, π_0, f, q):
　Let $h_f \subseteq h_0$ be all chunks in the given state for field f
　var $h'_f := \varnothing$ 　　　　　　　　　　　　　　/* Processed chunks */
　var $q_{needed} := q$ 　　　　　　　　　　　　/* Permissions still to take */
　foreach $(r.f \rightarrow [v_i(r), q_i(r)]) \in h_f$ **do:**
　　/* Determine the permissions to take from this chunk 　　　　　　*/
　　var $q_{current} := (\lambda r \cdot min(q_i(r), q_{needed}(r)))$

　　/* Decrease the permissions still needed 　　　　　　　　*/
　　$q_{needed} := (\lambda r \cdot q_{needed}(r) - q_{current}(r))$

　　/* Add an updated chunk to the processed chunks 　　　　　*/
　　$h'_f := h'_f \cup \{r.f \rightarrow [v_i(r), (q_i(r) - q_{current}(r))]\}$
　end

　/* Check that sufficient permissions were removed 　　　　　*/
　check $\pi_0 \models \forall r \cdot q_{needed}(r) = 0$

　return $(h_0 \backslash h_f) \cup h'_f$

Fig. 3. The remove operation. The argument q maps references to permission amounts. The operation checks that the symbolic heap contains at least $q(r)$ permission for each location $r.f$ and removes it.

remove takes as inputs an initial symbolic heap h_0 and path conditions π_0, a field name f, and a function q that yields for each reference r the permission amount for location $r.f$ to be removed. **remove** fails with a verification error if the initial heap does not contain the permissions in q, and otherwise returns an updated symbolic state. This is achieved by iterating over all available chunks for field f, greedily taking as much of the still-required permissions (q_{needed}) as possible from the current chunk ($q_{current}$). Updating the chunks is expressed via pointwise-defined functions describing the corresponding permission amounts;

they involve permission arithmetic, but no existential quantifiers, and can be handled efficiently by the underlying SMT solver. After this iteration, remove checks that all requested permissions have been removed.

In our array example (Fig. 1), we exhale the second precondition before each recursive call; this requires finding the appropriate permissions from the (single) quantified chunk in the state at this point, and removing them. Dually, when exhaling the postcondition at the end of the method body, all permissions from both of the two quantified chunks yielded by the recursive calls must be removed: the iteration in the remove algorithm achieves this.

Note that remove's permission accounting is precise, which is important for soundness and completeness: it maintains the invariant that (for all r), the difference between the permissions held in the original state and those requested via parameter q is equal to the difference between those held in the updated state and those still needed. If the operation succeeds, we know (from the last check) that those still needed are exactly 0, from which we conclude that precisely the correct amounts were subtracted.

3.3   Integrating Predicates with Iterated Separating Conjunctions

Predicates are a standard feature of verification tools for permission logics (including the Viper infrastructure on which our implementation is built); they integrate simply with our support for ISCs. Figure 4 shows an example of a predicate definition, parameterised by a set of nodes, that defines a graph in terms of ISCs and closure properties over the given set of nodes. Viper requires explicit ghost operations to exchange a predicate instance $P(e)$ for its body (via an operation **unfold** $P(e)$), and vice versa (via an operation **fold** $P(e)$); this is a standard way to handle possibly-recursive predicates. In terms of the underlying verifier, an operation **fold** $P(e)$ essentially corresponds to **exhale** $P_{body}(e)$ followed by **inhale** $P(e)$, and dually for **unfold** $P(e)$. Since our support for ISCs is expressed in terms of inhale and exhale rules, it naturally integrates with Viper's existing way of handling predicates; our implementation supports predicates with ISCs and pure quantifiers in their bodies, as illustrated by the graph predicate.

Our implementation does not yet support predicates inside ISCs, but our presented technique extends straightforwardly to support this. Inhaling an ISC which ranges over predicate instances yields, just as for accessibility predicates for fields, a new quantified chunk. An **unfold** of a predicate belonging to such a chunk can be handled by exhaling the predicate instance (removing it from the chunk's permissions), and then inhaling the predicate's body. Folding an instance inhales a quantified predicate chunk that provides permissions to the single instance. We plan to extend our implementation to also support this feature combination, which will allow one to denote an unbounded number of predicate instances.

```
predicate Graph(nodes: Set[Ref]) {
       (forall n: Ref :: n in nodes ==> acc(n.left))
    && (forall n: Ref :: n in nodes ==> acc(n.right))
    && (forall n: Ref :: n in nodes && n.left != null ==> n.left  in nodes)
    && (forall n: Ref :: n in nodes && n.right != null ==> n.right in nodes)
}
```

Fig. 4. A predicate defining a graph in terms of ISCs and closure properties over a given set of nodes (that form the graph).

4   Treatment of Symbolic Values

So far we have addressed the first three technical challenges described in Sect. 2 by presenting a novel heap representation for ISCs together with algorithms that let the verifier efficiently add, as well as check for and remove permissions. In this section we present our solution to the remaining two challenges, concerned with the evaluation and framing of expressions.

4.1   Symbolic Evaluation of Heap-Dependent Expressions

Quantified chunks $r.f \mapsto [v(r), q(r)]$ represent value information via the value map v. The existence of such a chunk in a symbolic heap allows the evaluation of a read of field f for any receiver in the domain of the heap chunk, to an application of the value map. Intuitively, v represents a partial function from this domain to values (of the type of the field f). Since SMT solvers typically do not natively support partial functions, we model value maps as under-specified total functions from the receiver reference (the field f is fixed) to the type of f. We *apply* these functions only to references whose f field location is in the chunk's domain. This is why the **exhale** algorithm (Fig. 2) does not need to explicitly remove information about the values stored in the locations whose permissions are removed; the underlying total function still represents appropriate values for the new (smaller) domain.

Summarising Value Maps. Inhaling permissions adds a fresh heap chunk with a fresh value map (see Fig. 2). Therefore, a symbolic heap may contain multiple chunks for the same field, each with its own value map. In the presence of fractional permissions, the domains of these chunks may overlap such that the value of one location $x.f$ may be represented by multiple value maps. Similarly, the value of $x.f$ may be represented by multiple maps when the receiver x is quantified over and the permissions to different instantiations of the quantifier are recorded in different chunks. Therefore, all of these value maps need to be considered when evaluating such a field access.

In order to incorporate information from all relevant chunks, and provide a simple translation for field-lookups, we summarise the value maps for all chunks for a field f *lazily* before we evaluate an expression $e.f$. This summarisation is defined by the **summarise** operation in Fig. 5. For each quantified chunk with the

---

def summarise(h_0, f):
    Let $h_f \subseteq h_0$ be all quantified chunks in the given heap for field f
    Let v be a fresh value map
    var $def := \varnothing$ /* Value summary path conditions */
    var $perm := \lambda r \cdot 0$ /* Permission summary */
    foreach $(r.f \rightarrow [v_i(r), q_i(r)]) \in h_f$ **do:**
        $def := def \cup \{\forall r \cdot 0 < q_i(r) \Rightarrow v(r) = v_i(r)\}$ /* (VMDEFEQ) */
        $perm := \lambda r \cdot (perm(r) + q_i(r))$
    end
    return $(v, def, perm)$

Fig. 5. The summarise operation introduces a fresh value map for field f and constrains it according to the value maps of all heap chunks for f. It also returns a function summarising the permissions held for the field f.

appropriate field, it equates a newly-introduced value map with the value map in the chunk at all locations in the chunk's domain. Analogously, it builds up a permission expression summarising the permissions held per receiver, across all heap chunks for the field f; we use this permission expression to check whether a field access is permitted.

Note that the definition of summarise does not depend on path conditions, only on the symbolic heap; it can be computed without querying the SMT solver. Our implementation memoizes summarise, avoiding the duplication of the function declarations and path conditions defining the value and permission maps.

Symbolic Evaluation. Symbolic evaluation of expressions is defined by an operation eval, which takes a symbolic heap, path conditions, and an expression, and yields updated path conditions and the symbolic value of the expression; the cases for field lookup and pure quantifiers are given in Fig. 6 (some additional cases can be found in Appendix A). Using the summarise operation, we can simply define the evaluation of a field lookup, as shown first in Fig. 6. To evaluate such an expression, we check that at least some permission to the field location is held in the current symbolic heap, and use the value map generated by summarise to define the value of the field lookup. Via the path conditions generated by summarise, any properties known about the value maps of any of the corresponding quantified chunks will also be known about the resulting symbolic value. In each reachable state, these properties are consistent, which implies in particular that there exists a value for the field lookup that satisfies all of them. Viper regularly checks for inconsistent path conditions and prunes the current program path if it detects an unreachable state.

Evaluating pure quantifiers is handled by replacing the bound variable with a fresh constant and evaluating the quantifier body. Additional path conditions generated during this recursive evaluation might mention the fresh constant; these are universally quantified over when returning the path conditions.

Inhale, Exhale, and Field Writes. Inhaling and exhaling pure boolean expressions is implemented by first symbolically evaluating the expression and then either adding the resulting symbolic expression to the path conditions or checking it, respectively (see Appendix A).

A field write $e_1.f := e_2$ is desugared as: **exhale acc**$(e_1.f)$; **inhale acc**$(e_1.f)$; **inhale** $e_1.f == e_2$. The exhale checks that the heap has the required permission and removes it; the inhales create a new chunk with the previously-removed permission and constrain the associated value map such that it maps receiver e_1 to the value of e_2. For example, the field write a[left] := to in Fig. 1 is executed in a symbolic heap with a single quantified chunk that provides full permissions to each array location. After the field write has been executed, the heap contains two quantified chunks: the initial one, still providing full permissions to each array location *except for* a[left] (and with an unchanged value map), and a second one that provides permissions to a[left] only, with a fresh value map representing the updated value.

$\text{eval}(h_0, \pi_0, e.f) \rightsquigarrow$
  var $(\pi_1, \underline{e}) := \text{eval}(h_0, \pi_0, e)$
  var $(v, def, perm) := \text{summarise}(h_0, f)$
  check $\pi_1 \models 0 < perm(\underline{e})$
  return $(\pi_1 \cup def, v(\underline{e}))$

$\text{eval}(h_0, \pi_0, \textbf{forall } x :: e(x)) \rightsquigarrow$
  Let y be a fresh symbolic constant
  var $(\pi_1, \underline{e}(y)) := \text{eval}(h_0, \pi_0, e(y))$
  return $(\{b \in \pi_1 \mid y \notin FV(b)\} \cup \{\forall x \cdot (\bigwedge_{b \in \pi_1, y \in FV(b)} b[x/y])\}, \forall x \cdot \underline{e}(x))$

Fig. 6. Symbolic evaluation of field reads and pure quantifiers.

4.2 Framing Heap-Dependent Expressions

Permissions provide a straightforward story for framing the values of heap locations (and pure quantifiers over these): so long as the symbolic state contains *some* permission to a field location, its value will be preserved. However, framing heap-dependent functions is more complicated [8,20]. The value of a function can be framed so long as all locations the function depends on remain unchanged. To express a function's dependency on the heap, its precondition must require permission to all locations its implementation may read. For any given function application, the symbolic values of these locations are called the *snapshots* of the function application. Consequently, two function applications yield the same result if they take the same arguments and have equal snapshots. One can thus model a heap-dependent function at the SMT level by a function taking snapshots as additional arguments [20].

ISCs complicate this approach because a function whose precondition contains an ISC may depend on an unbounded set of heap locations. The values of these locations cannot be represented by a fixed number of snapshots. It is also not possible to represent them as a value map since these are modelled at the SMT level as total functions, causing two problems. First, requiring equality of total functions would include locations the heap-dependent function does not actually depend on; since the values for these locations are under-specified, the equality check would often fail even when the function value could be soundly framed. Second, a function cannot be used as a function argument, nor compared for equality in the first-order logic supported by SMT solvers.

We address the first problem by modelling snapshots as *partial* functions called *partial value maps*, and the second by applying *defunctionalisation* [17]. That is, we model a partial value map for a field f of type T as a value of an (uninterpreted) type PVM, together with a function $domain_f \colon PVM \to Set[Ref]$ for the domain of the partial value map, and a function $apply_f \colon PVM \times Ref \to T$ for the result of applying a partial value map to a receiver reference. We also include an extensionality axiom for partial value maps, allowing us to prove equality when two partial value maps are equal as partial functions.

Following the prior work, we model a heap-dependent function via a function at the SMT level, with a partial value map as additional snapshot argument for each ISC required in the function's precondition. For each application of such a function, we check that the current state contains all permissions required by the function precondition. If this is the case, we process each ISC in the precondition in turn. For an ISC for a field f, we employ the **summarise** operation (Fig. 5) to summarise the value information v for the field f in the current symbolic state, and introduce a fresh constant pvm of type PVM. We constrain $domain_f(pvm)$ to yield the set of references in the domain of the ISC, and for all receivers r in this domain, assume $apply_f(pvm, r) = v(r)$. pvm is then used as a snapshot argument to the translated function.

5   Controlling Quantifier Instantiations

When generating quantifiers for an SMT solver, it is important to carefully control their instantiation [8,11,13] by providing syntactic triggers. A quantifier $\forall x \cdot P(x)$ may be decorated with a *trigger* $\{f(x)\}$, which instructs the solver to instantiate x with a term e only if $f(e)$ is a term encountered by the solver during the current proof effort. Triggers must be chosen carefully: enabling too few instantiations may cause examples to fail unexpectedly, while too many may lead to unreliable performance or even non-termination of the solver (see also Sect. 6).

We carefully select triggers for all quantifiers generated by our technique (although we have omitted them from the presentation so far). Figure 7 shows three representative examples. The path condition VMDEFEQ relates the value map introduced by the **summarise** operation to the value maps of heap chunks (Fig. 5). The two triggers express alternatives: they allow instantiating the path condition if *either* of the two value maps have been applied to the term instantiating r. This design allows us to derive relationships between two evaluations of

$\forall r : \mathit{Ref} \cdot \{v(r)\}\{v_i(r)\}\ \ 0 < q_i(r) \Rightarrow v(r) = v_i(r)$	/* (VMDEFEQ) */
$\forall r : \mathit{Ref} \cdot \{e^{-1}(r)\}\ \ \underline{c}(e^{-1}(r)) \Rightarrow \underline{e}(e^{-1}(r)) = r$	/* (INV-1) */
$\forall x : T \cdot \{e(x)\}\ \ \underline{c}(x) \Rightarrow e^{-1}(\underline{e}(x)) = x$	/* (INV-2) */

Fig. 7. Example triggers used in our SMT encoding.

an expression, which introduce two summary value maps. Instantiating VMDE-
FEQ in both directions allows us to relate these value maps via the value maps
of heap chunks.

The next two examples define the inverse function of a receiver expression
(see Fig. 2). The trigger $e^{-1}(r)$ for INV-1 is essential for relating occurrences of
the inverse function to the original expression e. The case of INV-2 is almost sym-
metrical, but with extra technicalities. Since e comes from the source program,
it may not be an expression allowed as a trigger. Trigger terms must typically
include at least one function application (if $e(x)$ were simply x, this could not
be used), and no built-in operators such as addition. In the former case, we use
$v(x)$ as a trigger, where v is the value map of the relevant chunk; the quantifier
will then be instantiated whenever we look up a value from the chunk, which
is when we need the definition of the inverse function. In the latter case, we
resort to allowing the underlying tools select trigger terms, which may lead to
incompleteness. However, we did not observe any such incompletenesses in our
experiments.

Instantiating either of the two axioms INV-1 and INV-2 gives rise to potentially new function application terms suitable for triggering the other axiom. For
example, when instantiating INV-2 due to a term of the shape $e(x)$, we learn the
equality $e^{-1}(\underline{e}(x)) = x$ in which the function application $e^{-1}(\underline{e}(x))$ matches the
trigger for the INV-1 axiom. Instantiating this axiom, in turn, will provide the
equality $\underline{e}(e^{-1}(\underline{e}(x))) = \underline{e}(x)$. Note however, that this will not cause an indefinite sequence of instantiations of these two axioms (a so-called matching loop):
SMT solvers consider quantifier instantiations *modulo* known equalities. Thus,
the function application $\underline{e}(e^{-1}(\underline{e}(x)))$ does not give rise to a *new* instantiation of
INV-2, since the term to be matched against the quantified variable $(e^{-1}(\underline{e}(x)))$
is already known to be equal to x, which was used for the prior instantiation.

6   Evaluation

We have implemented our technique as an extension of the Viper verification
infrastructure [14]; the implementation is open source and can be tried online [1].
To evaluate the performance of our technique, we ran experiments with three
kinds of input programs: (1) 9 hand-coded verification problems involving arrays
and graphs, including our running example (see the Viper examples page [1] for
details), (2) 65 examples generated by the VerCors project at the University of
Twente [4], which uses our implementation to encode GPU verification problems,
and (3) 82 additional regression tests.

Program	Size (LOC)	Time (s)	w/o memoization	w/o triggers
`arraylist`	114	1.93	−7.29%	−16.53%
`quickselect`	132	2.51	+24.44%	−4.23%
`binary-search`	47	0.31	+14.15%	−8.94%
`graph-copy`	120	1.81	+14.93%	+21.21%
`graph-marking`	53	1.71	+41.29%	−30.95%
`longest-common-prefix`	34	0.19	+6.51%	−10.73%
`max-elimination`	59	0.50	+45.41%	−0.07%
`max-standard`	53	0.24	+16.40%	+2.43%
`parallel-replace`	56	0.27	+3.71%	−6.12%

Fig. 8. Performance evaluation of our implementation on verification challenges. Lines of code (LOC) does not include blank lines and comments. Column "Time (s)" gives runtimes of the base version of our implementation; columns "w/o memoization" and "w/o triggers" show the % difference in time relative to the base version.

Figure 8 shows the results for (1), and Fig. 9 those for (2) and (3). We performed our experiments on an Intel Core i7-4770 3.40 GHz with 16 GB RAM machine running Windows 7 × 64 with an SSD. The reported times are averaged over 10 runs of each verification (with negligible standard deviations). Timings do not include JVM start-up: we persist a JVM across test runs using the Nailgun tool.

Program Set	No. Files (#)	Size Mean (LOC)	Time Mean (s)	Time Max (s)	w/o memoization Mean (±)	w/o memoization Max (s)	w/o triggers Mean (±)	w/o triggers Max (s)
VerCors	65	104	0.72	11.81	+0.92%	15.71	-4.40%	8.83
Regressions	82	34	0.22	3.41	+0.58%	3.81	-2.24%	3.38

Fig. 9. Performance evaluation of our implementation on two sets of programs: the "VerCors" set contains (non-trivial) programs generated by the VerCors tool, "Regressions" contains (usually simple) regression tests; column "No. Files" displays the number of files per program set. All input files are available as part of the Viper test suite.

Our experiments show that our implementation is consistently fast: all examples verify in a few seconds. Since SMT encodings sometimes exhibit worse performance for *failed* verification attempts, we also tested 4 variants of each example from Fig. 8 in which we seeded errors; in all cases the errors were detected with lower runtimes (the verifier halts as soon as an error is detected).

To measure the effect of memoizing calls to `summarise`, we disabled this feature and measured the difference in runtimes over the same inputs. As shown in the "w/o memoization" columns, disabling this optimisation typically increases the runtime, but not enormously; a likely explanation for the relatively small difference is that `summarise` performs the iteration over quantified chunks efficiently, without querying the SMT solver. The number of quantified chunks in a given symbolic state is also typically kept small: the tool performs modular verification per method/loop body, and we eagerly remove any quantified chunks that no longer provide permissions (after an exhale).

To evaluate the importance of our use of triggers for controlling quantifier instantiations (see Sect. 5), we also compare with a variant of our implementation in which triggers are omitted, leaving this task to the underlying tools (that is, Viper and Z3 [6]). The relative times are shown in the "w/o triggers" columns. We observe that this variant typically *improves* verification time. However, the triggers chosen automatically by Viper and Z3 are too strict: 7 % of the programs (11 out of the 156 original programs) fail spuriously in this version. This, as well as a general reduction in quantifier instantiations, explains the effect on the runtime: the longest-running example in our base implementation (averaging 11.82 s) takes only 3 s without our triggers, but wrongly fails to verify. The longest-running example in the variant without triggers takes 8.83 s but also has a high standard deviation of 4.71 s, suggesting that performance also becomes unpredictable when triggers are selected automatically. The triggers that we choose thus avoid spurious errors and provide predictable, fast performance.

7   Conclusions and Future Work

We have presented the first symbolic execution technique that supports ISCs. This feature provides the possibility of specifying random-access data structures and provides an alternative mechanism to recursive definitions which is essential in the common case when a data structure can be traversed in multiple ways. Our technique generalises Smallfoot-style symbolic execution and is, thus, applicable to other verifiers for permission logics using this common implementation technique.

Two of the authors participated in the recent VerifyThis verification competition at ETAPS'16 (see http://etaps2016.verifythis.org/) using our implementation, and won the *Distinguished User-assistance Tool Feature* for the ISC support described in this paper: this prize was awarded for a feature that proved particularly useful during the competition.

As future work, we plan to build on our verification technique in four ways. First, we plan to extend our technique to support predicates under ISCs, as discussed in Sect. 3.3. Second, we plan to combine our verification technique with inference techniques that make use of ISCs, such as the shape analysis developed by Lee *et al.* [9]. Third, we plan to support **foreach** statements that perform an operation (*e.g.*, unfolding a predicate) on each instance of a quantifier without requiring a loop (and invariant). Such statements require permissions that can be expressed using ISCs. Fourth, we plan to integrate support for aggregates in pure assertions [11], which provide another means for specifying functional properties over locations described by an ISC.

A   Additional Definitions and Symbolic Execution Rules

Partial Value Maps. Figure 10 shows background definitions related to partial value maps (see Sect. 4.2), which are emitted to the SMT solver before the verification starts. The background definitions include a type PVM and, per field declaration, a function $domain_f$ that denotes the domain of a partial value map, a function $apply_f$ that denotes applying a partial value map to a receiver to obtain the value of the corresponding field location, and an extensionality axiom stating that two partial value maps are equal if their domains agree and if they agree on the values in their domain.

---

1. Let FD be the set of all field declarations $f\colon T$ of a given program for which ISCs are used

2. Declare a type PVM

3. Declare a function $domain_f\colon PVM \to Set[Ref]$ per declaration $f\colon T \in FD$

4. Declare a function $apply_f\colon PVM \times Ref \to T$ per declaration $f\colon T \in FD$

5. Declare the following extensionality axiom per declaration $f\colon T \in FD$:
$$\forall pvm_1, pvm_2\colon PVM \cdot \{toSnap(pvm_1), toSnap(pvm_2)\}$$
$$domain_f(pvm_1) = domain_f(pvm_2) \wedge$$
$$\forall r\colon Ref \cdot r \in domain_f(pvm_1) \Rightarrow apply_f(pvm_1, r) = apply_f(pvm_2, r)$$
$$\Rightarrow pvm_1 = pvm_2$$

Fig. 10. Background definitions related to partial value maps (see Sect. 4.2). $domain_f$ denotes the domain of a partial value map, $apply_f$ its application to a reference.

The trigger of the extensionality axiom $\{toSnap(pvm_1), toSnap(pvm_2)\}$ ensures that the extensionality axiom is instantiated whenever it is necessary to reason about the equality of partial value maps that are used as snapshots. Wrapping partial value maps by $toSnap$ is necessary because Viper requires snapshots to uniformly be of type $toSnap$; function $toSnap$ embeds values into the $toSnap$ type (a corresponding inverse function exists as well). This external requirement (of Viper, not of our technique) turned out to be beneficial for us, since it allows choosing triggers that are permissive, yet yield good performance.

Inhaling and Exhaling Pure Assertions. Figure 11 shows the symbolic execution rules for inhaling and exhaling potentially heap-dependent (but pure) assertions such as pure quantifiers. Both rules use **eval** to evaluate the assertion; the result is then added to the path conditions or asserted to hold in the current state, respectively.

$$\begin{array}{l}
\mathbf{inhale}(h_0,\ \pi_0,\ e) \rightsquigarrow \\
\quad \mathbf{var}\ (\pi_1, \underline{e}) := \mathbf{eval}(h_0,\ \pi_0,\ e) \\
\quad \mathbf{return}\ (h_0, \pi_1 \cup \{\underline{e}\}) \\
\\
\mathbf{exhale}(h_0,\ \pi_0,\ e) \rightsquigarrow \\
\quad \mathbf{var}\ (\pi_1, \underline{e}) := \mathbf{eval}(h_0,\ \pi_0,\ e) \\
\quad \mathbf{check}\ \pi_1 \vDash \underline{e} \\
\quad \mathbf{return}\ (h_0, \pi_1)
\end{array}$$

Fig. 11. Symbolic execution rules for inhaling and exhaling pure assertions.

Symbolic Evaluation of Expressions. Figure 12 shows selected symbolic execution rules for evaluating expressions. Evaluating an implication $e_1 \Rightarrow e_2$ starts by evaluating e_1, and temporarily assuming $\underline{e_1}$ while evaluating e_2 (see also the discussion of Fig. 2 in Sect. 3.1). From the path conditions obtained from evaluating e_1 (π_δ), all instances of VMDEFEQ are extracted (π_v). The final set of path conditions, with which the verification proceeds (π_3), includes the path conditions obtained from the evaluation of e_1, all instances of VMDEFEQ that were obtained from evaluating e_2 (this allows memoizing `summarise` because value map definitions are always in scope, that is, are not nested under implications), and — conditionally on $\underline{e_1}$ — the remaining path conditions from evaluating e_2.

$$\begin{array}{l}
\mathbf{eval}(h_0,\ \pi_0,\ e_1 \Rightarrow e_2) \rightsquigarrow \\
\quad \mathbf{var}\ (\pi_1, \underline{e_1}) := \mathbf{eval}(h_0,\ \pi_0,\ e_1) \\
\quad \mathbf{var}\ (\pi_2, \underline{e_2}) := \mathbf{eval}(h_0,\ \pi_1 \cup \{\underline{e_1}\},\ e_2) \\
\quad \mathbf{var}\ \pi_\delta := \pi_2 \backslash (\pi_1 \cup \{\underline{e_1}\}) \\
\quad \mathbf{var}\ \pi_v := \{b \in \pi_\delta \mid b \text{ is instance of } \text{VMDEFEQ}\} \\
\quad \mathbf{var}\ \pi_3 := \pi_1 \cup \pi_v \cup \{\underline{e_1} \Rightarrow \bigwedge(\pi_\delta \backslash \pi_v)\} \\
\quad \mathbf{return}\ (\pi_3, \underline{e_1} \Rightarrow \underline{e_2}) \\
\\
\mathbf{eval}(h_0,\ \pi_0,\ \mathit{fun}(e_1,\dots,e_n)) \rightsquigarrow \qquad\qquad \text{/* } \mathit{fun} \text{ is heap-independent */} \\
\quad \mathbf{var}\ (\pi_1, \underline{e_1}) := \mathbf{eval}(h_0,\ \pi_0,\ e_1) \\
\quad \dots \\
\quad \mathbf{var}\ (\pi_n, \underline{e_n}) := \mathbf{eval}(h_0,\ \pi_{n-1},\ e_n) \\
\quad \mathbf{return}\ (\pi_n, \underline{\mathit{fun}(\underline{e_1},\dots,\underline{e_n})}) \\
\\
\mathbf{eval}(h_0,\ \pi_0,\ e_1 \wedge e_2) \rightsquigarrow \\
\quad \mathbf{var}\ (\pi_1, \underline{e_1}) := \mathbf{eval}(h_0,\ \pi_0,\ e_1) \\
\quad \mathbf{var}\ (\pi_2, \underline{e_\Rightarrow}) := \mathbf{eval}(h_0,\ \pi_1,\ e_1 \Rightarrow e_2) \\
\quad \mathbf{return}\ (\pi_2, \underline{e_1} \wedge \underline{e_\Rightarrow})
\end{array}$$

Fig. 12. Additional symbolic execution rules for evaluating pure expressions.

Viper's remaining symbolic execution rules for evaluating expressions did not need to be changed when we implemented our technique. For illustrative purposes, we show the rule for evaluating heap-*independent* functions (including arithmetic and other operators), and for evaluating short-circuiting conjunction.

References

1. Viper Online: Try examples in the browser. http://viper.ethz.ch/examples/
2. Berdine, J., Calcagno, C., O'Hearn, P.W.: Smallfoot: modular automatic assertion checking with separation logic. In: de Boer, F.S., Bonsangue, M.M., Graf, S., de Roever, W.-P. (eds.) FMCO 2005. LNCS, vol. 4111, pp. 115–137. Springer, Heidelberg (2006)
3. Birkedal, L., Torp-Smith, N., Reynolds, J.C.: Local reasoning about a copying garbage collector. In: Jones, N.D., Leroy, X. (eds.) POPL, pp. 220–231. ACM (2004)
4. Blom, S., Huisman, M.: The VerCors tool for verification of concurrent programs. In: Jones, C., Pihlajasaari, P., Sun, J. (eds.) FM 2014. LNCS, vol. 8442, pp. 127–131. Springer, Heidelberg (2014)
5. Boyland, J.: Checking interference with fractional permissions. In: Cousot, R. (ed.) SAS 2003. LNCS, vol. 2694, pp. 55–72. Springer, Heidelberg (2003)
6. de Moura, L., Bjørner, N.S.: Z3: an efficient SMT solver. In: Ramakrishnan, C.R., Rehof, J. (eds.) TACAS 2008. LNCS, vol. 4963, pp. 337–340. Springer, Heidelberg (2008)
7. Distefano, D., Parkinson, M.J.: jStar: towards practical verification for Java. In: OOPSLA, pp. 213–226. ACM (2008)
8. Heule, S., Kassios, I.T., Müller, P., Summers, A.J.: Verification condition generation for permission logics with abstract predicates and abstraction functions. In: Castagna, G. (ed.) ECOOP 2013. LNCS, vol. 7920, pp. 451–476. Springer, Heidelberg (2013)
9. Lee, O., Yang, H., Yi, K.: Automatic verification of pointer programs using grammar-based shape analysis. In: Sagiv, M. (ed.) ESOP 2005. LNCS, vol. 3444, pp. 124–140. Springer, Heidelberg (2005)
10. Leino, K.R.M.: Dafny: an automatic program verifier for functional correctness. In: Clarke, E.M., Voronkov, A. (eds.) LPAR-16 2010. LNCS, vol. 6355, pp. 348–370. Springer, Heidelberg (2010)
11. Leino, K.R.M., Monahan, R.: Reasoning about comprehensions with first-order SMT solvers. In: Shin, S.Y., Ossowski, S. (eds.) SAC, pp. 615–622. ACM (2009)
12. Leino, K.R.M., Müller, P.: A basis for verifying multi-threaded programs. In: Castagna, G. (ed.) ESOP 2009. LNCS, vol. 5502, pp. 378–393. Springer, Heidelberg (2009)
13. Moskal, M.: Programming with triggers. In: SMT. ACM International Conference Proceeding Series, vol. 375, pp. 20–29. ACM (2009)
14. Müller, P., Schwerhoff, M., Summers, A.J.: Viper: a verification infrastructure for permission-based reasoning. In: Jobstmann, B., et al. (eds.) VMCAI 2016. LNCS, vol. 9583, pp. 41–62. Springer, Heidelberg (2016). doi:10.1007/978-3-662-49122-5_2
15. Parkinson, M., Bierman, G.: Separation logic and abstraction. In: Palsberg, J., Abadi, M. (eds.) POPL, pp. 247–258. ACM (2005)
16. Piskac, R., Wies, T., Zufferey, D.: GRASShopper—complete heap verification with mixed specifications. In: Ábrahám, E., Havelund, K. (eds.) TACAS 2014. LNCS, vol. 8413, pp. 124–139. Springer, Heidelberg (2014)
17. Reynolds, J.C.: Definitional interpreters for higher-order programming languages. In: ACM Annual Conference, ACM 1972, vol. 2, pp. 717–740. ACM (1972)
18. Reynolds, J.C.: Separation logic: a logic for shared mutable data structures. In: LICS. IEEE Computer Society Press (2002)

19. Smans, J., Jacobs, B., Piessens, F.: Implicit dynamic frames: combining dynamic frames and separation logic. In: Drossopoulou, S. (ed.) ECOOP 2009. LNCS, vol. 5653, pp. 148–172. Springer, Heidelberg (2009)

20. Smans, J., Jacobs, B., Piessens, F.: Heap-dependent expressions in separation logic. In: Hatcliff, J., Zucca, E. (eds.) FMOODS 2010, Part II. LNCS, vol. 6117, pp. 170–185. Springer, Heidelberg (2010)

21. Smans, J., Jacobs, B., Piessens, F.: Implicit dynamic frames. ACM Trans. Program. Lang. Syst. **34**(1), 2:1–2:58 (2012)

22. Smans, J., Jacobs, B., Piessens, F.: VeriFast for Java: a tutorial. In: Clarke, D., Noble, J., Wrigstad, T. (eds.) Aliasing in Object-Oriented Programming. LNCS, vol. 7850, pp. 407–442. Springer, Heidelberg (2013)

23. Yang, H.: An example of local reasoning in BI pointer logic: the Schorr-Waite graph marking algorithm. In: Proceedings of the SPACE Workshop (2001)

From Shape Analysis to Termination Analysis in Linear Time

Roman Manevich[1]([✉]), Boris Dogadov[2], and Noam Rinetzky[2]

[1] Ben-Gurion University of the Negev, Beer-Sheva, Israel
romanm@cs.bgu.ac.il
[2] Tel Aviv University, Tel Aviv, Israel
{borisdog,maon}@post.tau.ac.il

Abstract. We present a novel algorithm to conservatively check whether a (recursive) heap-manipulating program terminates. Our algorithm can be used as a post-processing phase of any shape analysis satisfying some natural properties. The running time of the post-processing phase is linear in the size of the output of the chosen shape analysis.

The main idea is to partition the (unbounded but finite) set of allocated objects in every state into a bounded set of regions, and track the flow of objects between heap regions in every step of the program. The algorithm proves the existence of the well-founded relation over states by showing that in every loop iteration at least one object (which was allocated before entering the loop) moves to a strictly lower-ranked heap region. The partitioning of objects into regions, the flow of objects between regions, and the ranks of regions are computed automatically from the output of the underlying shape analysis. Our algorithm extends the state of the art in terms of complexity, the class of supported data structures, and its generality.

We successfully applied a prototype of our analysis to prove termination of a suite of benchmarks from existing literature, including (looping, recursive, and concurrent) list manipulating programs, looping list-sorting programs, and looping programs that manipulate trees and graphs. The overhead of the termination phase in our experiments is at most 14 % of the overall analysis time.

1 Introduction

Proving termination of heap manipulating programs is both important and challenging. System codes, whose reliability is crucial for the stack of software built on top of them, often use low-level manipulation of linked data structures to gain efficiency. Proving termination requires synthesizing ranking functions that correlate two different types of unbounded data—data structure invariants and the number of loop iterations. This in turn requires tracking highly complex shape-numeric invariants [14,19].

This work was funded by EU FP7 project ADVENT (308830) and by the Broadcom Foundation and Tel Aviv University Authentication Initiative.

S. Chaudhuri and A. Farzan (Eds.): CAV 2016, Part I, LNCS 9779, pp. 426–446, 2016.
DOI: 10.1007/978-3-319-41528-4_23

Almost all existing approaches (with Brotherson et al. [8,9] as a notable exception) address the undecidable problem of proving termination of heap-manipulating programs by reducing it to another undecidable problem, e.g., proving termination of a numeric program [4,5,19], proving termination of a term-rewriting system [21], or proving the termination of a constraint-logic program [27]. In contrast, we take a direct approach. In the first phase, we apply any program-wide shape analysis that partitions the heap into finitely many heap regions and computes the following two relations: (i) an abstract transition relation, and (ii) an abstract relation that tracks how program statements cause individual objects to change membership in heap regions. In the second phase, we conservatively check termination by solving a linear time problem over these two relations. By decoupling the reasoning used to synthesize heap invariants from the reasoning used for checking termination, we gain the following notable advantages:

- We avoid the need to track complex heap measures during the shape analysis.
- Our termination checking phase is agnostic to most details of the programming language. Its only requirement is that the loops form a hierarchical tree structure.
- Our termination checking phase can be latched on top of any shape analysis, which satisfies certain natural assumptions. This makes our approach quite flexible, allowing to adapt the shape analysis to a given class of programs and data structures[1] and to support combined shape domains [28,29].
- Our algorithm handles recursive procedures quite precisely via the call stack-as-list approach [24,25]. As far as we know, we are the first to automatically prove termination of recursive heap-manipulating procedures with side-effects.
- We can apply summarization to the result of the shape analysis phase. Then, we can check the termination of each loop and procedure only with respect to these summaries in a modular way.

Overview of Our Approach. The termination analysis begins by processing the abstract transition relation computed by the underlying shape analysis to produce a bounded graph which conservatively tracks the flow of objects between heap regions. The nodes of the graph are pairs of abstract states and regions. The graph contains two kind of edges, pertaining to over- and under- approximation information: *evolution edges* and *must-evolution edges*. The former over-approximates the object flow information by refining every abstract transition into a set of *evolution edges* going from every region in the source abstract state to every region in the target abstract state which *may* contain some of its objects, while the latter under-approximates the flow information by producing a similar set of evolution edges which records *must flow* information.

---

[1] For example, by choosing separation logic approaches for programs manipulating inductive data structures and shape graph approaches for programs manipulating arbitrary graph data structures.

Using the (may) evolution graph, we compute an acyclic graph, called the *condensation graph*, by collapsing strongly-connected components and removing self-loops. The condensation graph entails a well-founded relation over heap regions: Every region is given a *rank* based on its depth in the condensation graph, and as the latter is acyclic and the number abstract states and regions is bounded, there is a bounded number of ranks. This well-founded relation can be point-wise lifted to a well-founded relation over abstract states which maps every region in every state to its rank. The resulting relation is preserved by any abstract transition (i.e., the either stays the same of strictly decreases). To prove that every loop in the program terminates, we find for every cycle in the abstract transition relation terminates, a *cutting set*—a set of transitions that strictly decrease this relation in every iteration through the cycle. Specifically, our algorithm looks for a cutting set containing only must-evolution edges.

Main Contributions. The main contributions of this paper are summarized below:

1. **Novel Well-founded Relation Over Heaps.** We show how to use the result of a shape analysis to construct a well-founded relation over the transitions of any heap-manipulating program (Sect. 5). This avoids the need to synthesize a different well-founded relation for each program. It also allows us to dynamically find the best set of cut points in the abstract transition relation, in contrast to existing analyses that choose them a priori.

2. **Generic Framework.** Our algorithm (Sect. 3) is parameterized by (the atomic statements of) the programming language (Sect. 2) and a class of shape analyses satisfying very weak and natural assumptions (Sect. 4). It is independent of the iteration strategy used by the shape analysis, e.g., whether it is forward or backward, compositional [10], and whether it uses widening. This allows us to mix and match existing shape analyses, and take advantage of any advances in this field by simply replacing the underlying shape analysis. We utilize this flexibility to support recursion (Sect. 6).

3. **Featherweight Reasoning.** Our termination checking phase analyzes loops and recursive procedures separately by summarizing their behavior. Its overall running time is linear time in the size of the program and the output of the shape analysis. The predictable performance makes it an appealing upgrade for existing shape analyses.

5. **Experimental Evaluation.** We have implemented a prototype of our analysis and applied it to a suite of benchmarks (Sect. 7). Our analysis successfully handles programs operating on inductive data structures as well as a garbage-collection benchmark operating on arbitrary graphs, programs with recursive procedures, and intricate examples introduced by previous works. We have also proved lock-freedom for concurrent programs manipulating linked lists with a constant number of threads.

2   Programming Language and Running Example

We formalize our results using a simple imperative programming language for sequential procedure-less programs, which we later extend to handle (recursive) procedures and bounded parallelism. We assume that the reader is familiar with the way programs are represented using *control-flow graphs* (see, e.g., [1,20]), and only define the necessary terminology.

Syntax. A program $P = (V, E, v_{entry}, v_{exit}, c)$ is a *control-flow graph (CFG)*: Nodes $v \in V$ correspond to *program points* and edges $e \in E$ indicate possible transfer of control. Every node v is associated with a primitive command $c(v)$. P starts its execution at program point v_{entry} and terminates at v_{exit}. We assume that the program has a *reducible* CFG, i.e., every loop has a single *entry node*, which we refer to as the *loop header*. For simplicity, we assume that every loop has a unique entry node which is also its unique *exit node*, and identify loops by their headers. We also assume E does not contain self loops, i.e., $\forall v \in V. (v, v) \notin E$.

We say that $L = (V', E', v'_{entry}, v'_{exit}, c|_{V'})$ is the *sub-CFG* of P pertaining to V' if $\{v'_{entry}, v'_{exit}\} \subseteq V' \subseteq V$, $E' = E \cap V' \times V'$, v'_{entry} is the only node in V' into which control can flow in P from program points outside V' and v'_{exit} is the only node in V' from which control can leave V'. We denote the entry node and exit nodes of a sub-CFG L by $Entry(L)$ and $Exit(L)$, respectively. We denote the set of sub-CFGs pertaining to the natural loops[2] in the CFG of P by $\text{Loops}(P)$.

Our technique is independent of the choice of primitive commands; we only require that they can be handled by the underlying shape analysis. Thus, we leave this set unspecified. In our examples, we use a set of typical commands for heap-manipulating programs: assignments between variables, dynamic allocation and deallocation of objects, (possibly destructive) accesses to fields of objects, and conditionals involving pointer expressions. The meaning of these commands is standard (see, e.g., [23]).

Operational Semantics. The concrete semantics of a program is defined as a *concrete transition relation* $T \subseteq \Sigma \times \Sigma$ over a set of *concrete states* $\sigma \in \Sigma$. We assume an unbounded set $o \in \mathcal{O}$ of *object identifiers* (*objects* for short). We only expect that a concrete state $\sigma = \langle v, A, F, \ldots \rangle$ records the value of the program counter, denoted by $v(\sigma) = v$, the finite, but unbounded, set of *allocated* objects, denoted by $A(\sigma) = A$, and the unbounded set of *free* (unallocated) objects, denoted by $F(\sigma) = F$. Concrete transitions induce a *concrete evolution relation*. That is, a relation that for each $(\sigma, \sigma') \in T$ connects the objects in σ to the corresponding objects in σ'[3]. We place no other restrictions on the form of states or on the transition relation.

---

[2] Intuitively, a natural loop is the CFG-analogue of a `while` loop: It has a single *header* (entry) node, and every two natural loops are either nested, disjoint, or share the header node. See [1].

[3] Intuitively, this relation is identity, although in reality a garbage collector can relocate objects in memory.

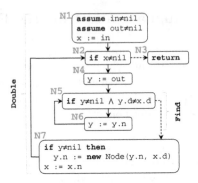

Fig. 1. CFG for `Double` (with extended basic blocks). Dashed edges represent false condition branches.

Running Example. In the rest of the paper, we exemplify our analysis using a simple program in a Java-like language whose control-flow graph (CFG) is shown in Fig. 1. The program operates over two disjoint acyclic singly-linked lists pointed-to by `in` and `out`, respectively. List elements are declared as

<code>class Node { Node n; int d; }</code> .

The outer loop scans the `in` list and uses the inner loop, shown by the sub-CFG `Find`, to find an identical element in the `out` list. If it finds one, it splices a copy of that element next to it. The sub-CFG of the outer loop is consists of the nodes in the CFG except N1 and N3, and its header is N2. The sub-CFG of the inner loop consists of the nodes N5 and N6, and its header is N5.

3   Termination Analysis

This section defines our termination analysis, which is shown as pseudo-code in Fig. 2.

The analysis is based on the following principles: (i) using a partition-based shape analysis (Sect. 3.1) to approximate the concrete transition relation and to approximate the flow of objects between heap regions by a so-called *evolution relation*; (ii) using the flow of objects between heap regions to define a well-founded relation[4] over heap regions and then lift it to a well-founded relation over the abstract heap descriptors (Sect. 3.2); (iii) using the well-founded relation to discover a *loop cut* for each loop—a set of transitions that strictly decrease the well-founded relation and must be taken in each loop iteration (Sect. 3.3); and (iv) summarizing loops to handle loop nesting (Sect. 3.4).

3.1   Shape Analysis

Our termination analysis is built on top of an underlying shape analysis, which is first applied to the entire program (OBJECTFLOWTERMCHECK line 1).

---

[4] A relation is well-founded if it has no infinite descending chains.

OBJECTFLOWTERMCHECK(P) {
1    $(\tau, \text{ev}) \longleftarrow$ SHAPEANALYSIS(P)
2    $L_1, \ldots, L_n \longleftarrow$ LOOPS(P)
3    $(\overline{\tau}[L_1, \ldots, L_n], \overline{\text{ev}}[L_1, \ldots, L_n]) \longleftarrow$ SUMMARIZE(P, τ, ev)
4   **foreach** $i = 1..n$ **do**
5   // Compute well-founded relation over regions, for the loop-specific evolution relation.
6        $\text{ev}_\prec \longleftarrow$ EVOLUTIONTOWF$(\overline{\text{ev}}[L_i])$
7        $\tau_\circlearrowleft \longleftarrow \overline{\tau}[L_i]$ // Get loop-specific abstract transition relation.
8   // Remove decreasing abstract transitions.
9   **foreach** $(s, s') \in \tau_\circlearrowleft$ **do**
10   **if** $\exists([(s, \rho)], [(s', \rho')]) \in \text{ev}_\prec(s, s')$ **then**
11              $\tau_\circlearrowleft \longleftarrow \tau_\circlearrowleft \setminus (s, s')$ //since $s \prec s'$
12        $NonDecreasingCycles \longleftarrow \{b \in \text{SCC}(\tau_\circlearrowleft) \mid |b| > 1\}$
13   **if** $NonDecreasingCycles \neq \emptyset$ **then**
14   Print "Loop L may not terminate!"
   }

EVOLUTIONTOWF(ev_L) {
1    $\{[r_1], \ldots, [r_m]\} \longleftarrow$ SCC(MAY$(\text{ev}_L))$
2   // Merge region ranks possibly containing loop-allocated objects.
3   **foreach** $[r_i] \in \{[r_1], \ldots, [r_m]\}$ **do**
4   **if** $(\rho_{free}, r_i) \in \text{ev}_L^*$ **then**
5           $[\rho_{free}] \longleftarrow [\rho_{free}] \cup [r_i]$
6   // Maintain strictly-decreasing evolution edges.
7    $\text{ev}_\prec \longleftarrow \text{ev}_L$
8   **foreach** $((s, \rho), (s', \rho')) \in \text{ev}_\prec$ **do**
9   **if** $[(s, \rho)] = [(s', \rho')] \vee \neg$MUST$((s, \rho), (s', \rho'))$ **then**
10          $\text{ev}_\prec \longleftarrow \text{ev}_\prec \setminus \{((s, \rho), (s', \rho'))\}$
11   **return** $\text{ev}_\prec$
   }

Fig. 2. Soundly checking termination. MAY(ev) and MUST(ev) return the subset of evolution may edges and evolution must edges, respectively

$x, z \in \text{Var}$	Variables
$v \in V$	CFG nodes
$E ::= x \mid \text{nil}$	Expressions
$P ::= E = E \mid \neg P$	Simple pure formulae
$Q ::= \text{true} \mid P \mid Q \wedge Q$	Pure formulae
$A ::= (x \mapsto E) \mid \text{ls}(E, E)$	Atomic spatial formulae
$H ::= A \mid \text{emp} \mid H * H$	Spatial formulae
$\langle v, Q \wedge H \rangle$	Symbolic heaps
$\text{ls}(E, F) = E \mapsto F \vee \exists z . E \mapsto z * \text{ls}(z, F)$	

Fig. 3. Symbolic heaps

The shape analysis must produce two relations—an abstract transition relation and an (abstract) *evolution relation*. The abstract transition relation is a finite graph whose nodes are (abstract) heap descriptors and edges overapproximate the concrete transition relation between the concrete heaps they represent. A heap descriptor consists of a finite set of *heap regions* (or simply *regions*), which partition the set of objects in each concrete heap it represents. The evolution relation is a (finite) graph whose nodes are the regions in the heap descriptors. The edges (over- and under-) approximate the flow of objects between the regions of any two heap descriptors related by an abstract transition. To identify a heap region ρ in a specific heap descriptor s, we write (s, ρ).

To exemplify our analysis, we assume basic familiarity with shape analysis based on separation logic [3] and use the analysis of singly-linked lists [12]. In this analysis, the heap descriptors are represented by *symbolic heaps* and the heap regions are represented by *spatial formulae*, both of which are defined in Fig. 3.

Example 1. Figure 4 shows a concrete transition from state σ to state σ', resulting from executing the statement y:=y.n. The objects in each state are partitioned as shown by the spatial formulae annotations. The red edges that connect corresponding objects comprise the so-called concrete evolution relation. Specifically, notice that the transition moves the object e from the region ls(y, nil) to the region ls(out, y).

To approximate the concrete transition relation for a given statement, a separation logic-based analysis applies a sequence of derivation rules. To approximate the concrete evolution relation, each derivation rule must be augmented with two types of edges between the regions of the pre and post symbolic heaps. A may edge means that an object in the source region may exist in the destination region. A must edge means that at least one object in the source region must exist in the destination region. To maintain soundness, may edges can be overapproximated and must edges can be underapproximated.

Figure 5 shows (a simplified subset of) such derivation rules used in analyzing the Find loop. For the given rules, the set of evolution may edges and the set of evolution must edges are equal. The double-lined arrows stand for the bijection between the spatial formulae appearing in the pre formula and the corresponding spatial formulae appearing in the post formula.

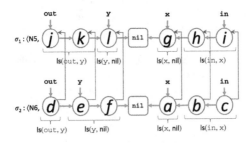

Fig. 4. A concrete transition annotated with evolution edges and spatial formulae

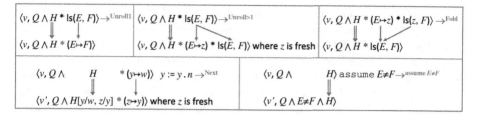

Fig. 5. Derivation rules augmented with abstract evolution edges. For the statement rules, we have that $(v, v') \in E$ and $c(v)$ is the statement at hand

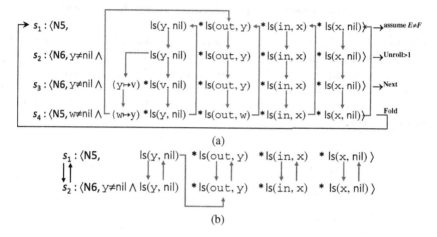

Fig. 6. (a) Symbolic execution augmented with evolution edges, and (b) the resulting transition relation and evolution relation

Figure 6(a) shows how the symbolic heap s_2 is derived from s_1 and how s_1 is derived from s_2 via the intermediate symbolic heaps s_3 and s_4 (redundant variables are removed after each rule application). By composing the relations (using natural join) across the intermediate states of the symbolic execution, we obtain the abstract transitions edges $(s_1, s_2), (s_2, s_1)$ and the evolution relation shown in Fig. 6(b).

The edges $(s_1, s_2), (s_2, s_1)$ form a cycle in the abstract transition relation. *How do we show that every execution represented by this cycle terminates?*

3.2   From Shape Analysis to a Well-Founded Relation

Consider a concrete execution whose states are represented by s_1 and s_2. Every concrete transition represented by the abstract transition (s_2, s_1) shrinks the region $\mathsf{ls}(\mathsf{y}, \mathsf{nil})$ of s_2 by moving an object (e in our example) to the region $\mathsf{ls}(\mathsf{out}, \mathsf{y})$ of s_1 (i.e., from the suffix of the list to its prefix, relative to y). Furthermore, this transition appears infinitely often in every infinite path that contains this cycle. Since no objects flow into this region other than from itself, after taking this transition a number of times that is bounded by the number of cells in the out list, this region becomes empty and the execution must exit the cycle.

In **EvolutionToWF**, line 1, the procedure accepts the evolution relation induced by the transitions between CFG nodes of a loop and uses the may edges to compute its strongly-connected components in linear time [11]. It then produces a so-called *condensation graph* by collapsing the set of regions in each component to a single node and removing self-loops. This results in a finite and acyclic graph, which is therefore a well-founded relation. The *region rank*, or simply *rank*, of a region (s, ρ), denoted $[(s, \rho)]$, is the component in the condensation to which it belongs. We write $[(s, \rho)] \preceq [(s', \rho')]$ if $[(s', \rho')]$ is reachable from $[(s, \rho)]$ in the condensation graph. Figure 7 shows the condensation graph induced by s_1 and s_2.

The well-founded relation $\cdot \preceq \cdot$ induces a well-founded relation over the concrete states represented by the abstract transition relation. Intuitively, we map each object o in a concrete state to the rank of the region representing o, denoted by $rank(o)$. We then lift this relation to pairs of concrete states related by the execution of a statement by comparing the objects in the post-state to the objects in the pre-state.

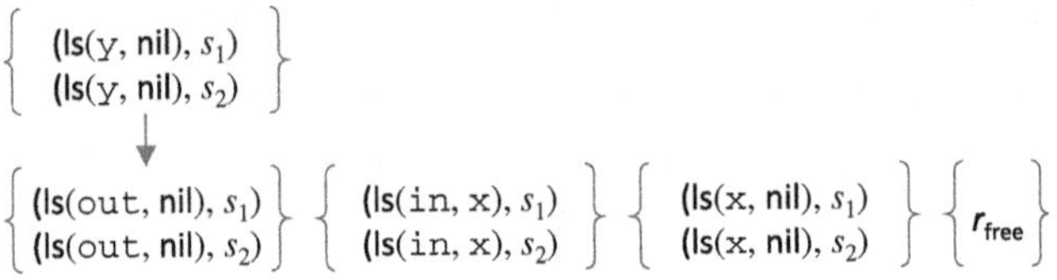

Fig. 7. The condensation graph induced by the evolution edges between s_1 and s_2

Our reasoning depends on depleting regions. To account for this, care must be taken when objects are allocated inside a loop. To account for this, we introduce a special *free region* (not explicitly represented by the symbolic heaps) to represent the (infinite) region of unallocated objects. We merge its region rank with any region rank that may contain loop-allocated objects (lines 2–5). This way, loop-allocated objects never decrease the relation.

By definition (Sect. 5), all concrete transitions preserve the resulting well-founded relation. To show termination, however, we need to show that this relation strictly decreases infinitely often for each cycle. For this purpose, we maintain only evolution must edges that decrease the well-founded relation (lines 6–10).

3.3   Computing Loop Cuts

Let L be a loop and $\tau(L) \subseteq \mathcal{S} \times \mathcal{S}$ be the abstract transition relation computed by the shape analysis for that loop. To show that L terminates, we follow this recipe: (i) find a well-founded relation $s \preceq s'$ over the heap descriptors, which is preserved by each transition (that is, either the relation stays the same or it strictly decreases); (ii) find a set $Cut(L) \subseteq \tau(L)$ (as large as possible) such that each transition in $Cut(L)$ strictly decreases $\preceq$; and (iii) test whether $Cut(L)$ forms a cut. That is whether $\tau(L) \setminus Cut(L)$ does not contain any cycles, in which case all executions represented by $\tau(L)$ must terminate.

The benefit of this approach is that each abstract transition can be tested independently. In our case, we only need to check (lines 8–14) whether the transition includes an edge returned by EVOLUTIONTOWF.

Contrast this with approaches [5] that synthesize loop-specific rank functions. Those usually choose a priori a set of CFG nodes as loop cutpoints (usually the loop header) and try to establish that transitions leaving these cutpoints decrease the rank. If that fails, e.g., due to the level of abstraction at those points, an alternative set must be searched for. Our approach finds the set of cutpoints at the fine granularity of abstract transitions. Since this set is maximal, all alternative choices have been explored in one shot. This is possible only because we have constructed a well-founded relation that is guaranteed to be preserved by all (concrete and abstract) transitions.

In our example, the evolution edge $((\mathsf{ls}(\mathsf{y},\mathsf{nil}), s_2),\ (\mathsf{ls}(\mathsf{out},\mathsf{y}), s_1))$ decreases the rank of every concrete state represented by s_2 and therefore the abstract transition (s_2, s_1) forms a loop cut.

3.4   Employing Modular Reasoning

To show that a program terminates, we can first infer a sound specification for each loop, e.g., as a Hoare triple, by a program-wide analysis. We can then reason about the termination of each loop separately by: (i) using specifications for its internal loops, and (ii) assuming internal loops terminate. If all loops have been proven to terminate this way, the entire program terminates.

ObjectFlowTermCheck obtains the set of sub-CFGs corresponding to program loops (line 2). Those can be found by linear time loop-reconstruction algorithms based on the dominance. The algorithm then proceeds to produce a loop-specific version of the abstract transition relation and the evolution relation for each loop L. This is achieved by the recursive procedure SUMMARIZE (line 3), which works as follows. It computes for each heap descriptor at the loop entry the heap descriptors it reaches at the loop exit. This can be done in linear time by a breadth-first search by following the abstract transition relation. Similarly, the reachability relation can be computed in linear time for the evolution relation. When a heap descriptor stored at the entry of an inner loop L' is encountered, SUMMARIZE executes for L' and caches its result—a pair of relations between the entry of L' and its exit. It uses the cached relation of L' to compute the result for L. Finally, SUMMARIZE returns for each loop L the pair of relations where inner loops are treated as atomic steps by using their entry-to-exit summarized relations. Finally (lines 12–14), if a loop cannot be determined to terminate, we emit a warning.

Conceptually, the well-founded relations of nested loops yield a lexicographic order. However, summarization lets us avoid reasoning about this lexicographic order explicitly. Instead, it is constructed incrementally in reverse order to the nesting level of the loops. The resulting verification is loop-modular: The outer loop is verified to terminate under the (proven) assumption that the inner loop terminates. However, loop-modularity comes with a price: When verifying the termination of the outer loop we cannot use must-flow edges of the inner loop, and vice versa.

Using the summary for Find, we apply our algorithm to the outer loop of Fig. 1 and establish that it terminates.

The overall running time of our algorithm is linear in the size of the program CFG P, the size of the abstract transition relation τ, and the size of the evolution relation ev.

We note that our reasoning can only be applied to loops whose number of iterations is linearly bounded by the number of objects that exist upon entry (this is because the rank of an object can decrease at most by a number of times equal to the height of the condensation graph, which is a static constant). In practice, this does not seem to be a limitation as the overwhelming majority of programs we have looked at have linear loops and the small number of super-linear loops (such a fixed-point loops) do not seem to be amenable to automation.

4   Partition-Based Shape Analysis

Our algorithm for proving termination is parametric in the underlying shape analysis, which is expected to satisfy three natural properties:

1. The analysis should represent (possibly unbounded) sets of states by *finite* sets of *abstract states*, and provide an over-approximation of the program's transition relation by means of a *finite abstract transition relation* between abstract states.
2. Every abstract state should induce a partitioning of (the unbounded set of) the allocated objects in every state it represents into a finite set of *regions*. Furthermore, the analysis should allow to deduce an *evolution relation* [30] which tracks the flow of objects between regions in every transition.

Abstract Semantic Domains	
$s \in \mathcal{S}$	Abstract states
$S \in \mathfrak{S} \subseteq 2^{\mathcal{S}}$	Abstract domain
$\rho \in \mathcal{R}$	Region identifiers
$\tau \subseteq \mathcal{S} \times \mathcal{S}$	Abstract transition relation
$\mathsf{ev}, \hat{e} \subseteq (\mathcal{S}, \mathcal{R}) \times (\mathcal{S}, \mathcal{R})$	Evolution relation
Concretization Functions	
$\gamma : \mathfrak{S} \to 2^{\Sigma}$	Concretization function
$\gamma^R : (\mathcal{S} \times \Sigma) \rightharpoonup (\mathcal{R} \to 2^{\mathcal{O}})$	Region concretization function

Fig. 8. Summary of the abstract semantic domains and expected operations

3. Given an abstract transition pertaining to a command that allocates memory, the analysis should be able to determine which regions in the post-state may contain newly allocated objects. Similarly, for a command that deallocates memory, it should be able to determine which regions in the pre-state may contain objects deallocated by the command.

In the rest of the section, we formalize the expected properties of the underlying shape analysis and describe the construction of the *evolution relation*. Figure 8 summarizes the semantic domains and the operations assumed on them.

4.1 Shape Analysis

We assume that the underlying shape analysis uses an abstract domain $\mathfrak{S}$, ranged over by S, whose elements are finite sets of *abstract states*. We denote the (arbitrary but *finite*) set of all possible abstract states by $\mathcal{S}$, and range over it by s. We are not concerned by the way the analysis works, only that it provides a *concretization function* γ which determines which (concrete) states every set $S \in \mathfrak{S} \subseteq 2^{\mathcal{S}}$ of abstract states represents. We expect that the latter work in a pointwise manner, i.e., $\gamma(S) = \bigcup_{s \in S} \gamma(\{s\})$. That is, the set of states represented by S is the union of the states represented by its members. In addition, we expect abstract states to record the value of the program counter, i.e., all the (concrete) states represented by an abstract state s have the same value for the program counter, and all the abstract states in a set $S \in \mathfrak{S}$ record the same value of the program counter.

Definition 1 (Shape Domain). *A* shape domain $(\mathfrak{S}, \gamma)$ *is comprised of a set of sets of abstract states* $\mathfrak{S} \subseteq 2^{\mathcal{S}}$ *and a concretization function* $\gamma : \mathfrak{S} \to 2^{\Sigma}$ *mapping sets of abstract states to sets of (concrete) states, such that for any* $S \in \mathfrak{S}$ *the following holds:*

$$\gamma(S) = \bigcup_{s \in S} \gamma(\{s\}) \text{, and}$$

$$\forall s_1, s_2, \sigma_1, \sigma_2. (\{s_1, s_2\} \subseteq S \wedge \sigma_1 \in \gamma(\{s_1\}) \wedge \sigma_2 \in \gamma(\{s_2\})) \implies v(\sigma_1) = v(\sigma_2).$$

Recall that the semantics of the program is described using a transition relation between states. We expect that the underlying shape analysis computes an over-approximation of this relation as a relation between abstract states.

Definition 2 (Abstract Transition Relation). *Let* $(\mathfrak{S}, \gamma)$ *be a shape domain. An* abstract transition relation $\tau \subseteq \mathcal{S} \times \mathcal{S}$ *is a binary relation over abstract states.* T conservatively represents *a concrete transition relation* T *if*

$$T \subseteq \{(\sigma_1, \sigma_2) \mid (s_1, s_2) \in \tau, \sigma_1 \in \gamma(\{s_1\}), \sigma_2 \in \gamma(\{s_2\})\}.$$

4.2   Partition-Based Shape Analysis

Partition-based shape analyses *utilize abstract states which induce* a finite partitioning of the (the unbounded set of) allocated objects in every state they represent into a finite set of regions. The regions induced by an abstract state often have a semantic meaning, e.g., different regions may correspond to different data structures. However, for our purpose, such a meaning is of no importance. We only care that for a given program, the number of regions induced by any abstract state is finite. We abstract away from the particular details of this kind of partition-based abstractions using the notion of a *region concretization function* γ^R. Formally, we assume to be given a finite set of *regions identifiers* $\mathcal{R}$, ranged over by the metavariable ρ, and use them to identify subsets of the dynamically allocated objects in a state. γ^R maps an abstract state s and a concrete state σ represented by it to a function from region identifiers to (the possibly empty) the set of objects they represent. For technical reasons, we assume that $\mathcal{R}$ includes a specially designated region identifier ρ_{free}, which represents the free (unallocated) memory locations.

Definition 3 (Partition-Based Shape Domains). *A* partition-based shape domain $\mathcal{A} = (\mathfrak{S}, \gamma, \gamma^R)$ *is comprised of a shape domain* $(\mathfrak{S}, \gamma)$ *and a* region concretization function $\gamma^R : (\mathfrak{S} \times \Sigma) \to (\mathcal{R} \to 2^{\mathcal{O}})$, *such that for every abstract state* $s \in \mathfrak{S}$ *and any concrete state* $\sigma \in \gamma(s)$, *the following holds:*

1. *The free region represents the unallocated objects:* $\gamma^R(s, \sigma, \rho_{free}) = F(\sigma)$, *and*
2. *Every object is represented by exactly one region:*

$$\forall o \in \mathcal{O}. \exists! \rho \in \mathcal{R}. o \in \gamma^R(s, \sigma, \rho).$$

The definition formalizes our intention that an abstract state s induces a partitioning of the objects of every concrete state σ it represents. For example, if a heap containing a single linked list, then all the objects comprising the list may be in one region or in two regions, separating, e.g., the head of the list from its tail. However, it is not possible for an object to appear in two different regions. The partitioning of allocated objects is parametric in the chosen shape domain. By introducing the free region, we ensure that all the objects, and not only the allocated ones, are associated with a region. In our experiments, a region is comprised of a connected set of objects. However, for our purposes, a region may contain an arbitrary set of objects.

The success of a shape analysis algorithm to prove interesting properties often depends on its ability to record properties which are common to all the objects that reside in the same region. For example, in TVLA [26], it is often crucially important to track the reachability relation between heap allocated object, e.g., that all the elements in the list pointed-to by a variable out can be reached from it by following a finite number of n-pointer fields. To be able to record such information, the partitioning induced by abstract states is dynamic—changes to the state might lead objects to flow from one region to another.

Perhaps the most important property that we require from the underlying shape analysis is that it should be possible to deduce an *evolution relation* [30], which tracks the flow of objects between the regions of abstract states related by an abstract transition. We have shown an example of how to compute this relation for separation logic. TVLA uses a similar approach.

Definition 4 (May Evolve Relation). *Let* $(\mathfrak{S}, \gamma, \gamma^R)$ *be a partition-shape domain. A* may evolution relation $\textbf{\textit{ev}} \subseteq (\mathcal{S}, \mathcal{R}) \times (\mathcal{S}, \mathcal{R})$ *is a binary relation over pairs of abstract states and region identifiers. We denote the* abstract transition relation underlying $\textbf{\textit{ev}}$ by

$$\tau(\textbf{\textit{ev}}) \stackrel{def}{=} \{(s_1, s_2) \mid ((s_1, \rho_1), (s_2, \rho_2)) \in \textbf{\textit{ev}}\} \ .$$

The evolution relation $\textbf{\textit{ev}}$ conservatively represents *a concrete transition relation* T *if*

1. T *is conservatively represented by* $\tau(\textbf{\textit{ev}})$.
2. *There is a transition from* (s_1, ρ_1) *to* (s_2, ρ_2) *if an object in a state represented by* s_1 *in region* ρ_1 *flows to region* ρ_2 *in a state represented by* s_2:

$$\forall \sigma_1, \sigma_2, s_1, s_2, \rho_1, \rho_2. \, \big((\sigma_1, \sigma_2) \in T \wedge \sigma_1 \in \gamma(\{s_1\}) \wedge \sigma_2 \in \gamma(\{s_2\}) \wedge \\ \gamma^R(s_1, \sigma_1)(\rho_1) \cap \gamma^R(s_2, \sigma_2)(\rho_2) \neq \emptyset)\big) \implies ((s_1, \rho_1), (s_2, \rho_2)) \in \textbf{\textit{ev}}.$$

The evolution relation records the way objects *may* flow between regions. The last requirement we place is the ability to (conservatively) determine that some of the evolution transitions correspond to *must* flow information, i.e., that an object actually moves from one region to another.

Definition 5 (Must Evolve Relation). *Let* $(\mathfrak{S}, \gamma, \gamma^R)$ *be a partition-based shape domain,* $\hat{e}$ *an evolution relation, and* T *be a concrete transition relation.* $\hat{e}$ conservatively under-approximates *the flow of objects in* T *if*

$$\forall \sigma_1, \sigma_2, s_1, s_2, \rho_1, \rho_2. \, \big(((s_1, \rho_1), (s_2, \rho_2)) \in \hat{e} \wedge (\sigma_1, \sigma_2) \in T \wedge \\ \sigma_1 \in \gamma(\{s_1\}) \wedge \sigma_2 \in \gamma(\{s_2\})\big) \implies \gamma^R(s_1, \sigma_1)(\rho_1) \cap \gamma^R(s_2, \sigma_2)(\rho_2) \neq \emptyset) \ .$$

5   Establishing Well-Founded Relations

Our termination algorithm ensures that a program P terminates by: (i) establishing a well-founded relation over the pre- and post- states of every transition in P's concrete transition relations T, and (ii) attempting to prove the existence of a cutting set of transitions that strictly decrease the relation.

We now describe how to construct this well-founded relation from the abstract transition relation τ and the evolution relation $\textbf{\textit{ev}}$, and how to detect decreasing transitions via the must-evolve relation $\hat{e}$, computed using a partition-based shape domain $\mathcal{A} = (\mathfrak{S}, \gamma, \gamma^R)$.

Establishing a Well-Founded Relation Over Regions. Given the (finite) evolution relation **ev**, we construct the graph induced by its strongly connected components. Formally, every node in this graph corresponds to an equivalence class of pairs $r = (s, \rho)$ of abstract states and region identifiers. We refer to such a pair as an *abstract region* (region for short). Recall that our algorithm verifies the termination of every loop in the program separately. It does so by tracking the flow of objects which were allocated at the entry to the loop. To prevent us from considering objects which are allocated inside the loop in our termination argument, we collapse together all the nodes that contain a (s, ρ) pair which is reachable in the evolution relation from the free region of some input abstract state into a single ρ_{free} region. We refer to the resulting graph as the *condensation graph* and to its nodes as *region ranks*, and denote the region rank corresponding to a region r by $[r]$. We say that a region r is *less than or equal to* a region r', denoted $r \preceq r'$, if $[r']$ is reachable from $[r]$.

Lemma 1. *The relation $r \preceq r'$ is well-founded.*

Establishing a Well-Founded Relation Across Loop Iterations. We define a relation $\preceq$ between states that occur in T by lifting the relation between region rank to objects in a pointwise manner. Note that we do not care about relating states that do not occur in T and recall that a state encodes the value of the program location. Thus, it is sufficient to only define a relation between pairs of states $(\sigma_1, \sigma_2) \in T$ that appear as transitions in T and then take its transitive closure.

Let s be an abstract state and $\sigma \in \gamma(\{s\})$ a state represented by s. We define the *rank map* of σ according to s, denoted by $rank_{s,\sigma}$ to be a mapping from objects to region ranks according to the partitioning induced by s:

$$rank_{s,\sigma}(o) = (s, \rho), \text{ where } o \in \gamma^R(s, \sigma, \rho).$$

Let $(\sigma_1, \sigma_2) \in T$ be a concrete transition of P. We say that an abstract transition (s_1, s_2) *represents* (σ_1, σ_2) if $\sigma_1 \in \gamma(\sigma_1)$ and $\sigma_1 \in \gamma(\sigma_1)$. We say that σ_1 is *less than or equal* to state σ_2, denoted by $\sigma_1 \preceq_1 \sigma_2$, if there exists an abstract transition $(s_1, s_2) \in \tau$ such that for every $o \in \mathcal{O}$, it holds that $rank_{s_1,\sigma_1}(o) \leq rank_{s_2,\sigma_2}(o)$. We write $\sigma_1 \prec_1 \sigma_2$ if $\sigma_1 \preceq_1 \sigma_2$ and $\sigma_2 \not\preceq_1 \sigma_1$. We define the binary relation $\cdot \preceq \cdot$ as the reflexive transitive closure of the *smaller or equal* relation $\cdot \preceq_1 \cdot$ induced by T.

Lemma 2. *The relation $\sigma_1 \preceq \sigma_2$ is well-founded, and if $(\sigma_1, \sigma_2) \in T$ then $\sigma_1 \preceq \sigma_2$.*

Theorem 1. *Let T^+ denote the (irreflexive) transitive closure of T. If the loop contains a cutting set of transitions, then the relation defined as*

$$\sigma_1 \ll \sigma_2 \overset{def}{=} \{\sigma_1 \preceq \sigma_2 \mid (\sigma_1, \sigma_2) \in T^+ \land v(\sigma_1) = v(\sigma_2)\}$$

(that is, σ_2 is the result of executing at least one loop iteration and reaching the same program location) is well-founded.

6   Interprocedural Analysis

We now briefly discuss the extension of our approach to verify termination of recursive heap-manipulating programs. We forbid mutual-recursion and assume procedures have local variables, but no input parameters nor return values[5]. Syntactically, every procedure call is represented by a *call node* and a *return node* in the program's CFG. Every call node of p has a control-flow edge associated with a *call* command connecting it to the entry node of p's sub-CFG, and the exit node of the latter is connected to each of p's return nodes via a control-flow edge associated with a *return* command. The operational semantics is extended to handle procedures via reduction: we treat the call stack as a heap-allocated list. This allows treating recursive procedures as loop commands that explicitly manipulate the call stack. This kind of reduction has been employed successfully in previous shape analysis algorithms to verify safety properties [24, 25]. As far as we are aware, we are the first to employ it to verify termination.

A disadvantage of this approach is that it does not allow us to take advantage of the modular structure of the program— the underlying shape analysis becomes a whole program analysis and has to cope with an additional heap-allocated data structure. Our approach for verifying termination is, however, loop-modular, and thus can still treat procedures in a modular way.

7   Implementation and Experimental Evaluation

We implemented our algorithm on top of the existing shape analysis of TVLA, a parametric framework for shape analysis based on 3-Valued-Logic [17, 26], and used it to verify termination for the suite of benchmarks listed in Table 1. The experiments were performed on a machine with a 2.5 GHz *i7* Intel processor and 16 GB memory. The **Time** column measures the overall time of the shape analysis and the termination analysis combined. The **overhead** column lists the fraction of the time of the analysis spent to prove termination. As expected, the termination analysis is rather efficient.

We extended our programming language to handle bounded parallelism by allowing the program's CFG to have multiple pairs of entry and exit nodes. Every pair corresponds to a thread: The entry node corresponds to the program location of the thread when the program starts. The program terminates when every thread reaches its exit nodes. We assume that the sub-CFG pertaining to different threads are not connected. We record in every state the program location of every thread, and define the operational semantics to be the interleaving of primitive commands executed by different threads.

The suite of benchmarks consists of a variety of programs, concurrent and single-threaded, both recursive and iterative, flat and deeply nested loops. We handle several classic sorting algorithms, trees and graphs algorithms. We implemented and verified 16 out of the 21 benchmarks used to evaluate MUTANT [5],

---

[5] Mutually recursive procedures can be handled by merging them into a single recursive procedure, and parameter transfer by using specially-designated global variables.

which we had access to. One of the 16 benchmarks has a termination bug in which a lasso is created in a linked list, preventing traversing loop from ever reaching back to the head, and thus making it iterate forever. Our analysis correctly warned against non-termination. Some other interesting examples which were successfully verified for termination include Deutsch-Schorr-Waite tree-traversal algorithm [18] which involves double-reversal of links, the phases of a Mark-and-sweep garbage collection algorithm, the Even-Odd-marking [16] program which marks the elements of a singly-linked list as odd or even regarding their distance from the *end* of the list. We successfully prove termination of some concurrent programs including Treiber stack and CAS-based queue. A faulty implementation of the Treiber stack was correctly warned for non-termination.

Table 1. Benchmarks, analysis times, relative overhead over the original shape analysis times, and loop-nesting depth

Benchmark	Time (sec.)	Overhead	ND
a. Shallow programs manipulating acyclic lists			
Search, Insert, Reverse, Delete-all, Merge-sorted	≤0.7	≤0.1%	1
b. Deeply nested programs manipulating acyclic lists			
Bubble-sort	5.1	14%	2
Insertion-sort	0.9	1%	2
Insertion-sort with malloc	1.1	2.7%	2
Odd-even-marking	0.2	5.1%	2
Nested-loop-depth-4	4.4	4.5%	4
c. Shallow programs manipulating cyclic lists			
Mutant 1–16	0.113	0.1%	1
Search, Insert	≤0.1	≤0.1%	1
d. Recursive programs manipulating acyclic lists			
Search, Insert, Append, Reverse, Delete	≤0.3	≤0.3%	1
Merge	38.9	0.5%	1
e. Programs manipulating binary trees			
Insert-to-sorted-tree	0.9	1%	1
Delete-from-sorted-tree	42.1	6%	1
Deutsch-Schorr-Waite	14.5	4.8%	1
f. Programs manipulating graphs			
Mark-and-sweep	0.8	1.25%	1
g. Concurrent programs (lock-freedom)			
CAS Merge two lists (2 threads)	9.21	4%	1
Treiber stack (2 threads)	1.4	2.5%	1
Treiber stack (3 threads)	21.2	13%	1
Faulty Treiber stack (2 threads)	1.6	1.25%	1

8   Related Work

In this section, we discuss and compare our work with other approaches for verifying termination of *heap-manipulating programs*. This body of work can broadly be classified according to the following dimensions: (i) lattice of heap invariants and supported data structures, and (ii) type of "heap measures" used for reasoning about termination.

In terms of supported program features, we are the only ones to support side-effecting recursive procedures. However, we completely abstract away integers.

Approaches Based on Inductive Heap Invariants. Approaches based on separation logic [4,5,8,9,19] and tree automata [16] are restricted to programs operating on inductively-defined data structures, preventing them from handling programs operating on graphs of unbounded treewidth such as arbitrary graphs. Our algorithm is parametric in the underlying shape analysis and can therefore be used both with separation logic and 3-valued shape analysis. Our implementation uses 3-valued shape analysis as the underlying domain to prove termination of programs manipulating both inductively-defined data structures as well as arbitrary graphs.

Both Berdine et al. [4,5] and Brotherson et al. [8,9] use the number of unfoldings of inductively-defined definitions as a basis for their reasoning. Berdine et al. [4,5] modify a separation logic-based analysis to track changes in the number of unfoldings of inductive predicates and produce a numeric program whose termination implies the termination of the original program. The termination of the numeric program can be checked by termination proving tools for numeric programs. Brotherson et al. [8] develop a proof framework for cyclic proofs where termination is done by directly relating (cyclic) inference trees with inductive predicates. Brotherson and Gorogiannis [9] introduce a method for synthesizing inductive predicates, allowing them to automatically adapt to the data structures appearing in a program.

Magill et al. [19] develop a flexible analysis that simultaneously tracks both shape invariants and related numeric measures such as the sizes of lists and trees. They generate a numeric program whose termination proof implies termination of the original program. Proving termination of the numeric program is done by using tools dedicated for that purpose (ARMC-LIVE).

Tracking numeric properties is both expensive and requires making modifications to the shape analysis. Proving termination of numeric programs is undecidable in general and expensive in practice. Our algorithm avoids these problems by directly processing the result of the shape analysis in linear time. We note that computing the evolution relation is relatively simple and efficient.

Haberhmehl et al. [16] use shape analysis based on tree automata to generate a counter automaton that simulates the original program. They use counterexample-guided abstraction refinement to obtain a high degree of automation (and to prove relative completeness for a subclass of programs). They track measures suitable for termination of tree manipulation such as tree size, height, and distance of pointers from the root. However, they only handle tree rotations and do not handle dynamic allocation.

Approaches Based on FO^{TC} Shape Invariants. A family of analyses approximate the shape of the heap via predicates expressible in first-order logic with transitive closure (FO^{TC}). These enable to indirectly capture some recursive data structures as well as reason about arbitrary data structures in a sound manner.

Podelski et al. [22] present an analysis for inferring necessary preconditions for termination of list-manipulating programs. Their analysis starts with a coarse heap abstraction and proves termination by translation to numeric programs. If an abstract counterexample is found, the heap abstraction is refined. The heap abstraction is converted to a numeric program which tracks the lengths of heap paths between two pointer variables.

Gulwani et al. [14] develop an abstract interpretation framework for tracking numerical relations betweens the sizes of heap regions, and use it to manually obtain ranking functions for bubble-sort and the mark and sweep garbage collector benchmark. One disadvantage of combining shape and size information (other than the expensive cost incurred by tracking numeric properties and performing partial reduction between the shape domain and numeric domain) is the unpredictability brought by widening operations that are usually necessary for the numeric sub-domain. Additionally, the termination of some programs, e.g., Odd-even-marking [16], does not depend on the sizes of heap regions.

Albert et al. [2] and Fausto et al. [27] develop heap abstractions based on sharing, cyclicity, and aliasing and use access path lengths to prove termination. Technically, they translate Java byte code to constraint logic programs (CLP) where the actual termination reasoning is done. Giesl et al. [21] define a shape analysis based on sharing, aliasing, and reachability patterns. This allows them to analyze programs manipulating integers and tree-shaped data structures and prove their termination by reduction to term rewriting systems (TRS). The termination measures available by TRS go beyond region sizes (e.g., flattening a tree). They later extend their technique to handle certain cyclic data structure patterns [6] and recursive procedures without side-effects [7]. Their analysis has been implemented in the **AProVE** tool [13], which analyzes both Java and C programs.

The main limitation of the last three approaches is the rigidity of the heap abstraction—adapting the abstraction to precisely handle new data structures and new data structure manipulation patterns requires reworking the analysis. In particular, proving termination for programs manipulating arbitrary graphs seems to be out of reach. In contrast, our algorithm is not tied down to any specific shape analysis technique, allowing us to take advantage of advances in the field of shape analysis, e.g., compositional analysis [10], and automatic synthesis of inductive predicates [9,15]. Our implementation on top of TVLA allows us to quickly adapt to new data structures by refining the abstraction with new predicates (soundness is automatically guaranteed). Finally, our treatment of recursion allows us to quite precisely track intricate properties between the heap and the call stack.

Efficiency. As far as we know, our algorithm is the only one that operates in linear time with respect to an underlying shape analysis. This is due to two factors—the properties of the well-founded relation our analysis constructs and our modular treatment of loops and recursive procedures.

Acknowledgments. We thank the anonymous reviewers for their detailed comments. We thank Josh Berdine and Amir Ben-Amram for useful discussions.

References

1. Aho, A.V., Sethi, R., Ullman, J.D.: Compilers: Principles,Techniques and Tools. Addison-Wesley, Reading (1988)
2. Albert, E., Arenas, P., Codish, M., Genaim, S., Puebla, G., Zanardini, D.: Termination analysis of Java bytecode. In: Barthe, G., de Boer, F.S. (eds.) FMOODS 2008. LNCS, vol. 5051, pp. 2–18. Springer, Heidelberg (2008)
3. Berdine, J., Calcagno, C., O'Hearn, P.W.: Symbolic execution with separation logic. In: Yi, K. (ed.) APLAS 2005. LNCS, vol. 3780, pp. 52–68. Springer, Heidelberg (2005)
4. Berdine, J., Chawdhary, A., Cook, B., Distefano, D., O'Hearn, P.W.: Variance analyses from invariance analyses. In: ACM SIGPLAN-SIGACT Symposium on Principles of Programming Languages, pp. 211–224 (2007)
5. Berdine, J., Cook, B., Distefano, D., O'Hearn, P.W.: Automatic termination proofs for programs with shape-shifting heaps. In: Ball, T., Jones, R.B. (eds.) CAV 2006. LNCS, vol. 4144, pp. 386–400. Springer, Heidelberg (2006)
6. Brockschmidt, M., Musiol, R., Otto, C., Giesl, J.: Automated termination proofs for Java programs with cyclic data. In: International Conference on Computer Aided Verification, pp. 105–122 (2012)
7. Brockschmidt, M., Otto, C., Giesl, J.: Modular termination proofs of recursive Java bytecode programs by term rewriting. In: International Conference on Rewriting Techniques and Applications, pp. 155–170 (2011)
8. Brotherston, J., Bornat, R., Calcagno, C.: Cyclic proofs of program termination in separation logic. In: ACM SIGPLAN-SIGACT Symposium on Principles of Programming Languages, pp. 101–112 (2008)
9. Brotherston, J., Gorogiannis, N.: Cyclic abduction of inductively defined safety and termination preconditions. In: Müller-Olm, M., Seidl, H. (eds.) Static Analysis. LNCS, vol. 8723, pp. 68–84. Springer, Heidelberg (2014)
10. Calcagno, C., Distefano, D., O'Hearn, P.W., Yang, H.: Compositional shape analysis by means of bi-abduction. J. ACM **58**(6), 26 (2011)
11. Cormen, T.H., Leiserson, C.E., Rivest, R.L., Stein, C.: Introduction to Algorithms, 3rd edn. MIT Press, Cambridge (2009)
12. Distefano, D., O'Hearn, P.W., Yang, H.: A local shape analysis based on separation logic. In: Hermanns, H., Palsberg, J. (eds.) TACAS 2006. LNCS, vol. 3920, pp. 287–302. Springer, Heidelberg (2006)
13. Gies, J., et al.: Proving termination of programs automatically with AProVE. In: Demri, S., Kapur, D., Weidenbach, C. (eds.) IJCAR 2014. LNCS, vol. 8562, pp. 184–191. Springer, Heidelberg (2014)
14. Gulwani, S., Lev-Ami, T., Sagiv, M.: A combination framework for tracking partition sizes. In: ACM SIGPLAN-SIGACT Symposium on Principles of Programming Languages, pp. 239–251 (2009)

15. Guo, B., Vachharajani, N., August, D.I.: Shape analysis with inductive recursion synthesis. In: ACM SIGPLAN conference on Programming Language Design and Implementation, pp. 256–265 (2007)
16. Habermehl, P., Iosif, R., Rogalewicz, A., Vojnar, T.: Proving termination of tree manipulating programs. In: Namjoshi, K.S., Yoneda, T., Higashino, T., Okamura, Y. (eds.) ATVA 2007. LNCS, vol. 4762, pp. 145–161. Springer, Heidelberg (2007)
17. Lev-Ami, T., Sagiv, M.: TVLA: a framework for implementing static analyses. In: Palsberg, J. (ed.) SAS 2000. LNCS, vol. 1824, pp. 280–301. Springer, Berlin (2000)
18. Loginov, A., Reps, T., Sagiv, M.: Automated verification of the Deutsch-Schorr-Waite tree-traversal algorithm. In: Yi, K. (ed.) SAS 2006. LNCS, vol. 4134, pp. 261–279. Springer, Heidelberg (2006)
19. Magill, S., Tsai, M., Lee, P., Tsay, Y.: Automatic numeric abstractions for heap-manipulating programs. In: ACM SIGPLAN-SIGACT Symposium on Principles of Programming Languages, pp. 211–222 (2010)
20. Muchnick, S.S.: Advanced Compiler Design and Implementation. Morgan Kaufmann Publishers Inc., San Francisco (1997)
21. Otto, C., Brockschmidt, M., von Essen, C., Giesl, J.: Automated termination analysis of Java bytecode by term rewriting. In: International Conference on Rewriting Techniques and Applications, pp. 259–276 (2010)
22. Podelski, A., Rybalchenko, A., Wies, T.: Heap assumptions on demand. In: Gupta, A., Malik, S. (eds.) CAV 2008. LNCS, vol. 5123, pp. 314–327. Springer, Heidelberg (2008)
23. Rinetzky, N., Ramalingam, G., Sagiv, M., Yahav, E.: On the complexity of partially-flow-sensitive alias analysis. ACM Trans. Program. Lang. Syst. 30(3), 13:1–13:28 (2008)
24. Rinetzky, N., Sagiv, M.: Interprocedural shape analysis for recursive programs. In: Wilhelm, R. (ed.) CC 2001. LNCS, vol. 2027, pp. 133–149. Springer, Heidelberg (2001)
25. Rival, X., Chang, B.-Y.E.: Calling context abstraction with shapes. In: ACM SIGPLAN-SIGACT Symposium on Principles of Programming Languages, pp. 173–186 (2011)
26. Sagiv, M., Reps, T., Wilhelm, R.: Parametric shape analysis via 3-valued logic. ACM Trans. Program. Lang. Syst. 24(3), 217–298 (2002)
27. Spoto, F., Mesnard, F., Payet, E.: A termination analyzer for Java bytecode based on path-length. ACM Trans. Program. Lang. Syst. 32(3), 8:1–8:70 (2010)
28. Toubhans, A., Chang, B.-Y.E., Rival, X.: Reduced product combination of abstract domains for shapes. In: Giacobazzi, R., Berdine, J., Mastroeni, I. (eds.) VMCAI 2013. LNCS, vol. 7737, pp. 375–395. Springer, Heidelberg (2013)
29. Toubhans, A., Chang, B.-Y.E., Rival, X.: An abstract domain combinator for separately conjoining memory abstractions. In: Müller-Olm, M., Seidl, H. (eds.) Static Analysis. LNCS, vol. 8723, pp. 285–301. Springer, Heidelberg (2014)
30. Yahav, E., Reps, T.W., Sagiv, S., Wilhelm, R.: Verifying temporal heap properties specified via evolution logic. In: European Symposium on Programming, pp. 204–222 (2003)

RV-Match: Practical Semantics-Based Program Analysis

Dwight Guth[1(✉)], Chris Hathhorn[1,3(✉)], Manasvi Saxena[1,2(✉)],
and Grigore Roşu[1,2(✉)]

[1] Runtime Verification Inc., Urbana, USA
{dwight.guth,chris.hathhorn,manasvi.saxena,
grigore.rosu}@runtimeverification.com
[2] University of Illinois at Urbana-Champaign,
Urbana, USA
[3] University of Missouri, Columbia, USA

Abstract. We present RV-Match, a tool for checking C programs for undefined behavior and other common programmer mistakes. Our tool is extracted from the most complete formal semantics of the C11 language. Previous versions of this tool were used primarily for testing the correctness of the semantics, but we have improved it into a tool for doing practical analysis of real C programs. It beats many similar tools in its ability to catch a broad range of undesirable behaviors. We demonstrate this with comparisons based on a third-party benchmark.

Keywords: C11 · Programming language semantics · Undefined behavior · Static analysis · Abstract interpretation

1 Introduction

The $\mathbb{K}$ semantic framework[1] is a program analysis environment based on term rewriting [1]. Users define the formal semantics of a target programming language and the $\mathbb{K}$ framework provides a series of formal analysis tools specialized for that language, such as a symbolic execution engine, a semantic debugger, a systematic checker for undesired behaviors (model checker), and even a fully fledged deductive program verifier. Our tool, RV-Match, is based on the $\mathbb{K}$ framework instantiated with the publicly-available C11 semantics[2] [6,7], a rigorous formalization of the current ISO C11 standard [10]. We have specially optimized RV-Match for the execution and detection of errors in C programs.

Unlike modern optimizing compilers, which have a goal to produce binaries that are as small and as fast as possible at the expense of compiling programs that may be semantically incorrect, RV-Match instead aims at mathematically rigorous dynamic checking of programs for strict conformance with

---

[1] http://kframework.org.

[2] https://github.com/kframework/c-semantics.

© Springer International Publishing Switzerland 2016
S. Chaudhuri and A. Farzan (Eds.): CAV 2016, Part I, LNCS 9779, pp. 447–453, 2016.
DOI: 10.1007/978-3-319-41528-4_24

the ISO C11 standard. A strictly-conforming program is one that does not rely on implementation-specific behaviors and is free of the most notorious feature of the C language, *undefined behavior*. Undefined behaviors are semantic holes left by the standard for implementations to fill in. They are the source of many subtle bugs and security issues [9].

Running RV-Match. Users interface with RV-Match through the kcc executable, which behaves as a drop-in replacement for compilers like gcc and clang. Consider a file undef.c with contents:

```
int main(void) {
        int a;
        &a+2; }
```

We compile the program with kcc just as we would with gcc or clang. This produces an executable named a.out by default, which should behave just as an executable produced by another compiler—for strictly-conforming, valid programs. For undefined or invalid programs, however, kcc reports errors and exits if it cannot recover:

```
$ kcc undef.c
$ ./a.out
Error: UB-CEA1
Description: A pointer (or array subscript) outside the
 bounds of an object.
Type: Undefined behavior.
See also: C11 sec. 6.5.6:8, J.2:1 item 46
   at main(undef.c:2)
```

In addition to location information and a stack trace, kcc also cites relevant sections of the standard [10].

2   Practical Semantics-Based Program Analysis

Unlike similar tools, we do not instrument an executable produced by a separate compiler. Instead, RV-Match directly interprets programs according to a formal operational semantics. The semantics gives a separate treatment to the three main phases of a C implementation: compilation, linking, and execution. The first two phases together form the "translation" semantics, which we extract into an OCaml program to be executed by the kcc tool. The kcc tool, then, translates C programs according to the semantics, producing an abstract syntax tree as the result of the compilation and linking phases. This AST then becomes the input to another OCaml program extracted from the execution semantics.

The tool on which we have based our work was originally born as a method for testing the correctness of the operational semantics from which it was extracted [7], but the performance and scalability limitations of this original version did not make it a practical option for analysis of real programs. To this end, we have improved the tool on several fronts:

- *OCaml-based execution engine.* We implemented a new execution engine that interprets programs according to a language semantics 3 orders of magnitude faster than our previous Java-based version. For this improvement in performance, we take advantage of the optimized pattern-matching implemented by the OCaml compiler, a natural fit for $\mathbb{K}$ Framework semantics. In the course of this work, we uncovered and fixed a few limitations of the OCaml compiler itself in dealing with very large pattern match expressions.[3]
- *Native libraries.* Previous versions of our tool required all libraries to be given semantics (or their C source code) before they could be interpreted. We now support linking against and calling native libraries, automatically marshalling data to and from the representation used in the semantics.
- *Expanded translation phase.* In our C semantics, we now calculate the type of all terms, the values of initializers, and generally do more evaluation of programs during the translation phase. Previously, much of this work was duplicated during execution.
- *Error recovery and implementation-defined behavior.* We have implemented error recovery and expanded support for implementation-defined behavior. Programs generated by older versions of kcc would halt when encountering undefined or implementation-defined behavior. Our new version of kcc gives semantics for many common undefined behaviors so the interpreter can continue with what was likely the expected behavior after reporting the error. Similarly, we have added support for implementation profiles, giving users an easy way to parameterize the semantics over the behaviors of common C implementations.
- *Scope of errors.* We have also expanded the breadth of the errors reported by kcc to include bad practices and errors involving standard library functions.[4]

These improvements have allowed kcc to build and analyze programs in excess of 300k lines of code, including the BIND DNS server.

Performance evaluation. For an idea of the extent of the performance enhancements over previous versions of our tool, consider this simple program that calculates the sum of integers between 0 and 10000:

```
#include <stdio.h>
int main(void) {
        int i, sum = 0;
        for (i = 0; i < 10000; ++i) sum += i;
        printf("Sum: %d\n", sum); }
```

---

[3] See   http://caml.inria.fr/mantis/view.php?id=6883   and   http://caml.inria.fr/mantis/view.php?id=6913.

[4] For a summary of the kinds of errors kcc will report, see https://github.com/kframework/c-semantics/blob/master/examples/error-codes/Error_Codes.csv.

In the table below, we compare the time in seconds to compile and run this program five times with an old version of our tool[5] [9] to our new version using our OCaml execution engine. The first and second rows report the average time for five compilations and runs,[6] respectively, and the third reports the sum of all runs plus the average compilation time to simulate the case of a compiled test being run on different input.

	Old kcc	New kcc	Change
Avg. compile time	13 s	2 s	−85%
Avg. run time	816 s	11 s	−99%
All runs + avg. comp.	4092 s	59 s	−99%

3   Evaluation

Of course, many other tools exist for analyzing C programs. In this section, we compare RV-Match with some popular C analyzers on a benchmark from Toyota ITC. We also briefly mention our experience with running our tool on the SV-COMP benchmark. The other tools we consider:

- *GrammaTech CodeSonar* is a static analysis tool for identifying "bugs that can result in system crashes, unexpected behavior, and security breaches" [8].
- *MathWorks Polyspace Bug Finder* is a static analyzer for identifying "run-time errors, concurrency issues, security vulnerabilities, and other defects in C and C++ embedded software" [11].
- *MathWorks Polyspace Code Prover* is a tool based on abstract interpretation that "proves the absence of overflow, divide-by-zero, out-of-bounds array access, and certain other run-time errors in C and C++ source code" [12].
- *Clang UBSan, TSan, MSan, and ASan (version 3.7.1)* are all `clang` modules for instrumenting compiled binaries with various mechanisms for detecting undefined behavior, data races, uninitialized reads, and various memory issues, respectively [5].
- *Valgrind Memcheck and Helgrind (version 3.10.1, GCC version 4.8.4)* are tools for instrumenting binaries for the detection of several memory and thread-related issues (illegal reads/writes, use of uninitialized or unaddressable values, deadlocks, data races, etc.) [13].
- *The CompCert C interpreter (version 2.6)* uses an approach similar to our own. It executes programs according to the semantics used by the CompCert compiler [3] and reports undefined behavior.

---

[5] Version 3.4.0, with $\mathbb{K}$ Framework version 3.4.

[6] These tests were run on a dual CPU 2.4 GHz Intel Xeon with 8 GB of memory. On more memory-intensive programs, we see an additional order of magnitude or more improvement in performance.

- *Frama-C Value Analysis (version sodium-20150201)*, like Code Prover, is a tool based on static analysis and abstract interpretation for catching several forms of undefinedness [4].

Tool		Static memory	Dynamic memory	Stack-related	Numerical	Resource management	Pointer-related	Concurrency	Inappropriate code	Misc.	Avg. (unweighted)	Avg. (weighted)
RV-Match (kcc)	DR	100	94	100	96	93	98	67	*0*	63	79	82
	FPR	100	100	100	100	100	100	100	–	100	100	100
	PM	100	97	100	98	96	99	82	*0*	79	89	91
GrammaTech CodeSonar	DR	100	89	*0*	48	61	52	70	46	69	59	68
	FPR	100	100	–	100	100	96	77	99	100	97	98
	PM	100	94	*0*	69	78	71	73	67	83	76	82
MathWorks Bug Finder	DR	97	90	15	41	55	69	*0*	28	69	52	62
	FPR	100	100	85	100	100	100	–	94	100	98	99
	PM	98	95	36	64	74	83	*0*	51	83	71	78
MathWorks Code Prover	DR	97	92	60	55	20	69	*0*	1	83	53	53
	FPR	100	95	70	99	90	93	–	97	100	94	95
	PM	98	93	65	74	42	80	*0*	10	91	71	71
UBSan + TSan + MSan + ASan (clang)	DR	79	16	95	59	47	58	67	*0*	37	51	47
	FPR	100	95	75	100	96	97	72	–	100	93	95
	PM	89	39	84	77	67	75	70	*0*	61	69	67
Valgrind + Helgrind (gcc)	DR	9	80	70	22	57	60	72	2	29	44	42
	FPR	100	95	80	100	100	100	79	100	100	95	97
	PM	30	87	75	47	76	77	76	13	53	65	65
CompCert interpreter	DR	97	29	35	48	32	87	58	17	63	52	51
	FPR	82	80	70	79	83	73	42	83	71	74	76
	PM	89	48	49	62	52	80	49	38	67	62	63
Frama-C Value Analysis	DR	82	79	45	79	63	81	7	33	83	61	66
	FPR	96	27	65	47	46	40	100	63	49	59	55
	PM	89	46	54	61	54	57	26	45	63	60	60

Fig. 1. Comparison of tools on the 1,276 tests of the ITC benchmark. The numbers for the GrammaTech and MathWorks tools come from [14]. (Color figure online)

- Highlighting indicates the best score in a category for a particular metric.
- DR, *FPR*, and PM are, respectively, the detection rate, $100 - FPR$ (the complement of the false positive rate), and the productivity metric.
- The final average is weighted by the number of tests in each category.
- Italics and a dash indicate categories for which a tool has no support.

The Toyota ITC benchmark [14]. This publicly-available[7] benchmark consists of 1,276 tests, half with planted defects meant to evaluate the defect rate capability of analysis tools and the other half without defects meant to evaluate the false positive rate. The tests are grouped in nine categories: static memory, dynamic memory, stack-related, numerical, resource management, pointer-related, concurrency, inappropriate code, and miscellaneous.

We evaluated RV-Match along with the tools mentioned above on this benchmark. Our results appear in Fig. 1 and the tools we used for our evaluation are available online.[8] Following the method of [14], we report the value of three metrics: DR is the detection rate, the percentage of tests containing errors where the error was detected; $FPR = 100 - FPR$, where FPR is the false positive rate; and PM is a productivity metric, where $PM = \sqrt{DR \times FPR}$, the geometric mean of DR and FPR.

Interestingly, and similar to our experience with the SV-COMP benchmark mentioned below, the use of RV-Match on the Toyota ITC benchmark detected a number of flaws in the benchmark itself, both in the form of undefined behavior that was not intended, and in the form of tests that were intended to contain a defect but were actually correct. Our fixes for these issues were accepted by the Toyota ITC authors and we used the fixed version of the benchmark in our experiments. Unfortunately, we do not have access to the MathWorks and GrammaTech static analysis tools, so in Fig. 1 we have reproduced the results reported in [14]. Thus, it is possible that the metrics scored for the other tools may be off by some amount.

The SV-COMP benchmark suite. This consist of a large number of C programs used as verification tasks during the International Competition on Software Verification (SV-COMP) [2]. We analyzed 1346 programs classified as correct with RV-Match and observed that 188 (14 %) of the programs exhibited undefined behavior. Issues ranged from using uninitialized values in expressions, potentially invalid conversions, incompatible declarations, to more subtle strict aliasing violations. Our detailed results are available online.[9]

4 Conclusion

We have presented RV-Match, a semantics-based ISO C11 compliance checker. It does better than the other tools we considered in terms of its detection rate, and note that it reports *no false positives*. Also, we think our experience with finding undefined behavior even in the presumed-correct programs of the above benchmarks demonstrates our tool's usefulness.

We do not claim, however, that our approach is simply better than the approaches represented by the other tools. We see our technology as a complement to other approaches. Static analysis tools, for example, are more forgiving

---

[7] https://github.com/Toyota-ITC-SSD/Software-Analysis-Benchmark.

[8] https://github.com/runtimeverification/evaluation/tree/master/toyota-itc-benchmark.

[9] https://github.com/runtimeverification/evaluation/tree/master/svcomp-benchmark.

in terms of analyzing code that does not even compile, so they can help find errors earlier. They also typically analyze all code in one run of the tool. On the other hand, our tool, like all tools performing dynamic analysis, generally requires the program to actually execute in order to detect most errors. Our tool also limits itself to the code that is actually executed, so it is best combined with existing testing infrastructure (e.g., by running unit tests with `kcc`).

References

1. Roşu, G., Şerbănuţă, T.F.: An overview of the K semantic framework. J. Log. Algebr. Program. **79**(6), 397–434 (2010). doi:10.1016/j.jlap.2010.03.012
2. Beyer, D.: Reliableand reproducible competition results with BenchExec and witnesses. In: Chechik, M., Raskin, J.-F. (eds.) Tools and Algorithms for the Construction and Analysis of Systems: 22nd International Conference (TACAS 2016), (Report on SV-COMP 2016), pp. 887–904 (2016). ISBN: 978-3-662-49674-9, doi:10.1007/978-3-662-49674-9_55
3. Campbell, B.: An executable semantics for CompCert C. In: Hawblitzel, C., Miller, D. (eds.) CPP 2012. LNCS, vol. 7679, pp. 60–75. Springer, Heidelberg (2012)
4. Canet, G., Cuoq, P., Monate, B.: A value analysis for C programs. In: Conference Source Code Analysis and Manipulation (SCAM 2009), pp. 123–124. IEEE (2009). doi:10.1109/SCAM.2009.22
5. Clang: Clang 3.9 documentation. http://clang.llvm.org/docs/index.html
6. Ellison, C.: A formal semantics of C with applications. Ph.D. thesis, University of Illinois, July 2012. http://hdl.handle.net/2142/34297
7. Ellison, C., Roşu, G.: An executable formal semantics of C with applications. In: ACM SIGPLAN-SIGACT Symposium on Principles of Programming Languages (POPL 2012), pp. 533–544 (2012). doi:10.1145/2103656.2103719
8. GrammaTech: CodeSonar. http://grammatech.com/products/codesonar
9. Hathhorn, C., Ellison, C., Roşu, G.: Defining the undefinedness of C. In: 36th Conference on Programming Language Design and Implementation (PLDI 2015) (2015)
10. ISO/IEC JTC 1, SC 22, WG 14. ISO/IEC 9899:2011: Programming Language C Technical report International Organisation for Standardization (2012)
11. MathWorks: Polyspace Bug Finder. http://www.mathworks.com/products/polyspace-bug-finder
12. MathWorks: Polyspace Code Prover. http://www.mathworks.com/products/polyspace-code-prover
13. Nethercote, N., Seward, J.: Valgrind: a framework for heavy-weight dynamic binary instrumentation. In: ACM SIGPLAN Conference on Programming Language Design and Implementation (PLDI 2007), pp. 89–100. ACM (2007). doi:10.1145/1250734.1250746
14. Shiraishi, S., Mohan, V., Marimuthu, H.: Test suites for benchmarks of static analysis tools. In: The 26th IEEE International Symposium on Software Reliability Engineering (ISSRE 2015), Industrial Track (2015)

Timed and Hybrid Systems

Under-Approximating Backward Reachable Sets
by Polytopes

Bai Xue[1,2]($\boxtimes$), Zhikun She[1], and Arvind Easwaran[2]

[1] School of Mathematics and Systems Science, Beihang University, Beijing, China
`zhikun.she@buaa.edu.cn`
[2] Nanyang Technological University, Singapore, Singapore
{`xuebai,arvinde`}`@ntu.edu.sg`

Abstract. Under-approximations are useful for falsification of safety properties for nonlinear (hybrid) systems by finding counter-examples. Polytopic under-approximations enable analysis of these properties using reasoning in the theory of linear arithmetic. Given a nonlinear system, a target region of the simply connected compact type and a time duration, we in this paper propose a method using boundary analysis to compute an under-approximation of the backward reachable set. The under-approximation is represented as a polytope. The polytope can be computed by solving linear program problems. We test our method on several examples and compare them with existing methods. The results show that our method is highly promising in under-approximating reachable sets. Furthermore, we explore some directions to improve the scalability of our method.

Keywords: Polytopic under-approximations · Backward reachable sets · Nonlinear systems

1 Introduction

Reachability analysis, which involves constructing reachable sets, is a central component of model checking. It plays an important role in automatic verification and falsification of safety properties for continuous nonlinear and hybrid systems [2,3]. It has been utilized in diverse applications such as artificial pancreas [4,5] and robotic systems [6]. Over the past few years, a lot of attention has been given to construct over-approximations of reachable sets of nonlinear systems, i.e., abstraction methods [7,8], simulation based methods [9] and Taylor series expansions [10,11]. Nevertheless, much less attention has been given to the problem of finding under-approximations. Actually, under-approximations of reachable sets are also important to compute because of a variety of applications in engineering domains. For example, they can be used for designing

B. Xue—This work is based on Bai Xue's Ph.D. thesis from Beihang University [1].
Z. She— The work of Zhikun She was partly supported by NSFC-11422111 and NSFC-11371047.

S. Chaudhuri and A. Farzan (Eds.): CAV 2016, Part I, LNCS 9779, pp. 457–476, 2016.
DOI: 10.1007/978-3-319-41528-4_25

robust artificial pancreas [5,12]. Computing under-approximations of backward reachable sets can help find a set of feasible states such that every trajectory originating from it will definitely enter a specified region (e.g., normal blood glucose ranges) at a specified time instant. They can be used to prove attractive properties by checking if all the trajectories originating from them will stay in them forever and eventually enter some specified desired sets [13]. They can also be used for falsification by checking if the under-approximation intersects the unsafe sets[1] [3]. Also, under- and over-approximations of reachable sets can provide an indication of the precision of an estimate of the exact reachability region [4]. In contrast to over-approximation problems, methods for computing under-approximations are far from being developed. One of main reasons may lie in the fact that the problem is more difficult than the one of computing over-approximations [14].

We in this paper propose a linear programming based approach combining validated numerical methods for ordinary differential equations for finding polytopic under-approximations of backward reachable sets, under the assumption that the target region is a simply connected compact set. The basic procedure for computing the under-approximation mainly consists of three steps. The first step is to compute an enclosure of the boundary of the backward reachable set based on validated numerical techniques for ordinary differential equations. The second step is to obtain a polytope, which contains the enclosure obtained in the first step, and the last step is to shrink this polytope based on linear programming to yield an under-approximation of the backward reachable set. The contributions of this paper are summarized as follows:

1. We show how a polytopic under-approximation of the backward reachable set can be obtained by solving linear programming problems. We first construct a polytopic over-approximation of the reachable set based on the reachable set's boundary and validated numerical techniques for ordinary differential equations, then contract this over-approximation to obtain a polytopic under-approximation by solving linear programs.
2. We implement our approach based on linear programming solver GLPK[2] and the validated ordinary differential equation solver VNODE-LP [24], test and compare it with the method of Korda et al. [22] based on several examples. The experiment results show that our approach is highly promising in under-approximating reachable sets for some cases. Furthermore, we explore some directions toward making our method scale well based on an example involving a seven-dimensional biological system.

Related Work

Several techniques have been proposed for computing under-approximations of reachable sets for linear systems, e.g., [14–16]. However, they cannot be easily extended to handle non-linear systems. Under-approximations of reachable sets

---

[1] If the under-approximation intersects the unsafe sets, then the system is definitely unsafe.

[2] http://www.gnu.org/software/glpk/.

for nonlinear systems have been discussed elsewhere (e.g., [17] and [21]), but a feasible solution is not given. Recently, some methods have been proposed to compute under-approximations of reachable sets for nonlinear systems.

Sum-of-squares programming based methods are proposed to compute inner approximations of reachable sets for polynomial dynamical systems in [22,37]. Unfortunately, the present status of semi-definite programming solvers is not so advanced. The numerical problems produced by these solvers often lead to unreliable results for some cases. On the contrary, our method relies on linear programming and validated numerical methods for ordinary differential equations, thus making our method more reliable. A Taylor model backward flow-pipe method is presented to compute under-approximations in [23]. However, the algorithm in [23], in which an interval constraint propagation technique is employed to verify the connectedness of an already obtained basic semi-algebraic set, for finding implicit Taylor models such that the semi-algebraic set formed by them is simply-connected[3] is not complete generally[4]. In our method, the procedure employing interval constraint propagation techniques to enclose the boundary of the reachable set is complete.

As mentioned previously, polytopic under-approximations permits the analysis of some specified properties such as the falsification of safety properties using reasoning in the theory of linear arithmetic. Interval under-approximations received increasing attention recently [18,19]. A method based on modal intervals with affine forms is proposed to under-approximate reachable sets using intervals for continuous nonlinear systems modelled by ordinary differential equations [20]. However, our method provides a way to characterize under-approximations of reachable sets using general polytopes, reducing the conservativeness induced by interval representations in the construction of reachable sets.

The structure of this paper is as follows. Some basic definitions related to backward reachable sets as well as an introduction to convex polytopes is introduced in Sect. 2. Our approach of computing under-approximations, together with its computational complexity, is presented in Sect. 3. Several numerical examples with a detailed discussion of our approach and comparison with the method in [22] are provided in Sect. 4. Finally, we conclude our paper in Sect. 5.

2 Preliminary

In this paper, the following notations are used. Vectors are denoted by boldface letters (e.g., $\boldsymbol{x}$). For a set Δ, its complement, interior, closure and boundary are denoted by Δ^c, Δ°, $\overline{\Delta}$ and $\partial\Delta$ respectively. Further, $\mathbb{U}(\boldsymbol{x};\epsilon) = \{\boldsymbol{y} : \|\boldsymbol{y} - \boldsymbol{x}\| < \epsilon, \epsilon > 0\}$ represents an ϵ−neighbourhood of the vector $\boldsymbol{x}$.

---

[3] A set is simply connected if there are no holes in it to prevent the continuous shrinking of each closed arc to a point.

[4] An algorithm is complete, implying that it guarantees to find a solution if there is one.

2.1   Backward Reachable Sets

Consider a nonlinear system of the form

$$\dot{x} = f(x), \tag{1}$$

where $x = (x_1, \cdots, x_n)' \in \mathbb{R}^n$, and $f(x) \colon \mathbb{R}^n \to \mathbb{R}^n$ is $(p-1)$-time continuously differentiable and $p \geq 1$. We also assume f is locally Lipschitz continuous. Thus for a given set $\mathcal{X}$ that is a simply connected compact set, the existence and uniqueness of the trajectory with $x(0) = x_0$ and $x_0 \in \mathcal{X}$ will be assured over some time interval $[-\sigma_{\mathcal{X}}, \sigma_{\mathcal{X}}]$ with $\sigma_{\mathcal{X}} > 0$. Further, the trajectory of System (1) is defined to be $\phi(t; x_0) = x(t)$, where $x(t)$ is the solution of System (1) satisfying the initial condition $x(0) = x_0$. Furthermore, the backward and forward reachable sets of a simply connected compact set TR for the time duration T are defined as follows.

Definition 1. *Given System (1), a set TR that is a simply connected compact set and a finite time duration $T \leq \sigma_{TR}$, the backward reachable set of TR for the time duration T is defined to be $\Omega_b(T; \text{TR}, f) = \{x_0 | \phi(T; x_0) \in \text{TR}\}$ and the forward reachable set of TR for the time duration T is defined to be $\Omega_f(T; \text{TR}, f) = \{x | x = \phi(T; x_0) \text{ and } x_0 \in \text{TR}\}$.*

Remark 1. According to Definition 1, the map $\phi(t; \cdot) : \text{TR} \subseteq \mathbb{R}^n \to \Omega_f(t; \text{TR}, f)$ (or, $\Omega_b(t; \text{TR}, f) \to \text{TR}$) is bijective and continuous for $t \in [0, T]$ under the Lipschitz condition of f.

It is intractable to obtain these reachable sets for nonlinear systems since they generally do not have a closed-form solution. However, as mentioned previously, it is sufficient to consider an under-approximation of the backward reachable set, denoted as UAB, for certain applications such as artificial pancreas [12].

Definition 2. *Given System (1), a set TR that is a simply connected compact set and a finite time duration T, an UAB of TR for the time duration T is a nonempty subset of $\Omega_b(T; \text{TR}, f)$.*

Obviously, all trajectories originating from UAB will definitely enter TR after a time duration T, although there may be trajectories not in UAB that also enter TR after the time duration T. The under-approximation is equivalent to a region attracting to a target region, but a variant of the classical region of attraction containing an equilibrium.

2.2   Convex Polytopes

Convex polyhedra over reals (rationals) are a natural representation of sets of states for the verification of hybrid systems [25–27]. A convex polytope is a set in $\mathbb{R}^l$ that can be regarded as the set of solutions to the system of linear inequalities $Aw + C \leq B,^5$ where $A = (a_{ij})_{m \times l}$ is a $m \times l$ matrix, $w = (w_1, \ldots, w_l)'$ is a $l \times 1$ vector, $C = (c_1, \ldots, c_m)'$ and $B = (b, \ldots, b)'$ are both $m \times 1$ vectors.

---

[5] A convex polytope is formulated in this form for the convenience of the presentation of our approach in Sect. 3.

A convex polytope $P = \{w : Aw + C \le B\}$ has the following property, where the matrix A is full row rank.

Property 1. Let P be compact and its interior P° be not empty, then P and P° are both simply connected sets with the same boundary $\partial P = \{w \in P : \vee_{i=1}^{m}[\sum_{j=1}^{l} a_{ij}w_j + c_i = b]\}$.

Based on Property 1, the following two lemmas can be obtained, which are further illustrated in Fig. 1.

Lemma 1. *Assume $P = \{w : Aw + C \le B\}$ is a compact convex polytope. If U is a compact set such that its boundary is a subset of the compact convex polytope P, then P is an over-approximation of the set U.*

Proof. Since U is a compact set, there exists $y_i = (y_{i1}, \ldots, y_{il})' \in U$ such that $\sum_{j=1}^{l} a_{ij}w_j + c_i$ reaches its maximum value $\texttt{MAX}_i$ in U at this point, where $i = 1, \ldots, m$. Obviously, $U \subseteq P$ is equivalent to $\texttt{MAX}_i \le b$ for $i = 1, \ldots, m$. Thus it is enough to prove that $\texttt{MAX}_i \le b$ for $i = 1, \ldots, m$.

Assuming that there exists an index $i \in \{1, \ldots, m\}$ such that $\texttt{MAX}_i > b$, we derive a contradiction as follows. Since $\partial U \subseteq P$ and $Aw + C \le B$ for $\forall w \in P$, then $y_i \in U^\circ$. If $U^\circ = \emptyset$, a contradiction is obtained; Otherwise, let $\Omega = \{w : Aw + C \le \texttt{MAX}\}$, where $\texttt{MAX} = (\texttt{MAX}_i, \ldots, \texttt{MAX}_i)'$. By Property 1, we obtain that $y_i \in \partial\Omega$. Thus for an arbitrary but fixed positive number ϵ, there exists $z = (z_1, \ldots, z_l)' \in \mathbb{U}(y_i; \epsilon)$ such that $\sum_{j=1}^{l} a_{ij}z_j + c_i > \texttt{MAX}_i$. Also, since $y_i \in U^\circ$, there exist $\epsilon_1 > 0$ and $w_0 = (w_{01}, \ldots, w_{0l})' \in \mathbb{U}(y_i; \epsilon_1) \subseteq U$ such that $\sum_{j=1}^{l} a_{ij}w_{0j} + c_i > \texttt{MAX}_i$, contradicting the fact that $\sum_{j=1}^{l} a_{ij}w_j + c_i$ reaches its maximum $\texttt{MAX}_i$ in U at the point y_i. Thus, $\texttt{MAX}_i \le b$ for $i = 1, \ldots, m$. That is, P is an over-approximation of the set U.

Lemma 2. *Assume O is a simply connected compact set and $P = \{w : Aw + C \le B\}$ is a compact convex polytope. If the boundary of the set O is a subset of the enclosure of the complement of the polytope P, and the intersection of the interior of the set O and the interior of the set P is not empty, then the set P is an under-approximation of the set O.*

Proof. Since $P = \{w : Aw + C \le B\}$ is compact, P° and P are simply connected sets with the same boundary $\partial P = \{w \in P : \vee_{i=1}^{m} \sum_{j=1}^{l} a_{ij}w_j + c_i = b\}$.

Assuming that $y \in P$ is a point such that $y \notin O$, we derive a contradiction as follows.

Case 1: $y \in P^\circ$. Since $O^\circ \cap P^\circ \ne \emptyset$, there exists $y_0 \in O^\circ \cap P^\circ$. Thus there exists a path q in P°, connecting y and y_0. Due to the assumption that $y \notin O$, there exists $y_1 \in q$ such that $y_1 \in \partial O$ and $y_1 \in P^\circ$, contradicting the assumption that $\partial O \subseteq \overline{P^c}$.

Case 2: $y \in \partial P$. Since $y \notin O$ and O is compact, there exists a $\delta > 0$ such that $P^\circ \cap \mathbb{U}(y; \delta) \neq \emptyset$ and $\mathbb{U}(y; \delta) \cap O = \emptyset$. Thus there exists z_1 such that $z_1 \in P^\circ \cap \mathbb{U}(y; \delta)$ and $z_1 \notin O$. Then, similar to the above case, a contradiction is derived.

Thus, we conclude that the set P is an under-approximation of the set O.

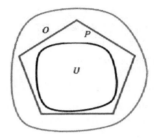

Fig. 1. An illustration for Lemmas 1 and 2. (blue curve – the boundary of the set O in Lemma 1; red curve – the boundary of the convex polytope P; black curve – the boundary of the set U in Lemma 2.) (Color figure online)

Based on the above two lemmas, an approach to compute a polytopic UAB is proposed in the section that follows.

3   Under-Approximating Backward Reachable Sets

In this section an approach is proposed to compute an UAB of a compact simply connected target region TR after the time duration T. The UAB is represented by a polytope.

3.1   Computing Under-Approximations

In this subsection an approach for computing an UAB of TR for the time duration T is detailed. The framework to compute an UAB of a simply connected compact set TR for the time duration T in our method involves the following steps,

1. a time grid $0 = t_0 < t_1 < \ldots < t_N = T$ is adopted with a step size h;
2. starting with $U_0 = $ TR, we compute a compact polytope U_1, which is an UAB of TR for the time duration h;
3. starting from the kth UAB, we advance our approximation to a compact polytopic UAB U_{k+1};
4. U_N is what we want to obtain.

Assume that we have already obtained a compact polytope U_k, where U_k is an UAB of TR for the time duration t_k. A compact polytopic UAB for the time duration $k+1$ is constructed through the following steps:

(a) compute a set Ω_{k+1}, which is an union of a collection of intervals, such that $\partial\Omega_b(h; U_k, \boldsymbol{f}) \subseteq \Omega_{k+1}$, as discussed below;
(b) compute a compact polytope $O_{k+1} = \{\boldsymbol{x} : A\boldsymbol{x} + C \le B\}$ such that $\Omega_{k+1} \subseteq O_{k+1}$;
(c) contract O_{k+1} to obtain $U_{k+1} = \{\boldsymbol{x} : A\boldsymbol{x} + C \le B^u\}$ such that $\Omega_{k+1} \subseteq \overline{U^c_{k+1}}$ and $U^\circ_{k+1} \cap (\Omega_b(h; U_k, \boldsymbol{f}))^\circ \ne \emptyset$.

In order to prove that U_{k+1} obtained by the steps (a) $\sim$ (c) is also a simply connected compact set and is a subset of $\Omega_b(h; U_k, \boldsymbol{f})$, we first introduce a fundamental theorem behind our method based on the fact that $\phi(t; \cdot) : \Omega_b(t; \Delta, \boldsymbol{f}) \mapsto \Delta$ is a homeomorphism between two topological spaces $(\Delta, \mathcal{T}_\Delta)$ and $(\Omega_b(t; \Delta, \boldsymbol{f}), \mathcal{T}_{\Omega_b(t; \Delta, \boldsymbol{f})})$.

Theorem 1. [28,29] *If $\Delta \subseteq \mathbb{R}^n$ is a simply connected compact set, then $\Omega_b(t; \Delta, \boldsymbol{f})$ is also a simply connected compact set and $\partial\Omega_b(t; \Delta, \boldsymbol{f}) = \Omega_b(t; \partial\Delta, \boldsymbol{f})$.*

Based on Theorem 1, we have the following lemma stating that U_{k+1} is a simply connected compact UAB of U_k for the time duration h.

Lemma 3. *If U_k is a simply connected compact set, then U_{k+1} obtained by our framework is also a simply connected compact set satisfying $U_{k+1} \subseteq \Omega_b(h; U_k, \boldsymbol{f})$.*

Proof. Since U_k is a simply connected compact set, $\Omega_b(h; U_k, \boldsymbol{f})$ is also a simply connected compact set according to Theorem 1. Also, since O_{k+1} in our framework is a simply connected compact set, we obtain that U_{k+1} is a simply connected compact set.

Regarding $\partial\Omega_b(h; U_k, \boldsymbol{f}) \subseteq \Omega_{k+1} \subseteq \overline{U^c_{k+1}}$ and $U^\circ_{k+1} \cap (\Omega_b(h; U_k, \boldsymbol{f}))^\circ \ne \emptyset$, we conclude that $U_{k+1} \subseteq \Omega_b(h; U_k, \boldsymbol{f})$ according to Lemma 2.

From Lemma 3, we can deduce that U_N is an UAB of TR for the time duration T, as stated in Theorem 2.

Theorem 2. *Given a nonlinear system of the form (1), if $U_0 = $ TR is a simply connected compact set, U_N obtained by our computational framework is an UAB of TR for the time duration $t = T$.*

In the sections that follow, we detail how to compute Ω_{k+1}, O_{k+1} and U_{k+1} in the steps (a) $\sim$ (c).

3.1.1 Computing Ω_{k+1} and O_{k+1}

In this subsection, we describe how to compute Ω_{k+1} and O_{k+1} in the steps (a) and (b) respectively in our computational framework.

Firstly, we introduce a proposition stating that the backward reachable set of System (1) can be obtained by computing the corresponding forward reachable set of its reverse system, as described in the following.

Proposition 1. [21] $\Omega_f(h; \mathcal{X}, -\boldsymbol{f}) = \Omega_b(h; \mathcal{X}, \boldsymbol{f})$, where $\mathcal{X} \subseteq \mathbb{R}^n$.

From Proposition 1, we observe that $\Omega_f(h; U_k, -\boldsymbol{f})$ instead of $\Omega_b(h; U_k, \boldsymbol{f})$ can be used for performing computations in our computational framework, where $k = 0, \ldots, N - 1$. Thus, we can equivalently compute a set Ω_{k+1} such that $\partial \Omega_f(h; U_k, -\boldsymbol{f}) \subseteq \Omega_{k+1}$. Also, the fact that the boundary of $\Omega_f(h; U_k, -\boldsymbol{f})$ corresponds to the boundary of U_k under the map $\phi(h; \cdot)$ according to Theorem 1 is observed. Thus Ω_{k+1} is obtained based on ∂U_k. According to these observations, an approach to computing Ω_{k+1} is presented, as described in the following.

1. For a given ϵ_M, we use the interval Branch and Bound methods (e.g., [30]) to obtain a set of compact intervals $\{s_j, j = 1, \ldots, M_k\}$ such that $\partial U_k \subseteq \cup_{j=1}^{M_k} s_j$, where M_k is the number of intervals and each interval s_j is of the form $[\underline{x}_1, \overline{x}_1] \times \ldots \times [\underline{x}_n, \overline{x}_n]$ satisfying $|\overline{x}_l - \underline{x}_l| \leq \epsilon_M$.
2. For $j = 1, \ldots, M_k$, we use interval reachability analysis based methods (e.g., [24]) to obtain a compact interval I_j such that $\Omega_f(h; s_j, -\boldsymbol{f}) \subseteq I_j$. Thus, $\Omega_{k+1} = \cup_{j=1}^{M_k} I_j$ is what we want.

The above procedure for computing Ω_{k+1} is denoted by $\mathtt{Boundary}(h, U_k, \epsilon_M)$.

Remark 2. In the procedure $\mathtt{Boundary}(h, U_k, \epsilon_M)$, ϵ_M is used to restrict the size of boxes enclosing ∂U_k. As ϵ_M becomes smaller, the volume of the obtained boxes becomes smaller and the resulting Ω_{k+1} becomes less conservative, but the computational burden increases.

The procedure $\mathtt{Boundary}(h, U_k, \epsilon_M)$ for computing Ω_{k+1} is illustrated through the following example.

Example 1. Consider a model of an electromechnical oscillation of s synchronous machine [31],

$$\begin{cases} \dot{x}_1 = x_2 \\ \dot{x}_2 = 0.2 - 0.7 \sin x_1 - 0.05 x_2 \end{cases},$$

where $\mathtt{TR} = [-0.1, 0.1] \times [2.9, 3.1]$ and $T = 0.5$.
Computing Ω_1 when $h = 0.5$ and $\epsilon_M = 0.05$ is illustrated in Fig. 2.

Next, we compute a convex hull O_{k+1} such that $O_{k+1} \supseteq \Omega_{k+1}$, where $\Omega_{k+1} = \cup_{j=1}^{M_k} I_j$. Let v_j be the set of vertices of the interval I_j and $v = \cup_{j=1}^{M_k} v_j$. We get a polytope $O_{k+1} = \{\boldsymbol{x} : A\boldsymbol{x} + C \leq B\}$ of v using convex hull algorithm (e.g., [33]), where $A = (a_{ij})_{m \times n}$ and $B = (b, \ldots, b)'$. This procedure for computing O_{k+1} is denoted by $\mathtt{Polytope}(\Omega_{k+1})$.

Since I_j is compact for $j = 1, \ldots, M_k$, v is a bounded set, and as a consequence O_{k+1} is bounded and thus compact. Also, since every box I_j is also a convex hull of v_j, every $\boldsymbol{x} \in I_j$ can be formulated as $\sum_{l=1}^{2^n} \lambda_l \boldsymbol{v}_{j,l}$, where $\boldsymbol{v}_{j,l} \in v_j$, $\lambda_l \geq 0$ for $l = 1, \ldots, 2^n$ and $\sum_{l=1}^{2^n} \lambda_l = 1$. Thus $\boldsymbol{x} \in O_{k+1}$ holds, implying that $\cup_{j=1}^{M_k} I_j \subseteq O_{k+1}$. Now we conclude that O_{k+1} in the step (b) is computed.

Remark 3. According to Lemma 1 in Subsect. 2.2, the convex hull O_{k+1} is an over-approximation of the backward reachable set of U_k for the time duration h.

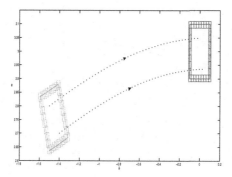

Fig. 2. An illustration for computing Ω_1. (red boxes – Ω_1 including $\partial\Omega_b(T; \text{TR}, \boldsymbol{f})$; green points – $\partial\Omega_b(T; \text{TR}, \boldsymbol{f})$) obtained by simulation methods; black points – some simulation trajectories originating from $\Omega_b(T; \text{TR}, \boldsymbol{f})$ over the time interval $[0, 0.5]$; purple curve – ∂TR; blue boxes – $\cup_j s_j$ including ∂TR.) (Color figure online)

3.1.2   Computing an Under-Approximation U_{k+1}

This section focuses on computing a polytopic under-approximation U_{k+1} (step (c) in our computational framework) by solving linear programming problems.

After obtaining $\Omega_{k+1} = \cup_{j=1}^{M_k} I_j$ and $O_{k+1} = \{\boldsymbol{x} : A\boldsymbol{x} + C \leq B\}$ in steps (a) and (b) based on the method in Subsect. 3.1, we shrink O_{k+1} to yield U_{k+1} by solving linear programming problems. The computations consist of two steps, as described below.

1. For $j = 1, \ldots, M_k$, we solve the following linear optimization problem:

$$\begin{aligned}
\text{minimize} \quad & b_j \\
\text{s. t.} \quad & A\boldsymbol{x} + C \leq B_j, \\
& b_j \leq b, \\
& \boldsymbol{x} \in I_j,
\end{aligned} \tag{2}$$

where $B_j = (b_j, \ldots, b_j)'$. Since $b_j \leq b$, we can obtain that $\{\boldsymbol{x} : A\boldsymbol{x} + C \leq B_j\} \subseteq \{\boldsymbol{x} : A\boldsymbol{x} + C \leq B\}$.
2. We denote $min\{b_j, j = 1, \ldots, M_k\}$ by b^u and $(b^u, \ldots, b^u)'$ by B^u respectively. If $\{\boldsymbol{x} : A\boldsymbol{x} + C \leq B^u\} \neq \emptyset$, it is denoted by U_{k+1}. The case that U_{k+1} is empty is discussed in Sect. 4. Note that U_{k+1} is just a candidate of what we want.

The above procedure for U_{k+1} is denoted by $\texttt{Contraction}(\Omega_{k+1}, O_{k+1})$, which is illustrated in the following example.

Example 2. For Example 1, computing U_1 when $\epsilon_M = 0.05$ and $h = 0.5$ is illustrated in Fig. 3, where $T = 0.5$.

Since $U_{k+1} \subseteq O_{k+1}$, U_{k+1} is compact. However, we cannot conclude that U_{k+1} is an UAB of U_k for the time duration h. In order to further ensure that U_{k+1} is an under-approximation of $\Omega_b(h; U_k, \boldsymbol{f})$, we need to verify whether U_{k+1}

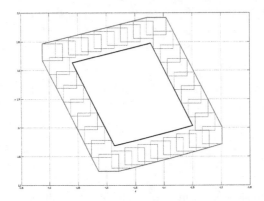

Fig. 3. An illustration for computing Ω_1. (red boxes – Ω_1 including $\partial\Omega_b(T;\mathtt{TR},\boldsymbol{f})$; green curve – ∂O_1; black curve – ∂U_1.) (Color figure online)

satisfies the condition as described in the step (c) in our computational framework, i.e., verify whether $\Omega_{k+1} \subseteq \overline{U_{k+1}^c}$ and $U_{k+1}^\circ \cap (\Omega_b(h; U_k, \boldsymbol{f}))^\circ \neq \emptyset$ holds.

For the constraint $\Omega_{k+1} \subseteq \overline{U_{k+1}^c}$, we can ensure it by the following lemma.

Lemma 4. $\Omega_{k+1} \subseteq \overline{U_{k+1}^c}$, where Ω_{k+1} and U_{k+1} are respectively obtained based on the procedures $\mathtt{Boundary}(h, U_k, \epsilon_M)$ and $\mathtt{Contraction}(\Omega_{k+1}, O_{k+1})$.

Proof. Since $U_{k+1} = \{\boldsymbol{x} : A\boldsymbol{x} + C \leq B^u\}$, where $A = \left(a_{ij}\right)_{m\times n}$, $C = (c_1,\ldots,c_m)'$, $B^u = (b^u,\ldots,b^u)'$, $b^u = \min\{b_j, j = 1,\ldots,M_k\}$ and b_j is obtained by solving the optimization problem (2), we can obtain that for every $\boldsymbol{x} = (x_1,\ldots,x_n)' \in \cup_{j=1}^{M_k}I_j$, there exists an index $i \in \{1,\ldots,m\}$ such that $\sum_{j=1}^n a_{ij}x_j + c_i \geq b^u$, implying that $\boldsymbol{x} \notin \{\boldsymbol{x} : A\boldsymbol{x} + C < B^u\}$. Thus, $\Omega_{k+1} = \cup_{j=1}^{M_k}I_j \subseteq \overline{U_{k+1}^c}$.

In order to check whether $U_{k+1}^\circ \cap (\Omega_b(h; U_k, \boldsymbol{f}))^\circ \neq \emptyset$ holds, we first take a point $\boldsymbol{x} \in U_{k+1}^\circ = \{\boldsymbol{x} : A\boldsymbol{x} + C < B^u\}$, then apply interval methods (e.g., [24]) to get an interval enclosure $s_{\boldsymbol{x}}$ of $\phi(h; \boldsymbol{x})$, and check whether $s_{\boldsymbol{x}} \subseteq U_k$ holds. If the answer is positive, $U_{k+1}^\circ \cap (\Omega_b(h; U_k, \boldsymbol{f}))^\circ \neq \emptyset$ holds, as stated in Lemma 5. The procedure for checking $U_{k+1}^\circ \cap (\Omega_b(h; U_k, \boldsymbol{f}))^\circ \neq \emptyset$ is denoted by $\mathtt{Verification}(U_{k+1}^\circ \cap (\Omega_b(h; U_k, \boldsymbol{f}))^\circ)$.

Lemma 5. If $s_{\boldsymbol{x}} \subseteq U_k$, then $\boldsymbol{x}^6 \in U_{k+1}^\circ \cap (\Omega_b(h; U_k, \boldsymbol{f}))^\circ$ holds, where $s_{\boldsymbol{x}}$ and U_{k+1} are respectively computed based on the procedures $\mathtt{Verification}(U_{k+1}^\circ \cap (\Omega_b(h; U_k, \boldsymbol{f}))^\circ)$ and $\mathtt{Contraction}(\Omega_{k+1}, O_{k+1})$.

---

[6] Although $\boldsymbol{x}$ can be an arbitrary point belonging to U_{k+1}°, $\boldsymbol{x}$ has to be a point being away from ∂U_{k+1} due to the fact that $s_{\boldsymbol{x}}$ is an interval box rather a point and $s_{\boldsymbol{x}} \subseteq U_k$. This can be done by taking $\boldsymbol{x}$ being in $\{\boldsymbol{x} : A\boldsymbol{x} + C \leq B^u - \delta\}$, where $\delta > 0$.

Proof. Since $s_x \subseteq U_k$, $x \in \Omega_f(h; U_k, -f)$ and thus $x \in \Omega_b(h; U_k, f)$ holds. Also, according to the fact that $\partial \Omega_b(h; U_k, f) \subseteq \Omega_{k+1}$ and $\Omega_{k+1} \subseteq \overline{U_{k+1}^c}$, we obtain that $U_{k+1}^\circ \cap \partial \Omega_b(h; U_k, f) = \emptyset$, implying that $x \notin \partial \Omega_b(h; U_k, f)$. Thus, $x \in U_{k+1}^\circ \cap (\Omega_b(h; U_k, f))^\circ$.

Thus, if the boolean value returned by $\mathtt{Verification}(U_{k+1}^\circ \cap (\Omega_b(h; U_k, f))^\circ)$ is true, i.e., $U_{k+1}^\circ \cap (\Omega_b(h; U_k, f))^\circ \neq \emptyset$, then U_{k+1} obtained by the procedure $\mathtt{Contraction}(\Omega_{k+1}, O_{k+1})$ is an UAB of $\Omega_b(h; U_k, f)$.

Remark 4. In the procedure $\mathtt{Contraction}(\Omega_{k+1}, O_{k+1})$, $|\frac{b-b^u}{b-d}|$ can be used to evaluate the obtained UAB U_k, where d is the supremum such that $\{x : Ax + C < D\} = \emptyset$ and $D = (d, \ldots, d)'$[7]. As it approaches one, the under-approximation becomes increasingly conservative.

Thus our approach for computing a compact polytopic UAB is elucidated. We formally formulate our approach for computing an UAB of TR for the time duration T as Algorithm 1.

Algorithm 1. Computing an Under-Approximation

Input: Given system (1), a target region: TR, a time duration: T, a time step h such
   that $\frac{T-0}{h} \geq 1$ is an integer, ϵ_M: the size of intervals enclosing the boundaries, and
   ϵ: local error bounds.
Output: an UAB of TR for the time duration T.
1: $U_0 := \mathtt{TR}$;
2: **for** $i = 0 : 1 : N - 1$ **do**
3:    $\Omega_{i+1} := \mathtt{Boundary}(h, U_i, \epsilon_M)$;
4:    $O_{i+1} := \mathtt{Polytope}(\Omega_{i+1})$;
5:    $U_{i+1} := \mathtt{Contraction}(\Omega_{i+1}, O_{i+1})$;
6:    **if** $\mathtt{Verification}(U_{i+1}^\circ \cap (\Omega_b(h; U_i, f))^\circ)$ is false or $|\frac{b-b^u}{b-d}| > \epsilon$ **then**
7:       return "failed to obtain an UAB" and terminate;
8:    **end if**
9: **end for**
10: return an UAB U_N.

Remark 5. Our method, as formalised in Algorithm 1, can be applied to under-approximate forward reachable sets by performing forward computations on initial sets.

In order to enhance the understanding of our approach, an example is employed to illustrate Algorithm 1 as follows.

Example 3. Consider a model of an electromechanical oscillation of s synchronous machine,

$$\begin{cases} \dot{x}_1 = x_2 \\ \dot{x}_2 = 0.2 - 0.7 sin x_1 - 0.05 x_2 \end{cases},$$

where $\mathtt{TR} = [-0.1, 0.1] \times [2.9, 3.1]$ and $T = 3$.

---

[7] d can be obtained by solving the linear program: min d, s.t., $Ax + C \leq D$.

Let $h = 3$, $\epsilon_M = 0.0001$ and $\epsilon = 0.5$. Firstly, we compute $\Omega_1 = \cup_j I_j$ such that $\partial \Omega_b(T; \mathrm{TR}, \boldsymbol{f}) \subseteq \Omega_1$ based on the procedure $\mathtt{Boundary}(h, \mathrm{TR}, \epsilon_M)$ in Subsect. 3.1, where I_j is of the interval form. Secondly, we compute O_1 based on the procedure $\mathtt{Polytope}(\Omega_1)$ in Subsect. 3.1 such that $\Omega_1 \subseteq O_1$. Thirdly, we contract O_1 to obtain U_1 based on the procedure $\mathtt{Contraction}(\Omega_1, O_1)$ in Subsect. 3.1. Finally, we find a point $\boldsymbol{x} = (-8.08, 2.52) \in U_1^\circ$ and obtain $s_{\boldsymbol{x}} = [0.0082, 0.0083] \times [3.0181, 3.0182]$ based on the procedure $\mathtt{Verification}(U_1^\circ \cap (\Omega_b(h; \mathrm{TR}, \boldsymbol{f}))^\circ)$ in Subsect. 3.1. Since $s_{\boldsymbol{x}} \subseteq \mathrm{TR}$ and $|\frac{b-b^u}{b-d}| \approx 0.246621 \leq \epsilon$, where $b = 0$, $b^u = -0.008260$ and $d = -0.0334927$, U_1 is an UAB of TR for the time duration $T = 3$. The boundary of U_1 is depicted in Fig. 4.

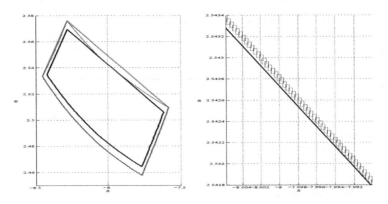

Fig. 4. An UAB for Example 3. (left: red boxes – Ω_1 including $\partial \Omega_b(3; \mathrm{TR}, \boldsymbol{f})$; green curve – ∂O_1; black curve – ∂U_1; right: a zoomed-in portion of the left figure.) (Color figure online)

3.2   Computational Complexity

In this subsection, the computational complexity of Algorithm 1 is discussed briefly. In the kth step, the branch-and-bound method for the problem of yielding some interval subdivisions to enclose ∂U_k is of exponential complexity $\mathcal{O}(\xi^n)$, where $\xi = \mathcal{O}(\frac{1}{\epsilon_M})$. The underlying interval Taylor series method is of polynomial complexity: the work is $\mathcal{O}(p^2)$ to compute the Taylor coefficients, where p is the order of the used Taylor expansion, and $\mathcal{O}(n^3)$ for performing linear algebra [32]. The complexity of applying simplex algorithms to solve the linear program (2) is $\mathcal{O}(nm_k)$ generally, where m_k is the number of linear constraints. The computational complexity of the convex hull algorithm (e.g., [33]) is $\mathrm{Con}_k = \mathcal{O}(2^n M_k \log r)$ for $n \leq 3$ and $\mathcal{O}(2^n M_k f_r / r + f_r)$ when $n > 3$, where $r \leq 2^n M_k$ is the number of vertices of O_{k+1}, $f_r = \mathcal{O}(r^{\lfloor \frac{n}{2} \rfloor} / \lfloor \frac{n}{2} \rfloor !)$ and $\lfloor \frac{n}{2} \rfloor$ is the floor function of $\frac{n}{2}$. Therefore, the total computational complexity of our method is $\sum_{k=0}^{N-1} \left(\mathcal{O}(\xi_k^n) + M_k(\mathcal{O}(p^2) + \mathcal{O}(n^3)) + M_k \mathcal{O}(nm_k) + \mathrm{Con}_k \right)$.

4 Examples, Discussions and Comparisons

Our approach is implemented based on the floating point linear programming solver GLPK running the Simplex algorithm and the validated ordinary differential equation solver VNODE-LP [24]. We evaluate it using five examples and compare it with the method of Korda et al. [22]. The results for Examples 4–7 can be found in Figs. 5, 6, 7 and 8 respectively. Table 1 presents details on parameters that control our approach. All these computations are performed on an i5-3337U 1.8 GHz CPU with 4 GB RAM running Ubuntu Linux 13.04.

4.1 Examples and Discussions

In this subsection our approach is evaluated using Examples 4–8, and parameters that control our approach are discussed using the first four examples. The results are illustrated in Figs. 4, 5, 6 and 7. Regarding the computational complexity analysis in Subsect. 3.2, our approach suffers from dimensional curse. In order to overcome this problem, we explore some future directions to make our approach more practical through Example 8.

Table 1. Performance of Algorithm 1 on Examples. Each benchmark is indexed by its example number. TR: target region, ϵ_M: bound for the size of intervals in the procedure Boundary(h, U_k, ϵ_M); ϵ: bound for $\left|\frac{b-b^u}{b-d}\right|$ in the procedure Contraction(Ω_{k+1}, O_{k+1}); h: step size; T :a specified time duration for UAB; Time: CPU time cost (seconds).

Ex	TR	ϵ_M	ϵ	h	T	Time
4	$[-0.1, 0.1] \times [-0.1, 0.1]$	0.001	0.5	0.5	10	34.29
4	$[-0.1, 0.1] \times [-0.1, 0.1]$	0.0002	0.5	0.5	10	266.58
5	$[0.3, 0.4] \times [0.5, 0.7]$	0.001	0.5	0.05	1.1	55.23
5	$[0.3, 0.4] \times [0.5, 0.7]$	0.0002	0.5	0.05	1.1	410.13
6	$[1.2, 1.5] \times [0.8, 1.1]$	0.001	0.5	0.5	10	23.04
6	$[1.2, 1.5] \times [0.8, 1.1]$	0.0001	0.5	0.5	10	911.40
7	$x_i \in [-0.1, 0.1],\ i = 1, \ldots, 3$	0.003	0.5	0.5	2.5	450.32
7	$x_i \in [-0.1, 0.1],\ i = 1, \ldots, 3$	0.003	0.5	2.5	2.5	66.56
8	$x_i \in [-0.015, 0.001],\ i = 1, \ldots, 7$	0.016	0.5	0.01	0.2	0.67

Example 4. Consider the system in Example 1 again

$$\begin{cases} \dot{x}_1 = x_2 \\ \dot{x}_2 = 0.2 - 0.7 sinx_1 - 0.05x_2 \end{cases}.$$

Example 5. Consider the Brusselator model [10],

$$\begin{cases} \dot{x}_1 = 1 + x_1^2 x_2 - 1.5x_1 - x_1 \\ \dot{x}_2 = 1.5x_1 - x_1^2 x_2 \end{cases},$$

Example 6. Consider the Van-der-Pol system,

$$\begin{cases} \dot{x}_1 = x_2 \\ \dot{x}_2 = -0.2(x_1^2 - 1)x_2 - x_1 \end{cases}.$$

Example 7. Consider the 3D-Lotka-Volterra System,

$$\begin{cases} \dot{x}_1 = x_1 x_2 - x_1 x_3 \\ \dot{x}_2 = x_2 x_3 - x_2 x_1 \\ \dot{x}_3 = x_3 x_1 - x_3 x_2 \end{cases}.$$

Note that $\Omega_b(2.5; \text{TR}, \boldsymbol{f}) \subseteq O_1$ in Fig. 8 according to Remark 3.

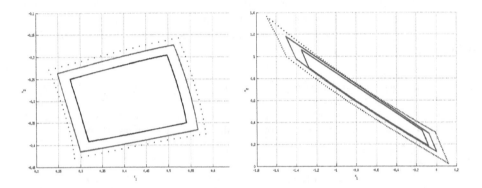

Fig. 5. ∂UAB for Example 4.(blue points $- \partial\Omega_b(10; \text{TR}, \boldsymbol{f})$ obtained by Runge-Kutta methods; red curve $- \partial U_{20}$ when $\epsilon_M = 0.0002$; green curve $- \partial U_{20}$ when $\epsilon_M = 0.001$.) (Color figure online)

Fig. 6. ∂UAB for Example 5. (blue points $- \partial\Omega_b(1.1; \text{TR}, \boldsymbol{f})$ obtained by Runge-Kutta methods; red curve $- \partial U_{22}$ when $\epsilon_M = 0.0002$; green curve $- \partial U_{22}$ when $\epsilon_M = 0.001$.) (Color figure online)

From the above four examples, we first observe that polytopes can represent reachable sets well for some nonlinear systems, e.g., Examples 4–7. Also, we observe that (1) when h is fixed, the resulting UAB becomes less conservative as ϵ_M becomes smaller (Examples 4–6); (2) when ϵ_M is fixed, a smaller h may lead to large errors. The underlying reason is that the under-approximation error in every iterative step will propagate through the computations (Example 7), similar to the well known wrapping effect in over-approximating reachable sets. The errors in the construction of under-approximations of reachable sets using our method result from three parts in every iteration. The first one is the computation of interval boxes enclosing the boundary of the target region. The second one is the computation of interval boxes enclosing the boundary of the

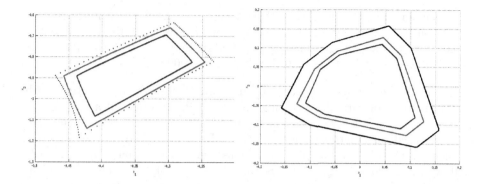

Fig. 7. ∂UAB for Example 6. (blue points – $\partial\Omega_b(10; \text{TR}, f)$ obtained by Runge-Kutta methods; red curve – ∂U_{20} when $\epsilon_M = 0.0001$; green curve - ∂U_{20} when $\epsilon_M = 0.001$.) (Color figure online)

Fig. 8. ∂UAB for Example 7. (black curve – ∂O_1 when $h = 2.5$; red curve – ∂U_1 when $h = 2.5$; green curve – ∂U_5 when $h = 0.5$.) (Color figure online)

backward reachable set based on the interval Taylor-series method and the last one is the computation of an polytopic under-approximation. It is well known that reachable sets of nonlinear systems are in general far from being convex, the last one contributes to the total error mainly. Especially, for the case that the returned under-approximation is empty in some iterative step, we could try a smaller ϵ_M and/or a different time step h. A smaller ϵ_M, which mitigates the error from the first source, will help to obtain a tighter Ω_{k+1}, eventually leading to a less conservative UAB. However, the computational cost increases. Therefore, in order to obtain a tighter Ω_{k+1}, reachability analysis methods which better control the wrapping effect should be considered (e.g., [10, 27]). This corresponds to the reduction of the error from the second source. As to the last error source resulting from polytopic approximations, an under-approximation of the semi-algebraic form instead of the polytopic form will be contemplated in our future study.

Example 8. Consider a seven-domensional biological system[8],

$$\begin{cases} \dot{x}_1 = -0.4x_1 + 5x_3x_4 \\ \dot{x}_2 = 0.4x_1 - x_2 \\ \dot{x}_3 = x_2 - 5x_3x_4 \\ \dot{x}_4 = 5x_5x_6 - 5x_3x_4 \\ \dot{x}_5 = -5x_5x_6 + 5x_3x_4 \\ \dot{x}_6 = 0.5x_7 - 5x_5x_6 \\ \dot{x}_7 = -0.5x_7 + 5x_5x_6 \end{cases} .$$

---

[8] The model is from http://ths.rwth-aachen.de/research/hypro/biological-model-i/.

Using an interval hull rather than a convex hull in every iterative step of Algorithm 1, we obtain that an UAB for the time duration $t = 0.2$ is $[-0.0152, 0.000] \times [-0.0169, 0.0011] \times [-0.0140, 0.0030] \times [-0.0141, 0.0001] \times [-0.0141, 0.0001] \times [-0.0138, 0.0014] \times [-0.0155, 0.000]$.

From Example 8, we observe that our approach scales well to systems with a large number of variables by using an interval hull instead of a convex hull in every iteration. However, this results in more conservative results, compared to that based on polytopic representations. In order to reduce the conservativeness brought by interval representations, while making our approach scale well, we will explore using oriented rectangular hulls [25], zonotopes [15] or symbolic orthogonal projections [34] to construct under-approximations in our future work. Furthermore, regarding that the boundary of a polytope is piecewise of the zonotope form, therefore the exact boundary of the polytope rather than interval subdivisions enveloping it obtained by Branch and Bound methods in every iteration can be used for computations directly using methods in [11, 27], thereby reducing the computational cost and further improving the scalability of our method.

4.2   Comparisons

In this section we will compare our method with the method of Korda et al. [22]. Due to a lot of input parameters such as sum-of-squares multipliers being coordinated in the method of Korda et al. [22], it is not trivial to find an optimal combination, thereby making fair comparisons difficult. Therefore, we try to explore some potential benefits of our method by comparing with this method.

Firstly, the method of Korda et al. [22] aims to compute inner approximations of the region of attraction for polynomial dynamical systems by solving sum-of-squares programming problems. The region of attraction is the set of all states that end in the target set at a given time without leaving a constraint set. In contrast, our method is not restricted to polynomial dynamical systems. That is, our method can deal with more general nonlinear systems such as Example 4 in Subsect. 4.1. Secondly, we compare the performances of the two methods based on Examples 5–8. Assume that the specified constraint sets for the four examples are $\{\boldsymbol{x} : 1.25^2 - (x_1 + 0.75)^2 - (x_2 - 0.65)^2 \geq 0\}$, $\{\boldsymbol{x} : 4 - x_1^2 - x_2^2 \geq 0\}$, $\{\boldsymbol{x} : 0.04 - x_1^2 - x_2^2 - x_3^2 \geq 0\}$ and $\{\boldsymbol{x} : 0.0125^2 - \sum_{i=1}^{7}(x_i + 0.0075)^2 \geq 0\}$ respectively. Actually, they are respectively the over-approximations of backward reachable sets of the target regions for these four examples. Using the method of Korda et al. [22], we can not obtain feasible solutions to any of the above examples based on the sum-of-squares programming solver YALMIP [35] with Sedumi [36]. Since there are a lot of sum-of-squares multipliers that are coordinated in advance, their degrees should be determined in advance for computations, improper mixing will result in unreliable results. The main underlying reason is that the present status of semi-definite programming solvers is not so advanced, as pointed out in [37]. The numerical problems produced by these solvers often result in unreliable results for some cases. We use Example 5 to illustrate this.

Although the solver YALMIP returns a "feasible" solution as shown in Fig. 9 for some mixing of sum-of-squares multipliers, the result is incorrect actually. On the contrary, our method relies on Interval methods to locate the boundary of the backward reachable set and linear programs to obtain an under-approximation in every iterative step, making our method more reliable.

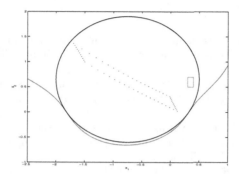

Fig. 9. An incorrect UAB for Example 5 obtained by the method of Korda et al. [22] due to numerical problems. (black curve – $\{x : 1.25^2 - (x_1 + 0.75)^2 - (x_2 - 0.65)^2 \geq 0\}$; red curve – the boundary of an incorrect under-approximation of $\Omega_b(1.1, \mathtt{TR}, f)$; green curve - $\partial \mathtt{TR}$; blue points – $\partial \Omega_b(1.1, \mathtt{TR}, f)$ obtained by Runge Kutta methods.) (Color figure online)

5   Conclusion

Given a nonlinear system and a target region of the simply connected compact type, we in this paper proposed a method by performing boundary analysis to obtain an UAB of the target region for a specified time duration. The UAB is represented as a polytope. The polytope can be obtained by combining validated numerical methods for ordinary differential equations and linear programs. Numerical results and comparisons with the method of Korda et al. [22] based on five examples were given to illustrate the benefits of our approach. The results show that our method has some significant benefits in under-approximating reachable sets for some cases. Furthermore, we explore some directions toward improving the scalability of our method.

Extending our method to compute under-approximations of reachable sets for nonlinear systems with time delay (e.g., [38]) is considered in our future work. Moreover, computing a bounded error approximation of the solution over a bounded time is another interesting investigation towards addressing under-approximation problems [39].

Acknowledgements. The authors are grateful to Prof. Martin Fränzle from Carl von Ossietzky Universität Oldenburg, Mr. Milan Korda from École Polytechnique Fédérale de Lausanne, Dr. Xin Chen from University of Colorado at Boulder for helpful discussions. Also, the authors are especially grateful to the anonymous reviewers for their valuable comments.

References

1. Xue, B.: Computing rigor quadratic lyapunov functions and underapproximate reachable sets for ordinary differential equations. Doctoral dissertation, Beihang University (2013)
2. Ratschan, S., She, Z.: Safety verification of hybrid systems by constraint propagation-based abstraction refinement. ACM Trans. Embed. Comput. Syst. **6**, 1–23 (2007)
3. Plaku, E., Kavraki, L.E., Vardi, M.Y.: Hybrid systems: from verification to falsification. In: Damm, W., Hermanns, H. (eds.) CAV 2007. LNCS, vol. 4590, pp. 463–476. Springer, Heidelberg (2007)
4. Herrero, P., Calm, R., Vehí, J., Armengol, J., Georgiou, P., Oliver, N., Tomazou, C.: Robust fault detection system for insulin pump therapy using continuous glucose monitoring. J. Diabetes Sci. Technol. **6**, 1131–1141 (2012)
5. Xue, B., Easwaran, A., Cho, N.: Towards robust artificial pancreas based on reachability analysis techniques. In: Workshop on Medical Cyber-Physical Systems (2015)
6. Althoff, M., Dolan, J.M.: Online verification of automated road vehicles using reachability analysis. IEEE Trans. Robot. **30**, 1–16 (2014)
7. Alur, R., Dang, T., Ivančić, F.: Progress on reachability analysis of hybrid systems using predicate abstraction. In: Maler, O., Pnueli, A. (eds.) HSCC 2003. LNCS, vol. 2623, pp. 4–19. Springer, Heidelberg (2003)
8. Asarin, E., Dang, T., Girard, A.: Hybridization methods for the analysis of nonlinear systems. Acta Inf. **43**(7), 451–476 (2007)
9. Huang, Z., Mitra, S.: Proofs from simulations and modular annotations. In: Proceedings of the 17th International Conference on Hybrid Systems: Computation and Control (HSCC 2014), pp. 183–192. ACM, New York (2014)
10. Chen, X., Ábrahám, E., Sankaranarayanan, S.: Taylor model flowpipe construction for non-linear hybrid systems. In: Proceedings of the 2012 IEEE 33rd Real-Time Systems Symposium (RTSS 2012), pp. 183–192. IEEE Computer Society, Washington (2012)
11. Althoff, M.: Reachability analysis of nonlinear systems using conservative polynomialization and non-convex sets. In: Proceedings of the 16th International Conference on Hybrid Systems: Computation and Control (HSCC 2013), pp. 173–182. ACM, New York (2013)
12. Revert, A., Calm, R., Vehi, J., Bondia, J.: Calculation of the best basal-bolus combination for postprandial glucose control in insulin pump therapy. IEEE Trans Biomed. Eng. **58**, 274–281 (2011)
13. Ratschan, S., She, Z.: Providing a basin of attraction to a target region of polynomial systems by computation of lyapunov-like functions. SIAM J. Control Optim. **48**(7), 4377–4394 (2010)
14. Kurzhanski, A.B., Varaiya, P.: Ellipsoidal techniques for reachability analysis: internal approximation. Syst. Control Lett. **41**, 201–211 (2000)

15. Girard, A., Le Guernic, C., Maler, O.: Efficient computation of reachable sets of linear time-invariant systems with inputs. In: Hespanha, J.P., Tiwari, A. (eds.) HSCC 2006. LNCS, vol. 3927, pp. 257–271. Springer, Heidelberg (2006)
16. Maidensa, J.N., Kaynamaa, S., Mitchell, I.M., Oishic, M.K., Dumonta, G.A.: Lagrangian methods for approximating the viability kernel in high-dimensional systems. Automatica **49**, 2017–2029 (2013)
17. Benvenuti, L., Bresolin, D., Casagrande, A., Collins, P., Ferrari, A., Mazzi, E., Sangiovanni-Vincentelli, A., Villa, T.: Reachability computation for hybrid systems with Ariadne. In: Proceedings of the 17th IFAC World Congress, vol. 41, pp. 8960–8965. IFAC Papers-OnLine (2008)
18. Goldsztejn, A., Jaulin, L.: Inner approximation of the range of vector-valued functions. Reliable Comput. **14**, 1–23 (2010)
19. Mullier, O., Goubault, E., Kieffer, M., Putot, S.: General inner approximation of vector-valued functions. Reliable Comput. **18**, 117–143 (2013)
20. Goubault, E., Mullier, O., Putot, S., Kieffer, M.: Inner approximated reachability analysis. In: Proceedings of the 16th International Conference on Hybrid Systems: Computation and Control (HSCC 2014), pp. 163–172. ACM, New York (2014)
21. Mitchell, I.M.: Comparing forward and backward reachability as tools for safety analysis. In: Bemporad, A., Bicchi, A., Buttazzo, G. (eds.) HSCC 2007. LNCS, vol. 4416, pp. 428–443. Springer, Heidelberg (2007)
22. Korda, M., Henrion, D., Jones, N.C.: Inner approximations of the region of attraction for polynomial dynamical systems. In: Proceedings of 9th IFAC Symposium on Nonlinear Control Systems, pp. 534–539 (2013)
23. Chen, X., Sankaranarayanan, S., Ábrahám, E.: Under-approximate flowpipes fornon-linear continuous systems. In: Proceedings of the 14th Conference on Formal Methods in Computer-Aided Design (FMCAD 2014), pp. 59–66. IEEE (2014)
24. Nedialkov, N.S.: VNODE-LP - a validated solver for initial value problems in ordinary differential equations. Technical report CAS-06-06-NN, Department of Computing and Software, McMaster University, Hamilton, Canada, L8S4K1 (2006). VNODE-LP is available at www.cas.mcmaster.ca/nedialk/vnodelp/
25. Stursberg, O., Krogh, B.H.: Efficient representation and computation of reachable sets for hybrid systems. In: Maler, O., Pnueli, A. (eds.) HSCC 2003. LNCS, vol. 2623, pp. 482–497. Springer, Heidelberg (2003)
26. Testylier, R., Dang, T.: NLTOOLBOX: a library for reachability computation of nonlinear dynamical systems. In: Van Hung, D., Ogawa, M. (eds.) ATVA 2013. LNCS, vol. 8172, pp. 469–473. Springer, Heidelberg (2013)
27. Eggers, A., Ramdani, N., Nedialkov, N.S., Fränzle, M.: Improving the SAT modulo ODE approach to hybrid systems analysis by combining different enclosure methods. Softw. Syst. Model. **14**, 121–148 (2015)
28. Massey, W.S.: A Basic Course in Algebraic Topology. Springer, New York (1991). Corollary 6.7
29. Khalil, H.K.: Nonlinear Systems, 3rd edn, p. 188. Prentice Hall, Upper Saddle River (2002)
30. Granvilliers, L., Benhamou, F.: Realpaver: an interval solver using constraint satisfaction techniques. ACM TOMS **32**(1), 138–156 (2006)
31. Susuki, Y., Koo, T.J., Ebina, H., Yamazaki, T., Ochi, T., Uemura, T., Hikihara, T.: A hybrid system approach to the analysis and design of power grid dynamic performance. Proc. IEEE **100**, 225–239 (2012)
32. Ramdani, N., Nedialkov, N.S.: Computing reachable sets for uncertain nonlinear hybrid systems using interval constraint-propagation techniques. Nonlinear Anal. Hybrid Syst. **5**, 149–162 (2011)

33. Barber, C.B., Dobkin, D.P., Huhdanpaa, H.: The quickhull algorithm for convex hulls. ACM Trans. Math. Softw. **22**, 469–483 (1996)
34. Hagemann, W.: Reachability analysis of hybrid systems using symbolic orthogonal projections. In: Biere, A., Bloem, R. (eds.) CAV 2014. LNCS, vol. 8559, pp. 407–423. Springer, Heidelberg (2014)
35. Löfberg, J.: YALMIP: a toolbox for modeling and optimization in MATLAB. In: Proceedings of the CACSD Conference, Taipei, Taiwan, pp. 284–289 (2004)
36. Sturm, J.F.: Using SeDuMi 1.02, a MATLAB toolbox for optimization over symmetric cones. Optim. Methods Softw. **11**, 625–653 (1999)
37. Wang, T., Lall, S., West, M.: Polynomial level-set method for polynomial system reachable set estimation. IEEE Trans. Autom. Control **58**(10), 2508–2521 (2013)
38. Zou, L., Fränzle, M., Zhan, N., Mosaad, P.N.: Automatic verification of stability and safety for delay differential equations. In: Kroening, D., Păsăreanu, C.S. (eds.) CAV 2015. LNCS, vol. 9207, pp. 338–355. Springer, Heidelberg (2015)
39. Majumdar, R., Prabhu, V.S.: Computing distances between reach flowpipes. In: Proceedings of the 19th International Conference on Hybrid Systems: Computation and Control (HSCC 2016), pp. 267–276. ACM, New York (2016)

Parsimonious, Simulation Based Verification of Linear Systems

Parasara Sridhar Duggirala[1](✉) and Mahesh Viswanathan[2]

[1] University of Connecticut, Mansfield, USA
psd@uconn.edu
[2] University of Illinois, Urbana-Champaign, Champaign, USA
vmahesh@illinois.edu

Abstract. We present a technique to verify safety properties of linear systems (possibly time varying) using very few simulations. For a linear system of dimension n, our technique needs $n + 1$ simulation runs. This is in contrast to current simulation based approaches, where the number of simulations either depends upon the number of vertices in the convex polyhedral initial set, or on the proximity of the unsafe set to the set of reachable states. At its core, our algorithm exploits the superposition principle of linear systems. Our algorithm computes both an over and an under approximation of the set of reachable states.

1 Introduction

Cyberphysical systems, that involve the close interaction of a computing device with a physical process, are most faithfully modeled as a hybrid system that exhibits both discrete and continuous changes to system state. The mathematical model of a hybrid system consists of a finite collection of *control modes* where the system state evolves continuously with time. Transitions between control modes are governed by constraints on the system state.

A commonly occurring special class of hybrid systems is one where the continuous dynamics in each control mode is mathematically described using a *time-varying linear differential equation* of the form

$$\dot{x} = A(t)x + B(t), \tag{1}$$

where $A(t)$ and $B(t)$ are matrices which may themselves be changing with time. While verifying invariant properties for such systems is known to be undecidable in general, the set of states reachable within bounded time (and bounded number of discrete steps) can be approximated with arbitrary precision. One of the core challenges in computing such bounded-time reachable sets is to compute the set of all states reachable within a time bound for a *single control mode* with no mode switches (often referred as continuous post).

There are two main approaches to computing the continuous post for a mode within time bound T. The first approach [7,12,18] exploits the linearity of the system dynamics. For continuous dynamics given by Eq. (1), let us denote by

© Springer International Publishing Switzerland 2016
S. Chaudhuri and A. Farzan (Eds.): CAV 2016, Part I, LNCS 9779, pp. 477–494, 2016.
DOI: 10.1007/978-3-319-41528-4_26

$\xi(x, t)$ the state at time t starting from x. It is well known that the state reached at time t when starting from $\alpha x_1 + (1 - \alpha)x_2$ ($0 \leq \alpha \leq 1$), a convex combination of states x_1 and x_2, is given by $\alpha \xi(x_1, t) + (1 - \alpha)\xi(x_2, t)$. Hence, if the initial set of states is a *convex, bounded polytope*, then the set of states reached at time t is the convex hull of the states reached from each vertex of the initial polytope. Further, the set of states reached *within* time t is over-approximated by bloating the convex hull of the vertices of the initial polytope and the vertices of the polytope of states reached at time t. The bloating factor, determined by a careful error analysis, depends on the length of time t. Thus to get a good approximation of the reach set within a time bound T, the interval $[0, T]$ is broken up into small steps adaptively [13, 22]. The cost of computing the reach set in this approach, therefore, depends on two things (1) the number of vertices in the initial polytope (which is exponential in the dimension of the system), and (2) the number of smaller intervals the time interval $[0, T]$ is divided into. The efficiency of this approach also depends on the data structure used to store the set of reachable states. Ellipsoids [17], convex polyhedra [12], zonotopes [14], support functions [18], polynomial zonotopes [2], and Taylor models [5], are some of the popular data structures used. Each of these data structures requires developing new algorithms for computing the reachable set for a given class of systems.

The second approach is a *simulation-based* approach [9, 10, 15]. Here, the initial set is partitioned into smaller neighborhoods, and the system is simulated from the center of each neighborhood. Based on the norms of matrices A and B, one can compute an envelope around each simulation trace that guarantees the containment of the trajectory starting from any point in a given initial partition. The reachable set is therefore over-approximated by a collection of simulation tubes. The quality of this set can be improved by computing a finer partitioning of the initial set. Thus, for a safe system, the number of simulations needed, depends on how far the unsafe set is from the reachable set; if it is far, a coarse initial partition suffices, and if it is close then we need a fine initial partition, which means many simulations. Though this approach may require significantly more simulations, it enjoys a couple of advantages over the previous approach. First, since this approach does not rely on convexity properties of linear systems, it can be used to analyze non-convex initial sets and time varying linear systems (where $A(t)$ and $B(t)$ change with time). Second, not only can it be used to prove safety, but also to find counterexamples.

Apart from these two approaches, a few theorem proving approaches have also been proposed [16, 20, 21, 23, 24, 26]. In these approaches one does not compute the set of reachable states, but rather prove that a certain safety property is satisfied. Therefore, this technique can be used for proving safety of non-convex and unbounded initial sets, but also requires additional manual effort.

Inspired by the simulation-based approach, we present a new approach for computing the reachable set for linear systems. Our approach combines the advantages of each of the above approaches. First, like the simulation-based approach, it can be used to analyze non-convex initial states, time-varying linear systems, and it can prove unsafety of systems in addition to safety. Second, and more importantly, it uses significantly fewer simulations — to compute the reachable set of an n-dimensional system, we need to simulate the system from only $n + 1$ initial states. This is in contrast to the potentially exponentially many vertices to be propagated in the non-simulation approach, and potentially much larger than exponentially-many simulations in the simulation-based approach. Third, our approach does not require any additional computation if the initial set changes, as long as the "center" of the set remains the same; what this means precisely will be become clearer later in this introduction as we describe our approach. Fourth, the previous two approaches only work for *bounded initial sets*. Our new approach, on the other hand, can handle unbounded initial sets. Finally, since our method only relies on simulations, it does not require a formal model, and can be used to analyze *black-box* systems.

The main idea behind our approach is to exploit what is sometimes called the *superposition principle*. Let us consider an n-dimensional system (i.e., continuous state is in $\mathbb{R}^n$) described by Eq. (1). For vectors $v_1, v_2, \ldots v_n$, initial "center" x_0, and constants $\alpha_1, \alpha_2, \ldots \alpha_n$, the superposition principle says that

$$\xi(x_0 + \sum_{i=1}^{n} \alpha_i v_i, t) = \xi(x_0, t) + \sum_{i=1}^{n} \alpha_i(\xi(x_0 + v_i, t) - \xi(x_0, t)) \qquad (2)$$

Thus, if the initial set is of the form $x_0 + \sum_{i=1}^{n} \alpha_i v_i$ where the coefficients $\bar{\alpha}$ belong to some set Δ, then the set of states reached at time t is given by $\xi(x_0, t) + \sum_{i=1}^{n} \alpha_i v_i'$ with $\bar{\alpha} \in \Delta$, where $v_i' = \xi(x_0 + v_i, t) - \xi(x_0, t)$.

Notice, that this representation of the states at time t, only requires us to find $\xi(x_0, t), \xi(x_0 + v_1, t), \ldots \xi(x_0 + v_n, t)$, which can be obtained by only $n + 1$ simulations. We call this representation of sets of states as the linear span of a center x_0 and basis vectors $\{v_i\}_{i=1}^{n}$ with coefficients $\bar{\alpha} \in \Delta$ *generalized star sets*. Such generalized star sets naturally generalize standard shapes like polytopes, ellipsoids, and non-convex sets. Using generalized star sets makes reachable set computation simple. Moreover, if the initial set changes because of a change in Δ, the superposition principle tells us that we don't need to do any additional simulations in order to represent the reachable set at time t. We show how this basic idea can be adapted to account for simulation errors, to construct both under and over approximations of the reachable set of states, efficiently.

Our experimental results substantiate our belief that this new approach can serve as the founding principle that underlies the next advance in the scalable analysis of time varying linear systems. Our method scales to high dimensional systems and beats all current verification technologies by at least an order of magnitude. This is not surprising given the obvious theoretical advantages it enjoys over past methods due to the reduced number of simulations it needs.

2   Preliminaries

We refer to states and vectors as elements in $\mathbb{R}^n$. We denote the ℓ^∞ norm of the vectors and states by $||\cdot||$. To avoid confusion we denote states by x_i and vectors by v_i. Given two states x_1 and x_2, the difference vector is defined as $v = x_2 - x_1$. Given a set $S \subseteq \mathbb{R}^n$, $\text{diameter}(S) \triangleq \sup\{||x - y|| \mid x, y \in S\}$. For a set $S \subseteq \mathbb{R}^n$, a point $x \in S$ is said to be a center if $\forall y \in S$. $||x - y|| \leq \text{diameter}(S)/2$. A set S may or may not have a center; convex sets do have a center. When a set S has a center there maybe many; we will abuse notation and use $\text{center}(S)$ to denote one picked by the axiom of choice. A predicate $P : \mathbb{R}^n \to \{\top, \bot\}$ denotes a set of vectors denoted by $[\![P]\!] = \{v \mid P(v) = \top\}$. We abuse notation and denote both the predicate P and the set $[\![P]\!]$ as P. The ball of radius δ around a state x is defined as $B_\delta(x) = \{y \mid ||x - y|| \leq \delta\}$; similarly, for a set $S \subseteq \mathbb{R}^n$, $B_\delta(S) = \cup_{x \in S} B_\delta(x)$. Given two vectors $p, q \in \mathbb{R}^k$ where $p = [p_1, p_2, \ldots, p_k]^T$ and $q = [q_1, q_2, \ldots, q_k]^T$, we say that $p \leq q$ if and only if $\forall i. \, p_i \leq q_i$. Given $x \in \mathbb{R}^n$ and $S \subseteq \mathbb{R}^n$, the set of difference vectors from x to S, is defined as $\text{diff}(S, x) \triangleq \{v \mid \exists x' \in S, v = x' - x\}$.

We will find it convenient to represent subsets of states using a representation that we call *generalized star sets*, which we define next.

Definition 1. *A* generalized star set *is a tuple* $\Theta = \langle x_0, V, P \rangle$ *where* $x_0 \in \mathbb{R}^n$ *is called the* center, *$V = \{v_1, v_2, \ldots v_m\}$ is a set of m ($\leq n$) vectors in $\mathbb{R}^n$ called the* basis, *and $P : \mathbb{R}^n \to \{\top, \bot\}$ is a predicate.*

A generalized star set Θ defines a subset of $\mathbb{R}^n$ as follows.

$$[\![\Theta]\!] = \{x \mid \exists \bar{\alpha} = [\alpha_1, \ldots, \alpha_m]^T \text{ such that } x = x_0 + \Sigma_{i=1}^n \alpha_i v_i \text{ and } P(\bar{\alpha}) = \top\}$$

Sometimes we will refer to both Θ and $[\![\Theta]\!]$ as Θ.

In the above definition of generalized star sets, the size of the vector set V will often be determined by the dimension of the set $[\![\Theta]\!]$ being defined, and the vectors will be linearly independent. However, we do not require this. Generalized star sets are a generalization of many natural sets of states. Depending on the predicate P, generalized star representation can define a variety of sets including non-convex sets and convex sets like polyhedra and ellipsoids. We provide some examples of such sets.

Example 1. Consider the 2-dimensional plane $\mathbb{R}^2$. Take $V = \{[1, 0]^T, [0, 1]^T\}$ the set of unit vectors along the two axes, and $x_0 = (3, 3)$.

Consider $g = [1, 1, 1, 1]^T$, and $P(\bar{\alpha}) = C\bar{\alpha} \leq g$ where $C = \begin{bmatrix} 1 & -1 & 0 & 0 \\ 0 & 0 & 1 & -1 \end{bmatrix}^T$

The generalized star set $\Theta = \langle x_0, V, P \rangle$ defines the rectangular set

$$[\![\Theta]\!] = B_1(3, 3) = \{(x, y) \mid 2 \leq x \leq 4 \wedge 2 \leq y \leq 4\}$$

On the other hand, defining $P(\bar{\alpha}) = (\alpha_1 - 3)^2 + (\alpha_2 - 3)^2 \leq 1$ defines the disc of radius 1 with center $(3, 3)$.

Consider a system described by the linear ODE

$$\dot{x} = A(t)x + B(t). \tag{3}$$

The solution of the above ODE with initial state x_0 is denoted as $\xi(x_0, t)$. For this solution $\frac{d}{dt}(\xi(x_0, t)) = A(t)\xi(x_0, t) + B(t)$ and $\xi(x_0, 0) = x_0$. For well defined linear time varying systems, the state at time t is given using the state transformation matrix $\Phi : \mathbb{R}_{\geq 0} \times \mathbb{R}_{\geq 0} \to \mathbb{R}^{n \times n}$ such that the trajectory at time t is given as

$$\xi(x_0, t) = \Phi(t, 0)x_0 + \int_0^t \Phi(t, s)B(s)ds. \tag{4}$$

Notice that for linear time invariant systems, the expression for $\Phi(t_2, t_1) = e^{A(t_2 - t_1)}$.

For performing simulation based verification, instead of using a numerical simulation which returns a sequence of states, we use *validated simulations* which returns a sequence of sets of states with the following guarantees.

Definition 2. *For a system described by Eq. (3), with closed form $\xi(x_0, t)$ given by Eq. (4), an (x_0, T, ϵ, h)-validated simulation of $\xi(x_0, t)$ is $\psi = (R_1, [t_0, t_1])$, $(R_2, [t_1, t_2])$, ..., $(R_k, [t_{m-1}, t_m])$ where $R_i \subseteq \mathbb{R}^n$ such that*

1. $\forall 1 \leq i \leq m, t_i - t_{i-1} \leq h, t_0 = 0, t_m = T$.
2. $\forall 1 \leq i \leq m, \forall t \in [t_{i-1}, t_i], \xi(x_0, t) \in R_i$.
3. $\forall 1 \leq i \leq m, \mathsf{diameter}(R_i) \leq \epsilon$.

The first condition enforces that the time step for each of these regions is bounded by h. The second condition enforces that for each interval $[t_{i-1}, t_i]$ the trajectory is contained within the region R_i. The third condition enforces that the diameter of each region is bounded by ϵ. Existing numerical solvers such as CAPD, and VNODE-LP can compute validated simulations which contain the trajectory. For these tools, the sets R_i are convex, polyhedral sets. Therefore, we assume that the subroutine $\mathsf{valSim}(x_0, T, h)$ returns $\langle \psi, \epsilon \rangle$ such that ψ is an (x_0, T, ϵ, h)-validated simulation (with R_i being convex). In addition, as $h \to 0$, $\epsilon \to 0$.

Definition 3. *For a system in Eq. (3), and initial set Θ, the set of states reachable within time bound T is $ReachSet_{\langle A,B \rangle}(\Theta, T) = \{\xi(x_0, t) | x_0 \in \Theta, 0 \leq t \leq T\}$. We drop A and B from the ReachSet when it is clear from the context.*

A set R_O is said to be an over-approximation *of the reachable states within time T if $ReachSet(\Theta, T) \subseteq R_O$. Analogously, R_U is said to be an under-approximation of the set of reachable states within time bound T, if $R_U \subseteq ReachSet(\Theta, T)$.*

Definition 4. *The system given in Eq. (3) is said to be safe for bounded time T from the initial state Θ and unsafe set U if $ReachSet(\Theta, T) \cap U = \emptyset$.*

3   Computing Reachable Sets from Simulations

In this section we outline how to compute reachable sets of n-dimensional linear systems, using at most $n + 1$ simulations. We begin (Sect. 3.1) by making an observation that is often called the *superposition principle*. This principle enables us to express the set of states reached at time t as a generalized star set, if the initial states is given as a generalized star set. In Sect. 3.2, we show how the superposition principle can be used to compute the set of reachable states, under the assumption that the exact trajectory from each initial state can be computed. Finally, in Sect. 3.3, we show how all of these ideas can used when we only have access to validated simulation engines.

3.1   Superposition Principle for Linear Systems

In order to explain the superposition principle, let us fix a system described by Eq. (3). Recall from Eq. (4), the solution is for the system is given as

$$\xi(x_0, t) = \Phi(t, 0)x_0 + \int_0^t \Phi(t, s)B(s)ds.$$

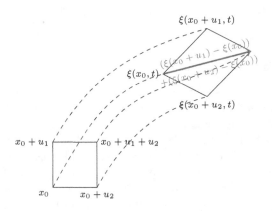

Fig. 1. Observe that the state reached at time t from $x_0 + u_1 + u_2$ is identical to $\xi(x_0, t) + (\xi(x_0 + u_1, t) - \xi(x_0, t)) + (\xi(x_0 + u_2, t) - \xi(x_0, t))$.

Consider two initial states x_0 and $x_0 + u_1$, for some vector u_1. From the solution given in Eq. (4), we have

$$\xi(x_0 + u_1, t) - \xi(x_0, t) = \Phi(t, 0)u_1 \tag{5}$$

For two vectors u_1 and u_2, and state x_0, from Eq. (4), we have

$$\xi(x_0 + \alpha_1 u_1 + \alpha_2 u_2)$$
$$= \Phi(t, 0)(x_0 + \alpha_1 u_1 + \alpha_2 u_2) + \int_0^t \Phi(t, s)B(s)ds$$
$$= [\Phi(t, 0)x_0 + \int_0^t \Phi(t, s)B(s)ds] + \alpha_1 \Phi(t, 0)u_1 + \alpha_2 \Phi(t, 0)u_2$$
$$= \xi(x_0, t) + \alpha_1 \Phi(t, 0)u_1 + \alpha_2 \Phi(t, 0)u_2$$
$$= \xi(x_0, t) + \alpha_1[\xi(x_0 + u_1, t) - \xi(x_0, t)] + \alpha_2[\xi(x_0 + u_2, t) - \xi(x_0, t)]$$

The above equation suggests that linear combinations of $\xi(x_0 + u_1, t) - \xi(x_0, t)$ and $\xi(x_0 + u_2, t) - \xi(x_0, t)$ gives us the difference between trajectories starting from initial state x_0 and $x_0 + \alpha_1 u_1 + \alpha_2 u_2$. This is illustrated in Fig. 1. Extending this observation to n vectors we have

$$\xi(x_0 + \Sigma_{i=1}^n \alpha_i u_i, t) = \xi(x_0, t) + \Sigma_{i=1}^n \alpha_i(\xi(x_0 + u_i, t) - \xi(x_0, t)). \quad (6)$$

3.2   Reach Sets from Exact Trajectories

In this section, we will outline how the superposition principle can be used construct the reachable states at a given time t. Let us fix an initial set given as a generalized star set $\Theta = \langle x_0, V, P \rangle$, where $V = \{v_1, v_2, \ldots v_m\}$. We begin by showing how to compute $Reach_t(\Theta)$, the set of states reached at time t; $Reach_t(\Theta)$ is defined precisely as follows.

$$Reach_t(\Theta) = \{\xi(x, t) \mid x \in [\![\Theta]\!]\}.$$

The reachable states at time t is computed by Algorithm 1 as a generalized star set.

---

input : Initial Set: $\Theta = \langle x_0, V, P \rangle$, Time instance: t
output: $Reach_t(\Theta)$

1 $x'_0 \leftarrow \xi(x_0, t)$;
2 **for** *each $v_i \in V$* **do**
3 $\quad$ $x'_i \leftarrow \xi(x_0 + v_i, t)$;
4 $\quad$ $v'_i \leftarrow x'_i - x'_0$;
5 **end**
6 $V' \leftarrow \{v'_1, \ldots, v'_m\}$;
7 $Reach_t(\Theta) \leftarrow \langle x'_0, V', P \rangle$;
8 **return** $Reach_t(\Theta)$;

Algorithm 1. Algorithm that computes the reachable set at time t from $n + 1$ simulations.

The algorithm in line 1 computes the state of trajectory starting from the initial state x_0 at time t as x'_0. The loop in lines 2 to 4 computes x'_i, the state of the trajectory starting from $x_0 + v_i$ at time t. The reachable set at time t is given as as generalized star set $\langle x'_0, V', P \rangle$, where $V' = \{v'_1, \ldots, v'_n\}$ with $v'_i = x'_i - x'_0$. Theorem 1 proves that the set returned is indeed the reachable set.

Theorem 1. *The set $Reach_t(\Theta)$ is the reachable set for Θ at time t.*

Proof. Let us consider the set of vectors $V' = \{v'_1, \ldots, v'_m\}$. Observe from Eq. (5) that $v'_i = \Phi(t, 0)v_i$.

$\quad$ A state y is reachable at time t, if y is the state reached at time t when starting from some initial state $x' \in [\![\Theta]\!]$. More formally, a state $y \in Reach_t(\Theta)$

if and only if $\exists \bar{\alpha} = [\alpha_1, \ldots, \alpha_m]^T$ such that $P(\bar{\alpha}) = \top$ and $y = \xi(x', t)$ where $x' = x_0 + \Sigma_{i=1}^n \alpha_i v_i$. From lines 1, 3, and 4, we have that

$$y = \xi(x_0, t) + \Sigma_{i=1}^n \alpha_i (\xi(x_0 + v_i, t) - \xi(x_0, t)).$$

Thus, $y \in \langle x'_0, V', P \rangle$ establishing the correctness of the algorithm.

We conclude this proof by observing that since $\Phi(t, 0)$ is an invertible matrix, V' is linearly independent set of vectors, if V is linearly independent.

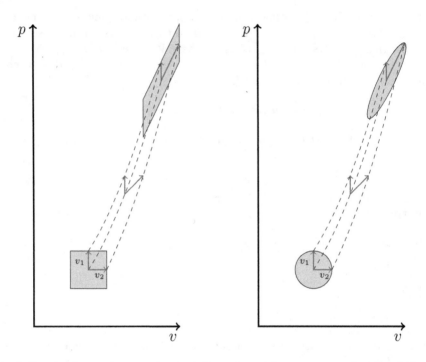

Fig. 2. Reachable set of car moving in 1-dimension with constant acceleration. In both graphs, car velocity v is plotted on the x-axis and position p is on the y-axis. The set of initial states and the set of reachable states at time 2 are shown in yellow. The vectors defining the sets is shown in red at time $0, 1$, and 2. On the left, the initial set is the ball of radius 1 with center $(3, 3)$ with respect to ℓ^∞-norm. On the right the initial set is the same except that the ball is defined with respect to the ℓ^2-norm. Notice that the evolution of the vectors that define the generalized star set is the same in both the left and the right. (Color figure online)

Example 2. Consider the simple example of a car moving in 1-dimension with constant acceleration of 2 units. Taking the state of the system to be the car position (p) and velocity (v), the dynamics can be described as

$$\dot{p} = v \qquad \dot{v} = 2$$

Consider the polyhedral initial set given as a generalized star set. In other words, $\Theta = \langle x_0, V, P \rangle$, where $x_0 = (3,3)$, $V = \{[1,0]^T, [0,1]^T\}$, $g = [1,1,1,1]^T$ and $P(\bar{\alpha}) = C\bar{\alpha} \leq g$ where $C = \begin{bmatrix} 1 & -1 & 0 & 0 \\ 0 & 0 & 1 & -1 \end{bmatrix}^T$ The evolution of the reachable set is shown in the left graph in Fig. 2. The reachable set at time 2 is given by the generalized star set $\Delta = \langle x_0', V', P \rangle$, where $x_0 = (7, 13)$, and $V' = \{[0,1]^T, [1,2]^T\}$. The only part that changes in the generalized star representation of the reachable set at time 2 is the center and the set of vectors.

Suppose we consider the initial set to be the disc of radius 1 with center $(3,3)$ as in Example 1. That is the initial set if given as $\langle (3,3), \{[1,0]^T, [0,1]^T\}, P \rangle$ where $P(\bar{\alpha}) = (\alpha_1 - 3)^2 + (\alpha_2 - 3)^2 \leq 1$. The evolution of the reachable set over time is shown on the right graph in Fig. 2. The reachable set at time 2 is described as $\langle (7,13), \{[0,1]^T, [1,2]^T\}, P \rangle$. Thus the way the center and the set of vectors change is the same for both the box and the disc initial sets. The evolution of the center and vectors is independent of the "shape" of the initial set. The difference in the reachable sets only arises because of the difference in the predicate used to describe the initial sets.

3.3   Computing Reachable Set from Validated Simulations

Algorithm 1 computes the reachable set at time t when the *exact* state of the $n+1$ trajectories starting from x_0, $x_0 + v_1$, $\ldots$, $x_0 + v_n$ at time t is known. However, computing the exact state requires computing the closed form expression for Φ. This expression Φ in the simplest case where $A(t)$ and $B(t)$ are time invariant matrices requires computing matrix exponentials and so the exact expression can only be computed for very special matrices. We now present a new technique in Algorithm 2 (based on Algorithm 1) for computing a formula with existential quantifiers that represents the overapproximation and the underapproximation of the reachable set of states.

Informally, instead of computing the exact trajectories starting from x_0, $x_0 + v_1$, $\ldots$, $x_0 + v_n$, we compute their validated simulations. We assume that all these validated simulations are *synchronized*, i.e., the number of intervals in all the validated simulations are the same. Although according to Definition 2, each of these validated simulations can have different time intervals and regions, we can split the required intervals further and generate new validated simulations such that all the $n + 1$ validated simulations have the same number of regions. We assume that there are m such regions in each validated simulation, i.e., the simulation from x_0, denoted as $\langle \psi^0, \epsilon \rangle \leftarrow \mathsf{valSim}(x_0, h, T)$ is such that $\psi^0 = (R_1^0, [t_0, t_1]), (R_2^0, [t_1, t_2]), \ldots,$ $(R_m^0, [t_{m-1}, t_m])$. The validated simulation $\langle \psi^i, \epsilon \rangle \leftarrow \mathsf{valSim}(x_0 + v_i, h, T)$ is such that $\psi^i = (R_1^i, [t_0, t_1]), \ldots, (R_m^i, [t_{m-1}, t_m])$.

input : Initial Set: $\Theta = \langle x_0, V, P \rangle$, Time bound: T
output: Overapproximation and underapproximation of the reachable set of
        states.

1   $\langle \psi^0, \epsilon^0 \rangle \leftarrow$ valSim(x_0, h, T);
2 **for** *each* $v_i \in V$ **do**
3 | $\langle \psi^i, \epsilon^i \rangle \leftarrow$ valSim$(x_0 + v_i, h, T)$;
4 **end**
5 **for** $j = 1 \ldots m$ **do**
6 | $OverReach[j] \leftarrow OA(R_j^0, R_j^1, \ldots, R_j^n, P)$;
7 | $UnderReach[j] \leftarrow UA(R_j^0, R_j^1, \ldots, R_j^n, P)$;
8 **end**
9 **return** $(OverReach, UnderReach)$;

Algorithm 2. Algorithm that computes the overapproximation and underapproximation of reachable set for each time interval.

Given $R_0, R_1, \ldots, R_n \subseteq \mathbb{R}^n$, $OA(R_0, R_1, \ldots, R_n, P)$ is a formula with quantifiers that represents an overapproximation of the reachable set is defined as:

$$OA \triangleq \{ \, x \mid \exists x_0 \in R_0, \exists v_i \in \mathsf{diff}(R_i, x_0), \exists \bar{\alpha}, $$
$$x = x_0 + \Sigma_{i=1}^n \alpha_i v_i \wedge P(\bar{\alpha}) = \top \, \} \tag{7}$$

Similarly $UA(R_0, R_1, \ldots, R_n, P)$ is a formula with quantifiers that represents an underapproximation of the reachable set is defined as:

$$UA \triangleq \{ \, x \mid \forall x_0 \in R_0, \forall v_i \in \mathsf{diff}(R_i, x_0), \exists \bar{\alpha}, $$
$$x = x_0 + \Sigma_{i=1}^n \alpha_i v_i, P(\bar{\alpha}) = \top \, \} \tag{8}$$

Theorem 2. *OverReach[j] and UnderReach[j] computed in line 6 and 7 give an overapproximation and underapproximation of the reachable set of states for the time interval $[t_{j-1}, t_j]$ respectively.*

Proof. The proof follows from the proof of Theorem 1.

Overapproximation: Consider the $Reach_t(\Theta)$ for some $t \in [t_{j-1}, t_j]$. A state $x \in Reach_t(\Theta)$ if and only if $\exists \bar{\alpha}$ such that $x = x_0' + \Sigma_{i=1}^n \alpha_i v_i', P(\bar{\alpha}) = \top$. From Definition 2, it follows that $x_0' \in R_j^0$ and $v_i' \in \mathsf{diff}(R_j^i, x_0')$. As the formula is existentially quantified, if follows that $x \in OverReach[j]$. Therefore, $\cup_{t \in [t_{j-1}, t_j]} Reach_t(\Theta) \subseteq OverReach[j]$.

Underapproximation: Consider a state $x \in UnderReach[j]$. Therefore, $\forall x_0' \in R_j^0, \forall v_i' \in \mathsf{diff}(R_j^i, x_0'), \exists \bar{\alpha}$, such that $x = x_0' + \Sigma_{i=1}^n \alpha_i v_i', P(\bar{\alpha}) = \top$. Now consider $Reach_t(\Theta)$ for some time instance $t \in [t_{j-1}, t_j]$. As x_0' and v_i' is universally quantified, it follows that $x \in Reach_t(\Theta)$. Therefore $UnderReach[j] \subseteq \cap_{t \in [t_{j-1}, t_j]} Reach_t(\Theta)$.

Remark 1. Algorithm 2 can be used for safety verification. Given an unsafe set of states U, one can check whether the overapproximation ($OverReach[i]$) and underapproximation ($UnderReach[i]$) computed in lines 6 and 7 has any state in unsafe set using SMT solvers like Z3. Moreover, this technique can prove that the system is unsafe and provide counterexamples from the model for SMT formula if satisfied.

Algorithm 2 has several advantages compared to the existing techniques for reachable set computation. First, the algorithm uses only $m + 1$ numerical simulations, where m is the number of vectors in the set V. Second, it can compute reachable set not just for convex sets, but also for non-convex sets. Third, the initial set can be unbounded. Finally, the algorithm can compute underapproximation of the reachable set as well. Typical reachable set computation techniques require that the initial set is bounded and convex and specified in a special form like convex polyhedra, zonotopes, or ellipsoids. Moreover, techniques for computing underapproximation require special computation techniques and bounding the error for underapproximation is a challenging problem.

Notice that the formulas for computing overapproximation OA in line 6 and underapproximation UA in line 7 contain product terms of α_i and v_i. Hence, even for special initial sets like convex polyhedra, checking system safety using OA or UA involves reasoning about bilinear constraints, which is NP-hard. Moreover, our representation of UA has alternating quantifiers which adds to the challenges. To overcome these issues, we present a new overapproximation of the reachable set with a quantifiable bounded error, for initial sets that have special geometric properties like bounded convex polyhedra or ellipsoids. While we will not present a new underapproximation that avoids quantifier alternation, we will present a technique that can efficiently detect unsafety.

4   Faster Reachable Set Computation for Special Initial Sets

In this section, we present an algorithm for computing the reachable set when the initial set is given as a bounded convex polyhedron or an ellipsoid. For the presentation used in this paper, the set considered will be a polyhedra if the predicate P is given by linear inequalities $Cx \leq d$. Consider a bounded polyhedral initial set represented as $\Theta \triangleq \langle x_0, V, C, d \rangle$ where $C \in \mathbb{R}^{k \times n}$ is a $k \times n$ matrix, $d \in \mathbb{R}^k$. Recall that the set it represents is $[\![\Theta]\!] = \{x \mid x = x_0 + \Sigma_{i=1}^n \alpha_i v_i, C\bar{\alpha} \leq d\}$. For a bounded polyhedral set $[\![\Theta]\!]$, one can pick a state x_0 in the set Θ and an orthonormal basis V such that $max\{||\alpha_i||\} \leq \frac{1}{n}$. We assume that such a representation of the initial set Θ is provided. We now present a technique to compute a polyhedral representation of the overapproximation of the reachable set represented by the formula OA with quantifiers.

For a given time interval, assume that $R_0, R_1, \ldots, R_n$ are the regions returned by the $n + 1$ validated simulations $(dia(R_i) \leq \epsilon)$ and $OA(R_0, R_1, \ldots, R_n, C, d)$ gives the overapproximation predicate, defined in Eq. (7). For polyhedral initial set, the only nonlinear term in Eq. (7) for OA is the product term $\alpha_i v_i$. To eliminate this product term, we pick a fixed v_i (defined below), estimate the error in the resulting set given this fixed basis, and *bloat* the polyhedron based on this error analysis.

Theorem 3. *Given regions $R_0, R_1, \ldots, R_n$, and the set $OA(R_0, R_1, \ldots, R_n, C, d)$ defined according to Eq. (7), we have $OA \subseteq B_\delta(R)$ where $R \triangleq \langle x_0, V, C, d \rangle$ where $x_0 = center(R_0)$, $V = \{v_1, \ldots, v_n\}$ where $v_i = center(R_i) - center(R_0)$ and $\delta = 3\epsilon$ and $\epsilon = max_{i=0}^n \{dia(R_i)\}$.*

Proof. Consider a state $x' \in OA(R_0, R_1, \ldots, R_n, C, d)$, then there exists $x'_0 \in R_0$, $x_1 \in R_1, \ldots, x_n \in R_n$ where $v'_i = x'_i - x'_0$ such that $x' \in R' \triangleq \langle x'_0, \mathcal{U}_2, C, d \rangle$, $\mathcal{U}_2 = \{v'_1, \ldots, v'_n\}$.

Since $x' \in R'$, $\exists \alpha_1, \ldots, \alpha_n$ such that $x' = x'_0 + \alpha_1 v'_1 + \ldots + \alpha_n v'_n$. Consider the corresponding state $x \in R$ such that $x = x_0 + \alpha_1 v_1 + \ldots + \alpha_n v_n$. The distance between x and x' is given as:

$$
\begin{aligned}
||x - x'|| &= ||x_0 + \alpha_1 v_1 + \ldots + \alpha_n v_n - (x'_0 + \alpha_1 v'_1 + \ldots + \alpha_n v'_n)|| \\
&= ||(x_0 - x'_0) + \alpha_1(v_1 - v'_1) + \ldots + \alpha_n(v_n - v'_n)|| \\
&\leq ||x_0 - x'_0|| + \Sigma_{i=1}^n ||\alpha_i|| \cdot ||v_i - v'_i|| \\
&\leq dia(R_0) + \Sigma_{i=1}^n ||\alpha_i|| \cdot ||x_i - x'_i + (x'_0 - x_0)|| \\
&\leq dia(R_0) + \Sigma_{i=1}^n ||\alpha_i|| \cdot (dia(R_i) + dia(R_0)) \\
&\leq dia(R_0) + \Sigma_{i=1}^n ||\alpha_i|| \cdot 2\epsilon \\
&\leq dia(R_0) + \Sigma_{i=1}^n max\{ ||\alpha_i|| \} \cdot 2\epsilon \\
&\leq \epsilon + n \cdot \frac{1}{n} \cdot 2\epsilon \\
&\leq 3\epsilon
\end{aligned}
$$

Hence, the maximum distance between any two states x and x' is bounded by δ where $\delta = 3\epsilon$ and $x \in R$. Therefore $x' \in B_\delta(R)$.

Therefore for checking safety, instead of performing quantifier elimination, one can perform the following computations: (1) Compute the polyhedron R with $center(R_0)$ as the center, $center(R_i) - center(R_0)$ as the basis vectors, and predicate given as linear inequalities $C\bar{\alpha} \leq d$. Bloat the polyhedron R by the amount δ. Check for common states between unsafe region U and $B_\delta(R)$. Theorem 3 proves that if $B_\delta(R) \cap U = \emptyset$ then the reachable set does not have any unsafe state and hence the result is guaranteed to be sound.

Notice that the proof also gives a technique for checking when the system is unsafe. If $\exists x \in R$ such that $B_\delta(x) \subseteq U$, then it follows that for any choice of x'_0 and the basis vectors $\mathcal{U}_2$, the corresponding state x' is in the unsafe set. Therefore, the system is unsafe.

The proof for Theorem 3 can be extended to any general bounded sets and not necessarily for polyhedra. However, checking the safety with respect to general sets is computationally harder than checking for polyhedra. We consider one special case where the initial set is an ellipsoid. An ellipsoid can be defined as $E \triangleq \langle x_0, V, C, 1 \rangle$ where $[\![E]\!] = \{x | x = x_0 + \alpha_1 v_1 + \ldots + \alpha_n v_n, \bar{\alpha}^T C \bar{\alpha} \leq 1\}$.

Corollary 1. *For initial set defined as $\Theta = \langle x_0, V, C, 1 \rangle$ and given regions $R_0, R_1, \ldots, R_n$ for computing $OA(R_0, R_1, \ldots, R_n, C, 1)$ in Eq. (7), $OA \subseteq B_\delta(R)$*

where $R \triangleq \langle x_0', V', C, 1 \rangle$ where $x_0' = center(R_0)$, $V' = \{v_1', \ldots, v_n'\}$ where $v_i' = center(R_i) - center(R_0)$ and $\delta = 3\epsilon$ and $\epsilon = max_{i=0}^n \{dia(R_i)\}$.

5   Extension to Hybrid Systems

In this section, we outline the extension of the algorithm to hybrid systems. In principle, the Algorithm 2 computes the set of reachable states for a given continuous linear system for a given time interval. Therefore, one can essentially apply the algorithm used in tools like Phaver and SpaceEx for computing the reachable set of states for a hybrid system. For simplicity, we assume that all the invariants for the modes and guards for discrete transitions to be convex polyhedra and all the reset mappings to be linear functions. Under this assumptions, we present the algorithm for reachable set computation for hybrid system.

The algorithm performs the following three steps iteratively until the time horizon for verification. First, for the given mode and a given initial set, the algorithm computes the reachable set for that mode from that initial set for the bounded time specified using Algorithm 2. Second, the reachable set is pruned by removing all the states that violate the invariant. Third and lastly, the reachable set is checked to satisfy any guards for discrete transitions, and if so, the initial states for the next mode are computed by applying the reset map of the states that satisfy the guard predicate. As the reachable set of states for a hybrid system at a given time might belong to two different modes, we track the discrete transitions using a queue of set and location pairs.

---

input : Hybrid System: $\mathcal{A}$, Initial Set: Θ, Initial mode: m_0, Time bound: T
output: Bounded time reachable set: $ReachSet_{\mathcal{A}}(\Theta, T)$
1 regionQueue $\leftarrow \langle \Theta, m_0 \rangle$;
2 **for** each $\langle \Theta, m \rangle$ in regionQueue **do**
3   reachMode $\leftarrow Alg2(\Theta, m)$;
4   reachMode $\leftarrow$ reachMode $\cap$ Invariant$_m$;
5   nextRegions $\leftarrow$ discreteTransitions(reachMode);
6      $ReachSet_{\mathcal{A}}(\Theta, T) \leftarrow$ reachMode $\cup ReachSet_{\mathcal{A}}(\Theta, T)$;
7   regionQueue.$append$(nextRegions);
8 **end**
9 **return** $ReachSet_{\mathcal{A}}(\Theta, T)$;

Algorithm 3. Algorithm that computes the reachable set for hybrid systems.

Algorithm 3 computes the reachable set for a hybrid system. As the problem in general is undecidable, the loop need not terminate. The main loop that performs the three key steps iteratively happens from line 2 to line 8. Line 3 computes the reachable set of states from Θ for the corresponding mode using Algorithm 2. Line 4 checks the invariant for the reachable set and line 5 computes the states reached after discrete transitions. Although we present the algorithm here, in this paper, we perform experiments on purely continuous system to demonstrate the efficiency of Algorithm 2.

6   Experiments

To demonstrate the applicability of the proposed approach, we have implemented this algorithm as an extension of the tool C2E2 [11]. C2E2 is a dynamic analysis tool that implements a simulation based verification algorithm for nonlinear hybrid systems where the model is annotated with discrepancy functions. Unlike C2E2, this approach would not require the linear systems model to be provided with a discrepancy function. For generating the validated simulations, C2E2 uses a validated numerical integration engine called CAPD [1]. As the systems considered in this paper are restricted to linear systems, instead of using CAPD, we use the numerical integration engine ODEINT[1], which is a part of BOOST libraries. Unlike CAPD, ODEINT does not provide validated simulations, therefore, for computing rigorous bounds on the numerical simulation, we use error analysis provided in [4] for the 4th order Runge-Kutta method that is used in our experiments.

The experimental section is divided into 3 parts. First, we verify the safety property of several high dimensional linear time invariant systems with polyhedral initial sets and polyhedral unsafe sets. For checking the intersection of the reachable set computed with the unsafe states, we use GLPK library[2]. Second, we consider several linear time varying systems. Finally, we verify safety property of linear time invariant systems with non-convex initial and unsafe sets and also for unbounded initial and unsafe sets. All experiments were performed on a system with i7 Quad-core processor with 8GB memory running Ubuntu 11.10.

6.1   High Dimensional Linear Time Invariant Systems

We compare the performance of our approach with the state-of-the-art tool for linear systems verification SpaceEx on several high dimensional linear systems. Though the reachability computation can be extended to hybrid systems (Sect. 5 in Appendix), our experiments here are restricted to continuous systems; we believe our main contribution is the algorithm for reachability for continuous systems with the extension to hybrid systems being standard. The experimental results are provided in Table 1. The tank system considered in Table 1 is one of the examples provided with SpaceEx. In this example, the water level in tank i is model as a continuous variable x_i. The tank i leaks into tank $i+1$ and the rate of leakage is proportional to the water level in tank i, making the system a linear system. The 28 dimensional helicopter system and the 9 dimensional insulin system are also part of the examples provided by SpaceEx. The platoon system is a controller for stabilizing a platoon of vehicles and is obtained from [19].

The experiments show that our approach outperforms SpaceEx by at least an order of magnitude. This is mainly because as the number of dimensions increases, the complexity of representing the reachable set of states as a support function increases exponentially. Whereas in our approach, the number of

---

[1] http://headmyshoulder.github.io/odeint-v2/.

[2] https://www.gnu.org/software/glpk/.

simulations performed only increases linearly with the number of dimensions and the representation of the reachable set is just a basis transformation of the representation of the initial set of states considered. Also, notice that the time taken for computing the validated simulations using the approach in [4] takes the majority of the verification time as opposed to checking the safety of reachable set. An advantage our approach enjoys over SpaceEx is that we can compute underapproximations and hence conclude that the system is unsafe and provide counterexamples. We however note that for the experiments in Table 1, the results reported by SpaceEx were indeed consistent with the results reported by our approach.

Table 1. Experimental results for verification of high dimensional linear time invariant systems. Vars: number of variables, TH: time horizon for verification, Sims: total number of simulations, Simu. time: time taken for simulations, Verif. result: result of verification. TO: time out for 5 min.

Benchmark	Vars.	TH	Sims.	Simu. time.	Verif. time	C2E2	SpaceEx	Verif. result
Insulin	8	10	9	0.157 s	0.049 s	0.206 s	8.07 s	Safe
Insulin	8	10	9	0.166 s	0.034 s	0.2 s	7.89 s	Unsafe
Platoon	10	25	11	0.337 s	0.019 s	0.356 s	TO	Safe
Platoon	10	25	11	0.323 s	0.019 s	0.342 s	TO	Unsafe
Tank-10	10	20	11	0.745 s	0.206 s	0.951 s	4.886 s	Safe
Tank-10	10	20	11	0.721 s	0.19 s	0.911 s	4.992 s	Unsafe
Tank-15	15	20	16	1.325 s	0.363 s	1.688 s	8.176 s	Safe
Tank-18	18	20	19	1.705 s	0.569 s	2.274 s	10.466 s	Safe
Helicopter	28	20	29	3.192 s	1.634 s	4.826 s	2m1.66s	Safe

6.2 Verifying Linear Time Varying Systems

Typical approaches for computing reachable set for linear time varying systems differ considerably from that of linear time invariant systems. Therefore, there is a lack of tools that are geared towards verifying linear time varying systems. For the experimental evaluation, we model the linear time varying system as a nonlinear system with *time* as a variable t and compare the results of our approach with the tool Flow* [6] that can verify nonlinear systems. The experimental results are provided in Fig. 3(a). The tank system in Fig. 3(a) is similar to the linear time invariant system, except that water is being pumped into Tank 1 at a rate that decreasing with time. Therefore, the differential equation governing the dynamics contains t^{-1} term which makes it non polynomial. The second example is a modified version of the uncertain linear system from [3].

The experiments show that our approach outperforms Flow* by at least an order of magnitude. Also, similar to SpaceEx, the time taken by Flow* increases exponentially as the number of dimensions in the system increases, whereas in

Benchmark.	Vars.	Flow*.	C2E2
Tank	2	1.56 s	0.132 s
Tank	4	4.28 s	0.198 s
Tank	6	9.41 s	0.287 s
Tank	8	18.73 s	0.356 s
Tank	10	33.67 s	0.484 s
LTV [3]	5	7.51 s	0.24 s
LTV	7	12.09 s	0.31 s
LTV	9	18.18 s	0.4 s

(a) Verifying linear time varying systems

Benchmark.	Dim.	TH.	Init. Set.	Res.	Time
ACC [25]	3	2	NC	Safe	2.185
ACC	3	2	UB	Safe	1.774
ACC	3	2	NC	Unsafe	1.11
ACC	3	2	UB	Unsafe	1.01
Tank	5	1	NC	Safe	2.717
Tank	5	1	UB	Safe	2.145
Tank	5	1	NC	Unsafe	1.722
Tank	5	1	UB	Unsafe	1.519

(b) Verifying nonconvex and unbounded initial sets.

Fig. 3. Verification of linear time varying systems and non-convex and unbounded initial sets. Res.: verification result. NC: nonconvex initial set, UB: unbounded initial set

our approach, the number of simulations required increases only linearly with the number of dimensions.

6.3 Non-convex and Unbounded Initial Sets

An advantage of our approach is that we can compute the reachable set when the initial set of states is non-convex and also when the initial set is unbounded. To demonstrate this, we compute reachable set of states for several benchmark examples given in Fig. 3(b). In these experiments, we consider non-convex and unbounded initial sets symbolically represented as conjunctions of polynomial inequalities. We use Z3 [8] SMT solver for performing quantifier elimination and inferring whether the system is safe or unsafe. As the complexity of quantifier elimination over reals is exponentially more than linear real arithmetic, the time taken for verification is more than for polyhedral initial sets even for low dimensional systems. Unlike the existing theorem proving based approaches which can verify non-convex or unbounded initial set that requires some manual effort, our approach is completely automatic.

6.4 Discussion

It is evident from Table 1 and Fig. 3(a), (b) that our approach outperforms the existing approaches. Furthermore, our technique works for computing both over-approximation and underapproximation for linear time invariant and linear time varying systems. In case of polyhedral initial and unsafe sets, notice from Table 1 that the time taken for verification is only a fraction of the time taken from simulations. Given two bounded polyhedral initial sets $\Theta_1 \triangleq \langle x_0, V, C_1, d_1 \rangle$ and $\Theta_2 \triangleq \langle x_0, V, C_2, d_2 \rangle$, with the same center x_0 and the same set of basis vectors V, the reachable set computation technique *need not* generate $n+1$ simulations Θ_1 and $n + 1$ simulations for Θ_2. Instead, it can *reuse* the same set of simulations runs used for Θ_1 and compute the reachable set for Θ_2 thus reducing the number of simulations *per* verification. This would also bring down the total time for verification as computing simulations is computationally more expensive than verifying safety. Furthermore, given k bounded polyhedral initial sets, $\Theta_1, \ldots, \Theta_k$, by performing k coordinate transformations one can represent these sets with a common center and basis vectors and the amortized number of simulations for verification would be $\frac{n+1}{k}$ where n is the number of dimensions of the system. This is a significant advantage of our approach as opposed to the reachable set computation performed by SpaceEx, where, a change in the initial set would require discarding the reachable set computed and recomputing the new reachable set from scratch.

References

1. Computer assisted proofs in dynamic groups (capd). http://capd.ii.uj.edu.pl/index.php
2. Althoff, M.: Reachability analysis of nonlinear systems using conservative polynomialization and non-convex sets. In: Proceedings of the 16th International Conference on Hybrid Systems: Computation and Control, pp. 173–182. ACM (2013)
3. Althoff, M., Le Guernic, C., Krogh, B.H.: Reachable set computation for uncertain time-varying linear systems. In: Proceedings of the 14th International Conference on Hybrid Systems: Computation and Control, pp. 93–102. ACM (2011)
4. Bouissou, O., Martel, M.: Grklib: a guaranteed runge kutta library. In: 12th GAMM-IMACS International Symposium on Scientific Computing, Computer Arithmetic and Validated Numerics, SCAN 2006, p. 8. IEEE (2006)
5. Chen, X., Abraham, E., Sankaranarayanan, S.: Taylor model flowpipe construction for non-linear hybrid systems. In: RTSS (2012)
6. Chen, X., Ábrahám, E., Sankaranarayanan, S.: Flow*: an analyzer for non-linear hybrid systems. In: Sharygina, N., Veith, H. (eds.) CAV 2013. LNCS, vol. 8044, pp. 258–263. Springer, Heidelberg (2013)
7. Chutinan, A., Krogh, B.H.: Computational techniques for hybrid system verification. IEEE Trans. Autom. Control **48**, 64–75 (2003)
8. de Moura, L., Bjørner, N.S.: Z3: an efficient SMT solver. In: Ramakrishnan, C.R., Rehof, J. (eds.) TACAS 2008. LNCS, vol. 4963, pp. 337–340. Springer, Heidelberg (2008)
9. Donzé, A., Maler, O.: Systematic simulation using sensitivity analysis. In: Bemporad, A., Bicchi, A., Buttazzo, G. (eds.) HSCC 2007. LNCS, vol. 4416, pp. 174–189. Springer, Heidelberg (2007)
10. Duggirala, P.S., Mitra, S., Viswanathan, M.: Verification of annotated models from executions. In: Proceedings of the 13th International Conference on Embedded Software (EMSOFT 2013), Montreal, Canada (2013)
11. Duggirala, P.S., Mitra, S., Viswanathan, M., Potok, M.: C2E2: a verification tool for stateflow models. In: Baier, C., Tinelli, C. (eds.) TACAS 2015. LNCS, vol. 9035, pp. 68–82. Springer, Heidelberg (2015)
12. Frehse, G.: PHAVer: algorithmic verification of hybrid systems past HyTech. In: Morari, M., Thiele, L. (eds.) HSCC 2005. LNCS, vol. 3414, pp. 258–273. Springer, Heidelberg (2005)

13. Frehse, G., Le Guernic, C., Donzé, A., Cotton, S., Ray, R., Lebeltel, O., Ripado, R., Girard, A., Dang, T., Maler, O.: SpaceEx: scalable verification of hybrid systems. In: Gopalakrishnan, G., Qadeer, S. (eds.) CAV 2011. LNCS, vol. 6806, pp. 379–395. Springer, Heidelberg (2011)
14. Girard, A.: Reachability of uncertain linear systems using zonotopes. In: Morari, M., Thiele, L. (eds.) HSCC 2005. LNCS, vol. 3414, pp. 291–305. Springer, Heidelberg (2005)
15. Julius, A.A., Fainekos, G.E., Anand, M., Lee, I., Pappas, G.J.: Robust test generation and coverage for hybrid systems. In: Bemporad, A., Bicchi, A., Buttazzo, G. (eds.) HSCC 2007. LNCS, vol. 4416, pp. 329–342. Springer, Heidelberg (2007)
16. Kong, S., Gao, S., Chen, W., Clarke, E.: dReach: δ-reachability analysis for hybrid systems. In: Baier, C., Tinelli, C. (eds.) TACAS 2015. LNCS, vol. 9035, pp. 200–205. Springer, Heidelberg (2015)
17. Kurzhanski, A.B., Varaiya, P.: Ellipsoidal techniques for reachability analysis: internal approximation. Syst. Control Lett. 41(3), 201–211 (2000)
18. Le Guernic, C., Girard, A.: Reachability analysis of hybrid systems using support functions. In: Bouajjani, A., Maler, O. (eds.) CAV 2009. LNCS, vol. 5643, pp. 540–554. Springer, Heidelberg (2009)
19. Makhlouf, I.B., Kowalewski, S.: Networked cooperative platoon of vehicles for testing methods and verification tools. In: Applied Verification for Continuous and Hybrid Systems. CPS-VO (2014)
20. Mitra, S., Archer, M.: PVS strategies for proving abstraction properties of automata. Electron. Notes Theor. Comput. Sci. 125(2), 45–65 (2005)
21. Platzer, A., Quesel, J.-D.: KeYmaera: a hybrid theorem prover for hybrid systems (system description). In: Armando, A., Baumgartner, P., Dowek, G. (eds.) IJCAR 2008. LNCS (LNAI), vol. 5195, pp. 171–178. Springer, Heidelberg (2008)
22. Prabhakar, P., Viswanathan, M.: A dynamic algorithm for approximate flow computations. In: Proceedings of the 14th International Conference on Hybrid Systems: Computation and Control, pp. 133–142. ACM (2011)
23. Prajna, S., Jadbabaie, A.: Safety verification of hybrid systems using barrier certificates. In: Alur, R., Pappas, G.J. (eds.) HSCC 2004. LNCS, vol. 2993, pp. 477–492. Springer, Heidelberg (2004)
24. Taly, A., Tiwari, A.: Deductive verification of continuous dynamical systems. In: IARCS Annual Conference on Foundations of Software Technology and Theoretical Computer Science, FSTTCS 2009, 15–17 December 2009, pp. 383–394. IIT Kanpur, India (2009)
25. Tiwari, A.: Approximate reachability for linear systems. In: Maler, O., Pnueli, A. (eds.) HSCC 2003. LNCS, vol. 2623, pp. 514–525. Springer, Heidelberg (2003)
26. Tiwari, A.: HybridSAL relational abstracter. In: Madhusudan, P., Seshia, S.A. (eds.) CAV 2012. LNCS, vol. 7358, pp. 725–731. Springer, Heidelberg (2012)

Counterexample Guided Abstraction Refinement for Stability Analysis

Pavithra Prabhakar[1(✉)] and Miriam García Soto[2]

[1] Kansas State University, Manhattan, KS, USA
pprabhakar@ksu.edu
[2] IMDEA Software Institute and Universidad Politécnica de Madrid, Madrid, Spain
miriam.garcia@imdea.org

Abstract. In this paper, we present a counterexample guided abstraction refinement (CEGAR) algorithm for stability analysis of polyhedral hybrid systems. Our results build upon a quantitative predicate abstraction and model-checking algorithm for stability analysis, which returns a counterexample indicating a potential reason for instability. The main contributions of this paper include the validation of the counterexample and refinement of the abstraction based on the analysis of the counterexample. The counterexample returned by the quantitative predicate abstraction analysis is a cycle such that the product of the weights on its edges is greater than 1. Validation involves checking if there exists an infinite diverging execution which follows the cycle infinitely many times. Unlike in the case of CEGAR for safety, the validation problem is not a bounded model-checking problem. Using novel insights, we present a simple characterization for the existence of an infinite diverging execution in terms of the satisfaction of a first order logic formula which can be efficiently solved. Similarly, the refinement is more involved, since, there is a priori no bound on the number of predecessor computation steps that need to be performed to invalidate the abstract counterexample. We present strategies for refinement based on the insights from the validation step. We have implemented the validation and refinement algorithms and use the stability verification tool AVERIST in the back end for performing the abstraction and model-checking. We compare the CEGAR algorithm with AVERIST and report experimental results demonstrating the benefits of counterexample guided refinement.

1 Introduction

Hybrid systems refer to systems exhibiting mixed discrete continuous behaviors. These manifest naturally in embedded control systems as a result of the interaction of embedded software, which executes in discrete steps, with physical systems, which evolve continuously in dense real-time. In particular, we consider switched hybrid systems [13] in which the continuous state does not change during a mode switching. These are apt for modeling supervisory control, wherein a supervisor continuously senses the state of a plant and takes mode change decisions based on that.

© Springer International Publishing Switzerland 2016
S. Chaudhuri and A. Farzan (Eds.): CAV 2016, Part I, LNCS 9779, pp. 495–512, 2016.
DOI: 10.1007/978-3-319-41528-4_27

In this paper, we focus on automated stability analysis of switched hybrid systems. Stability is a fundamental property in control system design and captures robustness of the system with respect to initial states or inputs. We consider a classical notion of stability, namely, *Lyapunov stability* with respect to an equilibrium point — a state of the system which does not change with time evolution. Intuitively, an equilibrium point is Lyapunov stable if the executions starting in a small neighborhood of the equilibrium point remain close to it.

The classical methods for stability analysis are based on exhibiting a function from the state-space to the non-negative reals called a Lyapunov function (see, for instance, [11]), that ensures that the value of the function decreases along any execution of the system. Automated methods for stability analysis rely on a template based search for a Lyapunov function. For instance, a polynomial function with coefficients as parameters is chosen as a candidate Lyapunov function. The parameters are computed by solving Linear Matrix Inequalities or Sum-of-Squares [17] programming which arise while encoding the constraints of the Lyapunov function.

One of the challenges with Lyapunov based methods is the ingenuity of the user required in choosing the right templates. An exhaustive search over all templates (for instance, polynomials of increasing degrees) becomes unmanageable for relative small degrees of polynomials. In [20,21], the authors present an alternate stability analysis method based on abstractions for a subclass of hybrid systems called polyhedral hybrid systems. Polyhedral hybrid systems are an interesting class of systems that can be used to abstract linear and non-linear hybrid systems [3,12]. The authors propose a quantitative predicate abstraction method that constructs a finite weighted graph, and analyse the latter for the existence of cycles with product of edge weights ≥ 1. The absence of such cycles indicates that the system is Lyapunov stable. It is suggested that better abstractions can be obtained by choosing a larger set of predicates. However, no efficient strategies for the selection of the same is discussed. Here we take the quantitative predicate abstraction based analysis a step further, and discuss strategies for refinement based on counterexample validation. This is popularly referred to as CEGAR (counterexample guided abstraction refinement [6]).

The main contributions of the paper are the validation and refinement algorithms. Validation consists of checking if an abstract counterexample actually corresponds to a concrete counterexample. In the context of safety analysis [6], an abstract counterexample typically consists of a finite sequence of abstract states or nodes in a finite graph from the initial state to an unsafe state. Validation consists of checking if there exists a finite execution of the system which follows the sequence of abstract states. However, the validation problem we encounter is not a bounded model-checking problem as above. Instead, it consists of checking if there exists an infinite diverging trajectory that follows the cycle infinitely many times. This property cannot, as is, be encoded as the satisfiability of a formula in a finitary logic. We provide a novel characterization of the existence of an infinite diverging execution in terms of the existence of a finite execution that follows the cycle once from a continuous state x to a continuous state y such that $y = \alpha x$ for some $\alpha > 1$. This provides an algorithmic procedure to perform validation, since, the latter can be encoded as the satisfiability problem of a first order logic formula, and efficiently solved.

Refinement in safety analysis consists of computing, iteratively, subsets of concrete states corresponding to abstract states that can reach the unsafe states. If the counterexample is spurious, one of the computed sets is empty, referred to as the point of refinement, and a refinement occurs by examining some local abstract states around this point of refinement. Since, the concrete counterexample required for validation has a finite length m, upper bounded by the abstract counterexample length, the point of refinement is reached within m steps. In the case of refinement for stability, we show that though a priori no such bound on the point of refinement exists, if the counterexample is spurious, it is definitely reached.

We propose two refinement strategies — one of which is applicable always, however, does not eliminate a large fraction of counterexamples; the other is applicable only in certain cases, but eliminates a large fraction of counterexamples. If the validation procedure infers that the counterexample not only does not have an infinite diverging execution corresponding to it, but also does not have any infinite executions corresponding to it; then our refinement algorithms ignores the edge weights and aims to "eliminate" the cycle. Otherwise, it considers the weights and only aims to reduce the weights on the cycle.

We have implemented the CEGAR algorithm, which uses AVERIST in the backend to perform the abstraction and model-checking steps of the CEGAR. We report experimental comparisons between the CEGAR algorithm and the AVERIST algorithm. For the latter, we consider refinement based on the naive strategy of uniformly adding new predicates. Our experimental results demonstrate the benefits of CEGAR both in terms of reduced computation time and smaller abstractions that result as a result of careful refinement in each iteration. Future work will consist of extending the CEGAR framework for stability analysis to more general classes of hybrid systems, and related notions such as asymptotic stability.

Related Work. We briefly discuss related work. There is a large body of work on Lyapunov function based stability analysis for linear and non-linear hybrid systems, see the surveys [4,14]. There is some work on automated verification of stability of linear systems by iteratively refining partitions [15,16,24], however, it is not an abstraction based approach and the refinements are not guided by counterexample analyses. CEGAR has been explored for safety verification of hybrid systems [2,5,18] and region stability analysis [8]. However, unlike Lyapunov and asymptotic stability, safety and region stability are bisimulation invariant properties. Recently, there is some work on learning the templates for Lyapunov functions [10].

2   Polyhedral Switched System (*PSS*)

A hybrid automaton [1] is a popular formalism for modeling mixed discrete-continuous behaviors. It extends the finite state automaton model for discrete dynamics by annotating the modes with differential equations or inclusions for modeling the physical systems. In addition, invariants on the modes and guards on the edges provides constraints that need to be satisfied during evolution and mode switching, respectively. A polyhedral switched system *PSS* is a special kind of hybrid automaton in which each mode is associated with a polyhedral differential inclusion and the invariants and guards are specified by linear constraints.

Definition 1. *A n-dimensional polyhedral switched system (PSS) is a tuple* $\mathcal{H} = (Loc, Edges, X, Flow, Inv, Guard)$, *where:*

- *Loc is a finite set of locations;*
- *Edges* $\subseteq$ *Loc* $\times$ *Loc is a finite set of edges;*
- $X = \mathbb{R}^n$ *is the continuous state-space;*
- *Flow* : *Loc* $\rightarrow$ *CPolySets*(n) *is the flow function;*
- *Inv* : *Loc* $\rightarrow$ *PolySets*(n) *is the invariant function; and*
- *Guard* : *Edges* $\rightarrow$ *PolySets*(n) *is the guard function.*

where PolySets(X) *denotes the set of all convex polyhedral subsets of X, and CPolySets*(X) *denotes the set of compact convex polyhedral sets.*

Notation. From now on, we will denote each of the elements in a *PSS* $\mathcal{H}$, with $\mathcal{H}$ as a subscript, for instance, the invariant function will be referred to as $Inv_\mathcal{H}$.

Example. Figure 1 shows a 3-dimensional polyhedral switched system along the $x-y$ plane when the value along the z-axis is taken to be 1. Essentially, the polyhedral sets from A to F are pyramids centered at $x = 0, y = 0$. V_A through V_F represent the polyhedra in the polyhedral differential inclusions corresponding to the regions A to F. We assume that $\dot{z} = 1$ everywhere. A sample execution of the system is shown using a sequence of directed thin lines.

A switched system starts evolving in a mode $q \in Loc$ and a continuous state x. In this mode q, the continuous state evolves inside $Inv(q)$ such that the differential of the evolution at any time lies within $Flow(q)$. If (q_1, q_2) is an edge of the system and the continuous state satisfies the guard, a switch from q_1 to q_2 can occur. The continuous state does not change during the mode switching. The semantics of a *PSS* $\mathcal{H}$ are given by the set of executions exhibited by the system.

Definition 2. *An execution σ of a PSS of dimension n is a triple (ι, η, γ), where ι is a sequence of time intervals $I_0, I_1, \ldots$ which refer to the times spent by the execution in a particular location, $\eta : \mathcal{I}(\iota) \rightarrow X$, where $\mathcal{I}(\iota) = \cup_i \iota(i)$, represents the continuous state at all times, and γ maps i to the location the execution evolves in during the interval I_i.*

An execution $\sigma = (\iota, \eta, \gamma)$ of $\mathcal{H}$ is said to be *complete* if $\mathcal{I}(\iota)$ is $[0, \infty)$; otherwise, it is called *finite*. The set of all executions of $\mathcal{H}$ will be denoted by *Exec*($\mathcal{H}$), and the set of all complete executions by *CExec*($\mathcal{H}$).

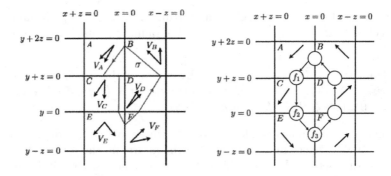

Fig. 1. (Left) Polyhedral switched system (Right) Abstract counterexample

2.1 Reachability Relations

We introduce certain predicates related to reachability which we will need in the sequel. Let us fix an n-dimensional PSS $\mathcal{H}$, two locations q_1 and q_2 in $Loc_{\mathcal{H}}$, and three polyhedral sets P_1, P_2 and P over $\mathbb{R}^n$ for the rest of the section.

$$ReachRel_{\mathcal{H}}((q_1, P_1), P, (q_2, P_2)) = \{(x, y) \in \mathbb{R}^n \times \mathbb{R}^n \mid \exists \text{ finite execution } \sigma = (\iota, \eta, \gamma)$$
$$\in Exec(\mathcal{H}), \mathcal{I}(\iota) = [0, T], x = \eta(0) \in P_1, y = \eta(T) \in P_2, \eta(t) \in P \; \forall t \in (0, T),$$
$$\gamma(0) = q_1 \text{ and } \gamma(Last(dom(\iota))) = q_2\}$$

It captures the set of points $(x, y) \in P_1 \times P_2$ such that there exists an execution which starts at (q_1, x) and ends at (q_2, y) and remains in P at all intermediate time points. It is shown in [21] that the $ReachRel_{\mathcal{H}}$ is computable and can be represented as a $2n$-dimensional polyhedral set. Next, we define the predecessor and successor operators denoted by $pre_{\mathcal{H}}$ and $post_{\mathcal{H}}$, and their weighted counterparts $wpre_{\mathcal{H}}$ and $wpost_{\mathcal{H}}$, respectively.

– $pre_{\mathcal{H}}((q_1, P_1), P, (q_2, P_2)) = \{x \in P_1 \mid \exists y \in P_2 : (x, y) \in ReachRel_{\mathcal{H}}((q_1, P_1),$
   $P, (q_2, P_2))\}$
– $post_{\mathcal{H}}((q_1, P_1), P, (q_2, P_2)) = \{y \in P_2 \mid \exists x \in P_1 : (x, y) \in ReachRel_{\mathcal{H}}((q_1, P_1),$
   $P, (q_2, P_2))\}$

– $wpre_{\mathcal{H}}((q_1, P_1), P, w, (q_2, P_2)) =$
   $= \{x \in P_1 \mid \exists y \in P_2, (x, y) \in ReachRel_{\mathcal{H}}((q_1, P_1), P, (q_2, P_2)), \frac{\|y\|}{\|x\|} = w\}$
– $wpost_{\mathcal{H}}((q_1, P_1), P, w, (q_2, P_2)) =$
   $= \{y \in P_2 \mid \exists x \in P_1, (x, y) \in ReachRel_{\mathcal{H}}((q_1, P_1), P, (q_2, P_2)), \frac{\|y\|}{\|x\|} = w\}$

Here, w is a positive real number and e $\|\cdot\|$ denotes the infinity norm of an element in $\mathbb{R}^n$.

3 Stability

In this section, we define a classical notion of stability in control theory, namely, Lyapunov stability. We consider stability of the system with respect to the origin $\bar{0}$, which we assume is an equilibrium point. Intuitively, Lyapunov stability captures the notion that an execution starting close to the equilibrium point remains close to it. Le $B_\epsilon(\bar{0})$ be an open ball of radius ϵ around $\bar{0}$, which denotes $\{x \mid ||x|| < \epsilon\}$.

Definition 3. *A PSS* $\mathcal{H}$ *is said to be* Lyapunov stable, *if for every* $\epsilon > 0$, *there exists a* $\delta > 0$ *such that for every execution* $\sigma = (\iota, \eta, \gamma) \in Exec(\mathcal{H})$ *with* $\eta(0) \in B_\delta(\bar{0})$, $\eta(t) \in B_\epsilon(\bar{0})$ *for every* $t \in \mathcal{I}(\iota)$.

Observe that Lyapunov is a local property whose satisfaction depends on the behaviors of the system in a small neighborhood around the origin. Hence, the only polyhedral sets of the *PSS* which play a role in stability analysis are those which contain the $\bar{0}$. Therefore, we will assume without loss of generality that the *PSS* is in a normal form [20, 21].

Definition 4. *A polyhedral set* P *is* closed under positive scaling *if for every* $x \in P$ *and* $\alpha > 0$, $\alpha x \in P$.

Definition 5. *A PSS* $\mathcal{H}$ *is in* normal form *if for every* $q \in Loc$ *and for every* $e \in Edges$, $Inv_\mathcal{H}(q)$ *and* $Guard_\mathcal{H}(e)$ *are positive scaling closed.*

4   Counterexample Guided Abstraction Refinement

In this section, we present the CEGAR framework for stability analysis. The algorithm is summarized in Algorithm 1. First, we briefly review the abstraction and model-checking algorithms for stability analysis of polyhedral switched systems from [21]. Then, we present the new validation and refinement algorithms.

4.1   Abstraction

The abstraction procedure is a modification of the standard predicate abstraction [9] which constructs a finite state system using a finite set of predicates, which simulates the concrete system. It was shown in [19] that stability is not preserved by simulation and instead stronger notions which strengthen the simulation relation with continuity conditions are required. Hence, the abstraction procedure in [20] constructs a finite weighted graph as illustrated in Fig. 1. More precisely, the vertices of the graph correspond to pairs of location and facet of the partition (instead of the regions). An edge exists between two vertices if there exists an execution from one pair of location and facet to the other by remaining in the common region of the facets. Further, the weights on the edges store quantitative information, which track by what factor the execution moves closer to the origin when it reaches the target facet as compared to where it started on the source facet. Next, we present the formal construction of the abstract system, for what we introduce some auxiliary definitions.

Definition 6. *A polyhedral partition* $\mathcal{P}$ *of* $X \subseteq \mathbb{R}^n$ *is a finite set of closed convex polyhedral sets,* $\{P_1, \ldots, P_k\}$, *such that* $X = \cup_{i=1}^{k} P_i$ *and* $interior(P_i) \cap interior(P_j) = \emptyset$, *for* $1 \leqslant i, j \leqslant k$.

Algorithm 1. CEGAR for stability analysis

Require: $\mathcal{H}, \mathcal{P}, \mathcal{F}$
Ensure: Stable/Unstable
 1: **if** $Check\text{-}explosion(\mathcal{H}, \mathcal{P})$ **then**
 2:     **return** Unstable
 3: $\mathcal{A} = Abs(\mathcal{H}, \mathcal{P}, \mathcal{F})$
 4: **while true do**
 5:     $\pi := Model\text{-}checking(\mathcal{A})$
 6:     **if** π not counterexample **then**
 7:         **return** Stable
 8:     $\psi := Encode\text{-}\psi_\pi(m > 1)$
 9:     **if** $Check\text{-}satisfiability(\psi)$ **then**
10:         **return** Unstable
11:     **else**
12:         $\psi := Encode\text{-}\psi_\pi(m \leqslant 1)$
13:         **if** $Check\text{-}satisfiability(\psi)$ **then**
14:             $\mathcal{A} := Weighted\text{-}refinement(\mathcal{A}, \pi)$
15:         **else**
16:             $\mathcal{A} := Refinement(\mathcal{A}, \pi)$

The elements of a polyhedral partition are referred to as regions. A polyhedral partition is said to *respect* a *PSS* $\mathcal{H}$ if for every $P \in \mathcal{P}$, $q \in Loc_\mathcal{H}$ and $e \in Edges_\mathcal{H}$, either $P \subseteq Inv_\mathcal{H}(q)$ or $P \cap Inv_\mathcal{H}(q) = \emptyset$ and either $P \subseteq Guard_\mathcal{H}(e)$ or $P \cap Guard_\mathcal{H}(e) = \emptyset$.

Definition 7. *A facet partition $\mathcal{F}$ of a polyhedral partition $\mathcal{P}$ is a polyhedral partition of $\cup_{P \in \mathcal{P}} \partial(P)$, where $\partial(P)$ is the boundary of P.*

Definition 8. *Let us fix a concrete PSS $\mathcal{H}$. Let $\mathcal{P}$ be a polyhedral partition of X and $\mathcal{F}$ be a facet partition of $\mathcal{P}$. The abstract system is the finite weighted graph $Abs(\mathcal{H}, \mathcal{P}, \mathcal{F}) = (V, E, W)$ defined as follows.*

- $V = Loc \times \mathcal{F}$.
- $E \subseteq V \times \mathcal{P} \times V$ is $\{((q_1, f_1), P, (q_2, f_2)) \mid ReachRel((q_1, f_1), P, (q_2, f_2)) \neq \emptyset\}$.
- $W : E \to \mathbb{R}_{\geq 0} \cup \{\infty\}$, such that for $e = ((q_1, f_1), P, (q_2, f_2)) \in E$,

$$W(e) = \sup\{\|y\|/\|x\| \mid (x, y) \in ReachRel((q_1, f_1), P, (q_2, f_2))\}$$

The weight computation on the edges of the abstract graph can be constructed by solving an optimization problem on the reachability relation polyhedral set [20,21].

4.2 Model-Checking and Counterexample Generation

For every execution of the concrete system, there is a path in the weighted graph such that the product of the weights of its edges is an upper bound on the scaling of the execution - the ratio of the distance of its end point from the origin to the distance of its starting point from the origin. Therefore, the following theorem provides sufficient conditions on the finite weighted graph which imply stability of the concrete system. We say that a region is exploding in $\mathcal{H}$ if there exists an execution which always remains in the region and diverges (goes arbitrarily far from the origin). Consider a partition $\mathcal{P}$ which respects $\mathcal{H}$, then for every region $P \in \mathcal{P}$ there exists $q \in Loc_{\mathcal{H}}$ such that $P \subseteq Inv_{\mathcal{H}}(q)$. The region P is exploding in $\mathcal{H}$ in the case of $P \cap Flow_{\mathcal{H}}(q) \neq \emptyset$. Given a path π, let $W(\pi)$ denote the product of the weights on the edges of π.

Theorem 1 [21]. *Let $\mathcal{H}$ be a PSS, $\mathcal{P}$ be a polyhedral partition respecting $\mathcal{H}$ and $\mathcal{F}$ be a facet partition of $\mathcal{P}$. Then, the PSS $\mathcal{H}$ is Lyapunov stable if for every simple cycle π, $W(\pi) \leq 1$ and there is no region in $\mathcal{P}$ which explodes in $\mathcal{H}$.*

The conditions on the abstract system can be efficiently checked [20,21]. The model-checking procedure will either return that $\mathcal{H}$ is stable or in the case that the abstract system does not satisfy the conditions of Theorem 1 return an abstract counterexample in the form of a simple cycle with weight >1 or say that the system has an exploding region. In the first case, we know that the system is stable, and in the third case, it is unstable. For the second case, the CEGAR algorithm proceeds to the validation phase.

Example. Consider the 3-dimensional *PSS* shown in Fig. 1 (Left). Now, the picture on the right shows part of the abstract system. The nodes are superimposed over the facets they represent and the edges show the existence of an execution between such facets evolving through the common polyhedral set. For instance, we observe that there exists an execution from facet f_1 to f_2 evolving through the polyhedron C. The cycle shown is an abstract counterexample since the weight associated with it is greater than 1. Validation will check if there exists an actual execution along the cycle which can witness instability.

Remark 1. The conditions in Theorem 1 are, in fact, both necessary and sufficient in the case of 2-dimensional *PSS*s [23], however, it is only sufficient in 3 or more dimensions. There are two reasons for the conservativeness. First, the edges are not transitively closed, because they are existential with respect to the executions in the concrete system. More precisely, existence of an execution from a facet f_1 to f_2 and an execution from f_2 to f_3 does not imply that there is a single execution which goes from f_1 to f_2 to f_3. Secondly, a similar transitivity may not hold on the weights. Suppose that the weight on the edge from f_1 to f_2 is w_1 and from f_2 to f_3 is w_2. There exists an execution from some point in f_1 to some point in f_2 with scaling w_1 and an execution from some point in f_2 to a point in f_3 with weight w_2. However, there may not be a single execution from f_1 to f_3 through f_2 such that the scaling corresponding to the prefix from f_1 to f_2 is w_1, while that from f_2 to f_3 is w_2.

4.3   Validation

We present some preliminaries and define the validation problem. Next, the validation procedure and its theoretical basis are presented.

Definition 9. *A simple cycle* π *in* $Abs(\mathcal{H}, \mathcal{P}, \mathcal{F})$ *is an* abstract counterexample *if* $W(\pi) > 1$.

A. Validation Problem. Validation consists of checking if the abstract counterexample corresponds to a violation of stability in the concrete system. Let us fix a counterexample $\pi = (q_0, f_0), P_0, (q_1, f_1), P_1, \ldots, (q_{k-1}, f_{k-1}), P_{k-1}, (q_0, f_0)$ of $\mathcal{A} = Abs(\mathcal{H}, \mathcal{P}, \mathcal{F})$. The following definition states a connection between the abstract counterexample and the executions in the concrete system.

Definition 10. *An execution* $\sigma = (\iota, \eta, \gamma)$ *of* $\mathcal{H}$ *is said to* follow *the abstract counterexample* π *of* $\mathcal{A} = Abs(\mathcal{H}, \mathcal{P}, \mathcal{F})$, *denoted* $\sigma \rightsquigarrow \pi$, *if there exists a non-decreasing sequence of times* $0 = t_0, t_1, t_2, \ldots$ *such that* $\eta(t_i) \in f_{i \bmod k}$, $\eta(t) \in P_i$ *for* $t \in [t_{(i-1) \bmod k}, t_{i \bmod k}]$ *and* $(\eta(t_i), \eta(t_{i+1})) \in ReachRel((q_i, f_i), P_i, (q_{i+1}, f_{i+1}))$. *Further,* σ *is said to* follow π respecting the weights, *denoted* $\sigma \overset{w}{\rightsquigarrow} \pi$, *if in addition*

$$\frac{||\eta(t_{i+1})||}{||\eta(t_i)||} = W((q_{i \bmod k}, f_{i \bmod k}), P_{i \bmod k}, (q_{(i+1) \bmod k}, f_{(i+1) \bmod k})).$$

The following notion captures the violation of Lyapunov stability along π. The abstract counterexample π is a witness to the violation of Lyapunov stability by the concrete system $\mathcal{H}$ if there exist executions with arbitrary scaling which follow the cycle respecting the weights.

$$(C1) \; \exists \epsilon > 0, \forall \delta > 0, \exists \sigma \in Exec(\mathcal{H}) \text{ such that}$$

$$\sigma \overset{w}{\rightsquigarrow} \pi, \; \eta(0) \in B_\delta(\bar{0}), \exists t \in \mathcal{I}(\iota), \eta(t) \notin B_\epsilon(\bar{0})$$

The next proposition states that the above condition in fact implies that there is a complete execution along π.

Proposition 1. *Condition (C1) is equivalent to the existence of a complete execution* σ *of* $\mathcal{H}$ *such that* $\sigma \overset{w}{\rightsquigarrow} \pi$.

While (C1) can be validated exactly, a refinement corresponding to (C1) tries to eliminate just the executions which follow the weights on the edges of π exactly. In order to accelerate the progress in the CEGAR iterations, we consider a stronger validation problem, where we do not require the execution to follow the weights, but still be diverging.

Definition 11. *An abstract counterexample* π *is said to be* spurious *if there does not exist a divergent complete execution* σ *such that* $\sigma \rightsquigarrow \pi$.

Validation problem: Given an abstract counterexample π, is π spurious?

B. Validation Procedure. The crux of the validation procedure is to reduce the problem of checking the existence of infinite executions to that of finite executions. Hence, for $m \in \mathbb{R}_{\geq 0}$ we define a predicate $\psi_\pi(m)$, which captures the set of points $x_0, \ldots, x_k$ such that x_k can be reached from x_0 by following the cycle once, and $x_k = m x_0$.

$$\psi_\pi(m) := \exists x_0, x_1, \ldots, x_k \in \mathbb{R}^n : x_k = m x_0, \forall 0 \leq i < k,$$

$$x_i \in f_i, (x_i, x_{i+1}) \in ReachRel((q_i, f_i), P_i, (q_{i+1}, f_{i+1})).$$

Next, we state the main theorem for validation.

Theorem 2. *The following holds for the abstract counterexample π:*

V1 $\exists m > 1 : \psi_\pi(m) \Rightarrow \exists \sigma \in CExec(\mathcal{H}) : \sigma \rightsquigarrow \pi \wedge \sigma$ *diverges.*
V2 $\nexists m : \psi_\pi(m) \Rightarrow \nexists \sigma \in CExec(\mathcal{H}) : \sigma \rightsquigarrow \pi.$
V3 $\exists m : \psi_\pi(m) \wedge \nexists m > 1 : \psi_\pi(m) \Rightarrow$
    $\exists \sigma \in CExec(\mathcal{H}) : \sigma \rightsquigarrow \pi \wedge \nexists \sigma \in CExec(\mathcal{H}) : \sigma \overset{w}{\rightsquigarrow} \pi.$

Remark 2. Condition V1 implies that when there exists $m > 1$ such that $\psi_\pi(m)$ holds, the system is unstable. Condition V2 states that when there exist no m at all such that $\psi_\pi(m)$ is true, then the counterexample has no complete executions following it, and hence, is spurious. Condition V3 implies that there is no complete execution following π which respects the weight, however, there is some complete execution (diverging or not).

Before proving the result above, we introduce some definitions and a fixpoint theorem that we will use to establish an intermediate result. Let $\pi = (q_0, f_0), P_0, (q_1, f_1), P_1, \ldots, (q_{k-1}, f_{k-1}), P_{k-1}, (q_0, f_0)$ be an abstract counterexample of $\mathcal{A}$. Let $PreReach^i(S_0)$, for some $S_0 \subseteq f_0$, denote the set of points from which there is a sequence of length i following π which starts at S_0. Similarly, let $WPreReach^i(S_0)$ denote the points from which the executions also respect the weights. We introduce the formal definitions below. *PreReach* is defined as follows:

- $PreReach^0(S_0) = S_0$.
- For $i > 0$, $PreReach^i(S_0) = pre_\mathcal{H}((q_j, f_j), P_j, (q_{j+1}, PreReach^{i-1}(S_0)))$, where $j = k - (i \bmod k)$.

In addition to *WPreReach* we also define *WPostReach*.

- $WPreReach^0(S_0) = S_0$.
- $WPreReach^i(S_0) = wpre_\mathcal{H}((q_j, f_j), P_j, w_j, (q_{j+1}, WPreReach^{i-1}(S_0)))$, where $w_j = W((q_{j-1}, f_{j-1})(q_j, f_j))$, $i > 0$ and $j = k - (i \bmod k)$.
- $WPostReach^0(S_0) = S_0$.
- $WPostReach^i(S_0) = wpost_\mathcal{H}((q_j, f_j), P_j, w_j, (q_{j+1}, WPostReach^{i-1}(S_0)))$, where $w_j = W((q_{j-1}, f_{j-1})(q_j, f_j))$, $i > 0$ and $j = i \bmod k$

Theorem 3 (Kakutani's fixed point theorem). *Let $S \subseteq \mathbb{R}^n$ be a non empty, compact and convex set. Let $H : S \to 2^S$ be a set-valued function whose graph $\{(s, s') : s' \in H(s)\}$ is a closed set, and for all $s \in S$, $H(s) \neq \emptyset$ and convex. Then H has a fixed point, which means $\exists s^* \in S : s^* \in H(s^*)$.*

The existence of such kind of fixed point provides us a strategy for proving the next result.

Proposition 2. *If there exists $\sigma \in CExec(\mathcal{H})$ such that $\sigma \overset{w}{\leadsto} \pi$, then there exists a value m greater than 1 such that $\psi_\pi(m)$ holds.*

Proof. Suppose $\sigma \in CExec(\mathcal{H})$ such that $\sigma \overset{w}{\leadsto} \pi$. Let us first define a set of starting points for divergent executions following π respecting the weights. $Kernel(\pi) = \{x \in f_0 \mid \exists \sigma = (\iota, \eta, \gamma) \in CExec(\mathcal{H}) : \eta(0) = x, \sigma \overset{w}{\leadsto} \pi\}$.

$Kernel(\pi)$ is a closed convex set which is positive scaling closed. This follows from the following facts. Firstly, the facet f_0 is closed, convex and positive scaling closed, since it is a facet from a polyhedral partition respecting a PSS $\mathcal{H}$ in normal form. Next, the set $Kernel(\pi)$ is the intersection of $WPreReach^i(f_0)$ for $i \geqslant 0$ which is a multiple of k, the length of the counterexample π. (This depends on the fact that the set $Z = \bigcap_{i \bmod k = 0} WPreReach^i(f_0)$ has the property that $Z \subseteq PreReach^k(Z)$). Finally, the $WPreReach$ and intersection operations preserve the closedness, the convexity and the positive scaling property.

Consider a set-valued function G from f_0 to f_0 which maps $x_0 \in f_0$ to the set $WPostReach^k(x_0)$. Define $S = \{x \mid ||x|| \leq 1, x \in Kernel(\pi)\}$. Since $Kernel(\pi)$ is non-empty, convex, closed and closed under positive scaling, we obtain that S is non-empty, compact and convex. Compactness follows from the assumption that $Kernel(\pi)$ is closed and the set $||x|| \leq 1$ is compact, and hence, their intersection S is compact. The convexity of S follows from the fact that it is the intersection of the set $Kernel(\pi)$ and the set $||x|| \leq 1$, both of which are convex.

Define K as an upper bound for the scaling of the executions following π for one iteration and respecting the weights, so the ones from f_0 to $WPostReach^k(f_0)$, being k the length of π. Define the set valued function H from S to 2^S, which maps $x \in S$ to the set $\{\frac{y}{K} \mid y \in G(x)\}$.

Note that the graph $\{(x, y) \mid y \in G(x)\}$ is a closed set. Consider a sequence of points $(x_0, y_0), (x_i, y_i), \ldots$ which belong to the graph and converge to (x, y). Then x will be in the domain of the graph because of closedness of f_0. And $y \in G(x)$ because of compactness and linearity of every polyhedral set $Flow(q)$ for $q \in Loc$ which represents the dynamics.

Next, we show that H has a fixed point. For this, we apply the Kakutani's fixed point theorem. Since H defined above satisfies the hypothesis of Kakutani's theorem, there exists $s^* \in S$ such that $s^* \in H(s^*)$. Then, Note that $s^* \in \frac{G(s^*)}{K}$, it is $Ks^* \in G(s^*)$. Then the sequence of points $s^*, Ks^*, K^2s^*, \ldots$ holds $\psi_\pi(K)$, and $K > 1$ because it is an upper bound on the $W(\pi)$ and π is a counterexample, and $K^{j+1}s^* \in WPostReach^k(K^js^*)$ for every $j \geqslant 0$.   □

Next, we prove Theorem 2. Suppose π is an abstract counterexample.

V1 Suppose there exists $m > 1$ and $x_0, \ldots, x_k \in \mathbb{R}^n$ such that for all $0 \le i < k$, $x_i \in f_i$ and $(x_i, x_{i+1}) \in ReachRel((q_i, f_i), P_i, (q_{i+1}, f_{i+1}))$, and $x_k = mx_0$. Then consider the infinite execution $\nu = x_0, \ldots, x_{k-1}, mx_0, \ldots, mx_{k-1}, m^2 x_0, \ldots, m^2 x_{k-1}, \ldots$ such that $(m^j x_i, m^j x_{i+1}) \in ReachRel((q_i, f_i), P_i, (q_{i+1}, f_{i+1}))$ for every $j \ge 0$ because of linearity of the flows. Construct with such points and π an execution σ such that $\sigma \leadsto \pi$. Note that σ diverges, since $m > 1$.

V2 It can show by using a similar argument that in the proof of Proposition 2 but defining $Kernel(\pi)$ as $\{x \in f_0 \mid \exists \sigma = (\iota, \eta, \gamma) \in CExec(\mathcal{H}) : \eta(0) = x, \sigma \leadsto \pi\}$.

V3 Suppose there exists $0 < m \le 1$ and $x_0, \ldots, x_k \in \mathbb{R}^n$ such that for all $0 \le i < k$, $x_i \in f_i$ and $(x_i, x_{i+1}) \in ReachRel((q_i, f_i), P_i, (q_{i+1}, f_{i+1}))$, and $x_k = mx_0$. Then consider the infinite execution $\nu = x_0, \ldots, x_{k-1}, mx_0, \ldots, mx_{k-1}, m^2 x_0, \ldots, m^2 x_{k-1}, \ldots$. Construct with such points and π an execution σ such that $\sigma \leadsto \pi$. Note that there does not exist σ respecting the weights in π because in case of existence we would get a contradiction due to Proposition 2.   □

4.4 Refinement

First, we formalize the refinement problem. Then, we present different strategies for refinement by considering the reason for the spuriousness of the abstract counterexample.

A. Refinement Problem. We first introduce the notion of refinement.

Definition 12. *Given two abstract systems for $\mathcal{H}$, $\mathcal{A} = Abs(\mathcal{H}, \mathcal{P}, \mathcal{F}) = (V, E, W)$ and $\mathcal{A}' = Abs(\mathcal{H}, \mathcal{P}, \mathcal{F}') = (V', E', W')$, $\mathcal{A}'$ is said to be a refinement of $\mathcal{A}$, if there exists a mapping $\alpha : V' \to V$ such that if $(v_1, P, v_2) \in E'$, then $(\alpha(v_1), P, \alpha(v_2)) \in E$, and $W'(v_1, P, v_2) \le W(\alpha(v_1), P, \alpha(v_2))$.*

Next we associate a set of triples with an abstract system which captures the potential executions and scalings along the edges.

Definition 13. *Given an abstract system $\mathcal{A} = (V, E, W)$ of $\mathcal{H}$, $Pot(\mathcal{A}) = \{((q_1, x), w, (q_2, y)) \mid \exists((q_1, f_1), P, (q_2, f_2)) \in E, x \in f_1, y \in f_2, ||y||/||x|| = w \le W((q_1, f_1), P, (q_2, f_2))\}$.*

Definition 14. *An abstract system $\mathcal{A}'$ of $\mathcal{H}$ is a strict refinement of an abstract system $\mathcal{A}$ of $\mathcal{H}$, if $\mathcal{A}'$ is a refinement of $\mathcal{A}$ and $Pot(\mathcal{A}')$ is a strict subset of $Pot(\mathcal{A})$.*

Refinement problem: Given the concrete system $\mathcal{H}$, an abstract system $\mathcal{A}$ of $\mathcal{H}$ and a spurious abstract counterexample of $\mathcal{A}$, namely π, find a strict refinement $\mathcal{A}'$ of $\mathcal{A}$.

Remark 3. Observe that if $\mathcal{F}'$ is a facet partition which is strictly finer than $\mathcal{F}$, then $Abs(\mathcal{H}, \mathcal{P}, \mathcal{F}')$ is a refinement of $Abs(\mathcal{H}, \mathcal{P}, \mathcal{F})$, however, it may not be a strict refinement of $Abs(\mathcal{H}, \mathcal{P}, \mathcal{F})$. Hence, it is crucial to exploit the spuriousness of the abstract counterexample π to construct a finer facet partition $\mathcal{F}'$ such that $\mathcal{A}' = Abs(\mathcal{H}, \mathcal{P}, \mathcal{F}')$ is a strict refinement of $\mathcal{A}$.

B. Refinement Procedure. We present two different strategies for refinement based on the reason for the spuriousness. First, we show that non-existence of a complete execution along π (respecting the weights) implies that the *PreReach* (*WPreReach*) computation terminates.

Theorem 4. *Consider a PSS $\mathcal{H}$, an abstract system $\mathcal{A}$ of $\mathcal{H}$ and a counterexample π. Then*

R1 *If $\nexists \sigma \in CExec(\mathcal{H})$ such that $\sigma \rightsquigarrow \pi \Rightarrow PreReach^i(f_0) = \emptyset$ for some i.*
R2 *If $\nexists \sigma \in CExec(\mathcal{H})$ such that $\sigma \overset{w}{\rightsquigarrow} \pi \Rightarrow WPreReach^i(f_0) = \emptyset$ for some i.*

From Theorem 2, there are two reasons for spuriousness corresponding to Conditions V2 and V3. Statements R1 and R2 suggest the refinement strategies corresponding to V2 and V3.

Refinement strategy when the premise of V2 holds. Let ι be the smallest index such that $PreReach^\iota(f_0)$ empty. Note that $S_1 = PreReach^{\iota-1}(f_0)$ is not empty. Let the value $\hat{k} = k - (\iota \bmod k)$. Also, $(\hat{k}+1) \bmod k$ is the index of the facet which contains S_1. It also implies that the set $S_2 = post_{\mathcal{H}}((q_{\hat{k}}, f_{\hat{k}}), P_{\hat{k}}, (q_{(\hat{k}+1) \bmod k}, f_{(\hat{k}+1) \bmod k}))$ which is also a subset of $f_{(\hat{k}+1) \bmod k}$ has an empty intersection with S_1. Refinement corresponds to refining the facet $f_{(\hat{k}+1) \bmod k}$ into $\{f^1, f^2\}$ such that it separates S_1 and S_2, that is, $S_1 \subseteq f^1$ and $S_2 \subseteq f^2$, and $S_1 \cap f^2 = \bar{0}$ and $S_2 \cap f^1 = \bar{0}$. Such a splitting is always possible since S_1 and S_2 are two closed convex polyhedral sets whose intersection contains only $\bar{0}$ and hence, there exists a hyperplane which separates them.

An illustration of the refinement is shown in Fig. 2. The system is partitioned by the two polyhedral sets C and E, in which the flow direction is determined by the dashed lines, pointing from facet f_1 to facet f_2 and from f_2 to facet f_3. Observe that after performing predecessor operation on f_3 once we reach S_2 in f_2, and predecessor reach set of S_2 in f_1 becomes empty. From f_1 the succes-

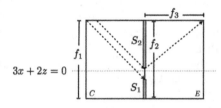

Fig. 2. Refinement

sor reach set is computed and intersected with f_2, obtaining S_1. The two sets S_1 and S_2 are almost disjoint but for $\bar{0}$ so they can be separated by a hyperplane. A choice of a separating hyperplane is $3x + 2z = 0$.

Proposition 3. *The abstract system $Abs(\mathcal{H}, \mathcal{P}, \mathcal{F}')$ is a strict refinement of the abstract system $Abs(\mathcal{H}, \mathcal{P}, \mathcal{F})$, where $\mathcal{F}' = (\mathcal{F} \backslash \{f_{(\hat{k}+1) \bmod k}\}) \cup \{f^1, f^2\}$.*

Proof. It follows from the fact that there is an edge from $(q_{\hat{k}}, f_{\hat{k}})$ to $(q_{(\hat{k}+1) \bmod k}, f^2)$, but no edge from $(q_{\hat{k}}, f_{\hat{k}})$ to $(q_{(\hat{k}+1) \bmod k}, f^1)$.

Refinement strategy when the premise of V3 holds. The refinement is similar to the previous case, except that all the operators are replaced by their weighted counterparts, that is, *PreReach* is replaced by *WPreReach* and *post* by *wpost*. The following proposition implying progress is similar to Proposition 3, however, the proof relies on the reduction of the weight rather than the removal of an edge.

Proposition 4. *The abstract system Abs$(\mathcal{H}, \mathcal{P}, \mathcal{F}')$ is a strict refinement of the abstract system Abs$(\mathcal{H}, \mathcal{P}, \mathcal{F})$, where $\mathcal{F}' = (\mathcal{F} \backslash \{f_{(\hat{k}+1) \bmod k}\}) \cup \{f^1, f^2\}$.*

Proof. Note that the weight of the edge $((q_{\hat{k}}, f_{\hat{k}}), P_{\hat{k}}, (q_{(\hat{k}+1) \bmod k}, f^1))$, if it exists, is less than the weight $w_{\hat{k}}$, the weight of the edge $((q_{\hat{k}}, f_{\hat{k}}), P_{\hat{k}}, (q_{(\hat{k}+1) \bmod k}, f_{(\hat{k}+1) \bmod k}))$.

Algorithm 1 summarizes the validation and refinement procedures. Line 8 checks if there exists an infinite diverging trajectory by constructing the formula $\psi_\pi(m > 1)$. If it is satisfiable, then a counterexample is found. If not, a refinement is required. However, to determine the type of refinement, the satisfiability of the formula $\psi_\pi(m \leq 1)$ is checked. If it is not satisfiable, then no infinite execution corresponding to the abstract counterexample exists, and we proceed with a non-weighted refinement. However, if $\psi_\pi(m \leq 1)$ is satisfiable, we know that an infinite execution exists, but we cannot conclude that it is diverging, hence, we proceed with a weighted refinement in Line 14.

5   Implementation

The validation procedure and the refinement strategies have been implemented in Python 2.7.3. We use Z3 SMT solver [7] for the validation, that is, checking the satisfiability of the formulas in Theorem 2; and use Parma Polyhedra Library (PPL) for performing polyhedral operations such as reachability computations in the refinement process. We also use AVERIST [22] for the abstraction and model-checking algorithms from [20].

We illustrate our CEGAR algorithm on a particular class of polyhedral switched systems. The experiments are inspired by the example described in Fig. 1. The 3-dimensional experiments consist of the same locations as the one in the example where the configurations of the flow function *Flow* are modified. The 4 and 5-dimensional experiments are obtained by extending every element of the example to higher dimensions.

Some of our results are summarized in Table 1. Here, *Exp* refers to the experiment number, *Dim* to the dimension of the concrete system (number of continuous variables) and *Stab* states whether the concrete system is Lyapunov stable (Y) or not (N). *Ans* is the output of the CEGAR algorithm, which can be stable (S) (when the model-checking succeed), unstable (NS) (when the validation succeeds) or no answer (NA) (if the system does not terminate in a pre-set time). *Regions* is the number of regions in the polyhedral partition. *IT* refers to the number of iterations of the CEGAR loop before termination, *Ref* indicates if weighted refinement strategy has been applied for some iteration, *Pre* states only

Table 1. Experimental results for CEGAR algorithm

Exp	Dim	Stab	Ans	Regions	IT	Ref	Size	A time	MC time	Val time	Ref time	Time
1	3	Y	S	163	3	Pre	75	18.75	0.01	0.03	0.03	20.02
2	3	Y	S	287	11	Pre	153	196	0.23	0.84	0.30	204.50
3	3	N	NS	135	1	-	−	0	0	0	0	0.15
4	3	Y	NA	59	11	WPre	123	119.32	0.25	0.94	2.44	130.91
5	3	N	NS	9	1	-	16	0.30	ε	0.13	0	0.55
6	3	Y	S	151	2	WPre	74	12.55	ε	0.17	0.07	5.72
7	3	Y	S	179	4	Pre	87	31.63	0.02	0.03	0.04	33.62
8	3	Y	S	291	11	Pre	157	249.40	0.38	0.57	0.39	269.11
9	4	Y	S	537	3	Pre	341	312	0.32	0.32	0.10	319.42
10	4	Y	S	865	7	Pre	601	1543	2.13	1.18	0.28	1582.33
11	5	Y	S	1706	3	Pre	1365	4208	4.32	0.51	0.12	4252

Table 2. Comparison of AVERIST and CEGAR technique

			AVERIST				CEGAR technique			
Exp	Dim	Stab	Answer	Regions	Runs	Time	Answer	Regions	IT	Time
2	3	Y	NA	85250	6	10658.26	S	287	11	204.50
2	3	Y	NA	4034	4	857.23	NA	59	11	130.91
3	3	Y	NA	4035	4	181.32	S	151	2	5.72
4	3	Y	NA	4035	4	187.24	S	179	4	33.62
5	4	Y	NA	27201	3	4728.61	S	537	3	319.42

predecessor reach computation and *WPre* indicates some weighted predecessor reach computation has been performed. *Size* refers to the number of nodes in the final weighted graph. The time for abstraction, *A time*, model-checking, *MC time*, validation, *Val time* and refinement, *Ref time*, are shown along with the total time *Time*. All the times are in seconds, and ε indicates a value smaller than 0.001.

A limit on the number of CEGAR iterations has been set to 11, but it can be set to any arbitrary value. The CEGAR procedure terminates on most of the examples that we are reporting. In the case of experiment 4 we do not obtain any answer, while in the case of experiments 3 and 5 we obtain instability. In the experiment 3, we observe instability due to an exploding region, therefore all the times are zero. In the experiment 5, the refinement is not performed because the validation algorithm returns the existence of a concrete counterexample. Our experiments illustrate that the CEGAR framework is practically feasible, since the times added by the validation and refinement procedures can be neglected if considering the total times.

Next, we compare the CEGAR algorithm with AVERIST. AVERIST allows specification of predicates as well as built-in automated methods for generating uniform predicates based on an input granularity value. In our comparison, we run our examples on AVERIST by iteratively increasing the number of predicates using this feature. Our CEGAR algorithm on the other hand applies the new refinement strategies based on the returned counterexamples for adding the predicates. We choose the termination criterion for CEGAR to be a bound of 11 on the number of iterations, and for AVERIST, we stop when the running time is more than 5 times the total time taken by the CEGAR algorithm. We compared all the examples in Table 1 with AVERIST, however, we present only a representative subset of them in Table 2. In Table 2, *Exp* refers to the experiment number, *Dim* to the dimension of the concrete system and *Stab* states whether the concrete system is Lyapunov stable (Y) or not (N). *Answer* is the algorithmic output, which can be stable (S), unstable (NS) or no answer (NA). *Regions* is the number of regions in the last polyhedral partition. *Runs* refers to the number of times AVERIST is run with an incremented number of uniform predicates, *IT* refers to the number of iterations of the CEGAR loop before termination and *Time* is the total time. As we observe from the experiments, AVERIST does not terminate on any of the examples within time 5 times that of the CEGAR algorithm. It shows that uniformly partitioning may be slower since the new predicates added are not necessarily useful towards constructing the right abstractions that are successful in stability analysis.

6   Conclusions

In this paper, we developed a counterexample guided abstraction refinement framework for the stability analysis of polyhedral switched systems. This approach explores the search space systematically by using counterexamples. To the best of our knowledge, this is the first CEGAR framework for stability analysis. Instantiating the CEGAR algorithm for stability analysis is non-trivial, since the notion of a counterexample is more involved, and the refinement is more expensive. Future work will focus on extending the ideas in the paper to more general classes of switched systems.

Acknowledgements. This work is partially supported by the Marie Curie Career Integration Grant no. 631622 and the NSF CAREER award no. 1552668 to Pavithra Prabhakar and by the research grant no. BES-2013-065076 from the Spanish Ministry of Economy and Competitiveness to Miriam García Soto.

References

1. Alur, R., Courcoubetis, C., Henzinger, T.A., Ho, P.: Hybrid automata: an algorithmic approach to the specification and verification of hybrid systems. In: Grossman, R.L., Nerode, A., Ravn, A.P., Rischel, H. (eds.) Hybrid Systems. LNCS, vol. 736, pp. 209–229. Springer, Heidelberg (1992)
2. Alur, R., Dang, T., Ivanvcić, F.: Counter-example guided predicate abstraction of hybrid systems. In: Garavel, H., Hatcliff, J. (eds.) TACAS 2003. LNCS, vol. 2619, pp. 208–223. Springer, Heidelberg (2003)

3. Bogomolov, S., Frehse, G., Greitschus, M., Grosu, R., Pasareanu, C., Podelski, A., Strump, T.: Assume-guarantee abstraction refinement meets hybrid systems. In: Yahav, E. (ed.) HVC 2014. LNCS, vol. 8855, pp. 116–131. Springer, Heidelberg (2014)
4. Branicky, M.S.: Stability of hybrid systems: state of the art. In: Conference on Decision and Control, pp. 120–125 (1997)
5. Clarke, E.M., Fehnker, A., Han, Z., Krogh, B., Ouaknine, J., Stursberg, O., Theobald, M.: Abstraction and counterexample-guided refinement in model checking of hybrid systems. Int. J. Found. Comput. Sci. 14(4), 583–604 (2003)
6. Clarke, E.M., Grumberg, O., Jha, S., Lu, Y., Veith, H.: Counterexample-guided abstraction refinement. In: Emerson, E.A., Sistla, A.P. (eds.) CAV 2000. LNCS, vol. 1855, pp. 154–169. Springer, Heidelberg (2000)
7. de Moura, L., Bjørner, N.S.: Z3: an efficient SMT solver. In: Ramakrishnan, C.R., Rehof, J. (eds.) TACAS 2008. LNCS, vol. 4963, pp. 337–340. Springer, Heidelberg (2008)
8. Duggirala, P.S., Mitra, S.: Abstraction refinement for stability. In: International Conference on Cyber-Physical Systems, pp. 22–31 (2011)
9. Graf, S., Saidi, H.: Construction of abstact state graphs with PVS. In: Grumberg, O. (ed.) CAV 1997. LNCS, vol. 1254, pp. 72–83. Springer, Heidelberg (1997)
10. Kapinski, J., Deshmukh, J.V., Sankaranarayanan, S., Arechiga, N.: Simulation-guided lyapunov analysis for hybrid dynamical systems. In: Proceedings of the International Conference on Hybrid Systems: Computation and Control, pp. 133–142 (2014)
11. Khalil, H.K.: Nonlinear Systems. Prentice-Hall, Upper Saddle River (1996)
12. Kourjanski, M., Varaiya, P.: Stability of hybrid systems. In: Alur, R., Henzinger, T.A., Sontag, E.D. (eds.) Hybrid Systems III. LNCS, vol. 1066, pp. 413–423. Springer, Heidelberg (1995)
13. Liberzon, D.: Switching in Systems and Control. Birkhäuser, Boston (2003)
14. Lin, H., Antsaklis, P.J.: Stability and stabilizability of switched linear systems: a survey of recent results. IEEE Trans. Autom. Control 54(2), 308–322 (2009)
15. Möhlmann, E., Theel, O.E.: Stabhyli: a tool for automatic stability verification of non-linear hybrid systems. In: Proceedings of the International Conference on Hybrid Systems: Computation and Control, pp. 107–112 (2013)
16. Oehlerking, J., Burchardt, H., Theel, O.: Fully automated stability verification for piecewise affine systems. In: Bemporad, A., Bicchi, A., Buttazzo, G. (eds.) HSCC 2007. LNCS, vol. 4416, pp. 741–745. Springer, Heidelberg (2007)
17. Parrilo, P.A.: Structure semidefinite programs and semialgebraic geometry methods in robustness and optimization. Ph.D. thesis, California Institute of Technology, Pasadena, CA, May 2000
18. Prabhakar, P., Duggirala, P.S., Mitra, S., Viswanathan, M.: Hybrid automata-based CEGAR for rectangular hybrid systems. In: Giacobazzi, R., Berdine, J., Mastroeni, I. (eds.) VMCAI 2013. LNCS, vol. 7737, pp. 48–67. Springer, Heidelberg (2013)
19. Prabhakar, P., Dullerud, G.E., Viswanathan, M.: Pre-orders for reasoning about stability. In: Proceedings of the International Conference on Hybrid Systems: Computation and Control, pp. 197–206 (2012)
20. Prabhakar, P., Soto, M.G.: Abstraction based model-checking of stability of hybrid systems. In: Sharygina, N., Veith, H. (eds.) CAV 2013. LNCS, vol. 8044, pp. 280–295. Springer, Heidelberg (2013)
21. Prabhakar, P., Soto, M.G.: An algorithmic approach to stability verification of polyhedral switched system. In: American Control Conference (2014)

22. Prabhakar, P., Soto, M.G.: AVERIST: an algorithmic verifier for stability. Electron. Notes Theor. Comput. Sci. **317**, 133–139 (2015)

23. Prabhakar, P., Viswanathan, M.: On the decidability of stability of hybrid systems. In: Proceedings of the International Conference on Hybrid Systems: Computation and Control (2013)

24. Yfoulis, C.A., Shorten, R.: A numerical technique for stability analysis of linear switched systems. In: Alur, R., Pappas, G.J. (eds.) HSCC 2004. LNCS, vol. 2993, pp. 631–645. Springer, Heidelberg (2004)

Symbolic Optimal Reachability in Weighted Timed Automata

Patricia Bouyer$^{(\boxtimes)}$, Maximilien Colange,
and Nicolas Markey

LSV – CNRS, ENS Cachan,
Université Paris Saclay, Cachan, France
{bouyer,colange,markey}@lsv.fr

Abstract. Weighted timed automata have been defined in the early 2000 s for modelling resource-consumption or -allocation problems in real-time systems. Optimal reachability is decidable in weighted timed automata, and a symbolic forward algorithm has been developed to solve that problem. This algorithm uses so-called *priced zones*, an extension of standard zones with *cost functions*. In order to ensure termination, the algorithm requires clocks to be bounded. For unpriced timed automata, much work has been done to develop sound abstractions adapted to the forward exploration of timed automata, ensuring termination of the model-checking algorithm without bounding the clocks. In this paper, we take advantage of recent developments on abstractions for timed automata, and propose an algorithm allowing for symbolic analysis of all weighted timed automata, without requiring bounded clocks.

1 Introduction

Timed automata [AD94] have been introduced in the early 1990s as a powerful model to reason about (the correctness of) real-time computerized systems. Timed automata extend finite-state automata with several clocks, which can be used to enforce timing constraints between various events in the system. They provide a convenient formalism and enjoy reasonably-efficient algorithms (e.g. reachability can be decided using polynomial space), which explains the enormous interest that they raised in the community of formal verification.

Hybrid automata [ACHH93] can be viewed as an extension of timed automata, involving hybrid variables: those variables can be used to measure other quantities than time (e.g. temperature, energy consumption,...). Their evolution may follow differential equations, depending on the state of the system. Those variables unfortunately make the reachability problem undecidable [HKPV98], even in the restricted case of stopwatches (i.e., clocks that can be stopped and restarted).

Weighted (or priced) timed automata [ALP01,BFH+01] have been proposed in the early 2000s as an intermediary model for modelling resource-consumption

This work was partly supported by ERC project EQualIS (FP7-308087) and FET project Cassting (FP7-601148).

S. Chaudhuri and A. Farzan (Eds.): CAV 2016, Part I, LNCS 9779, pp. 513–530, 2016.
DOI: 10.1007/978-3-319-41528-4_28

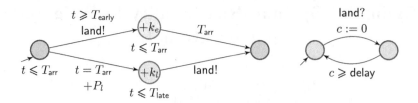

Fig. 1. A (simplified) model of the Aircraft Landing System [LBB+01]: aircrafts (left) have an optimal landing time T_{arr} within a possible landing interval $[T_{early}, T_{late}]$. The aircraft can speed up (which incurs some extra cost, modelled by k_e) to land earlier than T_{arr}, or can delay landing (which also entails some penalties, modelled by P_l and k_l). Some delay has to occur between consecutive landings on the same runway, because of wake turbulence; this is taken into account by the model of the runways (right).

or -allocation problems in real-time systems (*e.g.* optimal scheduling [BLR05]). Figure 1 displays an example of a weighted timed automaton, modelling aircrafts (left) that have to land on runways (right). In (single-variable) weighted timed automata, each location carries an integer, which is the rate by which the hybrid variable (called *cost* variable hereafter) increases when time elapses in that location. Edges may also carry a value, indicating how much the cost increases when crossing this edge. Notice that, as opposed to (linear) hybrid systems, the constraints on edges (a.k.a. *guards*) only involve clock variables: the extra quantitative information measured by the *cost* is just an observer of the system, and it does not interfere with the behaviors of the system.

Optimal cost for reaching a target, and associated almost-optimal schedules, can be computed in weighted timed automata [ALP01, BFH+01, BBBR07]. The proofs of these results rely on region-based algorithms (either priced regions [BFH+01], or corner-point refinements [ALP01, BBBR07]). Similarly to standard regions for timed automaton [AD94], such refinements of regions are not adapted to a real implementation. A symbolic approach based on priced zones has been proposed in [LBB+01], and later improved in [RLS06]. Zones are a standard symbolic representation for the analysis of timed-automata [BY03, Bou04], and priced zones extend zones with cost functions recording, for each state of the zone, the optimal cost to reach that state. A forward computation in a weighted timed automaton can be performed using priced zones [LBB+01]: it is based on a single-step Post-operation on priced zones, and on a basic inclusion test between priced zones (inclusion of zones, and point-to-point comparison of the cost function on the smallest zone). The algorithmics has been improved in [RLS06], and termination and correctness of the forward computation is obtained for weighted timed automata *in which all clocks are bounded*. Bounding clocks of a weighted timed automaton can always be achieved (while preserving the cost), but it may increase the size of the model. We believe that a better solution is possible: for timed automata and zones, a lot of efforts have been put into the development of sound abstractions adapted to the forward exploration of timed automata, ensuring termination of the model-checking algorithms without bounding clocks [BY03, BBFL03, BBLP06, HKSW11, HSW12].

In this paper, we build on [LBB+01, RLS06], and extend the symbolic algorithm to general weighted timed automata, without artificially bounding the clocks of the model. The keypoint of our algorithm is an inclusion test between *abstractions* of priced zones, computable from the (non abstracted) priced zones themselves. It can be seen as a priced counterpart of a recently-developed inclusion test over standard zones [HSW12]: it compares abstractions of zones without explicitly computing them, which has shown its efficiency for the analysis of timed automata. We prove that the forward-exploration algorithm using priced zones with this inclusion test indeed computes the optimal cost, and that it terminates. We also propose an algorithm to effectively decide inclusion of priced zones. We implemented our algorithm, and we compare it with that of [RLS06].

Related Work. The approach of [LBB+01, RLS06] is the closest related work. Our algorithm applies to a more general class of systems (unbounded clocks), and always computes fewer symbolic states on bounded models (see Remark 1); also, while the inclusion test of [RLS06] reduces to a mincost flow problem, for which efficient algorithms exist, we had to develop specific algorithms for checking our new inclusion relation. We develop this comparison with [RLS06] further in Sect. 6, including experimental results.

Our algorithm can be used in particular to compute best- and worst-case execution times. Several tools propose WCET analysis based on timed automata: TIMES [AFM+03] uses binary-search to evaluate WCET, while Uppaal [GELP10] and METAMOC [DOT+10] rely on the algorithm of [RLS06] mentioned above; in particular they require bounded clocks to ensure termination. A tentative workaround to this problem has been proposed in [ARF14], but we are uncertain about its correctness (as we explain with a counter-example in [BCM16]).

All proofs are available in the research report [BCM16].

2   Weighted Timed Automata

In this section we define the weighted (or priced) timed automaton model, that has been proposed in 2001 for representing resource consumption in real-time systems [ALP01, BFH+01].

We consider as time domain the set $\mathbb{R}_{\geqslant 0}$ of non-negative reals. We let X be a finite set of variables, called *clocks*. A *(clock) valuation* over X is a mapping $v : X \to \mathbb{R}_{\geqslant 0}$ that assigns to each clock a time value. The set of all valuations over X is denoted $\mathbb{R}_{\geqslant 0}^{X}$. Let $t \in \mathbb{R}_{\geqslant 0}$, the valuation $v + t$ is defined by $(v + t)(x) = v(x) + t$ for every $x \in X$. For $Y \subseteq X$, we denote by $[Y \leftarrow 0]v$ the valuation assigning 0 (respectively $v(x)$) to every $x \in Y$ (respectively $x \in X \setminus Y$). We write $\mathbf{0}_X$ for the valuation which assigns 0 to every clock $x \in X$.

The set of *clock constraints* over X, denoted $\mathcal{C}(X)$, is defined by the grammar $g ::= x \sim c \mid g \wedge g$, where $x \in X$ is a clock, $c \in \mathbb{N}$, and $\sim \in \{<, \leqslant, =, \geqslant, >\}$.

Clock constraints are evaluated over clock valuations, and the satisfaction relation, denoted $v \models g$, is defined inductively by $v \models (x \sim c)$ whenever $v(x) \sim c$, and $v \models g_1 \wedge g_2$ whenever $v \models g_1$ and $v \models g_2$.

Definition 1. *A* weighted timed automaton *is a tuple* $\mathcal{A} = (X, L, \ell_0,$ Goal, E, weight) *where* X *is a finite set of clocks,* L *is a finite set of locations,* $\ell_0 \in L$ *is the initial location,* Goal $\subseteq L$ *is a set of goal (or final) locations,* $E \subseteq L \times \mathcal{C}(X) \times 2^X \times L$ *is a finite set of edges (or transitions), and* weight $: L \cup E \to \mathbb{Z}$ *is a weight function which assigns a value to each location and to each transition.*

In the above definition, if we omit the weight function, we obtain the well-known model of *timed automata* [AD90, AD94]. The semantics of a weighted timed automaton is that of the underlying timed automaton, and the weight function provides quantitative information about the moves and executions of the system.

   The semantics of a timed automaton $\mathcal{A} = (X, L, \ell_0, \text{Goal}, E)$ is given as a timed transition system $\mathcal{T}_\mathcal{A} = (S, s_0, \to)$ where $S = L \times \mathbb{R}_{\geq 0}^X$ is the set of configurations (or states) of $\mathcal{A}$, $s_0 = (\ell_0, \mathbf{0}_X)$ is the initial configuration, and $\to$ contains two types of moves:

- delay moves: $(\ell, v) \xrightarrow{t} (\ell, v + t)$ if $t \in \mathbb{R}_{\geq 0}$;
- discrete moves: $(\ell, v) \xrightarrow{e} (\ell', v')$ if there exists an edge $e = (\ell, g, Y, \ell')$ in E such that $v \models g$, $v' = [Y \leftarrow 0]v$.

   A run ϱ in $\mathcal{A}$ is a finite sequence of moves in the transition system $\mathcal{T}_\mathcal{A}$, with a strict alternation of delay moves (though possibly 0-delay moves) and discrete moves. In the following, we may write a run $\varrho = s \xrightarrow{t_1} s_1' \xrightarrow{e_1} s_1 \xrightarrow{t_2} s_2' \xrightarrow{e_2} s_2 \ldots$ more compactly as $\varrho = s \xrightarrow{t_1, e_1} s_1 \xrightarrow{t_2, e_2} s_2 \cdots$. If ϱ ends in some $s = (\ell, v)$ with $\ell \in \text{Goal}$, we say that ϱ is *accepting*. For a configuration $s \in S$, we write Runs$(\mathcal{A}, s)$ the set of accepting runs that start in s.

   In the following we will assume timed automata are non-blocking, that is, from every reachable configuration s, there exist some delay t, some edge e and some configuration s' such that $s \xrightarrow{t, e} s'$ in $\mathcal{A}$.

   We can now give the semantics of a weighted timed automaton $\mathcal{A} = (X, L, \ell_0, \text{Goal}, E, \text{weight})$. The value weight$(\ell)$ given to location ℓ represents a cost rate, and delaying t time units in a location ℓ will then cost $t \cdot \text{weight}(\ell)$. The value weight$(e)$ given to edge e represents the cost of taking that edge. Formally, the cost of the two types of moves is defined as follows:

$$\begin{cases} \text{cost}\left((\ell, v) \xrightarrow{t} (\ell, v + t)\right) = t \cdot \text{weight}(\ell) \\ \text{cost}\left((\ell, v) \xrightarrow{e} (\ell', v')\right) = \text{weight}(e) \end{cases}$$

A *run* ϱ of a weighted timed automaton is a run of the underlying timed automaton. The cost of ϱ, denoted cost(ϱ), is the sum of the costs of all the simple moves along ϱ.

Example 1. We consider the weighted timed automaton $\mathcal{A}$ depicted in Fig. 2 (left). When a weight is non-null, we add a corresponding decoration to the location or to the transition. A possible run in $\mathcal{A}$ is:

$$\varrho = (\ell_0, 0) \xrightarrow{0.1} (\ell_0, 0.1) \xrightarrow{e_1} (\ell_1, 0.1) \xrightarrow{e_3} (\ell_3, 0.1) \xrightarrow{1.9} (\ell_3, 2) \xrightarrow{e_5} (\odot, 2)$$

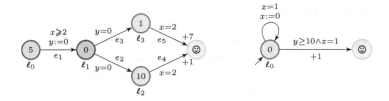

Fig. 2. Examples of weighted timed automata

The cost of ϱ is $\mathsf{cost}(\varrho) = 5 \cdot 0.1 + 1 \cdot 1.9 + 7 = 9.4$ (the cost per time unit is 5 in ℓ_0, 1 in ℓ_3, and the cost of transition e_5 is 7).

The Optimal-Reachability Problem

For this model we are interested in the optimal-reachability problem, and in the synthesis of almost-optimal schedules. Given a weighted timed automaton $\mathcal{A} = (X, L, \ell_0, \mathsf{Goal}, E, \mathsf{weight})$, the optimal cost from $s = (\ell, v)$ is defined as:

$$Optcost_{\mathcal{A}}(s) = \inf_{\varrho \in \mathsf{Runs}(\mathcal{A}, s)} \mathsf{cost}(\varrho)$$

If $\epsilon > 0$, a run $\varrho \in \mathsf{Runs}(\mathcal{A}, s)$ is ϵ-*optimal* whenever $\mathsf{cost}(\varrho) \leq Optcost_{\mathcal{A}}(s) + \epsilon$.

We are interested in $Optcost_{\mathcal{A}}(s_0)$, simply written as $Optcost_{\mathcal{A}}$, when s_0 is the initial configuration of $\mathcal{A}$. It is known that $Optcost_{\mathcal{A}}$ can be computed in polynomial space [ALP01, BFH+01, BBBR07], and that almost-optimal schedules (that is, for every $\epsilon > 0$, ϵ-optimal schedules) can also be computed.

The solutions developed in the aforementioned papers are based on refinements of regions, and a symbolic approach has been proposed in [LBB+01, RLS06], which extends standard zones with cost functions: this algorithm computes the optimal cost in weighted timed automata with nonnegative weights, assuming the underlying timed automata are *bounded*, that is, there is a constant M such that no clock can go above M. This is without loss of generality w.r.t. optimal cost, since any weighted timed automaton can be transformed into a bounded weighted timed automaton with the same optimal cost; it may nevertheless increase the size of the model, and more importantly of the state-space which needs to be explored (it can be exponentially larger). We believe that a better solution is possible: for timed automata and zones, a lot of efforts have been put into the development of sound abstractions adapted to the forward exploration of timed automata, ensuring termination of the model-checking algorithm without bounding clocks [BY03, BBFL03, BBLP06, HKSW11, HSW12].

Building on [LBB+01, RLS06], we extend the symbolic algorithm to general weighted timed automata, without assuming bounded clocks. The keypoint of our algorithm is an *abstract* inclusion test between priced zones. It can be seen as a priced counterpart of a recently-developed abstract inclusion test over standard zones [HSW12]; this test compares abstractions of zones without explicitly computing them, and has shown its efficiency for the analysis of timed automata. We prove that the symbolic algorithm using priced zones and this inclusion test indeed computes the optimal cost, and that it terminates.

3   Symbolic Algorithm

In this section we briefly recall the approach of [LBB+01,RLS06], and explain how we extend it to the general model, explaining which extra operation is required. The rest of the paper is devoted to proving correctness, effectiveness and termination of our algorithm.

3.1   The Symbolic Representation: priced Zones

Let X be a finite set of clocks. A *zone* is a set of valuations defined by a generalized constraint over clocks, given by the grammar $\gamma ::= x \sim c \mid x - y \sim c \mid \gamma \wedge \gamma$, where $x, y \in X$ are clocks, $c \in \mathbb{Z}$, and $\sim \in \{<, \leqslant, =, \geqslant, >\}$. Zones and their representation using Difference Bound Matrices (DBMs in short) are the standard symbolic data structure used in tools implementing timed systems [BY03,Bou04].

To deal with weighted timed automata, zones have been extended to priced zones in [LBB+01]. A *priced zone* is a pair $\mathcal{Z} = (Z, \zeta)$ where Z is a zone, and $\zeta \colon \mathbb{R}_{\geqslant 0}^X \to \mathbb{R}$ is an affine function. In a symbolic state $(\ell, \mathcal{Z})$, the cost function ζ is meant to represent the optimal cost so far (that is, $\zeta(v)$ is the optimal cost so far for reaching configuration (ℓ, v)). In [LBB+01], it is shown how one can simply represent priced zones, and how these can be used in a forward-exploration algorithm. The algorithm is shown as Algorithm 1, and we parametrize it by an inclusion test $\preceq$ between priced zones.

Let $\mathcal{A} = (X, L, \ell_0, \mathsf{Goal}, E, \mathsf{weight})$ be a weighted timed automaton. The algorithm makes a forward exploration of $\mathcal{A}$ from $(\ell_0, \mathcal{Z}_0)$ with $\mathcal{Z}_0 = (Z_0, \zeta_0)$, where Z_0 is the initial zone defined by $\bigwedge_{x \in X} x = 0$ and ζ_0 is identically 0 everywhere. Then, symbolic successors are iteratively computed, and when the target location is reached, the minimal cost given by the priced zone is computed (for a priced zone $\mathcal{Z} = (Z, \zeta)$, we note $infCost(\mathcal{Z}) = \inf_{v \in Z} \zeta(v)$), and compared to the current optimal value (variable COST). An inclusion test between priced zones

---

Algorithm 1. Symbolic algorithm for optimal cost, with inclusion test $\preceq$

---

1   COST $\leftarrow \infty$
2   PASSED $\leftarrow \emptyset$
3   WAITING $\leftarrow \{(\ell_0, \mathcal{Z}_0)\}$
4   **while** WAITING $\neq \emptyset$ **do**
5   $\quad$ select $(\ell, \mathcal{Z})$ from WAITING
6   $\quad$ **if** $\ell \in \mathsf{Goal}$ *and* $infCost(\mathcal{Z}) <$ COST **then**
7   $\quad\quad$ COST $\leftarrow infCost(\mathcal{Z})$

8   $\quad$ **if** *for all* $(\ell, \mathcal{Z}') \in$ PASSED, $\mathcal{Z} \npreceq \mathcal{Z}'$ **then**
9   $\quad\quad$ add $(\ell, \mathcal{Z})$ to PASSED
10 $\quad\quad$ add $\mathsf{Post}(\ell, \mathcal{Z})$ to WAITING

11 **return** COST

---

is performed, which allows to stop the exploration from $(\ell, \mathcal{Z})$ when $\mathcal{Z} \preceq \mathcal{Z}'$ and $(\ell, \mathcal{Z}')$ already appears in the set of symbolic states that have already been explored. In [RLS06], the algorithm uses the following inclusion test $\in$, which refines the inclusion test of [LBB+01]: inclusion $\mathcal{Z} \in \mathcal{Z}'$ holds whenever $Z \subseteq Z'$ and $\zeta(v) \geq \zeta'(v')$ for every $v \in Z$. As shown in [RLS06], this algorithm computes the optimal cost in $\mathcal{A}$, provided it terminates, and this always happens when the weights in $\mathcal{A}$ are nonnegative, and when all clocks in $\mathcal{A}$ are bounded.

In the present paper, we define a refined inclusion test $\sqsubseteq$ between priced zones, which will enforce termination of Algorithm 1 even when clocks are not upper-bounded, and, to some extent, when costs are negative.

We now give some definitions which will allow to state the correctness of the algorithm. Given a timed automaton $\mathcal{A}$, a location ℓ and a priced zone $\mathcal{Z} = (Z, \zeta)$, we say that $(\ell, \mathcal{Z})$ is *realized* in $\mathcal{A}$ whenever for every valuation $v \in Z$, and for every $\epsilon > 0$, there exists a run ϱ from the initial state $(\ell_0, \mathbf{0}_X)$ to (ℓ, v), such that $\zeta(v) \leqslant \mathrm{cost}(\varrho) \leq \zeta(v) + \epsilon$. For a location ℓ, a priced zone $\mathcal{Z} = (Z, \zeta)$ and a run ϱ starting in a configuration s, we say that ϱ *ends in* $(\ell, \mathcal{Z})$ if ϱ leads from s to a configuration (ℓ, v) with $v \in Z$ and $\mathrm{cost}(\varrho) \geqslant \zeta(v)$. The post operation Post on priced zones used in Algorithm 1 is described in [LBB+01]. Its computation is effective (see [LBB+01]), and is such that (see [RLS06]):

- every $(\ell, \mathcal{Z}) \in \mathsf{Post}^*(\ell_0, \mathcal{Z}_0)$ is realized in $\mathcal{A}$, where Post^* denotes the iteration of the Post operator;
- for every run ϱ from a configuration s to a configuration s', and every mixed move τ from s', if ϱ ends in $(\ell, \mathcal{Z})$, then $\varrho\tau$ ends in an element of $\mathsf{Post}(\ell, \mathcal{Z})$.
- for every run ϱ from $(\ell_0, \mathbf{0}_X)$, there exists $(\ell, \mathcal{Z}) \in \mathsf{Post}^*(\ell_0, \mathcal{Z}_0)$ such that ϱ ends in $(\ell, \mathcal{Z})$ (this is a consequence of the previous property).

The purpose of this work is to propose an inclusion test $\sqsubseteq$ such that the following three properties are satisfied:

1. *(Termination)* Algorithm 1 with inclusion test $\sqsubseteq$ terminates;
2. *(Soudness w.r.t. optimal reachability)* Algorithm 1 with inclusion test $\sqsubseteq$ computes the optimal cost for reaching Goal;
3. *(Effectiveness)* There is an algorithm deciding $\sqsubseteq$ on priced zones.

We now present our inclusion test, and show its soundness for optimal reachability. We then turn to effectiveness (Sect. 4), and then to termination (Sect. 5).

3.2 The Inclusion Test

Our inclusion test is inspired by the inclusion test on (pure) zones proposed in [HSW12].[1] We start by recalling an equivalence relation on valuations. We assume a function $M \colon X \mapsto \mathbb{N} \cup \{-\infty\}$ such that $M(x)$ is larger than any constant against which clock x is compared to in the (weighted) timed automata

---

[1] Contrary to pure reachability, we cannot use the preorder $\preceq_{LU}$ (which distinguishes between lower-bounded constraints and upper-bounded constraints) [BBLP06], since it does not preserve optimal cost (not even optimal time).

under consideration. Let v and v' be two valuations in $\mathbb{R}_{\geq 0}^{X}$. Then, $v \equiv_M v'$ iff for every clock $x \in X$, either $v(x) = v'(x)$, or $v(x) > M(x)$ and $v'(x) > M(x)$. We note $[v]_M$ the equivalence class of v under $\equiv_M$.

Lemma 2. *If $v \equiv_M v'$, then, for any $\ell \in L$, $Optcost_\mathcal{A}(\ell, v) = Optcost_\mathcal{A}(\ell, v')$.*

We now define our inclusion test for two priced zones $\mathcal{Z} = (Z, \zeta)$ and $\mathcal{Z}' = (Z', \zeta')$; it is parameterized by M, which gives upper bounds on clocks:

$$\mathcal{Z} \sqsubseteq_M \mathcal{Z}' \text{ iff } \forall v \in Z, \ \forall \epsilon > 0, \ \exists v' \in Z' \text{ s.t. } v \equiv_M v' \text{ and } \zeta'(v') \leq \zeta(v) + \epsilon.$$

Theorem 3. *When using $\sqsubseteq_M$, provided Algorithm 1 terminates, it is sound w.r.t. optimal reachability (the returned cost is the optimal one).*

Remark 1. Remember that the inclusion test $\Subset$ of [RLS06] requires $Z \subseteq Z'$ and, for every $v \in Z$, $\zeta(v) \geq \zeta'(v)$. It is easily seen that $\mathcal{Z} \Subset \mathcal{Z}'$ implies $\mathcal{Z} \sqsubseteq_M \mathcal{Z}'$ for any M; hence the branches are always stopped earlier in our algorithm (which uses $\sqsubseteq_M$) than in the original algorithm of [RLS06] (which uses $\Subset$). Moreover, $\Subset$ does not ensure termination of the forward exploration when clocks are not bounded: on the automaton of Fig. 2 (right), where the optimal time to reach the right state is 10, the forward algorithm successively computes zones $x \leq 1 \wedge n \leq y - x \leq n + 1$, for every integer n. Any two such zones are always incomparable (for $\Subset$).

4   Effective Inclusion Check

In this section we show that we can effectively check the inclusion test $\sqsubseteq_M$ of priced zones. For the rest of this section, we fix two priced zones $\mathcal{Z} = (Z, \zeta)$ and $\mathcal{Z}' = (Z', \zeta')$, and a function M. To improve readability, we write $\equiv$ and $\sqsubseteq$ in place of $\equiv_M$ and $\sqsubseteq_M$.

4.1   Formulation of the Optimization Problem

We first express the inclusion of the two priced zones as an optimization problem.

Lemma 4. $\mathcal{Z} \sqsubseteq \mathcal{Z}' \iff \sup_{v \in Z} \inf_{\substack{v' \in Z' \\ v' \equiv v}} \zeta'(v') - \zeta(v) \leqslant 0.$

Note that $\mathcal{Z} \sqsubseteq \mathcal{Z}'$ already requires some relation between zones Z and Z': indeed, for the above inclusion to hold, it should be the case that for every $v \in Z$, there exists some $v' \in Z'$ such that $v \equiv v'$. Interestingly, this corresponds to the test on (unpriced) zones developed in [HSW12] (with $L = U = M$); this can be done efficiently (in time quadratic in the number of clocks) as a preliminary test [HSW12, Theorem 34].

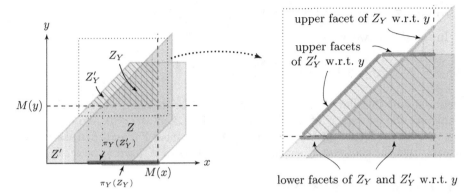

Fig. 3. Two-dimensional zones Z and Z', and sub-zones Z_Y and Z'_Y for $Y = \{x\}$.

Fig. 4. Simple facets of Z_Y and Z'_Y w.r.t. clock y.

Remark 2. The constraint $v \equiv v'$ is not convex, and we have a bi-level optimization problem to solve. Hence common techniques for convex optimization, such as dualization [BV04], do not directly apply to the above problem. Still, it is possible to transform it into finitely many so-called *generalized semi-infinite optimization problems* (GSIPs) [RS01] (using Z_Y's as defined later in this section). As far as we know, such problems do not have dedicated efficient algorithmic solutions. We thus propose a more direct solution, that benefits from the specific structure of our problem (see for instance Sect. 4.3); it provides a feasible way to solve our optimization problems, hence to decide $\sqsubseteq$ on priced zones.

In order to compute the above optima, we transform our problem into a finite number of optimization problems that are easier to solve. Let $Y \subseteq X$. A zone Z is M-bounded on Y if, for every $v \in Z$, $\{x \mid v(x) \leqslant M(x)\} = Y$. We note Z_Y the restriction of Z to its M-bounded-on-Y component: $Z_Y = Z \cap \bigcap_{x \in Y}(x \leqslant M(x)) \cap \bigcap_{x \notin Y}(x > M(x))$. Note that Z_Y may be empty, and that the family $(Z_Y)_{Y \subseteq X}$ forms a partition of Z. We also define $\mathcal{Z}_Y$ as the priced zone (Z_Y, ζ). We define the natural projection $\pi_Y : \mathbb{R}^X_{\geq 0} \to \mathbb{R}^Y_{\geq 0}$, which associates with $v \in \mathbb{R}^X_{\geq 0}$ the valuation $v' \in \mathbb{R}^Y_{\geq 0}$ that coincides with v on Y.

Lemma 5. *The following two properties are equivalent:*

(i) for every $v \in Z$, there is $v' \in Z'$ such that $v' \equiv v$
(ii) for every $Y \subseteq X$, $\pi_Y(Z_Y) \subseteq \pi_Y(Z'_Y)$.

This allows to transform the initial optimization problem into finitely many optimization problems.

Lemma 6.

$$\sup_{\substack{v \in Z \ v' \in Z' \\ v' \equiv v}} \inf \zeta'(v') - \zeta(v) = \max_{Y \subseteq X} \sup_{\substack{v \in Z_Y \ v' \in Z'_Y \\ v' \equiv v}} \inf \zeta'(v') - \zeta(v).$$

Corollary 7. $\mathcal{Z} \sqsubseteq \mathcal{Z}'$ *iff for every* $Y \subseteq X$, $\mathcal{Z}_Y \sqsubseteq \mathcal{Z}'_Y$

In the sequel, we write

$$S(\mathcal{Z}, \mathcal{Z}', Y) = \sup_{v \in Z_Y} \inf_{\substack{v' \in Z'_Y \\ v' \equiv v}} \zeta'(v') - \zeta(v)$$

Lemma 4 and Corollary 7 suggest an algorithm for deciding whether $\mathcal{Z} \sqsubseteq \mathcal{Z}'$: enumerate the subsets Y of X, and prove that $S(\mathcal{Z}, \mathcal{Z}', Y) \le 0$. We now show how to solve the latter optimization problem (for a fixed Y), and then show how we can drive the choice of Y so that not all subsets of X have to be analyzed.

4.2   Computing $S(\mathcal{Z}, \mathcal{Z}', Y)$

We show the following main result to compute $S(\mathcal{Z}, \mathcal{Z}', Y)$, which produces a simpler optimization problem, allowing to decide the inclusion of two priced zones, on parts where cost functions are lower-bounded.

Theorem 8. *Let* $\mathcal{Z} = (Z, \zeta)$ *and* $\mathcal{Z}' = (Z', \zeta')$ *be two non-empty priced zones, and let* $Y \subseteq X$ *be such that* $\pi_Y(Z_Y) \subseteq \pi_Y(Z'_Y)$ *and* ζ *and* ζ' *are lower-bounded on* Z_Y *and* Z'_Y *respectively. Then we can compute finite sets* $\mathcal{K}_Y$ *and* $\mathcal{K}'_Y$ *of zones over* Y, *and affine functions* ζ_F *and* $\zeta'_{F'}$ *for every* $F \in \mathcal{K}_Y$ *and* $F' \in \mathcal{K}'_Y$ *s.t.:*

$$S(\mathcal{Z}, \mathcal{Z}', Y) = \max_{F \in \mathcal{K}_Y} \max_{F' \in \mathcal{K}'_Y} \sup_{u \in F \cap F'} \zeta'_{F'}(u) - \zeta_F(u). \tag{1}$$

The idea behind this result is to first rewrite $S(\mathcal{Z}, \mathcal{Z}', Y)$ into:

$$S(\mathcal{Z}, \mathcal{Z}', Y) = \sup_{u \in \pi_Y(Z_Y)} \left[\left(\inf_{\substack{v' \in Z'_Y \\ \pi_Y(v') = u}} \zeta'(v') \right) - \left(\inf_{\substack{v \in Z_Y \\ \pi_Y(v) = u}} \zeta(v) \right) \right]$$

which decouples the dependency of v' on v. The algorithm then uses the notion of facets (introduced in [LBB+01]), which corresponds to the boundary of the zone w.r.t. a clock (if W is the zone, a facet of W w.r.t. x is $\overline{W} \cap (x = n)$ or $\overline{W} \cap (x - y = m)$ whenever $x \bowtie n$ or $x - y \bowtie m$ is a constraint defining W). Given a clock $x \in X \setminus Y$, we consider the facets of Z_Y w.r.t. x that minimize, for any $w \in \pi_{X \setminus \{x\}}(Z_Y)$, the function $v \mapsto \zeta(v)$ when $\pi_{X \setminus \{x\}}(v) = w$. The restriction of ζ on such a facet is a new affine function, which we can compute. We then iterate the process for all clocks in $X \setminus Y$. We do the same for ζ'. This yields the result claimed above: sets $\mathcal{K}_Y$ and $\mathcal{K}'_Y$ are sets of projections of facets over Y.

Facets are zones, and so are their projections on Y and intersections thereof. Additionally, all functions ζ_F and $\zeta'_{F'}$ are affine; hence the supremum in Eq. (1) is reached at some vertex u_0 of zone $F \cap F'$, for some facets F and F'. By construction of ζ_F and $\zeta'_{F'}$, we get

$$S(\mathcal{Z}, \mathcal{Z}', Y) = \inf_{\substack{v' \in Z'_Y \\ \pi(v') = u_0}} \zeta'(v') - \inf_{\substack{v \in Z_Y \\ \pi(v) = u_0}} \zeta(v)$$

In particular, u_0 has integral coordinates. We end up with the following result, which will be useful for proving the termination of Algorithm 1:

Corollary 9. *Let* $\mathcal{Z} = (Z, \zeta)$ *and* $\mathcal{Z}' = (Z', \zeta')$ *be two non-empty priced zones, and let* $Y \subseteq X$ *be such that* $\pi_Y(Z_Y) \subseteq \pi_Y(Z'_Y)$ *and* ζ *and* ζ' *are lower-bounded on* Z_Y *and* Z'_Y *respectively. Then the following holds:*

$$S(\mathcal{Z}, \mathcal{Z}', Y) = \max_{\substack{u_0 \in \pi_Y(\overline{Z_Y}) \\ u_0 \in \mathbb{N}^Y}} \left[\min_{\substack{v' \in Z'_Y \\ v' \equiv u_0}} \zeta'(v') - \min_{\substack{v \in Z_Y \\ v \equiv u_0}} \zeta(v) \right]$$

The requirement for lower-bounded priced zones in Theorem 8 is crucial in the proof. But the case when this requirement is not met can easily be handled separately, so that $\sqsubseteq$ can always be effectively decided:

Lemma 10. *Let* $\mathcal{Z} = (Z, \zeta)$ *and* $\mathcal{Z}' = (Z', \zeta')$ *be two non-empty priced zones.*

- *If* ζ *is not lower-bounded on* Z *but* ζ' *is lower-bounded on* Z', *then* $\mathcal{Z} \not\sqsubseteq \mathcal{Z}'$.
- *Let* $Y \subseteq X$ *such that* $\pi_Y(Z_Y) \subseteq \pi_Y(Z'_Y)$. *If* ζ' *is not lower-bounded on* Z'_Y, *then* $\mathcal{Z}_Y \sqsubseteq \mathcal{Z}'_Y$.

Corollary 11. *Let* $\mathcal{Z} = (Z, \zeta)$ *and* $\mathcal{Z}' = (Z', \zeta')$ *be two priced zones. Then we can effectively decide whether* $\mathcal{Z} \sqsubseteq \mathcal{Z}'$.

4.3   Finding the Right Y

Applying Lemma 6, the main obstacle to efficiently decide $\sqsubseteq_M$ is to find the appropriate Z_Y in which the sought supremum is reached. Unless good arguments can be found to guide the search towards the best choice for Y, an exhaustive enumeration of all the Y's will be required.

Example 2. We consider the zone Z defined by the constraints $x \geqslant 0$, $y \geqslant 1$, $x \leqslant y$ and $y \leqslant x + 2$. We fix $M(x) = 2$ and $M(y) = 3$. We then consider $Z' = Z$. The zone Z is equipped with a constant cost function ζ. In Fig. 5(a), Z' is attached $\zeta'(x, y) = x + y$, and the expression of the function $f(v) = \inf_{v' \in Z', \, v' \equiv_M v} \zeta'(v')$ is given in each Z_Y, for $Y \subseteq X$. It is then easy to see that the supremum of f is reached at the point $(2, 3)$, in the middle of the zone. In Fig. 5(b), we take $\zeta'(x, y) = 2x - y$, and the expression of the function $f(v) = \inf_{v' \in Z'. \, v' \equiv_M v} \zeta'(v')$ is given in each Z_Y. The supremum of f is then reached at the point $(2, 2)$, on the border, but not at a corner of the zone. The latter example also shows that f is not continuous on the whole zone Z.

Nevertheless, in many cases, we will be able to guide the search of the Z_Y where the sought optimal is to be found. The following development focuses on the zone, not on the cost function. Given a zone Z, we define a preorder $\preceq$ on the clocks, such that if $Z_Y \neq \emptyset$, then Y is downward-closed for $\preceq$. In other words, whenever $x \preceq y$, $y \in Y$ and $Z_Y \neq \emptyset$, then $x \in Y$. The knowledge of $\preceq$ can be a precious help to guide the enumeration of non-empty Z_Y's. Indeed, if $Z_Y \neq \emptyset$, Y is downward-closed for $\preceq$, and candidates for Y are thus found by enumerating the antichains of $\preceq$. In particular, if $\preceq$ is total, then there are at most $|X| + 1$ sets Y such that $Z_Y \neq \emptyset$.

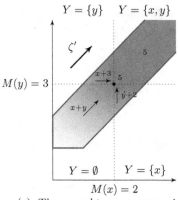
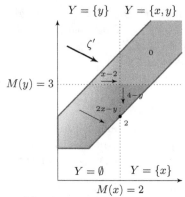

(a) The sought supremum is reached in the middle of the zone.

(b) The sought supremum is reached on the border of the zone.

Fig. 5. The supremum may lie in the middle of zones or facets

To be concrete, let $X_{\leq M}$ and $X_{>M}$ be the (disjoint) sets of clocks x such that $Z \subseteq (x \leq M(x))$ and $Z \subseteq (x > M(x))$, respectively. We define the relation $\preceq_Z$ as the least relation satisfying the following conditions:

- for each $x \in X_{\leq M}$, for each $y \in X$, $x \preceq_Z y$;
- for each $y \in X_{>M}$, for each $x \in X$, $x \preceq_Z y$;
- for all $x, y \in X \setminus (X_{\leq M} \cup X_{>M})$, $Z \subseteq (x - y \leq M(x) - M(y))$ implies $x \preceq_Z y$.

Note that, since $\preceq_Z$ is the least relation satisfying the above conditions, we have $x \not\preceq_Z y$ when (a) $x \in X_{>M}$ and $y \in X \setminus X_{>M}$, and when (b) $x \in X \setminus X_{\leq M}$ and $y \in X_{\leq M}$. It is then not difficult to show that $\preceq_Z$ is a preorder such that: $y \in X_{\leq M}$ and $x \preceq_Z y$ implies $x \in X_{\leq M}$, and $x \in X_{>M}$ and $x \preceq_Z y$ implies $y \in X_{>M}$.

Lemma 12. *Let $Y \subseteq X$ such that $Z_Y \neq \emptyset$. Then Y is downward-closed for $\preceq_Z$.*

The preorder $\preceq_Z$ can be computed in polynomial time, since it only requires to check emptiness of zones, which can be done in time polynomial in $|X|$ (cubic in $|X|$ with DBMs for instance).

We recall that, if Z is a zone generated in a timed automaton where only resets of clocks to 0 are allowed, for any pair of clocks x, y, it cannot be the case that Z crosses the diagonal hyperplane of equation $x = y$.

Proposition 13. *If Z is generated by a timed automaton, and all clocks have the same bound M, then $\preceq_Z$ is total.*

Proof. Let x and y be two clocks. Since Z is generated by a timed automaton, it is contained either in the half-space of equation $[x \leq y]$, or in the one of equation $[x \geq y]$. By definition of $\preceq_Z$, and since $M(x) = M(y)$, the former entails $x \preceq_Z y$, and the latter $y \preceq_Z x$. Any two clocks are thus always comparable, and $\preceq_Z$ is therefore total. ∎

Under the assumptions of Proposition 13, there are polynomially many subsets $Y \subseteq X$ to try. Note that these assumptions are easily realized by taking $\widetilde{M} = \max_{x \in X} M(x)$ as the unique maximal constant for all the clocks. Formally, $\sqsubseteq_{\widetilde{M}}$ is an under-approximation of the exact version of $\sqsubseteq_M$. This approximation does not hinder correctness, and illustrate the trade-off between the complexity of the inclusion procedure and the number of priced zones that will be explored.

5 Termination of the Computation

In this section we prove termination of our algorithm, by exhibiting an appropriate well-quasi-order. We fix a timed automaton $\mathcal{A}$ and a maximal-constant function M (for every clock $x \in X$, the integer $M(x)$ is larger than any constant with which clock x is compared in $\mathcal{A}$).

Proposition 14. $\sqsubseteq$ *is a preorder (or quasi-ordering).*

We now consider the "converse" preorder $\sqsupseteq$, defined over priced zones by $\mathcal{Z}' \sqsupseteq \mathcal{Z}$ iff $\mathcal{Z} \sqsubseteq \mathcal{Z}'$. We show that $\sqsupseteq$ is a *well quasi-ordering (wqo)*. Thus the relation $\sqsupseteq$ has no infinite antichain, which entails termination of Algorithm 1.

We now gather the results to exhibit a sufficient condition for $\sqsupseteq$ to be a wqo.

Theorem 15. *For every $\mu \in \mathbb{Z}$, $\sqsupseteq$ is a well-quasi-order on (non-empty) priced zones whose cost functions are either not lower-bounded, or lower-bounded by μ.*

Corollary 16. *Algorithm 1 terminates on weighted timed automata, which generate priced zones with a uniform lower bound on the cost functions,*

We can argue that infinite antichains for $\sqsupseteq$ generated by a forward exploration of $\mathcal{A}$ actually corresponds to infinite paths in $\mathcal{A}$ with cost $-\infty$. While this condition can be decided (using the corner-point abstraction of [BBL08]), we do not want to check this as a preliminary step, since this is as complex as computing the optimal cost. Furthermore, symbolically, this would amount to finding a cycle of symbolic states which is both ω-iterable [JR11, DHS+14] and cost-divergent; this is a non-trivial problem. We can nevertheless give simple syntactic conditions for the condition to hold: this is the case of weighted timed automata with non-negative weights (this is the class considered in [LBB+01, RLS06]); let T_ℓ be the minimum (resp. maximum) delay that can be delayed in ℓ if location ℓ has positive (resp. negative) cost: if along any cycle of the weighted timed automaton, the sum of the discrete weights and of each T_ℓ.weight(ℓ) is nonnegative, then the above condition will be satisfied; this last condition encompasses all the acyclic weighted timed automata, like all scheduling problems [BLR05].

6 Experimental Results

We have implemented a prototype, TiAMo, to test our new inclusion test. It is based on the DBM library of Uppaal (in C++),[2] which features the inclusion

---

[2] http://people.cs.aau.dk/~adavid/UDBM/.

test of [RLS06]. We added our inclusion test (also in C++). This core is then wrapped in OCaml code, in which the main algorithm is written. The source code is publicly available online: http://git.lsv.fr/colange/tiamo.

As we have seen, termination in presence of negative costs is not guaranteed. We thus limited our experiments to models with positive costs only.

TiAMo is able to prune the state space using the best cost so far. Concretely, it would not explore states whose cost exceeds the current optimal cost. This can dramatically reduce the state space to explore, but is sound only when all costs in the model are non-negative. On such models, the user can provide a hint, a known cost to TiAMo (obtained for example by a reachability analysis, or by other independent techniques) to be used to prune the model. Moreover, TiAMo reports, during the computation, the best known cost so far. Such values are upper bounds on the sought optimum, and may be interesting to get during long computations.

A direct comparison between TiAMo and Uppaal[3] (or Uppaal-CORA[4]) is difficult: the source code of Uppaal (and Uppaal-CORA) is not open, and it is often hard to know what is precisely implemented. For instance, on the unbounded automaton of Fig. 2, the algorithm described in [LBB+01, RLS06] does not terminate. Depending on the way it is queried (asking for the fastest trace, or with an inf query), Uppaal terminates or runs forever on this model.

In order to measure the impact of the inclusion test on the algorithm, we decided to compare the performance of TiAMo running one or the other inclusion test ($\in$ or $\sqsubseteq$). Our primary concern is to compare the number of (symbolic) states explored, and the number of inclusion tests performed.

We run our experiments with and without pruning activated. Deactivated pruning allows to measure the impact of the choice of the inclusion test itself. It is also more representative of the behavior that can be expected on models with negative costs, for which pruning is not sound.

The models. We briefly describe the models used in our experiments. The first two are case studies described on the web page of Uppaal-CORA.

The Aircraft Landing System (ALS) problem has been described in Fig. 1: it consists in scheduling landings of aircrafts arriving to an airport with several runways, subject to timing constraints. Early and late arrivals induce a cost, which is to be minimized globally. We use the original version form Uppaal-CORA, with two runways and 10 aircrafts. The model has 5 clocks (one global clock, plus two per runway) and 14, 000 discrete states.

In the Energy-optimal Task-graph Scheduling (ETS) problem, several processors having different speeds and powers are to be used to perform interdependent tasks. The aim is to optimize energy consumption for performing the given set of tasks within a certain delay. The model we used for our experiments is the one described in [BFLM11, Example 3]. It has 2 clocks (one per CPU) and 55 discrete states.

---

[3] http://www.uppaal.org/.

[4] http://people.cs.aau.dk/~adavid/cora/.

Table 1. Experimental results

			# Waiting	# Passed	# stored	# tests	# succ. tests	time (s.)
ASL	+P	⊑	11,820	4,785	9,324	3.7×10^{05}	13,676	0.3
		∈	32,322	13,036	26,555	2.9×10^{06}	32,263	0.7
	-P	⊑	1.7×10^{06}	1.5×10^{06}	6.9×10^{05}	8.1×10^{08}	1.2×10^{07}	312.7
		∈	TO	TO	TO	TO	TO	TO
ETS	+P	⊑	107	84	83	174	66	0.0
		∈	664	606	590	17,684	455	0.0
VRPTW	+P	⊑	6.0×10^{05}	4.8×10^{05}	5.6×10^{05}	6.2×10^{06}	1.7×10^{05}	11.3
		∈	1.5×10^{06}	1.3×10^{06}	1.4×10^{06}	9.1×10^{07}	7.0×10^{05}	27.5
	-P	⊑	1.3×10^{06}	1.3×10^{06}	1.3×10^{06}	2.5×10^{07}	7.0×10^{05}	23.9
		∈	5.8×10^{06}	5.8×10^{06}	5.4×10^{06}	1.1×10^{09}	1.9×10^{06}	111.2
unbound.	+P	⊑	14	13	14	135	3	0.0
		∈	TO	TO	TO	TO	TO	TO
	-P	⊑	14	14	14	135	3	0.0
		∈	TO	TO	TO	TO	TO	TO

In the Vehicle Routing Problem with Time Windows (VRPTW) problem, a fleet of vehicles with limited capacity is to be scheduled to deliver goods to customers. Deliveries should respect the customers preferred time windows. We use the version downloadable from the Uppaal-CORA website, with a few syntactical modifications to account for the limits of the parser of TiAMo. The cost function used in this example is a combination of the distance travelled by the vehicles, the time to achieve deliveries, and the demand satisfied on time. The model considers 3 vehicles and 7 customers, and has 4 clocks (one for each vehicle and a global clock) and about $150,000$ discrete states.

Finally, we also ran TiAMo on the model Fig. 2, to illustrate that ⊑ handles unbounded models. This model has two clocks and two discrete states.

Exploration Strategies. TiAMo implements several strategies to explore the symbolic state space. We retain here only the one called SBFS, a modification of BFS based on the observation that, if s subsumes s', the successors of s' are subsumed by successors of s. Successors of s are thus explored first, until all successors of s' in the Waiting list are subsumed. This is a very naive implementation of a strategy proposed in [HT15]. The strategy has two variants, depending on whether pruning is activated (+P) or not (−P). For the ETS problem, both yield very similar results, so we chose to only present +P.

Experimental Results. The results are summed up in Table 1. For each model, and for different combinations of inclusion test and exploration strategy, we indicate the number of symbolic states added to the Waiting list, added to the Passed list, as well as the number of tests (successful or not) that have been performed. We also indicate the maximal size of the list Passed; although not detailed in Algorithm 1, the tool ensures that Passed remains an antichain. This minimizes the number of inclusion tests. When a new element is added to the Passed list, all elements of Passed subsumed by the new one are removed, so that the size of Passed does not necessarily increase.

The mention "TO" means that the computation does within the time bound of 120 min. We observe that $\sqsubseteq$ always explores fewer states than $\Subset$, for any given exploration strategy. Though this was expected (recall Remark 1), we believe the reduction is impressive. It is significant even for small models (such as ETS). The case of ALS with no pruning shows that the higher complexity of $\sqsubseteq$ can be largely compensated by the reduction in the size of the state space to explore. On the model of Fig. 2, our inclusion $\sqsubseteq$ ensures termination, while $\Subset$ does not.

7 Conclusion

In this paper we have built over a symbolic approach to the computation of optimal cost in weighted timed automata [LBB+01, RLS06], by proposing an inclusion test between priced zones. Using that inclusion test, the forward symbolic exploration terminates and computes the optimal cost for all weighted timed automata, regardless whether clocks are bounded or not. The idea of this approach is based on recent works on pure timed automata [HSW12], where a clever inclusion test "replaces" any abstraction computation during the exploration.

We will pursue our work with extensive experimentations using our tool TiAMo. We will also look for more dedicated methods for specific application domains, like planning problems.

References

[ACHH93] Alur, R., Courcoubetis, C., Henzinger, T.A., Ho, P.-H.: Hybrid automata: an algorithmic approach to specification and verification of hybrid systems. In: Grossman, R.L., Nerode, A., Ravn, A.P., Rischel, H. (eds.) HS 1993. LNCS, vol. 736, pp. 209–229. Springer, Heidelberg (1993)

[AD90] Alur, R., Dill, D.L.: Automata for modeling real-time systems. In: Paterson, M.S. (ed.) ICALP 1990. LNCS, vol. 443, pp. 322–335. Springer, Heidelberg (1990)

[AD94] Alur, R., Dill, D.L.: A theory of timed automata. Theoret. Comput. Sci. **126**(2), 183–235 (1994)

[AFM+03] Amnell, T., Fersman, E., Mokrushin, L., Pettersson, P., Yi, W.: TIMES: a tool for schedulability analysis and code generation of real-time systems. In: Larsen, Kim Guldstrand, Niebert, Peter (eds.) FORMATS 2003. LNCS, vol. 2791, pp. 60–72. Springer, Heidelberg (2004)

[ALP01] Alur, R., La Torre, S., Pappas, G.J.: Optimal paths in weighted timed automata. In: Di Benedetto, M.D., Sangiovanni-Vincentelli, A.L. (eds.) HSCC 2001. LNCS, vol. 2034, pp. 49–62. Springer, Heidelberg (2001)

[ARF14] Al-Bataineh, O., Reynolds, M., French, T.: Finding best and worst case execution times of systems using difference-bound matrices. In: Legay, A., Bozga, M. (eds.) FORMATS 2014. LNCS, vol. 8711, pp. 38–52. Springer, Heidelberg (2014)

[BBBR07] Bouyer, P., Brihaye, T., Bruyère, V., Raskin, J.-F.: On the optimal reachability problem. Form. Methods Syst. Des. **31**(2), 135–175 (2007)

[BBFL03] Behrmann, G., Bouyer, P., Fleury, E., Larsen, K.G.: Static guard analysis in timed automata verification. In: Garavel, H., Hatcliff, J. (eds.) TACAS 2003. LNCS, vol. 2619, pp. 254–270. Springer, Heidelberg (2003)

[BBL08] Patricia, B., Brinksma, E., Larsen, K.G.: Optimal infinite scheduling for multi-priced timed automata. Form. Methods Syst. Des. **32**(1), 2–23 (2008)

[BBLP06] Behrmann, G., Bouyer, P., Larsen, K.G., Pelànek, R.: Zone based abstractions for timed automata exploiting lower and upper bounds. Int. J. Softw. Tools Technol. Transf. **8**(3), 204–215 (2006)

[BCM16] Bouyer, P., Colange, M., Markey, N.: Symbolic optimal reachability in weighted timed automata. Technical report abs/1602.00481, CoRR (2016). http://arxiv.org/abs/1602.00481

[BFH+01] Behrmann, G., Fehnker, A., Hune, T., Larsen, K.G., Pettersson, P., Romijn, J.M.T., Vaandrager, F.W.: Minimum-cost reachability for priced timed automata. In: Di Benedetto, M.D., Sangiovanni-Vincentelli, A.L. (eds.) HSCC 2001. LNCS, vol. 2034, pp. 147–161. Springer, Heidelberg (2001)

[BFLM11] Bouyer, P., Fahrenberg, U., Larsen, K.G., Markey, N.: Quantitative analysis of real-time systems using priced timed automata. Commun. ACM **54**(9), 78–87 (2011)

[BLR05] Behrmann, G., Larsen, K.G., Rasmussen, J.I.: Optimal scheduling using priced timed automata. ACM Sigmetrics Perform. Eval. Rev. **32**(4), 34–40 (2005)

[Bou04] Bouyer, P.: Forward analysis of updatable timed automata. Form. Methods Syst. Des. **24**(3), 281–320 (2004)

[BV04] Boyd, S., Vandenberghe, L.: Convex Optimization. Cambridge University Press, Cambridge (2004)

[BY03] Bengtsson, J.E., Yi, W.: On clock difference constraints and termination in reachability analysis of timed automata. In: Dong, J.S., Woodcock, J. (eds.) ICFEM 2003. LNCS, vol. 2885, pp. 491–503. Springer, Heidelberg (2003)

[DHS+14] Deshpande, A., Herbreteau, F., Srivathsan, B., Tran, T.-T., Walukiewicz, I.: Fast detection of cycles in timed automata. Technical report abs/1410.4509, CoRR (2014). http://arxiv.org/abs/1410.4509

[DOT+10] Dalsgaard, A.E., Chr, M., Olesen, M.T., Hansen, R.R., Larsen, K.G.: METAMOC: modular execution time analysis using model checking. In: Proceedings of 10th International Workshop on Worst-Case Execution Time Analysis (WCET 2010). OpenAccess Series in Informatics (OASIcs), vol. 15, pp. 113–123. Schloss Dagstuhl-Leibniz-Zentrum fuer Informatik (2010)

[GELP10] Gustavsson, A., Ermedahl, A., Lisper, B., Pettersson, P.: Towards WCET analysis of multicore architectures using UPPAAL. In: Proceedings of 10th International Workshop on Worst-Case Execution Time Analysis (WCET 2010). OpenAccess Series in Informatics (OASIcs), vol. 15, pp. 101–112. Schloss Dagstuhl-Leibniz-Zentrum fuer Informatik (2010)

[HKPV98] Henzinger, T.A., Kopke, P.W., Puri, A., Varaiya, P.: What's decidable about hybrid automata? J. Comput. Syst. Sci. **57**(1), 94–124 (1998)

[HKSW11] Herbreteau, F., Kini, D., Srivathsan, B., Walukiewicz, I.: Using non-convex approximations for efficient analysis of timed automata. In: Proceedings of 30th Conference on Foundations of Software Technology and Theoretical Computer Science (FSTTCS 2011). LIPIcs, vol. 13, pp. 78–89. Leibniz-Zentrum für Informatik (2011)

[HSW12] Frédéric Herbreteau, B., Srivathsan, I.W.: Better abstractions for timed automata. In: Proceedings of 27th Annual Symposium on Logic in Computer Science (LICS 2012), pp. 375–384. IEEE Computer Society Press (2012)

[HT15] Herbreteau, F., Tran, T.-T.: Improving search order for reachability testing in timed automata. In: Sankaranarayanan, S., Vicario, E. (eds.) FORMATS 2015. LNCS, vol. 9268, pp. 124–139. Springer, Heidelberg (2015)

[JR11] Jaubert, R., Reynier, P.-A.: Quantitative robustness analysis of flat timed automata. In: Hofmann, M. (ed.) FOSSACS 2011. LNCS, vol. 6604, pp. 229–244. Springer, Heidelberg (2011)

[LBB+01] Larsen, K.G., Behrmann, G., Brinksma, E., Fehnker, A., Hune, T., Pettersson, P., Romijn, J.M.T.: As cheap as possible: efficient cost-optimal reachability for priced timed automata. In: Berry, G., Comon, H., Finkel, A. (eds.) CAV 2001. LNCS, vol. 2102, pp. 493–505. Springer, Heidelberg (2001)

[RLS06] Rasmussen, J.I., Larsen, K.G., Subramani, K.: On using priced timed automata to achieve optimal scheduling. Form. Methods Syst. Des. 29(1), 97–114 (2006)

[RS01] Rückmann, J.-J., Stein, O.: On linear and linearized generalized semi-infinite optimization problem. Ann. Oper. Res. 101(1–4), 191–208 (2001)

Automatic Reachability Analysis for Nonlinear Hybrid Models with C2E2

Chuchu Fan[1]([✉]), Bolun Qi[1], Sayan Mitra[1], Mahesh Viswanathan[1],
and Parasara Sridhar Duggirala[2]

[1] University of Illinois, Urbana-Champaign, Urbana, USA
{cfan10,bolunqi2,mitras,vmahesh}@illinois.edu
[2] University of Connecticut, Mansfield, USA
psd@uconn.edu

Abstract. C2E2 is a bounded reachability analysis tool for nonlinear dynamical systems and hybrid automaton models. Previously it required users to annotate each system of differential equations of the hybrid automaton with *discrepancy functions*, and since these annotations are difficult to get for general nonlinear differential equations, the tool had limited usability. This version of C2E2 is improved in several ways, the most prominent among which is the elimination of the need for user-provided discrepancy functions. It automatically computes piece-wise (or local) discrepancy functions around the reachable parts of the state space using symbolically computed Jacobian matrix and eigenvalue perturbation bounds. The special cases of linear and constant rate differential equations are handled with more efficient algorithm. In this paper, we discuss these and other new features that make the new C2E2 a usable tool for bounded reachability analysis of hybrid systems.

1 Introduction

C2E2 is a tool for checking bounded time invariant properties of nonlinear hybrid automaton models through reachability analysis. A hybrid automaton combines ordinary differential equations (ODE) and with guarded-command program fragments, and is seen as a convenient mathematical formalism for describing a variety of cyber-physical systems. Since nonlinear differential equations often do not have analytical solutions, C2E2 implements a simulation-based approach for over-approximating the reachable states of a system of ODEs. This involves: (a) generating numerical simulations of the ODE from a finite set of representative initial states that cover the whole (uncountably many) initial set, say Θ, (b) bloating each of these simulations by *some factor* such that the bloated tubes together over-approximate the reachable states from Θ, and (c) checking if this computed over-approximation is adequate for proving invariance; otherwise, add more representative initial states to obtain a more precise over-approximation and repeat from (a).

This work was in part supported by the grants CCF 1422798 and CNS1054247 from the National Science Foundation.

S. Chaudhuri and A. Farzan (Eds.): CAV 2016, Part I, LNCS 9779, pp. 531–538, 2016.
DOI: 10.1007/978-3-319-41528-4_29

The previous version of C2E2 [10,11] relied on the user to provide the bloating factor, formally called a *discrepancy function*, required in step (b). For linear ODEs, one could, in principle, find discrepancy functions automatically from the dynamics of the system, but for general nonlinear systems this is not the case. The primary improvement we present in this new version of C2E2 [1] relieves the user from this burden. We have implemented the algorithm presented in [13] which computes a piece-wise (or local) discrepancy function for the ODE. This algorithm is *on-the-fly* or *lazy* in that it only computes the discrepancy function around parts of the state-space that are known to be reachable (from step (a)). For linear models the new implementation automatically computes a global discrepancy function. Automatic handling of systems with constant dynamics, and a technique to carry-out coordinate transformation are also implemented to improve the overall performance of C2E2. The new C2E2 can automatically verify and find counter-examples in interesting nonlinear and linear hybrid systems created using Stateflow[TM]: for example, a 5-dimensional highly nonlinear benchmark model of a powertrain control system [17], an auto-passing control system with 6 modes, and a 28-dimensional linear model of a helicopter [22].

2   Related Tools

Several automatic verification tools for hybrid models have been developed over the past two decades and they have been used in verifying numerous systems. Uppaal [20], HyTech [15] and SpaceEx [14] target timed automata, rectangular hybrid automata, and linear hybrid automata, respectively. Nonlinear dynamical and hybrid models are handled by d/dt [4], Flow* [6], dReach [19], CORA [3], and Ariadne [5]. S-Taliro [21] finds counter-examples in complex and realistic models using Monte-carlo techniques and provides probabilistic guarantees. STRONG [7] is a MATLAB toolbox for analysis of linear hybrid systems and it uses a Lyapunov function-based approach.

The simulation-based verification algorithm implemented in C2E2 is closest in spirit to the Matlab-based Breach tool [8]. Breach uses sensitivity analysis of the ODEs (related to our notion of discrepancy function) to verify signal temporal logic (STL) properties. Sensitivity analysis is known to be sound for linear ODEs and for more complex models Breach uses numerical procedures for estimating the Jacobian matrix of the system. This enables it to handle complex models at the expense of rigorous guarantees. The new version of C2E2 computes discrepancy functions from symbolically computed Jacobian matrix of the ODEs. This gives soundness and relative completeness guarantees, but restricts its application to ODEs with continuously differentiable right hand sides.

3   New Features in C2E2

The architecture of C2E2 is shown in Fig. 1. The GUI-based front end parses the input hybrid model which has to be given either as a Stateflow model (.mdl) or as an XML file (.hyxml). The front end produces (i) an executable for producing validated simulations for each system of ODEs for the hybrid automaton, (ii) a specification of the candidate invariant properties to be checked, and (iii) a newly implemented function for symbolically evaluating the Jacobian matrix for each system of ODEs in the hybrid model. The front end provides a property editor which checks syntactic correctness of properties as they are typed. After the back end produces verification results, which includes the reach set and possibly counter-example, these objects can be plotted using the front end as well (see Fig. 2).

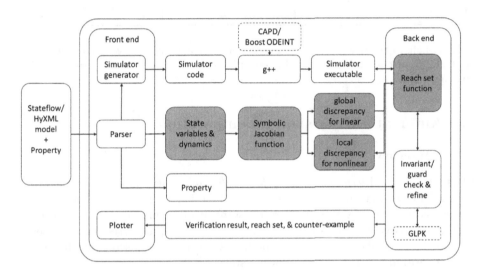

Fig. 1. Architecture of C2E2: The colored blocks are newly implemented. Improvements in existing blocks are discussed in Sect. 4.2.

The Jacobian function and the simulator are used by the new back end for computing reachable states using the approach described in Sect. 1. If the system or a discrete location of the hybrid system is linear (which is automatically checked by the front end), then the Jacobian matrix is used to compute a global discrepancy function once and for all. Otherwise, the back end iteratively calls the simulator as well as the Jacobian function, to over-approximate the reachable states over small time intervals (more details are given in Sect. 4).

The rest of the functions in the back end work with the computed reach set to check for the guards of the hybrid automaton. It also checks if the candidate invariant properties are provably satisfied or violated. Based on these decisions the main verification loop decides to (a) return results to the front end, or (b) start over the process by refining the initial set of states, or (c) start simulations from a new set of initial states in a new mode (that is, with a new system of ODEs).

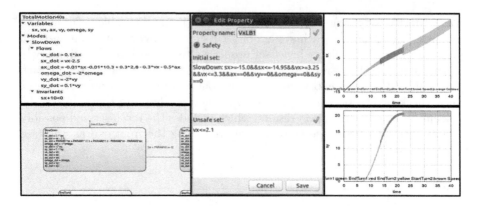

Fig. 2. Left to right: figures showing a snippet of partial auto-passing control model in C2E2 front end and Stateflow^{TM}, property dialog, plots of reachable set for auto-passing control model.

4   Automatic Discrepancy Computation

4.1   Overview

The block labeled *local discrepancy for nonlinear* in Fig. 1 implements the algorithm for computing piece-wise discrepancy function for general nonlinear ODEs using Jacobian matrix and Lipschitz constant. It takes one simulation trajectory and initial partition size as input at one time, and produces a sequence of coefficients. These coefficients define the piece-wise exponential discrepancy function. The algorithm consists of the following steps:

(a) First, using the Lipschitz constant a coarse over-approximation of the reachable set up to a short time horizon T_s is constructed. Let this set be S.

(b) The largest eigenvalue $\lambda_{max}\left((J(s_0) + J^T(s_0))/2\right)$ of the symmetric part of the Jacobian matrix $J(s_0)$ at the center s_0 of S is computed.

(c) From $\lambda_{max}\left((J(s_0) + J^T(s_0))/2\right)$ an upper bound b of the eigenvalue of the symmetric part of all the Jacobian matrices $J(s), s \in S$ is computed. This uses a theorem from matrix perturbation theory and involves bounding the terms of the symbolic Jacobian over S.

(d) The upper bound b (possibly negative) defines the discrepancy function $\beta(t) = \beta'(t_0)e^{b(t-t_0)}$ over the simulation time interval $[t_0, t_0 + T_s]$, where $\beta'(\cdot)$ is the previous piece of the discrepancy function. Using this piece-wise discrepancy function an over-approximation of the reachable set is computed.

The soundness of the algorithm comes from the fact that the computed bound b over a certain region S provides an exponential bound on the distance of any two trajectories in that region.

4.2 Implementation and Enhancements

We discuss the design decisions made in implementing the above mentioned functions and how they impact C2E2.

Symbolic Jacobian Computation. From the parse tree generated by the front end, the state variables and ODEs for each location of the hybrid automaton are extracted. For an ODE $\frac{dx}{dt} = f(x)$, where f is a vector valued function, the Jacobian matrix $J(x)$ is the matrix of partial derivatives $J_{ij}(x) = \frac{\partial f_i}{\partial x_j}$. We use the Python Sympy[1] library for computing derivatives of f symbolically. This library handles a general class of functions and as a result our implementation of symbolic Jacobian computation works for all standard polynomial, trigonometric, exponential and logarithmic functions. Our approach works for complicated models like the powertrain benchmark [17,18] which has more than 30 nonlinear terms in f. C2E2 compiles the symbolic Jacobian matrices into a Python module, which is then used to evaluate their numerical values.

Discrepancy Function Computation. To compute local discrepancy functions on-the-fly, the upper bound of the eigenvalues of (the symmetric part of) Jacobian matrices and the upper bound of the matrix perturbations are obtained along the simulation traces using Python linear algebra library[2].

The local discrepancy function module communicates with the reach set function, takes simulation traces and initial set, and returns a local discrepancy function designed specially for the given simulation trace. In C2E2, we provide multiple simulator options: the validated simulator CAPD [2] as well as the standard ODE solver in the Boost library[3].

Global Discrepancy for Linear ODEs. For linear time invariant hybrid models, the entries in the symbolic Jacobian matrix are constants. Thus, the local discrepancy function will be the same as the global one. C2E2 takes advantage of this fact and evaluates the Jacobian matrix just once and computes a global exponential discrepancy function to be used throughout, instead of on-the-fly local discrepancy. For example, analysis of the 28-dimensional linear model of the helicopter with this approach completes in seconds.

Automatic Handling of Constant Dynamics. Often hybrid models have timers and other variables that evolve at a constant rate with time. The ODEs for such systems have the form:

$$\begin{cases} \frac{dx}{dt} = f(x) \\ \frac{dy}{dt} = k \end{cases}$$

where k is a constant and y changes at that constant rate with time. Although the simple dynamics of y should make it easier to compute its reach set—at

---

[1] http://www.sympy.org/en/index.html.

[2] http://docs.scipy.org/doc/numpy/reference/routines.linalg.html.

[3] https://headmyshoulder.github.io/odeint-v2/.

any time t, $y(t) = y(0) + kt$—our discrepancy-based algorithm has problems dealing with such systems. These constant-rate variables introduce all 0 rows and all 0 columns in the Jacobian matrix. This not only increases the dimension of the system, but also introduces extra conservatism in the estimation of the eigenvalues. For example, the Jacobian matrix of such systems has 0 eigenvalue even when the rest of the system is stable. The new C2E2 mitigates this problem by automatically decomposing the system by handling the constant-rate part independently.

For example, the Cardiac cell model in [11] uses a timer $\frac{d(\text{timer})}{dt} = 1$ to transit between the location where stimulate is on and the location where it is off. Systems with such constant dynamics are detected and decomposed automatically. That is, C2E2 will first compute the reach set of $\frac{dx}{dt} = f(x)$ using our standard technique, then bloat $y(t)$ by δ_y for $\frac{dy}{dt} = k$, where δ_y is the size of initial set for variable y.

Coordinate Transformation. Coordinate transformation can help produce less conservative over-approximations of the reach set. Coordinate transformations are done automatically in the new C2E2 in the following manner: first, Jacobian matrix is transformed to the real Jordan form by a similarity transformation, and then the similarity transformation matrix is used to perform the linear coordinate transformation. Such transformation decreases the conservatism of exponential bound (the factor b mentioned in Sect. 4.1), but comes at the price of a constant multiplicative factor in $\beta(t)$. C2E2 allows the users to set a parameter in the GUI that helps explore this trade off.

Other Enhancements. We re-implemented the reach set plotter for C2E2 which now uses gnuplot and is much faster. It also shows unsafe regions and counter-example segments. C2E2 now comes with testing scripts and a command line interface. The tests check the reach sets computed on a new installation against the corresponding reference versions computed in our lab machine. Examples inputs and outputs are documented in the website[4].

Detailed comparison of the performance of the new C2E2 with other verification tools will be presented in a future paper and in the tool's website. In several examples, it performs favorably in comparison with Flow*[6]. For example, it verifies a 10 dimensional nonlinear cardiac cell model from [16] (Fig. 1) in less than 10 s where Flow* took 500 s. The dynamics is given by, for example,
$f_1(x_1, x_2, u_1, u_2, stim) = -0.9x_1^2 - x_1^3 - 0.9x_1 - x_2 + 10(u_1 + u_2 - 2x_1) + stim$
and $f_2(x_1, x_2) = x_1 - 2x_2$, with $S_{on} = 5$ and $S_{off} = 20$.

5   Discussion of Performance and Conclusions

The new version of C2E2 comes with a growing set of interesting example models such as a powertrain control system with highly nonlinear dynamics, a 28-dimensional linear helicopter, a hybrid auto-passing control model with 6 locations, a cardiac cell model and others. Although some of these (for example, the

---

[4] http://publish.illinois.edu/c2e2-tool/example/.

powertrain control system model [9,12]) had been verified earlier, those analyses involved hand-crafting special functions inside C2E2 for computing Jacobian matrices, handling constant dynamics, etc. The new C2E2 checks the examples automatically, without the need for annotations, typically in minutes.

A single reach set computation by bloating a single simulation trace using discrepancy computation usually takes less than one second for nonlinear systems with 5–6 dimensions or linear systems, up to a time horizon of 10 s.

The verification time of each example, of course, depends on the complexity of the system, the distance of the unsafe set from the reachable set, the stability of the dynamics, and the time horizon.

In summary, this paper presents several new features implemented in C2E2, the most prominent one being an algorithm for computing discrepancy functions for linear, nonlinear, and constant ODEs. These features make the new C2E2 a more usable tool for verifying nonlinear hybrid models while preserving the original soundness and relative completeness guarantees.

References

1. C2E2 Webpage. http://publish.illinois.edu/c2e2-tool/
2. Computer Assisted Proofs in Dynamic Groups (CAPD). http://capd.ii.uj.edu.pl/index.php
3. Althoff, M.: An introduction to cora 2015. In: ARCH (2015)
4. Asarin, E., Dang, T., Maler, O.: The $\mathbf{d/dt}$ tool for verification of hybrid systems. In: Brinksma, E., Larsen, K.G. (eds.) CAV 2002. LNCS, vol. 2404, pp. 365–370. Springer, Heidelberg (2002)
5. Balluchi, A., Casagrande, A., Collins, P., Ferrari, A., Villa, T., Sangiovanni-Vincentelli, A.L.: Ariadne: a framework for reachability analysis of hybrid automata. In: MTNS. Citeseer (2006)
6. Chen, X., Ábrahám, E., Sankaranarayanan, S.: Flow*: an analyzer for non-linear hybrid systems. In: Sharygina, N., Veith, H. (eds.) CAV 2013. LNCS, vol. 8044, pp. 258–263. Springer, Heidelberg (2013)
7. Deng, Y., Rajhans, A., Julius, A.A.: STRONG: a trajectory-based verification toolbox for hybrid systems. In: Joshi, K., Siegle, M., Stoelinga, M., D'Argenio, P.R. (eds.) QEST 2013. LNCS, vol. 8054, pp. 165–168. Springer, Heidelberg (2013)
8. Donzé, A.: Breach, a toolbox for verification and parameter synthesis of hybrid systems. In: Touili, T., Cook, B., Jackson, P. (eds.) CAV 2010. LNCS, vol. 6174, pp. 167–170. Springer, Heidelberg (2010)
9. Duggirala, P.S., Fan, C., Mitra, S., Viswanathan, M.: Meeting a powertrain verification challenge. In: Kroening, D., Păsăreanu, C.S. (eds.) CAV 2015. LNCS, vol. 9206, pp. 536–543. Springer, Heidelberg (2015)
10. Duggirala, P.S., Mitra, S., Viswanathan, M.: Verification of annotated models from executions. In: EMSOFT, p. 26. IEEE Press (2013)
11. Duggirala, P.S., Mitra, S., Viswanathan, M., Potok, M.: C2E2: a verification tool for stateflow models. In: Baier, C., Tinelli, C. (eds.) TACAS 2015. LNCS, vol. 9035, pp. 68–82. Springer, Heidelberg (2015)
12. Fan, C., Duggirala, P.S., Mitra, S., Viswanathan, M.: Progress on powertrain verification challenge with C2E2. In: ARCH (2015)

13. Fan, C., Mitra, S.: Bounded verification with on-the-fly discrepancy computation. In: Finkbeiner, B., et al. (eds.) ATVA 2015. LNCS, vol. 9364, pp. 1–8. Springer, Heidelberg (2015). doi:10.1007/978-3-319-24953-7_32

14. Frehse, G., Le Guernic, C., Donzé, A., Cotton, S., Ray, R., Lebeltel, O., Ripado, R., Girard, A., Dang, T., Maler, O.: SpaceEx: scalable verification of hybrid systems. In: Gopalakrishnan, G., Qadeer, S. (eds.) CAV 2011. LNCS, vol. 6806, pp. 379–395. Springer, Heidelberg (2011)

15. Henzinger, T.A., Ho, P.-H., Wong-Toi, H.: Hytech: a model checker for hybrid systems. In: Grumberg, O. (ed.) CAV, pp. 460–463. Springer, Heidelberg (1997)

16. Huang, Z., Fan, C., Mereacre, A., Mitra, S., Kwiatkowska, M.: Invariant verification of nonlinear hybrid automata networks of cardiac cells. In: Biere, A., Bloem, R. (eds.) CAV 2014. LNCS, vol. 8559, pp. 373–390. Springer, Heidelberg (2014)

17. Jin, X., Deshmukh, J.V., Kapinski, J., Ueda, K., Butts, K.: Benchmarks for model transformations and conformance checking. In: ARCH (2014)

18. Jin, X., Deshmukh, J.V., Kapinski, J., Ueda, K., Butts, K.: Powertrain control verification benchmark. In: HSCC, pp. 253–262. ACM (2014)

19. Kong, S., Gao, S., Chen, W., Clarke, E.: dReach: δ-reachability analysis for hybrid systems. In: Baier, C., Tinelli, C. (eds.) TACAS 2015. LNCS, vol. 9035, pp. 200–205. Springer, Heidelberg (2015)

20. Larsen, K.G., Pettersson, P., Yi, W.: Uppaal in a nutshell. Int. J. Softw. Tools Technol. Transf. (STTT) 1(1), 134–152 (1997)

21. Nghiem, T., Sankaranarayanan, S., Fainekos, G., Ivancić, F., Gupta, A., Pappas, G.J.: Monte-carlo techniques for falsification of temporal properties of non-linear hybrid systems. In: HSCC, pp. 211–220. ACM (2010)

22. Skogestad, S., Postlethwaite, I.: Multivariable Feedback Control-Analysis, Design: Solution Manual Part i (2005)

Author Index

Printed in the United States
by Bookmasters

Printed in the United States
By Bookmasters